# Digital Transformation and Entrepreneurial Innovation for Sustainable Business


Reshmy Krishnan
*Muscat College, Oman*

Araby Madbouly Ahmed Hussain
*Muscat College, Oman*

Buthaina Yahya Al Kharousi
*Muscat College, Oman*

Nitha Mary
*Muscat College, Oman*



IGI Global
Scientific Publishing
Publishing Tomorrow's Research Today

| | |
|---|---|
| Vice President of Editorial | Melissa Wagner |
| Director of Acquisitions | Mikaela Felty |
| Director of Book Development | Jocelynn Hessler |
| Production Manager | Mike Brehm |
| Cover Design | Jose Rosado |

Published in the United States of America by
IGI Global Scientific Publishing
701 East Chocolate Avenue
Hershey, PA, 17033, USA
Tel: 717-533-8845 | Fax: 717-533-7115
Website: https://www.igi-global.com E-mail: cust@igi-global.com





Library of Congress Cataloging-in-Publication Data

LCCN: 2026032938 (CIP Data Pending)
ISBN13: 9798260031797
Isbn13Softcover: 9798260031803
EISBN13: 9798260031810
British Cataloguing in Publication Data
A Cataloguing in Publication record for this book is available from the British Library.

# Table of Contents

# Detailed Table of Contents



Artificial Intelligence and Emerging Technologies as Enablers of Innovation very critical issues that need more attention in our entrepreneurship and innovation. This chapter will explore the topic and declared in more details all the basic technologies. The collaboration between humans and machines: enhanced intellect Make the case that the future is not about replacing people with AI, but about using AI to make people better at what they do. AI does data processing and pattern detection, which lets people focus on strategy, creativity, and empathy. A group of strong new technologies are coming together to change the way businesses and people interact in the modern world. This chapter examines the roles of artificial intelligence (AI), big data, the Internet of Things (IoT).



The digital world is significantly reshaping entrepreneurship by introducing innovation and competition across industries. This transformation involves utilizing technologies such as artificial intelligence, cloud computing, and data analytics, posing both opportunities and challenges for entrepreneurs. The chapter explores how digital tools influence entrepreneur behavior, strategy, leadership, and business models, using case studies of startups like Airbnb, Uber, and Tesla. It emphasizes the faster recognition of opportunities and the shift towards experience-centric value generation. Additionally, the chapter discusses future skills, platform-based business models, sustainability, and essential startup tips. It concludes that successful entrepreneurship will hinge on blending human creativity with technological intelligence while fostering inclusive, sustainable digital ecosystems to empower entrepreneurs with profitable ventures..

Fintech services play a dynamic role in the evolution and growth of SMEs by providing support, contributing, sponsoring, and investing in facilities. Providing fintech services is increasingly difficult due to numerous issues, including privacy and security concerns, and an inconsistent understanding of electronic platforms. The research study examines the impact of a business entity's activities on the willingness to use online services, with trust in technology as a mediating factor. A reliability test has been conducted using Cronbach's Alpha to assess the internal consistency of the gathered information. Democratic details have been collected and interpreted accordingly. The mediating role of the trust factor would help determine the adoption of fintech services. It presents insights into how fintech services could unify into SME activities. This study would also help policymakers and service providers reduce barriers to trust, thereby ensuring the successful integration of fintech services into corporate operations.



The research explores how crowdfunding integrates financing and digital marketing, enabling entrepreneurs to directly engage with consumers and investors, thereby expanding access to capital and market participation. A qualitative case study approach was adopted, using document analysis and an extensive literature review covering crowdfunding, e-commerce, digital marketing, and digital consumer behavior. The findings indicate that Kickstarter provides a transparent and interactive environment where producers can secure funding, market their products, and obtain real-time consumer feedback. While the platform lowers financial entry barriers and enhances market engagement, it also presents challenges such as increased competition, consumer fatigue, and algorithm-driven visibility inequalities. Overall, the study concludes that although crowdfunding contributes to the democratization of finance and marketing, structural and behavioral limitations restrict its full potential, highlighting the need for improved platform governance and regulatory frameworks.



This chapter analyzes how tiny, locally rooted enterprises maneuver through modern market challenges by employing adaptive techniques that reconcile commercial viability with wider societal obligations. This chapter examines the interplay between entrepreneurial behaviors and technology-driven market communication within the local café sector, highlighting their role in fostering long-term value development. The discourse amalgamates theoretical viewpoints and contemporary empirical findings to delineate principal economic impediments, social and cultural conflicts, and environmental limits encountered by small firms. Strategic approaches are examined, encompassing business model reconfiguration, platform-based involvement, community-focused practices, and resource-efficient operations. The chapter delineates prospective research avenues for new technologies and effect assessment in small enterprises. This chapter provides a cohesive viewpoint that connects firm-level strategy with local development and ethical business practices in service-oriented sectors.



To improve sustainability frameworks in developing economies, it is important to understand how small and medium-sized business (SME) owners behave. Although

factors. Feature importance analysis identifies unemployment benefits and country-specific influences (e.g., Germany, India) as key factors shaping policy outcomes.

# Preface

## INTRODUCTION

Digital transformation has fundamentally reshaped the landscape of entrepreneurship, creating unprecedented opportunities for innovation, competitiveness, and sustainable business growth. Advances in artificial intelligence, big data analytics, cloud computing, financial technologies, digital platforms, and the Internet of Things are enabling organizations to rethink traditional business models and develop new approaches to value creation. These technologies are empowering entrepreneurs to respond more effectively to rapidly evolving markets, optimize operations, improve customer engagement, and address complex economic, environmental, and societal challenges. As businesses increasingly operate within interconnected digital ecosystems, entrepreneurial success depends not only on technological adoption but also on the ability to innovate responsibly and sustainably.

As editors, we recognize that digital transformation is not solely a technological phenomenon but a strategic and organizational journey that influences leadership, governance, finance, marketing, sustainability, and stakeholder engagement. Entrepreneurs today are expected to balance profitability with social responsibility, environmental stewardship, and ethical governance while navigating dynamic digital environments. Sustainable business therefore requires integrating technological innovation with responsible decision-making, resilient organizational cultures, and long-term value creation. This evolving landscape calls for multidisciplinary perspectives capable of bridging entrepreneurship, digital innovation, sustainability, and public policy.

This volume brings together contributions from researchers and practitioners across diverse disciplines and international contexts to examine how digital transformation is redefining entrepreneurship and sustainable business development. The chapters collectively explore technological innovation, digital finance, entrepreneurial leadership, sustainability adoption, corporate governance, responsible marketing, nature-inspired innovation, financial systems, and public policy. Through conceptual discussions, empirical investigations, historical analyses, and comparative studies, the volume provides comprehensive insights into the opportunities and challenges associated with building innovative, digitally enabled, and sustainable enterprises.

## CHAPTER OVERVIEW

**Chapter 1** introduces the foundational role of artificial intelligence and emerging digital technologies in driving entrepreneurial innovation. The chapter examines how AI, big data, the Internet of Things, and related technologies enhance decision-making, foster creativity, and enable organizations to achieve greater efficiency while supporting collaborative human–machine innovation.

**Chapter 2** explores entrepreneurship within the digital economy by examining platform innovation, entrepreneurial leadership, and sustainable business models. Through contemporary case studies, the chapter demonstrates how digital transformation enables entrepreneurs to recognize opportunities, create customer-centered value, and develop resilient enterprises within rapidly evolving digital ecosystems.

**Chapter 3** investigates the adoption of financial technology services among small and medium-sized enterprises. Focusing on the mediating role of trust in technology, the chapter analyzes how fintech solutions influence business performance and provides practical insights for policymakers and service providers seeking to encourage greater digital financial inclusion.

**Chapter 4** examines crowdfunding as an innovative financing mechanism in the digital era. Using Kickstarter as a representative platform, the chapter explores how digital platforms democratize entrepreneurial finance while simultaneously highlighting governance challenges, market competition, and algorithmic inequalities affecting entrepreneurial visibility.

**Chapter 5** focuses on entrepreneurial innovation and digital marketing within locally rooted coffee businesses. The chapter illustrates how adaptive business strategies, digital engagement, community participation, and environmentally responsible practices contribute simultaneously to economic growth, social development, and environmental sustainability.

**Chapter 6** examines the behavioral dimensions of sustainability adoption among small and medium-sized enterprise owners. Through a longitudinal qualitative investigation, the authors demonstrate how attitudes toward sustainability evolve over time and identify the cognitive, emotional, and social factors that influence the successful integration of circular economy and enterprise risk management practices.

**Chapter 7** explores the relationship between corporate social responsibility, board governance, and corporate tax strategies. The chapter demonstrates how effective governance structures and responsible corporate practices strengthen organizational performance while contributing to broader sustainability objectives and transparent fiscal management.

**Chapter 8** investigates corporate social responsibility awareness within the tourism and hospitality workforce. Emphasizing the importance of education, organizational culture, and employee engagement, the chapter illustrates how translating CSR principles into daily organizational practice strengthens sustainability performance and service excellence.

**Chapter 9** introduces biomimicry as a strategic framework for sustainable competitive advantage. By integrating nature-inspired design principles with strategic management theory, the chapter demonstrates how organizations can enhance innovation, resilience, resource efficiency, and responsible technological development through regenerative business practices.

**Chapter 10** presents the concept of Boundary Pushing Entrepreneurship through the historical context of the Prohibition Era in the United States. The chapter illustrates how entrepreneurs operating under severe constraints employed creativity, resilience, and unconventional strategies to develop innovative business models, offering valuable insights for modern entrepreneurial practice.

**Chapter 11** examines the influence of monetary policy on banking sector performance by analyzing the impact of interest rate changes on Indian bank stock returns. The chapter provides empirical evidence regarding financial market behavior while offering practical implications for investors, financial institutions, and policymakers.

**Chapter 12** concludes the volume by evaluating G20 policy initiatives designed to promote sustainable economic growth. Applying advanced machine learning techniques, the chapter compares policy implementation across member countries, identifies key determinants of successful outcomes, and demonstrates how predictive analytics can strengthen evidence-based policymaking for sustainable development.

## CONCLUSION

The contributions assembled in this volume demonstrate that digital transformation and entrepreneurial innovation have become inseparable drivers of sustainable business development. Across diverse industries and institutional contexts, the chapters reveal how emerging technologies, innovative business models, responsible leadership, and strategic adaptation enable organizations to create economic value while simultaneously advancing social well-being and environmental sustainability. Collectively, the contributors illustrate that entrepreneurial success in the digital era depends upon balancing technological progress with ethical governance, organizational resilience, and long-term societal impact.

A central theme emerging throughout this collection is that sustainable innovation extends far beyond technological capability. The effective application of digital technologies requires trust, responsible governance, inclusive leadership, supportive policy environments, and continuous organizational learning. Whether addressing fintech adoption, digital marketing, corporate social responsibility, crowdfunding, biomimicry, or sustainability-oriented entrepreneurship, the chapters consistently emphasize the importance of integrating innovation with accountability, transparency, and stakeholder engagement. Such integration is essential for ensuring that digital transformation contributes meaningfully to inclusive economic growth and sustainable development.

As editors, we hope that Digital Transformation and Entrepreneurial Innovation for Sustainable Business serves as a valuable reference for researchers, educators, entrepreneurs, business leaders, policymakers, and students seeking to understand the evolving relationship between digital innovation and sustainable enterprise. We further hope that the diverse perspectives presented throughout this volume inspire continued interdisciplinary collaboration, encourage responsible entrepreneurial practices, and stimulate future research that advances digitally enabled, resilient, and socially responsible business ecosystems. Ultimately, we believe that the convergence of entrepreneurship, technology, and sustainability offers extraordinary opportunities for shaping a more innovative, equitable, and sustainable global economy.

Editors

**Reshmy Krishnan**
*Muscat College, Oman*

**Araby Ahmed Hussain**
*Muscat College, Oman*

**Buthaina Al Kharousi**
*Muscat College, Oman*

**Nitha Mary**
*Muscat College, Oman*

# Chapter 1
# Artificial Intelligence and Emerging Technologies as Enablers of Innovation

**Ghaliya Alfarsi**
http://orcid.org/0000-0001-5038-0302
*Al-Buraimi University College, Oman*

## ABSTRACT

*Artificial Intelligence and Emerging Technologies as Enablers of Innovation very critical issues that need more attention in our entrepreneurship and innovation. This chapter will explore the topic and declared in more details all the basic technologies. The collaboration between humans and machines: enhanced intellect Make the case that the future is not about replacing people with AI, but about using AI to make people better at what they do. AI does data processing and pattern detection, which lets people focus on strategy, creativity, and empathy. A group of strong new technologies are coming together to change the way businesses and people interact in the modern world. This chapter examines the roles of artificial intelligence (AI), big data, the Internet of Things (IoT).*

## 1. INTRODUCTION

### 1.1. Setting the Scene: The Fourth Industrial Revolution

The present period is characterized by the convergence of the physical, digital, and biological realms, setting it apart from the preceding three industrial revolutions the first one mechanization, second mass production, and third automation (Truong

DOI: 10.4018/979-8-2600-3179-7.ch001

et al., 2023; Skilton & Hovsepian, 2018). Talk about how the rate of change is speeding up instead than staying the same.

### 1.2. What Does “Innovation Enablers” Mean?

The technologies are more than just products; they are basic platforms. They are “enablers” because they make it easier for new ideas to come up, open up new possibilities for products and services such as Netflix's recommendation engine, make processes better such as predictive maintenance in manufacturing, and change the way businesses work such as Uber's platform model (Sahai & Rath, 2021; Al Farsi et al., 2019; AlSinani et al., 2020)

The Goals and Plan for the Chapter to clearly describe what the reader will learn: how to comprehend the core technologies, how to look at their synergistic effects, how to look at their effects on specific industries, and how to think critically about the problems and trends that will come up in the future.

## 2. THE HISTORICAL AND TECHNOLOGICAL BACKGROUND

The Roots of the Digital Age and the first computers and automation (1940s–1960s): Programmable computers like ENIAC are the initial step. This time period saw the idea of automating complicated calculations, moving from mechanical processing to electronic data processing. The Dartmouth Workshop (1956) was the first major research project in artificial intelligence. It looked at symbolic AI and rule-based systems (Kang et al., 2024; Bolón-Canedo et al., 2024; Mohanarajesh, 2024).

The growth of the internet and connection (1970s–1990s): The creation of ARPANET and later the public internet made it possible for people all over the world to share information. This was the first step toward cloud computing, transferring large amounts of data, and eventually the Internet of Things. The World Wide Web makes it easier for everyone to get information (Truong & Papagiannidis, 2022).

Mobile and ubiquitous computing (2000s–2010s): The rise of smartphones put a powerful computer in everyone's pocket. This faster connection produced huge new data streams (such location and app usage) and set consumer expectations for rapid services on demand. “The app economy” was the first step toward platform-based business models that are now possible thanks to new technology (Jouppi et al., 2023;Wu,2022). .

Data explosion, What makes current AI work. From not enough to too much: For a long time, storing data was expensive and processing power was limited. The dramatic drop in the cost of digital storage (Kryder's Law) and Moore's Law trajectory for rising processing power have made these problems go away. used to live in a world where data was hard to find, but now live in a world where there is too much of it.

The problem with unstructured data, at first, data was mostly ordered (in databases, for example, in rows and columns). The internet, social media, sensors, and multimedia have all become more common, which has resulted to a huge amount of unstructured data (pictures, videos, audio, social media postings, and texts)(Al Sideir et al., 2020; Voronkova et al., 2023; Hamad & Jawad, 2024; Diesen, 2021). This was too complicated for regular software to examine, therefore more complex artificial intelligence methods like deep learning were needed.

Big changes and probable breakthroughs. The cloud computing revolution: The rise of on-demand computing resources like AWS, Azure, and Google Cloud constituted a huge change. It has made it possible for both startups and big businesses to run complicated AI models and store petabytes of data without having to spend a lot of money on hardware up front. The "utility model" of computing is the algorithmic leap: From symbolic AI to deep learning: Early AI (symbolic AI) had a hard time dealing with how unclear things are in the real world. Neural networks and deep learning made a comeback in the 2010s, thanks to important research like AlexNet in 2012 and the availability of big labeled datasets like ImageNet. These technologies were able to do tasks like recognizing images and voice better than people. This was the first time that artificial intelligence could be used in real life and make money (Mourtzis, 2021; Oke, 2025). Deep Learning is a specialized subset of Machine Learning that uses artificial neural networks (ANNs) with multiple layers (hence "deep") to learn complex patterns in data. Inspired by the structure and function of the human brain, these networks are particularly effective at processing raw data like images, audio, and text, extracting features automatically without explicit programming (Al Farsi, G. (2023). Neural Networks: Composed of interconnected "neurons" organized in layers (input, hidden, and output layers). Each connection has a weight, and neurons activate based on weighted sums of their inputs. During training, these weights are adjusted to minimize errors. Deep Architectures: The "deepness" comes from having many hidden layers, allowing the network to learn hierarchical representations of data. For example, in an image, early layers might detect edges, middle layers shapes, and later layers complex objects. Convolutional Neural Networks (CNNs), Primarily used for Computer Vision tasks like image recognition, object detection, facial recognition, and medical image analysis. They are adept at identifying spatial hierarchies in data. MachineTranslation: Automatically translating text from one language to another (e.g.,Google Translate). Speech Recognition, Converting spoken language into written text (e.g., voice assistants like Siri, Alexa). Text Summarization, Condensing long documents into shorter, coherent summaries. Chatbots and Virtual Assistants, Understanding user queries and providing relevant responses. The open-source ecosystem, The popularity of open-source software frameworks like TensorFlow, PyTorch, and Scikit-learn has made it much easier for people to get started with AI development. Researchers and developers from all around the world can build on each other's work, which speeds up the rate of new ideas.

The debut of the 4G/LTE network made the mobile experience know today possible. The ongoing development of 5G networks promises far faster speeds and, most importantly, very low latency, which is necessary for real-time control of autonomous systems and the huge number of devices connected to the Internet of Things.

## A Change in Mindset: From Linear to Exponential.

The end of linear thinking, Linear forecasts were commonly used in traditional corporate and innovation strategies. The coming together of these technologies has a bigger and faster effect. More IoT devices, for instance, create more data, which leads to stronger AI models. These models then make IoT networks smarter and more efficient. This nonlinear growth is a key feature of the present tech landscape and a big reason why it is so disruptive (Mthombeni, 2024; Yu & Jiang, 2024). The concept of the IoT can be traced back to the late 1990s, but it has only truly taken off in recent years due to several convergent factors: the miniaturization and cost reduction of sensors, the proliferation of wireless connectivity (Wi-Fi, Bluetooth, 5G), the exponential growth of cloud computing, and the advanced analytical capabilities offered by AI and Big Data. These factors have made it economically and technically feasible to connect virtually any physical object to the internet, transforming mundane items into intelligent data-generating entities. Having explored Artificial Intelligence as the cognitive engine, Big Data as the essential fuel, the Internet of Things as the pervasive sensory network, and Blockchain as the foundational layer of trust and immutability, it becomes clear that their individual powers, while significant, are merely precursors to their combined, exponential potential. The true revolution in innovation arises not from each technology operating in isolation, but from their strategic and often seamless integration. This convergence creates intelligent, connected, data-rich, and verifiable ecosystems that redefine what is possible across industries.

The interplay among these technologies can be visualized as a highly sophisticated, interconnected system such as:

1. IoT as the Data Generator: Billions of IoT devices ceaselessly gather vast amounts of real-time data from the physical world. These "eyes and ears" provide granular insights into processes, environments, and behaviors that were previously opaque or inaccessible. This data includes everything from sensor readings on machinery to geographical location data, environmental conditions, and user interaction

patterns. Without the IoT, much of the contextual data needed for truly intelligent systems would simply not exist or would be collected manually and inconsistently.

2. Big Data as the Data Enabler and Organizer: The sheer volume, velocity, and variety of data flowing from IoT devices (and other sources like web interactions, enterprise systems, and social media) necessitates Big Data infrastructure. Big Data technologies are crucial for ingesting, storing, processing, and managing this torrent of information.

3. Automated Trust with Smart Contracts: AI-driven decisions or IoT-triggered events can be linked to smart contracts on a blockchain. This enables automated, trustless execution of agreements (e.g., releasing payment when an IoT sensor verifies product delivery) without intermediaries.

## Illustrative Synergies: How They Work Together

Let's consider a few high-level examples to understand this powerful cooperation such as:

## Autonomous Vehicles

IoT, Sensors (cameras, lidar, radar, GPS) on the vehicle constantly collect vast amounts of real-time data about the environment (traffic, road conditions, pedestrians, other vehicles).

Big Data, This continuous stream of sensor data is processed locally (edge computing) and also transmitted to the cloud, where massive historical datasets are stored and analyzed to train and refine AI models.

AI, Deep Learning algorithms (Computer Vision, Reinforcement Learning) process the IoT data to perceive the environment, predict actions of other agents, plan routes, and make split-second driving decisions. Reinforcement Learning RL is a type of ML where an agent learns to make decisions by performing actions in an environment. It tries different moves, and if a move leads to a better board state (closer to winning), it receives a reward. If it leads to a worse state, it receives a penalty. Over many iterations, it learns optimal strategies. Computer Vision is an AI field that trains computers to "see" and interpret visual information from the world in a way similar to human vision. AI field that trains computers to Image Classification: Categorizing an entire image (e.g., "this is a cat"). Object Detection: Identifying specific objects within an image and locating them with bounding boxes (e.g., "there is a car at X,Y coordinates"). Facial Recognition: Identifying individuals from images or video. Autonomous Navigation: Enabling self-driving cars to "see" roads, pedestrians, and obstacles. Quality Control: Automated inspection of products on a production line. Common Applications: Robotics (teaching robots to perform tasks), autonomous driving, game playing (e.g., AlphaGo mastering Go), resource management, and complex control systems. Algorithms: Q-learning, SARSA, Deep Q-Networks (DQN). Blockchain: Could be used for secure, immutable logging of vehicle maintenance records, insurance claims, or even for secure vehicle-to-vehicle (V2V) communication to authenticate data exchanges and establish trust in a decentralized network of self-driving cars.

- **Smart Grid Management:**

o **IoT:** Smart meters in homes and sensors in power substations, transmission lines, and renewable energy sources (solar panels, wind turbines) continuously monitor energy consumption, production, and grid health.

o **Big Data:** These enormous, high-velocity datasets are ingested and analyzed to understand energy demand patterns, identify inefficiencies, and predict potential points of failure.

o **AI:** Machine Learning algorithms optimize energy distribution, predict fluctuations from renewable sources, balance supply and demand in real-time, and identify anomalies indicative of faults or cyber-attacks.

o **Blockchain:** Could facilitate secure, transparent peer-to-peer energy trading between prosumers (producers + consumers) or manage a decentralized record of renewable energy credits, enhancing trust and auditability in energy transactions.

- **Precision Agriculture:**

o **IoT:** Drones and ground-based sensors collect granular data on soil moisture, nutrient levels, crop health, weather conditions, and pest presence across vast farmlands.

o **Big Data:** This diverse data (images, sensor readings, historical weather data) is processed and stored in analytics platforms.

o **AI:** Machine Learning models analyze the Big Data to recommend precise irrigation schedules, optimal fertilizer application, early pest detection, and yield prediction, tailoring interventions to specific areas of a field.

o **Blockchain:** Can provide an immutable record of crop provenance, organic certifications, irrigation and pesticide usage, ensuring transparency and trust for consumers and supply chain partners, and potentially enabling automated payments via smart contracts upon verified delivery of produce.

## 3. LOOKING AT BASIC TECHNOLOGIES

Artificial Intelligence: The wide field of study that tries to copy how people think and act. There is a difference between narrow AI (which is made for one goal, like recognizing faces) and general AI (which is a theoretical level of intelligence).

Machine learning is a part of artificial intelligence that deals with algorithms that learn from data without being told how to do so. Talk about supervised learning (using labeled data, like spam filtering), unsupervised learning (using unlabeled data, like customer segmentation), and reinforcement learning (using rewards and punishments to learn, like AI in games) (Yu & Jiang, 2024; Rose, 2016; Goldschmidt, 2017).

Deep learning is a type of machine learning that uses neural networks with several layers. It works well with unstructured data like text (natural language processing), voice (speech recognition), and photos (computer vision).

### 3.1. Big Data and Smart Analytics

The three V's are: Volume (the huge amount of data), Velocity (the pace at which data is created and processed), and Variety (the different types of data, such as structured, unstructured, and semi-structured). Some models add value and truthfulness (data quality).

Maturity of analytics: A description of progress: Descriptive (What happened? Dashboards, reports), Diagnostic (Why did it happen? - Deep dive, discovery), Predictive (What will happen? - Forecasting, machine learning models), Prescriptive (What should I do? - Optimization, recommendation engines).

If Artificial Intelligence represents the brain of innovation, then **Big Data** unequivocally serves as its fuel, its sensory input, and its primary learning material. The proliferation of digital devices, online interactions, ubiquitous sensors, and automated systems has led to an explosion in the volume, velocity, and variety of data generated globally. This deluge of information, far exceeding the capabilities of traditional data processing applications, is what define as Big Data.

The concept of Big Data is not merely about having a lot of data; it's about the ability to store, process, analyze, and derive insights from datasets that are too large or complex for conventional data-processing software. Its true value lies not just in the sheer quantity but in what organizations do with the data – how they analyze it to gain new perspectives, make more informed decisions, and drive strategic innovations. The characteristics that define Big Data are often encapsulated by the "Vs," which have evolved over time to encompass a more comprehensive understanding:

1. **Volume:** This is the most obvious characteristic. Big Data refers to datasets that are of an exceptionally large size, often measured in terabytes, petabytes,

exabytes, and beyond. This volume is constantly growing, driven by everything from social media interactions to IoT device readings.

  - o Example: A major e-commerce platform collects terabytes of data daily from customer browsing history, purchase records, reviews, and interactions. A large Hadron Collider experiment generates petabytes of data from particle collisions.

2. **Velocity:** This refers to the speed at which data is generated, collected, and processed. In many Big Data scenarios, data arrives continuously and rapidly, demanding real-time or near real-time processing to derive timely insights.
   - o Example: Stock market data streams in milliseconds, requiring immediate analysis for algorithmic trading. IoT sensors in a smart factory transmit data every second, necessitating rapid processing for predictive maintenance.
3. **Variety:** Big Data encompasses a wide range of data types, both structured and unstructured.
   - o **Structured Data:** Highly organized, easily searchable, and stored in databases (e.g., customer names, addresses, credit card numbers in a CRM system).
   - o **Unstructured Data:** Has no predefined format or organization, making it harder to process and analyze using traditional methods (e.g., text from social media posts, emails, customer service call recordings, images, video files).
   - o **Semi-structured Data:** Contains tags or markers to enforce hierarchical grouping, but does not conform to the rigid structure of relational databases (e.g., XML files, JSON documents).
   - o Example: A healthcare system might combine structured patient demographics, semi-structured electronic health records, and unstructured doctor's notes and medical images.
4. **Veracity:** This refers to the quality, accuracy, and trustworthiness of the data. With vast volumes and varieties of data, ensuring its veracity becomes a significant challenge. Low-quality data can lead to flawed analyses and poor decisions.
   - o Example: Noisy sensor readings from an IoT device, inconsistencies in customer input across different platforms, or deliberate misinformation on social media all impact data veracity. Robust data governance and cleansing processes are critical.
5. **Value:** Ultimately, the purpose of collecting and processing Big Data is to derive actionable insights and generate value. Data alone is just raw material; its true worth is realized when it informs strategy, optimizes operations, or creates new products and services.

- Example: Analyzing traffic patterns (Volume, Velocity) from GPS devices (Variety) with known accuracy (Veracity) to develop more efficient public transport routes, saving time and fuel (Value).

## Data Acquisition, Storage, Processing, and Analytic:

Harnessing Big Data requires a sophisticated ecosystem of technologies and methodologies:

1. **Data Acquisition:** This involves collecting data from its myriad sources. This can include:
   - **Transactional Systems:** CRM, ERP, e-commerce platforms.
   - **IoT Devices:** Sensors, smart appliances, industrial machinery.
   - **Web and Social Media:** User interactions, clickstreams, posts, comments.
   - **External Sources:** Public datasets, market intelligence, geospatial data.
   - **Streaming Data:** Real-time collection from high-velocity sources.
2. **Data Storage:** Traditional relational databases struggle with the volume and variety of Big Data. Modern solutions include:
   - **NoSQL Databases:** Non-relational databases designed to handle large volumes of unstructured or semi-structured data (e.g., MongoDB for document storage, Cassandra for wide-column stores).
   - **Data Lakes:** Centralized repositories that store raw data in its native format, without prior structuring, until it's needed for analysis. This offers flexibility but requires careful management.
   - **Data Warehouses:** Optimized for analytical queries on structured data, often containing transformed and integrated data from various sources.
   - **Distributed File Systems:** Technologies like Hadoop Distributed File System (HDFS) designed to store extremely large files across clusters of commodity hardware.
3. **Data Processing:** Transforming raw data into a usable format for analysis. This often involves:
   - **Batch Processing:** Processing large volumes of data collected over a period (e.g., daily sales reports). Technologies like Apache Hadoop MapReduce are foundational here.
   - **Stream Processing:** Analyzing data as it arrives in real-time, critical for high-velocity scenarios (e.g., fraud detection, anomaly alerts). Technologies like Apache Kafka, Apache Spark Streaming, and Flink are commonly used.

- **Data Cleansing and Transformation (ETL/ELT):** Extracting data from sources, transforming it to meet quality and format requirements, and loading it into a target system.

4. **Data Analytics:** Applying statistical methods, machine learning algorithms, and other computational techniques to uncover patterns, trends, and insights.
   - **Descriptive Analytics:** What happened? (e.g., reporting, dashboards).
   - **Diagnostic Analytics:** Why did it happen? (e.g., root cause analysis).
   - **Predictive Analytics:** What will happen? (e.g., forecasting, risk assessment, customer churn prediction – heavily reliant on ML).
   - **Prescriptive Analytics:** What should I do? (e.g., recommendations for optimal actions – often involves AI-driven decision systems).

## Role of Cloud Computing and Distributed Systems

The sheer demands of Big Data processing have made **Cloud Computing** an indispensable enabler. Cloud platforms (e.g., AWS, Azure, Google Cloud Platform) provide:

- **Scalability:** On-demand access to massive computing and storage resources, allowing organizations to scale infrastructure up or down as needed without huge upfront capital investments.
- **Cost-Effectiveness:** Pay-as-you-go models reduce operational expenses.
- **Accessibility:** Global access to data and processing capabilities.
- **Managed Services:** Cloud providers offer a wide array of pre-built Big Data services (e.g., managed Hadoop, Spark, data warehousing solutions), simplifying deployment and management.

**Distributed Systems** are also fundamental. Big Data workloads are often too large for a single machine, so they are broken down and processed across clusters of interconnected computers. Frameworks like Apache Hadoop and Apache Spark are designed specifically for this distributed processing, enabling parallel computation and fault tolerance.

## The Indispensability of Big Data for AI

The symbiosis between Big Data and AI is profound and bidirectional:

- **Fuel for AI:** Big Data provides the massive, diverse, and often high-velocity datasets that are essential for training complex AI models, particularly in Machine Learning and Deep Learning. Without vast amounts of data, AI models cannot learn to recognize patterns, make accurate predictions, or generate realistic content.

- **AI for Big Data:** AI and ML algorithms are, in turn, critical tools for making sense of Big Data. They enable automated anomaly detection, pattern recognition, predictive modeling, and natural language processing on unstructured data at scales that would be impossible for human analysts. AI helps extract the "value" from the "Vs."

## 3.2. Internet of Things (IoT)

Components: Describe the ecosystem, which includes sensors and devices for collecting data, connectivity (Wi-Fi, 5G, LPWAN) for sending data, data processing (in the cloud or at the "edge"), and a user interface for human involvement.

Function: Its main job is to connect the real world with the digital world by collecting huge amounts of real-time data from physical items. This data is what powers AI and analytics.

## 3.3. Distributed Ledger Technology (DLT) and Blockchain Technology

Basic principles: decentralization (no one central authority), immutability (records can't be changed after the fact), transparency (everyone can see the transactions), and consensus (a way to agree on transaction verification).

Self-executing contracts with terms put right into the code are called "smart contracts." It makes and enforces agreements without any middlemen.

There are other uses for blockchain technology besides cryptocurrencies, such as proof of supply chain, digital identification, secure voting systems, and decentralized finance (DeFi).

## 3.4. Other Important Characteristics That Help

Cloud computing gives you the on-demand computing power and storage you need to run these technologies that need a lot of data.

Fifth-generation networks give you the fast, low-latency connections you need for real-time Internet of Things and AI apps, including self-driving cars.

Robots are the physical version of artificial intelligence and do things in the actual world.

## 4. THE COMBINED POWER OF DIFFERENT TECHNOLOGIES COMING TOGETHER

How the Internet of Things gives artificial intelligence big data to work with

Big data is created by IoT devices on the manufacturing floor that collect terabytes of operational data. This information is used by AI models to figure out when machines will break down (predictive maintenance). This makes a closed system where data leads to smart actions.

### 4.1. AI Serves as the "Brain" for Robots and Other Autonomous Systems

The self-driving automobile employs sensors like cameras and LiDAR (Internet of Things) to see what's around it. Artificial intelligence (AI), notably computer vision and deep learning, uses this data to make decisions about steering, braking, and accelerating in real time. This controls the vehicle's robots.

### 4.2. Blockchain to Protect and Verify Data From IoT and AI

IoT sensors keep an eye on the temperature in the pharmaceutical supply chain. Writing this information to the blockchain makes a record that can't be changed and can be checked. This makes sure that the data hasn't been changed, which builds trust in the AI system that might be watching to make sure rules are being followed.

Case study: ecosystem of smart cities. Give an example from actual life: smart traffic management. IoT cameras and sensors keep an eye on traffic flow. Artificial intelligence uses this information to change the timing of traffic lights in real time. Smart contracts (Blockchain) can automatically tax citizens for traffic jams, and all transactions are kept safe on a distributed ledger. Blockchain for Secure Health Records and Data Exchange, While AI and IoT generate and process health data, Blockchain offers a transformative solution for managing this sensitive information with unparalleled security, privacy, and interoperability.

- **Secure Electronic Health Records (EHRs):** Storing patient health records on a private or consortium blockchain creates an immutable, timestamped audit trail of all changes and accesses. Patients can control who views their data (e.g., giving temporary access to a new specialist). To enhances data security, protects patient privacy, and gives patients true ownership and control over their medical history.
- **Interoperable Data Exchange:** Blockchain can facilitate secure and standardized sharing of patient data across different healthcare providers, hos-

pitals, and research institutions, overcoming the perennial problem of fragmented and siloed health information. This improves care coordination and reduces redundant tests.

- **Supply Chain for Pharmaceuticals:** Tracking the provenance of drugs from manufacturing to patient delivery on a blockchain can combat counterfeit medications, ensure drug authenticity, and streamline recall processes.
- **Clinical Trial Data Management:** Recording clinical trial data on a blockchain ensures its integrity and immutability, enhancing trust in research results and preventing data manipulation.
- **Medical Research Consortia:** Allowing multiple research organizations to securely share and analyze de-identified patient data on a blockchain, accelerating discovery while maintaining privacy.

## 4.3. The Synergistic Future of Healthcare Innovation

Imagine a future where:

- An **IoT wearable** continuously monitors your vital signs, feeding data into a **Big Data** platform.
- An **AI algorithm** detects a subtle change indicative of a developing condition before symptoms appear.
- This AI then triggers a **smart contract on a blockchain** to alert your doctor (with your permission), who then accesses your secure, immutable **EHR (also on blockchain)**.
- Based on your genomic data (processed by **Big Data**) and the AI's insights, a **personalized, predictive treatment plan** is initiated, perhaps delivered by an AI-powered home assistant.

This integrated vision of healthcare leverages the strengths of each technology: IoT provides the real-time insights from the physical body, Big Data manages and aggregates vast health information, AI derives intelligence and actionable recommendations, and Blockchain ensures the privacy, security, and integrity of all patient data. The result is a healthcare system that is not only more efficient and cost-effective but fundamentally more patient-centric, proactive, and capable of extending and improving human life. The convergence promises to redefine healthcare delivery, making it truly personalized, predictive, preventive, and participatory.

## 5. CHANGES THAT ARE SPECIFIC TO AN INDUSTRY

Artificial intelligence in diagnosis: Algorithms that look at MRI pictures can find malignancies as well as radiologists can.

Internet of Things (remote monitoring): Wearable gadgets like smartwatches keep an eye on patients' vital signs all the time and let doctors know if anything seems off.

Blockchain (for health records): It lets patients control their own data and lets providers share it safely and with permission.

### 5.1. Fintech and Insurtech in Finance and Banking

Artificial Intelligence (Fraud Detection): Machine learning algorithms look at transaction patterns in real time to find signs of fraud.

Payments on the blockchain make cross-border settlements faster, cheaper, and more open, and they don't need correspondent banks.

Big data (credit assessment): Looks into unusual data sources, such utility payments and social media, to figure out if "unbanked" people may get credit.

### 5.2. Industry 4.0 and Manufacturing

Smart factories: Machines that are connected to the Internet of Things talk to each other to make manufacturing lines better.

Artificial Intelligence (Predictive Maintenance) can determine when equipment is going to break down before it does, which cuts down on downtime. Digital twins are virtual copies of real things or processes that may be used to run simulations and make things work better without affecting the real system (Putzier, 2017; De Valence, 2022; Shalwani, 2021).

### 5.3. Logistics, Retail, and the Supply Chain

Using the Internet of Things and blockchain technology to monitor a product from its raw ingredients to the store shelf and make sure it is real and ethically sourced (like fair trade coffee).

Artificial Intelligence (Demand Forecasting): Uses sales data, weather, and social trends to guess what people will want in the future and make sure there is enough stock on hand.

Recommendation engines are AI algorithms that make purchasing more personal by showing you things like "customers who bought this also bought others"

## 5.4. The Energy, Agriculture, and Other Industries

Drones (part of the Internet of Things) fly over the fields and take pictures. Then, artificial intelligence looks at the pictures and figures out how much water and pesticides to use in each region.

Smart grids: IoT sensors keep the supply and demand for energy in balance and make it easy to use renewable sources (Tiwari, 2022; Cox, 2014; Grinin & Grinin, 2016).

# 6. DIFFICULTIES, DANGERS, AND MORAL ISSUES

The process of gathering the huge amounts of data needed for AI makes people worry about privacy issues like facial recognition and data breaches. Talk about rules like the General Data Protection Regulation (GDPR) (Mhlanga, 2023; Barros, 2019; Upadhyaya, 2024).

## 6.1 Fair Artificial Intelligence and Algorithmic Bias

If AI learns from biased historical data, it will keep those biases alive and make them stronger. For example, this may happen with hiring algorithms or loan approvals. The necessity for varied data and "explainable artificial intelligence" (XAI) (Folmer, E.,et al. (2020); Fiok, K., et al. 2022 ; Weingärtner, T. (2019).

Automation is taking over certain regular jobs, like data entry, but it is also spawning new ones, like AI ethics and data scientist. The immediate necessity for rehabilitation and continuous education (Olayinka, 2021; Gupta & Quamara, 2020; Hu, 2014).

## 6.2. Impact on the Environment

Big AI models and various blockchain consensus processes, such proof of work, use a lot of energy. Talk about the shift to more energy-efficient options, such proof of stake (Wang et al., 2018; Frempong et al., 2022; Al-Hadhrami & Hussain, 2020).

6.3. Rules and laws from the government and other organizations Regulatory and governmental frameworks. Technology moves faster than the law does. Talk about the need for new rules to control digital currencies, self-driving cars, and AI (Mohamed, 2019; Slama et al., 2015; Albouq, 2022).

## 7. DISCUSSION AND CONCLUSION

The chapter meticulously lays out the individual characteristics and capabilities of Artificial Intelligence (AI), Big Data, the Internet of Things (IoT), and Blockchain, subsequently demonstrating how their convergence unlocks exponential value.

### Example of Constructive Integrative: Factory Smart as a Cross Department Innovation Platform

The convergence of Artificial Intelligence (AI), Big Data, the Internet of Things (IoT), and blockchain can be understood by considering a single illustrative case - the smart factory. The integrated smart factory acts as an organizational ecosystem. This comparison allows us to show how information flows between all parts of an organization — from production and logistics to quality control, maintenance, finance, HR and executive management. By using the smart factory as a framework for discussing digital transformation, we can demonstrate that digital transformation replaces previous technologies with new technologies — as well as changing how the organization operates. Digital transformation is driven by interconnected systems and data-driven decision-making. Within a smart factory, IoT sensors continuously collect real-time operational data from machines, production lines, inventory systems, and environmental conditions. This data is transmitted continuously to a centralized data analysis platform, where AI algorithms analyze the data and provide insights such as similar patterns, prediction of possible equipment failure, optimization of production scheduling, and improvements in energy efficiency. Big data technologies are used to support the storage, processing and interpretation of large quantities of structured and unstructured data generated in the smart factory ecosystem. Finally, blockchain technology can be used to provide secure and verifiable records of supply chain transactions, equipment maintenance logs, and product traceability.

All departments are interconnected to form an enterprise-wide digital infrastructure where information flows across the organization with little to no interruption, and decision-making is collaborative and based on facts/evidence. The application of the smart factory is particularly useful because it demonstrates that emerging technologies are interrelated (synergy) rather than siloed (isolated innovation). For example, predictive maintenance is dependent on IoT devices for machine data; a big data platform for managing real-time data streams; and artificial intelligence models for predicting future failures before they happen. Once a machine has been repaired, the blockchain verifies that the maintenance occurred (maintenance history) and holds all suppliers and service providers accountable for their actions. Therefore, instead of requiring one technology to drive innovation, innovation is generated from the integration and alignment of multiple layers of technology that work together under the same organizational framework. From an organization's perspective, this convergence of technologies will drastically alter historical management structures and operational governance. Departments that previously functioned separately will be required to collaborate through interconnected digital systems that require greater coordinating efforts, shared data standards, and integrated decision-making processes. Thus, this change creates new governance issues regarding (1) ownership of the data; (2) responsibilities for protecting the data; (3) responsible use of artificial intelligence; and (4) compliance with regulations.

For instance, in a fully digitized environment, determining who has the authority for operational data, how sensitive data is to be shared between departments and how to monitor algorithmic results is becoming increasingly complex.

Moreover, the concept of smart factories entails various strategic and human-centric issues. It is essential to empower employees and management integrative into concepts of digital competence that emphasize the intersection of technical competency, analytical and managerial ability. In addition to developing digital competency, organizational leaders will need to manage the balance between increased efficiencies achieved through automation and concerns regarding worker displacements, surveillance of employees by way of digital technologies, and bias in automated decision-making processes. With workforces relying increasingly on interconnected digital technologies, evolved governance frameworks should incorporate qualities such as transparency, accountability, ethical compliance, and resilience to the technological risks posed by cyber-attacks and failures associated with digital infrastructures. Thus, the use of smart factory as an example of integrative practical application has very strong conceptual linkage across all functional or departmental divisions and creates a better analytical view of how emerging technologies collectively contribute to the transformation of innovation ecosystems and allow organizations to successfully transform actual tangible materials into digitized artifacts through technical and governance, organizational adaptation and responsible management practices.

## 8. RESULT

1. **Artificial Intelligence (AI),** Positioned as the "brain of innovation," AI encompasses Machine Learning (supervised, unsupervised, reinforcement learning), Deep Learning (CNNs, RNNs, Transformers), Natural Language Processing (NLP), Computer Vision, Robotics, and Generative AI (López, et al., 2023; Vermesan & Bacquet, 2022). It excels at automation, optimization, prediction, personalization, augmentation, and content creation (Miller, 2019; Kumar & Metta, 2024; Tamimi & Ellis, 2009).

2. **Big Data,** Described as the "fuel for intelligent systems," Big Data is characterized by its Volume, Velocity, Variety, Veracity, and Value (Pavunraj et al., 2025). The chapter details the ecosystem required for handling Big Data: acquisition, storage (NoSQL, data lakes, data warehouses), processing (batch, stream), and analytics (descriptive, diagnostic, predictive, prescriptive), heavily relying on cloud computing and distributed systems. Its indispensability for training AI models is highlighted (Wah, 2025; Malik et al., 2021).
3. **Internet of Things (IoT),** Referred to as the "senses of the digital world," IoT connects billions of devices that collect, transmit, and exchange data. Its architecture involves devices/sensors, a connectivity layer, a data processing layer (edge and cloud), and an application layer. Benefits include real-time data generation, automation, efficiency, predictive capabilities, enhanced decision-making, and new products/services, despite challenges in security, interoperability, and data management (Qian, 2021).

## 9. COMPONENTS AND ARCHITECTURE OF IOT

A typical IoT ecosystem comprises several layers, working in concert to collect, process, and act upon data:

1. **Things (Devices/Sensors):** These are the physical objects equipped with sensors, actuators, and embedded computing capabilities(Han et al., 2020)
   - o **Sensors:** Collect data from the environment (e.g., temperature, humidity, light, motion, pressure, GPS location, heart rate).
   - o **Actuators:** Respond to commands to take physical action (e.g., turning a light on/off, adjusting a thermostat, opening a valve).
   - o **Embedded Computing:** Small microcontrollers or processors that handle local data processing and communication.
   - o Examples: Smart thermostats, connected cars, industrial machinery sensors, smartwatches, agricultural soil sensors, smart city cameras.
2. **Connectivity Layer:** This layer is responsible for transmitting the data collected by the "things" to the next stage of the IoT architecture. Various communication protocols and networks are used depending on factors like data volume, range, power consumption, and latency requirements (Madine et al., 2020).
   - o **Short-Range:** Bluetooth, Wi-Fi, Zigbee (for smart homes, personal devices).
   - o **Medium-Range:** Cellular (4G, 5G), LoRaWAN, NB-IoT (for smart cities, agriculture, industrial IoT).
   - o **Long-Range:** Satellite communication (for remote areas).

- o **Gateways:** Often serve as a bridge, aggregating data from multiple local devices and translating it into a format suitable for wider network transmission, often to the cloud. They can also perform initial data filtering and processing.

3. **Data Processing Layer (Edge and Cloud):** Once data is transmitted, it needs to be processed. This often involves a hybrid approach:
   - o **Edge Computing:** Processing data closer to the source (at the "edge" of the network, e.g., on the IoT device itself or a local gateway).
     - ▪ Benefits: Reduces latency (critical for real-time applications like autonomous vehicles), conserves bandwidth (by sending only filtered or aggregated data to the cloud), enhances security (by processing sensitive data locally), and allows for disconnected operations.
     - ▪ Example: A factory sensor detects a critical anomaly and triggers an immediate shutdown without waiting for cloud processing.
   - o **Cloud Computing:** Centralized processing and storage in remote data centers.
     - ▪ Benefits: Scalability for massive data storage and complex analytics (leveraging Big Data technologies), access to powerful AI algorithms, and unified data management across geographically dispersed devices.
     - ▪ Example: Historical temperature data from thousands of smart thermostats is analyzed in the cloud to identify energy consumption patterns across a city.

**Application Layer:** This is where the processed data is transformed into actionable insights and delivered to end-users or other systems through dashboards, mobile apps, or enterprise software.

- o Example: A farmer monitors soil moisture levels and remotely controls irrigation systems via a smartphone app. A city planner uses a dashboard to visualize traffic flow data and optimize signal timings.

## 10. KEY ENABLERS AND BENEFITS OF IOT

- **Real-time Data Generation:** IoT devices continuously stream data from the physical world, providing an unprecedented level of real-time visibility into operations, environments, and conditions. This granular data is a critical input for Big Data analytics and AI models.

- **Automation and Control:** Through actuators, IoT enables remote and autonomous control over physical processes. This ranges from simple smart home automation to complex industrial automation and robotic systems.
- **Efficiency and Optimization:** By monitoring performance, resource usage, and environmental factors, IoT helps identify inefficiencies, optimize processes, and reduce waste across diverse sectors.
- **Predictive Capabilities:** The continuous stream of sensor data, when analyzed with AI, allows for powerful predictive maintenance in machinery, early detection of issues in infrastructure, and proactive resource management.
- **Enhanced Decision-Making:** With real-time and granular data at their fingertips, decision-makers can react faster and make more informed choices, leading to improved outcomes.
- **New Products and Services:** IoT enables the creation of entirely new smart products (e.g., connected cars with advanced safety features) and innovative services (e.g., usage-based insurance, smart city management platforms).

## 11. CHALLENGES OF IOT

Despite its immense potential, IoT faces significant challenges:

- **Security and Privacy:** The vast number of interconnected devices creates a massive attack surface for cyber threats. Protecting sensitive data collected by IoT devices from unauthorized access and ensuring user privacy are paramount concerns.
- **Interoperability:** The lack of universal standards for communication and data exchange among diverse IoT devices and platforms can create fragmentation and hinder seamless integration.
- **Data Management:** The sheer volume and velocity of data generated by IoT devices pose significant challenges for storage, processing, and analysis, necessitating robust Big Data infrastructure.
- **Scalability:** Managing and maintaining billions of devices, ensuring their connectivity, and processing their data at scale requires sophisticated and resilient infrastructure.
- **Energy Consumption:** Many IoT devices operate on batteries, and ensuring long battery life while maintaining connectivity and processing capabilities is a continuous engineering challenge.

## 12. THE SYMBIOTIC RELATIONSHIP WITH AI AND BIG DATA

The IoT's role as the "senses" of the digital world is inextricably linked to AI and Big Data:

- **Data Provider:** IoT is the primary generator of the high-volume, high-velocity, and high-variety data that fuels Big Data repositories. Without IoT, AI models would lack real-time insights from the physical world.
- **Action Executor:** While AI processes and decides, IoT devices (through actuators) are often the means by which AI's decisions are executed in the physical world, enabling automated responses.

**Intelligent Edge:** The integration of AI algorithms into edge computing devices (Edge AI) allows for faster, more localized decision-making, reducing reliance on constant cloud connectivity and enhancing the autonomy of IoT systems. A cutting-edge area of AI, generative AI focuses on models that can create new, original content, rather than just classifying or predicting. It trained on vast datasets of existing content (text, images, audio, code), generative models learn the underlying patterns and structures. They can then generate novel outputs that resemble the training data but are entirely new. such as Generative Adversarial Networks (GANs), Variational Autoencoders (VAEs), and increasingly, large-scale Transformer models (like GPT-3, DALL-E, Midjourney). The Applications sucha as text Generation, Writing articles, stories, code, marketing copy, Image Generation: Creating photorealistic images from text descriptions, generating art, designing product concepts, Audio Generation: Synthesizing speech, composing music, Video Generation: Creating short video clips from text or images, Drug Discovery, Generating novel molecular structures.

AI's pervasive capabilities make it the "brain" of modern innovation. It empowers organizations to:

- **Automate:** Streamline repetitive and complex tasks, freeing human capital for higher-value activities.
- **Optimize:** Discover efficiencies, predict failures, and personalize experiences at a granular level.
- **Predict:** Forecast trends, anticipate market shifts, and mitigate risks with greater accuracy.
- **Personalize:** Deliver bespoke products, services, and content tailored to individual preferences.
- **Augment:** Enhance human decision-making and capabilities by providing intelligent insights and assistance.

- **Create:** Generate novel content, designs, and solutions, pushing the boundaries of creativity and problem-solving.

In essence, IoT provides the critical connection between the digital brain (AI) and the physical world, continuously feeding it data and enabling it to interact with its environment. It transforms inert objects into active participants in the digital economy, creating a pervasive intelligence that monitors, analyzes, and responds to the world around us.

## Key Features and Principles

- **Immutability:** This is perhaps the most defining characteristic. Once data is recorded on a blockchain, it is extremely difficult, if not impossible, to alter or remove it. This provides a high degree of data integrity and trustworthiness.
- **Transparency:** In public blockchains, every participant can view the entire transaction history. In private or permissioned blockchains, transparency can be configured to allow only authorized participants to view relevant data. This shared, verifiable record eliminates information asymmetry.
- **Decentralization:** The absence of a central authority means there's no single point of control or failure. This enhances security, resilience, and resistance to censorship.
- **Security:** Cryptographic principles underpin blockchain security. Transactions are digitally signed, and the chaining of blocks ensures that any attempt to tamper with past data would require recalculating all subsequent blocks and gaining control of a majority of the network's computing power (a "51% attack"), which is practically infeasible for large, public blockchains.
- **Consensus:** All participants must agree on the validity of transactions before they are added to the ledger, ensuring data consistency across the distributed network.
- **Disintermediation:** Blockchain can reduce or eliminate the need for intermediaries (banks, lawyers, escrow services) in transactions, potentially lowering costs, increasing speed, and streamlining processes.

4. **Blockchain,** Presented as the "trust layer of the digital economy," Blockchain is a distributed, decentralized, immutable ledger. Key features include cryptographic security, consensus mechanisms, transparency, disintermediation, and smart contracts for trustless automation. The chapter discusses public, private, and consortium blockchains Governed by a group of pre-selected organizations (e.g., a consortium of banks, or supply chain partners). They offer a balance between decentralization and control, with enhanced privacy and higher transaction speeds than public

blockchains., acknowledging challenges like scalability, energy consumption, and regulatory uncertainty. The despite its immense promise, blockchain technology faces several challenges:

- **Scalability:** Many public blockchains (especially PoW) struggle with transaction speed and throughput compared to centralized systems. This is an active area of research (e.g., Layer 2 solutions, sharding).
- **Energy Consumption:** Proof of Work (PoW) consensus mechanisms, like Bitcoin's, are notoriously energy-intensive, raising environmental concerns. PoS and other mechanisms address this.
- **Regulatory Uncertainty:** The decentralized and global nature of blockchain makes it challenging for traditional regulatory frameworks to adapt, leading to legal ambiguities in various jurisdictions.
- **Interoperability:** Different blockchains often operate in silos, making it difficult for them to communicate and exchange data seamlessly.
- **Complexity and Adoption:** Implementing blockchain solutions can be complex, requiring specialized expertise. Mass adoption is still in its early stages for many applications beyond cryptocurrencies.
- **Data Storage:** While transactions are small, the ledger grows indefinitely. Storing the entire chain can become burdensome for individual nodes.

## Types of Blockchains

The specific applications and desired levels of transparency and control determine the type of blockchain deployed:

- **Public Blockchains (Permissionless):** Anyone can join the network, participate in consensus, and view the ledger. High degree of decentralization and transparency (e.g., Bitcoin, Ethereum). Ideal for broad public trust applications.
- **Private Blockchains (Permissioned):** Participation is restricted and managed by a central entity. While still distributed and cryptographically secured, they offer less decentralization. Often used within a single organization for internal auditing or specific use cases where full public transparency is not desired.

## 13. DISCUSSION

The core discussion revolves around the **"Power of Synergy,"** where these technologies intersect to create "intelligent, connected, data-driven, and trusted" systems. The chapter argues that their combined effect is multiplicative, not merely additive, creating cohesive digital fabrics.

- Integrated Workflow:
  - o **IoT** acts as the primary data generator, providing real-time insights from the physical world.
  - o **Big Data** ingests, stores, processes, and organizes this vast, diverse, and high-velocity data.
  - o **AI** then extracts intelligence, identifies patterns, makes predictions, and automates decisions based on the structured data provided by Big Data.
  - o **Blockchain** ensures the integrity, authenticity, and provenance of the data, and enables automated, trustless execution of agreements via smart contracts, thus securing the entire ecosystem.
- **Illustrative Synergies (Examples):** The chapter provides concrete examples like autonomous vehicles (IoT sensors, Big Data processing, AI decision-making, Blockchain for V2V trust), smart grid management (IoT metering, Big Data analytics, AI optimization, Blockchain for energy trading), and precision agriculture (IoT sensors/drones, Big Data processing, AI recommendations, Blockchain for provenance).
- **Sectoral Deep Dive - Healthcare:** This section serves as a comprehensive case study, demonstrating the practical application of the synergy:
  - o **AI:** Revolutionizes diagnostics (medical imaging), drug discovery (target ID, molecule design, trial optimization), personalized treatment plans, and surgical robotics.
  - o **IoT:** Enables remote patient monitoring (wearables), proactive care, smart hospitals (asset tracking, inventory), connected medication devices, and elderly care.
  - o **Big Data:** Essential for population health management, epidemiological studies, personalized medicine research (genomics, EHRs), clinical trial acceleration, and operational efficiency within health systems.
  - o **Blockchain:** Provides solutions for secure and interoperable Electronic Health Records (EHRs), patient data control, pharmaceutical supply chain transparency (combating counterfeits), clinical trial data integrity, and secure research consortia.

## 1. AI for Diagnostics, Drug Discovery, and Treatment Optimization

- Advanced Diagnostics, They can analyze X-rays, MRIs, CT scans, and pathology slides with superhuman speed and often greater accuracy than human experts, detecting subtle anomalies indicative of diseases like cancer, diabetic retinopathy, or neurological disorders at earlier stages.
  - Example: Google's DeepMind has demonstrated AI models capable of identifying over 50 eye diseases from retinal scans as accurately as human specialists, and AI systems can detect breast cancer in mammograms with a reduced false-positive rate.
- **Drug Discovery and Development:** The traditional process of bringing a new drug to market is incredibly lengthy, expensive, and high-risk. AI is drastically accelerating this.
  - **Target Identification:** AI can analyze vast biological datasets (genomic, proteomic) to identify potential drug targets with higher precision.
  - **Molecule Design:** Generative AI models can design novel drug molecules with desired properties, vastly expanding the chemical space explored.
  - **Clinical Trial Optimization:** AI can identify ideal patient cohorts for clinical trials, predict trial outcomes, and monitor patient safety, reducing costs and accelerating timelines.
  - Example: Companies like Atomwise use deep learning to predict the binding affinity of small molecules to protein targets, significantly speeding up the early stages of drug discovery.
- **Personalized Treatment Plans:** AI can analyze a patient's unique genetic profile, medical history, lifestyle data, and treatment responses to recommend highly personalized therapies. This is particularly impactful in oncology, where AI can help select the most effective chemotherapy or immunotherapy regimen.
- **Robotics in Surgery:** AI-powered surgical robots enhance precision, minimize invasiveness, and reduce recovery times. While the robots perform the actions, AI guides their movements based on real-time data and surgeon input, adapting to anatomical variations. While not exclusively AI, modern robotics heavily relies on AI for tasks such as perception (using computer vision), navigation (path planning, obstacle avoidance), manipulation (fine motor control), and intelligent decision-making, allowing robots to perform complex tasks in dynamic environments.

## 2. IoT for Remote Patient Monitoring and Proactive Care:

The Internet of Things is extending healthcare beyond the clinic, enabling continuous monitoring and proactive interventions in patients' daily lives.

- **Wearable Devices and Remote Monitoring:** Smartwatches, fitness trackers, and specialized medical wearables (e.g., continuous glucose monitors, smart patches for vital signs) collect real-time data on heart rate, sleep patterns, activity levels, blood pressure, and more. This data is transmitted to healthcare providers.
    - Impact: Enables early detection of deteriorating conditions (e.g., arrhythmias, falls in the elderly), supports chronic disease management (diabetes, heart failure), and reduces hospital readmissions by allowing clinicians to intervene proactively.
- **Smart Hospitals and Clinics:** IoT sensors in healthcare facilities monitor equipment status, track assets (e.g., wheelchairs, IV pumps), manage inventory, and even monitor patient locations and movements. This improves operational efficiency and patient safety.
- **Connected Inhalers and Smart Pills:** Devices that track medication adherence (e.g., smart inhalers that record usage and location) or ingestible sensors that monitor internal physiological parameters and communicate with external devices.
    - Impact: Improves medication adherence, provides objective data for treatment efficacy, and allows for targeted interventions.
- **Elderly Care and Assisted Living:** IoT devices can monitor the safety and well-being of seniors living independently, detecting falls, monitoring activity patterns, and providing reminders for medication, offering peace of mind to families and caregivers.

## 3. Big Data for Population Health Management and Research:

The massive datasets generated by electronic health records (EHRs), IoT devices, genomic sequencing, clinical trials, and public health surveillance systems are the lifeblood of AI in healthcare. Big Data analytics unlocks insights into population health, disease patterns, and treatment efficacy.

- **Epidemiology and Public Health:** Analyzing large-scale patient data and public health records to identify disease outbreaks, track their spread, understand risk factors, and evaluate the effectiveness of public health interventions. This was critical during the COVID-19 pandemic.

- **Personalized Medicine Research:** Integrating genomic data, proteomic data, lifestyle information, and EHRs for millions of patients allows researchers to identify biomarkers for disease susceptibility, drug response, and adverse effects, driving the development of truly personalized therapies.
- **Clinical Research Acceleration:** Big Data analytics can identify suitable patients for clinical trials more efficiently, analyze trial results more rapidly, and discover unforeseen drug interactions or side effects.
- **Operational Efficiency:** Analyzing operational data within healthcare systems (e.g., patient flow, resource allocation, appointment scheduling) to optimize hospital administration, reduce wait times, and improve patient experience.

## 14. CONCLUSION

Quantum computing can tackle problems that regular computers can't, such finding new drugs and optimizing things that are exceedingly complicated.

Generative AI is AI that makes new things like words, graphics, and programs, like GPT-4 and DALL-E. It is changing the way creative industries work.

The collaboration between humans and machines: enhanced intellect

Make the case that the future is not about replacing people with AI, but about using AI to make people better at what they do. AI does data processing and pattern detection, which lets people focus on strategy, creativity, and empathy. A summary of the essential points: encouraging a culture of experimentation, putting money into data infrastructure, putting talent development and ethical principles first, and making a clear plan for digital transformation. Using technology to create sustainable and inclusive new ideas

A final and forceful summary makes it clear that these technologies are just tools. The ultimate value of it is defined by how well can guide its growth and use it to solve the biggest problems facing humanity and make the future more fair and affluent. As delve into the other emerging technologies, it will become increasingly clear how AI serves as the intelligence layer that derives meaning from data, orchestrates complex systems, and drives autonomous action, thereby acting as a pivotal enabler of innovation across virtually every sector. Its ability to learn, adapt, and create fundamentally changes what is possible, setting the stage for unprecedented levels of efficiency, insight, and disruptive potential when combined with other powerful digital tools.

## REFERENCES


Al Farsi, G. (2023, November). The Impact of Artificial Intelligence Technology in Learning Zones. In International Conference on Computational Intelligence (pp. 215-222). Singapore: Springer Nature Singapore.

Al-Hadhrami, Y., & Hussain, F. K. (2020). Real time dataset generation framework for intrusion detection systems in IoT. *Future Generation Computer Systems*, *108*, 414–423. DOI: 10.1016/j.future.2020.02.051

Albouq, S. S., Abi Sen, A. A., Almashf, N., Yamin, M., Alshanqiti, A., & Bahbouh, N. M. (2022). A survey of interoperability challenges and solutions for dealing with them in IoT environment. *IEEE Access : Practical Innovations, Open Solutions*, *10*, 36416–36428. DOI: 10.1109/ACCESS.2022.3162219

AlSinani, M. J., Kayed, A., & Al Farsi, G. (2020). Improving data security using modified LSB-based image steganography technique. *Journal of Hunan University Natural Sciences*, *47*(8).

Barros, A. C. P. (2019). *Industry 4 0 and Transversal Skills: Comparing Social Sciences and Stem Higher Education Graduates* (Master's thesis, Universidade do Porto (Portugal)).

Bolón-Canedo, V., Morán-Fernández, L., Cancela, B., & Alonso-Betanzos, A. (2024). A review of green artificial intelligence: Towards a more sustainable future. *Neurocomputing*, *599*, 128096. DOI: 10.1016/j.neucom.2024.128096

Cox, C. R. (2014). *Synthesizing the vertical and the horizontal: A world-ecological analysis of'the Industrial Revolution', Part I.* Portland State University.

De Valence, G. (2022). *Creative Destruction and Constructing The Built Environment: From the first industrial revolution to the fourth.* Construction Economics Research.

Diesen, G. (2021). Great power politics in the fourth industrial revolution.

Fiok, K., Farahani, F. V., Karwowski, W., & Ahram, T. (2022). Explainable artificial intelligence for education and training. *The Journal of Defense Modeling and Simulation*, *19*(2), 133–144. DOI: 10.1177/15485129211028651

Folmer, E., Ronzhin, S., Van Hillegersberg, J., Beek, W., & Lemmens, R. (2020). Business rationale for linked data at governments: A case study at the Netherlands' Kadaster data platform. *IEEE Access : Practical Innovations, Open Solutions*, *8*, 70822–70835. DOI: 10.1109/ACCESS.2020.2984691

Frempong, D., Akinboboye, O., Okoli, I., Afrihyia, E., Umar, M. O., Umana, A. U., Appoh, M., & Omolayo, O. (2022). Real-time analytics dashboards for decision-making using Tableau in public sector and business intelligence applications. *Journal of Frontiers in Multidisciplinary Research, 3*(2), 65–80. DOI: 10.54660/.IJFMR.2022.3.2.65-80

Goldschmidt, K. (2017). The fourth industrial revolution and human capital development. *Unpublished master's thesis, Rhodes University, Grahamstown, South Africa.*

Grinin, L., & Grinin, A. L. (2016). *The cybernetic revolution and the forthcoming epoch of self-regulating systems*. ООО" Издательство" Учитель".

Gupta, B. B., & Quamara, M. (2020). An overview of Internet of Things (IoT): Architectural aspects, challenges, and protocols. *Concurrency and Computation, 32*(21), e4946. DOI: 10.1002/cpe.4946

Hamad, B. M., & Jawad, M. K. (2024). The Fourth Industrial Revolution: A Historical and Conceptual Review. *Journal of Economics and Administrative Sciences, 30*(141), 154–172. DOI: 10.33095/gh3a7g38

Han, A., Isaacson, A., & Muennig, P. (2020). The promise of big data for precision population health management in the US. *Public Health, 185*, 110–116. DOI: 10.1016/j.puhe.2020.04.040 PMID: 32615477

Hu, Z. (2014). *Self-configuration, monitoring and control of physical entities via sensor and actuator networks* (Doctoral dissertation, Université Claude Bernard-Lyon I).

Jouppi, N., Kurian, G., Li, S., Ma, P., Nagarajan, R., Nai, L., & Patterson, D. A. (2023, June). Tpu v4: An optically reconfigurable supercomputer for machine learning with hardware support for embeddings. In *Proceedings of the 50th annual international symposium on computer architecture* (pp. 1-14). DOI: 10.1145/3579371.3589350

Kang, H. G., Moon, A., & Jeon, S. (2024). Examining the Generative Artificial Intelligence Landscape: Current Status and Policy Strategies. *Asia pacific journal of information systems, 34*(1), 150-190.

Kumar, A., & Metta, D. S. (2024). AI-driven precision oncology: Predictive biomarker discovery and personalized treatment optimization using genomic data. *Int J Adv Res Publ Rev, 1*(3), 21–38. DOI: 10.55248/gengpi.5.0224.0421

López, O. L., Rosabal, O. M., Ruiz-Guirola, D. E., Raghuwanshi, P., Mikhaylov, K., Lovén, L., & Iyer, S. (2023). Energy-sustainable IoT connectivity: Vision, technological enablers, challenges, and future directions. *IEEE Open Journal of the Communications Society, 4*, 2609–2666. DOI: 10.1109/OJCOMS.2023.3323832

Madine, M., Salah, K., Jayaraman, R., Battah, A., Hasan, H., & Yaqoob, I. (2022). Blockchain and NFTs for time-bound access and monetization of private data. *IEEE Access : Practical Innovations, Open Solutions, 10*, 94186–94202. DOI: 10.1109/ACCESS.2022.3204274

Malik, S. I., Tawafak, R. M., Alfarsi, G., Ashfaque, M. W., & Mathew, R. (2021). A model for enhancing algorithmic thinking in programming education using PAAM. *International Journal of Interactive Mobile Technologies, 15*(9), 37. DOI: 10.3991/ijim.v15i09.20617

Mhlanga, D. (2023). Exploring the evolution of artificial intelligence and the fourth industrial revolution an overview. *FinTech and Artificial Intelligence for Sustainable Development: The Role of Smart Technologies in Achieving Development Goals*, 15-39.

Miller, A. (2019). Permissioned and permissionless blockchains. *Blockchain for distributed systems security*, 193-204.

Mohamed, K. S. (2019). IoT physical layer: Sensors, actuators, controllers and programming. In *The Era of Internet of Things: Towards a Smart World* (pp. 21–47). Springer International Publishing. DOI: 10.1007/978-3-030-18133-8_2

Mohanarajesh, K. (2024). Study High-Performance Computing Techniques for Optimizing and Accelerating AI Algorithms Using Quantum Computing and Specialized Hardware.

Mourtzis, D. (2021). Towards the 5th industrial revolution: A literature review and a framework for process optimization based on big data analytics and semantics. *Journal of Machine Engineering, 21*(3), 5–39. DOI: 10.36897/jme/141834

Mthombeni, Z. M. (2024). A quantitative analysis of public attitudes towards the fourth industrial revolution: An integrated technology adoption model in South Africa. *Doctoral dissertation*.

Oke, J. A., Karimzadeh, S., Oviroh, P. O., Ukoba, K., Imoisili, P. E., & Jen, T. C. (2025). *Smart Materials and Energy in the Fourth Industrial Revolution*. CRC Press. DOI: 10.1201/9781003604488

Olayinka, O. H.Olalekan Hamed Olayinka. (2021). Big data integration and real-time analytics for enhancing operational efficiency and market responsiveness. *Int J Sci Res Arch, 4*(1), 280–296. DOI: 10.30574/ijsra.2021.4.1.0179

Pavunraj, D., Kumar, A. M., & Anbumaheshwari, K. (2025). AI in personalized treatment planning. In *AI insights on nuclear medicine* (pp. 117–142). IGI Global Scientific Publishing. DOI: 10.4018/979-8-3373-1275-0.ch006

Putzier, M. L. (2017). *The readiness of the South African private and public sector for the fourth industrial revolution*. Nelson Mandela University.

Qian, K., Zhang, Z., Yamamoto, Y., & Schuller, B. W. (2021). Artificial intelligence internet of things for the elderly: From assisted living to health-care monitoring. *IEEE Signal Processing Magazine*, *38*(4), 78–88. DOI: 10.1109/MSP.2021.3057298

Rose, G. (Ed.). (2016). *The fourth industrial revolution: A Davos reader*. Foreign Affairs.

Sahai, A. K., & Rath, N. (2021). Artificial intelligence and the 4th industrial revolution. In *Artificial intelligence and machine learning in business management* (pp. 127–143). CRC Press. DOI: 10.1201/9781003125129-8

Santos, L., Cunha, B., Fé, I., Vieira, M., & Silva, F. A. (2021). Data processing on edge and cloud: A performability evaluation and sensitivity analysis. *Journal of Network and Systems Management*, *29*(3), 27. DOI: 10.1007/s10922-021-09592-x

Shalwani, M. (2021). *Insights into The Topic of The Fourth Industrial Revolution* (Doctoral dissertation, Khalifa University).

Skilton, M., & Hovsepian, F. (2018). *The 4th industrial revolution*. Springer Nature. DOI: 10.1007/978-3-319-62479-2

Slama, D., Puhlmann, F., Morrish, J., & Bhatnagar, R. M. (2015). *Enterprise IoT: Strategies and Best practices for connected products and services*. O'Reilly Media, Inc.

Tamimi, N. A., & Ellis, P. (2009). Drug development: From concept to marketing! *Nephron. Clinical Practice*, *113*(3), c125–c131. DOI: 10.1159/000232592 PMID: 19729922

Tiwari, S. P. (2022). Re-emergence of Asia in the New Industrial Era. *Technium Soc. Sci. J.*, *29*, 471–480. DOI: 10.47577/tssj.v29i1.6103

Truong, Y., & Papagiannidis, S. (2022). Artificial intelligence as an enabler for innovation: A review and future research agenda. [Jouppi, N., Kurian]. *Technological Forecasting and Social Change*, *183*, 121852. DOI: 10.1016/j.techfore.2022.121852

Truong, Y., Schneckenberg, D., Battisti, M., & Jabbouri, R. (2023). Guest editorial: Artificial intelligence as an enabler for entrepreneurs: an integrative perspective and future research directions. *International Journal of Entrepreneurial Behaviour & Research*, *29*(4), 801–815. DOI: 10.1108/IJEBR-04-2023-033

Upadhyaya, N. (2024). Artificial intelligence in web development: Enhancing automation, personalization, and decision-making. *Artificial Intelligence*, *4*(1), 534–540.

Vermesan, O., & Bacquet, J. (Eds.). (2022). *Cognitive hyperconnected digital transformation: Internet of things intelligence evolution*. CRC Press. DOI: 10.1201/9781003337584

Voronkova, V., Vasyl'chuk, G., Nikitenko, V., Kaganov, Y., & Metelenko, N. (2023). Transformation of digital education in the era of the fourth industrial revolution and globalization.

Wah, J. N. K. (2025). Revolutionizing surgery: AI and robotics for precision, risk reduction, and innovation. *Journal of Robotic Surgery*, *19*(1), 47. DOI: 10.1007/s11701-024-02205-0 PMID: 39776281

Wang, L., Ma, Y., Yan, J., Chang, V., & Zomaya, A. Y. (2018). pipsCloud: High performance cloud computing for remote sensing big data management and processing. *Future Generation Computer Systems*, *78*, 353–368. DOI: 10.1016/j.future.2016.06.009

Weingärtner, T. (2019, November). Tokenization of physical assets and the impact of IoT and AI. In *European Union Blockchain Observatory and Forum* (Vol. 10, pp. 1-16).

Wu, C. J., Raghavendra, R., Gupta, U., Acun, B., Ardalani, N., Maeng, K., ... & Hazelwood, K. (2022). Sustainable ai: Environmental implications, challenges and opportunities. Proceedings of machine learning and systems, 4, 795-813.

Yu, Y., & Jiang, Y. (2024). *Understanding the Digital Revolution and Its Influences*. Springer. DOI: 10.1007/978-981-97-4939-3

Chapter 2

# Digital Transformation and Entrepreneurship in the Digital Economy:
## Platform Innovation, Sustainability, and Entrepreneurial Leadership

**D. Indhumathi**
http://orcid.org/0009-0000-1720-3996
*SASTRA (Deemed to be) University, SRC, Kumbakonam, India*

**Hariharan Muruganantham**
http://orcid.org/0009-0000-3953-3582
*SASTRA (Deemed to be) University, SRC, Kumbakonam, India*

## ABSTRACT

*The digital world is significantly reshaping entrepreneurship by introducing innovation and competition across industries. This transformation involves utilizing technologies such as artificial intelligence, cloud computing, and data analytics, posing both opportunities and challenges for entrepreneurs. The chapter explores how digital tools influence entrepreneur behavior, strategy, leadership, and business models, using case studies of startups like Airbnb, Uber, and Tesla. It emphasizes the faster recognition of opportunities and the shift towards experience-centric value generation. Additionally, the chapter discusses future skills, platform-based business models, sustainability, and essential startup tips. It concludes that suc-*

DOI: 10.4018/979-8-2600-3179-7.ch002

*cessful entrepreneurship will hinge on blending human creativity with technological intelligence while fostering inclusive, sustainable digital ecosystems to empower entrepreneurs with profitable ventures..*

## 1. INTRODUCTION

Digital technologies have revolutionized the entrepreneurial landscape by creating new opportunities and opportunities for innovation. Technologies like Artificial Intelligence (AI), cloud computing, blockchain, big data analytics, the Internet of Things (IoT), and digital platforms (Schumpeter, 1942; Drucker, 1985; Teece, 2007) have become a growing concern for entrepreneurship, which has traditionally been linked to innovation, opportunity recognition, risk-taking, and value creation. These technologies are not just enabling business functions but are a key enabler for business transformation, changing the way businesses are born, run and scaled.

Digital transformation is defined as the use of digital technologies to create changes in the processes, business models and customer relations of organizations that significantly impact the way in which they create value and are a source of their competitive advantage (Vial, 2019; Verhoef et al., 2021). Digital transformation in entrepreneurship is not just about technology adoption, but also involves shifts in entrepreneurial behavior, strategic decision-making, leadership patterns, and involvement in digital ecosystems. Today, the reliance on digital infrastructures and data-driven innovation is growing as entrepreneurs are looking for ways to find opportunities, make operational decision making more efficient, interact with customers, and act swiftly on ever-changing market demands.

Digital entrepreneurship has revolutionized the traditional ways of doing business and markets. Start-ups like Airbnb, Uber, Amazon, and Tesla show the power of digital platforms and data-based systems to reinvent or revolutionize industries and to expand rapidly throughout the world. Digital enterprises are fundamentally different from businesses that rely on physical inventory and local operations, and they are able to scale efficiently through the network effects, platform ecosystems and real-time analytics (Parker, Van Alstyne, & Choudary, 2016; de Reuver, Sørensen, & Basole, 2018). The entrepreneurial success is now highly reliant on digital literacy, technological adaptability, and innovation combined with data decision making.

At the same time, digital transformation has opened the doors to more opportunities for sustainability and inclusive entrepreneurship. The use of technologies, including the Internet of Things, blockchain, and predictive analytics, can help in the implementation of environmentally sustainable practices by enhancing resource management and minimizing waste, while providing greater transparency in supply chains (Bican & Brem, 2020). Meanwhile, digital platforms, mobile technologies, and digital payment systems open up new opportunities for women entrepreneurs, rural businesses, and disadvantaged groups, and they remove obstacles by facilitating access to markets, financial services, and entrepreneurial circles.

India, as an emerging economy, is a clear example of the relevance and significance of digital entrepreneurship. Digital entrepreneurial ecosystems have grown in leaps and bounds with the penetration of internet, cheap mobile devices and Government initiatives like Digital India and Unified Payments Interface (UPI). The examples of Zomato, Paytm, Byju's and Zerodha are some of the Indian startups that demonstrate how digital technologies are enabling scalable and innovative business models across various sectors like finance, education, logistics and e-commerce.

However, digital transformation comes with its own set of challenges. Issues that entrepreneurs encounter include issues of cybersecurity, data privacy, algorithmic bias, the digital inequality, and reliance on dominant digital platforms. Over-dependence on third parties could decrease the autonomy of entrepreneurs and make their business vulnerable to unpredictable regulatory and algorithmic changes imposed by third-party platforms. Moreover, unequal access to digital infrastructure and technological literacy persist and are inhibiting participation in digital entrepreneurship, especially in rural and underserved areas.

In the digital transition of entrepreneurial contexts, leadership and resilience are thus becoming more and more important. Businesses need to cope with the fast pace of technological advancement, fluctuating customer needs and market volatility. Companies that had more digital capabilities were generally more resilient and better able to keep their operations going in times of disruption, as was seen during the COVID-19 pandemic.

While the literature addresses digital business models, innovation ecosystem or sustainability, many studies pay attention to one of the dimensions of digital entrepreneurship but not to the integrated understanding of the multiple impacts of digital transformation on the behavior, leadership, inclusiveness and innovation of entrepreneurs. Further, not much has been said about emerging economies like India. Thus, a wider conceptual knowledge regarding digital entrepreneurship and its consequences is needed.

This chapter seeks to fill this gap by analysing the digital transformation of entrepreneurship in terms of opportunities, business model innovation, sustainability, platform interaction, and entrepreneurial leadership. The chapter takes a qualitative conceptual approach using a systematic review of literature, with examples drawn from the world and India's digital enterprises.

The chapter has been divided into nine sections. The theoretical frameworks, study methodology, digital transformation and entrepreneurial change, platform ecosystems, sustainability, leadership, implications, study limitations and future directions are discussed in the introduction followed by the major findings of the study.

# 2. LITERATURE REVIEW AND THEORETICAL FOUNDATION

## 2.1 Entrepreneurship Theory and Digital Transformation

Entrepreneurship, as an integral part of economic development, innovation and competitiveness has been known for long. The classical theories of entrepreneurship focus on the role of the entrepreneur in detecting opportunities, bringing innovations to market, and managing uncertainty and resources. For Schumpeter (1942), entrepreneurship was a phenomenon of "creative destruction", in which entrepreneurs take advantage of innovation and technological change to upset the market structure. From this point of view, entrepreneurship is one of the many ways to bring about economic development by bringing innovative and efficient products, processes and business models to the market in place of the old. Schumpeter's framework is still very relevant today — digital technologies are still transforming industries and redefining competitive environments.

Entrepreneurship theory emphasizes innovation and the importance of recognizing opportunities and being able to adapt strategically. Drucker (1985) stated that entrepreneurs are searching systematically for change and that they are exploiting new opportunities that arise from the technology, economic and social changes. Likewise, Leibenstein (1979) has underscored the entrepreneur's ability to respond to market inefficiencies and gaps and pointed out that the entrepreneur is successful when he or she can recognize unexploited resources and unmet customer demands. These theoretical principles are more and more important in digital environments since the transformation of technology constantly generates new demands, market structures and customer behavior.

The dynamic capabilities framework also plays a role in the understanding of entrepreneurship in digitally transforming economies. Teece (2007) gave a definition of dynamic capabilities as the capacity of the organization to adapt to opportunities, to adapt them in an effective way, and to reconfigure resources continuously to meet changing environments. This is exactly what digital entrepreneurs need as they need to adjust quickly to technological disruption, changing customer expectations and fierce competition. To compete in digital ecosystems, businesses must have flexible organizations, fast cycles of innovation, and processes of strategic decision making that rely on data.

Digital transformation is an extension of traditional theories on entrepreneurship, incorporating technological infrastructures and digital ecosystems as the core elements of entrepreneurship. According to Vial (2019), digital transformation is a process by which the organizations use digital technologies to improve their operations, generate value, and strengthen their strategic capabilities. Likewise, Verhoef et al. (2021) stress on the reconfiguration of the organization, the innovation of the business model, and the integration of customers' technology, rather than just new technology. These interpretations illustrate how fundamentally digital transformation is changing entrepreneurial processes and entrepreneur's strategic behavior.

Digital technologies have also reshaped the speed and scale of entrepreneurship. The digital enterprise can scale quickly by leveraging platform-based ecosystems, cloud computing, and digital connectivity throughout the world, unlike traditional businesses which typically need an extensive physical infrastructure and localized operations. Today, entrepreneurs have access to digital tools and online platforms that enable them to connect with international markets, automate processes and integrate real-time customer data. As a result, entrepreneurship is becoming more and more data-driven, networked and ecosystem reliant.

## 2.2 Digital Entrepreneurship

Digital entrepreneurship is the cross of entrepreneurship and digital technology. It is about entrepreneurship that is deeply embedded in the use of digital infrastructure, online platforms, data analytics and technological innovation in the recognition of opportunities, creation of business and delivery of value, and growth of the organization (Nambisan, 2017). Digital entrepreneurship is not the same as traditional entrepreneurship, as digital technologies are not only used to support business operations, but they also constitute the core of the business model.

Digital entrepreneurship has been supported by technological advancements like cloud computing, artificial intelligence, blockchain, mobile internet, social media, and digital payment solutions. These technologies help to lower the costs of operations, expand scale, enhance market reach, and allow entrepreneurs to directly connect with customers and stakeholders. Digital tools are becoming more and more important for the creation of platform-based business models, delivery of digital services, automated processes and the customization of customer experiences for entrepreneurs.

According to Nambisan (2017), digital entrepreneurship has lower barriers to entry, quicker experiments and constant innovation. Digital tools allow startups to quickly prototype concepts, gather customer feedback on the fly, and quickly adjust products and services. It therefore enables new business models characterized by agility of business practice and the iterative development of innovations which are fundamentally different from the linear business development models.

The importance of digital ecosystems is also highlighted in the research on digital entrepreneurship. In order to account for the relationships of entrepreneurs with technological infrastructures, digital institutions, online communities and platform networks, Sussan and Acs (2017) introduced the concept of the digital entrepreneurial ecosystem. Entrepreneurial success is now more and more reliant on the capacity to make use of networks, entry to digital sources and navigate effective within interconnected technological environments in these ecosystems.

Platform-based business models have also helped to drive the development of digital entrepreneurship. Platform-based infrastructures that connect producers, consumers, service providers, and other actors can be used to build a scalable digital venture; as seen with companies like Airbnb, Uber, Amazon, and Alibaba. Platforms create network effects: the more users that join the more value will be added to the platform (Parker, Van Alstyne & Choudary, 2016). This is what makes digital enterprises so scalable and castles small in the need for traditional physical assets.

Meanwhile, digital entrepreneurship comes with new challenges in terms of strategy and operation. The algorithms, data ownership policies and technological infrastructures of dominant businesses in digital ecosystems are often essential for entrepreneurs working with them. According to Nambisan and Baron (2021), the nature of dependency on the platform governance structures can result in role conflict, performance pressure and less strategic autonomy for the entrepreneurs involved in the digital ecosystem. Thus, digital entrepreneurship has its opportunities and constraints, which affect entrepreneurial decision-making and sustainability.

## 2.3 Platform Ecosystems and Business Model Innovation

Platform ecosystems are at the heart of digital entrepreneurship and modern business innovation. A digital platform can be seen as a technology platform that enables interactions between various groups of users, such as consumers, producers, service providers and advertisers (de Reuver, Sørensen, & Basole, 2018). Platform-based entrepreneurship enables firms to create value by facilitating exchanges, interactions, and network participation rather than solely producing physical goods or services.

The platform economy has revolutionized the way business is done. Typical value chain of a conventional business is a linear chain from the producers to the consumers. Platform businesses, on the other hand, are those that establish multi-sided markets, where users both create and consume value. According to Parker, Van Alstyne, and Choudary 2016, platform ecosystems thrive on network effects, digital connectivity, and flows of data to grow fast and gain competitive edge.

The business model innovation has thus become one of the important characteristics of digital entrepreneurship. According to Osterwalder and Pigneur (2010), business models are systems that should detail how organisations generate, communicate and collect value. In digital spaces, entrepreneurs continue to build business models that have become more flexible, scalable, and data-centric, with an emphasis on the customer experience, subscriptions, joining the digital ecosystem, and digital interactions. Engagement, personalisation, data monetisation, and collaborative innovation are key elements of digital business models.

Digital transformation is also helping businesses to experiment and pursue agility in business model development. Real-time analytics and digital feedback systems allow entrepreneurs to constantly experiment with pricing strategies, marketing methods, operational structures, and customer engagement techniques. The ability to adjust quickly to market dynamics and customer preferences is a key advantage of this versatility.

Platform ecosystems also are fraught with risks and limitations, though. Third party platforms can create a reliance on algorithms, ranking systems, commission rates, and data policies for third party entrepreneurs. However, according to Lehdonvirta (2025), over-dependence on platforms may limit the autonomy of entrepreneurs and make them more susceptible to changes in regulations or algorithms. Unexpected changes in platform policies can result in loss of visibility or market access for businesses. As a result, entrepreneurs are increasingly looking for hybrid approaches where they are involved in platforms but have their own digital channels as well.

Another crucial element of platform ecosystems is data governance. The digital landscape has transformed how businesses operate, making data a key differentiator in shaping customer insights, behavioral analytics, and algorithmic recommendations, which are vital to competitive positioning and business performance. This means that entrepreneurs must have skills in data management, cybersecurity, digital ethics, and compliance with regulations.

## 2.4 Sustainability and Inclusive Entrepreneurship

Sustainability and inclusivity are emerging new facets of digital entrepreneurship. To get a clear picture of contemporary entrepreneurship it is not enough to consider only profitability or expansion of the market; social responsibility, environmental sustainability and equity in development are equally considered. These wider entrepreneurs' goals are supported by digital technologies to a great degree.

Sustainable entrepreneurship is a concept that defines an entrepreneurial activity that is beneficial to the economy, to the environment, and to society. Digital technologies can facilitate sustainable entrepreneurship by increasing operational efficiency, waste reduction, optimisation of the use of resources and transparency in supply chains. Through the use of technologies such as IoT, blockchain, cloud computing and predictive analytics, companies can track and control energy use, minimize carbon footprints, optimize logistics, and practice circular economy (Bican & Brem, 2020).

Green innovation is also enabled through digital transformation. Digital technologies can enable entrepreneurs to create environmentally friendly products and services, to enhance remote collaboration, to cut down on paper processes and to optimise transportation systems. In sustainable sourcing and supply-chain management, blockchain technologies also provide additional traceability and accountability. The world is increasingly aware of the importance of addressing environmental issues, and it is seen as a strategic imperative and competitive advantage to consider sustainable digital entrepreneurship.

Besides sustainability, inclusiveness is one of the significant topics of the research in digital entrepreneurship. Digital technologies lower the costs associated with entrepreneurship in terms of access to information, markets, financial systems, and communication networks. Woman entrepreneurs, rural businesses and marginalized groups can access digital platforms and mobile technologies to engage in economic activities and innovation systems more actively.

Inclusion of mobile Internet and digital payment systems has been particularly strengthened by emerging economies. Digital marketplaces are a great opportunity to help small business expand its reach without having to invest in an extensive branch network. Likewise, social commerce and mobile-based entrepreneurialism foster entrepreneurial self-employment, micro-entrepreneurship and community-driven innovation.

But the level of digital inclusion is still not homogeneous in different regions and social groups. Even today, the digital divide remains a barrier to entrepreneurial involvement in many rural or under-served communities because of the lack of adequate Internet access, digital literacy and technological infrastructure. OECD (2021) underlines that access to digital is not equal and that if digital transformation strategies are not supported by inclusive policies and investments, these inequalities will be exacerbated.

Issues of ethics also come into play in the context of sustainable and inclusive entrepreneurship in the digital era. Artificial Intelligence, automation and big data analytics can create privacy, surveillance, algorithmic bias and job displacement issues. For entrepreneurs, this means becoming responsible innovators who must navigate the competing demands of innovation and ethical responsibility, transparency, and stakeholder welfare.

The literature shows that digital entrepreneurship is a multi-faceted phenomenon with technological innovation, business model transformation, ecosystem participation, sustainability and social inclusion. The theoretical ideas outlined in this section offer a conceptual framework for interpreting the impact of digital transformation on entrepreneurial actions, strategies and economic ecosystems in the current society.

## 3. RESEARCH METHODOLOGY

### 3.1 Research Design

The chapter is conceptual and takes a qualitative research approach using a systematic review and thematic synthesis of literature regarding digital entrepreneurship, digital transformation, platform ecosystems, sustainability and inclusive innovation. The methodology is not designed to test hypotheses but rather to synthesis knowledge in an empirical analysis to develop a coherent conceptual analysis of the impact of digital transformation on entrepreneurship.

The systematic review approach was chosen due to the uniqueness of the field, the digital entrepreneurship, being fast moving and interdisciplinary. Current studies are spread throughout the realm of entrepreneurship research, innovation management, information systems, sustainability research and the digital business literature. Thus, a systematic review allows the convergence of the scattered knowledge and the emergence of paradigms, theories and trends.

A set of illustrative business examples of digital enterprises from around the globe and in India have also been included in the chapter to give a context to the conceptual discussions. These examples are not chosen as cases studies that are treated as case studies in and of themselves, but are selected to illustrate how the theoretical themes manifest in "real-world" entrepreneurial contexts.

### 3.2 Literature Review Process

We have used a systematic method in the literature review process in order to be transparent, consistent and relevant with regard to the papers. A selection of academic research studies was in the main considered, as they cover a period of time that was characterized by a dramatic acceleration of digital transformation, platform economies, the use of artificial intelligence, and digitally enabled entrepreneurship(2015-2025). Prior to this time; several theories on entrepreneurship and classical Entrepreneurship works were included as foundations of theoretical understanding.

The review procedure comprised four stages – identification, screening, eligibility and thematic synthesis.

The sources used in the identification phase were major academic databases and publishers such as Scopus, Web of Science, Google Scholar, ScienceDirect, Springer, Emerald, Wiley and Taylor & Francis. The COEs and policy reports from organisations like OECD, UNCTAD, the World Bank and the European Commission were also incorporated to provide overviews of the ecosystem and policies.

The keywords used in the search process included: "digital entrepreneurship" and "digital transformation." The most common users' key words were:

- Digital entrepreneurship
- Digital transformation
- Platform economy
- Platform ecosystems

Development of artificial intelligence and entrepreneurship.

- Business model innovation
- Sustainable entrepreneurship
- Inclusive innovation
- Entrepreneurial resilience
- Digital leadership
- Digital ecosystems
- Entrepreneurship and AI
- Digital business models
- Entrepreneurial ecosystems

Interest in using a wider number of technology relevant keywords rather than using only artificial intelligence was crucial to ensure that the research did not focus solely on a technological aspect. Hence, research related to cloud computing, blockchain, IoT, big data analytics, digital platform, and mobile technologies were also taken into account.

## 3.4 Scoring Systems

The inclusion and exclusion criteria were formulated to match the literature that was reviewed, in order to make the literature of good quality and of relevance.

### Inclusion Criteria

The review included:

- Peer-reviewed journal articles
- Recent books and edited volumes containing scholarly articles and edited conference proceedings.
- Reputable conference proceedings
- The use of institutional and policy reports.

- English-language publications
- Advances in the direct fields of entrepreneurship and digital transformation.
- Direct contributions in these fields of science such as entrepreneurship and digital transformation.
- Research on digital business models, digital innovation, sustainability, inclusivity or entrepreneurial digital ecosystems.

### Exclusion Criteria

The review excluded:

- For any non-academic blogs and opinion articles, email the visitor editor at visitors.
- Writing research papers that do not have an entrepreneurial component.
- Technical Engineering papers of a very technical nature which may have no relevance for entrepreneurship
- Duplicate publications
- Articles that are either conceptually or analytically unproductive with regard to the study of digital entrepreneurship being published in.

During the process of researching for the database, an initial set of some 320 publications was identified. Following screening of abstracts for relevance and cleaning of the duplicates, 148 publications remained and were suitable for in-depth review. In full-text analysis and thematic assessment, 85 proper studies were selected by filtering the most relevant to counsel, namely those whose content was very relevant. After the full text analysis and thematic evaluation, about 85 studies were selected for conceptual synthesis and discussion because of their significant content.

## 3.4 Thematic Analysis

The thematic synthesis of literature and the elucidation of the same conceptual patterns was performed by a manual thematic analysis approach. Thematic analysis was chosen since it can be used to analyse large data volumes, present in a qualitative nature, into coherent themes of analysis.

The analysis was done in a staged manner. To identify the concepts repeated and the new ones of digital entrepreneurship, first open coding was performed. These first codes focused on themes like opportunity recognition, digital business models, platform dependency, sustainability, leadership adaptability, innovation ecosystems, resilience and digital inclusion.

Second, a process of axial coding that brought together related concepts as larger thematic categories was used. In the process several thematic and strong points arose:

- Digital transformations and entrepreneurial actions,
- Content partner and innovation in business models on platform ecosystems
- Sustainability entrepreneurship and inclusive entrepreneurship
- The ability to exhibit entrepreneurial leadership and resilience
- Ethical and regulatory issues
- Future entrepreneurial competencies

The coding and theming process was undertaken by hand enabling flexibility of interpretation and inter-conceptualization across interdisciplinary studies. The manual coding process allowed for a more in-depth comparison of the personal experiences drawn from the literature and theory on entrepreneurship, information systems and sustainability.

## 3.5 Use of illustrative business examples for integration

The chapter includes examples of digital businesses from not only around the world, but also from India to reinforce the understanding of the context. The purposive selection of examples like Airbnb, Uber, Amazon, Zerodha, Byju's, Paytm, Tesla, and Zomato included different segments, industry paradigms, businesses, and entrepreneurial ecosystems.

The chosen examples showcase the impact of digital transformation on opportunity recognition, platform engagement, scaling the operations, customer engagement, and sustainable innovation. Importantly, these examples are no empirical studies based on primary data that would have been gathered. Others are instead used analytically to facilitate conceptual arguments that come from the literature review.

It had the added advantage of Indian examples as India is one of the fastest expanding digital entrepreneurial ecosystems in the world. To boost digital entrepreneurship in India, the government has launched several initiatives including Digital India, development of digital payment system, low-cost Internet and increasing investments from startups in the overall digital business ecosystem. Thus, some of the fundamental characteristics of digital entrepreneurship are important to understand in the Indian context to draw out certain inferences about digital entrepreneurship in the emerging markets of the rest of the world.

## 3.6 Methodological Contribution and Limitations

The methodological approach will help the chapter in many ways. Thanks to its multidisciplinary approach by the synthesis of entrepreneurship theory, digital transformation research, sustainability research, and platform ecosystem literature, this book offers a first-of-its-kind understanding of entrepreneurship in the contemporary era. Second, the thematic synthesis method helps the synthesis of fragmented knowledge from various disciplines into a logical conceptual framework.

The methodology also facilitates a theoretical integration with technological transformation and entrepreneurial behavior, leadership, sustainability, inclusivity and resilience. The integration is especially relevant in the context of digital entrepreneurship due to the increasing influence and interaction between technological, social, economic and institutional aspects.

There are some drawbacks, however. It is conceptual and not much based on empirical written field investigation, but mostly on secondary literature. As such, the results are not statistically generalizable. Furthermore, all digital technologies are dynamic and innovative and there might have been technological advances and business models that can keep shifting beyond the scope of time period that is covered in this chapter.

Nevertheless, the methodology offers a robust conceptual starting point for grasping the implications of digital transformation on the entrepreneurial processes, business models and innovation landscapes.

# 4. ENTREPRENEURIAL CHANGE AND DIGITAL TRANSFORMATION

## 4.1 Opportunity Recognition in the Digital Economy

Digital transformation fundamentally has shaped the way entrepreneurs discover and analyse business opportunities. The search for traditional business opportunities relied on market observations, experience, and personal contacts that occurred locally. However, digital entrepreneurship increasingly involves real time data, online interactions, predictive analytics and digital platforms in capturing new trends and new customer needs.

Entrepreneurs can harness large amounts of data from customers and the market through artificial intelligence, social media tracking, cloud-based computing systems and big data technologies and have them analysed in a timely manner. Digital tools allow entrepreneurs to track consumer activity, create ground-up purchasing patterns, and evaluate their competitors' strategies, as well as forecast alterations in market demand. This data-driven approach improves entrepreneurial decision making and helps to minimise uncertainty when evaluating an opportunity.

Entrepreneurs can also mount experiments quickly with digital technologies. They can rapidly put together minimum viable products, send the products to end-users via the internet, and make ongoing changes to products and services that incorporate actual feedback. This cycle enables enterprises to continuously innovate and adapt to evolving consumer needs promptly.

Platform ecosystems also help in recognition of entrepreneurial opportunities. When it comes to providers of customer base as well as digital infrastructures, digital marketplaces like Amazon, Shopify, Airbnb and app-based ecosystems opened up a whole new world for entrepreneurs in no time at all. Entrepreneurs can thus find niche markets more efficiently and scale up innovations more efficiently in the traditional business setting.

Digital entrepreneurship has also made it feasible for micro entrepreneurs and small business entities to take part in a wider range of economic activities. Internet and social networking, digital payment and e-commerce have created an environment where people and startups can be entrepreneurs with minimal initial capital investment. As a consequence, digital transformation increases the participation and, above all, the democratization of innovation participation from entrepreneurs.

But there are challenges in opportunity recognition in digital environments, too. Rapid speed of technology changing drives competition and shorter innovation cycle. To stay competitive in today's digital world, entrepreneurs have to be always on the case and aware of the various digital trends, technological disruptions and consumer behavior change. Hence, it is becoming more and more important to be flexible, techno literate, and open to learning opportunities.

## 4.2 Digital Business Model Innovation

Entrepreneurial business models have dramatically changed due to digital transformation. Old business models were always asset and product intensive, linear, and for a geographically limited range. Digital business models, by contrast, focus on platform engagement, embedding into ecosystems, customer experiences and creating value from data.

Business model innovation is the act of reframing how value is created, delivered and captured through the process of innovation by entrepreneurs. Digital technologies enable the creation of flexible and scalable business frameworks which can respond quickly to market shifts and transformations. Indeed, in digitally transformed entrepreneurial contexts, there are any number of cloudification-based design patterns that are gaining currency, such as subscription models, sharing economy platforms, digital marketplaces, freemium services or on-demand business models.

One of the most important evolutions in Digital Entrepreneurship is the Platform-based model. Digital platforms, like Airbnb and Uber, provide value because they enable user interactions without hosting ownership or management instead. Network effects play a crucial role for these platform ecosystems, as the value and reach of the ecosystem grows with the number of participants.

In addition, Digital business model innovations allow entrepreneurs to customize user experiences. Insights provided by AI tools, such as analytics, recommendation systems, and customer data platforms, enable companies to tailor products and services to meet their customers' preferences and leverage marketing strategies for enhanced effects. Personalization also increases customer engagement, customer satisfaction, and competitive position.

In addition, a fundamental quality of digital business models is its functional scalable. Cloud Computing and Digital infrastructures save business in many ways when compared to a traditional business and lower operation costs. However, entrepreneurs can rapidly grow and expand to international markets without significant infrastructure investments.

Concurrently, digital business model innovation brings in strategic risks. Entrepreneurs can get tied up in external digital platforms, algorithms, and technological infrastructures. Business in the platform can be greatly affected by platform governance policies, data ownership policies, and ranking algorithms. This has led to online platforms being increasingly used in conjunction with building brands and developing proprietary web channels.

## 4.3 Operational agility & Entrepreneurial efficiency

Digital changes have helped entrepreneurs to become more efficient in operating their businesses, more connected with each other and more coordinated in real time. Cloud platforms, AI driven automation, enterprise resource planning, and digital collaboration solutions make transactional tasks easier to do and make administration more efficient.

These days repetitive tasks for inventory management, customer services, accounting, logistics and marketing can all be automated. Precision, lowered operational expenses, and the ability to devote more effort to strategic initiatives like market extension and innovation are the key advantages of automation.

The use of cloud-based technologies also enhances operational agility, facilitating remote work, digital collaboration, and decentralized business operations. This allows entrepreneurs and workers to organize affairs both geographically and access common digital resources and communication systems in real time. However, Digital operational agility became more crucial during the COVID-19 pandemic as many businesses had to make a quick transition to online service delivery and remote operations.

The digital transformation also makes data-driven decision making easier. A growing number of entrepreneurs are deploying dashboards, analytical tools, and predictive systems to track business performance, assess customer engagement and pinpoint inefficiencies in business operations. This analytical function aids in making strategic plans and increases the responsiveness of the organization.

While these benefits are there, there are also cybersecurity concerns and technological vulnerabilities as a result of the operational digitalization.

## 4.4 Value Co-Creation and Customer-Centric Entrepreneurship

Unlike product-centric approaches, digital transformation has brought a new way of creating value for the entrepreneur – a customer-centric, and experience-oriented one. In the traditional business setting, companies have mainly created value within the company and offered products or services to consumers in linear processes. However, in the online world, consumers are increasingly active in the value creation process through online interaction, feed-back support systems, review, social media interaction and participation in platforms.

Breaking the cycle of customer and stakeholder interactions is possible with the use of digital technologies. Social media, online communities and digital feedback mechanisms enable a two-way dialogue between businesses and customers, enabling companies to gain insights into customer preferences and develop creative solutions.

Custom data is a strategic value in the value co-creation. Data can be used by entrepreneurs to study customer behavior, preferences, and engagement patterns, which can then be leveraged to make informed decisions about how to enhance products, services, and user experience. These algorithms can boost customer satisfaction and foster long-term customer loyalty by delivering personalized marketing campaigns and customer service systems.

This form of entrepreneurship, heavily grounded in experience is especially significant in platform-based economy. Customers are now not just considering businesses based on their product quality, but also on their convenience, personalization, transparency and digital experience. Players like Netflix, Spotify, Airbnb, and Amazon have shown that customer-focused experiences in digital environments can yield great positive results – both in terms of competitive advantages and customer loyalty.

Value co-creation also plays its impact role in innovation. User input and online forums can help entrepreneurs uncover new concepts, enhance the development process, and act quickly when customer needs evolve. That is a collaborative way, which can make the organization can be adjusted proactively and are able to invent new things continuously.

However, there are also privacy, surveillance and moral issues with customer-driven digital entrepreneurship. The digital interactions of businesses with customers provide ample opportunities to gather a ton of data, making issues of transparency, data security and ethical practices important. Therefore responsible data governance is becoming more and more part of the digital entrepreneurial strategy.

In summary, digital transformation transforms entrepreneurship, by changing opportunity recognition, business model innovation, operational efficiency and creation of value to customers. Such shifts reflect the need for entrepreneurs to navigate the digital landscape, embrace technology for flexibility, and adapt their strategies to the power of data in today's business world.

# 5. PLATFORM ECOSYSTEMS, SUSTAINABILITY, AND INCLUSIVE ENTREPRENEURSHIP

## 5.1 Platform-Based Entrepreneurship

Platform based entrepreneurship is one of the most relevant consequences of the Digital transformation. Digital platforms generate value through an interaction with the other elements within the business, whether consumers, producers, service providers, or others. Digital platforms create value through an interaction with others in the business, including a customer (consumer), a producer, a service provider, or others; unlike traditional linear business models. Business models like Amazon's, Airbnb, Uber, Alibaba's, and Shopify's illustrate the ability to rapidly scale businesses using a connected digital ecosystem.

Value generated by digital platforms comes from network effects, ecosystems and value added from data analytics. Tasks like getting to larger customer bases, lowering running expenses, and expanding crosswords markets are what entrepreneurs can benefit from using this. Issues such as gaining access to larger market bases, lower running costs, and international expansion are what entrepreneurs can benefit from using this. Additionally, platform ecosystems foster collaboration with businesses, developers, customers, and service providers who are actively engaged in each other's digital environments on an ongoing basis which promotes innovative opportunities that are collaboratively developed.

This is what I mean by the word "risks": there are risks with platform entrepreneurship too. It is possible for companies to become so reliant on platform algorithms, ranking systems, commissions, and governance policies determined by technology giants that they lose their independence. Alterations in platform standards may have a big impact on entrepreneurs' visibility, access to customers, and income generation. Within digital ecosystems too, there is intensive competition as entry barriers are quite low and thus making it accessible to all around the globe.

There are additional influences on platform-based entrepreneurship: data governance and cybersecurity. As consumers are increasingly data-rich, customer analytics and digital data is a frequent tool used by entrepreneurs in order to boost the efficiency of their products, personalize offerings and gain market competitiveness. This means that companies need to juggle innovation and privacy, ethical responsibility and regulatory needs.

## 5.2 Sustainability and Green Digital Innovation

There has been a focus on aspects of sustainability in digital entrepreneurship. Digital technologies can aid in environmentally responsible innovation by making the operations more efficient and effective, preventing waste, optimizing logistics, and improving resource management. AI, IoT, blockchain, and cloud computing are technologies that aid businesses in tracking energy consumption, promoting supply-chain transparency, and implementing circular economy applications.

Sharing economy and collaborative consumption models are also an example of digital entrepreneurship and its contribution to sustainable consumption. Ride-sharing, peer-to-peer economies, co-working and online rental services make better use of resources and minimise over-production and waste costs.

Concurrently, digital systems raise problems regarding electronic waste, technological obsolescence and power-hungry data centres. Entrepreneurs therefore, are increasingly been asked to take the principles of sustainability into their innovation strategies and decision-making processes.

## 5.3 Entrepreneurship and Digital Accessibility: Inclusive Business Models

Digital transformation has managed to open up new avenues of inclusive entrepreneurship, to the extent that it lowers geographic, infrastructural and market access constraints. Mobile technologies, digital payment systems, social media, and e-commerce platforms can facilitate women entrepreneurs, rural enterprises, freelancers/and or small businesses in the participation in the economic activities.

Financial technology innovations, digital payment platforms like UPI, have, in the emerging economies like India, made financial inclusion and digital commerce participation more robust. Business owners can reach customers, do business and market products without having to build a lot of buildings.

Still, the opportunities that exist fall short of digital democracy. Even today there is a disparity between entrepreneurship participation in underserved communities and access to Internet connectivity, digital know-how, and technological resources. Government and institutions are, therefore, important in promoting inclusive infrastructure of digital post, start-up training and affordable Internet connectivity.

### 5.4 Question of ethics and risks in digital environments

There are also cybersecurity and privacy concerns with digital entrepreneurship, algorithmic bias and platform dependence issues. Organizations are becoming more aware of the data they are gathering and analysing about customers, which brings with it responsibilities for transparency, ethical use, and safeguarding that data.

Another strategic weak point for entrepreneurs is operating on third-party digital platforms, where visibility and performance may be impacted by policy changes or changes in algorithms. Therefore, an ethical governance and cyber security readiness, in addition with the ability of responsible entrepreneurship, are also central aspects of digital entrepreneurship.

Platform ecosystems, sustainability and inclusiveness are interconnected facets of today's digital entrepreneurship.

## 6. LEADERSHIP AND ENTREPRENEURIAL RESILIENCE IN THE DIGITAL ERA

### 6.1 Digital leadership and entrepreneurial adaptability

Leadership needs have evolved a lot as a result of digital transformation. The focus of traditional entrepreneurial management was mostly strategic planning, financial management, operational coordination and competitiveness. Yet, in the digitally transformed world, entrepreneurs need to be technologically adaptable, innovative, data-informed and be eager to learn.

Digital leadership is the capacity to manage effectively in a technologically dynamic environment, one that is dominated by rapid innovation, uncertainty and digital disruption. Leaders of digital ecosystems need to navigate the technological fluctuations, and at the same time tackle customer expectations, agility in operations and ethical requirements.

An essential element of digital leadership is being adaptable. but opportunities for technological innovation are becoming shrinking, and the entrepreneurial challenge is to keep track of new technology, shifting preferences, and shifts in competitive situations. If businesses aren't ready to keep up some may become irrelevant and out of the selling game.

Equally as crucial are keeping up with digital literacy and technological savvy for entrepreneurs. With the advent of AI, data analytics, automation systems, digital platforms, and the growing complexities of cybersecurity, there is a more significant need than ever to know how to use AI effectively in decision making and innovation management.

Moreover collaboration and eco-system management are two essential aspects of leadership for digital entrepreneurship. As more companies become entrepreneurs, they find themselves at the centre of a network of customers, platform providers, developers, suppliers, investors, and digital communities. The need for effective digital leadership means there is a need for communication skills, stakeholder engagement and collaboration and innovation skills.

Ethical leadership is crucial in the digital world. Ethical considerations for using data, protecting private information, managing AI systems, ensuring sustainability, and employee automation are all emerging challenges for entrepreneurs. Thus, it is essential that responsible leadership practice is adopted to build trust from stakeholders and achieve long-term organizational legitimacy.

## 6.2 Entrepreneurial Resilience in Dynamic Environments

The Strength of Entrepreneurial and Organisational Capacity to Respond to Time of Change and Inequality" outlines the term Resilience. Entrepreneurship has been accelerated, with entrepreneurial opportunities, as well as technological uncertainties, rising along with the advent and progress of digital transformation. Resilience is a key capability in the context of entrepreneurial opportunities and technological uncertainties that have emerged with digital transformation.

Digital adaptability during the COVID-19 pandemic illustrated that those businesses that had an effective remote system in place tended to be more successful in keeping their businesses running, through implementation on a remote system, ecommerce, digital communications and providing services online. Cloud solutions, analytics platforms and collaborative digital solutions enhance business agility and reactivity.

How adaptable, how life-long learners, how innovative and how strategically diversified are resilient entrepreneurs. The variety and complexity of digital mobility and multiple revenue streams, as well as operational models, pose a threat to businesses' vulnerability to disruptions and dependence on platforms.

Effectively managing cybersecurity, getting technologically prepared and maintaining adaptable organizational culture to adjust to the evolving market dynamics are also key to becoming resilient.

## 6.3 Human-Centred Innovation and Future Entrepreneurial Competencies

While the context of Digital Transformation is squarely in technology, Human-Centred Innovation is still critical for entrepreneurial success. Technological solutions aren't enough to ensure sustainable business performance. Innovation processes should incorporate into them creativity, empathy, ethical sense and social perception.

Human centred entrepreneurship puts at the heart of the design of the product, service and business model that meets real human needs and society needs. The impact of customer experience, accessibility, trust and feeling in a customer's emotions is becoming an increasingly significant determinant of entrepreneurs' competitiveness in digital markets.

The entrepreneurial skills that are to come in the future, will thus be fused by technological knowledge with human and strategic abilities. Digital literacy, AI integration, strategic adaptability, problem solving, sustainability management, communication, and interdisciplinary collaboration will be important skills for entrepreneurs.

Creativity and critical thinking will continue to be at the forefront as more routine operational tasks are automated. Business people with the ability to think creatively, comprehend much more intricate social challenges, and devise solutions which are centred on the customer will probably have greater degrees of long term competitiveness.

Lifelong learning is also becoming more and more relevant in the economies transitioning to the digital world. Owning a business demands the acquisition of new technology and a readiness to change with the changing business footing and other changes. Digital education features, including online education platforms, digital training systems, innovation networks, then are becoming increasingly important for entrepreneurial development.

Further, future entrepreneurship will be more interdisciplinary and global. Entrepreneurs will be required to overcome issues of industry, culture, and technology, as well as face challenges from around the world: climate change, digital inequality, cybersecurity, sustainable development, and so on.

In conclusion, leadership and resilience are critical aspects of successful digital entrepreneurship. Businesses that can "do the right thing," show strategic agility, be innovative and be "people oriented" have a higher chance of winning in the hyper-changing digital business age.

# 7. DISCUSSION AND IMPLICATIONS

## 7.1 Theoretical Implications

The results of this chapter suggest an absolutely new look on entrepreneurship in the digital age. Noble's theories of entrepreneurship emphasized the concepts of innovation, opportunity recognition, resource mobilization, and competitive advantage in the context of basically stable industrial contexts. Current developments of digital ecosystems, platform economies, artificial intelligence and data-centric business models have however vastly broadened the scope and complexity of entrepreneurial activities.

The key theoretical contribution of this chapter is the emphasis on entrepreneurship as process and space, in terms of an ecosystem approach and technology-mediated approach. No longer isolated in their own pockets, entrepreneurs must now extend beyond their own markets to work through digital ecosystems of platforms, customers, developers, investors, data infrastructures, and technical networks. Business success therefore is increasingly driven by the innovation-power of the individual but, crucially, also by their capacity to act successfully in extended digital networks.

The chapter also helps advance the digital entrepreneurship body of knowledge by connecting with the entrepreneurial theory framework, platform ecosystem framework, digital transformation and sustainability research. Often such dimensions are studied individually in existing research, but this leads to a disjointed theory of the dimensions. The chapter is designed to act as a synthesis of these perspectives, showing that digital entrepreneurship is multi-dimension and affected by at the same time technological, economic, institutional, environmental and social factors. Another important theoretical implication concerns the changing nature of entrepreneurial opportunity recognition. Traditional opportunity recognition theories often emphasized market observation, resource gaps, and industrial changes. In digitally transformed economies, however, opportunities increasingly emerge from data analytics, digital connectivity, platform interactions, and algorithmic insights. This transformation suggests that entrepreneurial cognition and strategic decision-making are increasingly shaped by technological systems and digital information flows.

The findings additionally reinforce the relevance of dynamic capabilities theory within digital entrepreneurship. Entrepreneurs must continuously sense technological opportunities, seize emerging innovations, and reconfigure organizational resources in response to rapidly changing environments. Adaptability, agility, and continuous learning therefore become essential strategic capabilities.

The chapter also contributes to sustainability and inclusive entrepreneurship literature by highlighting the role of digital technologies in supporting social inclusion, resource efficiency, and environmentally sustainable innovation. Digital entrepreneurship should therefore not be understood solely as a profit-oriented activity but also as a mechanism for addressing broader societal and developmental challenges.

Finally, the discussion emphasizes that digital entrepreneurship introduces important ethical and governance considerations. Issues related to algorithmic bias, data privacy, cybersecurity, digital inequality, and platform dependency demonstrate that entrepreneurship in digital economies involves significant institutional and ethical dimensions that require further theoretical exploration.

## 7.2 Managerial Implications

The lessons which can be drawn from the results of this chapter have implications for entrepreneurs and business leaders. First of all, digital transformation is no longer an option, but a must if it is to be a competitive and viable business in the long term. Online infrastructure, innovations and technological skills are areas in which entrepreneurs need to invest.

Secondly, business model innovations and organisational agility are strategic. Business models that are flexible and scalable, backed by data, automation and customer-focused digital experiences should be implemented by every entrepreneur.

Third, the need to improve security of business data, better data governance and ethical leadership. Customer trust and organisational legitimacy is growing more impacted by responsible innovation, transparency and sustainability.

Finally, entrepreneurs need to implement strategies for a resilient approach in terms of diversifying revenue flows, linking to an adaptive organizational culture, facilitating collaboration within the ecosystem.

## 7.3 Policy and Societal Implications

Implications of digital entrepreneurship seem to extend beyond the policy or societal realm. The government, educational institutions, regulation bodies and development bodies are key players in designing a digital entrepreneurial ecosystem and technological inclusive growth.

One of the key policy considerations is Digital infrastructure development. The availability of reliable Internet access, cost-effective digital technologies, cloud capabilities and secure digital payment methods is crucial to enable entrepreneurial engagement and innovation. Policymakers need to thus prioritize investments in the digital economy – especially in rural and un-served areas.

Other policy priorities include digital literacy and entrepreneurial education. The technological knowledge, digital competences and innovation skills are necessary for entrepreneurs to be able to fully engage in digital economies. This means that, in addition, universities and training institutions should make digital entrepreneurship, digital literacy with AI, sustainability issues and innovation management part of the curricula and education programmes.

Other key results include the need for accessible digital policies. Digital transformation supports entrepreneurial opportunities but also entails unequal access to technology and digital education that can deepen socio-economic inequalities. Inclusive entrepreneurship should therefore be encouraged by targeted funding schemes, digital skill development programs, women entrepreneurship programs, rural innovation support and accessibility to affordable Internet, through government support.

In addition, regulatory frameworks also need ongoing evolution in alignment with technological change. Issues around data privacy, cybersecurity, digital monopolies, AI governance, platform labour rights and algorithmic accountability are some of the challenges that policymakers must address increasingly. Any regulations should strike a balance between the interests of consumers, market fairness, ethical concerns, and incentivizing innovation.

Sustainability policies also have a significant impact on shaping the future digital entrepreneurship. Governments and international bodies are increasingly promoting environmental sustainability solutions based on new business models and innovations known as green entrepreneurship, investments in renewable energy, circular economy and reporting on sustainability.

Further, the Indian context is significant for specifying policy implications, as India is seeing fast growth of digital entrepreneurship through schemes like Digital India, Start-up India, fintech upswing and digital payment systems. The moves highlight the potential for a coordinated infrastructure investment, policy and digital inclusion strategy to drive entrepreneurial growth and innovation.

Overall, the discussion highlights that digital entrepreneurship is a technological and economic phenomenon, but also an institutional, educational, ethical and societal phenomenon, and that requires cooperation in governance and strategy over the longer-term.

## 8. LIMITATIONS AND FUTURE RESEARCH DIRECTIONS

While this chapter is a complete discussion of digital transformation and entrepreneurship, some limitations should be noted.

First, the chapter's conceptual; it is not based on primary research, but is rather based on the secondary sources. Results from the study are thus not statistically representative. Empirical studies such as surveys, interviews, case studies or longitudinal analysis of digital enterprises could be a source of strengthening the understanding of future studies.

Secondly, with the rapid advancement of technology there is constant change in the field of digital entrepreneurship. While the technologies presented here are foundational to the future of entrepreneurship, emerging technologies like Generative Artificial Intelligence, sophisticated automation, quantum computing, Web3 platforms and environments, and Metaverse could completely transform the landscape of entrepreneurship outside of the scope of this timeframe.

Third, the chapter uses case scenarios from India as well as other digital companies around the world, but does not offer an in-depth comparative analysis between the different countries or digital businesses. Future research could thus delve into the cross-national variations in the digital entrepreneurship ecosystem, regulatory frameworks, national innovation cultures and entrepreneurial outcomes.

Another constraint is that digital entrepreneurship studies are a very interdisciplinary body of work. Field involves seminars and schools on entrepreneurship research, information systems, innovation management, sustainability research, economics and organizational theory. This blended method ensures comprehensive conceptual knowledge, but can also result in terminological, conceptual, and methodological variations.

Further studies are needed on the longer-term social and ethical consequences of digital entrepreneurship. There is need to engage with the issue of AI governance and the justice of digital inequality and algorithmic bias, as well as cyber security, changing workforce, and platform monopolies, from a scholarly perspective.

Another aspect of digital entrepreneurship that could further be explored in research is how digital entrepreneurship and sustainability are connected. Issues of green innovation, circular economy systems, sustainable digital infrastructures, and environment friendly technological development will probably be playing more and more of a role in this regard.

Moreover, issues related to AI-driven environments constitute another promising line of research in the field of entrepreneurial leadership. Automated business and creativity, ethical considerations, emotions, social responsibility, and business owners' balancing act are worth investigation for scholars.

In concluding, future research may focus on the entrepreneurial strategies for coping in very uncertain digital environments within a context of technological, geopolitical, cyber threat, and global economic uncertainty.

Notwithstanding the aforementioned limitations, this chapter resonates with the wider digital entrepreneur literature, offering an integrated framework of concepts that unite digital transformation, entrepreneurship, sustainability, inclusivity, leadership and resilience.

## 9. CONCLUSION

The digital transformation has over-the-top redefined the entrepreneurship by redefining the path entrepreneurs discover on opportunities, develop, engagement with customers and create value on it. In the era of technological advancements, like AI, cloud computing, digital platforms, blockchain and analytics, innovation has been driven and participation in the ecosystem has become crucial, as has been the need for operational agility and data-driven decision making.

This chapter illustrated the importance of digital entrepreneurship beyond technology adoption. It goes beyond changes in entrepreneurial attitudes and business to better sustainability and resilience, leadership behaviours, inclusion and organization. Platform ecosystems provide scalability opportunities for innovation and market growth and digital tools are enhancing customer engagement, efficiencies, and entrepreneur accessibility.

It also featured a number of key issues related to digital entrepreneurship, such as cybersecurity risks, platform dependency, digital inequality, ethical AI usage, and data governance concerns. The challenges discussed here reflect the intersection between technology and social, institutional, and ethical change, as well as digital entrepreneurship.

The chapter used a systematic literature search, literature synthesis, and thematic synthesis to identify the findings and an illustrative example provided by global and Indian digital enterprises was used. The multi-disciplinary research process allowed for the synthesis of the theory of entrepreneurship, digital transformation research, sustainability studies and platform ecosystem views in one coherent conceptual framework.

The results highlight some implications. Giving more importance to the entrepreneurial development capability of being innovative, adaptable to technology, digitally literate and resilient in the spirit of leadership. Use policy to support development of digital infrastructure and inclusive entrepreneurship initiatives, cybersecurity governance and digital education systems. There is a need for ongoing research on emerging issues like AI-enabled entrepreneurship, sustainable digital ecosystems, entrepreneurial resilience, and ethical entrepreneurship.

In the end, digital transformation is transforming the definition of what entrepreneurship is. Technology innovation, ethical responsibility, sustainability, adaptability and value added in a human-centric manner is what will be more and more important traits for the future entrepreneurial success in these rapidly changing times.

## REFERENCES


Bican, P. M., & Brem, A. (2020). Digital business model, digital transformation, digital entrepreneurship: Is there a sustainable "digital"? *Sustainability (Basel), 12*(13), 5239. DOI: 10.3390/su12135239

de Reuver, M., Sørensen, C., & Basole, R. C. (2018). The digital platform: A research agenda. *Journal of Information Technology, 33*(2), 124–135. DOI: 10.1057/s41265-016-0033-3

Drucker, P. F. (1985). *Innovation and entrepreneurship*. Harper & Row.

Lehdonvirta, V. (2025). *Cloud empires: How digital platforms are overtaking the state and how we can regain control*. MIT Press.

Leibenstein, H. (1979). A branch of economics is missing: Micro-micro theory. *Journal of Economic Literature, 17*(2), 477–502.

Nambisan, S. (2017). Digital entrepreneurship: Toward a digital technology perspective of entrepreneurship. *Entrepreneurship Theory and Practice, 41*(6), 1029–1055. DOI: 10.1111/etap.12254

Nambisan, S., & Baron, R. A. (2021). On the costs of digital entrepreneurship: Role conflict, stress, and venture performance in digital platform-based ecosystems. *Journal of Business Research, 125*, 520–532. DOI: 10.1016/j.jbusres.2019.06.037

OECD. (2021). *The digital transformation of SMEs*. OECD Publishing.

Osterwalder, A., & Pigneur, Y. (2010). *Business model generation*. John Wiley & Sons.

Parker, G. G., Van Alstyne, M. W., & Choudary, S. P. (2016). *Platform revolution: How networked markets are transforming the economy and how to make them work for you*. W. W. Norton & Company.

. Schumpeter, J. A. (1942). Capitalism, socialism and democracy. Harper & Brothers.

Sussan, F., & Acs, Z. J. (2017). The digital entrepreneurial ecosystem. *Small Business Economics, 49*(1), 55–73. DOI: 10.1007/s11187-017-9867-5

Teece, D. J. (2007). Explicating dynamic capabilities: The nature and microfoundations of sustainable enterprise performance. *Strategic Management Journal, 28*(13), 1319–1350. DOI: 10.1002/smj.640

Verhoef, P. C., Broekhuizen, T., Bart, Y., Bhattacharya, A., Dong, J. Q., Fabian, N., & Haenlein, M. (2021). Digital transformation: A multidisciplinary reflection and research agenda. *Journal of Business Research, 122*, 889–901. DOI: 10.1016/j.jbusres.2019.09.022

Vial, G. (2019). Understanding digital transformation: A review and a research agenda. *The Journal of Strategic Information Systems, 28*(2), 118–144. DOI: 10.1016/j.jsis.2019.01.003

# Chapter 3
# A Study on the Intention to Use FinTech Services and Its Business Performance:
## The Mediating Role of SME Trust in Technology

**Krishna Murthy Meesaala**
http://orcid.org/0000-0001-8989-8862
*College of Economics and Business Administration, University of Technology and Applied Sciences, Oman*

**Mohamed RiyazhKhan**
*University of Technology and Applied Sciences, Oman*

**Talib Khalifa Hamad Al Saadi**
*University of Technology and Applied Sciences, Oman*

**Ravi Vinod Kumar Sharma**
http://orcid.org/0000-0002-2507-7800
*University of Technology and Applied Sciences, Oman*

**Varalakshmi Subramani**
http://orcid.org/0009-0009-3009-8807
*Mazoon College, Oman*

DOI: 10.4018/979-8-2600-3179-7.ch003

## ABSTRACT

*Fintech services play a dynamic role in the evolution and growth of SMEs by providing support, contributing, sponsoring, and investing in facilities. Providing fintech services is increasingly difficult due to numerous issues, including privacy and security concerns, and an inconsistent understanding of electronic platforms. The research study examines the impact of a business entity's activities on the willingness to use online services, with trust in technology as a mediating factor. A reliability test has been conducted using Cronbach's Alpha to assess the internal consistency of the gathered information. Democratic details have been collected and interpreted accordingly. The mediating role of the trust factor would help determine the adoption of fintech services. It presents insights into how fintech services could unify into SME activities. This study would also help policymakers and service providers reduce barriers to trust, thereby ensuring the successful integration of fintech services into corporate operations.*

## 1. INTRODUCTION

Fintech services, which are upsetting, have been growing and improving operational efficiency, supporting decision-making, and managing the financial development of SMEs. Fintech services help overcome issues that have existed for a long time, viz., limited access to capital mobilisation, inefficient financial management, and the density of financial activities in peer-to-peer lending, online banking, blockchain, and other mobile banking transactions. (Chowdhury, E. K., & Chowdhury, R 2024; Sharma & Sharma 2019). SMEs are using fintech services to a limited extent, even though they could potentially use them. The most important factor in fintech services is a lack of confidence in the technological arena (Begum, A., Gaytan, J. C. T., & Ahmed, G. (2023) & Kilani, et. al., 2023). Trusting technology is a significant factor in identifying customer intention and its use of innovative technologies (Yang, Tong & Zhang, Xun, (2022). Trust in technology includes the reliability of the service provider, the transparency of the service provider's platform, and the security of the data transformation (D.Y. Kim, et al., 2008). The association among intention to use fintech services, trust in technology, and business performance addresses a gap in prevailing knowledge about fintech services. Significantly less research is available on SMEs' trust in technology mediating the association between the intention to use fintech services and business performance. By exploring the underlying forces of SMEs, this research study intends to shed light on the factors influencing adoption in the serious activity. Since the turn of the millennium, the majority of commercial transactions have been completed through FinTech methods (Luan Vardari and Kujtim Hameli 2025). FinTech is therefore essential to sustainable growth and economic development in a variety of sectors. Trust and societal acceptance have a major positive impact, even while the advantages of using FinTech services do not directly raise client pleasure. FinTech firms have been essential in advancing financial inclusion, especially for underbanked and unbanked groups. This growth promotes sustainable development, economic activity, and poverty alleviation (Ozili, 2018). So. FinTech is essential to the growth of the country and the progress of society.

## 1.1. Significance of the study

In modern years, all banking and financial transaction have occurred by Fintech (FinTech) methodology. Because of rapid growth of technology and online businesses make our business transactions easy. The worldwide revolution and application of financial technology transaction (FinTech) internationally has obviously impacted knowledge paradigms within human communities and accelerated the energetic development of capital markets and other banking transactions. This study also covered how worldwide FinTech innovations and applications have greatly impacted human communities' understanding and sped up the rapid growth of developing capital markets in six Taiwanese municipalities (Shuen-Lin Jeng et al. 2025). FinTech is the new innovative method of financial transaction services to the banking sector and global business transaction, its roles are pivotal turn to the Indian and global scenario. After the new revaluation of Indian money, especially return of some Indian currency notes the FinTech role is very tremendous most of the customers are using the different mode of digital transaction in Fintech (Garima Srivastava et al. 2025). The rapid development of financial technology (FinTech) has transformed the structure and dynamics of the global financial sector. FinTech refers to the integration of innovative digital technologies with financial services to enhance the efficiency, accessibility, and convenience of financial transactions (Gai et al., 2018). Digital financial platforms that reduce the cost of transactions, increase financing accessibility, and simplify financial management procedures are especially beneficial to small and medium-sized businesses (SMEs) (Liu et al., 2020). Financial technology serves as a strategic catalyst for an entity's growth, development, and sustainability, as well as its technology transformation. Analysing past research on participants' use of financial technology is vital to shaping business performance. The study examines the area requiring further research, emphasising theoretical and rational outcomes, and offers a systematic overview of the latest academic discoveries. It is very important to consider the importance of this study in relation to the FinTech adoption by SMEs (Small and Medium-sized Enterprises). On the one hand, the use of financial technologies brings a lot of changes and improvements into the financial industry worldwide, on the other hand, many SMEs cannot use FinTech solutions because of various reasons, such as concerns about the level of security, issues related to privacy, and high costs. It is essential to underline that this study pays attention to the role played by trust in technology adoption among SMEs and reveals how the mediation by trust could improve the process of FinTech adoption. Moreover, it should be noted that SMEs are responsible for economic development of countries all over the world, and FinTech adoption among them will positively affect their economic growth in the long run. Therefore, this study highlights the factors influencing the process of FinTech adoption among SMEs, and, thus, allows determining some aspects of this adoption. The current study presents a theoretical framework of TAM, UTAUT, and trust model which could help people understand the process of adoption. This study also discusses the problem of intention. Intention has been regarded as one of the main reasons behind the failure of SMEs to utilize the adopted technology. The SMEs often make decisions based on social networks, peer groups, and recommendations provided by financial institutions. Although they have intentions to adopt the technology, such intentions do not guarantee actual usage. Additionally, the study examines the role of technological trust in mediating the relationship between intention and adoption of the technology in SMEs.

## 1.2 Statement of the Problem and Research Gap

The regulatory framework and economic environment would affect fintech services worldwide. Characteristics that influence the adoption of fintech services in developing nations vary with affordability and accessibility (Z. Liu, Z et al., 2024). Research on fintech in the MENA region is minimal, and this is a research gap that could improve knowledge of fintech obligations across different SMEs. Though the progress of fintech services is embraced by and extends to SMEs, too many questions remain unanswered. This study seeks to address these gaps by exploring how trust in technology and, by extension, the SMEs' victory affects SMEs' target to implement FinTech services. Identifying and addressing the gaps will enhance understanding of the features that support fintech adoption and SME success. Huge studies also indicate that SMEs' intention to use FinTech services is predominantly driven by perceived platform security and the service provider's reputation (Mathur, H.P., 2022). Since trust lowers the perceived risk of using digital stages, SMEs are very willing to adopt them and integrate them into their operations. Likewise, research studies have shown that SMEs that trust FinTech platforms tend to demonstrate improved business performance, including lowering costs, more efficient financial management, and easier access to finance (Arner et al., 2015). Trust in FinTech services may help SMEs make better decisions, manage their funds more optimally, and, ultimately, enhance profitability (Kang, J. (2018).

## 1.3 Objectives of the study

1. To analyse significant relationship among the intention to use fintech services and trust in technology.
2. To examine the significance relationship among the business performance and intention to adopt fintech services.
3. To identify the association among business performance and intention to use fintech services mediating trust in technology

## 1.4 Hypothesis of the study

H1: The intention to use FinTech services is in direct and significant positive relation with technological trust.
H2: There is a positive relationship between business performance and the intention to adopt FinTech services.
H3: Trust in technology mediates the association between business performance and the intention to use FinTech services.

# 2. REVIEW OF LITERATURE

FinTech, or financial technology, has become a disruptive force that is changing the world of financial services. FinTech is the use of digital technologies to offer financial services and solutions that improve consumer experience, accessibility, and effectiveness (Arner, Barberis & Buckley, 2017). FinTech's expansion has been fueled by a number of international reasons. FinTech adoption has been aided by the spread of digital payment methods, growing internet access, and rising smartphone usage (World Bank, 2022). Additionally, start-ups have been able to penetrate sectors that have historically been dominated by banks because to legislative reforms that promote innovation and competition. FinTech's growth and international expansion have also been expedited by the increase of venture capital investments (EY Global FinTech Report, 2021). As businesses and consumers quickly moved toward online financial transactions to minimize in-person contacts, the COVID-19 epidemic further accelerated digital transformation (Khatri & Srivastava, 2022). FinTech applications are found in many different areas of the financial services business. Peer-to-peer transfers, bill payments, and retail purchases are all made easier by digital wallets and mobile money solutions. Peer-to-peer platforms and digital credit scoring increase the availability of loans for people and small enterprises by evaluating applicants using alternative data (Jagtiani & Lemieux, 2018). Robo-advisors in wealth management provide low-cost automated investment services, opening up investing to a wider range of people. Data analytics is being used by insurtech companies to provide personalized insurance solutions and expedite the processing of claims (Stoeckli, Dremel & Uebernickel, 2018). In Summary, by enhancing customer satisfaction, reducing cost, and improving convenience, financial technology is yet to liberalize the traditional financial segment. Technological improvement, legal support, and improving online engagement have supported its development and growth. Financial Technology is expected to enhance development and financial support as it grows, but it also faces challenges in cybersecurity, implementation, and consumer security and privacy. Thus, to optimize its growth factors and lower related difficulties, the current study and smart policymaking will be very significant.

As digital banking platforms, mobile payment systems, peer-to-peer lending, and algorithm-driven investment services become more widely available, businesses and individuals are moving away from traditional financial institutions and toward technology-driven options (Varga, 2017). Because of this, it is now crucial for researchers and business professionals to understand users' motivations to utilize FinTech services. Technology acceptance theories like the Unified Theory of Acceptance and Use of Technology (UTAUT) and the Technology Acceptance Model (TAM) are frequently used to explain user intention to embrace FinTech services. According to these frameworks, adoption behavior is significantly influenced by perceived utility, usability, security, trust, and social influence (Davis, 1989; Venkatesh et al., 2003). Furthermore, psychological elements like perceived risk and trust continue to be crucial, particularly in financial settings where client confidence is impacted by security concerns (Lee, 2009). Consequently, examining these factors sheds light on how FinTech service providers might improve customer retention and engagement. Adoption of FinTech services has important effects on business performance in addition to consumer behavior. Businesses that use FinTech solutions frequently see increases in customer satisfaction, operational effectiveness, service personalization, and competitive advantage (Nicoletti, 2017). A combination of improved online technologies in the financial industry, aimed at augmenting effectiveness and respondents' experience, is called Financial Technology (Gai et al., 2018; Arner et al., 2017).

The embracement of FinTech tools and activities, for instance, the insistence on P2P techniques, online money, and blockchain technology, among others, has become more evident in recent years as a game-changer for small businesses (SMEs). As basic drivers of employment and economic development, SMEs frequently face financial management issues, high transaction costs, and limited access to finance (Ozili, 2018; Liu et al., 2020). Behavioural elements are the most important factors in building trust in technology, rather than other factors, which cannot guarantee technology adoption, as shown in past studies (Begum et al., 2023; Kilani et al., 2023). It is significant to identify the association among the intention to use fintech services, trust in one's technological knowledge, and other organisational performance indicators. The effort to accept FinTech services and trust in technology are closely related, as evidenced by numerous research studies. In monetary perspectives, risk, privacy, security, and trust are prevalent, and trust is identified as a basic component of technology acceptance (Lee, 2009; Pavlou, 2003). Technical know-how trust is a user's faith in the credibility, safety, transparency, and authenticity of technical expertise in policies and dealers (McKnight et al., 2002; Kim et al., 2008). Usage and usability are significant elements in creating behavioural intent, as supported by various theories of technical support acceptance, viz., the unified theory of acceptance and use of technology (UTAUT) and the technological know-how approach (Davis, 1989; Venkatesh et al., 2003). Regardless, researchers in the academic community argue that these models are very limited in exploring fintech services until the trust factor is considered an important aspect. (Gefen et al., 2003; Rahi et al., 2019). High levels of trust in technological use motivate various participants to engage in different transactions across fintech services, reducing ambiguity. Sharma, S. K., & Sharma, M. (2019) reinforce the understanding that trust has a significant effect on the use of online banking, enhancing confidence in operational security. Likewise, Yang, Tong & Zhang, Xun (2022) depicted that trust in technology, a significant element in financial technology embracement, comprises the financial aspect of a promising financial system. Trust is considered an important factor, even though SMEs have limited resources and little tolerance for financial losses. Trust in technology is more associated with the development of the purpose of using fintech. The existing literature review provides substantial support for the hypothesis, emphasising that the intention to use fintech services is positive and important, and is related to trust in technology.

Extensive research on the selected topic has been conducted to understand the association between nosiness performance and the acceptance of fintech services. Moreover, literature reviews will not, on their own, enhance performance. Performance activities require the efficient use of technological capabilities in operations, whereas the objective is to maintain readiness and receptivity to financial technology adoption, as affirmed by Huang et al. (2021). Despite findings from various research studies, it is suggested that there is a positive association between fintech services and business performance, particularly when optimal conditions exist in administration and technology. The association between the embracement of fintech services and business performance could not be identified as direct, as it operates through intermediaries, as per past studies on similar topics. Third parties act as a bridge between the intention to create financial technology and tangible business performance, which is trust in technology, as indicated by researchers McKnight et al. (2002) and Schnackenberg & Tomlinson (2016). Trust in technology reduces psychological issues and encourages people to adopt more online approaches for important activities. Performance and fintech adoption are associated, with the trust factor in technology serving as a predominant mediating role, as observed in empirical research by Huang et al. (2021). This describes the trust-in-technology factor that improves the effectiveness of fintech use. Kang (2018) found that SMEs that trust digital solutions achieve better results, making more effective, perfect, and consistent financial decisions.

A large body of literature has been reviewed on fintech services and their implementation, but these questions are not addressed in various studies of SMES. This gap will be examined in terms of the role of intention to use fintech services, the trust factors of fintech services, and business performance. (Liébana-Cabanillas, F., et. al., 2018) Have highlighted the objectives of SMEs and their goals to understand the problems with trust factors and technological activities that would influence service adoption. The fintech services have not been addressed as part of the embracement of SMEs (Chaudhary et al., 2024). Psychological factors are explored in the context of fintech services for SMEs, providing insights. Several studies have examined the association between SMEs' adoption of fintech services and the readiness of financial services (Chaudhary et al., 2024). Huang et al. (2021) addressed a gap in the current research by demonstrating that trust is a highly influential mediator across many fintech services. Adopting FinTech service approaches through experimentation, as SMEs must first overcome security, trust, and perceived costs associated with new technology. Many studies regarding FinTech adoption in SMEs emphasize certain factors affecting the process, such as the perceived usefulness and ease of use of the technology, social influence, and facilitation conditions (Davis, 1989; Venkatesh et al., 2003). Nevertheless, these studies have mainly focused on individuals and big companies, and there is little literature that discusses FinTech adoption by SMEs. This paper seeks to extend the current body of knowledge by considering the role of trust in determining the process of adoption, especially within the financial industry, where security of information is important. While TAM and UTAUT frameworks have been employed in many cases to examine the adoption of technologies, the concept of trust theory needs to be incorporated in the analysis in case of FinTech adoption among SMEs. Trust in FinTech service providers is very important for SMEs because they cannot dedicate any resources to information technology-based security measures. Privacy-related issues and problems like data theft and cyber-crime greatly influence SMEs' FinTech adoption process (Gefen et al., 2003). It is recommended that a combined model using TAM, UTAUT, and trust theories may lead to more fruitful results.

## 3. RESEARCH METHODOLOGY

This research chapter investigates the relationships among the variables considered in the study: intention to use fintech services, SMEs' business performance, and trust in technological factors. The study has been carried out by preparing a well-structured questionnaire to obtain information from SMEs on their intention to use fintech services, trust in technology, and business performance. A five-point Likert scale used, with options ranging from strongly disagree to agree strongly. The Questionnaire has been circulated both offline and online, as required, using convenient sampling techniques. The data necessary for the study gathered from the target respondents and examined and analysed using well-known statistical tools. The research study used to summarise the demographic variables of the sample respondents, including age, gender, educational qualifications, and years of business experience. Descriptive statistical tools help identify the mean and standard deviation to assess the distribution of respondents and to examine the significant factors in the study. Correlation is an important statistical technique to identify the intensity and direction of association between different variables selected for the study. Reliability test is used in the study to determine the stability, reliability and consistency of questionnaire. Frequency tables were prepared to shape, review and categorise the variables. Regression analysis is one of the important statistical technique utilized to analyse the association among a dependent variable and one or more independent variables and to predict the fluctuations influencing the results. Regression analysis is utilised in the study to analyse how and why independent variables in the study impact on dependent variables with the help of mediating variables. For this paper, the researchers adopted a quantitative research methodology and conduct surveys to find out the impact of FinTech adoption intention, trust in technology, and business performance among SMEs. The survey questionnaire is developed in order to collect data from SMEs regarding their perception toward the FinTech services offered to them. The questions in the survey were based on four constructs – security, privacy, perceived cost, and behavioural intention. The survey used a five-point Likert scale to gather consistent responses from the participants. Sampling was done through convenience sampling, where this strategy helps in accessing the SMEs within the region. Researchers understand that this is not the best strategy for sampling because there exists the danger of sampling bias. Future researchers can make use of random sampling or even stratified sampling to enhance generalization and increase external validity. Regarding data analysis, PLS structural equation modelling (PLS-SEM) was used to analyse the relationships among the variables used in this paper. The use of this tool ensures that complex models are tested using many constructs while considering the measurement error in the process.

## 3.1 Ethical Standards

The research study is focused on SMEs, the target audience, to provide the required information through a questionnaire. It is ensured that the personal data of the respondent SMEs will be kept confidential, and respondents may withdraw at any time without difficulty, as the information will be used only for academic purposes.

# 4. DATA ANALYSIS, FINDINGS, AND CONCLUSION

## 4.1 Frequency Table

*Table 1.*

| Gender of an Entrepreneur | | | | | |
|---|---|---|---|---|---|
| | | Frequency | Percent | Valid Percent | Cumulative Percent |
| Valid | Male | 161 | 49.2 | 49.2 | 49.2 |
| | Female | 166 | 50.8 | 50.8 | 100.0 |
| | Total | 327 | 100.0 | 100.0 | |

Source: Questionnaire

The above table 1 indicates that the gender distribution among entrepreneurial participants was 161 (49.2%) male and 166 (50.8%) female entrepreneurs.

*Table 2.*

| Age Group of an Entrepreneur | | | | | |
|---|---|---|---|---|---|
| | | Frequency | Percent | Valid Percent | Cumulative Percent |
| Valid | 25-30 Years | 61 | 18.7 | 18.7 | 18.7 |
| | 31-40 Years | 114 | 34.9 | 34.9 | 53.5 |
| | above 40 Years | 152 | 46.5 | 46.5 | 100.0 |
| | Total | 327 | 100.0 | 100.0 | |

Source: Questionnaire

The above table 2 shows that 152 respondents (46.5%) are 40 or older, 114 (34.9%) are 31–40, and 61 (18.7%) are 25–30.

*Table 3.*

| **Education Level of an Entrepreneur** | | | | | |
|---|---|---|---|---|---|
| | | **Frequency** | **Percent** | **Valid Percent** | **Cumulative Percent** |
| Valid | School | 32 | 9.8 | 9.8 | 9.8 |
| | Diploma | 136 | 41.6 | 41.6 | 51.4 |
| | Bachelor | 103 | 31.5 | 31.5 | 82.9 |
| | Others | 56 | 17.1 | 17.1 | 100.0 |
| | Total | 327 | 100.0 | 100.0 | |

Source: Questionnaire

The table 3 shows that most entrepreneurs have post-secondary education: 136 (41.6%) hold diplomas, and 103 (31.5%) hold bachelor's degrees. Others have different degrees (17.1%) or only school education (9.8%).

*Table 4.*

| **Annual Income of an Entrepreneur** | | | | | |
|---|---|---|---|---|---|
| | | **Frequency** | **Percent** | **Valid Percent** | **Cumulative Percent** |
| Valid | 6000 Rials | 28 | 8.6 | 8.6 | 8.6 |
| | 6001 Rials to 12000 Rials | 27 | 8.3 | 8.3 | 16.8 |
| | 12001 Rials to 24000 Rials | 159 | 48.6 | 48.6 | 65.4 |
| | Above 24000 Rials | 113 | 34.6 | 34.6 | 100.0 |
| | Total | 327 | 100.0 | 100.0 | |

Source: Questionnaire

The above table 4 shows the annual income of an entrepreneur. The income distribution represents almost half of the participants, 159 entrepreneurs, possessing (48.6%) fall under the substantial income category of 12000 rials to 24000 rials, whereas 113 entrepreneurs holding (34.6%) are categorised as above 24000 rials. 28 respondents (8.6%) account for the entrepreneurs in the income category of 6000 rials annually, followed by 27 respondents (8.3%) in the income category of 6001 rials to 12000 rials annually.

*Table 5.*

| Experience of Entrepreneur | | | | | |
|---|---|---|---|---|---|
| | | Frequency | Percent | Valid Percent | Cumulative Percent |
| Valid | Below 5 Years | 66 | 20.2 | 20.2 | 20.2 |
| | 6 to 10 years | 202 | 61.8 | 61.8 | 82.0 |
| | 10-15 Years | 59 | 18.0 | 18.0 | 100.0 |
| | Total | 327 | 100.0 | 100.0 | |

Source: Questionnaire

The above table 5 shows the experience of entrepreneurs. The majority of the entrepreneurs who responded to the questionnaire 202 (61.8%) had experience of six to ten years as entrepreneurs, followed by 66 (20.2%) of the entrepreneurs had experience of less than five years, with the least experience of 59 respondents accounting for (18%) had experience of ten to fifteen years as entrepreneurs.

## 4.2.Reliability Test

*Table 6.*

| Name of Variables | No of items | Cronbach's Alpha |
|---|---|---|
| Intention to use Fintech Services | 5 | 0.972 |
| Fintech Services helps to monitor with long-term reliability | 5 | 0.950 |
| Business Performance | 5 | 0.835 |

Source: Questionnaire

*Table 7.*

| Reliability Statistics | |
|---|---|
| Cronbach's Alpha | N of Items |
| .978 | 18 |

Source: Questionnaire

The above tables 6 & 7 shows the researchers prepared a 15-item questionnaire, which was subjected to reliability analysis, yielding high internal consistency (Cronbach's alpha = 0.978). This reliability test is widely used to identify the scale of reliability by examining the level of correlation between the constructs. The value of 0.70 is assumed as acceptable, 0.80 depicts very good reliability, and a value above

0.70 is assumed as acceptable. The above table shows that 0.80 indicates very good reliability and consistency, and values greater than 0.90 indicate very good internal consistency and reliability.

## 4.3 Descriptive Statistics

*Table 8.*

| Descriptive Statistics | | | | | | | | | | |
|---|---|---|---|---|---|---|---|---|---|---|
| | N | Minimum | Maximum | Mean | Std. Deviation | Variance | Skewness | | Kurtosis | |
| | Statistic | Statistic | Statistic | Statistic | Statistic | Statistic | Stats | Std. Error | Stats | Std. Error |
| Intention | 327 | 1 | 5 | 3.48 | 1.145 | 1.312 | -1.338 | .135 | .489 | .269 |
| Trust | 327 | 1 | 5 | 3.46 | 1.002 | 1.004 | -1.211 | .135 | .606 | .269 |
| BP | 327 | 1 | 5 | 3.59 | .765 | .586 | -.978 | .135 | 1.195 | .269 |
| Valid N (listwise) | 327 | | | | | | | | | |

Source: Questionnaire

The above table 8 shows the descriptive statistics for the aim to practice the fintech services expose an overall optimistic character respondents concerning the practise of fintech results. Five point Likert's scale shows statistical mean value of 3.48 specified that participants an average, tend to agree, signifying a predominantly positive behavioural intention. This suggests that significant fraction of the sample views fintech services as beneficial or appealing. The study shows 1.145 as standard deviation that explore important type in responses, signifying heterogeneity in adoption attentiveness, some respondents may endure hesitant or uncertain, whether due to perceived hazards, unusualness, or regulatory anxieties. The study emphasises the variance of 1.312 indicating a positive central tendency stating the variances are still important. The negative skewness of (-1.338) explores that majority of the participants selected greater values on the scale depicting a vigorous desire to use fintech services which is greater prevalent than the weak intention. Kurtosis value of (0.489) highlights a peak distribution in contract to normal curve. This indicating the participants are focused on the average values with a less frequency of extreme participants. . The skewness of -1.211 indicates negative skewness, dispersion, and a prevalence of high trust values, indicating a positive relationship with the technological classification. Kurtosis is 0.606, indicating a moderate leptokurtic distribution and suggesting less clustering of opinions at the average level among participants. The study also shows that business performance has a maximum mean of 3.59, indicating a positive assessment by the participants. This helps to identify constructs, namely efficiency, profitability or competitiveness above the average. A small standard deviation (0.765) supports minimum-variance forecasting and a high level of unanimity among participants in assessing business performance. The variance value of (0.586) subsequently validates that the participants are very close to the mean values. Dispersion shows the highest level of consensus among the selected variables, suggesting standardised business performance across regular organisational experiences. The skewness value of 0.978 indicates moderately negative skewness, with a higher proportion of high business performance values than lower ones. Participants' perceptions of negative performance were considered unusual. The kurtosis value of 1.195 indicates a leptokurtic distribution with a prominent peak.

## 4.4. Correlations

*Table 9.*

**Correlations**

| | | Intention to use Fintech Services | Trust in Technology | Business Performance |
|---|---|---|---|---|
| Intention to use Fintech Services | Pearson Correlation | 1 | .883** | .752** |
| | Sig. (2-tailed) | | .000 | .000 |
| | N | 327 | 327 | 327 |
| Trust in Technology | Pearson Correlation | .883** | 1 | .830** |
| | Sig. (2-tailed) | .000 | | .000 |
| | N | 327 | 327 | 327 |
| Business Performance | Pearson Correlation | .752** | .830** | 1 |
| | Sig. (2-tailed) | .000 | .000 | |
| | N | 327 | 327 | 327 |

Source: Questionnaire
**. Correlation is significant at the 0.01 level (2-tailed).

The correlation analysis explores the association between intention to use fintech services, trust in technology and business performance on the basis of data collection from 327 participants. Correlation coefficient analysis of Pearson's used to find the intensity and tendency of these correlations and the output shows a very strong, positive and statistically important on the three forms showing the variables are very closely related and moving in the same tendency. The correlation coefficient among the variables intention to use fintech services and trust in technology is very strong with the values of ($r=0.883$, $p < 0.01$). The values signify the greater values trust in technology are strongly related with a higher intention to use fintech services. Rationally the participants observe fintech services are very much protected, consistent and technologically vigorous and they are more probable to embrace and continue the usage of those services. The degree of this association emphasises trust as a significant factor in fintech adoption and aligns with theoretical approaches that position technological trust as a central experience of interactive purpose in digital and fintech perspectives. The relationship between the intention to use fintech services and business performance is also very strong and positive ($r = 0.752$, $p < 0.01$). The study also shows that SMEs' responses indicate a higher intention to explore adopting fintech services to achieve better business performance. The research indicates that the intent to adopt fintech services is very closely related to the questionnaire statement of heightened efficiency, yield, cost-cutting, or a moderate incentive. Thus, the correlation does not imply causation; the relationship between fintech readiness and openness to technological improvement is a significant factor associated with improved business outcomes. The association among trust in technology and business performance is strongly positive ($r = 0.830$, $p < 0.01$).

## 4.5 Regression Analysis

*Table 10.*

| R | R-sq | MSE | F | Df1 | DF2 | P |
|---|---|---|---|---|---|---|
| 0.830 | 0.689 | 0.314 | 718.622 | 1.000 | 325.000 | 0.000 |
| Model | Coeff | SE | T | P | LLCI | ULCI |
| Constant | -0.442 | 0.149 | -2.970 | 0.003 | -0.735 | -0.149 |
| Intention to use fintech services | 1.086 | 0.041 | 26.807 | 0.000 | 1.007 | 1.166 |

Source: Questionnaire

The above table 10 presents a regression analysis treating trust in technology as one of the study's outcome variables to evaluate how the intention to use fintech services influences it. The R value is 0.830, and the R-square is 0.689, demonstrating strong explanatory power. Thus, it is illustrated about 68.9% of the variation in trust in technology is caused by the variable intention to use fintech services. This suggests a strong relationship between the user's purpose and their level of trust in fintech-connected technology. The model's strong influence is indicated by a very high F value ($F = 718.622$, $p < 0.001$). Regression models provide a better fit than no predictors. Coefficient values for the regression, which align with users' wishes to use fintech services, are positive and statistically significant (β = 1.086, p < 0.001), suggesting a substantial increase in users' trust in technology, which is correlated with an increase in the wish to use fintech services.

*Table 11.*

| R | R-sq | MSE | F | Df1 | DF2 | P |
|---|---|---|---|---|---|---|
| 0.884 | 0.782 | 0.288 | 579.946 | 2.000 | 324.000 | 0.000 |
| Model | Coeff | SE | T | P | LLCI | ULCI |
| Constant | -0.143 | 0.145 | -0.987 | 0.324 | -0.427 | 0.142 |
| Business Performance | 0.091 | 0.070 | 1.303 | 0.193 | -0.046 | 0.228 |
| Trust in Technology | 0.952 | 0.053 | 17.910 | 0.000 | 0.848 | 1.057 |

Source: Questionnaire

The above table 11 shows the intention to use fintech services and trust in technology, which are used together as regressors in the model. The model's explanatory power shows an R value of 0.884 and an R-square of 0.782, indicating that 78.2% of the variance in business performance is accounted for by the two variables. A greater proportion of variance accounted for by the above model suggests that psychological factors related to fintech services affect organisational goal outcomes. The above models depict the overall picture of the study, which is important as demonstrated by statistical significance (F = 579.946, p < 0.001). A significant predictor of business performance across the full set of variables is trust in technology, as indicated by a beta of 0.952 (p < 0.001). This study demonstrates that performance is primarily improved by increased trust in technology, which is enabled by efficient business transactions and safer online transactions. The beta values shows (β = 0.091, p = 0.193), when trust in technology occurs the intention to use fintech services do not have any relationship impact on the business performance even the values are positive, the less significance value recommends when the trust in technology is measured, the intention to use fintech services do not require to have positive results by itself.

## Mediation Effects

*Table 12.*

| Effect | Coefficient | Se | T | P | LLCI | ULCI |
|---|---|---|---|---|---|---|
| Direct Effect (Intention to use fintech services-Business Performance) | -0.002 | 0.056 | -0.039 | 0.969 | -0.112 | 0.108 |
| Indirect Effect (Intention to use fintech services-Trust in Technology-Business Performance) | 0.522 | 0.087 | - | - | 0.364 | 0.705 |
| Total Effect | 0.520 | 0.024 | 21.844 | 0.001 | 0.473 | 0.567 |
| (Intention to use fintech services – Trust in Technology) | 0.849 | 0.019 | 44.880 | 0.001 | 0.812 | 0.886 |
| (Trust in Technology-Business Performance) | 0.615 | 0.061 | 10.084 | 0.001 | 0.495 | 0.735 |

The above table 12 shows the mediation effect of trust in technology: the mediating variable influences intention to use fintech services, which, in turn, influences business performance. The statistical test for mediating variables addresses the type, direct, and indirect consequences at a very high level. In conclusion, the intention to use technology to improve performance had a positive and significant influence on business performance, with a beta value of $\beta = 0.520$ ($p < 0.001$). The association between the intention to use fintech services and business performance is not statistically significant at the same level as the beta and p values indicate (-0.002 and 0.969, respectively), because the regression model includes trust in technology as a mediating factor. Whereas the bootstrapped model includes zero (LLCI = 0.364, ULCI = 0.705), the indirect effect of intention to use fintech activities on business activities via trust in technology is strong and statistically significant ($\beta = 0.522$). The values suggest a very strong mediation effect. The indirect influence demonstrates that the intention to use fintech services has a much greater, positive impact on trust in technology, while its impact on business performance is significant. The statistical results were also validated by the mediation variable with the significance among intention to use fintech services and trust in technology ($\beta = 0.849$, $p < 0.001$), and the association between trust in technology and business performance is statistically significant with the values of ($\beta = 0.615$, $p < 0.001$).

## 5. FINDINGS

It is concluded that the entrepreneurial activity in the study is not male controlled and it is evenly balanced. Majority of the respondents participated for the study belongs to the age group of above 40 years. Majority of the entrepreneurs holding formal post foundation education. Majority of the entrepreneurs earns substantial income per annum with stable financial status. Most of the respondents had experience of six to ten years as entrepreneurs in the fintech activities. This Cronbach's Alpha shows 0.978 implying the scale executing an exceptional level of reliability. The study used fifteen variables with an instrument that is mostly coherent and consistent and deliberated structure. Participants opinions were constant and constant signifying minimal random measurement error. High order of reliability ensures confidence in establishing accurate and dependable in collecting data, establishing suitable scale for accurate experimental testing. Internal consistency of the instrument is especially important to identify the complex constructs namely fintech adoption, trust in technology or business performance. The descriptive analysis shows the participants are focused on the average values with a less frequency of extreme participants. The values impose the intention to embrace fintech services is mostly favourable, a part of the participants remains hesitant. The analysis shows the distribution of characteristics are reasonable and helps that the variance is suitable for supplementary results consisting structural equation models to examine its antecedents and results. The study also depicts an average group of participants perceive that the trust factors are fairly consistent than compared broadly different. This relationship mostly implies shared contextual factors namely widespread use of intention to use technology or a same state of digital infrastructure. The trust in technology described as well demonstrated within the samples selected along with few fluctuations. It shows an extremely strong explanatory selected variables in the study that investigates technology embracement. Majority of the respondents' values are closer to mean which shows the strength of the robust consensus. Business performance is consistently and positively observed among the participants demonstrating it as a consistent and responsible construct for the further research analysis from the analytical perspective along with the attributes. Definite kurtosis specifies a common functioning conditions or united organisational outcomes. The descriptive values shows that the business performance is perceived positive and consistent that strengthens its usage as an explanatory variable in the study assessing its relationship with fintech adoption or trust in technology. The correlation coefficient results establish the higher trust in technological usage is strongly correlated with greater levels of business performance. This correlation would shows the element that entities and participants those trusting online system are more enthusiastically integrated to the business transactions, related to productive effectiveness, enhanced determination underpins the tactical significant of constructing and managing technological trust to accomplish sustainable professional achievement. All the variables which are reported in the study are significant statistically with a value of 0.01 level, depicting derived relationships are not likely to have arose by prospect. High correlated values also recommends that the variables are not only considered close but also interdependent in a broader fintech embracement framework. Regression analysis shows all variables are held constant, and a one-unit increase in intention leads to a 1.086-unit increase in trust in technology. Thus, with a greater inclination to use the service, SMEs are more likely to improve trust in the technology setup supporting the fintech services. Intention to use fintech services is not only a result of trust in technology but also an important driver of technological confidence. In conclusion, the output provides strong evidence supporting the hypothesis that the intent and technological trust of fintech services is connected. The study also demonstrates that the intention to use fintech services does not have a direct relationship with business performance, but it does indirectly support the reconstruction of behaviour towards technological factors. The results of the study suggest that trust in technology has more direct and significant implications for predicting business performance than the intention to use technology. The benefit achieved by businesses extends beyond users' intention to control activities and also encompasses their intention to demonstrate trust, ensuring that business activities influence technology outcomes appropriately. The study shows that the variable trust in technology plays an important mediating role, as it is strongly linked to both the intention to use technology and business performance. The study also examines the association between the intention to use fintech services and business performance, which is fully explained by the variable trust in technology. In general, the intention to use fintech services can improve business results when integrated with technology systems. The study summarises that trust in technology serves as a link between fintech service use intentions and business performance. The desire to use fintech services helps establish a relationship with online financial solutions, but it has not ensured good business performance. In this situation, the trust in technology established through the variable intention to make the business follows through the accomplishment of fintech services. The findings obtained in this research have shown a positive correlation between intention to adopt FinTech services and business performance. The results have revealed that SMEs showing high intentions to adopt FinTech have had high financial performance, efficient operations, and good access to credit. On top of all this, trust on technology has been found to positively moderate the relationship above. Further, the findings support the significance of TAM and UTAUT since usefulness and ease of use predicted SMEs' intention to adopt FinTech products. Nonetheless, perceived cost stood out as a hindrance to FinTech adoption, especially for SMEs operating in the developing world where they feared high subscription costs, transaction fees, and training costs. Nevertheless, behavioural intentions have proved to be key in determining actual adoption if there is sufficient trust and usefulness of the product. In order to determine the impact of FinTech adoption on SME performance, future research should consider longitudinal studies in order to understand how these two relate over time. The current research has provided strong associational evidence but longitudinal research will allow for better insights to be obtained on FinTech adoption process in SMEs. Qualitative research can also be done to enhance the understanding of FinTech adoption among SMEs. Another area of further research can be in examining cross-cultural variations on FinTech adoption due to differing cultural perceptions and regulatory frameworks around technology. For instance, SMEs operating in developing countries might be constrained by some unique factors such as lack of appropriate infrastructure, policy environment, and even cultural beliefs against using digital finance systems. Future studies can build on these unique characteristics to generate recommendations that would suit the FinTech providers and relevant policy makers.

## 6. CONCLUSION

The study explores to identify whether the trust in technology as a mediator of the association among the tendency of SMEs to use fintech activities and its execution. The questionnaire has been distributed to three hundred and twenty seven participants who are SMEs and the data was analysed for checking the reliability and consistency by using Cronbach's Alpha test, descriptive analysis, correlation coefficients, regression and mediation exploration. The output of the analysis signified a very strong and positive association among the business performance, technological acceptance and intention to embrace the financial technological activities. Regression analysis in the study explores the impact of using fintech which extensively predicted the trust in technology. While foreseeing the business performance two variables namely intention to use fintech services and the trust in technology with high regression value shows a very strong predictor. Moreover the output from mediation analysis accounts that trust in technology affects greater on the performance of SMEs. The study also shows the minimum direct influence on the business performance mediated variable affects positive significance. Typically, embracement of financial technology is not just with the intention but also very strong trust in technology is required to perceive the system. The respondents and policymakers have to concentrate on crating trust to SMEs by enhancing the cybersecurity and privacy safeguards, enhancing transparent procedures, providing trustworthy activities, demonstrating easy pathways to reduce the conflicts and support customers. Moreover, Further research studies are suggested to perceive the risk activities, cost factors, trust issues to adopt financial inclusion and SMEs affordability. It is suggested to have future research studies with large respondents and use detailed studies to identify the variation in different time periods. The paper contributes to FinTech adoption research by examining the mediation effect of trust in the association between intention to use FinTech and performance of SMEs. Using an integrated TAM-UTAUT-trust model framework, the research offers a robust explanation of factors that influence FinTech adoption behaviour in small firms. The results reveal that the extent to which SMEs adopt FinTech depends largely on their level of trust in technology. Therefore, FinTech providers should focus on ensuring adequate security of their products in order to encourage their adoption among SMEs. The findings further show that high adoption rates will positively impact the performance of SMEs. The study further draws attention to the challenges that hinder the adoption of FinTech technology in emerging markets, where the cost and security factors are perceived as major deterrents. Policymakers and FinTech providers need to resolve such issues for increased adoption by SMEs.

## 7. REFERENCES


Arner, D. W., Barberis, J., & Buckley, R. P. (2015). The evolution of FinTech: A new post-crisis paradigm? *SSRN*, *47*(4), 1271–1319. DOI: 10.2139/ssrn.2676553

Arner, D. W., Barberis, J., & Buckley, R. P. (2017). FinTech and RegTech. *Northwestern Journal of International Law & Business*, *37*(3), 371–414.

Begum, A., Gaytan, J. C. T., & Ahmed, G. (2023). The nexus between technology and innovation: A sustainable development model. In *2023 International Conference on Business Analytics for Technology and Security (ICBATS)* (pp. 1–8). IEEE.

Chowdhury, E. K., & Chowdhury, R. (2024). Role of financial inclusion in human development: Evidence from Bangladesh, India and Pakistan. *Journal of the Knowledge Economy*, *15*(1), 3329–3354. DOI: 10.1007/s13132-023-01366-x

Davis, F. D. (1989). Perceived usefulness, perceived ease of use, and user acceptance of information technology. *Management Information Systems Quarterly*, *13*(3), 319–340. DOI: 10.2307/249008

Gai, K., Qiu, M., & Sun, X. (2018). A survey on FinTech. *Journal of Network and Computer Applications*, *103*, 262–273. DOI: 10.1016/j.jnca.2017.10.011

Gefen, D., Karahanna, E., & Straub, D. W. (2003). Trust and TAM in online shopping: An integrated model. *Management Information Systems Quarterly*, *27*(1), 51–90. DOI: 10.2307/30036519

Huang, R., Kale, S., Paramati, S. R., & Taghizadeh-Hesary, F. (2021). The nexus between financial inclusion and economic development: Comparison of old and new EU member countries. *Economic Analysis and Policy*, *69*, 1–15. DOI: 10.1016/j.eap.2020.10.007

Jagtiani, J., & Lemieux, C. (2018). The roles of alternative data and machine learning in FinTech lending: Evidence from the LendingClub consumer platform (Working Paper). Federal Reserve Bank of Philadelphia.

Jeng, S.-L. (2025). *FinTech rankings of six Taiwan municipalities*. Asia Pacific Management Review. DOI: 10.1016/j.apmrv.2025.100398

Kang, J. (2018). Mobile payment in FinTech environment: Trends, security challenges, and services. *Human-Centric Computing and Information Sciences*, *8*(1), 1–16. DOI: 10.1186/s13673-018-0155-4

Khatri, S., & Srivastava, H. (2022). COVID-19 and digital finance adoption. *Journal of Financial Services*, *12*(2).

Kilani, A. A.-H. Z., Kakeesh, D., Al-Weshah, G. A., & Al-Debei, M. M. (2023). Consumer post-adoption of e-wallet: An extended UTAUT2 perspective with trust. *Journal of Open Innovation*.

Kim, D. Y., Park, J., & Morrison, A. M. (2008). A model of traveller acceptance of mobile technology. *International Journal of Tourism Research, 10*(5), 393–407. DOI: 10.1002/jtr.669

Lee, M.-C. (2009). Factors influencing the adoption of internet banking: An integration of TAM and TPB with perceived risk and perceived benefit. *Electronic Commerce Research and Applications*, *8*(3), 130–141. DOI: 10.1016/j.elerap.2008.11.006

Liébana-Cabanillas, F., Sánchez-Fernández, J., & Muñoz-Leiva, F. (2014). Antecedents of the adoption of new mobile payment systems: The moderating effect of age. *Computers in Human Behavior, 35*, 464–478. DOI: 10.1016/j.chb.2014.03.022

Liu, X., Manzoor, A., Wang, C., Zhang, L., & Manzoor, Z. (2020). The role of FinTech in sustainable banking: A review. *Sustainability*, *12*(24), 10591.

Liu, Z., Qi, Z., Tian, Q., Clark, J. S., & Zhang, Z. (2024). The impact of digital finance on farmers' adoption of eco-agricultural technology: Evidence from rice–crayfish co-cultivation technology in China. *Preprints*.

Mathur, H. P. (2022). Conceptual development of factors driving FinTech adoption by farmers. Purushartha: A Journal of Management. *Ethics and Spirituality*, *15*(1), 39–50.

McKnight, D. H., Choudhury, V., & Kacmar, C. (2002). Developing and validating trust measures for e-commerce: An integrative typology. *Information Systems Research, 13*(3), 334–359. DOI: 10.1287/isre.13.3.334.81

Nicoletti, B. (2017). *The future of FinTech*. Springer. DOI: 10.1007/978-3-319-51415-4

Ozili, P. K. (2018). Impact of digital finance on financial inclusion and stability. *Borsa Istanbul Review*, *18*(4), 329–340. DOI: 10.1016/j.bir.2017.12.003

Pavlou, P. A. (2003). Consumer acceptance of electronic commerce: Integrating trust and risk with the technology acceptance model. *International Journal of Electronic Commerce*, *7*(3), 101–134. DOI: 10.1080/10864415.2003.11044275

Rahi, S., Mansour, M. M. O., Alghizzawi, M., & Alnaser, F. M. (2019). Integration of UTAUT model in internet banking adoption context: The mediating role of performance expectancy and effort expectancy. *Journal of Research in Interactive Marketing*, *13*(3), 411–435. DOI: 10.1108/JRIM-02-2018-0032

Schnackenberg, A. K., & Tomlinson, E. C. (2016). Organizational transparency: A new perspective on managing trust in organization–stakeholder relationships. *Journal of Management*, *42*(7), 1784–1810. DOI: 10.1177/0149206314525202

Sharma, S. K., & Sharma, M. (2019). Examining the role of trust and quality dimensions in the actual usage of mobile banking services: An empirical investigation. *International Journal of Information Management*, *44*, 65–75. DOI: 10.1016/j.ijinfomgt.2018.09.013

Srivastava, G., Mishra, S., & Nigam, N. (2025). Digital transformation in FinTech: Redefining wealth creation and investment. In *Digital transformation in finance*. Emerald Publishing., DOI: 10.1108/978-1-83662-188-120251013

Stoeckli, E., Dremel, C., & Uebernickel, F. (2018). Exploring characteristics and transformational capabilities of InsurTech innovations to understand insurance value creation in a digital world. *Electronic Markets*, *28*(3), 287–305. DOI: 10.1007/s12525-018-0304-7

Vardari, L., & Hameli, K. (2025). Perceived benefits, trust and social influence in FinTech: Pathways to adoption and satisfaction in a developing economy. *Global Knowledge, Memory and Communication*. Advance online publication. DOI: 10.1108/GKMC-02-2025-0137

Varga, D. (2017). FinTech, the new era of financial services. *Budapest Management Review*, *48*(11), 22–32. DOI: 10.14267/VEZTUD.2017.11.03

Venkatesh, V., Morris, M. G., Davis, G. B., & Davis, F. D. (2003). User acceptance of information technology: Toward a unified view. *Management Information Systems Quarterly*, *27*(3), 425–478. DOI: 10.2307/30036540

Vives, X. (2017). *The impact of FinTech on banking*. European Economy—Banks, Regulation, and the Real Sector.

World Bank. (2022). FinTech and the future of finance.

Yang, T., & Zhang, X. (2022). FinTech adoption and financial inclusion: Evidence from household consumption in China. *Journal of Banking & Finance*, *145*, 106668. DOI: 10.1016/j.jbankfin.2022.106668

Zhou, T. (2012). Understanding users' initial trust in mobile banking: An elaboration likelihood perspective. *Computers in Human Behavior*, *28*(4), 1518–1525. DOI: 10.1016/j.chb.2012.03.021

# Chapter 4
# Democratizing Finance With Kickstarter's Crowdfunding in the Digital Era

**Alaattin Parlakkılıç**
http://orcid.org/0000-0002-6834-6839
*Ufuk University, Turkey*

## ABSTRACT

*The research explores how crowdfunding integrates financing and digital marketing, enabling entrepreneurs to directly engage with consumers and investors, thereby expanding access to capital and market participation. A qualitative case study approach was adopted, using document analysis and an extensive literature review covering crowdfunding, e-commerce, digital marketing, and digital consumer behavior. The findings indicate that Kickstarter provides a transparent and interactive environment where producers can secure funding, market their products, and obtain real-time consumer feedback. While the platform lowers financial entry barriers and enhances market engagement, it also presents challenges such as increased competition, consumer fatigue, and algorithm-driven visibility inequalities. Overall, the study concludes that although crowdfunding contributes to the democratization of finance and marketing, structural and behavioral limitations restrict its full potential, highlighting the need for improved platform governance and regulatory frameworks.*

DOI: 10.4018/979-8-2600-3179-7.ch004

## 1. INTRODUCTION

The rapid expansion of online shopping and its transformative effects on consumer behavior has become one of the most widely discussed topics in recent academic literature. With the advancement of digital technologies and increasing internet penetration, consumers have shifted from traditional brick-and-mortar purchasing habits toward more flexible, convenient, and personalized online shopping experiences. This transition has not only reshaped consumption patterns but has also fundamentally altered the dynamics of supply chains, marketing strategies, and competitive structures within markets. Particularly during the COVID-19 pandemic, the necessity of social distancing accelerated the adoption of e-commerce, making it an essential component of daily life rather than a complementary alternative. As a result, businesses across industries were compelled to digitize their operations, and consumers became increasingly reliant on digital platforms for their everyday needs.

Parallel to these developments, the concept of Industry 5.0 has emerged as a new paradigm, emphasizing the integration of advanced technologies with human-centric values. Unlike Industry 4.0, which primarily focuses on automation and efficiency, Industry 5.0 highlights collaboration between humans and intelligent systems, prioritizing personalization, sustainability, and societal well-being. Within this framework, digital platforms have evolved into ecosystems where not only transactions but also innovation, collaboration, and value co-creation take place. One of the most notable outcomes of this transformation is the rise of crowdfunding platforms, which have redefined how entrepreneurial ventures are financed and brought to market.

Among these platforms, Kickstarter has gained particular prominence as a pioneering example of reward-based crowdfunding. Founded with the intention of democratizing access to capital, Kickstarter enables creators to present their ideas directly to potential backers without relying on traditional financial intermediaries such as banks or venture capital firms. This model allows individuals with creative and innovative ideas—who might otherwise struggle to secure funding—to reach a global audience and obtain the necessary financial support. At the same time, investors, often referred to as backers, gain the opportunity to participate in the early stages of product development, thereby influencing innovation processes and market trends. The increasing popularity and success of platforms like Kickstarter have attracted significant academic interest, as they represent a shift toward more inclusive and decentralized economic systems (Jafari, Azarian, & Yu, 2022).

The crowdfunding financing model has thus become an indispensable mechanism for fostering innovation and entrepreneurship. It reduces entry barriers for new market participants and encourages experimentation by distributing financial risk among a large number of contributors. In the absence of such models, many innovative ideas might remain unrealized due to limited access to traditional funding sources. Consequently, crowdfunding not only supports individual entrepreneurs but also contributes to broader economic development by stimulating competition and diversification within markets. As emphasized by Shneor, Flåten, and Zhao (2020), crowdfunding serves as a catalyst for creativity, enabling a more dynamic and inclusive innovation ecosystem.

Moreover, crowdfunding platforms facilitate direct interaction between producers and consumers, thereby reshaping traditional roles within the marketplace. In this context, consumers are no longer passive recipients of products; instead, they actively participate in the development process by providing feedback, financial support, and social validation. This participatory approach enhances transparency and trust while also allowing creators to test market demand before committing to large-scale production. As a result, crowdfunding platforms function not only as financing tools but also as marketing and validation mechanisms.

Kickstarter, in particular, exemplifies this multifaceted role. The platform hosts a wide range of projects across categories such as technology, design, arts, and gaming, each accompanied by detailed descriptions, funding goals, and reward structures. The data generated by these projects—including funding amounts, success rates, and backer engagement—offers valuable insights into consumer preferences and market dynamics. Researchers have increasingly utilized such data to analyze factors influencing project success, including campaign design, social media presence, and communication strategies (John, John, & Han, 2022). These analyses contribute to a deeper understanding of how digital environments shape economic behavior and decision-making processes.

Despite the growing body of research on crowdfunding, there remains a relative scarcity of comprehensive studies that examine these platforms from a holistic perspective, particularly in terms of their implications for market democratization. This study aims to address this gap by focusing on platforms established for the implementation of the crowdfunding financing model, with a specific emphasis on Kickstarter. The research examines the entire ecosystem of the platform, including the diversity of projects, the interaction between stakeholders, and the financial outcomes associated with different types of campaigns. By analyzing these elements, the study seeks to provide a more nuanced understanding of how crowdfunding platforms influence both producer and consumer activities.

The scope of this study is limited to commercial activities conducted online through the crowdfunding model. The participants involved—both producers and consumers—are assumed to possess a certain level of digital literacy and familiarity with digital marketing tools. This assumption is the effectiveness of crowdfunding campaigns often depends on the ability of creators to leverage digital channels for promotion and engagement. Therefore, the intersection of crowdfunding and digital marketing constitutes a central focus of this research.

In this context, Kickstarter serves as a case study for examining the convergence of crowdfunding and digital marketing within the broader e-commerce environment. The platform not only enables financial transactions but also provides tools for storytelling, branding, and community building. These features allow creators to establish emotional connections with potential backers, thereby increasing the likelihood of campaign success. At the same time, backers benefit from early access to innovative products and the satisfaction of supporting creative endeavors.

The primary aim of this study is to analyze the innovations introduced by the Kickstarter platform and to evaluate their impact on producer and consumer activities. More specifically, the research explores how the integration of crowdfunding and digital marketing contributes to the democratization of the trade environment. By lowering barriers to entry and facilitating direct interaction between stakeholders, Kickstarter and similar platforms have the potential to create more equitable and inclusive markets. However, it is also important to critically examine potential challenges, such as information asymmetry, project failure risks, and unequal visibility among campaigns.

In conclusion, the rise of crowdfunding platforms represents a significant shift in the way economic activities are organized and conducted in the digital age. As e-commerce continues to evolve, understanding the mechanisms and implications of these platforms becomes increasingly important for both academics and practitioners. This study contributes to the existing literature by providing a comprehensive analysis of Kickstarter as a representative example of crowdfunding innovation, with particular emphasis on its role in reshaping market dynamics and promoting democratization.

## 2. THEORETICAL FRAMEWORK

The theoretical framework of this research is grounded in the interplay between industrial revolutions and the evolution of marketing paradigms, both of which have continuously reshaped production systems, consumption patterns, and market structures. Industrial revolutions have not only transformed how goods and services are produced but have also fundamentally influenced how they are marketed and delivered to consumers. Each phase of industrial development has introduced new technological capabilities that expand firms' ability to reach, understand, and interact with their target audiences. Consequently, marketing has evolved from a product-oriented function into a complex, data-driven, and interactive system that emphasizes customer engagement, personalization, and co-creation.

Within this broader transformation, digitalization plays a central role. The transition from traditional to digital environments has significantly altered the nature of economic interactions, enabling real-time communication and reducing the distance between producers and consumers. In this context, crowdfunding platforms have emerged as innovative tools that embody the convergence of production, financing, and marketing processes. Among these platforms, Kickstarter represents a prominent example, functioning not only as a funding mechanism but also as a digital marketing and market validation tool.

Kickstarter, the focal platform of this study, emerged during the Industry 4.0 era and aligns closely with the principles of Marketing 4.0, which emphasize the integration of digital technologies into marketing strategies (Kauffman & Naldi, 2020). Industry 4.0 introduced cyber-physical systems, automation, and advanced data analytics into production processes, enabling firms to operate more efficiently and respond more rapidly to market demands. Simultaneously, Marketing 4.0 facilitated the transition from traditional, one-way communication models to interactive, multi-channel engagement strategies. This shift allowed consumers to actively participate in the marketing process, influencing product development, branding, and distribution.

The rise of e-commerce is a critical component of this transformation. Historically, commerce was constrained by physical boundaries, but digital platforms have eliminated these limitations, allowing transactions to occur anytime and anywhere. During the COVID-19 pandemic, this shift accelerated dramatically, reinforcing the importance of online environments in everyday economic activities. Consumers now rely on digital channels not only for purchasing products but also for gathering information, comparing alternatives, and sharing feedback. As noted by De', Pandey, and Pal (2020), digital platforms have transformed consumers into active participants who can directly communicate their preferences and expectations to producers.

This participatory role of consumers has profound implications for marketing theory and practice. Traditional marketing models, which viewed consumers as passive recipients of promotional messages, are no longer sufficient to explain contemporary market dynamics. Instead, modern marketing emphasizes interaction, engagement, and value co-creation. Digital marketing, as a key enabler of this transformation, provides tools and techniques that facilitate continuous communication between producers and consumers. Social media platforms, data analytics, and personalized advertising strategies allow firms to build stronger relationships with their audiences and respond more effectively to their needs.

In this regard, Kickstarter serves as a unique integrative platform that connects crowdfunding, digital marketing, and e-commerce within a single ecosystem. The platform enables creators to present their projects, communicate their value propositions, and engage directly with potential backers. At the same time, it provides valuable data on consumer behavior, preferences, and engagement patterns. This data is not only beneficial for producers seeking to optimize their campaigns but also for consumers who rely on social proof and community feedback when making funding decisions. As Rangaswamy et al. (2020) emphasize, such platforms create a dynamic interaction environment in which information flows bidirectionally, enhancing transparency and trust.

## 2.1 Phases of Marketing

The evolution of marketing can be understood as a response to technological advancements and changing consumer expectations. Each phase of marketing reflects a distinct set of assumptions about the role of the consumer, the nature of competition, and the strategic priorities of firms. These phases are closely linked to the stages of industrial development, highlighting the interdependence between production systems and marketing practices.

The emergence of technologies such as the Internet of Things (IoT), the Internet of Services, cyber-physical systems, and smart factories has fundamentally redefined production processes. These technologies enable seamless communication between machines, systems, and humans, creating highly flexible and adaptive production environments. The Industry 5.0 paradigm builds upon these developments by emphasizing human-centricity, sustainability, and resilience. Unlike Industry 4.0, which prioritizes automation and efficiency, Industry 5.0 seeks to integrate human creativity and intelligence with advanced technologies, resulting in more personalized and meaningful products and services (Saracel & Aksoy, 2020; Yücebalkan, 2020).

Although Industry 5.0 is often described as a future-oriented concept, its principles are already observable in current practices. Many firms are adopting hybrid models that combine the efficiency of automated systems with the flexibility of human input. This approach enables the production of customized goods that cater to individual preferences while maintaining cost-effectiveness. As Dombrowski and Wagner (2014) suggest, such models support a more responsive and customer-oriented production system.

The historical development of marketing begins with Marketing 1.0, which emerged in the 1950s and focused primarily on mass production and cost efficiency. During this period, markets were largely supply-driven, and the primary objective of firms was to produce standardized goods at scale and distribute them as widely as possible. Marketing was considered a functional activity aimed at facilitating product distribution, with little emphasis on consumer needs or preferences. Communication was unidirectional, relying on traditional media channels such as television, radio, and print. Consumers played a passive role, and competition was driven by aggressive advertising and pricing strategies (Büyükkalaycı & Karaca, 2019).

The transition to Marketing 2.0 marked a significant shift toward a more consumer-oriented approach. This phase was driven by increased competition, market saturation, and the proliferation of information technologies. As consumers gained access to more information and a wider range of product choices, they became more selective and demanding. Firms responded by adopting segmentation and targeting strategies, focusing on understanding customer needs and delivering tailored value propositions. Marketing became more interactive and emotionally engaging, emphasizing customer satisfaction and brand loyalty (Jara et al., 2012).

Marketing 3.0 further expanded this perspective by recognizing consumers as holistic individuals with emotional, social, and ethical dimensions. In this phase, companies began to align their brand identities with broader societal values, such as sustainability, social responsibility, and ethical practices. The focus shifted from purely economic transactions to creating meaningful relationships and contributing to societal well-being. As Kotler, Kartajaya, and Setiawan (2010) argue, Marketing 3.0 represents a values-driven approach that seeks to address the aspirations and concerns of modern consumers.

The advent of digital technologies gave rise to Marketing 4.0, which integrates online and offline interactions within a unified framework. This phase is characterized by the use of big data, artificial intelligence, and advanced analytics to understand consumer behavior and deliver personalized experiences. Real-time communication and customer engagement have become central to marketing strategies, requiring firms to adopt more agile and responsive approaches. Marketers must possess a diverse set of skills, including data analysis, content creation, and digital communication. As highlighted by Durukal (2019) and Ertuğrul and Deniz (2018), Marketing 4.0 emphasizes the importance of customer experience and the ability to deliver value at the right time and place.

In this context, crowdfunding platforms like Kickstarter exemplify the principles of Marketing 4.0 by enabling direct interaction between producers and consumers. Campaign creators use storytelling, social media integration, and data-driven strategies to attract and engage backers. At the same time, consumers actively participate in the marketing process by sharing feedback, promoting campaigns, and influencing outcomes.

Looking ahead, Marketing 5.0 represents the next stage in this evolution, characterized by the integration of emerging technologies such as artificial intelligence, machine learning, blockchain, and augmented reality into marketing strategies. These technologies have the potential to further enhance personalization, improve decision-making processes, and create more immersive customer experiences. According to Draganov et al. (2018), Marketing 5.0 will enable firms to anticipate consumer needs more accurately and deliver highly customized solutions in real time.

In conclusion, the evolution of marketing reflects a continuous adaptation to technological and societal changes. From mass production to personalized experiences, and from passive consumption to active participation, marketing has undergone profound transformations that have redefined the relationship between producers and consumers. Within this dynamic landscape, platforms like Kickstarter serve as critical nodes that integrate multiple dimensions of modern marketing, making them essential subjects for academic investigation.

The concepts applied in this study align primarily with the **Industry 4.0** and **Marketing 4.0** paradigms. The Kickstarter platform represents an ideal convergence point of e-commerce, crowdfunding, and digital marketing. Its planning structure reflects digital marketing strategies, and its financing approach aligns with the crowdfunding model. Table 1 below illustrates the evolution of marketing in parallel with the industrial revolutions.

*Table 1. The marketing changes based on the industrial revolutions*

| Marketing Phase / Feature | Marketing 1.0 | Marketing 2.0 | Marketing 3.0 | Marketing 4.0 | Marketing 5.0 |
|---|---|---|---|---|---|
| **Industrial Era** | Industry 1.0 | Industry 2.0 | Industry 3.0 | Industry 4.0 | Industry 5.0 |
| **History** | 1870-1900 | 1900-1950 | 1950-1980 | 1980-2030 | 2030 and beyond |
| **Focus** | Sales | Customer | Values generation | Satisfaction of emotions | Machine-individual integration |
| **basis** | limited production | fabrication production | Mass production | Automation | Personalized-intelligent manufacturing |
| **Products** | Agriculture and craft | Basic need products | Technological products | high-tech products | Virtual reality products |
| **nature** | traditional marketing | Pre-modern marketing | modern marketing | Post-modern marketing | Post-digital marketing |
| **Marketing Communication Management** | One-way communication | traditional communication | Web 2.0 | digital communication | Artificial intelligence communication |

(Alankuş, 2021, p. 101) .

Until recently, e-commerce was considered a supplementary element within manufacturers' broader business strategies, primarily functioning as an additional sales channel rather than a core strategic component. However, with the rapid acceleration of technological innovation, widespread internet accessibility, and the development of supportive legal and regulatory frameworks, e-commerce has progressively shifted toward the center of corporate strategy. It is now widely recognized as a fundamental driver of competitiveness, innovation, and market expansion in the digital economy (Carpenter, 2011). In contemporary business environments, firms are no longer able to treat digital channels as optional; instead, they must integrate them into all levels of strategic planning, including marketing, logistics, customer relationship management, and product development.

One of the most critical enablers of this transformation has been advancements in information and communication technologies (ICT). These technologies have significantly reduced transaction costs, improved communication speed, and enhanced access to global markets. ICT has also facilitated the emergence of new business models such as platform-based economies, subscription services, and digital marketplaces. As a result, entrepreneurs are now able to develop and scale innovative business ideas with relatively lower entry barriers compared to traditional offline markets. Numerous empirical studies have confirmed a positive relationship between ICT development and productivity growth in manufacturing and service industries, highlighting the importance of digital infrastructure in sustaining economic development.

Despite these advantages, the early stages of e-commerce adoption were characterized by several structural and organizational challenges. Many firms struggled with integrating digital systems into their existing operations due to a lack of technical expertise, insufficient IT infrastructure, and unclear digital business models. Employees often lacked the necessary training to operate in digital environments, which led to inefficiencies and delayed implementation processes. Furthermore, uncertainties regarding cybersecurity, online payment systems, and consumer trust further slowed down initial adoption rates. These challenges were particularly evident among small and medium-sized enterprises (SMEs), which often lacked the financial and technical resources required for digital transformation.

Over time, however, the increasing dominance of digital technologies in global markets has forced organizations to overcome these barriers. Governments and private institutions have invested heavily in digital infrastructure, while educational programs have improved digital literacy among both employees and consumers. As a result, e-commerce has experienced exponential growth and has become a key component of global trade. Today, digital platforms are not only used for product sales but also for marketing, branding, customer engagement, and data analytics, making them essential tools for competitive advantage.

A significant contribution to understanding the development of the e-commerce sector in emerging economies was provided by the TÜSİAD report (2017), which emphasized the importance of identifying structural prerequisites for sustainable digital growth. According to the report, critical factors such as digital literacy, logistics efficiency, data security, payment infrastructure, and regulatory transparency are essential for maximizing the potential of e-commerce ecosystems (Kantarcı et al., 2017). Without these foundational elements, the full benefits of digital transformation cannot be realized, particularly in developing markets where institutional frameworks may still be evolving.

In addition to macroeconomic benefits, e-commerce provides substantial opportunities for small businesses and individual entrepreneurs. By reducing dependency on physical infrastructure and traditional distribution channels, digital platforms allow smaller firms to access wider markets and compete with larger corporations on more equal terms. This democratization of market access has contributed to increased entrepreneurial activity and innovation. Moreover, e-commerce enables firms to collect and analyze large volumes of consumer data, which can be used to optimize pricing strategies, improve product design, and enhance customer satisfaction.

Another important feature of e-commerce is its ability to facilitate direct and continuous communication between producers and consumers. Unlike traditional retail systems, where feedback is often delayed or indirect, digital platforms allow consumers to instantly share their opinions, experiences, and preferences. This creates a dynamic feedback loop that enables firms to adjust their offerings in real time. As Soydal (2006) argues, this transformation effectively turns consumers into active participants in the production and innovation process, rather than passive recipients of goods and services. In this sense, e-commerce not only changes how products are sold but also fundamentally reshapes how they are designed and developed.

In conclusion, e-commerce has evolved from a supplementary sales channel into a central component of modern economic systems. Its integration with ICT, digital marketing, and data analytics has redefined traditional business models and created new opportunities for innovation and growth. However, the full potential of e-commerce can only be realized through continued investment in infrastructure, education, and regulatory development. As digital transformation continues to accelerate, e-commerce will remain a key driver of global economic integration and market democratization.

When classified by supply and demand relationships, e-commerce applications can take several forms. As shown in Table 2, these models include business-to-business (B2B), business-to-consumer (B2C), consumer-to-consumer (C2C), and others. The focus of this study is on the **B2C model**, where products and services are delivered directly from producers to consumers through digital platforms.

*Table 2. E-commerce models*

| | **State** | **Company** | **Consumer** | **Artificial intelligence** |
|---|---|---|---|---|
| **State** | G2G | G2B | G2C | G2A |
| **Company** | B2G | B2B | B2C | B2A |
| **Consumer** | C2G | C2B | C2C<br>P2P | C2A |
| **Artificial intelligence** | A2G | A2B | A2C | A2A |

## 2.3 Digital Marketing

As of 2022, approximately 70% of the global population has access to the internet, representing a dramatic increase compared to less than 1% in 1995 (Internet Live Stats, 2022). This unprecedented growth in digital connectivity has fundamentally reshaped communication patterns, consumption habits, and production systems across the world. The expansion of internet infrastructure, mobile technologies, and social media platforms has enabled businesses to interact with consumers in real time and across geographical boundaries. As a result, digital marketing has become a central pillar of modern business strategy, replacing many traditional marketing approaches that were previously dependent on physical channels and mass communication methods.

Digital marketing can be broadly defined as the use of digital channels, platforms, and technologies to promote products and services, engage with consumers, and generate measurable business outcomes. Unlike traditional marketing, which relies heavily on one-way communication, digital marketing enables interactive, data-driven, and personalized engagement between firms and consumers. This shift has transformed consumers from passive recipients of marketing messages into active participants in the marketing process, capable of influencing brand perception and product development through feedback, reviews, and online behavior.

The development of a structured digital marketing strategy typically involves several key stages: analysis, planning, execution, interaction, and conversion (Gökşin, 2018). The analysis stage focuses on understanding market conditions, consumer behavior, and competitive dynamics using digital data sources. In the planning phase, firms define objectives, target audiences, and communication strategies. Execution involves the implementation of digital campaigns across various channels, while interaction refers to ongoing engagement with users through platforms such as social media, email, and websites. Finally, the conversion stage evaluates the effectiveness of campaigns in terms of sales, engagement, or other performance indicators. These stages form a continuous cycle, where feedback from consumers is used to refine future strategies.

The evolution of digital marketing is closely linked to technological innovation and changing consumer expectations. In the context of Marketing 4.0, businesses increasingly aim to deliver personalized and context-specific experiences to consumers. This requires the integration of advanced technologies such as artificial intelligence, big data analytics, and machine learning into marketing processes. As digital ecosystems become more complex, firms are expected to diversify their marketing channels and adopt more sophisticated tools to remain competitive. Common digital marketing tools include search engine optimization (SEO), social media marketing, email marketing, mobile marketing, affiliate marketing, pay-per-click

(PPC) advertising, viral marketing, gamification, and location-based marketing. More recently, crowdfunding platforms have also emerged as an important digital marketing channel, combining financial engagement with promotional activity (Rangaswamy et al., 2020).

Kickstarter represents a particularly significant example of the convergence between digital marketing and crowdfunding. Unlike traditional e-commerce platforms, Kickstarter integrates funding mechanisms with marketing functions, allowing creators to validate ideas while simultaneously promoting them to potential backers. One of the key advantages of this model is the ability to gather real-time feedback from users, which enables creators to adjust their strategies quickly and efficiently. This reduces market uncertainty and minimizes financial risk associated with product development (White, Habib, & Hardisty, 2019). Additionally, the platform's digital structure allows for flexible working arrangements and global accessibility, enabling entrepreneurs to reach international audiences without the constraints of physical distribution channels.

However, the increased accessibility and democratization of digital marketing also intensify competition among content creators and entrepreneurs. As more projects compete for attention in digital environments, visibility becomes a critical success factor. This leads to a highly competitive ecosystem where campaigns must be carefully designed, strategically promoted, and continuously optimized. At the same time, the abundance of choices available to consumers can lead to cognitive overload and decision fatigue, making it more difficult for users to evaluate and select among alternatives (Faruk, Rahman, & Hasan, 2021).

The COVID-19 pandemic further accelerated the transformation of digital marketing practices. Lockdowns, social distancing measures, and restrictions on physical interaction significantly altered consumer behavior and purchasing patterns. During this period, demand for online services, digital entertainment, e-learning platforms, and food delivery applications increased substantially. Conversely, demand for physical luxury goods and in-person services declined due to health concerns and mobility restrictions (Martinelli et al., 2021). These changes highlighted the importance of digital resilience and adaptability in marketing strategies.

In the post-pandemic era, these behavioral shifts have had lasting effects on both consumers and producers. Companies have increasingly adopted hybrid marketing models that combine online and offline strategies to meet evolving consumer expectations. Kickstarter's business model has proven particularly adaptable in this context, as it aligns with the growing preference for digital interaction, early product access, and community-based decision-making (Alankuş, 2021). The platform's ability to integrate storytelling, funding, and marketing within a single digital ecosystem makes it a powerful tool in the contemporary marketing landscape.

## 2.4 Crowdfunding

While reaching a target audience is essential for entrepreneurial success, securing adequate funding remains one of the most significant challenges for startups and early-stage ventures. Traditionally, entrepreneurs have relied on personal savings, family networks, friends, angel investors, or venture capital firms to finance their projects. However, these conventional funding sources are often limited, highly competitive, and inaccessible to many innovators, particularly those without strong financial or professional networks. Globalization and digital transformation have intensified competition in entrepreneurial ecosystems, increasing the need for alternative financing models that can support a broader range of projects (Çağlar, 2019).

Crowdfunding has emerged as a transformative financing model that leverages digital platforms to connect entrepreneurs directly with potential investors. This model eliminates traditional financial intermediaries and enables individuals to contribute small amounts of capital toward projects they find valuable or interesting. Crowdfunding ecosystems typically involve three main actors: the project initiator (entrepreneur), the contributor (investor or backer), and the digital platform that facilitates interaction between them. These platforms serve as both financial intermediaries and communication channels, playing a crucial role in project visibility and success.

Crowdfunding models are generally classified into two main categories: non-financial (rewards-based and donation-based) and financial (equity-based and debt-based) crowdfunding (Fettahoğlu & Khusayan, 2017; Sakarya & Bezirgan, 2018). Non-financial crowdfunding includes donation-based models, where contributors do not expect any return, and reward-based or pre-order models, where contributors receive non-monetary incentives such as early access to products or exclusive benefits. Platforms such as GoFundMe, Kiva, Kickstarter, and Indiegogo represent prominent examples of these models.

Financial crowdfunding, on the other hand, involves monetary returns for investors. Debt-based crowdfunding, also known as peer-to-peer lending, allows individuals to lend money directly to borrowers through platforms such as Lending Club, Funding Circle, and Prosper, often with lower interest rates and reduced transaction costs compared to traditional banking systems. Equity-based crowdfunding enables investors to acquire ownership stakes in startups, with platforms such as Crowdcube, FundedByMe, and MicroVentures facilitating these transactions. This model provides entrepreneurs with access to capital while offering investors the potential for financial returns.

Crowdfunding offers several advantages for both entrepreneurs and investors. For entrepreneurs, it provides access to alternative funding sources, reduces dependency on traditional financial institutions, and enables market validation before product launch. It also enhances visibility and marketing reach, as successful campaigns often generate media attention and consumer interest. For investors, crowdfunding offers opportunities to support innovative projects, diversify investment portfolios, and participate in early-stage ventures that were previously inaccessible.

Despite these advantages, crowdfunding also presents certain risks and limitations. Many campaigns fail to reach their funding goals, leading to project discontinuation or financial losses for entrepreneurs. Additionally, issues such as intellectual property risks, project delays, and fraud can undermine trust in crowdfunding platforms. From an investor perspective, liquidity constraints and a lack of regulatory protection may pose significant challenges. Cybersecurity risks also represent an emerging concern, as digital platforms are vulnerable to data breaches and fraudulent activities (Kirby & Worner, 2014).

In conclusion, crowdfunding has emerged as a powerful alternative financing mechanism that complements traditional financial systems. By democratizing access to capital and enabling direct interaction between entrepreneurs and investors, it plays a critical role in fostering innovation and entrepreneurship in the digital economy.

## 3. RESEARCH METHOD

This study adopts a **qualitative research design** to analyze the relationship between crowdfunding and digital marketing on platforms like Kickstarter. Data were collected through **document analysis**, a widely used qualitative method when direct observation or interviews are not feasible. Sources included empirical studies, academic journals, periodicals, books, statistical reports, and open-access data.

The research employs the **case study method**, a qualitative technique that enables in-depth examination of a specific phenomenon or context. This approach is particularly useful for defining complex systems and holistically understanding their dynamics. The study was conducted in multiple stages: (1) defining the research problem, (2) determining the research scope, (3) collecting relevant documents and data, and (4) analyzing findings in alignment with the theoretical framework.

This approach allows for an intensive exploration of how Kickstarter functions within the broader context of e-commerce, digital marketing, and crowdfunding, particularly in light of post-pandemic changes in consumer behavior and technological adoption.

## 4. ANALYSIS OF THE KICKSTARTER PLATFORM

The rapid development of internet technologies has fundamentally transformed not only traditional commerce but also the structure and dynamics of entrepreneurial ecosystems. In the digital age, e-commerce platforms have significantly accelerated the pace of business activities, enabling entrepreneurs to launch, promote, and scale their ventures with unprecedented speed and flexibility. The internet has evolved into a central infrastructure for economic exchange, functioning simultaneously as a marketplace, communication channel, and financing mechanism. Within this environment, entrepreneurial activity has shifted from localized and resource-intensive processes to globally accessible and digitally mediated systems. As a result, the boundaries between producers, consumers, and investors have become increasingly blurred.

In contemporary digital economies, the internet serves both as the starting point and the endpoint of commercial transactions. Entrepreneurs increasingly rely on digital platforms not only to market their products but also to secure initial funding and validate market demand. This shift has given rise to innovative business models in which consumers are no longer passive buyers but active participants in the production and financing process. In such models, individuals who contribute financially to a project often become its first customers, early adopters, and even co-developers. Kickstarter represents one of the most prominent examples of this convergence of roles, integrating crowdfunding, marketing, and product development into a unified digital ecosystem.

Kickstarter is a reward-based crowdfunding platform that enables entrepreneurs, artists, designers, and innovators to present their ideas to a global audience. The platform covers a wide range of categories, including technology, art, film, music, publishing, gaming, journalism, food, and design. Creators are allowed to upload project descriptions, prototypes, videos, and funding goals, which are then made accessible to potential backers worldwide. If users find the project appealing or valuable, they can pledge financial support in exchange for non-monetary rewards such as early product access, exclusive editions, or acknowledgments. This model eliminates the need for traditional intermediaries such as banks or venture capital firms, thereby democratizing access to funding.

From an entrepreneurial perspective, Kickstarter provides a highly valuable alternative financing mechanism, particularly for individuals and small businesses that face difficulties in accessing conventional financial institutions. Traditional funding sources often require collateral, credit history, or established business performance, which can be significant barriers for early-stage innovators. Kickstarter, on the other hand, allows entrepreneurs to bypass these barriers by directly engaging with potential users. This direct-to-consumer funding model reduces entry barriers and fosters a more inclusive innovation environment. According to Mollick (2014), crowdfunding platforms like Kickstarter significantly increase the likelihood of entrepreneurial experimentation by lowering financial risk and enabling market validation prior to product launch.

From the consumer's perspective, Kickstarter introduces a fundamentally new form of participation in the product development process. Unlike traditional e-commerce systems, where consumers only interact with finished products, Kickstarter users engage with projects at their earliest stages. Backers can follow project updates, view prototypes, and monitor development progress in real time. In many cases, they also provide feedback that directly influences product design and functionality. This interactive relationship transforms consumers into co-creators, enhancing their emotional and psychological attachment to the product. As Gerber and Hui (2013) note, crowdfunding platforms foster a sense of community and shared ownership, which strengthens user engagement and trust.

One of the most significant advantages of this model is its ability to reduce uncertainty in the market. In traditional e-commerce, consumers often face information asymmetry because they cannot physically inspect or test products before purchasing. Kickstarter mitigates this issue by providing detailed project descriptions, visual prototypes, and transparent funding goals. Additionally, the platform's funding structure ensures that projects are only executed if they reach their financial targets, reducing the risk of incomplete or unsuccessful product development. This "all-or-nothing" funding mechanism increases accountability and minimizes financial risk for both creators and backers (Belleflamme, Lambert, & Schwienbacher, 2014).

Kickstarter also plays a critical role in shaping modern marketing practices. The platform integrates storytelling, digital communication, and community building into a single marketing ecosystem. Successful campaigns are often characterized by strong narratives, emotional appeal, and effective use of multimedia content such as videos and graphics. These elements are essential for attracting attention in highly competitive digital environments where thousands of projects compete for visibility. Moreover, social media integration allows creators to expand their reach beyond the platform itself, leveraging external networks to drive traffic and funding.

Another important aspect of Kickstarter's ecosystem is its data-generating capacity. Every interaction on the platform—such as pledges, comments, shares, and updates—produces valuable behavioral data that can be analyzed to understand consumer preferences and market trends. Researchers and practitioners increasingly use this data to identify success factors in crowdfunding campaigns. For instance, factors such as campaign duration, funding goal size, communication frequency, and social media engagement have been shown to significantly influence campaign outcomes (Cordova, Dolci, & Gianfrate, 2015).

Despite its advantages, Kickstarter also presents several challenges and limitations. One of the most significant issues is project failure. A substantial proportion of campaigns fail to deliver promised products on time or within expected quality standards. This can lead to dissatisfaction among backers and damage trust in the platform. Additionally, intellectual property risks are a concern, as public disclosure of project ideas may expose creators to imitation or theft. Financial risks also exist for backers, as crowdfunding investments are typically not legally protected in the same way as traditional financial instruments. Furthermore, the increasing number of campaigns has led to information overload, making it difficult for users to evaluate and differentiate between projects.

Another critical challenge is competition intensity. As the platform grows, creators must invest more effort into marketing and visibility strategies to stand out. This has led to the professionalization of crowdfunding campaigns, where success increasingly depends on marketing expertise rather than purely innovative ideas. In this sense, Kickstarter has evolved from a simple funding platform into a highly competitive digital marketplace where branding, communication, and audience engagement play crucial roles.

In conclusion, Kickstarter represents a transformative innovation in the fields of e-commerce, crowdfunding, and digital marketing. By integrating financing, communication, and product development into a single platform, it has redefined traditional entrepreneurial processes. The platform not only democratizes access to capital but also enhances consumer participation and market transparency. However, its effectiveness depends on a range of factors including campaign design, user engagement, and market competition. As digital economies continue to evolve, platforms like Kickstarter will remain central to understanding the future of entrepreneurship and consumer behavior.

Unlike conventional online sales models, where consumers typically make decisions based on static product listings, the Kickstarter model relies on transparency and continuous communication. Entrepreneurs must convincingly present their concepts—often in early or draft form—and earn the support of potential backers. There is little room for incomplete or misleading representations, as funding success hinges directly on the perceived value and credibility of the project. This fosters a highly transparent and trust-based commercial ecosystem, as illustrated in Figure 1 (not shown here).

In summary, Kickstarter operates not only as a crowdfunding platform but also as a dynamic digital marketplace that merges financing and marketing. It empowers creators to build communities around their projects while simultaneously providing consumers with a sense of ownership and participation in product development.

*Figure 1. The diagram shows the production and marketing phases. (Guan et al., 2020, p. 3)*

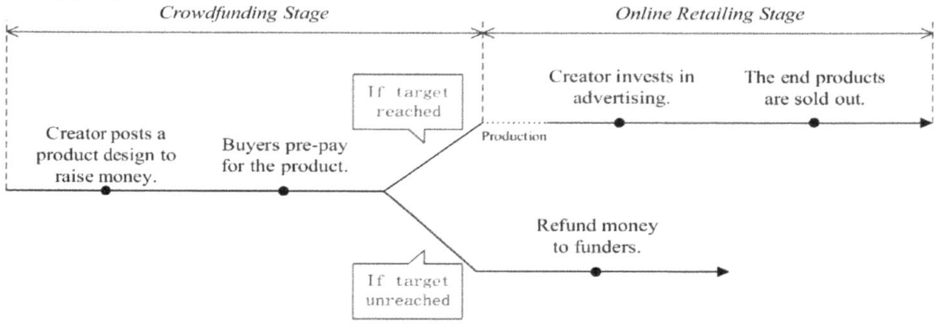


It is possible to find many interesting subcategories and projects on Kickstarter, including film and video, technology, games, broadcasting, music, design, fashion, art, food, crafts, photography, comics, theatre, journalism, and dance. As of May 2022, 220,558 projects have been successfully funded on the platform. These projects raised a total investment of $6,623,308,921 from 21,061,804 backers, of whom 7,153,230 supported two or more projects. In total, 558,135 projects were initiated, yielding a success rate of approximately 39.73%. Successful projects include 28,331 that raised less than $1,000; 117,455 between $1,000 and $9,999; 31,965 between $10,000 and $19,999; 33,238 between $20,000 and $99,999; 8,922 between $100,000 and $999,999; and 647 projects raising over $1,000,000 (Kickstarter Stats, 2022).

Given these figures, producers face several risks, including rejection by the audience, intense competition, poor timing, and insufficient funds during preliminary preparations. While the risk of being disliked is universal across all businesses and products, products must be refined and differentiated to compete effectively in today's e-commerce environment, where anyone can become a producer or seller. Consequently, manufacturers must work harder than before to create innovative, interesting, and unique products.

Preliminary preparation involves not only assessing and mitigating these risks but also marketing activities such as advertising, editorial planning, mass audience building, and market research. The availability of funding at this stage influences all subsequent processes. To maximize visibility, manufacturers incorporate promotional and audience-building efforts into their strategies. The participatory financing model transforms audiences into buyers and supporters, making mass building critical to ensuring product sales.

To minimize risks, producers must prepare extensively before initiating crowdfunding campaigns. Potential backers are typically engaged through social media, online forums, virtual communities, angel investors, or personal networks. Neglecting these preparatory steps increases marketing risks and diminishes the likelihood of achieving desired outcomes. Correspondingly, the literature reports a growing number of studies supporting entrepreneurial ventures through crowdfunding models. Guan et al. (2020) explain:

"Our results shed light on the creator's best decisions regarding crowdfunding pricing policies when faced with different buyers and market conditions. Intuitively, if he envisions a small end market in the normal sales phase, the creator will opt for a high crowdfunding price to raise more targeted money, at the risk of failing crowdfunding campaigns and subsequent sales activity. Conversely, if envisioning a larger end market, the creator will face a tradeoff between low and high prices to successfully advertise in the casual sales environment following crowdfunding campaigns" (p. 2).

Success factors on Kickstarter include active follower engagement, the speed at which projects reach minimum funding goals, and recognition by Kickstarter employees through the "Project We Love" designation. Studies reveal that about 5% of active followers typically support a project financially. Followers are often recruited via social media during mass building in the preliminary phase, with advertising playing a complementary role. One of the most challenging steps is building an audience on Kickstarter's "Coming Soon" page, which allows only a single product image for promotion. Since this is insufficient for comprehensive marketing, creators subsequently develop detailed product pages featuring visuals, slogans, and personal introductions, fostering a stronger connection with potential backers.

Kickstarter employs proprietary algorithms similar to other platforms, with staff reviewing projects to assess funding potential and eligibility for additional features like the "Project We Love" badge. This designation boosts project visibility and funding by algorithmically prioritizing them within the platform. Kickstarter's business model depends on a commission from successful projects, incentivizing the platform to highlight promising campaigns.

## Kickstarter explicitly states its mission to democratize market access:

"Our mission is to help bring creative projects to life. We believe that art and creative expression are necessary for a healthy and vibrant society and that the space for creation must be protected. We don't want the art elite and entertainment executives to define our culture; we want creative people, even those who have never done anything before, to get behind the wheel. We help creators connect directly with their communities and put the power where it belongs. We are so committed to our mission that we have written it into our business model. In 2015, we became a Community Benefit Company as a for-profit company that prioritizes positive results for society as well as our stakeholders, incorporating our values into our operations and promoting arts and culture" (About Kickstarter, 2022).

While this democratizing goal is commendable, it is important to critically assess the extent to which it has been realized for both producers and supporters. Research shows that when multiple projects with low funding goals launch simultaneously, funders can distribute their support across projects where budgets permit. However, projects with large funding targets face intense competition and tend to receive less backing (Chen, 2021).

Supporter behavior is pivotal; approximately one-third of backers support multiple projects. These repeat backers tend to follow specific creators and demonstrate loyalty by valuing those creators' products more highly. Kickstarter acknowledges this dynamic:

"Some creators like Critical Role, TLC, and The Smithsonian Institution already had huge fan bases. But a limited number of projects are as promising as small-scale silent meditation plaques or early versions of Phoebe Waller-Bridge's Fleabag" (About Kickstarter, 2022).

While some creators launch with established fan bases, others build their communities through successful campaigns. Nevertheless, market monopolization phenomena observed outside digital marketing also manifest on Kickstarter. Regardless of the platform's democratic design, ultimate success depends heavily on the preferences and decisions of buyers/supporters. Hence, achieving a truly democratic marketplace is challenging unless Kickstarter's algorithms ensure equitable treatment of all projects.

## 5. DISCUSSION

This study examined the crowdfunding financing model through the broader frameworks of industrial revolutions, marketing evolution, and digital economy transformations, with a specific focus on the Kickstarter platform. The findings demonstrate that crowdfunding has become a significant mechanism in reshaping entrepreneurial finance, particularly by democratizing access to capital and integrating financial processes with digital marketing strategies. In the context of rapid e-commerce expansion—especially during and after the COVID-19 pandemic—platforms such as Kickstarter have emerged as hybrid ecosystems where producers, consumers, and investors interact in a continuously evolving digital environment. This section situates the findings within existing literature and critically evaluates areas of convergence, divergence, and theoretical implications.

## 5.1 Crowdfunding and Democratization: Promise and Paradox

One of the most widely discussed contributions of crowdfunding is its potential to democratize entrepreneurial finance. The findings of this study strongly support the argument that crowdfunding reduces dependency on traditional financial intermediaries such as banks, venture capital firms, and institutional investors. This perspective is consistent with Mollick (2014), who characterizes crowdfunding as a disruptive innovation that lowers entry barriers for entrepreneurs and expands access to capital for individuals who would otherwise be excluded from traditional funding systems. Similarly, Howell, Niessner, and Yermack (2017) emphasize that crowdfunding platforms enhance inclusivity by directly connecting innovators with a dispersed pool of small-scale investors.

However, the results of this study also reveal that the democratizing effect of crowdfunding is not absolute. Instead, it is constrained by underlying market dynamics, user behavior, and platform structures. This aligns with Burtch, Carnahan, and Greenwood (2018), who argue that social capital plays a crucial role in determining crowdfunding success. Projects initiated by individuals with pre-existing networks, reputational advantages, or strong online presence are significantly more likely to succeed than those without such advantages. This creates an uneven playing field, despite the theoretical openness of crowdfunding platforms.

Moreover, the analysis supports Chen (2021), who highlights that intense competition among simultaneous campaigns can reduce the visibility of smaller or less-promoted projects. On platforms like Kickstarter, where thousands of projects compete for attention, algorithmic recommendation systems and user browsing behavior often concentrate exposure on already popular campaigns. This phenomenon reinforces a "rich-get-richer" dynamic, where successful projects attract more visibility and funding, while less visible projects struggle to gain traction. The present study confirms that although crowdfunding platforms are designed to democratize access, structural inequalities and behavioral biases limit the extent of this democratization.

Therefore, crowdfunding represents a paradoxical system: it expands access to financial opportunities while simultaneously reproducing certain inequalities found in traditional markets. This duality suggests that democratization in digital economies is not a linear process but rather a conditional and context-dependent outcome.

## 5.2 Comparisons to Traditional Financing Models

The findings of this study also contribute to the ongoing academic discussion on the evolution of entrepreneurial finance. Crowdfunding is not a replacement for traditional financing systems but rather a complementary mechanism that fills critical funding gaps, particularly for early-stage ventures. This view is supported by Cumming and Johan (2019), who argue that crowdfunding plays an important role in financing startups that are considered too risky or unproven for venture capital or bank lending.

In this study, Kickstarter is shown to function as both a financing tool and a market validation platform. Entrepreneurs are able to raise capital while simultaneously testing demand for their products. This dual function aligns with Agrawal, Catalini, and Goldfarb (2015), who emphasize that crowdfunding reduces information asymmetry between entrepreneurs and investors by enabling early-stage product visibility. Unlike traditional financing systems, where investors rely heavily on financial projections and business plans, crowdfunding allows backers to observe prototypes, updates, and user engagement in real time.

Furthermore, the interactive nature of crowdfunding platforms enhances transparency and trust. Backers can monitor project progress, communicate with creators, and provide feedback throughout the development process. This participatory structure reduces uncertainty and creates a more dynamic investment environment. However, it also shifts responsibility toward entrepreneurs, who must maintain continuous communication and accountability to sustain investor confidence.

Overall, the study confirms that crowdfunding represents a hybrid financial model that integrates funding, marketing, and product validation into a unified system. This distinguishes it fundamentally from traditional financing models, which separate these functions into distinct institutional processes.

## 5.3 The Role of Digital Marketing in Crowdfunding Success

Another key finding of this study is the critical role of digital marketing in determining crowdfunding success. The results demonstrate that effective crowdfunding campaigns are heavily dependent on strategic digital communication, audience engagement, and pre-launch marketing efforts. This finding is consistent with Gerber and Hui (2013), who identify social visibility, storytelling, and emotional engagement as key motivational factors influencing backer participation.

Digital marketing tools such as social media platforms, video content, influencer marketing, and search engine optimization significantly enhance campaign visibility. In addition, platform-specific features such as Kickstarter's "Project We Love" badge function as algorithmic amplifiers that increase exposure and credibility. These mechanisms demonstrate that crowdfunding success is not solely determined by product quality but also by marketing effectiveness and communication strategy.

Kuppuswamy and Bayus (2018) further support this view by showing that active engagement with backers—through updates, comments, and promotional campaigns—significantly increases funding probability. The present study confirms that successful campaigns often involve extensive preparation before launch, including audience building, branding, and social media outreach. This pre-campaign phase is critical for generating early momentum, which in turn influences platform algorithms and user trust.

However, the findings also highlight important challenges associated with digital marketing in crowdfunding environments. One of the most significant issues is consumer fatigue, which arises from the overwhelming number of campaigns competing for attention. As noted by Faruk, Rahman, and Hasan (2021), excessive exposure to promotional content can lead to reduced engagement and decision paralysis among consumers. This study supports these findings, indicating that while digital marketing expands reach, it also increases cognitive load for potential backers.

Additionally, the increasing professionalization of crowdfunding campaigns has intensified competition. Entrepreneurs are now required to possess advanced marketing skills, including content creation, data analytics, and audience segmentation. This shift suggests that crowdfunding success is increasingly dependent on marketing expertise rather than purely innovative ideas, potentially disadvantaging creators with limited marketing resources.

## 5.4 Synthesis and Implications

Overall, the findings of this study suggest that crowdfunding platforms like Kickstarter operate at the intersection of finance, marketing, and digital innovation. They represent a significant evolution in entrepreneurial ecosystems, where value creation is no longer confined to traditional institutional boundaries. Instead, it emerges from continuous interaction between multiple stakeholders within digital environments.

Theoretically, this study contributes to the literature by reinforcing the idea that crowdfunding is both an enabler of democratization and a reproducer of digital inequalities. Practically, it highlights the importance of digital marketing capabilities for entrepreneurial success in crowdfunding environments. Policymakers and platform designers should consider mechanisms that reduce visibility inequality and improve access for less-established creators.

## 5.6 Impact of the COVID-19 Pandemic on Crowdfunding Dynamics

The COVID-19 pandemic has had a profound and multifaceted impact on global economic systems, particularly in the domains of e-commerce, digital marketing, and crowdfunding. This study confirms that the pandemic acted as a major catalyst accelerating the digital transformation of entrepreneurial finance and consumer behavior. As physical mobility restrictions, lockdown measures, and social distancing policies were implemented worldwide, traditional commercial activities were significantly disrupted. In this context, digital platforms such as Kickstarter became essential tools for maintaining economic continuity and enabling entrepreneurial survival.

The findings of this study align closely with Martinelli et al. (2021), who highlight a significant shift in consumer behavior during the pandemic toward online purchasing and digital engagement. Consumers increasingly relied on digital platforms not only for essential goods but also for entertainment, education, and lifestyle products. This behavioral transformation led to increased demand for innovative and digitally accessible products, many of which were introduced and funded through crowdfunding platforms. Kickstarter, in particular, benefited from this shift, as creators who were unable to access traditional retail or investment channels turned to digital crowdfunding as an alternative financing mechanism.

Moreover, the pandemic accelerated the diversification of e-commerce product categories. As noted by Alankuş (2021), sectors such as online education, remote work technologies, digital entertainment, and health-related innovations experienced substantial growth. This study supports these findings by demonstrating that crowdfunding platforms adapted rapidly to these emerging demands. Kickstarter campaigns increasingly reflected pandemic-related needs, including home fitness equipment, remote collaboration tools, and educational technologies. This adaptability underscores the resilience of crowdfunding systems in times of economic crisis.

The pandemic also reshaped consumer motivations and participation patterns in crowdfunding ecosystems. Economic uncertainty and increased digital literacy encouraged more individuals to engage in online investment behaviors, even at small financial scales. At the same time, creators faced heightened pressure to communicate transparency, trustworthiness, and social relevance in their campaigns. As a result, storytelling and community engagement became even more critical components of successful crowdfunding strategies.

Overall, the COVID-19 pandemic not only disrupted traditional economic systems but also accelerated the structural integration of crowdfunding into mainstream digital economies. However, it also highlighted the vulnerability of digital platforms to sudden shifts in consumer behavior, emphasizing the need for continuous adaptation and innovation in platform design and governance.

## 5.7 Algorithmic Influence and Market Fairness

A significant and relatively underexplored dimension of crowdfunding ecosystems is the role of platform algorithms in shaping project visibility and funding outcomes. This study identifies algorithmic curation as a critical factor influencing fairness and competition within Kickstarter's ecosystem. While crowdfunding platforms are often perceived as open and democratic marketplaces, algorithmic mechanisms used to rank, recommend, or highlight projects can significantly influence user attention and funding success.

This observation is consistent with Zvilichovsky, Inbar, and Barzilay (2018), who demonstrate that platform algorithms and visibility structures play a decisive role in determining which projects receive funding. Projects that are featured on homepage listings, recommendation feeds, or category highlights tend to receive disproportionately higher attention and funding compared to those without algorithmic exposure. This creates structural advantages that may not necessarily reflect the intrinsic quality or innovation of the project itself.

The findings of this study further suggest that features such as Kickstarter's "Project We Love" badge or similar editorial selections can amplify existing inequalities within the platform. While these mechanisms are intended to guide users toward high-quality projects, they may inadvertently reinforce "winner-takes-all" dynamics, where already popular projects continue to attract disproportionate support. This phenomenon is particularly problematic in highly competitive categories where thousands of projects compete for limited user attention.

These insights align with Bradford (2012), who argues that digital platform governance requires greater transparency and accountability to ensure equitable access for all participants. Without clear and fair algorithmic governance, crowdfunding platforms risk reproducing inequalities similar to those found in traditional financial systems, despite their decentralized structure.

Furthermore, algorithmic influence raises important ethical and regulatory questions. Users are often unaware of how ranking systems operate, which projects are prioritized, or how visibility is determined. This lack of transparency can undermine trust in crowdfunding ecosystems and reduce perceived fairness. Therefore, there is a growing need for policy interventions that ensure algorithmic accountability, transparency, and fairness in digital marketplaces.

## 5.8 Future Research and Policy Implications

The findings of this study highlight several important directions for future research and policy development. One key area is the need to better understand behavioral mechanisms that influence backer decision-making in crowdfunding environments. While existing studies, such as Mollick and Kuppuswamy (2014), have examined social influence and trust dynamics, further research is needed to explore how platform design elements shape user behavior at a deeper level.

Experimental studies could be conducted to analyze how changes in platform features—such as visibility algorithms, recommendation systems, or reward structures—affect funding outcomes. Such research would provide valuable insights into how crowdfunding ecosystems can be designed to promote greater inclusivity and reduce inequality. Additionally, comparative studies across different crowdfunding platforms could help identify best practices in governance and user engagement.

From a policy perspective, regulatory frameworks may be necessary to ensure transparency and fairness in crowdfunding ecosystems. Belleflamme, Lambert, and Schwienbacher (2014) emphasize that effective regulation should balance innovation with investor protection and market integrity. In this context, policymakers could consider requiring platforms to disclose algorithmic criteria, funding risk levels, and project success statistics more clearly to users.

Another promising avenue is the integration of emerging technologies such as blockchain into crowdfunding systems. As suggested by Draganov et al. (2018), blockchain technology could enhance transparency, traceability, and trust in crowdfunding transactions by providing decentralized and immutable records of financial flows and project updates. However, while blockchain offers theoretical advantages, its practical implementation in large-scale crowdfunding platforms still requires further empirical validation.

In addition, future research could explore hybrid financing models that combine crowdfunding with traditional venture capital or institutional investment. Such hybrid systems may offer greater stability and scalability while preserving the inclusivity benefits of crowdfunding.

## 6. CONCLUSION

This study has examined the role of crowdfunding, particularly through the Kickstarter platform, within the broader context of industrial revolutions and marketing evolution. Positioned at the intersection of Industry 4.0 and Marketing 4.0, Kickstarter represents a transformative innovation in entrepreneurial finance, combining digital technologies, participatory engagement, and market-driven validation mechanisms. The platform demonstrates how e-commerce ecosystems can integrate financing and marketing functions, thereby reshaping traditional business models.

The findings indicate that crowdfunding has become an essential mechanism for supporting entrepreneurship, particularly for small-scale innovators who face barriers in accessing conventional financial systems. By enabling direct interaction between creators and backers, Kickstarter fosters a participatory economic model in which consumers actively influence product development. This reduces information asymmetry, enhances transparency, and strengthens user engagement.

However, despite these advantages, the study also identifies several structural limitations. Increasing competition among projects, reliance on social networks, and algorithmic filtering mechanisms contribute to unequal visibility and funding outcomes. These factors suggest that while crowdfunding platforms promote inclusivity in principle, they may still reproduce certain inequalities in practice. The presence of established networks and audience advantages further reinforces disparities in campaign success.

In conclusion, crowdfunding represents a powerful and innovative model that integrates finance, marketing, and digital technology to support creative and entrepreneurial activity. Nevertheless, achieving a fully democratic and equitable crowdfunding ecosystem requires ongoing improvements in platform governance, algorithmic transparency, and regulatory oversight. Future research should continue to explore these challenges to ensure that crowdfunding platforms evolve in ways that maximize both innovation and fairness in the digital economy.

## REFERENCES


Agrawal, A., Catalini, C., & Goldfarb, A. (2015). Crowdfunding: Geography, social networks, and the timing of investment decisions. *Journal of Economics & Management Strategy*, *24*(2), 253–274. DOI: 10.1111/jems.12093

Alankuş, S. (2021). Digital transformation of crowdfunding platforms in post-pandemic economy. *Journal of Digital Economy Studies*, *4*(2), 110–120.

Belleflamme, P., Lambert, T., & Schwienbacher, A. (2014). Crowdfunding: Tapping the right crowd. *Journal of Business Venturing*, *29*(5), 585–609. DOI: 10.1016/j.jbusvent.2013.07.003

Bradford, C. (2012). Crowdfunding and the democratization of finance. *Harvard Business Law Review*, *2*(1), 85–120.

Burtch, G., Carnahan, S., & Greenwood, B. N. (2018). Can you sell me a secret? Social capital and crowdfunding performance. *Management Science*, *64*(2), 939–958.

Büyükkalaycı, M., & Karaca, Y. (2019). Marketing evolution and digital transformation in marketing strategies. *Journal of Marketing Thought*, *6*(2), 460–472.

Çağlar, E. (2019). Crowdfunding and entrepreneurial finance in digital age. *Entrepreneurship Research Journal*, *9*(1), 15–28.

Carpenter, M. (2011). E-commerce and digital transformation in business strategy. *Business Horizons*, *54*(2), 181–190.

Chen, Y. (2021). Platform competition and crowdfunding inequality. *Information Economics and Policy*, *55*, 100897.

Cordova, A., Dolci, J., & Gianfrate, G. (2015). The determinants of crowdfunding success: Evidence from technology projects. *Procedia: Social and Behavioral Sciences*, *181*, 115–124. DOI: 10.1016/j.sbspro.2015.04.872

Cumming, D., & Johan, S. (2019). Crowdfunding and entrepreneurial finance. *Oxford Review of Economic Policy*, *35*(3), 488–509.

De', R., Pandey, N., & Pal, A. (2020). Impact of digital surge during COVID-19 pandemic: A viewpoint on research and practice. *International Journal of Information Management*, *55*, 102171. DOI: 10.1016/j.ijinfomgt.2020.102171 PMID: 32836633

Dombrowski, U., & Wagner, T. (2014). Mental strain as field of action in the 4th industrial revolution. *Procedia CIRP*, *17*, 100–105. DOI: 10.1016/j.procir.2014.01.077

Draganov, M., Tsankov, N., & Petkova, D. (2018). Marketing 5.0: The future of marketing in digital transformation era. *Economic Alternatives*, *3*, 1–10.

Durukal, H. (2019). Big data analytics and marketing transformation in Industry 4.0. *Procedia Computer Science*, *158*, 1624–1631. DOI: 10.1016/j.procs.2019.09.227

Ertuğrul, İ., & Deniz, E. (2018). Big data and marketing analytics: A new approach in Industry 4.0. *International Journal of Social Sciences and Education Research*, *4*(2), 230–240.

Faruk, M., Rahman, M., & Hasan, S. (2021). Consumer decision fatigue in digital environments. *Journal of Consumer Behaviour*, *20*(3), 450–462.

Fettahoğlu, A., & Khusayan, A. (2017). Crowdfunding models and financial innovation. *Finance & Banking Review*, *5*(1), 55–70.

Gerber, E. M., & Hui, J. (2013). Crowdfunding: Motivations and deterrents for participation. *ACM Transactions on Computer-Human Interaction*, *20*(6), 1–32. DOI: 10.1145/2530540

Gökşin, E. (2018). Digital marketing strategy development stages. *Marketing Science Review*, *12*(1), 20–30.

Howell, S. T., Niessner, M., & Yermack, D. (2017). Initial coin offerings: Financing growth with cryptocurrency token sales. *Review of Financial Studies*, *33*(9), 3925–3970. DOI: 10.1093/rfs/hhz131

Internet Live Stats. (2022). Internet usage statistics. Retrieved from https://www.internetlivestats.com

Jafari, A., Azarian, M., & Yu, H. (2022). Crowdfunding platforms and market democratization: Evidence from Kickstarter. *Journal of Business Research*, *142*, 100–112. DOI: 10.1016/j.jbusres.2021.12.034

Jara, A. J., Parra, M. C., & Skarmeta, A. F. (2012). Marketing 2.0 and consumer behavior in digital environments. *Procedia Computer Science*, *10*, 852–858. DOI: 10.1016/j.procs.2012.06.115

John, K., John, T. A., & Han, Y. (2022). Success factors in reward-based crowdfunding campaigns: Evidence from Kickstarter. *Electronic Commerce Research and Applications*, *52*, 101110. DOI: 10.1016/j.elerap.2021.101110

Kantarcı, Ö., Başaran, B., & Kılınç, M. (2017). *Türkiye'de e-ticaretin gelişimi ve geleceği*. TÜSİAD Yayınları.

Kauffman, R. J., & Naldi, M. (2020). Digital transformation in crowdfunding platforms and online markets. *Electronic Commerce Research and Applications, 41*, 100969. DOI: 10.1016/j.elerap.2020.100969

Kirby, E., & Worner, S. (2014). Crowd-funding: An infant industry growing fast. *IOSCO Research Report*, 23–35.

Kotler, P., Kartajaya, H., & Setiawan, I. (2010). *Marketing 3.0: From products to customers to the human spirit*. Wiley. DOI: 10.1002/9781118257883

Kuppuswamy, V., & Bayus, B. L. (2018). Crowdfunding creative ideas: The dynamics of project backers. *Management Science*, *64*(3), 1005–1026.

Martinelli, E., Acciaro, M., & Ferrari, C. (2021). COVID-19 and changes in consumer behavior. *Transport Policy*, *106*, 1–10.

Mollick, E. (2014). The dynamics of crowdfunding: An exploratory study. *Journal of Business Venturing*, *29*(1), 1–16. DOI: 10.1016/j.jbusvent.2013.06.005

Mollick, E. (2014). The dynamics of crowdfunding: An exploratory study. *Journal of Business Venturing*, *29*(1), 1–16. DOI: 10.1016/j.jbusvent.2013.06.005

Mollick, E., & Kuppuswamy, V. (2014). After the campaign: Outcomes of crowdfunding. *Management Science*, *60*(5), 1–18.

Rangaswamy, A., Moch, N., Felten, C., & van Bruggen, G. (2020). The role of crowdfunding platforms in innovation ecosystems. *Journal of Interactive Marketing*, *51*, 1–16. DOI: 10.1016/j.intmar.2020.01.003

Sakarya, S., & Bezirgan, M. (2018). Financial crowdfunding mechanisms and startup financing. *Journal of Business Research-Turk*, *10*(3), 123–138.

Saracel, N., & Aksoy, E. (2020). Industry 5.0 and human-centered production systems. *Journal of Industrial Engineering*, *31*(4), 112–120.

Shneor, R., Flåten, B. T., & Zhao, L. (2020). *Advances in crowdfunding: Research and practice*. Palgrave Macmillan. DOI: 10.1007/978-3-030-46309-0

Soydal, İ. (2006). E-commerce and consumer participation in digital markets. *Journal of Social Sciences*, *6*(3), 548–560.

Turkish Industry and Business Association (TÜSİAD). (2017). *Digital transformation and e-commerce ecosystem report*. TÜSİAD Publications.

White, R., Habib, R., & Hardisty, D. (2019). Crowdfunding success and feedback mechanisms. *JMR, Journal of Marketing Research*, *56*(4), 621–635.

Yücebalkan, B. (2020). Human-centered production in Industry 5.0 era. *Journal of Engineering and Technology Management*, *56*, 101567.

Zvilichovsky, D., Inbar, Y., & Barzilay, O. (2018). Playing both sides of the market: Success factors in crowdfunding. *Management Science*, *64*(9), 3810–3829.

## KEY TERMS AND DEFINITIONS

**Algorithmic Visibility:** A data-driven ranking mechanism that determines the order in which projects are presented to users on digital platforms, directly impacting success.

**Consumer Participation:** An interaction-based market behavior where consumers are actively involved in product development, feedback, and financing processes.

**Crowdfunding:** A financing model that enables entrepreneurs to raise funds from investors, conduct marketing, and receive consumer feedback through digital platforms; innovative, participatory online.

**Democratization of Marketing:** An approach that refers to producers and consumers interacting on equal terms, participating in decision-making processes, and expanding market access.

**Digital Marketing:** A strategic process encompassing the delivery of products and services to target audiences, establishing interaction, and influencing purchasing behavior using digital channels.

**E-Commerce:** The entirety of commercial activities that enable the buying and selling of goods and services over the internet, bringing producers and consumers together in a digital environment.

**Industry 4.0:** An industrial revolution that aims to increase efficiency and flexibility by integrating automation, big data, and cyber-physical systems into production processes.

**Industry 5.0:** A human-centered, personalized production-oriented industrial approach based on the collaboration of human creativity and intelligent machines.

**Kickstarter Platform:** A global digital platform that provides funding and marketing support to entrepreneurs by promoting their projects, operating with a reward-based crowdfunding model.

**Social Capital:** Refers to the contribution of individuals' relationship networks, trust levels, and community support to economic and entrepreneurial success.

# Chapter 5
# Entrepreneurial Innovation and Digital Marketing for Local Coffee Shops:
## Driving Economic, Social, and Environmental Sustainability

**Doni Sugianto Sihotang**
http://orcid.org/0009-0008-5222-4475
*Universitas Negeri Jakarta, Indonesia*

**Usep Suhud**
http://orcid.org/0000-0002-1728-0737
*Universitas Negeri Jakarta, Indonesia*

**Agung Wahyu Handaru**
http://orcid.org/0000-0003-0198-8041
*Universitas Negeri Jakarta, Indonesia*

**Ali Imaduddin Futuwwah**
http://orcid.org/0000-0002-4422-7579
*Faculty of Economic and Business, Muhammadiyah University of Surabaya, Indonesia*

**Achmad Nur Wahyu Kartiko**
*Universitas Airlangga, Indonesia*

**Edi Fitriana Afriza**
*Siliwangi University, Indonesia*

## ABSTRACT

*This chapter analyzes how tiny, locally rooted enterprises maneuver through modern market challenges by employing adaptive techniques that reconcile commercial viability with wider societal obligations. This chapter examines the interplay between entrepreneurial behaviors and technology-driven market communication within the local café sector, highlighting their role in fostering long-term value development. The discourse amalgamates theoretical viewpoints and contemporary empirical findings to delineate principal economic impediments, social and cultural*

DOI: 10.4018/979-8-2600-3179-7.ch005

*conflicts, and environmental limits encountered by small firms. Strategic approaches are examined, encompassing business model reconfiguration, platform-based involvement, community-focused practices, and resource-efficient operations. The chapter delineates prospective research avenues for new technologies and effect assessment in small enterprises. This chapter provides a cohesive viewpoint that connects firm-level strategy with local development and ethical business practices in service-oriented sectors.*

## INTRODUCTION: ENTREPRENEURIAL INNOVATION IN THE LOCAL COFFEE INDUSTRY

Entrepreneurial innovation in the local coffee market transcends mere product originality or artisanal distinction. In resource-limited settings, innovation serves as a strategic response to intensifying competition, digitalization, and sustainability-driven market demands (Sihotang, 2026). In contrast to international chains that leverage economies of scale, local coffee shops rely on adaptive, community-integrated strategies that integrate product development, business model reconfiguration, and consumer interaction mechanisms (Hernández-Perlines & Xu, 2023).

Extant research provides strong evidence of a favorable correlation between innovation and company success, especially when sustainability activities are included (Saeidi et al., 2021; Suhud et al., 2026). Nevertheless, a significant portion of this literature implicitly posits that innovation bolsters resilience and competitive advantage, while inadequately scrutinizing the structural vulnerabilities of small enterprises contending with cost volatility, supply chain instability, and capital limitations. In limited hospitality settings, innovation can both create differentiation and increase financial risk.

Two contrasting perspectives characterize current disputes. Sustainability-oriented innovation is perceived as a strategic advantage that enhances legitimacy, loyalty, and long-term competitiveness (Saeidi et al., 2021). It tacitly positions sustainability as an extra economic burden that could further pressure the already narrow profit margins of micro-enterprises. Although research emphasizes experiential branding and narrative distinctiveness (Hernández-Perlines & Xu, 2023), there is a paucity of studies that specifically examine the economic sustainability of these innovations over time.

Moreover, while the local coffee industry is characterized as a microcosm of lifestyle entrepreneurship and community-oriented value generation, there is insufficient integration among entrepreneurial innovation, digital marketing proficiency, and the three dimensions of sustainability within small service ecosystems. The analytical gap is not in establishing the significance of innovation, but in elucidating its functioning amongst concurrent economic, social, and environmental challenges.

This chapter reinterprets entrepreneurial innovation as a strategic balancing act rather than an inherently advantageous outcome, situated within the structural trade-offs unique to local coffee firms.

## 2. DIGITAL MARKETING AS A STRATEGIC ENABLER FOR SUSTAINABILITY

Digital marketing has transcended its conventional role as a promotional tool and has increasingly emerged as a strategic facilitator of sustainability across economic, social, and environmental dimensions. Digital marketing provides scalable, cost-effective, and data-driven strategies for entrepreneurial enterprises and small firms, especially in resource-limited environments, to generate value while aligning business expansion with sustainable development goals. Unlike traditional marketing methods, digital platforms enable companies to clearly communicate sustainability pledges, engage stakeholders interactively, and collaboratively generate value with consumers and communities.

From an economic standpoint, digital marketing fosters sustainability by expanding market access, improving operational efficiency, and enhancing long-term competitiveness. Data analytics, social media marketing, and search-based advertising enable companies to target niche segments precisely, minimize client acquisition costs, and improve resource allocation efficiency. Empirical research indicates that digital marketing capabilities enhance firm performance and resilience, particularly in small and medium-sized firms (SMEs), by facilitating swift adaptation to market fluctuations and consumer feedback (Chatterjee et al., 2021; Wibowo et al., 2023). The strategic application of digital tools promotes sustainable economic results by cultivating reliable revenue streams and diminishing reliance on resource-intensive marketing methods.

Digital marketing enhances social sustainability by promoting stakeholder participation, inclusivity, and community development. Interactive platforms like social media facilitate two-way communication between companies and consumers, employees, and local communities, thereby enhancing trust and relational capital. Digital storytelling and cause-related initiatives enable businesses to express societal values, bolster local identities, and advocate for ethical consumerism. Recent studies demonstrate that digitally mediated interactions enhance perceived authenticity and social legitimacy, which are essential for maintaining enduring relationships with socially conscious consumers (Bhattacharya et al., 2022; Martínez-Cañas et al., 2024; Suhud et al., 2025).

Digital marketing enhances environmental sustainability by dematerializing marketing efforts and advocating for eco-conscious consumption behaviors. The transition from print advertising to digital platforms decreases paper consumption and waste, while digital nudging and information disclosure enhance consumer knowledge of sustainable products and practices. Research indicates that digital communication techniques significantly influence pro-environmental attitudes and purchasing intentions, especially when sustainability claims are credible and data-driven (Tölkes & Butzmann, 2022; Yang et al., 2021).

These elements establish digital marketing as a strategic asset that incorporates sustainability into the essence of entrepreneurial decision-making. Digital marketing serves not merely as a supplementary communication tool but also empowers companies to synchronize financial goals with the development of social value and environmental stewardship. This viewpoint emphasizes the necessity of perceiving digital marketing not solely as a tactical tool, but as a transformative force that fosters sustainable entrepreneurship in increasingly intricate and competitive landscapes.

## 3. CHAPTER OBJECTIVES AND STRUCTURE

This chapter aims to provide a comprehensive and integrated understanding of how entrepreneurial innovation, supported by digital marketing capabilities, contributes to economic, social, and environmental sustainability within local coffee shops. As sustainability-oriented entrepreneurship and digital transformation continue to reshape competitive environments, small and locally embedded enterprises face increasing pressure to remain economically viable while simultaneously responding to social expectations and environmental responsibilities. Within this context, the chapter seeks to bridge theoretical perspectives and practical insights by examining how local coffee shops navigate these challenges through innovation and digitally enabled strategic practices.

More specifically, this chapter pursues three primary objectives. First, it seeks to conceptualize entrepreneurial innovation as a multidimensional construct encompassing product, process, and business model innovation. Second, it examines digital marketing as a strategic capability that facilitates the transformation of innovation into sustainable value creation. Third, it evaluates how the interaction between entrepreneurial innovation and digital marketing contributes to integrated sustainability outcomes across economic, social, and environmental dimensions. In doing so, the chapter responds to growing scholarly calls for context-sensitive and integrative approaches to sustainability research within entrepreneurship and small business studies (Audretsch et al., 2023; Cohen & Muñoz, 2021).

A secondary objective is to contribute to the existing body of knowledge by focusing on local coffee shops as a relevant yet underexplored context within sustainability and entrepreneurship research. Previous studies frequently concentrate on large corporations, manufacturing industries, or technology-intensive sectors, while small service-oriented businesses remain comparatively overlooked. Local coffee shops represent a valuable setting for examining sustainability-oriented entrepreneurship because they combine commercial activities with community engagement, ethical sourcing practices, cultural identity preservation, and environmentally responsible operations. Consequently, this chapter aims not only to advance theoretical understanding but also to generate practical insights for entrepreneurs, managers, policymakers, and other stakeholders seeking to strengthen sustainable local economies through entrepreneurial initiatives.

To achieve these objectives, the chapter is organized into several interconnected sections that collectively build a coherent conceptual narrative. Following this introduction, Section 2 (Literature Review) examines the theoretical foundations of entrepreneurial innovation, digital marketing, and sustainability. This section critically reviews the contemporary literature and establishes the conceptual basis for understanding the relationships among these constructs within small-business ecosystems. The review also identifies key debates, challenges, and knowledge gaps that justify the development of an integrated perspective.

Section 3 (Research Design/Methodology) explains the conceptual review approach adopted in the chapter. It outlines the procedures for identifying, selecting, analyzing, and synthesizing relevant scholarly literature, thereby ensuring methodological transparency and academic rigor. This section clarifies how theoretical insights and empirical evidence were integrated to develop the chapter's conceptual framework and thematic analysis.

Section 4 (Results) presents the synthesized findings derived from the literature review. The discussion focuses on major economic, social, and environmental challenges faced by local coffee shops, including financial vulnerability, platform dependence, pressures to transform digitally, sustainability-related operational constraints, and strategic trade-offs between growth and authenticity.

Section 5 (Discussion) interprets these findings within broader theoretical and practical contexts. The discussion highlights how entrepreneurial innovation and digital marketing capabilities can be strategically deployed to address sustainability challenges while balancing economic performance, social legitimacy, and environmental responsibility.

Section 6 (Conclusions) summarizes the key insights generated throughout the chapter and presents dedicated subsections on practical implications, limitations, and future research directions. These subsections provide recommendations for practitioners and scholars and identify opportunities to advance sustainability-oriented entrepreneurship research.

Finally, Section 7 (Key Terms and Definitions) presents the principal concepts utilized throughout the chapter, including entrepreneurial innovation, digital marketing capability, sustainability, platform dependency, community entrepreneurship, and related constructs. Together, these sections provide a structured and comprehensive examination of how entrepreneurial innovation and digital marketing can support sustainable development within local coffee shop ecosystems.

# LITERATURE REVIEW

## 1. Concept of Entrepreneurial Innovation

Entrepreneurial innovation is commonly defined as the deliberate introduction of new products, processes, services, or business models to exploit opportunities amid uncertainty. Contemporary scholarship extends this perspective by conceptualizing innovation as a dynamic capability rooted in experimentation, resource recombination, and continuous adaptation to changing environmental conditions (Foss & Saebi, 2020; Mirabeau et al., 2022). Rather than relying solely on technological advancement, entrepreneurial innovation often emerges from the creative use of existing resources to address unmet customer needs and respond to market disruptions. This perspective is particularly relevant for small enterprises operating under resource constraints, where innovation often takes incremental rather than radical forms.

Sustainability-oriented research further positions entrepreneurial innovation as a mechanism for simultaneously generating economic, social, and environmental value (Bergset & Fichter, 2022; Vuorio et al., 2023). Existing studies generally emphasize the positive relationship between innovation and organizational performance, suggesting that innovative firms are better equipped to achieve competitive advantage, legitimacy, and long-term resilience. However, this dominant perspective reflects an underlying assumption that innovation inherently produces favorable outcomes. Such a view has been increasingly challenged by scholars who argue that innovation may also introduce financial uncertainty, implementation costs, and operational complexity, particularly in small businesses with limited resources and managerial capacity.

A significant theoretical debate, therefore, exists between two contrasting perspectives: innovation as a driver of growth and as a source of risk. The growth-oriented perspective suggests that innovation enhances competitiveness, facilitates the recognition of opportunities, and strengthens sustainable performance (Bergset

& Fichter, 2022; Vuorio et al., 2023). Conversely, the risk-oriented perspective argues that innovation requires investments in new capabilities, technologies, and organizational processes that may exceed the absorptive capacity of small firms. Resource-constrained businesses often face substantial uncertainty regarding whether innovation investments will generate sufficient returns to justify their costs. Consequently, innovation may simultaneously function as a mechanism for value creation and a source of vulnerability, creating strategic tensions that are frequently overlooked in mainstream entrepreneurship literature.

Another important dimension concerns contextual embeddedness. Innovation processes are shaped by institutional environments, regional cultures, stakeholder relationships, and network configurations (de Medeiros et al., 2020; Hossain et al., 2021). Small enterprises typically rely on frugal, adaptive, and resource-efficient innovation practices rather than large-scale technological breakthroughs. From a capability perspective, entrepreneurial innovation represents a continuous process of opportunity sensing, resource mobilization, and strategic transformation (Foss & Saebi, 2020; Mirabeau et al., 2022).

Despite the growing body of literature, important research gaps remain. Existing studies predominantly focus on technology-intensive industries, high-growth ventures, and large organizational settings, leaving micro-enterprises and small service businesses comparatively underexplored. In particular, local coffee shops represent an understudied context where innovation must simultaneously address economic survival, community legitimacy, customer experience, and environmental responsibility. Consequently, there is a need for greater theoretical and empirical attention to how entrepreneurial innovation operates within resource-constrained service ecosystems and how entrepreneurs manage the trade-offs between growth, sustainability, and risk. This chapter addresses this gap by positioning entrepreneurial innovation not merely as a growth catalyst but as a strategic coordination mechanism that balances multiple sustainability objectives within local coffee business ecosystems.

## 2. Digital Marketing in Small and Local Businesses

Digital marketing is increasingly recognized as a strategic enabler that allows small businesses to enhance visibility, customer engagement, and market responsiveness in increasingly digitalized environments (Ainin et al., 2020; Drummond et al., 2022). Through social media platforms, online ordering systems, mobile applications, and digital advertising, small firms can reach broader audiences while operating with relatively limited marketing budgets. However, the growing dependence on digital technologies has also introduced governance, privacy, and strategic challenges that are often overlooked in discussions emphasizing the benefits of digital transformation. For local coffee shops and other small service businesses, digital capabilities not only improve performance but also expose firms to cybersecurity threats, data privacy concerns, and increasing dependence on digital platforms.

Data-driven marketing relies heavily on collecting customer information through loyalty programs, online transactions, social media interactions, and payment systems. Such information enables businesses to improve targeting accuracy, personalize customer experiences, and optimize customer lifetime value (Srinivasan & Swink, 2021; Kumar et al., 2021). Nevertheless, these advantages are accompanied by growing responsibilities related to data storage, consent management, and transparency. Many small businesses lack formal governance mechanisms for managing customer data, increasing their vulnerability to misuse, security breaches, and regulatory noncompliance.

A major theoretical debate in the digital marketing literature concerns platform empowerment versus platform dependency. The empowerment perspective argues that digital platforms reduce market entry barriers, democratize access to consumers, and enable small firms to compete with larger organizations despite limited resources (Ainin et al., 2020; Drummond et al., 2022). Through digital platforms, local businesses can achieve visibility, engage customers directly, and leverage analytics to improve decision-making. In contrast, the platform dependency perspective suggests that increasing reliance on digital ecosystems may reduce entrepreneurial autonomy and create structural asymmetries between platform owners and small businesses. Platform operators frequently control algorithms, customer data, commission structures, and visibility rules, limiting the strategic flexibility of firms that depend heavily on these systems. Consequently, digital marketing may simultaneously function as a source of empowerment and a mechanism of dependency.

Regulatory developments further complicate digital transformation efforts. Data protection frameworks such as the General Data Protection Regulation (GDPR) have influenced global expectations regarding explicit consent, data minimization, and user privacy. Even businesses operating outside Europe increasingly interact with digital platforms governed by these standards. Noncompliance may generate reputational damage, platform sanctions, or legal consequences. Furthermore, cybersecurity threats continue to expand as small firms rely on cloud-based services, external software providers, and online payment systems. Limited internal technological expertise often increases exposure to phishing attacks, ransomware incidents, and unauthorized access to customer information.

Trust therefore becomes a critical component of digital marketing effectiveness. Trust strengthens customer relationships, enhances community legitimacy, and contributes to long-term business sustainability (Bhattacharya et al., 2022; Martínez-Cañas et al., 2024). When customers perceive their personal information as mismanaged or inadequately protected, relational capital may deteriorate rapidly. Despite growing scholarly interest in digital marketing, significant research gaps remain. Existing studies predominantly focus on e-commerce firms, technology-intensive sectors, and large organizations, while small hospitality businesses receive comparatively limited attention. In particular, local coffee shops represent an underexplored context where digital marketing must simultaneously support customer engagement, preserve local authenticity, manage platform relationships, and maintain consumer trust. Consequently, future research should pay greater attention to how small hospitality enterprises balance digital opportunities with governance responsibilities and platform-related constraints.

## 3. Sustainability Dimensions in the Coffee Business

Sustainability has become a central concept in the global coffee industry due to growing concerns regarding economic resilience, social equity, and environmental degradation across coffee value chains. The coffee sector faces substantial sustainability challenges because of its dependence on agricultural resources, vulnerability to climate change, and complex networks involving smallholder farmers, intermediaries, processors, and retailers. Consequently, sustainability is increasingly understood as a multidimensional construct encompassing economic, social, and environmental dimensions that must be addressed simultaneously rather than independently.

From an economic perspective, sustainability in the coffee industry refers to the capacity to generate long-term value, maintain income stability, and strengthen resilience among producers and downstream businesses. Volatile coffee prices, rising production costs, and increasing market concentration create significant threats to economic viability, particularly for smallholder farmers and local coffee enterprises. Recent studies suggest that value-based differentiation, specialty coffee markets, and innovation-oriented strategies can enhance economic sustainability by increasing profit margins and reducing vulnerability to commodity price fluctuations (Borrella et al., 2022; Samoggia & Riedel, 2020). For local coffee shops, economic sustainability is closely linked to operational efficiency, ethical sourcing, and the ability to communicate value to increasingly conscious consumers.

Social sustainability emphasizes fairness, labor conditions, community development, and cultural preservation throughout the coffee value chain. Coffee production frequently relies on smallholder farmers who have limited bargaining power and are exposed to social vulnerabilities. Research highlights the importance of fair trade practices, direct trade relationships, and community-centered initiatives in improving livelihoods, strengthening social capital, and fostering trust among stakeholders (Dietz et al., 2021; Rueda et al., 2022). At the retail level, local coffee shops often serve as social spaces that foster inclusion, cultural expression, and community engagement, thereby extending social sustainability beyond production.

Environmental sustainability addresses challenges related to climate vulnerability, biodiversity loss, deforestation, waste generation, and resource consumption. Strategies such as shade-grown coffee production, agroforestry systems, waste reuse, and sustainable sourcing have been identified as mechanisms to reduce environmental impacts while preserving ecosystem services (Jezeer et al., 2021; Perfecto et al., 2023).

As illustrated in Figure 1, sustainability outcomes in local coffee enterprises arise from the interaction between entrepreneurial innovation and digital marketing capability within a context of resource constraints, platform dependence, and financial limitations. The framework highlights that economic, social, and environmental performance are interconnected outcomes rather than isolated objectives. Entrepreneurial innovation provides the strategic foundation through product, process, and business model innovation. At the same time, digital marketing capability acts as a mediating mechanism that transforms innovation into customer value, stakeholder engagement, and sustainability performance. The framework further emphasizes that local coffee businesses must continuously navigate tensions among digital expansion and authenticity, sustainability investments and short-term profitability, and platform visibility and entrepreneurial autonomy.

One of the most widely discussed contradictions is the sustainability-profitability paradox. Sustainability initiatives are often promoted as sources of competitive advantage, improved reputation, and long-term financial performance. However, for many small businesses, sustainability practices entail additional costs for certification, ethical sourcing, environmentally friendly packaging, and operational adjustments. While long-term benefits may exist, the short-term financial burden can create tensions between sustainability aspirations and business survival, particularly in resource-constrained enterprises. This tension is reflected in Figure 1 by the moderating influence of financial constraints on the relationship between innovation and sustainability outcomes.

A related debate concerns trade-offs among the three dimensions of sustainability. Actions that strengthen environmental performance may increase operating costs and reduce short-term profitability, while initiatives designed to maximize economic outcomes may weaken social or environmental commitments. Similarly, investments in social welfare programs may divert resources from environmental initiatives or business expansion. Although sustainability frameworks often emphasize synergy among dimensions, empirical evidence suggests that entrepreneurs frequently face difficult decisions involving competing priorities rather than mutually reinforcing outcomes. Existing research increasingly acknowledges these tensions, yet limited attention has been paid to understanding how small service-oriented businesses, such as local coffee shops, navigate sustainability trade-offs in practice. Consequently, a significant research gap remains regarding how to balance economic viability, social legitimacy, and environmental responsibility within resource-constrained coffee business ecosystems, a challenge that underpins the central logic of the integrative framework presented in Figure 1.

*Figure 1. Integrative Framework Linking Entrepreneurial Innovation, Digital Marketing Capability, and Sustainability Outcomes in Local Coffee Enterprises*

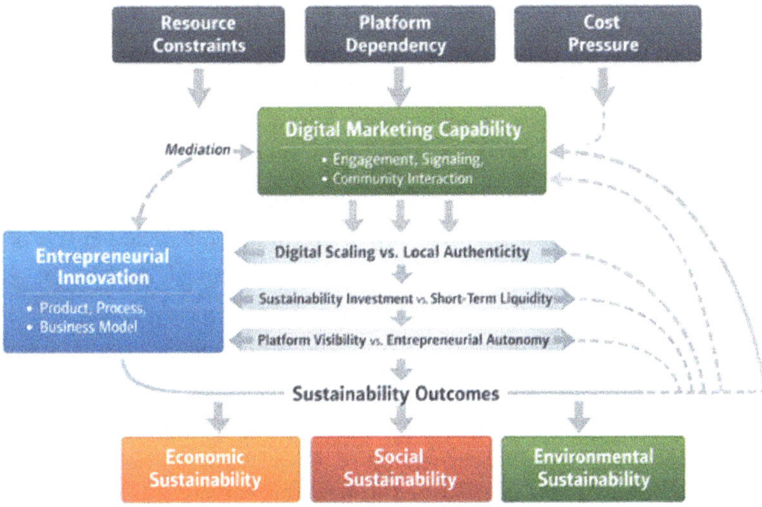


*Source: Author (2026)*

## METHODOLOGY

### 1. Research Approach

This chapter adopts an Integrative Literature Review and Conceptual Synthesis approach to develop a comprehensive understanding of how entrepreneurial innovation and digital marketing contribute to economic, social, and environmental sustainability in local coffee shops. An integrative literature review is appropriate because the topic spans multiple disciplinary domains, including entrepreneurship, digital marketing, sustainability, small business management, and hospitality studies. Unlike systematic reviews that primarily focus on narrowly defined research questions, the integrative approach enables the combination of theoretical perspectives, empirical findings, and conceptual insights from diverse streams of literature. This approach is particularly suitable for emerging and interdisciplinary topics where knowledge is fragmented across different academic fields. Through conceptual synthesis, the chapter seeks to identify recurring themes, theoretical relationships, and unresolved tensions related to innovation, digital transformation, and sustainability practices within local coffee business ecosystems. The objective is not merely to summarize existing studies but to develop an integrated framework that explains how entrepreneurial innovation and digital marketing capabilities interact to influence sustainability outcomes in resource-constrained service enterprises.

## 2. Literature Identification and Inclusion Criteria

The literature review focused on peer-reviewed journal articles indexed in the Scopus database and published between 2020 and 2025. The search process utilized combinations of keywords related to entrepreneurial innovation, digital marketing, sustainability, small and medium-sized enterprises, local businesses, hospitality enterprises, and the coffee industry. The search was designed to capture recent developments and emerging discussions on innovation-driven sustainability in small-business environments. To ensure quality and relevance, three inclusion criteria were applied. First, only peer-reviewed journal articles were considered. Second, publications had to be written in English. Third, studies were required to demonstrate direct relevance to entrepreneurship, digital marketing, sustainability, SMEs, local businesses, hospitality enterprises, or coffee-related business contexts. Studies focusing exclusively on large corporations, highly technical issues, or unrelated industrial sectors were excluded. Following the screening process, 68 peer-reviewed articles were selected for in-depth review and analysis.

## 3. Analytical Procedure

The analytical process followed four sequential stages. The first stage involved literature identification, during which potentially relevant publications were collected based on predefined search terms and database criteria. The second stage consisted of screening and selection, where articles were evaluated against the established inclusion criteria to ensure relevance and quality. The third stage involved thematic synthesis, in which the selected literature was systematically analyzed to identify recurring concepts, theoretical debates, challenges, contradictions, and emerging research trends related to entrepreneurial innovation, digital marketing, and sustainability. Particular attention was given to identifying relationships among economic, social, and environmental dimensions of sustainability within small business settings. The final stage involved developing a conceptual framework that integrated insights from the thematic synthesis into a coherent analytical model. This framework serves as the foundation for interpreting the findings presented in subsequent sections and for explaining how entrepreneurial innovation and digital marketing capabilities collectively contribute to sustainability outcomes in local coffee shop ecosystems.

## RESULTS

### 1. Economic Challenges in Local Coffee Shop Innovation

Local coffee shops depend on entrepreneurial innovation to remain competitive; nonetheless, innovation in micro-scale service firms is fundamentally shaped by economic instability. In contrast to major coffee chains that capitalize on economies of scale and diversified revenue streams, local coffee shops operate with limited liquidity, slim profit margins, and susceptibility to fluctuating input costs (Block et al., 2021; Cowling et al., 2023). Innovation signifies both the potential for distinction and a financial risk that may disrupt already-tenuous cash-flow frameworks.

A fundamental conflict arises between investment in innovation and cash flow vulnerability. Product experimentation, enhancements to digital infrastructure, sustainability-focused sourcing, and marketing strategies require initial financial investment and have unpredictable return timelines. Although incremental innovation is frequently recommended for small enterprises (Hwang & Kim, 2023), even minor modifications can strain cash flow during periods of significant revenue volatility. This presents a sequencing dilemma: companies must innovate to endure, yet investments in innovation may jeopardize short-term financial stability.

The restriction is exacerbated by increasing cost pressure. Volatile green bean prices, energy expenditures, and labor costs disproportionately impact small companies that lack negotiating leverage (Griffith et al., 2022). Sustainability initiatives, including biodegradable packaging and ethically sourced beans, can entail higher costs, creating a trade-off between sustainability commitment and profit preservation. Differentiation through sustainability may improve brand posture, but its financial returns are seldom immediate or guaranteed.

Digital scaling provides further economic intricacy. Enhancing visibility on online platforms may increase sales volume, yet platform commissions and advertising expenses can diminish profit margins. Thus, growth attained via digital means may ironically heighten reliance on intermediaries while diminishing profitability. This underscores the conflict between revenue growth and value acquisition.

Unforeseen repercussions may also occur. Excessive investment in innovation without corresponding digital capabilities may lead to poorly conveyed value propositions, hence diminishing the return on innovation. Conversely, an overemphasis on digital visibility may divert strategic focus from operational efficiency.

Consequently, economic obstacles to the creation of local coffee shops cannot be characterized exclusively as financial constraints. They signify systemic tensions among growth, sustainability, autonomy, and financial resilience. Innovation becomes a balancing act rather than a straightforward catalyst for performance.

The economic dimension underscores financial vulnerability and susceptibility to innovation risks, which are inextricably linked to wider social and relational processes. The subsequent section analyzes the impact of digital transformation on cultural identity, authenticity, and stakeholder trust within local coffee ecosystems.

## 2. Social and Cultural Tensions in Digital Transformation

The digital revolution of local coffee shops transcends mere technology adoption; it reconfigures social relationships, cultural identity, and the creation of experiential value. Although digital tools improve exposure and customer outreach (Srinivasan & Swink, 2021), they concurrently undermine the relational roots that characterize local coffee culture.

A major contradiction exists between digital scale and local authenticity. Coffee shops frequently gain a competitive edge through artisanal techniques, individualized service, and ingrained community stories. Algorithmic systems prioritize uniform formats, refined content methods, and expandable communications frameworks. As enterprises synchronize their communication with platform algorithms, a subtle homogenization may ensue. The quest for visibility jeopardizes the unique local identity that originally drew clients.

A secondary issue concerns platform dependency versus entrepreneurial independence. Platform ecosystems regulate algorithmic exposure, data ownership, and commission frameworks (Michaelidou et al., 2020). Although digital channels diminish entrance barriers, they may generate structural asymmetry in negotiating power. Entrepreneurs are increasingly reliant on visibility regulations beyond their control, which can restrict strategic autonomy.

The organization's social dynamics are also influenced. Digital transformation necessitates acquiring new competencies in analytics, content development, and consumer data management. This may result in role overload or digital weariness within small teams. Employees recruited for hospitality expertise may encounter identity conflict when tasked with digital marketing responsibilities. These internal frictions are inadequately examined yet signify unforeseen social repercussions of digitization.

Furthermore, technologically mediated interactions may diminish spontaneous face-to-face interactions, undermining the role of coffee shops as community hubs. Although digital communication enhances reach, it may diminish the profundity of social contact if not meticulously balanced.

The digital revolution has double effects: increased market accessibility and the potential degradation of relationship authenticity. Social sustainability in local coffee firms relies not only on digital presence but also on the strategic balance entrepreneurs maintain between scalability, cultural embeddedness, and autonomy.

Sustainability issues extend beyond social legitimacy and cultural embeddedness into operational and environmental areas. The following discussion examines the intersection of ecological responsibility with cost structures and resource limitations.

## 3. Environmental Sustainability and Operational Constraints

Environmental sustainability is increasingly anticipated in the coffee industry owing to climate vulnerability, waste generation, and heightened consumer awareness (Jezeer et al., 2021; Perfecto et al., 2023). Nonetheless, small coffee establishments face operational constraints that hinder their environmental commitment.

A fundamental conflict exists between sustainability efforts and financial constraints. Eco-friendly packaging, ethical sourcing, and circular waste management practices often entail higher procurement costs and greater supply chain complexity (Filimonau & De Coteau, 2020; Stylos et al., 2022). For companies with constrained margins, environmental enhancements may conflict with preserving liquidity.

Investments in energy efficiency pose an additional problem. Energy-efficient equipment reduces long-term operational expenses; however, the initial investment may exceed available funds. Small firms sometimes prioritize immediate cash stability over long-term environmental benefits, especially in volatile economic conditions.

Sustainability in the supply chain creates structural asymmetry. In contrast to multinational corporations, local retailers lack sufficient bargaining power to secure advantageous sustainable sourcing agreements. Thus, environmental commitment may rely on external collaborations rather than internal governance.

Unanticipated repercussions may also arise. Promoting sustainability without strong operational alignment risks damaging reputation if assertions are perceived as superficial. Conversely, implementing sustainability initiatives without effective communication may diminish customer recognition, thereby reducing strategic benefits.

Moreover, while eliminating physical promotion, digital marketing still relies on energy-intensive digital infrastructure. The ecological impact of digital operations is rarely acknowledged in small businesses' sustainability discussions, resulting in a conceptual oversight.

Environmental sustainability in local coffee firms should be seen as a restricted optimization problem. It entails negotiating operational feasibility, financial viability, and reputational expectations within structural constraints rather than achieving seamless integration.

## 4. Strategic Trade-Offs

The prior findings indicate that sustainability-focused innovation in local coffee shops is not a cohesive process but rather a series of negotiated compromises. These trade-offs function concurrently across economic, social, and environmental spheres, influenced by digital marketing proficiency.

This section provides two semi-anonymous instances from Indonesia, based on industry observations, secondary sources, and well-documented market trends in urban coffee ecosystems, to contextualize the prior theoretical discussion. These graphics depict the interplay among entrepreneurial innovation, digital marketing capabilities, and sustainability commitments within structural constraints in emerging-market contexts.

### Case 1: A Specialty Coffee Shop in Jakarta: Sequenced Integration and Strategic Equilibrium

A specialty coffee enterprise in South Jakarta implemented a staged innovation strategy prioritizing financial prudence and community involvement. The founders enhanced internal competencies prior to pursuing digital expansion. Ethically sourced beans from Indonesian smallholder farmers were promoted through genuine storytelling on social media, including user-generated content and barista-led brewing demonstrations. Digital marketing served as a mechanism for signaling value, so promoting sustainability narratives. Platform dependence was meticulously controlled by integrating food-delivery transparency with direct-order incentives to preserve consumer data. Environmental initiatives were implemented incrementally, including the adoption of compostable cups and energy-efficient equipment. The strategy exhibited a measured approach to innovation that harmonized sustainability obligations, fiscal stability, and genuine community engagement.

### Case 2: A Rapidly Expanding Urban Coffee Brand in Bandung: Visibility Lacking Structural Cohesion

A self-sufficient coffee enterprise in Bandung experienced rapid digital growth due to a transient surge in demand driven by social media visibility. Motivated by online interactions, the proprietors invested significantly in platform advertising, delivery improvements, and concurrent product development. Enhanced visibility on food delivery platforms increased order numbers, yet elevated commissions and discount campaigns diminished company margins. Simultaneously, sustainable packaging and seasonal beverages that utilize foreign ingredients increased expenses and operational complexity. The information on sustainability was inconsistent, undermining customers' understanding of price changes. Operational strain escalated as personnel managed internet orders, content generation, and in-store service. Ultimately, reliance on platforms and mismatched investments in innovation stretched budgets despite robust digital visibility.

### Analytical Perspectives from the Indonesian Context

The divergent Indonesian experiences corroborate the chapter's primary assertion: sustainability-focused innovation in local coffee businesses necessitates precise trade-off management. Success is contingent upon:

- Synchronizing innovation intensity with liquidity capacity
- Reconciling digital visibility with the maintenance of authenticity
- Administering platform exposure while preserving autonomy
- Systematically organizing sustainable investments accompanied by clear communication

Failure sometimes occurs when scaling decisions are made before structural preparedness is in place.

By anchoring the integrative framework in the realities of emerging markets, these examples illustrate that sustainable entrepreneurship in Indonesia's coffee ecosystem is not driven solely by resources or technology. It is strategically negotiated among economic vulnerability, cultural entrenchment, and platform-mediated market frameworks (Suhud et al., 2026).

## DISCUSSION

### 1. Entrepreneurial Innovation Strategies for Sustainability

Entrepreneurial innovation in local coffee businesses should be assessed not just by strategic positioning but also by financial viability. Sustainability-focused innovation enhances differentiation, but its economic feasibility depends on rigorous cost modeling and expected returns. For tiny coffee shops with narrow profit margins, investing in innovation necessitates a clear evaluation of return on investment (ROI).

A pragmatic financial perspective begins by distinguishing bctwccn capital expenditures (CAPEX) and operating expenditures (OPEX). Investments in energy-efficient espresso machines, enhancements to roasting equipment, or improvements in digital infrastructure signify initial capital commitments. In contrast, sustainable packaging, high-quality, ethical beans, and certification fees generally increase ongoing operational costs. In the absence of a comprehensive financial assessment, sustainability activities may jeopardize short-term liquidity.

The return on investment for innovation can be estimated using a streamlined formula:

ROI = (Incremental Revenue - Incremental Cost)/Innovation Investment

Introducing ethically produced beans at a 10% premium might elevate the average ticket value by 12% if communicated effectively. Nonetheless, if demand elasticity diminishes volume, the overall effect may turn negative. Consequently, pricing modifications must be underpinned by value communication via digital platforms.

Break-even analysis is essential. A coffee business spends USD 5,000 on an energy-efficient espresso machine, resulting in a monthly reduction of electricity costs by USD 250. The reimbursement duration would be:

Break-even period = Investment/Monthly Savings = 5,000/250 = 20 months

These assessments enable entrepreneurs to prioritize sustainability investments based on liquidity capabilities.

Frugal innovation tactics mitigate risk exposure. Incremental product experimentation through constrained batch testing reduces sunk costs. Collaborative purchasing arrangements with local vendors can stabilize procurement costs while enhancing social legitimacy.

These sustainability-oriented innovation strategies can also be interpreted through the lens of Dynamic Capability Theory, which emphasizes an organization's ability to sense opportunities, seize emerging possibilities, and transform resources in response to changing market conditions. The staged innovation pathway proposed in this chapter reflects these capabilities. During the early stage, the adoption of low-cost digital technologies and experimentation with frugal innovation practices enable coffee shop owners to identify market needs and operational inefficiencies, representing sensing capabilities. The implementation of customer analytics, loyalty systems, and digital relationship management during the growth stage reflects a focus on seizing capabilities, as entrepreneurs allocate resources to opportunities that strengthen competitiveness and customer retention. In the mature stage, the integration of ethical sourcing, circular economy practices, and sustainability-oriented branding demonstrates the capacity to transform by reconfiguring organizational resources and routines to support long-term sustainability objectives. Consequently, incremental adaptation should not be viewed merely as a cost-saving approach but as a strategic mechanism that enhances organizational resilience and responsiveness in uncertain business environments (Zhang et al., 2022; Kraus et al., 2022).

Furthermore, the strategic importance of sustainability-oriented innovation can be explained by the Resource-Based View (RBV), which holds that sustainable competitive advantage arises from valuable, rare, inimitable, and non-substitutable resources. For local coffee shops, competitive differentiation often depends on intangible assets rather than economies of scale. Relationships with local suppliers, community embeddedness, sustainability reputation, ethical sourcing practices, and locally rooted brand identities represent strategic resources that competitors cannot easily replicate. Collaborative innovation initiatives involving community organizations and local networks therefore create value beyond immediate operational benefits by strengthening social legitimacy and stakeholder trust. Similarly, sustainability-oriented branding and transparent sourcing practices can enhance customer loyalty and reinforce long-term competitive positioning. From an RBV perspective, sustainability initiatives should not be considered solely as additional operational costs but as investments in strategic resources that contribute to long-term business resilience and sustainable growth (Albort-Morant et al., 2021; Inigo & Albareda, 2020; Rosca et al., 2023).

Sustainability activities must be associated with revenue-generating processes. For example, verifiable sourcing may rationalize higher pricing if presented transparently. In the absence of communication, rising costs persist as internal liabilities rather than value-adding differentiators.

Sustainable entrepreneurial innovation in local coffee shops necessitates cohesive financial planning, cost modeling, and phased execution. The intensity of innovation must correspond with absorption capability to avert liquidity fragility. Sustainability is commercially feasible when underpinned by quantifiable return mechanisms rather than mere idealistic pledges.

## 2. Digital Marketing Practices for Sustainable Growth

Digital marketing in local coffee businesses should be regarded as an investment portfolio rather than merely a marketing expenditure. Although digital platforms provide scalability and visibility, their financial implications require systematic evaluation through return on investment (ROI) analysis and margin sensitivity assessment. Digital marketing expenditures commonly include paid advertising, platform commissions, content creation, loyalty program subscriptions, and analytics tools. These costs must be assessed against measurable performance indicators such as customer acquisition cost (CAC), customer lifetime value (CLV), conversion rates, and repeat purchase frequency. A structured assessment enables entrepreneurs to determine whether digital investments contribute to sustainable business growth or increase operational costs.

The ROI of digital campaigns can be expressed as:

ROI = (Customer Lifetime Value (CLV) – Customer Acquisition Cost (CAC)) / Customer Acquisition Cost (CAC)

For example, if a paid advertising campaign generates 200 new customers for USD 1,000, the CAC equals USD 5 per customer. Assuming an average CLV of

USD 40, the campaign demonstrates favorable return potential. However, profitability calculations become more complex when platform commissions and promotional incentives are taken into account. A reduction in net revenue caused by platform fees directly affects effective customer lifetime value and may significantly alter profitability projections.

Platform dependency introduces hidden cost layers. Delivery commissions ranging from 20–30% can substantially reduce contribution margins. For example, a beverage that generates a 60% gross margin through direct in-store sales may yield only 35% after platform deductions. Consequently, increasing digital orders without corresponding pricing adjustments may increase sales volume while simultaneously reducing overall profitability. This situation can be better understood through Platform Economy Theory, which suggests that digital platforms simultaneously create market access and structural dependency (Cutolo & Kenney, 2021; Nambisan et al., 2018). While platforms provide visibility, customer reach, and transaction infrastructure, they also control algorithms, customer data, commission structures, and transaction rules. This creates power asymmetries in which local coffee shops become increasingly dependent on platform governance systems. Algorithmic changes can influence customer reach and sales performance without direct entrepreneurial control, potentially reducing strategic autonomy and increasing vulnerability to external platform decisions (Hänninen et al., 2020; Cenamor et al., 2021).

Break-even analysis is equally important for subscription-based digital tools. A loyalty application costing USD 300 per month must generate revenue exceeding that amount to justify its adoption. If the average contribution margin per transaction is USD 2, the business must secure at least 150 additional transactions monthly to break even. Sustainability communication through digital platforms also carries financial implications. Transparent storytelling may support premium pricing and accelerate payback periods for investments in ethical sourcing or environmentally friendly packaging. Conversely, excessive discounting may erode perceived value and weaken brand positioning.

Digital marketing serves as a financial multiplier when strategically integrated with innovation and sustainability initiatives. From the perspective of Dynamic Capability Theory, successful digital marketing depends not only on technology adoption but also on an organization's ability to sense customer preferences, seize emerging opportunities, and transform organizational practices in response to market changes. The integration of customer analytics, online feedback, loyalty data, and digital experimentation enables entrepreneurs to refine marketing strategies and improve customer engagement continuously. These digital dynamic capabilities strengthen organizational adaptability, improve resource allocation, and enhance local coffee shops' ability to convert digital investments into sustainable competitive advantages (Vial, 2021; Zhang et al., 2022; Akter et al., 2023). Therefore, sustainable digital growth requires continuous monitoring of financial performance, controlled experimentation, and strategic management of platform dependence to ensure that increased visibility is accompanied by long-term profitability and resilience.

## 3. Integrating Economic, Social, and Environmental Goals

The integration of economic, social, and environmental objectives constitutes a fundamental challenge and opportunity for sustainability-oriented entrepreneurship. Historically, these dimensions have often been treated as competing priorities, with economic performance receiving greater attention than social welfare and environmental responsibility. However, Sustainable Entrepreneurship Theory argues that economic, social, and environmental value creation should be viewed as interconnected and mutually reinforcing objectives rather than independent outcomes. From this perspective, sustainability-oriented enterprises create value by simultaneously addressing market needs, societal expectations, and environmental concerns. For local coffee shops, the pursuit of sustainability therefore extends beyond profitability and encompasses community engagement, ethical sourcing, environmental stewardship, and long-term stakeholder value creation. This perspective provides a conceptual foundation for understanding why sustainability initiatives should be integrated into business strategy rather than treated as peripheral activities (Muñoz & Cohen, 2020; Shepherd & Patzelt, 2021; Kraus et al., 2020).

From an economic perspective, integration begins with redefining value creation beyond short-term profit maximization. Sustainable firms increasingly embed social and environmental benefits into their core value propositions, transforming sustainability into a source of competitive differentiation. Empirical evidence suggests that organizations adopting integrated sustainability strategies often achieve stronger financial performance through enhanced reputation, customer loyalty, and improved risk management (Eccles et al., 2020; Alsayegh et al., 2020). Consequently, economic objectives can be strengthened rather than compromised when aligned with broader sustainability goals.

Social objectives are integrated through stakeholder engagement, inclusive governance, and community-centered practices. Entrepreneurial ventures embedded within local environments possess unique opportunities to create social value by supporting local suppliers, promoting fair labor practices, and fostering spaces for social interaction and cultural expression. Previous studies demonstrate that stakeholder-oriented approaches strengthen trust, relational capital, and organizational resilience (Freeman et al., 2021; Hörisch et al., 2020). Social integration therefore serves both ethical and strategic purposes. From the perspective of the Resource-Based View (RBV), trust, community legitimacy, stakeholder relationships, and local embeddedness constitute valuable intangible resources that competitors find difficult to imitate. These resources contribute to sustainable competitive advantage by strengthening customer loyalty, enhancing reputation, and increasing stakeholder support during periods of uncertainty. Consequently, social sustainability should be viewed not only as a moral responsibility but also as a strategic asset that supports long-term organizational performance.

Environmental objectives are increasingly pursued through eco-innovation, resource efficiency, and circular economy practices. Rather than viewing environmental responsibility as a constraint, integrative approaches consider it a source of innovation and operational improvement. Research indicates that firms implementing environmental management systems and green innovation practices often achieve cost reductions, process efficiencies, and improved market positioning (Awan et al., 2021; Dangelico & Vocalelli, 2020). Environmental sustainability can therefore reinforce both economic and social objectives when effectively managed.

A key mechanism for integration is the adoption of holistic frameworks such as the Triple Bottom Line, shared value, and sustainable business model innovation. These approaches encourage entrepreneurs to evaluate synergies, trade-offs, and long-term consequences across sustainability dimensions. Effective integration, however, requires strong leadership commitment, organizational learning, and continuous adaptation. From the perspective of Dynamic Capability Theory, organizational learning, capability reconfiguration, and adaptive management enable firms to respond to changing stakeholder expectations and environmental conditions while maintaining strategic alignment. The ability to continuously reconfigure resources and processes allows local coffee shops to balance economic viability, social legitimacy, and environmental responsibility over time (Bocken et al., 2022; Lüdeke-Freund et al., 2020). Consequently, sustainable entrepreneurship is not achieved through isolated initiatives but through the ongoing coordination of multiple capabilities that transform sustainability trade-offs into sources of long-term resilience and competitive advantage.

## CONCLUSION

### 1. Summary

This chapter has analyzed the interconnected functions of entrepreneurial innovation and digital marketing in promoting economic, social, and environmental sustainability in local coffee shops. Entrepreneurial innovation is a multifaceted process encompassing product, process, and business model innovation, enabling small, locally anchored enterprises to generate value amid uncertainty and limited resources. Digital marketing is regarded as a strategic facilitator that enhances the effectiveness of innovation by expanding market reach, fostering stakeholder engagement, and improving operational efficiency. These two characteristics were shown to work synergistically, enabling local coffee shops to achieve sustainable expansion while preserving authenticity, a community focus, and environmental stewardship. The conversation emphasized that sustainability in the coffee industry should not be viewed as a single outcome but as an integrated framework in which economic viability, social value creation, and environmental stewardship are interdependent.

## 2. Theoretical Implication

This chapter enhances the sustainability and entrepreneurship literature by presenting an integrated framework that connects entrepreneurial innovation and digital marketing to the three dimensions of sustainability within a localized service setting. This chapter emphasizes local coffee shops, expanding current ideas typically centered on large firms or manufacturing, and illustrating how sustainability-oriented innovation operates within small-scale, community-based organizations. The chapter enhances conceptual comprehension by emphasizing the dynamic and context-dependent characteristics of innovation and digitalization in sustainability-focused entrepreneurship.

## 3. Practical Implication

This chapter offers practical implications for several stakeholders. For coffee shop owners, sustainability-oriented innovation should be implemented gradually through selective digitalization, ethical sourcing, and community engagement strategies that align with financial capacity. For local governments, support mechanisms such as digital capability training, sustainability incentives, and SME development programs can strengthen local entrepreneurial ecosystems. Digital platform providers should promote fair governance, transparency, and accessible analytics to reduce excessive platform dependency. Sustainability practitioners should encourage integrated approaches that balance economic viability, social legitimacy, and environmental responsibility within resource-constrained business environments.

## 4. Limitations and Future Studies

Several limitations should be acknowledged. First, this chapter is conceptual and relies on an integrative literature review rather than on primary empirical data. Second, the discussion focuses specifically on local coffee shops, which limits its generalizability to other industries and organizational contexts. Third, the analysis is predominantly based on Scopus-indexed literature, which may exclude relevant regional, practitioner, and non-English sources. Finally, contextual factors such as institutional environments, cultural differences, and technological readiness may influence sustainability outcomes beyond the scope of the present framework. Based on the limitations of this conceptual chapter, future research should empirically examine the relationships among entrepreneurial innovation, digital marketing, and sustainability outcomes using longitudinal, survey-based, or case-study approaches. Further studies should explore the implications of emerging technologies such as artificial intelligence, blockchain, and IoT for sustainable entrepreneurship. Research is also needed to develop SME-oriented sustainability measurement frameworks and to investigate sustainability-oriented innovation across diverse cultural, institutional, and emerging-market contexts (Dwivedi et al., 2021; Queiroz et al., 2021; Montiel & Delgado-Ceballos, 2021).

## ACKNOWLEDGMENT

The author acknowledges financial support from the Indonesian Ministry of Higher Education, Science, and Technology (Kemendiktisaintek) through the PMDSU (Pendidikan Magister menuju Doktor untuk Sarjana Unggul) program under Grant Numbers 0419/C3/DT.05.00/2025 and 083/C3/DT.05.00/PL/2025.

## REFERENCES

Ainin, S., Parveen, F., Moghavvemi, S., Jaafar, N. I., & Shuib, N. L. M. (2020). Factors influencing the use of social media by SMEs and their performance outcomes. *Industrial Management & Data Systems*, *120*(1), 187–207. DOI: 10.1108/IMDS-07-2019-0390

Akter, S., Wamba, S. F., Gunasekaran, A., Dubey, R., & Childe, S. J. (2023). How to improve firm performance using big data analytics capability and digital marketing capability. *International Journal of Production Economics*, *249*, 108497. DOI: 10.1016/j.ijpe.2022.108497

Albort-Morant, G., Leal-Rodríguez, A. L., & De Marchi, V. (2021). Absorptive capacity and relationship learning mechanisms as complementary drivers of green innovation performance. *Journal of Knowledge Management*, *25*(6), 1443–1463. DOI: 10.1108/JKM-01-2020-0071

Alsayegh, M. F., Rahman, R. A., & Homayoun, S. (2020). Corporate economic, environmental, and social sustainability performance transformation through ESG disclosure. *Sustainability (Basel)*, *12*(9), 3910. DOI: 10.3390/su12093910

Audretsch, D. B., Belitski, M., & Cherkas, N. (2023). Entrepreneurial ecosystems and sustainability transitions. *Small Business Economics*, *61*(2), 623–640. DOI: 10.1007/s11187-022-00666-4

Awan, U., Sroufe, R., & Kraslawski, A. (2021). Creativity enables sustainable development: Supplier engagement as a boundary condition. *Journal of Cleaner Production*, *298*, 126802. DOI: 10.1016/j.jclepro.2021.126802

Bergset, L., & Fichter, K. (2022). Green start-ups, A new typology for sustainable entrepreneurship and innovation research. *Journal of Innovation & Knowledge*, *7*(2), 100173. DOI: 10.1016/j.jik.2022.100173

Bhattacharya, C. B., Korschun, D., & Sen, S. (2022). Strengthening stakeholder–company relationships through mutually beneficial corporate social responsibility initiatives. *Journal of Business Ethics, 177*(2), 345–362. DOI: 10.1007/s10551-021-04863-9

Block, J. H., Colombo, M. G., Cumming, D. J., & Vismara, S. (2021). New players in entrepreneurial finance and why they are there. *Small Business Economics, 56*(3), 1–16. DOI: 10.1007/s11187-019-00227-9

Bocken, N. M. P., Short, S. W., Rana, P., & Evans, S. (2022). A literature and practice review to develop sustainable business model archetypes. *Journal of Cleaner Production, 65*, 42–56. DOI: 10.1016/j.jclepro.2013.11.039

Bocken, N. M. P., Weissbrod, I., & Tennant, M. (2022). Business model experimentation for sustainability: Evidence from SMEs. *Journal of Cleaner Production, 344*, 131035. DOI: 10.1016/j.jclepro.2022.131035

Borrella, I., Mataix, C., & Carrasco-Gallego, R. (2022). Smallholder farmers in the specialty coffee industry: Opportunities and constraints for economic sustainability. *Sustainability, 14*(3), 1376. DOI: 10.3390/su14031376

Cenamor, J., Parida, V., & Wincent, J. (2021). How entrepreneurial SMEs compete through digital platforms: The roles of digital platform capability and innovation. *Journal of Business Research, 124*, 384–397. DOI: 10.1016/j.jbusres.2020.11.058

Chatterjee, S., Chaudhuri, R., Vrontis, D., & Thrassou, A. (2021). Digital transformation of entrepreneurship and innovation: A bibliometric analysis. *Journal of Business Research, 135*, 575–588. DOI: 10.1016/j.jbusres.2021.06.048

Cohen, B., & Muñoz, P. (2021). Toward a theory of purpose-driven urban entrepreneurship. *Organization & Environment, 34*(2), 181–208. DOI: 10.1177/1086026619892345

Cowling, M., Brown, R., & Rocha, A. (2023). Did you save some cash for a rainy COVID-19 day? The crisis and SMEs. *International Small Business Journal, 41*(2), 187–210. DOI: 10.1177/02662426221104551 PMID: 35125601

Cutolo, D., & Kenney, M. (2021). Platform-dependent entrepreneurs: Power asymmetries, risks, and strategies in the platform economy. *The Academy of Management Perspectives, 35*(4), 584–605. DOI: 10.5465/amp.2019.0103

Dangelico, R. M., & Vocalelli, D. (2020). "Green marketing": An analysis of definitions, strategy steps, and tools. *Journal of Cleaner Production, 165*, 1263–1279. DOI: 10.1016/j.jclepro.2017.07.184

de Medeiros, J. F., Ribeiro, J. L. D., & Cortimiglia, M. N. (2020). Success factors for environmentally sustainable product innovation: A systematic literature review. *Journal of Cleaner Production, 270*, 122388. DOI: 10.1016/j.jclepro.2020.122388

Dietz, T., Börner, J., Förster, J. J., & von Braun, J. (2021). Governance of the coffee–forest frontier: Sustainability and social outcomes. *World Development, 137*, 105161. DOI: 10.1016/j.worlddev.2020.105161

Drummond, C., McGrath, H., & O'Toole, T. (2022). The impact of digital engagement on SME performance: The role of customer–brand relationships. *Journal of Business Research, 149*, 346–358. DOI: 10.1016/j.jbusres.2022.05.040

Dwivedi, Y. K., Hughes, D. L., Ismagilova, E., Aarts, G., Coombs, C., Crick, T., Duan, Y., Dwivedi, R., Edwards, J., Eirug, A., Galanos, V., Ilavarasan, P. V., Janssen, M., Jones, P., Kar, A. K., Kizgin, H., Kronemann, B., Lal, B., Lucini, B., & Williams, M. D. (2021). Artificial intelligence (AI): Multidisciplinary perspectives on emerging challenges, opportunities, and agenda for research. *International Journal of Information Management, 57*, 101994. DOI: 10.1016/j.ijinfomgt.2019.08.002

Eccles, R. G., Ioannou, I., & Serafeim, G. (2020). The impact of corporate sustainability on organizational processes and performance. *Management Science, 66*(11), 4889–4914. DOI: 10.1287/mnsc.2019.3451

Filimonau, V., & De Coteau, D. A. (2020). Food waste management in hospitality operations: A critical review. *Tourism Management, 78*, 104056. DOI: 10.1016/j.tourman.2019.104056

Foss, N. J., & Saebi, T. (2020). Business models and business model innovation: Between wicked and paradigmatic problems. *Long Range Planning, 53*(4), 101950. DOI: 10.1016/j.lrp.2019.101950

Freeman, R. E., Phillips, R., & Sisodia, R. (2021). Tensions in stakeholder theory. *Business & Society, 60*(2), 213–231. DOI: 10.1177/0007650318773750

Griffith, R., Levell, P., & O'Connell, M. (2022). How do food prices affect consumers and firms? Evidence from microdata. *Fiscal Studies, 43*(1), 1–28. DOI: 10.1111/1475-5890.12291

Hänninen, M., Smedlund, A., & Mitronen, L. (2020). Digitalization in retailing: Multi-sided platforms as drivers of industry transformation. *Baltic Journal of Management, 15*(2), 152–168. DOI: 10.1108/BJM-04-2017-0109

Hernández-Perlines, F., & Xu, W. (2023). Innovation, sustainability, and performance in small firms: The moderating role of entrepreneurial orientation. *Journal of Small Business Management, 61*(3), 987–1012. DOI: 10.1080/00472778.2021.1969653

Hörisch, J., Freeman, R. E., & Schaltegger, S. (2020). Applying stakeholder theory in sustainability management. *Organization & Environment, 33*(1), 1–23. DOI: 10.1177/1086026619831447

Hossain, M., Levänen, J., & Wierenga, M. (2021). Frugal innovation for sustainability: A systematic literature review. *Business Strategy and the Environment, 30*(4), 1707–1725. DOI: 10.1002/bse.2713

Hwang, J., & Kim, H. (2023). Cost pressure, innovation, and performance in small hospitality firms. *International Journal of Hospitality Management, 108*, 103352. DOI: 10.1016/j.ijhm.2022.103352

Inigo, E. A., & Albareda, L. (2020). Understanding sustainable innovation as a complex adaptive system. *Business Strategy and the Environment, 29*(7), 3143–3161. DOI: 10.1002/bse.2567

Jezeer, R. E., Santos, M. J., Boot, R. G. A., Junginger, M., & Verweij, P. A. (2021). Effects of shade and certification on coffee biodiversity and ecosystem services. *Agriculture, Ecosystems & Environment, 304*, 107140. DOI: 10.1016/j.agee.2020.107140

Kraus, S., Breier, M., Jones, P., & Hughes, M. (2022). Individual entrepreneurial orientation and new venture performance: The role of digital technologies. *International Journal of Entrepreneurial Behaviour & Research, 28*(1), 1–24. DOI: 10.1108/IJEBR-07-2021-0563

Kraus, S., Burtscher, J., Vallaster, C., & Angerer, M. (2020). Sustainable entrepreneurship orientation: A reflection on status-quo research. *Sustainability, 12*(12), 4873. DOI: 10.3390/su12124873

Kumar, V., Dixit, A., Javalgi, R. G., & Dass, M. (2021). Digital transformation of marketing: A multi-level framework. *Journal of the Academy of Marketing Science, 49*(1), 24–54. DOI: 10.1007/s11747-015-0426-9

Lüdeke-Freund, F., Gold, S., & Bocken, N. M. P. (2020). A review and typology of circular economy business model patterns. *Journal of Industrial Ecology, 24*(2), 331–345. DOI: 10.1111/jiec.12985

Martínez-Cañas, R., Ruiz-Palomino, P., Linuesa-Langreo, J., & Blázquez-Resino, J. J. (2024). Ethical marketing and consumer trust in the digital era. *Journal of Business Ethics, 189*(1), 115–132. DOI: 10.1007/s10551-023-05421-6

Michaelidou, N., Siamagka, N. T., & Christodoulides, G. (2020). Usage, barriers, and measurement of social media marketing: An exploratory investigation of small and medium B2B brands. *Industrial Marketing Management, 87*, 115–128. DOI: 10.1016/j.indmarman.2020.04.010

Mirabeau, L., Maguire, S., & Hardy, C. (2022). Bridging practice and process: A dynamic view of entrepreneurial innovation. *Organization Studies, 43*(6), 889–912. DOI: 10.1177/01708406211006846

Montiel, I., & Delgado-Ceballos, J. (2021). Defining and measuring corporate sustainability. *Organization & Environment, 34*(1), 1–30. DOI: 10.1177/1086026619871386

Muñoz, P., & Cohen, B. (2020). Sustainable entrepreneurship research: Taking stock and looking ahead. *Business Strategy and the Environment, 29*(3), 943–957. DOI: 10.1002/bse.2416

Nambisan, S., Siegel, D., & Kenney, M. (2018). updated relevance). On open innovation, platforms, and entrepreneurship. *Strategic Entrepreneurship Journal, 12*(3), 354–368. DOI: 10.1002/sej.1300

Perfecto, I., Vandermeer, J., & Philpott, S. M. (2023). Ecological complexity and sustainability in coffee agroecosystems. *Journal of Cleaner Production, 382*, 135301. DOI: 10.1016/j.jclepro.2022.135301

Queiroz, M. M., Telles, R., & Bonilla, S. H. (2021). Blockchain and supply chain sustainability: A systematic literature review. *Journal of Cleaner Production, 316*, 128301. DOI: 10.1016/j.jclepro.2021.128301

Rosca, E., Arnold, M., & Bendul, J. C. (2023). Business models for sustainable innovation – An empirical analysis. *Journal of Business Research, 156*, 113450. DOI: 10.1016/j.jbusres.2022.113450

Rueda, X., Garrett, R. D., & Lambin, E. F. (2022). Corporate investments in supply chain sustainability: Evidence from coffee sourcing. *Journal of Business Ethics, 176*(2), 319–336. DOI: 10.1007/s10551-020-04746-5

Saeidi, S. P., Sofian, S., Saeidi, P., Saeidi, S. P., & Saaeidi, S. A. (2021). How does corporate social responsibility contribute to firm financial performance? The mediating role of competitive advantage. *Journal of Business Research, 136*, 292–306. DOI: 10.1016/j.jbusres.2021.07.025

Samoggia, A., & Riedel, B. (2020). Coffee consumption and sustainability: Exploring consumer awareness and behavior. *Sustainability, 12*(8), 3235. DOI: 10.3390/su12083235

Shepherd, D. A., & Patzelt, H. (2021). Entrepreneurship and sustainability: New horizons. *Journal of Management Studies, 58*(1), 1–27. DOI: 10.1111/joms.12664

Sihotang, D. S. (2026). Digital Twins as an Enabler of Cognitive Enterprise Architecture: Reconfiguring Organizational Systems and Decision Intelligence. In *Transforming Physical Assets to Cognitive Enterprises With Digital Twins* (pp. 289–320). IGI Global Scientific Publishing., DOI: 10.4018/979-8-3373-9998-0.ch010

Srinivasan, R., & Swink, M. (2021). An investigation of visibility and flexibility as complements to supply chain analytics: An organizational information processing theory perspective. *Production and Operations Management*, *30*(2), 415–434. DOI: 10.1111/poms.13305

Stylos, N., Bellou, V., Andronikidis, A., & Vassiliadis, C. A. (2022). Linking environmental awareness to sustainable consumption in hospitality. *Journal of Sustainable Tourism*, *30*(2–3), 513–532. DOI: 10.1080/09669582.2020.1849234

Suhud, U., Boonkaew, S., Sihotang, D. S., Azinuddin, M., & Aujirapongpan, S. (2025). Bridging Social Responsibility and Sustainability: A Case Study of Modelling Tourist Citizenship Behaviour in Indonesia. *International Journal of Sustainable Development and Planning*, *20*(12), 5381–5393. DOI: 10.18280/ijsdp.201229

Suhud, U., Sihotang, D. S., Juliana, J., Azinuddin, M., Chanthawong, A., & Aujirapongpan, S. (2026). Eco-friendly souvenirs as a catalyst for sustainable tourism: Emotional and attitudinal perspectives. *Sustainable Futures : An Applied Journal of Technology, Environment and Society*, *11*, 101824. DOI: 10.1016/j.sftr.2026.101824

Tölkes, C., & Butzmann, E. (2022). Motivating pro-sustainability behavior: The potential of sustainability marketing. *Journal of Cleaner Production*, *343*, 130940. DOI: 10.1016/j.jclepro.2022.130940

Vial, G. (2021). Understanding digital transformation: A review and a research agenda. *The Journal of Strategic Information Systems*, *30*(2), 101695. DOI: 10.1016/j.jsis.2021.101695

Vuorio, A. M., Torkkeli, L., & Sainio, L. M. (2023). Entrepreneurial orientation, innovation, and sustainable performance. *Journal of Business Research*, *156*, 113482. DOI: 10.1016/j.jbusres.2022.113482

Wibowo, A., Chen, S. C., Wiangin, U., Ma, Y., & Ruangkanjanases, A. (2023). Customer behavior as an outcome of social media marketing: The role of trust and engagement. *Journal of Retailing and Consumer Services*, *71*, 103182. DOI: 10.1016/j.jretconser.2022.103182

Yang, M., Evans, S., Vladimirova, D., & Rana, P. (2021). Value uncaptured perspective for sustainable business model innovation. *Journal of Cleaner Production*, *290*, 125799. DOI: 10.1016/j.jclepro.2021.125799

Zhang, M., Zhao, X., Lyles, M., & Guo, H. (2022). Absorptive capacity and digital innovation: Evidence from SMEs. *Industrial Marketing Management, 102*, 105–117. DOI: 10.1016/j.indmarman.2021.12.007

## KEY TERMS AND DEFINITIONS

**Circular Economy:** An economic system that seeks to minimize waste and maximize resource efficiency through reuse, recycling, regeneration, repair, and closed-loop production and consumption processes.

**Community Entrepreneurship:** An entrepreneurial approach that creates economic value while simultaneously strengthening local communities through social participation, collaboration, cultural preservation, and inclusive development.

**Customer Engagement:** The degree of emotional, cognitive, and behavioral interaction between customers and a business, reflected through participation, communication, loyalty, advocacy, and co-creation activities.

**Digital Marketing Capability:** An organization's ability to utilize digital technologies, data analytics, online platforms, and digital communication tools to engage customers, improve market reach, and support strategic decision-making.

**Digital Transformation:** The strategic integration of digital technologies into organizational processes, business models, and customer interactions to improve efficiency, innovation, competitiveness, and value creation.

**Entrepreneurial Innovation:** The process through which entrepreneurs create, adapt, or reconfigure products, services, processes, or business models to generate value, respond to market changes, and enhance competitiveness under conditions of uncertainty.

**Ethical Sourcing:** The procurement of products and raw materials through practices that promote fairness, transparency, responsible labor conditions, environmental stewardship, and equitable treatment of suppliers.

**Local Coffee Shop:** A small or independently owned coffee business embedded within a local community that typically emphasizes personalized service, local identity, customer relationships, and community engagement.

**Platform Dependency:** A condition in which businesses become increasingly reliant on digital platforms for customer access, visibility, transactions, and market participation, potentially reducing strategic autonomy and increasing vulnerability to platform governance.

**Resource Efficiency:** The effective utilization of materials, energy, time, and financial resources to maximize value creation while minimizing waste, environmental impact, and operational inefficiencies.

**Stakeholder Engagement:** The process of involving customers, employees, suppliers, communities, governments, and other stakeholders in organizational activities, decision-making, and sustainability initiatives to create shared value and long-term relationships.

**Sustainability:** A multidimensional concept that emphasizes the balanced achievement of economic viability, social well-being, and environmental responsibility to ensure long-term value creation for present and future stakeholders.

**Sustainable Business Model:** A business model designed to create, deliver, and capture value while integrating economic, social, and environmental objectives into core organizational activities and decision-making processes.

**Sustainable Entrepreneurship:** An entrepreneurial approach that simultaneously pursues economic opportunities, social value creation, and environmental stewardship through innovative and sustainability-oriented business activities.

**Triple Bottom Line:** A sustainability framework that evaluates organizational performance across three interrelated dimensions: economic prosperity, social equity, and environmental protection.

# Chapter 6
# Behavioural Analysis of SME Owners Towards Sustainability Adoption

**Souvik Banerjee**
http://orcid.org/0000-0001-9988-8887
*Management Development Institute Murshidabad, India*

**Abhijit Pandit**
http://orcid.org/0000-0003-2122-3468
*School of Management & Commerce, Brainware University, Kolkata, India*

**Nabyendu Roy**
http://orcid.org/0009-0002-6469-9685
*Indepent Researcher, India*

**Merina Banerjee**
http://orcid.org/0009-0001-4974-5893
*Management Development Institute Murshidabad, India*

**Rajib Chowdhury**
http://orcid.org/0000-0002-4158-0625
*School of Business Administration, The Pennsylvania State University, USA*

## ABSTRACT

*To improve sustainability frameworks in developing economies, it is important to understand how small and medium-sized business (SME) owners behave. Although there has been significant research on the technical and financial obstacles to sustainability, there has been insufficient focus on the cognitive, emotional, and relational factors that influence owner responses to sustainability regulations. This*

DOI: 10.4018/979-8-2600-3179-7.ch006

*report is based on a long-term, multi-case research of ceramic small and medium-sized enterprise (SME) owners in rural West Bengal, India, who were exposed to a hybrid sustainability framework that combined Enterprise Risk Management (ERM) and Circular Economy (CE) practices. The study employs ethnographic interviews, participant observations, and process tracing across three waves to elucidate the belief systems, mental models, anxieties, motives, and social norms that affect the adoption of sustainability. The results show that owners' attitudes change from doubt and avoidance to inquiry, conditional acceptance, and finally internalisation.*

## INTRODUCTION

Policies and technologies alone would not be enough to help small and medium-sized businesses (SMEs) move towards sustainability (Alayón et al., 2022). The owner is at the centre of any small and medium-sized business. They are the one who makes decisions, runs the business, finances it, and manages risks (Hoyt & Liebenberg, 2015). The behaviour, attitudes, and mental models of the SME owner are very important in deciding whether sustainability frameworks are used, resisted, or changed, especially in rural and informal contexts. Even though this is a primary fundamental issue, the behavioural aspect of SMEs adopting sustainability is still not well-studied in academic research and policy practice. People commonly talk about technological, economic, and regulatory constraints as problems, but they don't talk as much about how small business owners think about risk, what they think about environmental responsibility and challenges, what they think about circularity, and how they feel about changing the paradigm.

This research tries to fulfill that gap, by doing a thorough indepth behavioural study of small and medium-sized business (SME) owners who are taking part in a long-term sustainability program based on the Enterprise Risk Management (ERM) and Circular Economy (CE) frameworks. The report is based on a three-wave qualitative field study with eleven pottery small and medium-sized enterprises (SMEs) in Duttapukur, West Bengal, India. The group learnt about ERM–CE tools in their own language and culture, and the facilitation was meant to encourage them to think about their own experiences rather than forcing them to use outside metrics. SME owners took part in semi-structured interviews, reflection workshops, process walk-throughs, and feedback sessions across the waves. This research is based on a lot of behavioural data that came from these interactions, such as, verbal expressions, metaphors, gestures, emotional reactions, resistance stories, and learning insights. This is in line with previous researches (Austin & Rahman, 2022; Pandey et al., 2024; Lundqvist, 2014).

This dataset did not show a simple split between adopters and non-adopters; instead, it showed a range of behaviours. At first, owners were sceptical of both the terminology of sustainability and the reasons why people were bringing it up. A lot of people thought that environmental issues were the job of regulators, NGOs, or city elites, and that they didn't have anything to do with the day-to-day problems of managing a kiln, coordinating workers, or getting pigments. Some were afraid that admitting to pollution or risk could lead to punishment or public shame. Some people thought that sustainability didn't fit with traditional crafts or that it needed resources that were out of their reach. But after just a few months of trying things out, thinking about them, and talking to their peers, these opinions started to change. People who had previously called risk registers "school paperwork" started making their own visual checklists. People who were worried that changing the colour of the product would make it less good started telling stories about safer colours as part of their brand. These changes weren't made because of pressure to follow the rules; they were made because of real-life experiences, learning from others, and growing confidence in oneself.

The goal of this study is to describe and analyse these behavioural patterns and figure out how small business owners mentally and emotionally move from being against sustainability to support it. The paper's goal is to broaden existing models of SME transformation beyond rational choice or resource-dependence models by focussing on the human aspects of ERM–CE adoption. It tries to show how belief systems, feelings, social conventions, identity, and lived experience all work together to form how owners act in the day to day life. By doing this, it adds to a growing corpus of research on sustainability that focusses on relational and behavioural aspects as key drivers of system change.

The next sections will go into details about the behavioural patterns, narrative trajectories, and social learning mechanisms that were seen in the Duttapukur cohort. The study will suggest a conceptual model called the ERM–CE Behavioural Continuum. It will end with some useful tips for creating interventions, facilitation protocols, and communication methods that are in line with the way SME owners behave. In the end, the study shows that small and medium-sized businesses (SMEs) adopting sustainability is not only a policy issue or a management problem; it is a human process that happens via trust, discovery, and changing what it means to be a responsible business owner at present.

The integration of sustainability in SMEs has become an international issue, especially in the developing economies where informal businesses are the predominant ones. Although previous studies have focused on technological obstacles, budgetary limitations and policy loopholes, behavioural aspects have not been fully investigated. The African and the Latin American research shows that SME owners tend to feel sceptical of sustainability, and that it is imposed on them, rather than being an opportunity. South Asia has disjointed supply chains and generational ownership structures that further complicate adoption (Saeed et al., 2019). It is on this context that this chapter contextualizes the behavioural analysis of SME owners in the greater context of entrepreneurial innovation, that behavioural change is an essential but neglected contributor to systemic change.

Theoretical lenses of sustainability adoption can be adopted to gain better understanding of behavioural adoption of sustainability. The Theory of Planned Behaviour by Ajzen (Ajzen, 1991) emphasizes the importance of attitudes, subjective norms and perceived behavioural control in influencing the decision made by the owners. The Diffusion of innovations by Rogers puts more emphasis on peer modelling and social networks playing a critical role in speeding up adoption. The institutional theory also describes the impacts of the legitimacy pressures and cultural norms on the reaction of SMEs to sustainability frameworks. But we can hardly find these behavioural theories combined with enterprise risk management (ERM) or circular economy (CE) practices in current research. That gap is filled in this chapter by showing how the behavioural triggers recognition, sensory validation, and peer demonstrations can be used in combination with ERM tools and CE tools to create a lasting change.

## METHODOLOGY

This behavioural study used a profoundly immersive, long-term, and qualitative approach to find out how small business owners in rural India react to the addition of sustainability practices, especially through a combination of Enterprise Risk Management (ERM) and Circular Economy (CE) frameworks. The research design was made to capture changing stories, emotional shifts, learning experiences, and social influence patterns at different stages of the transformation process, knowing that changing behaviour among SME owners is complex, specific to the situation, and happens over time. The strategy puts more weight on the lived experiences, implicit knowledge, and interpretive frameworks of SME owners than on metrics or evaluation rubrics that are set by others. This is in line with studies of Becerra-Bizarrón & Gomez-Bernal (2025),

The study took place in three separate waves between 2021 and 2025 in the Duttapukur pottery cluster in West Bengal, India. This place was picked because it has a lot of small, family-owned ceramic businesses that aren't official. The owners are involved in manufacturing things, taking risks, and making decisions on how to run the firm. The sample comprised eleven ceramic SME proprietors who voluntarily participated in a structured intervention program collaboratively developed with local facilitators. The people who were chosen to take part were chosen on purpose, not randomly. This made sure that people of all ages, business sizes, generations of ownership, and levels of experience with risk management or sustainability terminology were represented. It was important that all of the participants have only a little formal education in sustainability or business systems. This meant that any adoption or rejection of techniques was based on real participation and not on what they had learnt in school.

The research method was based on ethnographic and participatory action research. During the three waves, data gathering comprised semi-structured interviews, participant observation, shadowing work routines, reflexive workshops, risk mapping sessions, and narrative storytelling forms. There were 6 to 8 months difference between each wave, which gave people time to relearn from their experiences and see new habits in real life. The interviews were administered in the native Bengali dialect, and when necessary, they were translated into English for analysis. They were also taped with permission. Field notes, photos, and structured observation checklists made with local facilitators were used to keep track of observations. This multi-method strategy made sure that linguistic, visual, and behavioural evidence all pointed to the same thing.

The selection of the ethnographic and participatory action research was quite planned, as survey-based methods were, not applicable in low literacy and informal SME settings. Although quantitative research often simplifies the adoption of behaviour to the binary levels of adopters and non-adopters, this approach was able to capture subtle emotional changes, metaphors and identity redefinitions. Process tracing enabled mapping of causal paths and member-checking had been used to ensure interpretive validity. This immersive form of compliance audit offered deeper information on how behavioural thresholds and tipping points are realised in practice than conventional compliance audits.

One new part of the strategy was to using process tracing to find the causal processes that connect owner beliefs to changes in conduct. For instance, the study didn't only note whether a risk register was used; it also followed how the owner's view of "risk" changed over time, going from doubt to exploration to creating their own risk indicators. Also, emotional responses, from defensiveness to pride, were compared to actions that were either seen or reported, such making kilns safer, trying out different ways to store pigments, or changing work patterns to include rotation. This way of tracing processes helps us see the little changes that are often missed in research that use surveys.

Thc usc of narrative and metaphor analysis was another important part of the process. The study didn't employ Likert-scale questionnaires or set categories for attitudes. Instead, it focused on the metaphors that small business owners used to talk about sustainability, risk, tradition, and modernity. We didn't just look at phrases like "school homework," "scientific craftsmanship," or "the kiln speaks to us" as colours; we also saw them as means to understand how SME owners use culturally relevant analogies to make sense of abstract ideas. These expressions were meticulously coded and studied to uncover latent behavioural orientations and to pinpoint the emotional and social triggers of change.

There was a multi-stage interpretive procedures for analysing the data (Bocken et al., 2022; Bamel et al., 2019). First, all of the interviews and observations were written down and coded using open and axial coding methods, which are based on grounded theory. We put the codes into groups based on conduct, like "defensive disengagement," "conditional curiosity," "peer-modelling influence," and "identity redefinition." Then, these categories were mapped across time over the three waves to see if the owners' focus changed. We didn't force new themes into existing models; instead, we let them emerge from the data. This inductive method was necessary to make sure that the behavioural continuum shown in the results came from real-life practice and not just theoretical ideas.

Member-checking sessions, in which chosen SME owners were asked to read summaries of their behavioural narratives and confirm the interpretations, significantly strengthened the methodological rigour. These meetings often resulted in more explanations, revisions, or more in-depth discussions. When there were differences, the data were looked at again and marked with reflective remarks, that kept the owner's voice and intention while also acknowledging the researcher's point of view.

The study also included parts of behavioural facilitation mapping, that is a tool that has been changed to work in settings with minimal literacy and oral communication. The owners were given simplified maps of behavioural pathways (for example, demonstrating how choosing a safer pigment might lead to less complaints, which might lead to consumer praise). They were then asked to think about the roads they had taken or avoided. These maps were used for two things: to help people have deeper talks and to help the facilitators involved in the intervention figure out what was going on. They were not just theoretical frameworks.

To keep the research process non-extractive and to empower participants, participants were kept up to date on the results, and the SME owners were given multiple outputs, such as photo diaries, recognition certificates, and peer displays. This moral cycle of giving and receiving built trust, kept people interested, and helped the study show long-term behaviour changes.

The technique was crafted not only to assess the adoption of sustainable measures but also to elucidate the mechanisms, motivations, and timing of behavioural shifts. The study effectively captured the profound nuances of SME owner change through a qualitative, narrative-driven, and relationship-focused methodology, transcending mere compliance measures to unveil a narrative of discovery, agency, and identity reformation. This strategy has a lot of promise to be used in other informal SME groups in South Asia and abroad, especially when relationship issues and behavioural hesitations are a big part of the problem of sustainability (Tambunan, 2009).

## ANALYSIS OF RESULTS

The behavioural insight as derived from the longitudinal study of ceramic SME owners in Duttapukur, provide a profound understanding of the mindset, emotional dynamics, and social rationale influencing the approach to and internalisation of sustainability. Most proprietors were bit wary, as well as detached, and practical at the start of the intervention. Their responses to the first introduction of the ERM–CE framework were influenced by decades of dealing with bureaucratic ambiguity, market pressures that are informal in nature, and community-based labour ties. When people heard the phrase "sustainability," it made them think of compliance, outside meddling, or academic abstraction. Participating respondents often said things like "this is for the big factories, not for us" or "we know how to run our kiln; what can a checklist teach us?" These early statements didn't mean that people didn't like the ideas themselves; they were more like defensive scepticism based on past experiences with extractive interventions, random audits, or broken promises from government's programs.

But the interviews showed that there were underlying currents of worry, curiosity, and hope beneath their resistance at the outer-level . Many owners kept talking about problems they had with their operations that keep on happening, like sudden kiln failures, customer complaints about pigments, and quality that changed without warning. They thought these problems were caused by a lack of control, not bad luck. The first hints of behavioural openness showed up when the ERM lens was employed to look at these problems not as failures of the owner, but as systemic risks that could be acknowledged, predicted, and dealing mechanism is incorporated. When the risk register was offered first time as a wall chart with local language and colour-coded pictograms, many owners started to find "hotspots" in their everyday operations on their own. These were locations where things often went wrong but had never been written down or talked about openly. One owner who had said his procedure was "perfect" later told a story about a close call with pigment storage and moisture that he had never told his personnel about. Putting the risk on the wall and giving it a name not only made people think about it, but it also made them feel better and more willing to work together to solve issues.

One of the other thread common in owner stories was the fear of losing something—quality, consumer trust, or cultural identity—when adjusting based on the environment or risk. The idea of getting rid of some chemical tints was received with a lot of hostility at first. Owners said it was because of client preferences, aesthetic standards, or elder's wisdom. But when a peer owner did a live demonstration proving that a safer pigment not only kept the colour true but also made workers less likely to complain about eye irritation, several others did the same. The change in these behaviour were less about being persuaded by abstract ideas and more about seeing a trusted peer take on the risk and get better results. This shows how important social modelling and intra-cluster dissemination are in affecting the choices of owners. Interviews showed that owners often compared their activities not to rules or norms, but to what other respected members of the community were doing. When early adopters called improvements "modern tradition" or "scientific craftsmanship," other people were able to see sustainability in a new way, not as something strange but as something real.

It was found that the pride and recognition were also powerful motivators for behaviour. Owners who got printed photo diaries for their kiln improvements or who were asked to share their story in group reflection sessions showed clear signs of satisfaction and were more involved in the next waves. One owner who had first laughed on risk precautions started keeping a laminated sheet of kiln checkpoints and proudly presented it to clients who came to visit, saying that "our process is now scientific". The change from being defensive to taking ownership was not caused by rewards or punishments, but by the feeling of being seen, heard, and recognised as an astute inventor. The behavioural interviews showed that this kind of recognition not only made people proud but also changed their sense of self from "a survivor in a tough market" to "a responsible leader who brings dignity to the craft." These changes in identity lasted longer than any one technical fix and often led to changes in how owners treated workers, worked with suppliers, or talked about risks.

The last behavioural insight was how important it is to feel like one person can do something worthy. Owners who were confused by jargon or didn't know how to follow advice without support from others sometimes stopped or lost interest. On the other hand, people who were given small, local treatments that worked, like shielding a kiln vent or using a safer drying procedure, said they felt more confident and were more willing to try new things. The story in several interviews changed over time from "I don't have the time or ability" to "we can try this and see what happens," and then to "this is now part of how we work." The tipping points generally happened when owners saw real-time feedback—less smoke from the chimney, fewer reworks, and happier workers—and made the connection between these results and their own choices and new routines. During these times, the ERM–CE framework stopped being an outside agenda and became a way of thinking that people adopted, encouraging them to change their behaviour through positive feedback and more freedom.

These behavioural studies depict SME owners as introspective, emotionally perceptive, and socially responsive individuals who can undergo substantial transformation when engaged with respect and significance. The path of change is neither straight or even; it is formed by things like lived experience, trust in relationships, social modelling, recognition, and tiny victories. The next part will take these ideas and turn them into a framework for changing behaviour. It will also give suggestions for how to plan sustainability initiatives that fit with the psychology of the owner, the dynamics of the community, and the fact that change is an ongoing process.

*Table 1. Behavioural Stages and Sample Expressions*

| Stage | Representative Quote | Dominant Emotion |
|---|---|---|
| Defensive Disengagement | 'This is for big factories, not for us.' | Scepticism |
| Conditional Curiosity | 'If it works for them, maybe we can try.' | Cautious Interest |
| Practical Experimentation | 'Smoke was less after trying their method.' | Hope and Confidence |
| Identity Redefinition | 'Our process is now scientific.' | Pride and Stewardship |

The study found four main behavioural stages, which are shown in Table 1: Defensive Disengagement, Conditional Curiosity, Practical Experimentation and Identity Redefinition. A quote from a small business owner and the main emotional response that goes with that stage are given for each step. This table shows how the proprietors' mental state changed over time, from doubt to eventually taking care of sustainability principles.

*Table 2. Adoption Triggers by Owner Group*

| Trigger Type | Early Adopters (%) | Late Adopters (%) |
|---|---|---|
| Peer Demonstration | 90 | 50 |
| Facilitator Support | 70 | 85 |
| Visual Aids (e.g., Checklists) | 60 | 80 |
| Recognition Events | 85 | 60 |

Table 2 shows how several triggers affected the adoption habits of early and late adopters. It shows that peer demonstrations and recognition events worked very well for early adopters, but late adopters were more likely to respond to facilitator support and visual tools like checklists in their own language. This difference shows that owners at distinct levels of preparation require various kinds of help.

*Table 3. Behavioural Shifts by Wave*

| Wave | Avg. Risk Register Use (%) | Avg. Sustainability Language Use (%) | Observed Worker Participation (%) |
|---|---|---|---|
| Wave 1 | 15 | 5 | 20 |
| Wave 2 | 55 | 35 | 50 |
| Wave 3 | 85 | 75 | 80 |

Table 3 shows how people's behaviour changed over the three waves of the intervention. The usage of risk registers, the use of words connected to sustainability, and the participation of workers are all steadily rising. This table backs up the qualitative story of behavioural advancement with numbers and shows that it becomes easier to make sustainability a part of everyday life with greater exposure and support.

*Table 4. Emotional Responses by Behavioural Stage*

| Stage | Positive Emotion (%) | Negative Emotion (%) |
|---|---|---|
| Defensive | 10 | 80 |
| Curious | 40 | 50 |
| Experimenting | 70 | 25 |
| Redefining | 95 | 5 |

Table 4 shows how many good and negative feelings were shown at each stage of behaviour. When SME owners move from the Defensive stage to the Redefining stage, negative sentiments like fear and resistance go down a lot, while positive feelings like pride and confidence go up. This change in emotions is key to changing behaviour over time, and it explains why long-term involvement leads to more lasting results than short-term compliance efforts.

*Figure 1. Behavioural Practice Adoption Over Time*

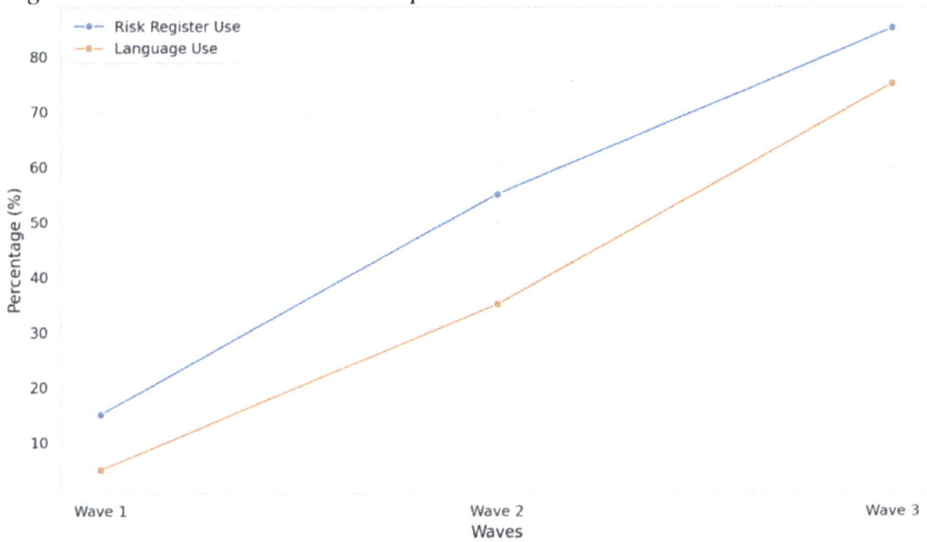


Figure 1 shows how the use of risk registers and the use of sustainability language have grown across the three waves. It demonstrates a consistent rising trend, which supports the idea that long-term exposure, peer modelling, and minor wins lead to more people internalising sustainability frameworks.

*Figure 2. Trigger Effectiveness by Adopter Group*

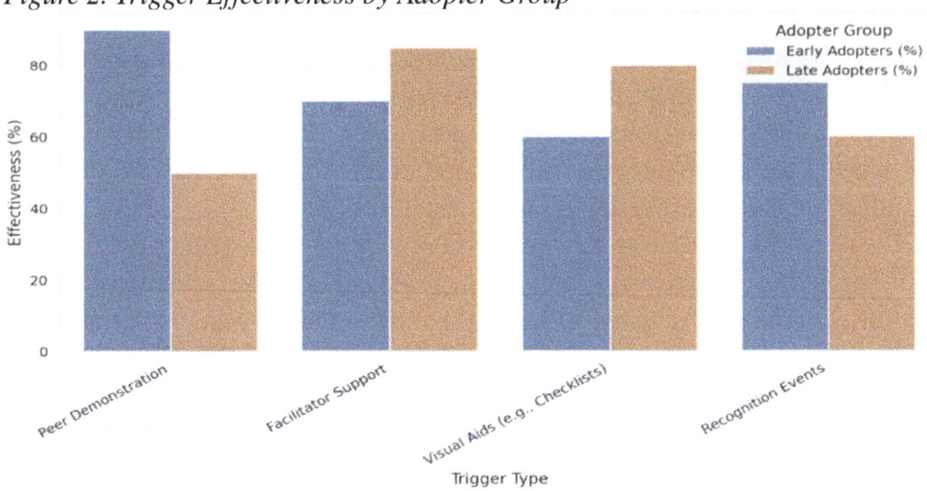

Figure 2 shows how early and late adopters think different adoption triggers work. Early adopters rated peer demonstrations and recognition events the highest, which suggests that their social capital in the community influenced others. On the other hand, visual tools and help from a facilitator were more helpful for late adopters who were unsure or doubtful, which shows that different techniques are needed for different groups.

*Figure 3. Emotional Trends Across Behavioural Stages*

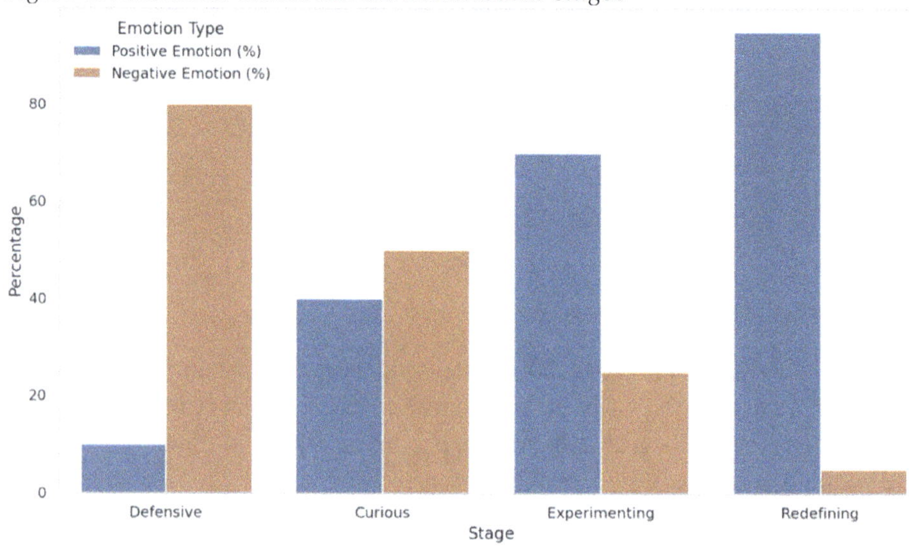


Figure 3 shows how people's emotional responses changed at each stage of conduct. As you move from the defensive to the redefined identity stage, your positive feelings get stronger, and negative feelings get weaker. This confirms that emotional and identity-based elements are very important in changing behaviour and that emotional support is just as important as technical training.

The results indicate the presence of barriers and enablers to sustainability adoption. The first opposition was due to fear of being punished by regulations, lack of relevance and fears of cultural identity. However, attitudes were slowly changed with enablers like peer demonstrations, facilitator support, and recognition events. Gender factors were rather subtle, with younger female owners being more open to experimentation and generational differences affecting the risk perception. Limits on resources, especially access to safer pigments, were frequent obstacles, and team problem-solving alleviated these obstacles. By juxtaposing these stories, the analysis highlights the fact that the adoption of behaviour is not linear and uniform but it depends on the social, emotional and contextual aspects.

## THEMATIC ANALYSIS

The common element in the behavioural journey of small business owners was about changing their view of sustainability from a burden imposed by the government to an emerging part of their own business identity. Instead, of adopting sustainability because it was required, owners started to make it a part of who they were as experts and artisans. The phrase "our process is now scientific," which is often used, really showed how this became part of their thinking. When owners saw tools like risk registers or cleaner kiln methods as improvements to their legacy rather than things that were forced on them, they began to "own" the idea of sustainability. This sense of ownership led to more involvement, also emotional investment, and long-term behaviour change, turning sustainability into a personal standard instead of a list of things to do.

The need for peer approval and the effects of social learning were also quite important. A lot of small business owners went from being curious but not sure to trying things out only after witnessing their colleagues succeed. Saying things like "if it works for them, maybe we can try" showed how important trust and reputation are inside a cluster. Owners who saw other people in the same socio-economic situation succeed felt more confident about making changes themselves. This kind of peer-led experimentation was more convincing than top-down compliance procedures because it used real-world examples that were relevant to the culture instead of abstract theory. It also changed how people thought about risk; something that used to feel like a gamble became a safe, shared practice backed up by the community's experience.

Sensory and experiential anchoring were very important for making early habit change stick. SME owners really cared about what they could see or feel, such less smoke coming from the kiln, more consistent products, or fewer complaints from workers. These real, sensory confirmations made the idea of sustainability seem more real and trustworthy than vague promises. Owners used terms like "smoke was less" and "better colours" again and again, which showed that they trusted their own senses more than written instructions or workshops. Change didn't happen because of far-off goals, but because of little, visible wins that made people think about cause and effect and gave them practical confidence.

During the early phases of the intervention, cognitive dissonance was quite apparent among SME proprietors. People generally thought of sustainability as something that only "big factories" or city elites care and talk about, and that had little to do with the daily task of making pottery in rural areas. Owners said they felt left out, which made them think that sustainability was elitist, impractical, or not that important. But many people started to make sense of this difference after spending more time with local facilitators, doing participatory risk mapping, and having community-driven conversations. The story changed over time from "this isn't for us" to "we can do it our way." This change meant going from comparing things to things outside of themselves to having trust in themselves. It changed sustainability from a foreign idea to a flexible practice based on their own living situation.

Emotion was a key part of the change in behaviour. At first, there were mostly feelings of doubt, dread, and avoidance. Owners feared being found out for their mistakes or being blamed for hazards they didn't grasp. But as the intervention went on and risk was seen to find out more about the problem instead than a way to punish people, the emotional tone changed. Hope, curiosity, and pride started to take the place of fear. This was seen in things like "let me show you my checklist," where overseeing and seeing the process became sources of pride instead of fear. Emotional reframing was a key part in helping people not just follow the rules but also realign their emotions with sustainability goals.

Language and semiotic translation also turned out to be important tools for bringing changes. In the beginning, standard terms for sustainability didn't always make sense to small business owners. But a semiotic bridge was built by using local metaphors, visual checklists, and oral narrative. People started using phrases like "school paperwork" to talk about how they kept their own records, and "scientific craftsmanship" became a common term to talk about output that was environmentally friendly and kept its cultural character. This change showed that sustainability was no longer a borrowed word; it had become part of the cluster's everyday language. Communication tactics that considered local language and signs were key to getting people to accept and stay involved over time.

Recognition was a strong way to encourage behaviour. Owners who were praised for their hard work, whether through printed picture diaries, public praise, or chances to speak in group workshops, felt validated in ways that went beyond commercial measures. They no longer saw themselves as just struggling business owners; they saw themselves as leaders in their communities and agents of change. This social support made them even more dedicated to sustainability. It pushed them to keep becoming better, help their peers, and incorporate sustainable thinking into more areas of their organisation. It also changed sustainability from a personal battle to a socially recognised success, making sure that changes would last longer across the cluster.

In addition to theoretical contributions, the research has practical implications to managers and facilitators of SMEs. To start with, demonstrations that are led by their peers should be given priority as it is more appealing than abstract training. Second, identity redefinition and maintenance of behavioural change can be supported by recognition mechanisms, like photo diaries or community awards. Third, facilitation protocols should be anchored by sensory validation (reduced smoke in the workplace, increased morale of the workers) to anchor the adoption in lived experience. Interventions aimed at policymakers must be based on respect of local metaphors and semiotic translations to make sustainability seem a form of scientific artisanship, and not a form of bureaucratic obedience. These managerial implications emphasise how behavioural innovation can be implemented in practice.

## FINDINGS

Based on the many behavioural observations from the long-term fieldwork in Duttapukur, a conceptual model comes to light that explains how SME owners deal with, oppose, try out, and eventually adopt sustainable frameworks. This model, which may be called the ERM–CE Behavioural Continuum, shows the range of cognitive and emotional stages that small business owners go through as they deal with sustainability practices in situations where they don't know what's going to happen, they must follow rules, and they are part of a culture. The approach doesn't assume that people would accept things in a rational, linear, logical way. Instead, it focusses on how behavioural change happens in small business ecosystems through experience, relationships, and repetition. There are certain attitudes, perceived hurdles, motivational triggers, and decision-making processes that are unique to each stage. These are impacted by both internal elements (like beliefs, emotions, and past experiences) and external pressure points (like peer behaviour, facilitation style, and market feedback).

The first step in the continuum is defensive disengagement. Here, owners are defensive of their current practices and sometimes see sustainability as something that outsiders force on them or as a threat to their freedom to run their businesses. People sometimes say things like "we have always done it this way" or "this is for big factories, not us." Scepticism is the main feeling, which comes from prior disappointments or a fear of being exposed. At this point, the SME owner feels that they don't have much influence, and sustainability is seen as either an abstract or hostile goal. When people try to use risk registers or CE terms, they generally avoid them or only use them symbolically. At this point, the behavioural job is not to compel change but to build trust and a sympathetic presence, recognising the owner's competence while gently bringing to light hidden hazards or inefficiencies through stories or observations.

The second step is conditional curiosity. People in this stage aren't sure yet if sustainability is worth it, but they are receptive to it in some cases, usually because they see their peers doing it, because they use familiar metaphors to explain it, or because they learn from their own problems. The way people make decisions changes from "this doesn't matter" to "this might help if it fits with what I am doing." There are conflicting feelings—some hope, some doubt—but the perceived risk of becoming involved is lower than it was before. Walk-throughs, photo diaries, and stories about similar businesses are examples of behavioural anchors that can be helpful starting points. Owners start to ask questions to learn more and may agree to try out small adjustments, such using different pigments or seeing how hot the kiln is. At this point, self-efficacy is still weak, so interventions should focus on low stakes testing and getting feedback right away.

The third step is to try things out in a practical way. Owners start to test ERM–CE processes here not because they believe in sustainability, but because early tests show useful effects, such fewer broken things, less smoke, and fewer worker complaints (Zhu et al., 2007). The way of thinking changes to "This is working for me, so I will keep doing it." Emotions get better, like pride, interest, and growing confidence. Owners can ask for more templates or start discussing their experiences with each other. At this point, facilitation needs to change from trying to convince people to work together to create things. This means giving personalised help, applauding minor achievements, and making time for people to think. Owners start to show behavioural momentum, where one change leads to another. For instance, keeping track of kiln accidents could lead to changes in labour schedules or new ways to store pigments.

The fourth step is to redefine oneself. At this stage, sustainability is no longer something the owner must do; it's a part of who they are. People see the business not merely to make money, but also as a place of safety, dignity, and social worth. Owners start to talk about their responsibilities as good employers, people who help keep the community healthy, or people who come up with new ideas in their field. Safety trainings, risk reviews, and CE audits become regular parts of a business life. Owners may also start coaching others or looking for ways to stand out in the market based on their practices. Pride, appreciation, and stewardship are the most important feelings. At this point, the way people behave changes permanently. External help becomes quite less important, and peer learning, community validation, and self-improvement become more important. Policy and support systems should see these owners as champions and invest in their roles as leaders, storytellers, and community members.

This behavioural continuum is not set in stone or one way. Depending on context shocks, facilitation gaps, or changing market conditions, owners may go forward, stay still, or even go back. The approach is useful because it may help plan sustainability solutions that fit with the owner's present level of behaviour. For instance, workshops that focus on technical standards would be good for those who are redefining their identity, but they might turn off people who are defensive and disengaged. In the same way, financial incentives may speed up experimenting, but they are unlikely to change deeply held views without recognition and relational support. The ERM–CE Behavioural Continuum is both a diagnostic and developmental tool. It lets facilitators, policymakers, and researchers meet SME owners where they are and help them through the process of becoming more sustainable.

This approach is based on a certain situation, but it can also be used in other SME ecosystems that are informal, traditional, and short on resources. It says that behaviour change comes from producing meaning, not from following orders; from discovery, not from following directions. When treated with care, humility and an understanding of the bigger picture, small business owners can and do become great stewards of sustainable business, coming up with new ideas from inside and leading from below.

## CONCLUSION

The end of this behavioural study found a fundamental truth that is often missed, in discussions about sustainability: change in small and medium-sized businesses starts with the owner's lived experience, thoughts, and feelings. These owners do not just passively follow policies or sit around doing nothing; they are active sense-makers who constantly read, reframe, and respond to social, economic, and environmental inputs. The Duttapukur pottery cluster shows that even when resources are very limited, people can change their behaviour to be more sustainable. This is often the case when, the frameworks introduced respect owner agency, build on their tacit knowledge, and provide real, experiential value.

The Enterprise Risk Management–Circular Economy (ERM–CE) integration process worked not simply because it was required, but because it was made more human. Facilitators listened to the owners, accepted their speed, changed the tools to fit their vernacular, and recognised small small accomplishments. This process changed doubt into interest, defensiveness into thoughtfulness, and being alone into being with others. By doing this, it set off a behavioural flywheel in which tiny changes at first led to new questions, social modelling made learning easier, and seeing results made people feel more capable. These dynamics show an important point: changing behaviour is less about getting over resistance and more about making it possible to discover. Owners did not give up on tradition; they looked at it through the eyes of modern responsibility. They did not say no to risk management; they just made it part of their everyday language. Sustainability became a part of their tale, not as a borrowed screenplay but as a new identity.

For practitioners who are building sustainable initiatives, the message is clear: put the individual first, not the rules. Start by learning about the owner's viewpoint, worries about how things work, and social references. Use metaphors, pictures, and stories from other people that make sense in your area. Instead of giving orders, ask questions that make people think. Start shared excursions instead of audits. Most importantly, do not only look at environmental outputs to see whether you are successful. Look at behavioural inflection points, including when the owners ask new questions, change their responsibilities, or teach others on their own. These kinds of events show that the mental and emotional substrate has changed, making it easier for long-term sustainability to take root.

The results show, that policymakers could change the way they think about investments, moving from heavy infrastructure and compliance enforcement to behavioural enablement. This involves paying for embedded facilitators, local peer networks, and projects that let people tell their own stories. It involves creating rewards based on behaviour (such as paperwork, group reflection, and exploration) rather than just hardware adoption. It also involves making feedback platforms where small business owners can track their success, compare themselves to others, and be proud of how far they've come. When it comes to fostering sustainability from the ground up, policy needs to understand that dignity, recognition, and identity are just as important as money.

Researchers should be more qualitative, longitudinal, and ethnographic in terms of methodologies to explore how small and medium-sized businesses change, according to this study. Quantitative indicators can, indicate what has changed, but only qualitative interaction elucidates how and why. Future research should investigate how behaviour changes across different industries, for examples textiles, food processing and services. It should also explore how gender, caste, age and exposure to technology affect how people think about sustainability. There is also need for cross-geography comparative studies to create a behavioural typology of small business owners and to see which combinations of incentives, peer learning, and facilitation work best to push people beyond behavioural thresholds.

Small and medium-sized business (SME) owners that adopt sustainability are not just following the rules; they are changing their behaviour through trust, reframing, and relational learning. The ERM–CE Behavioural Continuum is one method to map that journey and come up with ways to help that take its complexity into account. The Duttapukur ceramic entrepreneurs remind us that small businesses can do more than just make money. They can also help create a future where economic growth and environmental responsibility go hand in hand. This is line with existing literature (Gonçalves et al., 2022).

This chapter shows that the adoption of sustainability in SMEs is not a technical or regulatory only process but a behavioural way of innovating. ERM-CE Behavioural Continuum depicts how the owners shift between being defensive and identity redefinition by experiential learning, peer influence, and recognition. By redefining sustainability as an entrepreneurial identity, the research work adds to the overall theme of this book, that is, the effects of entrepreneurial innovation. Systemic change of informal economies can be triggered by behavioural change that has been fostered through culturally resonant facilitation. Subsequent studies are required to apply this framework to other industries and geographic areas etc. with the aim of understanding the intersection of behavioural innovation and digitalisation, supply chain resilience, and global sustainability agendas.

## REFERENCES


Ajzen, I. (1991). The theory of planned behavior. *Organizational Behavior and Human Decision Processes*, *50*(2), 179–211. DOI: 10.1016/0749-5978(91)90020-T

Alayón, C. L., Säfsten, K., & Johansson, G. (2022). Barriers and enablers for the adoption of sustainable manufacturing by manufacturing SMEs. *Sustainability (Basel)*, *14*(4), 2364. DOI: 10.3390/su14042364

Austin, A., & Rahman, I. U. (2022). A triple helix of market failures: Financing the 3Rs of the circular economy in European SMEs. *Journal of Cleaner Production*, *361*, 132284. DOI: 10.1016/j.jclepro.2022.132284

Bamel, N., Dhir, S., & Sushil, S. (2019). Inter-partner dynamics and joint venture competitiveness: A fuzzy TISM approach. *Benchmarking*, *26*(1), 97–116. DOI: 10.1108/BIJ-02-2018-0041

Becerra-Bizarrón, M. E., & Gomez-Bernal, J. R. (2025). Business sustainability practices in micro and small enterprises: A systematic review. *PLOS Sustainability and Transformation*, *4*(11), e0000140. DOI: 10.1371/journal.pstr.0000140

Bocken, N. M., Harsch, A., & Weissbrod, I. (2022). Circular business models for the fastmoving consumer goods industry: Desirability, feasibility, and viability. *Sustainable Production and Consumption*, *30*, 799–814. DOI: 10.1016/j.spc.2022.01.012

Gonçalves, B. D. S. M., Carvalho, F. L. D., & Fiorini, P. D. C. (2022). Circular economy and financial aspects: A systematic review of the literature. *Sustainability (Basel)*, *14*(5), 3023. DOI: 10.3390/su14053023

Hoyt, R. E., & Liebenberg, A. P. (2015). Evidence of the value of enterprise risk management. [Object Identifier ] [DOI]. *The Bank of America Journal of Applied Corporate Finance*, *27*(1), 41–47. DOI: 10.1111/jacf.12103

Lundqvist, S. A. (2014). An exploratory study of enterprise risk management: Pillars of ERM. *Journal of Accounting, Auditing & Finance*, *29*(3), 393–429. DOI: 10.1177/0148558X14535780

Pandey, V., Kumar, S., Gupta, S., & Khatri, N. (2024). Unlocking sustainability: Prioritizing barriers for SME success in India with AHP analysis. *Journal of Global Entrepreneurship Research*, *14*(1), 25. DOI: 10.1007/s40497-024-00395-3

Saeed, B. B., Afsar, B., Hafeez, S., Khan, I., Tahir, M., & Afridi, M. A. (2019). Promoting employee's proenvironmental behavior through green human resource management practices. *Corporate Social Responsibility and Environmental Management*, *26*(2), 424–438. DOI: 10.1002/csr.1694

Tambunan, T. T. H. (2009). *SMEs in Asian developing countries*. Springer., DOI: 10.1057/9780230250949

Zhu, Q., Sarkis, J., & Lai, K. H. (2007). Green supply chain management: Pressures, practices and performance within the Chinese automobile industry. *Journal of Cleaner Production*, *15*(11-12), 1041–1052. DOI: 10.1016/j.jclepro.2006.05.021

# Chapter 7
# Board busyness, Corporate Social Responsibility, and Firms' Tax Strategies

**Saleh F. A. Khatib**
http://orcid.org/0000-0001-7652-4191
*Sohar University, Oman*

## ABSTRACT

*This research investigates the relationship between social performance, board busyness, and tax incentives. We used a panel dataset from 4,831 non-financial firms across six Western European countries between 2015 and 2024. We found that companies with higher social responsibility are more likely to benefit from favorable tax incentives, affirming the fiscal value of corporate social responsibility. Board busyness positively moderates this relationship, especially among firms that comply with Global Reporting Initiative (GRI) standards. The result of this study highlights the strategic value of CSR in influencing fiscal outcomes. It also underscores the importance of governance quality and transparent social practices in enhancing the effectiveness of tax-related incentives. The findings remain consistent after running additional robustness checks using Generalized Method of Moments (GMM) and it offer practical implications for regulators and policymakers aiming to align corporate fiscal behavior with sustainability goals.*

DOI: 10.4018/979-8-2600-3179-7.ch007

## 1. INTRODUCTION

In recent years, corporate social performance (CSP) has gained increasing attention from both scholars and practitioners, particularly in the context of its strategic implications for firms' tax behavior and financial strategy. Among the many incentives that firms may consider when engaging in socially responsible behavior, favorable tax treatment remains a critical, albeit complex, economic consideration. As environmental, social, and governance (ESG) expectations intensify globally, firms are pressurized to integrate social responsibility into their core operations for sustainable and ethical business conduct. Tax incentives, as flexible policy tools, direct resources to innovative activities, boosting economic vitality and growth (C. Feng, 2024; K. Wu & Zheng, 2025). The synergistic effect of tax incentives provides a favorable environment for corporate innovation activities (Hu et al., 2025). The relationship between a firm's social engagement and its tax planning strategy has become a pressing issue, especially within the regulatory environments of Western European countries, where tax policies and sustainability standards are particularly stringent.

Figure 1 illustrates the yearly distribution of the overall social performance across European countries from 2015 to 2024. It should be noted that there was a steady increase in social performance scores from 2015 to 2018, peaking around 2018, followed by a consistent decline until 2021. This may reflect challenges posed by economic uncertainty, shifting regulatory priorities, or resource constraints, especially during the COVID-19 pandemic. This trend raises an important question: Do firms reduce their social investments in the face of financial and operational pressures, and what role do institutional incentives—particularly tax policies—play in shaping these decisions?

While prior research has overlooked the relationship between CSP and tax policies, recent studies has increasingly focused on how tax policies shape corporate behavior beyond mere compliance, particularly in contexts of innovation, sustainability, and governance. A growing body of literature affirms the positive influence of tax incentives on firm innovation and investment behavior, especially when they alleviate financial constraints and encourage long-term planning (Liu et al., 2024; Q. Wu et al., 2024; Zhao et al., 2024). For instance, Hu et al. (2025) argued that tax incentives significantly stimulate corporate innovation in China. Also, Li et al. (2024) maintained that tax incentives aimed at human capital accumulation enhance both the quality and scope of innovation by reducing firms' financial burdens related to training and development. Beyond innovation, other studies have focused on the association between tax incentives sustainability outcomes related to reputational advantages and stakeholder relations (Liu et al., 2024; Yin et al., 2025), digital transformation (Q. Feng et al., 2024; Fu et al., 2025), ESG investment decisions (Yin et al., 2025; Zhu et al., 2023), green innovation (C. Feng, 2024; Hu et al., 2025; Li et al., 2024), and supply chain perspective (K. Wu & Zheng, 2025). For example, Yin et al. (2025) argued that fiscal and tax incentives play a crucial role in supporting corporate green innovation and found that tax-based policies enhance ESG fulfillment, thereby contributing to firms' reputational and operational gains. However, there is no studies to consider the social and governance performance of corporate.

Corporate governance mechanisms play a central role in shaping such outcomes. In this context, the concept of board busyness, or the degree to which board members are simultaneously serving on multiple boards, emerges as an influential yet underexplored factor in moderating the CSP-taxation relationship. Overworked or "busy" boards may suffer from time constraints and diluted oversight capacity, thereby weakening their ability to monitor executive decisions (Fayad et al., 2024), including those related to tax strategy and CSR investments. While such boards may aim to reap the reputational and financial benefits associated with CSP, their limited attention may allow opportunistic or inconsistent behaviors to go unchecked. As such, understanding whether and how board busyness influences the association between social performance and tax incentives is critical for evaluating the effectiveness of corporate governance mechanisms in aligning sustainability goals with strategic financial outcomes.

This study seeks to address this gap by investigating the interplay between social performance, tax incentives, and board busyness from a sample of 4,831 non-financial firms in six major Western European countries—France, Germany, Italy, Sweden, Switzerland, and the United Kingdom—from 2015 to 2024. Drawing on agency theory and stakeholder perspectives, we hypothesize that firms with higher levels of social performance are more likely to benefit from tax incentives and that this relationship is contingent on the board's capacity to effectively govern, as proxied by board busyness.

*Figure 1. The social performance in Europe countries in the last ten years.*

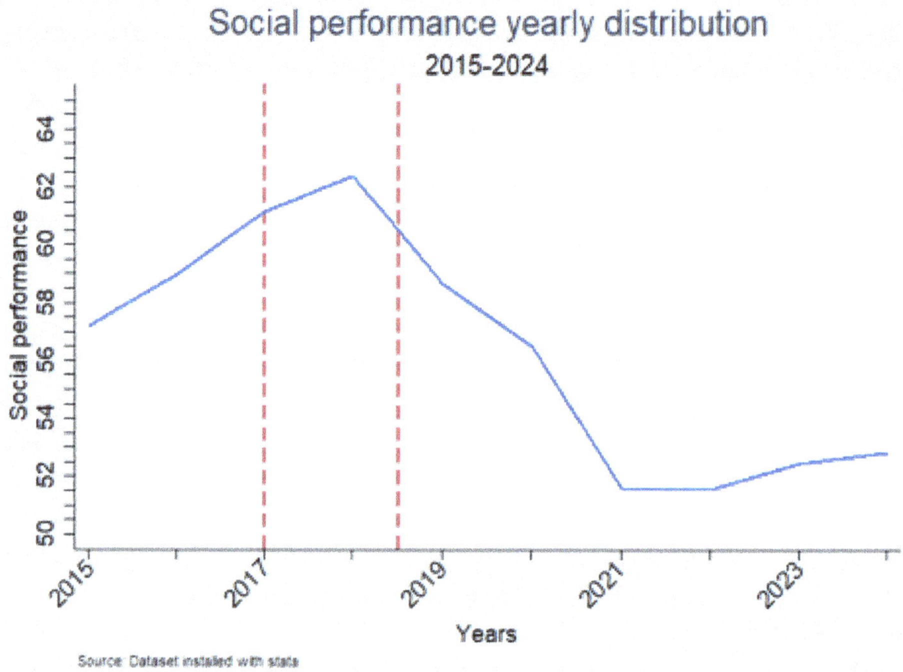


The contributions of this study are threefold. First, it enriches the literature on the CSP-tax strategy nexus by empirically testing the benefits of social responsibility in terms of tax outcomes, moving beyond conventional performance or reputational outcomes. In doing so, it addresses a critical but underexplored question: can social responsibility translate into tangible financial advantages via the tax system? Second, it introduces board busyness as a moderating variable, highlighting how overcommitted directors may dilute governance effectiveness in sustainability-tax alignment. It refines our understanding of how internal governance dynamics shape firms' ability to strategically capitalize on external institutional incentives. Third, the study is among the first to focus on Western European regulatory environments, which are characterized by both robust ESG expectations and relatively strict tax transparency regimes, thereby offering context-specific insights with broader applicability to similar institutional settings. Finally, the inclusion of GRI compliance as a contextual factor adds an important institutional layer, demonstrating how adherence to global reporting frameworks enhances the fiscal payoff of social engagement—an insight that is especially relevant for firms navigating sustainability reporting mandates such as the EU's Corporate Sustainability Reporting Directive (CSRD).

The remainder of this paper is structured as follows: Section 2 reviews the relevant literature and develops the hypotheses; Section 3 outlines the methodology and data; Section 4 presents the empirical results; and Section 5 concludes with policy implications and suggestions for future research.

## 2. SOCIAL PERFORMANCE STATUS IN EUROPE

Corporate Social Performance has evolved into a central component of responsible business conduct within the European context, driven by an intricate interplay of institutional regulation and stakeholder expectations. At the forefront of this evolution, the European Union has played a decisive role in institutionalizing the CSP agenda through progressive policy instruments, such as the Non-Financial Reporting Directive (NFRD), the CSRD, and the European Green Deal. These initiatives aim to embed transparency, sustainability, and ethical responsibility into corporate practice. Nevertheless, despite this policy momentum, the depth and authenticity of CSP engagement remain uneven across the region, revealing structural challenges in standardization and enforcement (García-Sánchez & Noguera-Gámez, 2017; Ioannou & Serafeim, 2019).

A critical factor underlying these disparities is Europe's highly heterogeneous institutional landscape. Northern and Western European countries—such as Germany, Sweden, and the Netherlands—exhibit more mature and embedded CSP systems. In these contexts, stakeholder-oriented corporate governance models have historically aligned corporate interests with broader societal goals, enabling CSP to become a fiduciary concern rather than a peripheral initiative (Matten & Moon, 2008; Oikonomou et al., 2020). By contrast, in Southern and Eastern European economies, CSP adoption is often constrained by weaker regulatory enforcement, lower civic pressure, and economic instability. These conditions foster environments where firms may engage in symbolic or selective forms of social responsibility rather than genuine, systemic engagement (Brammer et al., 2012; Fernandez-Feijoo et al., 2014).

Compounding this institutional variation is a persistent disconnect between CSP disclosure and actual performance outcomes. Although firms increasingly publicize social responsibility initiatives, such disclosures are frequently influenced by legitimacy-seeking behavior rather than substantive commitment to social impact. Michelon et al. (2015) and Searcy (2012) highlighted the prevalence of "decoupling," wherein firms comply with reporting expectations without internalizing the practices they endorse, particularly in sectors with high public scrutiny and limited internal accountability mechanisms. This performative CSP undermines the credibility of social reporting and raises concerns about superficial compliance and greenwashing.

Measurement inconsistencies further exacerbate the problem. Despite the proliferation of reporting frameworks (such as the GRI and recent EU-level taxonomy regulations) CSP measurement across European firms remains fragmented. The largely voluntary nature of these frameworks has allowed for broad discretion in what is reported and how it is framed, thereby limiting comparability across firms and countries and reducing the utility of CSP as a basis for performance evaluation or policy intervention (Hahn & Kühnen, 2013).

Moreover, recent disruptions have exposed the fragility of CSP commitment. As evidenced in Figure 1 of the manuscript, CSP levels across Europe rose consistently until 2018 but experienced a marked decline during the COVID-19 pandemic (2019–2021). This regression reflects the vulnerability of CSR initiatives during periods of macroeconomic stress, when corporate priorities shift toward liquidity preservation and cost minimization. Bai and Ho (2022) found that during the pandemic, firms reduced socially responsible investments despite earlier evidence linking CSP to reduced financial constraints and stronger stakeholder trust.

Within this context, a particularly salient dynamic emerges at the intersection of CSP and corporate taxation. European firms today navigate dual institutional pressures: the normative expectation to demonstrate social legitimacy and the regulatory imperative to maintain tax compliance. Consequently, CSP has evolved into a strategic lever not only for reputational capital but also for influencing fiscal treatment. Emerging empirical evidence (i.e., Jiang et al., 2024; Lu & Zhu, 2021) suggests that firms with higher CSP are more likely to receive favorable tax treatment, particularly when their social initiatives align with public policy goals. However, this intersection remains underexplored in scholarly research, which has primarily focused on social performance-related tax incentives.

## 2.1. Theoretical Background

Understanding how firms leverage CSP to influence fiscal outcomes, particularly tax incentives, requires a nuanced theoretical lens that captures both external institutional pressures and internal governance dynamics. This study draws on stakeholder theory, institutional theory, and agency theory to build an integrative framework explaining the relationship between CSP, tax incentives, and board busyness within the European corporate landscape.

Stakeholder theory posits that firms exist not solely to serve shareholders, but also to generate value for a broader set of stakeholders including governments, civil society, and employees (Freeman, 1984). Within this view, CSP is a strategic tool to manage stakeholder relations and reduce non-market risks (Donaldson & Preston, 1995). As empirical evidence suggests, firms with higher CSP often experience reputational advantages, improved risk management, and increased stakeholder trust—factors that enhance legitimacy and financial outcomes (Godfrey, 2005). From this perspective, governments may view socially responsible firms as valuable partners in achieving public policy objectives, thus offering preferential tax treatment as an incentive (Granda, 2021; Zhu et al., 2023; Wu et al., 2024).

Institutional theory further strengthens the rationale behind the CSP-taxation nexus by emphasizing how firms conform to institutional norms to gain legitimacy (DiMaggio & Powell, 1983). In the European context, regulatory pressures such as the EU's Non-Financial Reporting Directive (NFRD) and CSRD institutionalize expectations for CSP disclosures (Hahn & Kühnen, 2013; Ioannou & Serafeim, 2019). Firms operating in countries with robust institutional environments and civic pressure—such as Sweden or Germany—are more likely to embed CSP into their strategic objectives (Oikonomou et al., 2020). However, the institutional environment also interacts with the design and credibility of fiscal incentives. In countries with strong regulatory enforcement, tax incentives may serve as effective instruments to reward substantive, rather than symbolic, social engagement (Bai & Ho, 2022).

Agency theory introduces a critical governance lens, particularly relevant for analyzing the role of board busyness (Jensen & Meckling, 1976). Directors who serve on multiple boards may face time and resource constraints, reducing their effectiveness in monitoring managerial decisions (Fich & Shivdasani, 2006). While some studies argue that experienced and well-networked directors bring strategic advantages (Ferris et al., 2003), others find that board busyness undermines governance quality, leading to managerial opportunism or inattentiveness (Fayad et al., 2024). In the context of CSP, busy boards may fail to ensure alignment between social initiatives and corporate financial strategies, including the pursuit of tax advantages. Thus, board busyness serves as a moderating mechanism, influencing whether social investments are strategically leveraged for fiscal benefits.

Empirical research supports this governance-based interpretation. Michelon et al. (2015) demonstrated that firms with weaker governance structures are more likely to engage in symbolic CSR, whereas well-governed firms translate social initiatives into concrete outcomes. Similarly, Rehman et al. (2023) showed that shareholder protection interacts with CSP practices, affecting firm behavior across institutional contexts. Moreover, investor sentiment can incentivize CSR engagement when financial markets place a premium on sustainability, though this may result in "decoupling" if firms emphasize disclosure over implementation.

## 2.2. Social performance and tax incentives

Corporate social performance is increasingly regarded as a core component of a firm's strategic adaptation to external institutional and societal pressures that shift from shareholder-centric model toward a broader stakeholder-oriented framework

(Khatib, 2025b). Nevertheless, the extent to which such efforts yield direct financial benefits (particularly in the form of tax advantages) remains unclear. Prior literature posits that strong CSP may improve a firm's perceived legitimacy among regulatory authorities, thereby reducing the likelihood of intensive scrutiny and potentially facilitating access to fiscal incentives (Frynas & Stephens, 2015). Based on Stakeholder theory, firms hold accountability not only to shareholders but to a broader network of stakeholders, including regulators, employees, and local communities (Freeman, 1984), CSP can be interpreted as a proactive response to the expectations of these diverse constituencies.

From this perspective, enhanced social performance serves not merely as an ethical commitment but as a strategic mechanism for strengthening institutional legitimacy through proactive social responsible practices (e.g., environmental conservation, equitable labor policies, and community engagement) (Frynas & Stephens, 2015). such proactive strategies may result in a more favorable relationship with tax authorities, who may interpret socially responsible behavior as indicative of lower tax risk or greater alignment with public policy objectives. Furthermore, firms that demonstrate consistent contributions to societal welfare (i.e., investments in climate mitigation, community development, or inclusive labor practices) may be deemed more deserving of targeted tax relief as part of broader governmental efforts to incentivize sustainability transitions (Wu et al., 2024).

Empirical studies support this linkage (Putri et al., 2023). For example, Zhu et al. (2023) provide evidence that tax policies increasingly favor firms exhibiting verifiable environmental, social, and governance outcomes, including reduced carbon emissions, workforce diversity, and employee training initiatives. These findings suggest a growing policy alignment between ESG performance and fiscal policy instruments, reinforcing the view that CSP can function as both a reputational asset and a pathway to economic benefit through tax-related mechanisms.

**Hypothesis H1**: There is a relationship between social performance and tax incentives.

## 2.3. The Role of Board Busyness

Corporate social performance has been increasingly recognized as a strategic asset that may yield favorable tax outcomes, but the extent to which firms can translate their social investments into fiscal benefits depends heavily on the strength and structure of their internal governance mechanisms. Among these, board busyness (defined as the number of concurrent board memberships held by a director (Fayad et al., 2024; Teng et al., 2024)) emerges as a critical but understudied moderator in the CSP–tax incentive nexus.

Based on agency theory, which posits that effective board oversight is essential for aligning managerial decisions with shareholder interests (Jensen & Meckling, 1976). Directors who sit on multiple boards may bring valuable expertise, broadened networks, and institutional legitimacy, which can enhance a firm's ability to navigate complex regulatory environments—including those governing tax policies and ESG compliance (Fayad et al., 2024; Ferris et al., 2003; Jiraporn et al., 2009), and enhanced access to information regarding fiscal incentives (Karim et al., 2022). Such directors are likely to have broad exposure to best practices, knowledge of fiscal incentive programs, and relationships with regulators and policymakers that serve the companies in achieving their strategic goals (Hudson & Morgan, 2023; Trinh et al., 2019). From this perspective, the accumulated expertise may enhance the firm's ability to leverage CSP into tangible tax advantages by strategically leveraging their reputational capital, inter-organizational connections, and regulatory familiarity, especially in contexts where CSP is closely monitored and rewarded, such as under the EU's Corporate Sustainability Reporting Directive or GRI frameworks. For example, busy directors often sit on boards of firms in similar or overlapping industries, allowing them to cross-pollinate successful tax and ESG strategies, thus enabling more effective integration of social performance with fiscal planning. Trinh et al. (2019) found that the expertise and connections of busy outside directors lead to better decision-making, more efficient resource utilisation and more effective monitoring.

However, there is also a countervailing perspective. As suggested by Fich and Shivdasani (2006), excessively busy boards may suffer from "attention scarcity," limiting their capacity to monitor and support management in implementing CSP initiatives or aligning them with broader tax strategies. Trinugroho et al. (2023) further demonstrate that board busyness is negatively associated with firm performance, suggesting that overstretched directors may struggle to effectively engage in long-term sustainability planning or tax optimization efforts. In such cases, the governance inefficiency induced by board overload could weaken the strategic integration between social responsibility and tax planning, reducing the potential for favorable fiscal outcomes. Venkatesh et al. (2025) reported a nonlinear relationship between busy boards and firm performance.

**Hypothesis H2**: Board busyness moderates the relationship between social performance and tax incentives.

## 3. METHODOLOGY

Our sample is drawn from non-financial firms listed in six Western European countries—France, Germany, Italy, Sweden, Switzerland, and the United Kingdom—over the period from 2015 to 2024. We focus on Western Europe for two main reasons. First, these countries represent a diverse yet comparable institutional context characterized by robust ESG frameworks, mature capital markets, and tax regimes that increasingly integrate sustainability considerations. This regulatory environment provides a suitable backdrop for examining the interaction between social performance, tax incentives, and governance structures. Second, these jurisdictions are subject to the European Union's CSRD or equivalent national frameworks, creating both regulatory convergence and variation in CSP reporting standards that is ideal for cross-country comparative analysis.

We began with a population of 5,102 listed firms across the six countries. Financial institutions and insurance companies were excluded due to their unique capital structures, accounting frameworks, and regulatory oversight, which could distort the tax incentive structure and social performance metrics. We also excluded firms with incomplete financial data, missing governance indicators (such as board characteristics), or unavailable social performance scores. Further, we dropped firms that were not covered by Refinitiv ESG data or those with non-standard fiscal years.

After applying these criteria, the final sample consisted of 4,831 firms, yielding 38,926 firm-year observations. Industry distribution analysis shows that the majority of sample firms operate in the utilities and industrial sectors (18.38% each), followed by Manufacturing (16.5%), Technology (11.79%), and health care (10.86%). Table 1 provide summary of the sample distribution.

To measure tax incentives, we adopt two proxies: the effective tax rate (ETR) and tax savings from deferred tax liabilities, in line with recent literature. Social performance is operationalized using the social pillar scores obtained from the Thomson Reuters Eikon database. Board busyness is captured by the ratio of board seats held by outside directors. To address endogeneity concerns and dynamic panel bias, we employ two-stage least squares (2SLS) estimation, supplemented by Generalized Method of Moments (GMM) robustness checks with instrumental variables, mitigating potential correlated omitted variable issues and endogeneity problems (Cheng et al., 2014).

*Table 1. The sample distribution over countries and industries.*

| ICB Industry | Country | | | | | | |
|---|---|---|---|---|---|---|---|
| | France | Germany | Italy | Sweden | Switzerland | UK | Total |
| Basic Materials | 26 | 38 | 13 | 49 | 12 | 136 | 274 |
| Manufacturing | 164 | 130 | 123 | 137 | 33 | 209 | 798 |
| Consumer Staples | 38 | 32 | 19 | 32 | 16 | 61 | 197 |
| Energy | 26 | 21 | 15 | 23 | 5 | 95 | 186 |
| Health Care | 85 | 68 | 22 | 181 | 45 | 125 | 525 |
| Industrials | 139 | 123 | 114 | 187 | 72 | 249 | 883 |
| Real Estate | 55 | 51 | 13 | 68 | 26 | 78 | 290 |
| Technology | 95 | 117 | 52 | 143 | 19 | 143 | 570 |
| Telecommunications | 14 | 27 | 13 | 31 | 6 | 23 | 114 |
| Professional Services | 26 | 22 | 26 | 8 | 5 | 19 | 106 |
| Utilities | 94 | 328 | 52 | 186 | 140 | 89 | 888 |
| Total | 761 | 958 | 462 | 1046 | 377 | 1228 | 4831 |

## 3.1. Variables' Definition

To measure Social Performance (CSP), we rely on the social pillar scores extracted from the Refinitiv ESG database, one of the most recognized and widely used sources in ESG research (Ioannou & Serafeim, 2015; Oikonomou et al., 2020). These scores are constructed using over 100 key performance indicators that assess firms' human rights practices, employee welfare, diversity, product responsibility, and community engagement.[1] The use of the Refinitiv database ensures objectivity and comparability across firms and jurisdictions. Following prior literature, we normalize the social scores on a scale from 0 to 100, where higher values indicate stronger social performance. To mitigate year-specific and country-level effects, we standardize the scores within industry-country-year groups.

Tax Incentives are proxied using two widely adopted measures (see, Hu et al., 2025). First, we use the Effective Tax Rate (ETR), computed as the ratio of total tax expense to pre-tax income, consistent with previous research examining fiscal outcomes of corporate strategies (Gallemore et al., 2014; Wu et al., 2024). Second, we calculate Deferred Tax Benefits as the change in deferred tax liabilities scaled by total assets, capturing the impact of tax deferral mechanisms which can reflect tax relief linked to long-term investments, including those associated with CSR activities. Both proxies are drawn from the Thomson Reuters Eikon database.

Board Busyness (BUSY_BOD) is measured as the average number of external directorships held by each board member, excluding executives, in a given fiscal year. This approach follows the methodological standards (i.e., Trinh et al., 2019; Venkatesh et al., 2025), where boards are classified as "busy" when a majority of directors hold three or more directorships. This operationalization reflects the assumption that while moderate board engagement may benefit governance through knowledge spillover, excessive commitments may impair monitoring efficiency.

We also included several variables that control for potential confounding influences on both social performance and tax outcomes, consistent with the broader CSR and tax avoidance literature (Hu et al., 2025; Trinugroho et al., 2023; Venkatesh et al., 2025): firm size (SIZE), profitability (ROA), calculated as return on assets, to control for financial performance that may influence both tax strategies and CSP engagement, Leverage (LEV), Board size (IND_BOD), board gender diversity (GENDER), Cash holding (CASH), and GRI Compliance (GRI_FLAG), a binary indicator coded 1 if the firm reports following the Global Reporting Initiative guidelines, as a proxy for reporting transparency and alignment with international standards. Detailed definitions and measurement techniques for each variable are provided in Table 2.

*Table 2. The variable's measurements.*

| Variable Name | Symbol | Definition |
|---|---|---|
| Tax incentive | TIN1 | (Income tax expense - Deferred income tax expense) / Total profit. |
| | TIN2 | Income tax expense / Total profit. |
| Social performance | SOCIAL | social performance score representing firm's social responsibility activities. |
| Board busyness | BUSYN | Degree of affiliations or connections among board members. |
| Size | SIZE | Natural logarithm of total assets. |
| ROA | ROA | The degree of net income divided by total assets. |
| Leverage | LEV | Total debt divided by total equity. |
| Board size | BOSIZE | Number of directors on the company's board. |
| Gender diversity | GENDER | Percentage of female members on the board of directors. |
| Cash holding | CASH | The ratio of cash and cash equivalents to total assets. |
| Stock Return | RETURN | Annual stock return. |
| Loss | LOSS | Dummy variable indicating if the firm incurred a net loss (1 = Yes, 0 = No). |
| GRI Report Guidelines | GRI | Dummy variable indicating whether the firm follows GRI reporting guidelines (1 = Yes, 0 = No). |

## 4. RESULTS

Table 3 presents the descriptive statistics for the main variables used in the analysis. The mean of tax incentives variables suggests a moderate effective tax rates across firms. For the first tax incentive proxy (TIN1) is 0.535, with a standard deviation of 0.961, indicating moderate variation across firms in accessing tax reliefs. The second tax incentive proxy (TIN2) shows a slightly lower mean (0.453) and greater variability. The average social performance score (SOCIAL) is 54.82, suggesting a moderate level of CSR engagement across the sample, with a wide range from a minimum of 0.28 to a maximum of 98.2. This wide dispersion indicates significant heterogeneity in firms' social responsibility practices across countries and industries.

Regarding board characteristics, the average board busyness (BUSYN) score is 0.767, with a maximum value of 3.88. This suggests that, on average, directors hold less than one external directorship, though there are firms where directors serve on up to four other boards, raising potential concerns about oversight capacity. The average board size (BOSIZE) is approximately nine members, consistent with standard corporate governance practices in Western Europe. The average proportion of female directors (GENDER) is 29.2%, reflecting a relatively balanced gender representation in the boardroom, particularly in Scandinavian countries.

Firms in the sample are generally of medium to large size, with a mean log of total assets (SIZE) of 8.11. Leverage (LEV) averages 30.4%, and profitability (ROA) shows a mean of 0.266 but with high dispersion, indicating the presence of both highly profitable and loss-making firms. The mean value for the loss dummy (LOSS) is 0.114, meaning that approximately 11% of firms reported negative earnings during the observed period. Importantly, 98.9% of the firms report compliance with the GRI, reinforcing the reliability and comparability of CSP disclosures across the sample.

*Table 3. The descriptive statistics.*

| Variables | Mean | Std. Dev. | Min | Max | Skew. | Kurt. |
|---|---|---|---|---|---|---|
| TIN1 | 0.535 | 0.961 | 0.052 | 0.794 | 1.359 | 1.933 |
| TIN1 | 0.453 | 0.983 | -0.03 | 0.694 | 1.959 | 1.601 |
| SOCIAL | 54.82 | 24.348 | 0.28 | 98.2 | -0.252 | 2.1 |
| BUSYN | 0.767 | 0.61 | 0 | 3.88 | 0.956 | 3.747 |
| SIZE | 8.11 | 1.241 | 0.1 | 11.822 | -0.031 | 3.22 |
| ROA | 0.266 | 13.541 | -13.91 | 0.93 | -1.939 | 18.237 |
| LEV | 0.304 | 0.283 | 0 | 0.412 | 1.817 | 1.43 |
| BOSIZE | 9.087 | 3.728 | 1 | 30 | 1.042 | 4.205 |

continued on following page

*Table 3. Continued*

| Variables | Mean | Std. Dev. | Min | Max | Skew. | Kurt. |
|---|---|---|---|---|---|---|
| GENDER | 29.203 | 14.686 | 0 | 100 | -0.218 | 2.737 |
| CASH | 0.178 | 0.207 | 0.116 | 5.468 | 2.436 | 2.171 |
| RETURN | 0.532 | 32.789 | -1.01 | 4.769 | 3.206 | 11.617 |
| LOSS | 0.114 | 0.317 | 0 | 1 | 2.437 | 6.937 |
| GRI | 0.989 | 0.103 | 0 | 1 | -9.462 | 90.532 |

Detailed variable definitions and sources are provided in Table 2.

Figure 2 illustrates the temporal trend in social performance scores across countries. It shows a general upward trend in social performance scores across most countries until 2018. However, there was a noticeable decline of the trend between 2019 and 2021. This reflects the economic instability and disruptions brought on by the COVID-19 epidemic during this time, particularly in Sweden and the UK, where there was a notable drop. France consistently maintained higher social performance throughout the period, while Switzerland and Italy remained relatively stable after 2020.

*Figure 2. The social performance across countries.*

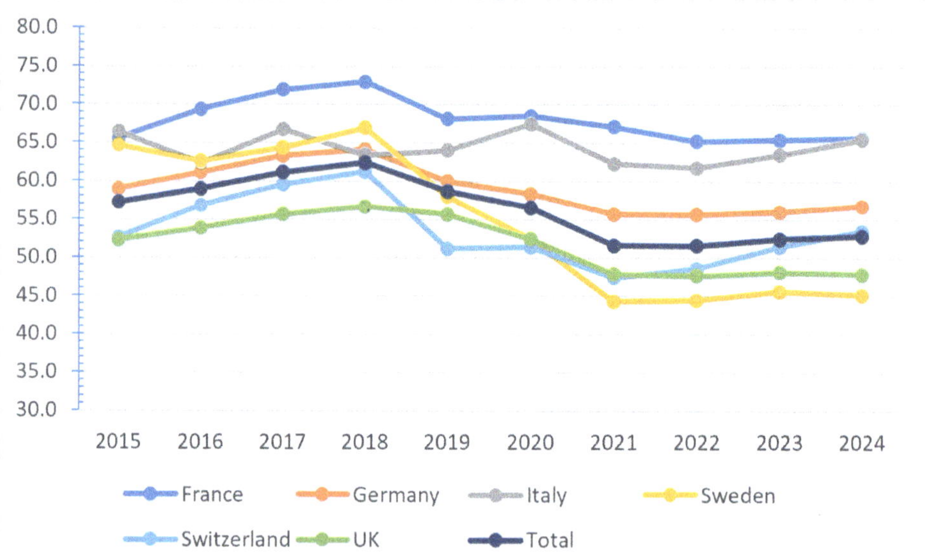


Table 4 reports the pairwise correlation matrix and the associated variance inflation factor (VIF) values. Social performance is positively and significantly correlated with both tax incentive proxies (r = 0.331*** for TIN1 and r = 0.215** for TIN2), suggesting that socially responsible firms tend to benefit more from tax-related advantages. This supports the hypothesis that CSR engagement may signal legitimacy and compliance, thus improving firms' standing with tax authorities or eligibility for fiscal support schemes. Board busyness is positively correlated with social performance (r = 0.345***), implying that directors serving on multiple boards are more likely to be affiliated with firms demonstrating higher levels of CSR activity. One possible interpretation is that well-connected board members bring sustainability norms and best practices from other firms, fostering greater CSR alignment. However, this relationship is explored further in interaction models to test the governance trade-offs associated with busyness. The correlation between board size and social performance is also strongly positive (r = 0.512***), and board gender diversity shows a moderate correlation with CSR outcomes (r = 0.335***). Firm size is, as expected, positively associated with both board attributes and social scores. All variance inflation factor (VIF) values are below 2.3, with a mean VIF of 1.294, suggesting that multicollinearity is not a concern in the regression models, as no correlation is larger than the commonly accepted level of 0.70, and the variance inflation factor is 1.52, so multicollinearity concerns are not raised (Wooldridge, 2015).

*Table 4. The Pairwise correlation matrix.*

| Variables | VIF | (1) | (2) | (3) | (4) | (5) | (6) | (7) | (8) | (9) | (10) | (11) | (12) |
|---|---|---|---|---|---|---|---|---|---|---|---|---|---|
| (1) TIN1 | - | 1.000 | | | | | | | | | | | |
| (2) TIN2 | - | 0.966*** | 1.000 | | | | | | | | | | |
| (3) SOCIAL | 1.503 | 0.331*** | 0.215** | 1.000 | | | | | | | | | |
| (4) BUSYN | 1.375 | 0.011 | -0.007 | 0.345*** | 1.000 | | | | | | | | |
| (5) SIZE | 2.274 | 0.372* | -0.004* | 0.677*** | 0.404*** | 1.000 | | | | | | | |
| (6) ROA | 1.04 | 0.212* | 0.011** | 0.006 | 0.013 | 0.003* | 1.000 | | | | | | |
| (7) LEV | 1.08 | 0.104** | -0.006* | 0.068*** | 0.012 | -0.036*** | -0.006* | 1.000 | | | | | |
| (8) BOSIZE | 1.762 | 0.340* | -0.009** | 0.512*** | 0.213*** | 0.635*** | -0.014** | 0.036*** | 1.000 | | | | |
| (9) GENDER | 1.172 | 0.018* | 0.007* | 0.335*** | 0.144*** | 0.262*** | -0.206 | 0.052*** | 0.283*** | 1.000 | | | |
| (10) CASH | 1.109 | 0.409* | 0.010 | -0.235*** | -0.070*** | -0.371*** | -0.012* | -0.005 | -0.166*** | -0.088*** | 1.000 | | |
| (11) RETURN | 1.013 | 0.151** | -0.001 | -0.022** | -0.012 | -0.014** | 0.016 | -0.101* | -0.019* | -0.019* | -0.005 | 1.000 | |
| (12) LOSS | 1.043 | 0.017 | 0.018* | 0.284*** | 0.187*** | 0.450*** | -0.053*** | -0.102 | 0.231*** | 0.039*** | -0.129*** | -0.006 | 1.000 |
| (13) GRI | 1.016 | 0.101 | 0.001 | 0.061*** | 0.035** | 0.053*** | 0.000 | 0.022 | 0.062*** | 0.075*** | -0.001 | 0.002 | -0.005 |

*, **, and *** indicate significance at the 0.1, 0.05, and 0.01 levels, respectively. Detailed variable definitions and sources are provided in Table 2.

## 4.1. Baseline Regression

To test empirically the impact of the social performance on tax incentives and the moderating effect of the board busyness, we use the following regression equation;

$$\text{Tax incentives}_{it} = \beta 0 + \beta_1 \text{Social}_{it} + \beta_n \text{ Control Variables}_{it} + \delta_i + \gamma_t + \epsilon_{it} \quad (1)$$

$$\text{Tax incentives}_{it} = \beta 0 + \beta_1 \text{Social}_{it} + + \beta_2 \text{ BUSYN}_{it} + \beta_3 \text{Social*BUSYN}_{it} + \beta_n \text{ Control Variables}_{it} + \delta_i + \gamma_t + \epsilon_{it} \quad (2)$$

Where tax incentives is measured using TIN1 and TIN2. Social refers to the firm's social performance score. BUSYN captures board busyness, measured by the average number of external board affiliations per director. The interaction term Social*BUSYN tests whether board busyness moderates the relationship between social performance and tax incentives. Control Variables include firm size, ROA, leverage, board size, gender diversity, cash holdings, stock return, loss indicator, and GRI compliance. $\delta_i$ denotes firm-fixed effects, $\gamma_t$ denotes year-fixed effects, and $\epsilon_{it}$ is the idiosyncratic error term.

The baseline regression results offer robust support for both hypotheses. Across all models, social performance (SOCIAL) is positively and significantly associated with tax incentives (TIN1 and TIN2), confirming Hypothesis H1. This implies that firms with stronger social responsibility practices are more likely to benefit from favorable tax outcomes. The coefficients range from 0.611 to 1.297 and are significant at the 1% and 5% levels, reinforcing the argument that CSP can enhance firm legitimacy in the eyes of tax authorities and improve access to fiscal benefits (Yin et al., 2025). Based on stakeholder theory which posits that firms responding effectively to a broad range of stakeholders (including governments) are better positioned to gain institutional favor (Freeman, 1984). Governments, acting as key stakeholders, may reward socially responsible firms through preferential tax treatments, as these firms contribute to broader societal goals. The findings suggest that regulatory authorities may already be rewarding ESG-compliant firms, intentionally or otherwise, through more favorable tax treatments. Firms, in turn, may perceive CSP as not merely a reputational or ethical choice, but a strategic fiscal asset, particularly under regulatory regimes where social outcomes are tied to policy benefits. The high and significant coefficients for GRI also imply that adherence to standardized reporting frameworks may further enhance these benefits, offering a path for firms to institutionalize and signal their CSP commitments.

The regression findings provide strong empirical support for Hypothesis H2, which posits that board busyness moderates the relationship between social performance and tax incentives. Specifically, the interaction term SOCIAL*BUSYN is positive and statistically significant in both specifications (0.367** and 0.402**, significant at the 5% level), indicating that the presence of busier boards strengthens the positive impact of social performance on tax incentives. Traditionally, agency theory would predict a negative consequence of board busyness, suggesting that directors serving on multiple boards may be overextended, leading to diminished monitoring capacity and weakened strategic oversight (Fich & Shivdasani, 2006). From this perspective, busy boards could be seen as a governance liability, especially in domains requiring attention and discretion, such as aligning social performance with fiscal strategy.

However, the positive and significant interaction found in this study challenges this conventional view and offers a more nuanced understanding. It suggests that under certain institutional conditions (such as those found in Western Europe) board busyness may operate as a resource rather than a constraint. This insight aligns more closely with the resource-based view (RBV), which contends that directors with extensive external affiliations may bring valuable intangible assets, such as reputational capital, regulatory insight, and inter-firm connections, which can be leveraged to convert CSP efforts into tangible fiscal outcomes like tax reliefs or exemptions. Moreover, in regulatory contexts that emphasize transparency and ESG accountability (such as those shaped by the EU's CSRD or GRI compliance) firms with well-connected and experienced board members may be better positioned to navigate the evolving nexus of sustainability and fiscal policy. These directors may possess deeper institutional knowledge, broader stakeholder access, and greater familiarity with policy instruments, all of which enhance the firm's ability to strategically align CSP activities with available tax incentives. This interpretation is further justified by the significant coefficient on the GRI variable, which implies that standardized reporting further strengthens the CSP–tax benefits relationship. Hence, busy directors operating in structured governance environments may not only compensate for oversight dilution but also amplify the strategic deployment of social performance initiatives for financial gain.

The tested models' goodness of fit is strong, as $R^2$ values ranging from 0.3166 to 0.4241, and the F-statistics are significant at the 1% level in all models, indicating a good overall explanatory power of the models. Diagnostic tests of Durbin and Wu-Hausman tests revealed that there is no evidence of endogeneity or misspecification.

*Table 5. The baseline regression result of tax incentive and social performance relationship.*

| | Tax incentive | | Alternative measure | |
|---|---|---|---|---|
| | (1) | (2) | (3) | (4) |
| | TIN1 | TIN1 | TIN2 | TIN2 |
| Lag (TIN1) | 0.119*** | 0.081*** | | |
| | (0.87) | (0.787) | | |
| Lag (TIN2) | | | 0.014*** | 0.109*** |
| | | | (0.361) | (0.327) |
| SOCIAL | 1.214** | 0.611*** | 1.297** | 0.655*** |
| | (0.243) | (0.25) | (0.259) | (0.27) |
| BUSYNESS | | 26.094** | | 28.751*** |
| | | (0.216) | | (0.241) |
| SOCIAL*BUSYN | | 0.367** | | 0.402** |
| | | (0.222) | | (0.244) |
| SIZE | -20.925*** | -5.603*** | -22.198*** | -5.757*** |
| | (-0.272) | (-0.476) | (-0.288) | (-0.492) |
| ROA | 0.403* | 0.166** | 0.415** | 0.163* |
| | (0.342) | (0.213) | (0.351) | (0.21) |
| LEV | 5.363*** | 4.173** | 5.629* | 4.631** |
| | (0.131) | (0.354) | (0.137) | (0.395) |
| BOSIZE | -0.25* | -0.345** | -0.274*** | -0.377* |
| | (-0.348) | (-0.491) | (-0.381) | (-0.541) |
| GENDER | -0.082* | -0.039* | -0.091** | -0.047* |
| | (-0.16) | (-0.113) | (-0.178) | (-0.134) |
| CASH | 3.746** | 4.553* | 3.508** | 4.739* |
| | (1.186) | (1.852) | (1.176) | (1.871) |
| RETURN | -0.629*** | -2.042** | -0.493** | -2.013** |
| | (-0.084) | (-0.43) | (-0.066) | (-0.426) |
| LOSS | 6.46* | 3.923 | 6.513* | 3.788 |
| | (0.503) | (1.041) | (0.506) | (1.01) |
| COVID | 0.725** | 1.686*** | 0.438** | 1.493* |
| | (0.128) | (0.414) | (0.077) | (0.368) |
| GRI | 14.637*** | 3.986* | 15.268** | 3.756** |
| | (0.264) | (0.143) | (0.275) | (0.136) |
| YEAR | Yes | Yes | Yes | Yes |

continued on following page

*Table 5. Continued*

| | Tax incentive | | Alternative measure | |
|---|---|---|---|---|
| | (1) | (2) | (3) | (4) |
| INDUSTRY | Yes | Yes | Yes | Yes |
| COUNTRY | Yes | Yes | Yes | Yes |
| Constant | 7.482*** | 7.818*** | 14.076*** | 6.457*** |
| | (0.288) | (0.119) | (0.307) | (0.114) |
| Obs. | 4831 | 4112 | 4644 | 4266 |
| R square | 0.4185 | 0.4241 | 0.3822 | 0.3166 |
| Adj_R square | 0.4097 | 0.4133 | 0.3712 | 0.3043 |
| F-test | (13,858) = 7.50 | (12,332) = 5.13 | (112,645) = 5.27 | (13,677) = 5.14 |
| Prob. (F-statistic) | 0.000 | 0.000 | 0.000 | 0.000 |
| Durbin (score) chi2(1) | 0.043 (p = 0.77) | 0.062 (p = 0.23) | 0.034 (p = 0.17) | 0.067 (p = 0.64) |
| Wu-Hausman | 0.088 (p = 0.19) | 0.045 (p = 0.37) | .075 (p = 0.69) | .063 (p = 0.45) |

Robust t-statistics are in parentheses. *, **, and *** indicate significance at the 0.1, 0.05, and 0.01 levels, respectively (two-tailed). Continuous variables are winsorized at the top and bottom 1 percent. Detailed variable definitions and sources are provided in Table 2.

## 4.2. Propensity Score Matching Analysis

To strengthen the robustness of our empirical findings and mitigate potential concerns related to selection bias, we conduct a Propensity Score Matching (PSM) analysis following the methodology proposed by Rosenbaum and Rubin (1983). In this framework, firms in the top quartile of the social performance index—those demonstrating the highest levels of CSP—are designated as the "treatment group." These are matched against firms from the remaining three quartiles (control group) using a nearest-neighbor algorithm based on a common support region. Matching is performed across a set of observable firm- and governance-specific covariates consistent with those employed in our primary regression analysis.

Table 6 presents the results of diagnostic testing before and after matching. The pre-matching results (Model 1) reveal statistically significant differences between the treatment and control groups on key covariates such as firm size (SIZE), return on assets (ROA), leverage (LEV), board size (BOSIZE), and gender diversity (GENDER), suggesting a possible imbalance in baseline characteristics. In contrast, the post-matching results (Model 2) show that these differences are largely attenuated and, in most cases, no longer statistically significant. The substantial reduction in the pseudo R-squared value from 0.301 to 0.029 further supports the validity of the matching process, indicating that the treatment and control groups are now well-balanced across observable dimensions.

Table 7 reports the results of the treatment effect regressions using the matched sample, with tax incentives (TIN1 and TIN2) as dependent variables. The coefficient for social performance remains strongly positive and statistically significant at the 1% level across both models, confirming that firms with higher CSP tend to benefit more from favorable tax treatment. Additionally, several control variables—such as ROA, GENDER, and COVID-period indicators—retain their expected signs and statistical significance, lending further support to the hypothesis that tax incentives are aligned with responsible corporate conduct. The consistency of the PSM results with our primary regression findings strengthens the conclusion that our observed relationships are unlikely to be artifacts of endogeneity or sample selection bias. This strengthens our conclusion that tax incentives can act as effective policy tools to encourage socially responsible business behavior.

*Table 6. Propensity score matching: Diagnostic testing*

| | **(1)** | **(2)** |
|---|---|---|
| **Variables** | **Pre-match<br>Treatment (High social performance)** | **Post-match<br>Treatment (High social performance)** |
| SIZE | 2.433*** (1.198) | 1.831(1.023) |
| ROA | 1.157** (0.047) | 0.945* (0.802) |
| LEV | 1.792* (1.622) | 0.871 (0.738) |
| BOSIZE | 2.739 (1.909) | 1.584** (1.537) |
| GENDER | 1.732* (1.428) | 2.732 (2.525) |
| CASH | -0.217 (-0.206) | -0.153 (-0.146) |
| RETURN | -1.272 (-1.101) | -0.587* (-0.553) |
| LOSS | 0.203*** (0.191) | 1.599 (1.457) |
| COVID | 0.213*** (0.199) | 0.324* (0.301) |
| GRI | 0.841 (0.656) | 0.651 (0.571) |
| Constant | 0.688*** (0.352) | 0.195 (0.225) |
| Observations | 4644 | 1921 |
| Pseudo R- squared | 0.301 | 0.029 |

*Table 7. Propensity score matching: The effect of social performance on tax incentives.*

| | (1) | | (2) |
|---|---|---|---|
| **Variables** | **TIN1** | | **TIN2** |
| Social performance | 4.173*** (0.354) | | 5.363*** (0.131) |
| SIZE | 2.785* (1.154) | | -1.019** (-1.011) |
| ROA | 0.149 (0.0441) | | 0.971 *** (0.861) |
| LEV | 0.843 (0.655) | | 0.862*(0.722) |
| BOSIZE | -2.869 (-1.944) | | -1.618** (-1.581) |
| GENDER | -1.651* (-1.491) | | -2.698* (-0.2.599) |
| CASH | 0.204 (0.194) | | 0.161* (0.152) |
| RETURN | -1.314 (-1.132) | | -0.601* (-0.581) |
| LOSS | 0.195*** (0.186) | | 1.637 (1.488) |
| COVID | 0.199*** (0.182) | | 0.317*** (0.288) |
| GRI | 0.863 (0.677) | | 0.666*** (0.582) |
| Constant | 0.403* (0.342) | | 0.166** (0.213) |
| Year | Yes | | Yes |
| Industry | Yes | | Yes |
| Country | Yes | | Yes |
| Observations | 4589 | | 4221 |
| Pseudo R- squared | 0.298 | | 0.315 |

## 4.3. Instrumental Variable Approach Using GMM

We conducted a robustness check applying the two-stage Generalized Method of Moments estimation to ensure the validity of the results presented in the baseline regression. This estimator helps further to ensure the elimination of any concerns of potential endogeneity, such as the reverse causality and omitted variable bias (Khatib, 2025a). We implement an IV approach with the industry-year median of social performance serving as the instrument. Specifically, the industry-year median is computed as the median CSP score of all other firms operating within the same two-digit SIC industry in a given year, excluding the focal firm. This serves as a valid instrument because it is expected to be highly correlated with a firm's own CSP due to shared institutional pressures, normative standards, and peer effects within industries, yet it is unlikely to directly influence the firm's tax incentive outcomes independent of the firm's own CSP decisions.

In the first stage, we employed the industry-year median value of social performance as an instrumental variable. It should be noted that firms are influenced by prevailing CSR norms within their sector but do not directly control the industry median itself. The first-stage results confirm a strong positive relationship between the instrument and the endogenous variable. We then use the fitted values from this regression to replace actual CSP in the second stage and re-estimate our main models. This instrument captures peer effects and industry-level pressure on CSR engagement while satisfying the relevance and exclusion conditions.

In line with the baseline 2SLS regression, Table 8 shows the results that confirm the positive and significant relationship between social performance and tax incentives. It also supports the moderating role of board busyness on this relationship. The interaction term (SOCIAL*BUSYN) remains positive and significant, indicating that even when accounting for endogeneity, firms with higher CSP and active board networks benefit more from favorable tax treatment. The consistency of these results reinforces the validity of our identification strategy and suggests that the observed CSP-tax incentive relationship is not driven by endogeneity concerns such as reverse causality or omitted variable bias.

*Table 8. The tax incentive and social performance results using GMM estimation.*

| | **Tax incentives** | | **Alternative** | |
|---|---|---|---|---|
| | **(1)** | **(2)** | **(3)** | **(4)** |
| | TIN1 | TIN1 | TIN2 | TIN2 |
| Lag (TIN1) | 1.248*** | 0.919*** | | |
| | (1.24) | (1.259) | | |
| Lag (TIN2) | | | 1.726*** | 1.379*** |
| | | | (0.398) | (0.473) |
| SOCIAL | 0.305* | 0.239** | 0.245*** | 0.193*** |
| | (0.626) | (0.67) | (0.676) | (0.734) |
| BUSYNESS | | 12.71** | | 10.083** |
| | | (0.739) | | (0.798) |
| SOCIAL * BUSYN | | 0.167*** | | 0.133* |
| | | (0.728) | | (0.784) |
| Controls | Included | Included | Included | Included |
| YEAR | Yes | Yes | Yes | Yes |
| INDUSTRY | Yes | Yes | Yes | Yes |
| COUNTRY | Yes | Yes | Yes | Yes |
| Constant | 25.184*** | 13.815*** | 20.093*** | 11.823*** |
| | (0.768) | (0.093) | (0.824) | (0.128) |
| Observations | 4822 | 4112 | 4640 | 4266 |

continued on following page

*Table 8. Continued*

| | Tax incentives | | Alternative | |
|---|---|---|---|---|
| | (1) | (2) | (3) | (4) |
| R-squared | 0.264 | 0.244 | 0.287 | 0.288 |
| Adj_R square | 0.253 | 0.216 | 0.266 | 0.252 |
| F-test | (9,191) =7.27 | (12,833) =5.83 | (12,397) =0.74 | (13,223) =4.94 |
| Prob. (F-statistic) | 0.000 | 0.000 | 0.000 | 0.000 |
| Wald $\chi2$ | 0.083*** | 0.087*** | 0.063*** | 0.034*** |
| Number of groups | 104 | 114 | 98 | 102 |
| Number of instruments | 94 | 89 | 91 | 87 |
| First-order autocorrelation (AR1) (p values) | 0.000 | 0.001 | 0.003 | 0.000 |
| Second-order autocorrelation (AR2) (p values) | 0.764 | 0.331 | 0.433 | 0.294 |
| Hansen J statistics (p values) | 0.51 | 0.44 | 0.23 | 0.61 |

Robust t-statistics are in parentheses. *, **, and *** indicate significance at the 0.1, 0.05, and 0.01 levels, respectively (two-tailed).

## 4.4. Does compliance with GRI affect the relationship?

Table 9 presents the results of subsample regressions aimed at evaluating whether adherence to the GRI standards moderates the relationship between corporate social performance (CSP), board busyness, and tax incentives. The findings indicate marked heterogeneity between firms that comply with GRI standards and those that do not, underscoring the critical role of sustainability reporting in shaping fiscal outcomes. Among GRI-compliant firms, social performance exhibits a consistently positive and statistically significant association with both measures of tax incentives (TIN1 and TIN2). Specifically, the coefficients for the SOCIAL variable are larger and more significant in the GRI-compliant subsample (e.g., 2.373*** and 1.017***) than in their non-compliant counterparts (0.277* and 0.134**). This disparity suggests that efforts in social responsibility are more likely to yield favorable tax treatment when coupled with transparent and standardized environmental, social, and governance (ESG) disclosures. These findings align with prior literature that emphasizes the legitimizing function of GRI-aligned reporting in enhancing corporate credibility and stakeholder trust, particularly with tax authorities (Yin et al., 2025; Zahid et al., 2022).

Furthermore, the interaction between board busyness and social performance appears more pronounced among GRI-compliant firms. The interaction terms are both positive and statistically significant (2.024** and 1.012**), whereas the corresponding estimates for non-GRI firms are smaller and less robust (1.165 and 0.038**). This evidence implies that within high-transparency reporting environments, even boards characterized by high external commitments may successfully harness CSP to obtain fiscal benefits. Such outcomes may be attributed to institutional expectations or the presence of external assurance mechanisms that validate CSR initiatives, thereby reinforcing the strategic utility of GRI-aligned disclosure practices.

*Table 9. Sub-sample regression result of tax incentive and social performance relationship.*

| | **GRI** | | | | **Non- GRI** | | | |
|---|---|---|---|---|---|---|---|---|
| | **(1)** | **(2)** | **(3)** | **(4)** | **(5)** | **(6)** | **(7)** | **(8)** |
| | TIN1 | TIN2 | TIN1 | TIN2 | TIN1 | TIN2 | TIN1 | TIN2 |
| Lag (TIN1) | 5.912*** | | 0.366*** | | 0.499*** | | 0.876*** | |
| | (0.548) | | (0.082) | | (0.51) | | (1.382) | |
| Lag (TIN2) | | 0.53*** | | 0.295*** | | 0.865*** | | 0.603*** |
| | | (0.552) | | (0.408) | | (1.156) | | (1.123) |
| SOCIAL | 1.242** | 1.018** | 2.373*** | 1.017*** | 0.277* | 0.134** | 1.343* | 0.199** |
| | (0.183) | (0.058) | (0.4) | (0.24) | (0.169) | (0.153) | (0.192) | (0.173) |
| BUSYNESS | | | 2.648*** | 3.805** | | | 1.172** | 1.554* |
| | | | (0.391) | (0.264) | | | (0.212) | (0.19) |
| SOCIAL * BUSYN | | | 2.024** | 1.012** | | | 1.165* | 0.038** |
| | | | (0.852) | (0.658) | | | (0.478) | (0.484) |
| Controls | Included | Included | Included | Included | Included | Included | Included | Included |
| YEAR | Yes | Yes | Yes | Yes | Yes | Yes | Yes | Yes |
| INDUSTRY | Yes | Yes | Yes | Yes | Yes | Yes | Yes | Yes |
| COUNTRY | Yes | Yes | Yes | Yes | Yes | Yes | Yes | Yes |
| Constant | 21.822** | 2.992*** | 2.019*** | 1.127*** | 23.928*** | 16.681** | 37.55** | 40.741** |
| | (0.177) | (0.102) | (0.852) | (0.658) | (0.07) | (0.049) | (0.478) | (0.484) |
| OBS | 4621 | 4388 | 4021 | 4221 | 4522 | 4388 | 4056 | 4187 |
| R square | 0.317 | 0.322 | 0.285 | 0.189 | 0.323 | 0.301 | 0.211 | 0.281 |
| Adj_R square | 0.301 | 0.299 | 0.272 | 0.179 | 0.319 | 0.294 | 0.208 | 0.276 |
| F-test | (11,163) =6.45 | (10,255) =7.32 | (9,737) =6.73 | (11,744) =3.43 | (10,242) =6.50 | (11,332) = 3.64 | (12,436) =4.27 | (11,74) =7.25 |
| Prob. (F-statistic) | 0.000 | 0.000 | 0.000 | 0.000 | 0.000 | 0.000 | 0.000 | 0.000 |

continued on following page

*Table 9. Continued*

| | GRI | | | | Non- GRI | | | |
|---|---|---|---|---|---|---|---|---|
| | **(1)** | **(2)** | **(3)** | **(4)** | **(5)** | **(6)** | **(7)** | **(8)** |
| Durbin (score) chi2(1) | 0.103 (p=0.62) | 0.342 (p=0.15) | 0.254 (p=0.43) | 0.266 (p=0.74) | 0.065 (p=0.24) | 0.204 (p=0.74) | 0.543 (p=0.45) | 0.166 (p=0.43) |
| Wu-Hausman | 0.054 (p=0.29) | 0.095 (p=0.37) | 0.014 (p=0.99) | 0.065 (p=0.64) | 0.074 (p=0.48) | 0.065 (p=0.37) | 0.085 (p=0.74) | 0.074 (p=0.77) |

Robust t-statistics are in parentheses. *, **, and *** indicate significance at the 0.1, 0.05, and 0.01 levels, respectively (two-tailed).

## 5. CONCLUSION

This study investigates the relationship between social performance, board busyness, and tax incentives. We apply both 2SLS and GMM estimation on a large panel of 4,831 non-financial firms across six Western European countries. The results offer strong evidence that firms with higher levels of social performance are more likely to benefit from favorable tax treatment. The findings also reveal that board busyness positively moderates this relationship. Hence, despite concerns about overcommitment busy boards can still contribute to translating social investments into fiscal benefits, particularly when institutional transparency mechanisms such as GRI reporting are followed.

The findings of this study underscore the importance of encouraging socially responsible behavior through fiscal incentives. Governments and tax authorities can consider linking tax benefits to credible ESG disclosures, such as those aligned with the Global Reporting Initiative. Tax regulators can formalize and expand CSR-linked incentive schemes by embedding clear ESG performance thresholds (e.g., GRI compliance, diversity standards, community engagement metrics) into eligibility criteria for corporate tax relief. This would institutionalize the positive externalities of CSR and ensure fairness in the allocation of fiscal benefits.This integration is particularly critical in today's business landscape, where stakeholders increasingly expect companies to operate ethically while efficiently managing their tax responsibilities.

The result also indicates that firms with strong social performance may be perceived as lower tax risks. Tax administrations could refine their risk assessment frameworks by integrating ESG indicators as soft controls in tax audits, reducing enforcement burdens on compliant firms and allowing more strategic resource deployment toward high-risk cases. The moderating effect of board busyness reveals a double-edged role of governance networks. On one hand, busy directors appear to leverage their external ties to enhance access to tax benefits through institutional familiarity and strategic spillovers. On the other hand, excessive board commitments may dilute oversight capacity. Firms aiming to maximize tax-related strategic outcomes from CSR investment should not indiscriminately increase board interlocks. Instead, they should balance experiential diversity with governance capacity, potentially setting internal limits on the number of board memberships per director or integrating workload assessment into nomination policies. Since the study found stronger tax outcomes among GRI-compliant firms with busy boards, investment in standardized ESG reporting frameworks can serve not only reputational but also fiscal functions. Thus, ESG departments should work more closely with tax strategy and legal compliance teams to synchronize CSR narratives with fiscal planning.

This study has several limitations. First, although it employs 2SLS and GMM to address endogeneity, there remains the possibility of omitted variable bias. Factors such as firm-level lobbying intensity, political connections, or prior tax audit history—which may influence both CSR and tax incentives—are not included due to data limitations. Second, board busyness is treated uniformly across countries, overlooking institutional differences in director workload norms and governance enforcement. Third, the measurement of tax incentives using effective tax rates may not fully capture discretionary tax arrangements or negotiated benefits, especially in multinational settings. Finally, causality direction remains difficult to establish definitively despite instrumental variable techniques.

## REFERENCES


Bai, M., & Ho, L. (2022). Corporate social performance and firm debt levels: Impacts of the covid-19 pandemic and institutional environments. *Finance Research Letters, 47*, 102968. DOI: 10.1016/j.frl.2022.102968 PMID: 35578609

Bassetti, T., Blasi, S., & Sedita, S. R. (2020). The management of sustainable development: A longitudinal analysis of the effects of environmental performance on economic performance. *Business Strategy and the Environment*, (May), 1–17. DOI: 10.1002/bse.2607

Brammer, S., Jackson, G., & Matten, D. (2012). Corporate Social Responsibility and institutional theory: New perspectives on private governance. *Socio-economic Review, 10*(1), 3–28. DOI: 10.1093/ser/mwr030

DiMaggio, P. J., & Powell, W. W. (1983). The Iron Cage Revisited: Institutional Isomorphism and Collective Rationality in Organizational Fields. *American Sociological Review, 48*(2), 147. DOI: 10.2307/2095101

Donaldson, T., & Preston, L. E. (1995). The Stakeholder Theory of the Corporation: Concepts, Evidence, and Implications. *Academy of Management Review, 20*(1), 65–91. DOI: 10.2307/258887

Fayad, A. A. S., Khatib, S. F. A., Abbas, A. F., Ghaleb, B. A. A., & Mousa, A. K. A. (2024). The determinants and consequences of board multiple directorships. *Corporate Governance (Bradford)*, (May). Advance online publication. DOI: 10.1108/CG-07-2023-0310

Feng, C. (2024). International tax incentives, cross-border research and development, and corporate innovation performance. *Finance Research Letters, 66*(December 2023), 105646. DOI: 10.1016/j.frl.2024.105646

Feng, Q., Ge, Y., & Zhao, L. (2024). Tax incentives and corporate digital transformation: Evidence from China's accelerated depreciation policy. *Journal of Asian Economics, 95*(June 2023), 101832. DOI: 10.1016/j.asieco.2024.101832

Fernandez-Feijoo, B., Romero, S., & Ruiz, S. (2014). Commitment to Corporate social responsibility measured through global reporting initiative reporting: Factors affecting the behavior of companies. *Journal of Cleaner Production, 81*, 244–254. DOI: 10.1016/j.jclepro.2014.06.034

Ferris, S. P., Jagannathan, M., & Pritchard, A. C. (2003). Too Busy to Mind the Business? Monitoring by Directors with Multiple Board Appointments. *The Journal of Finance, 58*(3), 1087–1111. DOI: 10.1111/1540-6261.00559

Fich, E. M., & Shivdasani, A. (2006). Are Busy Boards Effective Monitors? *The Journal of Finance*, *61*(2), 689–724. DOI: 10.1111/j.1540-6261.2006.00852.x

Freeman, R. E. (1984). *Stakeholder management: A strategic approach*. Pitman.

Frynas, J. G., & Stephens, S. (2015). Political Corporate Social Responsibility: Reviewing Theories and Setting New Agendas. *International Journal of Management Reviews*, *17*(4), 483–509. DOI: 10.1111/ijmr.12049

Fu, C., Luo, D., Zhang, J., & Li, W. (2025). Tax incentives, marketization level, and corporate digital transformation. *International Review of Economics & Finance*, *97*, 103777. DOI: 10.1016/j.iref.2024.103777

García-Sánchez, I., & Noguera-Gámez, L. (2017). Integrated Reporting and Stakeholder Engagement: The Effect on Information Asymmetry. *Corporate Social Responsibility and Environmental Management*, *24*(5), 395–413. DOI: 10.1002/csr.1415

Godfrey, P. C. (2005). The Relationship Between Corporate Philanthropy And Shareholder Wealth: A Risk Management Perspective. *Academy of Management Review*, *30*(4), 777–798. DOI: 10.5465/amr.2005.18378878

Granda, M. L. (2021). Tax haven ownership and business groups: Tax avoidance incentives in Ecuadorian firms. *Journal of Business Research*, *130*, 698–708. DOI: 10.1016/j.jbusres.2020.07.012

Hahn, R., & Kühnen, M. (2013). Determinants of sustainability reporting: A review of results, trends, theory, and opportunities in an expanding field of research. *Journal of Cleaner Production*, *59*, 5–21. DOI: 10.1016/j.jclepro.2013.07.005

Hu, S., Zhou, X., & Li, P. (2025). Tax incentives, market competition, and corporate innovation. *Finance Research Letters*, *77*(February), 107067. DOI: 10.1016/j.frl.2025.107067

Hudson, K., & Morgan, R. E. (2023). Board political ideological diversity and information exposure as antecedents to value creation and value appropriation. *Journal of Product Innovation Management*, *40*(6), 836–858. DOI: 10.1111/jpim.12688

Ioannou, I., & Serafeim, G. (2019). The Consequences of Mandatory Corporate Sustainability Reporting. In McWilliams, A., Rupp, D. E., Siegel, D. S., Stahl, G. K., & Waldman, D. A. (Eds.), *The Oxford Handbook of Corporate Social Responsibility* (pp. 451–489). Oxford University Press., DOI: 10.1093/oxfordhb/9780198802280.013.20

Jensen, M. C., & Meckling, W. H. (1976). Theory of the firm: Managerial behavior, agency costs and ownership structure. *Journal of Financial Economics*, *3*(4), 305–360. DOI: 10.1016/0304-405X(76)90026-X

Jiang, H., Hu, W., & Jiang, P. (2024). Does ESG performance affect corporate tax avoidance? Evidence from China. *Finance Research Letters, 61*, 105056. DOI: 10.1016/j.frl.2024.105056

Jiraporn, P., Singh, M., & Lee, C. I. (2009). Ineffective corporate governance: Director busyness and board committee memberships. *Journal of Banking & Finance, 33*(5), 819–828. DOI: 10.1016/j.jbankfin.2008.09.020

Karim, K. E., Li, J., Lin, K. J., & Robin, A. (2022). Do directors have style? Board interlock and accounting properties. *Journal of Business Finance & Accounting, 49*(1–2), 3–32. DOI: 10.1111/jbfa.12567

Khatib, S. F. A. (2025a). An assessment of methods to deal with endogeneity in corporate governance and reporting research. *Corporate Governance (Bradford), 25*(3), 606–630. DOI: 10.1108/CG-12-2023-0507

Khatib, S. F. A. (2025b). Social Trust, Environmental Violations, and Remedial Actions in China. *Social and Environmental Accountability Journal, 1–3*(1), 81–83. Advance online publication. DOI: 10.1080/0969160X.2025.2465948

Li, C., Chen, H., Xie, W., & Wang, P. (2024). Tax incentives for human capital accumulation and enterprise innovation quality: Evidence of a quasi-natural experiment in China. *Finance Research Letters, 70*(August), 106342. DOI: 10.1016/j.frl.2024.106342

Liu, J., Huang, B., & Hu, Y. (2024). The influence of tax incentives on market segmentation in the context of a unified national market. *Finance Research Letters, 65*(January), 105591. DOI: 10.1016/j.frl.2024.105591

Lu, C., & Zhu, K. (2021). Do tax expenses crowd in or crowd out corporate social responsibility performance? Evidence from Chinese listed firms. *Journal of Cleaner Production, 327*, 129433. DOI: 10.1016/j.jclepro.2021.129433

Matten, D., & Moon, J. (2008). "Implicit" and "Explicit" CSR: A Conceptual Framework for a Comparative Understanding of Corporate Social Responsibility. *Academy of Management Review, 33*(2), 404–424. DOI: 10.5465/amr.2008.31193458

Michelon, G., Pilonato, S., & Ricceri, F. (2015). CSR reporting practices and the quality of disclosure: An empirical analysis. *Critical Perspectives on Accounting, 33*, 59–78. DOI: 10.1016/j.cpa.2014.10.003

Nadeem, M., Gyapong, E., & Ahmed, A. (2020). Board gender diversity and environmental, social, and economic value creation: Does family ownership matter? *Business Strategy and the Environment, 29*(3), 1268–1284. DOI: 10.1002/bse.2432

Oikonomou, I., Yin, C., & Zhao, L. (2020). Investment horizon and corporate social performance: The virtuous circle of long-term institutional ownership and responsible firm conduct. *European Journal of Finance, 26*(1), 14–40. DOI: 10.1080/1351847X.2019.1660197

Putri, V. R., Zakaria, N. B., Said, J., & Azis, M. A. A. (2023). Do Foreign Ownership, Executive Incentives, Corporate Social Responsibility Activity and Audit Quality Affect Corporate Tax Avoidance? *Indian Journal of Corporate Governance, 16*(2), 218–239. DOI: 10.1177/09746862231205648

Searcy, C. (2012). Corporate Sustainability Performance Measurement Systems: A Review and Research Agenda. *Journal of Business Ethics, 107*(3), 239–253. DOI: 10.1007/s10551-011-1038-z

Teng, Y., Ma, Z., Liang, D., Song, S., & Zheng, Y. (2024). The moderating effect of national culture on board interlocks' impact on firm performance: A meta-analysis. *Journal of Business Research, 183*, 114816. DOI: 10.1016/j.jbusres.2024.114816

Trinh, V. Q., Elnahass, M., Salama, A., & Izzeldin, M. (2019). Board busyness, performance and financial stability: Does bank type matter? *European Journal of Finance, 26*(7–8), 774–801. https://doi.org/https://doi.org/10.1080/1351847X.2019.1636842

Trinugroho, I., Risfandy, T., Hanafi, M. M., & Sukmana, R. (2023). Busy commissioners and firm performance: Evidence from Indonesia. *International Journal of Emerging Markets, 18*(11), 5028–5048. DOI: 10.1108/IJOEM-01-2020-0007

Venkatesh, G., Kshatriya, S., & Bansal, S. (2025). Board Busyness and Firm Performance: An Emerging Market Perspective. *Corporate Governance, 33*(2), 231–245. DOI: 10.1111/corg.12600

Wu, K., & Zheng, K. (2025). Tax incentives, supply chain spillovers, and enterprise technological innovation. *International Review of Financial Analysis, 99*(January), 103930. DOI: 10.1016/j.irfa.2025.103930

Wu, Q., Wang, Y., & Shen, G. (2024). The green bonus of tax incentives: Evidence from China. *Journal of Economic Behavior & Organization, 227*(January), 106740. DOI: 10.1016/j.jebo.2024.106740

Yin, H., Zhang, L., Cai, C., Zhang, Z., & Zhu, Q. (2025). Fiscal & tax incentives, ESG responsibility fulfillments, and corporate green innovation performance. *International Review of Economics & Finance, 98*, 103838. DOI: 10.1016/j.iref.2025.103838

Zhao, L., Chong, K. M., Gooi, L. M., & Yan, L. (2024). Research on the impact of government fiscal subsidies and tax incentive mechanism on the output of green patents in enterprises. *Finance Research Letters, 61*(December 2023), 104997. DOI: 10.1016/j.frl.2024.104997

Zhu, N., Zhou, Y., Zhang, S., & Yan, J. (2023). Tax incentives and environmental, social, and governance performance: Empirical evidence from China. *Environmental Science and Pollution Research International, 30*(19), 54899–54913. DOI: 10.1007/s11356-023-26112-3 PMID: 36881223

## ENDNOTES

1 The database is compiled from publicly available information from approximately 900 sources yearly, including CSR and/or sustainability reports, firm's official websites, proxy filings, and reports from major news organisations globally. The database is compiled with 250 key performance indicators based on these sources (Bassetti et al., 2020; Nadeem et al., 2020).

# Chapter 8
# From Policy to Practice: CSR Awareness Among Tourism and Hospitality Workforce

**Elham Gharib Saghier**
*Faculty of Tourism and Hotels, Egypt*

**Kareem M. Selem**
http://orcid.org/0000-0003-2987-4134
*Faculty of Tourism and Hotels, Egypt*

## ABSTRACT

*The tourism and hospitality industry's corporate social responsibility (CSR) journey has evolved from a mere commitment to strategic integration and ethical obligation. CSR practice is based on the UN global compact and the sustainable development goals (SDGs). However, it continues to live within policy jargon boundaries, lacking understanding at the employee level. The focus of this chapter is to explore the understanding of CSR awareness in the tourism and hospitality industry. Prioritizing education and communication within the organizational culture to articulate policy into practice is key. Anchored in stakeholder theory, Carroll's CSR pyramid, and the triple bottom line, this chapter illustrates CSR and each employee's responsibility at each level of organizational hierarchy. This chapter discusses challenges in understanding tourism, development, and culture training. Therefore, this chapter focuses on professionalism in hospitality and service excellence as a conduit for creating CSR consciousness.*

DOI: 10.4018/979-8-2600-3179-7.ch008

## INTRODUCTION

Integrating corporate social responsibility (CSR) into business models became a priority for many organizations (Abidin et al., 2025). The tourism and hospitality industry felt this priority more than others, as it invests the most resources and time in international human interaction (Gao et al., 2025). It is an industry in which human engagement and bonding constitute the core of the business (Gupta et al., 2025). CSR advocacy hinges on the relationships and interconnectedness between businesses and communities (Cosa, 2024). Because of this relationship, business reputation hinges on trust, ethics, and community and environmental engagement (Gao et al., 2025). For the tourism and hospitality industry, CSR is about compliance, philanthropy, and achieving economic viability alongside social equity and environmental conservation (Khatter, 2025). CSR is a core component of the developed strategic plans, policies, and environmental sustainability goals (e.g., carbon footprint reduction, cultural heritage preservation, and ethical employment practices) (Montañés-Del Río et al., 2025).

International hotel chains (e.g., Marriott, Hilton, and Accor) have organized their hospitality businesses under international CSR initiatives (Macaveiu, 2025), focusing on sustainability management. However, frontline employee engagement and understanding of such initiatives at the operational level are primary concerns within such businesses (Gao et al., 2025). The growing importance of CSR awareness in the global tourism economy has become a moral and competitive necessity (von Weltzien Hoivik, 2025). Because many tourists are informed and socially aware, they will prefer to choose and spend money on strategically socially responsible brands (Baena & Cerviño, 2024). Ethical and sustainable business conduct expectations from governments, destination management organizations, and other non-business actors have also increased (von Weltzien Hoivik, 2025). However, translating macro commitments into employees' understanding at the micro level remains unsolved. Employee awareness of organizations' CSR, social, and environmental responsibilities is vital to addressing CSR strategy gaps when employees interface with stakeholders (Jiang et al., 2025). If employees are unaware of CSR objectives or view them as peripheral, CSR strategies will not be substantive (Shahzadi et al., 2024).

Suppose organizations have employees aware of CSR and engaged in socially responsible activities (Dong et al., 2024). In this vein, organizations will shape service delivery and stakeholder satisfaction (Abidin et al., 2025). CSR can move from concept to culture (von Weltzien Hoivik, 2025). Although tourism and hospitality organizations implement CSR initiatives and produce annual sustainability reports (Papafloratos et al., 2025), empirical research indicates that CSR practices are insufficiently embedded in daily operations (Baena & Cerviño, 2024; Montañés-Del Río et al., 2025). This gap goes beyond inadequate policies to understanding employee ownership and behavioral integration. For instance, hotels may have defined waste reduction policies. However, employees may not know how to separate recyclables, or may simply not be motivated (Cosa, 2024). Initiatives that support community development may also be seen as external to hospitality service philosophies (Moyeen & Mehjabeen, 2024).

This disconnection leads to unanswered questions: What do hospitality employees think of CSR? What drives their level of interest and participation? How do managers enable the operationalization of CSR into daily activities and decision-making? These questions are critical to advancing CSR and providing employees with a sense of social purpose that fosters a sense of belonging. CSR awareness within the workforce goes beyond ethical obligations and strengthens organizations' strategic positioning (Gidage & Bhide, 2024). Employees who are aware of the social and environmental nuances of hotel policies and practices are more likely to internalize and adhere to organizational values (Mansoor et al., 2025). Therefore, this may lead to more consistent service delivery and trust among stakeholders. Besides, CSR awareness at the employee level enables organizations' adaptive capacity to respond to external pressures (e.g., sustainability certifications, environmental laws, or changing audiences) (Reimer et al., 2024). It also advances organizations' employer positioning by positioning them as socially responsible and desirable workplaces (Gidage & Bhide, 2024).

Incorporating CSR awareness into HRM practices (e.g., recruitment, training, performance evaluation, and internal communication) can confer unique competitive advantages (Onyekwelu et al., 2024). For example, CSR awareness allows employee orientation programs to be designed so that new employees go beyond seeing themselves as service deliverers to become ambassadors of ethical and responsible hospitality (Reimer et al., 2024). In addition, innovation is advanced in such organizations as employees are more engaged in suggesting new community involvement initiatives (Alshukri et al., 2024) or eco-friendly practices beyond organizational limits (Papafloratos et al., 2025).

The importance of understanding CSR within the hospitality workforce can be examined through various theories (Gupta et al., 2025). While stakeholder theory focuses on the organization's responsibilities to various stakeholders (e.g., employees, customers, and society), Carroll's CSR pyramid outlines four dimensions of organizational responsibility: economic, legal, ethical, and philanthropic (Ramsbottom et al., 2025). This pyramid shows that organizations' CSR awareness should shift from compliance to moral obligations (Abidin et al., 2025). The triple bottom line (TBL) framework considers organizations' economic, social, and environmental aspects as equally interdependent (Nogueira et al., 2025). These theories indicate the need to align employee behaviors and actions with CSR to achieve complete sustainability within organizations.

In tourism and hospitality contexts, the intersection of CSR awareness and social learning theory arises because employees imitate superior behaviors through observation, reinforcement, and path-dependent organizational behaviors (Onyekwelu et al., 2024). This chapter analyzes how CSR awareness is created, communicated, and implemented among employees in the hospitality and tourism sectors. Specifically, this chapter seeks to:

- Describe the conceptual foundations of CSR theory within tourism and hospitality contexts.
- Examine existing policies on CSR and their effects on engaging employees within organizations.
- Determine obstacles that limit the practical understanding and execution of CSR initiatives.
- Provide research and case studies demonstrating the gap between policies and practice.
- Propose actionable ways to close this gap, focusing on training, stewardship, and the organization's ethos.

## 2. CONCEPTUAL FOUNDATIONS OF CSR IN TOURISM AND HOSPITALITY

### 2.1. Understanding CSR: Evolution and meaning

CSR began as a one-dimensional approach to incorporate a multidimensional business strategy of accountability, sustainability, and stakeholder action (Nguyen et al., 2025). In its earlier forms, CSR referred to organizations making donations and supporting community initiatives, philanthropy, and various forms of charity that improved corporate images (Abidin et al., 2025). Next, globalization, public scrutiny, and the growing environmental movement led to the emergence of CSR as a comprehensive, multidimensional approach that addresses economic, social, and environmental aspects (Ashurov et al., 2024). Nowadays, CSR incorporates economic, social, and environmental implications of corporate actions, day-to-day decision-making and organizational operations (Khan & Iqbal, 2024). The European Commission refers to CSR as firms' responsibility for their impacts on society (Resende et al., 2024).

Likewise, the World Business Council for Sustainable Development stated that CSR is businesses' continuing commitment to behave ethically and contribute to economic development (Wirba, 2024), cascading down to local communities. Thus, this showcases CSR as a strategic pillar for business sustainability and is ethically grounded. CSR assumes greater significance in tourism and hospitality since these industries influence local environments, economies, and cultures (Lee et al., 2025). Hotels and tourism businesses engage with local communities, draw on natural and cultural resources, and provide large-scale jobs for local employees (Baker, 2024). In this vein, CSR must go beyond the ethical balancing of environmental commitments to include social and labor equity, cultural engagement, and stewardship of local communities (Wirba, 2024).

## 2.2. Theoretical perspectives: Underpinning CSR

CSR refers to the systems and practices that organizations integrate to ensure they are socially responsible within their environments, communities, and the global economy (Faeni et al., 2025). The importance and interrelatedness of such systems must be studied and understood to enable organizations to integrate best practices for the optimal social performance (Rodrigues Coelho et al., 2025). CSR activities comprise social responsiveness, social reputation, and social commitments (Tawiah et al., 2025). In terms of ethical, legal, economic, and civic responsibilities, CSR must be understood in this context (Faeni et al., 2025). This chapter reviews and examines CSR frameworks in hospitality and tourism organizations.

### 2.2.1. Stakeholder theory

According to Awa et al. (2024), the primary concept of stakeholder theory is that each business is answerable to shareholders, employees, customers, suppliers, community members, and ecosystems. In tourism and hospitality contexts, stakeholder groups are notably wider, including local community members, tourists, local authorities, and international NGOs concerned with the environment (Đurić et al., 2025). Tourism and hotel businesses focused on profitability will likely risk their social license if they ignore employee well-being (Magdy & Salem, 2024). Claiming that organizations consider and satisfy their stakeholders' social and economic needs advocates (Awa et al., 2024). In this vein, employees psychologically engage with organizations and are motivated to implement sustainable practices that organizations have adopted (Czichos et al., 2025). Therefore, local suppliers and culturally beneficial initiatives enhance relations with communities and foster psychological engagement and support from organizations (Đurić et al., 2025).

### 2.2.2. Carroll's pyramid of CSR

Park and Rim (2025) describe CSR in four parts as a hierarchy of responsibilities: economic, legal, ethical, and philanthropic. This pyramid pragmatically assesses responsibility as eco-lodges' economic responsibility is maintaining viability through financially responsible operations (Ramsbottom et al., 2025). Legally, eco-lodges must comply with labor and safety regulations and treat employees and communities fairly. Philanthropically, they should invest in education and conservation (Abidin et al., 2025). Thus, Carroll's pyramid demonstrates multiple facets of CSR that are compatible with hospitality-oriented perspectives.

### 2.2.3. The triple bottom line framework

Nogueira et al. (2025) reframe business success in terms of TBL—people, planet, and profit. This multi-dimensional view shifts business success from a financial perspective to the interconnectedness of social, environmental, and economic dimensions. In the tourism and hospitality sectors, the TBL framework is evident in sustainable procurement, waste management, energy conservation, and community participation (Chiang, 2024). For instance, hotel chains can integrate profit and operational efficiency by managing renewable energy systems and ensuring equitable employee compensation (Khalil et al., 2024). Thus, TBL offers a comprehensive perspective on integrating businesses' performance with sustainability demands (Nogueira et al., 2025).

## 2.3. Dimensions of CSR in the tourism and hospitality context

Due to the unique nature of tourism and hospitality, CSR is multifaceted and interconnected (Ramsbottom et al., 2025). Economic, social, environmental, and cultural dimensions determine responsible business behavior within this sector.

### 2.3.1. Economic responsibility

Economic responsibility includes efficient operation, profit generation, and the advancement of local economic development (Leigh, 2024). For responsible tourism, this pertains to much more than profitability, extending to equitable distribution of benefits (Chauhan, 2025). Tourism income circulates ethically within local communities through fair procurement, fair pricing, and local supply chains (Chung & Day, 2024). The economic component of CSR also includes the absence of exploitative or parasitic pricing (Kumar, 2024), fostering ethical customer trust, transparency in financial dealings, and ethical marketing (Leigh, 2024).

### 2.3.2. Social responsibility

Social responsibility is associated with employee welfare, customers, and local communities in which organizations operate (Huang et al., 2024). In tourism and hospitality settings, this includes fair employment practices, ensuring safe environments, fostering and maintaining a culture of diversity and inclusion, and offering professional development opportunities (Abidin et al., 2025). For local communities, this could mean supporting education, healthcare, or infrastructure initiatives (Huang et al., 2024). Employees who are willing and able to provide integrated, valuable service are those who feel they are being appreciated in their workplaces (Baker, 2024).

### 2.3.3. Environmental responsibility

Environmental responsibility is a cornerstone of CSR for the tourism and hospitality industry (Nogueira et al., 2025). Hotels and other tourism facilities are major producers of water, energy, and waste (Mdoda et al., 2024). Hence, thorough ecological responsibility entails using energy-efficient technologies, minimizing waste, recycling, and adopting sustainable design. Adopting water-saving systems, eliminating single-use plastics, and sourcing food locally are becoming industry standards (Papallou et al., 2024). Many organizations use environmental certifications (e.g., Green Key, LEED, or EarthCheck) to formalize and integrate standards for sustainable practices (Hallas, 2024).

### 2.3.4. Cultural responsibility

Cultural responsibility regarding tourism refers to the obligation to protect destinations' cultural heritage (Pai et al., 2025). Thus, this is crucial in heritage and indigenous tourism, where the risk of cultural erosion from insensitive commercialization is high (Papallou et al., 2024). Organizations that emphasize CSR and work with local artisans encourage the preservation of traditional practices in tourism settings (Chauhan, 2025) and instill in their guests a sense of cultural respect for others. Cultural CSR preserves intangible cultural heritage while enriching tourist experiences, boosting destination authenticity and competitiveness (Jing & Loang, 2024).

## 2.4. Global frameworks and standards guiding CSR

To ensure uniform accountability, international organizations establish structures for implementing CSR across different destinations (Hallas, 2024). In tourism and hospitality, international frameworks shape this sector's policy development and reporting instruments.

### 2.4.1. United nations global compact

The UN Global Compact, launched in 2000, encourages businesses worldwide to adopt strategies aligned with ten universal principles on human rights, labor, the environment, and corruption (McCarty, 2024). Most hotel chains use compacts as the basis for their CSR reporting and benchmarking (Khalil et al., 2024).

### 2.4.2. ISO 26000: Guidance on social responsibility

ISO 26000 principles were published in 2010 and offer support for organizations to achieve responsible operations internationally (Garcia-Ortega et al., 2024). Thus, this covers the following seven core areas: governance, human rights, labor, environment, fair business, customers, and communities. These areas can serve as a basis for tourism and hospitality organizations to develop CSR policies (Pásková & Zelenka, 2024).

### 2.4.3. UNWTO global code of ethics for tourism

The United Nations World Tourism Organization (UNWTO) has established a global code of ethics for tourism to promote responsible tourism development (Rusu et al., 2024). It promotes safeguarding cultural heritage, environmental protection, and fair sharing of economic benefits with host communities (Khater et al., 2024). The global code of ethics for tourism encourages policymakers and practitioners to develop ethical tourism throughout value chains (Garcia-Ortega et al., 2024).

### 2.4.4. Global reporting initiative

The Global Reporting Initiative promotes sustainability reporting and transparency of economic, social, and environmental performances (Rusu et al., 2024). For the tourism and hospitality industry, the Global Reporting Initiative framework standards promote trust and ease of comparison in international markets (Ye et al., 2024). Stakeholders use the Global Reporting Initiative to assess CSR credibility promises and monitor its accountability (Uddin et al., 2024).

## 2.5. CSR and sustainable tourism development

CSR is an organizational framework through which sustainability principles are put to work (Hallas, 2024). Left unmanaged, tourism can lead to environmental degradation, overtourism, and commodification. If embedded in corporate DNA, CSR management safeguards against threats (Ye et al., 2024). For instance, hotels may go green in construction, collaborate with local NGOs on eco-tourism initiatives, and implement supply chain policies promoting fair trade (Akbari et al., 2025). Responsible tour operators encourage customers to follow customs, reduce waste while traveling, and promote environmental conservation (Uddin et al., 2024). Employee CSR awareness is crucial to the development of sustainable tourism (Hallas, 2024). Employees who perceive destinations' cultural and environmental value can manage guest behaviors, ensuring sustainability principles are applied in practice (Birinci et al., 2025).

# 3. CSR POLICIES IN TOURISM AND HOSPITALITY SECTORS

## 3.1. Introduction to CSR policy formulation in tourism and hospitality

CSR policies encapsulate organizations' values regarding ethics, sustainability, and social accountability (Pásková & Zelenka, 2024). Regarding tourism and hospitality, environmentally dependent industries, policies flow down to organizations that care about the social and ecological implications of their business operations (Murtaza et al., 2024). Such policies are tangible expressions of organizations' responsibilities to stakeholders (Akbari et al., 2025). In tourism and hospitality businesses, organizations' values and sustainability objectives (e.g., energy use, waste, health and safety, and social development within communities) are key points for developing CSR policies (Montañés-Del Río et al., 2025). Lastly, CSR policies are documented in corporate handbooks, the annual sustainability report, and employee training manuals (Pásková & Zelenka, 2024). Hence, policies and systems that underpin them depend on organizations' personnel and business culture. In tourism and hospitality businesses, CSR policies are driven by external forces (e.g., state- or international regulations, or target-market expectations) (Murtaza et al., 2024).

## 3.2. CSR policy development drivers in hospitality and tourism

The drivers influencing the formulation and development of CSR policies in the hospitality and tourism industry may arise from institutional, market, and organizational levels.

### 3.2.1. Institutional and regulatory pressures

According to institutional theory, organizations can be influenced by normative, coercive, and mimetic pressures (Wukich et al., 2024). Coercive pressures are regulatory and come from governments and international organizations (Panke & Stapel, 2024). For example, tourism ministries require hotels to obtain business licenses by adhering to specific sustainability certifications (Sriraksa et al., 2024). Normative pressures come from CSR-imbued ethics and industry standards developed by professional associations and educational institutions (Wukich et al., 2024). Lastly, competing organizations apply mimetic pressures by copying leading organizations' CSR initiatives to gain legitimacy and maintain competitive balance (Duan et al., 2025). Developed economies with a sizeable tourism industry use CSR-related instruments (e.g., environmental impact assessment, labor welfare laws, and anti-corruption laws) to enforce compliance (Panke & Stapel, 2024).

### 3.2.2. Market and consumer expectations

The shift towards responsible consumption in the tourism and hospitality sectors is undeniable (Taheri et al., 2024). Travelers assess destinations to stay based on environments, ethical sourcing of products, and integration with destination communities (Baena & Cerviño, 2024). This awareness among customers offers market-based incentives for integrating CSR into the organizational level (Taheri et al., 2024). In the absence of morally defensible practices, adopting policies on green operations (e.g., employment and cooperative community integration) will become necessary to diversify market competition (Baah et al., 2024). Moreover, major online travel agencies (e.g., Booking.com and TripAdvisor) have begun to incorporate sustainability into their business models (Vávrová et al., 2025). Such endorsements' visibility creates expectations that businesses will deliver on their stated values (Baah et al., 2024).

### 3.2.3. Corporate reputation and risk management

CSR policies serve to manage organizational reputation (Montañés-Del Río et al., 2025). With the rise of digital transparency, employees can easily access information about organizations' labor practices, their environmental treatment, and social ethics (Pásková & Zelenka, 2024). Well-crafted CSR policies can help organizations mitigate reputation risk by showing documented evidence of proactive responsibility (Montañés-Del Río et al., 2025). On the other hand, the absence of policies can lead to public outrage, derogatory social media commentary, and customer boycotts (Kumar, 2024). Given international hotel chains, the strategic importance of uniform policies across their different operational markets is crucial (Khalil et al., 2024). Such policies assume consistency, ethical behavior, and brand reliability, cultivating customer loyalty and confidence.

### 3.2.4. Leadership commitment and organizational culture

The internal culture of hospitality establishments shapes the extent and genuineness of CSR policies (Yikilmaz et al., 2025). Leadership commitment is often a driving force that translates ethical ideals into concrete plans (Pásková & Zelenka, 2024). Senior management that values social responsibility shapes HRM policies, employee training, evaluation, and compensation systems (Fawehinmi et al., 2024). Inclusivity and a sense of shared purpose at the tier level embolden employees to act on CSR objectives, completing the policy-practice connections (Yikilmaz et al., 2025).

## 3.3. Typologies of CSR policies in tourism and hospitality

CSR policies in the tourism and hospitality sector can be organized by organizational focus and operational model (Pásková & Zelenka, 2024). The following types exemplify the usual strategies employed by global and domestic entities:

### 3.3.1. Environmental sustainability policies

Green hotels, installing energy-saving lighting, and establishing recycling programs demonstrate sustainability improvements (Kalefa & Gado, 2024). Through the serve360 strategy, Marriott International has sustainability targets related to SDGs (e.g., achieving 100% renewable energy sourcing and reducing food waste by 50%) (Mensah et al., 2025). Boutique hotels will likely be built with local materials, use renewable energy, and promote biodiversity to conserve and offer community-based eco-lodges (Pourtaheri et al., 2024). Improving biodiversity and reducing usage to fulfill fulfillment requirements illustrates market positioning and operational cost improvements (Mensah et al., 2025).

### 3.3.2. Social equity and labor responsibility policies

Policies that meet social responsibility obligations focus on employees' fair treatment, safe workplaces, and equal working opportunities (Khalil et al., 2024). Such policies address various social and economic inequalities (e.g., inequity and discrimination, economic inequality, and wage gaps) (Fawehinmi et al., 2024). In the hospitality and tourism industry, economic opportunities are temporary, more diversified, and more susceptible to policy exploitation (Yikilmaz et al., 2025). Most civil society regulation policies in developing countries focus on local hiring and training to empower community capacity and reduce reliance on imported labor (Kalefa & Gado, 2024).

### 3.3.3. Community engagement and development policies

Sustainability in tourism and hospitality businesses entails integrating community development globally (Tabatabaei et al., 2025). Hence, this encompasses community support in education, healthcare, business, and culture. Thus, this may be through citizenship and collaboration on social development initiatives with NGOs or local government authorities (Đurić et al., 2025). For example, Accor's Planet 21 initiatives describe employees' volunteering efforts and support for local suppliers (Baker, 2024). Such policies serve to strengthen social cohesion, and brand loyalty deepens through emotional attachment and sentiment as local community members become key stakeholders in tourism destinations (Chen et al., 2025).

### 3.3.4. Ethical sourcing and supply chain policies

The tourism and hospitality industry operates through international supply chains; ethical procurement policies enforce ethical standards in labor, the sustainable and humane treatment of animals, and environmental protection (Rahman et al., 2024). To comply with human rights and anti-corruption standards, hotels have supplier codes of conduct (Moscariello et al., 2024). Environmental benefits of local procurement for food and beverage operations that ethically source from regional agriculture, while reducing transport-related emissions (Dhingra, 2025).

### 3.3.5. Cultural and heritage preservation policies

Policies aimed at preserving culture seek to honor and protect local practices, traditions, and historical resources (Reddy & Sailesh, 2024). The tourism industry is responsible for ensuring that its business activities do not undermine local culture (Chen et al., 2025). Adopting CSR that offers cultural sensitivity training promotes local art, and supports local indigenous entrepreneurship is an ethical and experiential blending (Tabatabaei et al., 2025).

## 3.4. Comparative perspectives: Developed and developing contexts

Global differences in CSR policies can be attributed to disparities in governance systems, resources, and culture (Mdoda et al., 2024). In Western economies, CSR policies are more systematically integrated into organizations' governance structures (Wirba, 2024). Regulatory laws and informed consumers are the driving forces behind policies mandating extensive reporting of CSR initiatives (Duan et al., 2025). For instance, European hotel groups are required to report and publish their sustainability reports in accordance with the Global Reporting Initiative (Guix et al., 2025). In contrast, developing policies and other emerging economies in the global south are characterized by informality and fragmentation (Ramos Farroñán et al., 2025). While their actions and policies are commendable, the lack of formal systems can stifle their scalability, monitoring, and transparency initiatives (Wirba, 2024). Regarding culture, the focus of CSR policies may be driven by the communities' social structure (Mdoda et al., 2024). International hotel chains, donor initiatives, and policy educational programs are cross-border initiatives to formalize policies and systems (Rezaei, 2025). The cross-border standardization of CSR policies is the first clear indication of the globalization of ethical practices in tourism and hospitality.

## 3.5. Implementation mechanisms and communication strategies

The practical impact of CSR policies depends on proper implementation and communication across tourism and hospitality organizations (Khatter, 2025). Implementation mechanisms include employee training programs, internal audits, performance indicator audits, and programs within incentive systems (Montañés-Del Río et al., 2025).

### 3.5.1. Training and development programs

Workshops, e-learning activities, and mentoring immerse employees in CSR policies (Ramos Farroñán et al., 2025). For example, take water-conserving practices training for housekeepers or sustainable sourcing training for chefs (Guix et al., 2025); employees are enabled to act responsibly within their job functions.

### 3.5.2. Internal communication and employee engagement

Consistent communication can help integrate individual actions with organizational CSR goals (Duan et al., 2025). The tourism and hospitality industry uses internal communication tools (e.g., newsletters, intranets, and CSR recognition programs) to celebrate CSR milestones (Chen et al., 2025). Including employees in organizing committees for CSR activities or volunteering events dramatically enhances engagement by converting awareness into active participation (Reddy & Sailesh, 2024).

### 3.5.3. Monitoring, reporting, and evaluation

Fundamental requirements for effective CSR policies are accountability, monitoring, and sustained reporting (Kandpal et al., 2024). Reporting metrics can include diversity ratios, community investments, or energy consumption per guest night (Reddy & Sailesh, 2024). Public reporting, independent audits, and sustainability certifications promote stakeholder trust and accountability (Duan et al., 2025). Reporting aligned with the SDGs, in which several hotel chains explain the nexus between corporate activities and the global goals they advance, illustrates impact communication (Ferrero-Ferrero et al., 2024).

## 3.6. Challenges in policy consistency and localization

Although policy adoption is ubiquitous, ensuring consistent CSR practices is problematic due to differences in culture and economics (Bux et al., 2024). Global hotel chains face the challenge of tailoring hotel policies to local community needs while maintaining corporate objectives (Khatter, 2025). For example, environmental policies tailored to urban hotels are unlikely to work for rural resorts with less developed infrastructure. Furthermore, training and mentoring the operational workforce in the hotel industry requires an understanding of local contexts, including literacy, cultural differences, and motivational issues (Zhao et al., 2025). Likewise, smaller independent hotels lack the financial and technical resources to develop comprehensive CSR policies (Alsheyab et al., 2024). These organizations will leave informal responsible practices strategically unframed without adequate guidance and incentives (Khatter, 2025).

## 4. CSR AWARENESS AMONG TOURISM AND HOSPITALITY WORKFORCE

### 4.1. Understanding CSR awareness in organizational contexts

Incorporating CSR within organizations is built on understanding employees' actions (Dong et al., 2024). In the tourism and hospitality industry, where interactions and human relations are a core component of service, transcending organizations' compliance is an absolute minimum (Baker, 2024). It shifts to the behavioral components of interaction, where human services associates within organizations manifest a compliant understanding of organizations' sustainability goals (Alsheyab et al., 2024). CSR awareness converges on a behavioral construct, is multidimensional, and incorporates cognitive, affective, and behavioral intentions (Zhao et al., 2025).

### 4.2. Workforce engagement in CSR success

In tourism and hospitality contexts, employees serve as organizations' ambassadors and implementers of CSR (Srivastava et al., 2025). Their attitude towards CSR determines whether actions are symbolic gestures or become embedded as core practices of organizational culture (Alsheyab et al., 2024). Consider hotels that promote and live by community engagement programs focused on environmental sustainability, working with socially disadvantaged communities (Turčinović et al., 2025) or that use systems to conserve energy within organizations (Reddy & Sailesh, 2024). Employee behaviors towards socially responsible actions (e.g., conserving water, reducing waste, recycling, and engaging with community social projects) determine the impact of such initiatives (Silva, 2024). Hence, the importance of CSR awareness remains ethical and operational, and builds corporate strategy integration into operational fronts (Turčinović et al., 2025).

### 4.3. Communication and training as enablers of CSR awareness

CSR communication in tourism and hospitality organizations goes beyond one-way information streams; it requires establishing communication, trust, and meaning (Srivastava et al., 2025). Most organizations use one-way communication channels (e.g., reports, newsletters, and posters) to adopt a top-down approach to raising CSR awareness (Nguyen et al., 2025). However, more productive systems include peer workshops, storytelling, and feedback, which cultivate a deeper, more ingrained awareness (Zamiri & Esmaeili, 2024). In the global hotel industry, corporate training is the most effective means of fostering CSR cultures in hospitality organizations, alongside other hospitality industry constants (Turčinović et al., 2025). Global hotel chains (e.g., Marriott International and Hilton) are integrated into the orientation and ongoing training of hospitality industry professionals, and the training objectives they implement (Khatter, 2025). Hilton and Marriott incorporate environmental management, community engagement, and ethics training at the employee level (Bernacchio et al., 2024).

Besides, contextual relevance underscores the necessity for localized training initiatives (Zamiri & Esmaeili, 2024). Differences in CSR training require an emphasis on local value norms (e.g., hospitality, respect, and communal responsibility) (Srivastava et al., 2025). In the Middle East and Africa, hospitality organizations are culturally and religiously motivated to engage in CSR as a form of generosity and stewardship, thereby improving acceptance, relevance, and resonance (Hamdi et al., 2024). On the other hand, the advent of digital learning tools has transformed CSR education. Employees download applications and e-learning modules that enable them to access sustainability policies, track their contributions, and report on best-practice sharing (Zamiri & Esmaeili, 2024). Such technologies reposition CSR knowledge from compliance with policies to dynamic learning (Hamdi et al., 2024).

## 4.4. Leadership and management practices in promoting CSR awareness

The primary influence on employees' understanding of CSR comes from leadership. Employees learn to take CSR to heart from transformational and ethical leaders (Zamiri & Esmaeili, 2024). Such leaders inspire vision, show empathy, and serve as moral examples. When leaders speak authentically about CSR, weaving in their personal stories and highlighting common goals, employees understand CSR as a central part of their organization's identity (Hamdi et al., 2024). Hospitality managers who practice socially responsible behavior have direct times when their employees are expected to emulate such behaviors (Mansoor et al., 2025). For example, department heads who regularly adopt ecologically responsible behavior or participate in socially directed community work influence employees to act. Employees are more motivated to engage in socially responsible acts when leadership explains expected socially responsible behaviors and their moral justifications (Guix et al., 2025).

The influence of these leaders is compounded by HRM policies when CSR is incorporated into recruitment, performance appraisal, and reward systems (Mansoor et al., 2025). Hiring practices based on corporate value frameworks focus on socially responsible candidates, while performance assessments and rewards justify CSR actions by recognizing contributions (Zamiri & Esmaeili, 2024). For example, hotels embed volunteer hours or sustainability initiatives into performance metrics (Papafloratos et al., 2025). Such HRM practices disseminate culturally embedded

CSR awareness and practices across hospitality and tourism organizations (Srivastava et al., 2025).

## 4.5. CSR awareness as a predictor of employee attitudes and behaviors

Research in the tourism and hospitality sector has found that employees who are invested in CSR have a positive impact on organizational commitment, trust, and identification (Mansoor et al., 2025; Nguyen et al., 2025). If employees perceive their organization as socially responsible, they are loyal and go the extra mile (Zamiri & Esmaeili, 2024). Employees' CSR awareness will prompt positive behaviors toward internal and external stakeholders (Nguyen et al., 2025). Internally, employees are more cooperative and collaborative while exercising appropriate fairness and ethics (Bernacchio et al., 2024). Employees aware of their organization's CSR principles are empathetic and culturally sensitive when serving guests (Papafloratos et al., 2025). Employees who understand organizations' CSR principles gain pride and a sense of purpose, helping lower turnover intentions (Schaefer et al., 2024). CSR awareness decreases employee turnover (Zamiri & Esmaeili, 2024). Employees ensure social responsibility and economically motivate organizations, acting as a protective shield for brand equity (Nguyen et al., 2025). In positive ways, economically and socially aligned brand equity results from the socially responsible commitment apprehended from turnover intention and CSR awareness (Turčinović et al., 2025).

## 4.6. Challenges in building CSR awareness in the hospitality workforce

Despite positive outcomes, achieving high levels of CSR awareness among the tourism and hospitality workforce remains challenging. This sector's high turnover, seasonal employment, and temporary jobs make continuous education about CSR less focused (Nguyen et al., 2025). Hospitality employees can be so absorbed in completing their work tasks that they consider CSR irrelevant (Peng & Liu, 2025). Employees who deal with customers often do not understand what their organizations do in terms of CSR (Huang et al., 2024). They have little knowledge of their organization's CSR efforts and less guidance on implementing them (Papafloratos et al., 2025). Multinational hospitality organizations hire employees from different cultures (Peng & Liu, 2025). Thus, this may lead to different understandings of issues and social responsibility frameworks. Building strategies toward culturally adaptive CSR awareness is essential (Nguyen et al., 2025). Most employees need limited incentives to enjoy balanced motivational frameworks (Peng & Liu, 2025).

Thus, CSR is most effective when integrated into performance management systems and articulated in terms of career growth and job satisfaction (Latan et al., 2022).

## 4.7. CSR awareness enchantment strategies

To grow understanding of CSR, a multifaceted, continuous effort involving communication, education, leadership, and acknowledgment is required (Baker, 2024). CSR must be included in organizations' mission and vision, and each employee must understand its connection to service quality and ethical hospitality. Employees participate in scenario-based training and simulation exercises in which they must make CSR decisions in real-life situations, thereby deepening their understanding of the concept. Employees are invited to propose and take charge of CSR activities and projects, which foster ownership and innovative thinking. Communicating employee CSR action success stories celebrates collective purpose and pride. CSR awareness is integrated into mobile apps, competitions, and other activities that foster continuous engagement. It is critical to integrate different departments (e.g., food and beverages, housekeeping, or marketing) to achieve CSR objectives.

## 4.8. Measuring and monitoring CSR awareness

Continuously improving CSR awareness requires quantification. Surveys, focus groups, and feedback channels can gauge employees' understanding, attitudes, and participation levels (Carlini & Grace, 2021)—constructed methods (e.g., CSR perception scale and employee social responsibility index facilitate awareness evaluation (Qin & Men, 2023). Regular evaluations help organizations understand knowledge and training gaps and adjust strategic communications (Baker, 2024). For instance, hotel chains might use annual CSR perception surveys to understand changes in employee engagement and revise initiatives (Choi & Choi, 2021). Correlating these evaluations with organizational performance metrics (e.g., employee retention, guest satisfaction, and sustainability) provides greater insight into the extent to which CSR is ingrained in tourism and hospitality organizations (Latan et al., 2022). Reporting results to employees and explaining the next steps demonstrates management's respect for their input (Qin & Men, 2023). Participatory feedback loops created by employees relaying assessment metrics reinforce the development aspect of awareness measurement (Carlini & Grace, 2021).

## 5. BARRIERS TO EFFECTIVE CSR AWARENESS AND IMPLEMENTATION

### 5.1. The policy–practice divide

Although CSR is recognized as critical in the tourism and hospitality sector, the gap between developing policies and engaging employees to enact them is one of the industry's weakest points (Latan et al., 2022). Organizations implement these policies to check a box in sustainability frameworks or to enhance their reputation (Aukhoon et al., 2024). Regulatory policies surrounding sustainability may give the impression that such efforts are meaningful and unlikely to change employee behaviors (Zervoudi et al., 2025). The policy–practice divide arises from a lack of organizational and cultural education, systemic issues, and a lack of will to instill CSR principles (Latan et al., 2022). This gap in understanding is damaging because most CSR initiatives are people-centered. Most innovative and valuable policies will fail if employees lack knowledge, attitude, and the will to act (Carlini & Grace, 2021).

### 5.2. Organizational barriers: Structure, culture, and prioritization

One significant barrier to CSR awareness is the internal structure and culture of hospitality organizations (Shin & Jang, 2025). Many organizations operate under hierarchical systems that rely on top-down communication (Abidin et al., 2025). Thus, this limits employees' understanding of CSR goals. Organizational policies are made at corporate headquarters with little consideration for frontline employees who interact with guests and handle operations (Rosenzweig et al., 2025). In fiercely competitive environments, hospitality organizations focus on profit, occupancy, and service speed (Aukhoon et al., 2024). Consequently, CSR is offered as a plug-in and is relegated to promotional use (Latan et al., 2022). When managers do not model CSR behaviors or when ethical conduct remains unchecked, employees receive a mixed message about organizations' CSR focus (Shin & Jang, 2025).

### 5.3. Managerial and leadership limitations

Although leadership commitment is fundamental to CSR implementation, hospitality managers are motivated and trained to push CSR forward (Rosenzweig et al., 2025). Thus, middle managers are key players in policy communication and employee motivation processes. However, their chief workload and most performance evaluations are geared toward short-term operational goals, leaving little time and focus for longer-term social objectives (Abidin et al., 2025). Thus, this is due to managers' prevailing attitudes, which tend to see CSR as talking down to employees, demotivating them, and fostering disengagement (Zervoudi et al., 2025). The lack of explicit leadership role modeling (e.g., leading community efforts or other participative sustainability initiatives) leaves a leadership void that CSR messages fail to fill. Although headquarters may defend ambitious sustainability and CSR goals, local managers often lack the resources and contextual knowledge to carry them out (Zervoudi et al., 2025). This strategic-operational gap creates ambiguity, leading to disarray in employee understanding and execution.

## 5.4. Educational and cognitive barriers

Employees' appreciation and understanding of CSR depend on how much they are taught and trained on it (Loos & Spraul, 2025). Unfortunately, CSR training is still patchy or absent in tourism and hospitality organizations in developing economies (Srivastava et al., 2025). Frontline employees might not appreciate the social and environmental consequences of their behaviors (Appe & Papyan, 2025). Furthermore, CSR is a complex concept involving abstract and remote issues (e.g., ethical governance, stakeholder relations, and environmental issues) (Latan et al., 2022). For example, housekeepers may not perceive their activities as contributing to achieving environmental targets, or restaurant employees may not appreciate social values of local sourcing (Appe & Papyan, 2025). Complex language is one barrier, and the use of CSR visuals and social games can improve the situation (Loos & Spraul, 2025). Instructors should use social games rather than classroom training to embed and reinforce CSR principles (Appe & Papyan, 2025).

## 5.5. Economic and resource constraints

Financial and resource constraints are serious obstacles to implementing CSR initiatives among small- and medium-sized tourism enterprises (Trupp et al., 2025). Unlike large hotel chains, small, locally situated organizations operate on limited budgets and prioritize immediate survival over long-term sustainability (Zervoudi et al., 2025). Hence, CSR efforts (e.g., environmental audits, community engagement, or simple activities) for employee training are often dismissed as unnecessary costs (Montañés-Del Río et al., 2025). When managers see CSR values, insufficient finances usually make training, purchasing sustainable resources, and allocating funds to pay volunteers unrealistic (Ni et al., 2024). This lack of investment fuels low CSR investment, reduces future willingness to invest, weakens and misinforms CSR awareness, and leads to poor performance (Trupp et al., 2025). While some constraints may be loosened through government subsidies and industry collaboration via grants, tax subsidies, and joint training initiatives (Ni et al., 2024), the lack of these means organizations will continue to operate with misinformation about CSR activities available to them in this industry (Montañés-Del Río et al., 2025).

## 5.6. Cultural and contextual factors

Given the global diversity of the hospitality workforce, understanding CSR will differ. Employees with diverse national, religious, and societal orientations may have divergent views on responsibility, ethics, and sustainability (Zervoudi et al., 2025). For instance, collectivist societies may lean towards collective responsibility, emphasizing community, whereas individualist cultures are likely to emphasize individual responsibility (Yang et al., 2024). In some cultures, CSR practices are donation-based philanthropy toward local nonprofits or charities and post-disaster giving (Appe & Papyan, 2025). This limited view of CSR misses its full potential to implement operational-level changes or improve environmental aspects of management (Meng et al., 2024).

Hospitality and tourism contexts have unique challenges in using temporary or migrant employees. Such employees may receive little to no orientation, making it difficult for them to align with organizations' long-term CSR vision and contributing to disengagement (Appe & Papyan, 2025). In certain cultures, there is a tendency toward hierarchical systems that mute employee voice in providing feedback on CSR, hindering constructive bottom-up change (Turčinović et al., 2025). Culturally sensitive and inclusive CSR strategies offer a better chance of success (Shahzadi et al., 2024). Stakeholders will appreciate efforts if CSR goals are set in locally meaningful, attainable scopes that involve shared moral constructs (e.g., stewardship and environmental care) (Meng et al., 2024).

## 5.7. Psychological and motivational barriers

Employees may see CSR initiatives as trivial to their jobs when they fail to form a personal attachment to CSR goals (Abdelraouf & Muharram, 2024). Employee motivation may dwindle when employees think their efforts are small to change hotels' footprints (Meng et al., 2024). Psychological barriers are present in organizations where hypocrisy governs behaviors (Shahzadi et al., 2024). When hotels preach CSR values, employees develop cynical attitudes, while exploitative practices, wastefulness, and profit-driven behaviors predominate (Ni et al., 2024). Distrust and crumbling trust bypass CSR efforts when cynicism governs employee attitudes (Meng et al., 2024). Thus, authentic alignment of words and actions sustains employee beliefs in CSR.

## 5.8. Regulatory and institutional barriers

External institutional factors influence the cultivation of CSR awareness (Nguyen et al., 2025), which is more prevalent in developing economies. In such economies, the absence of strong regulatory frameworks and enforcement leads to inconsistent and sporadic CSR practices (Kumar, 2024). Without clear national guidelines and industry standards, hospitality organizations lack benchmarks to frame CSR training and evaluation (Appe & Papyan, 2025). Moreover, tourism ministries and hotel associations seem more concerned with economic bottom lines (i.e., the number of visitors and jobs created) than with social and environmental impacts (Kumar, 2024). This institutional effect discourages organizations from investing in CSR development among their employees (Ni et al., 2024). Thus, this is compounded by the lack of collaboration between the tourism and hospitality industries, which limits progress in several countries. A lack of CSR literacy and sustainability management in hospitality programs means that graduates entering workplaces cannot be CSR champions (Kumar, 2024). This lack of alignment of institutional policies with education and industry incentives underscores the importance of systemic CSR integration.

# 6. EMPIRICAL EVIDENCE AND CASE STUDIES

## 6.1. The value of empirical insight

The tourism and hospitality workforce needs an explanation beyond frameworks to understand CSR awareness (Khatter, 2025). There have been various attempts to understand and implement CSR policies and employee awareness initiatives, with varying levels of success (Abdelraouf & Muharram, 2024). This part of the document integrates findings from the academic and professional literature on CSR awareness in tourism and hospitality organizations to explain and exemplify fostering, implementing, and evaluating (Khatter, 2025). Using international hotel chains and small local businesses as comparative cases, it identifies success factors, obstacles, and lessons that reconcile policy with practice (Nguyen et al., 2025).

## 6.2. Case Study 1: Marriott international's "spirit to serve" initiative

Marriott International's philosophy of CSR integrates the spirit to serve initiative, which is considered one of the most comprehensive frameworks in the hospitality industry relating employee engagement to community impact (Nguyen et al., 2025).

This initiative has five pillars (e.g., empathy for communities, environmental stewardship, ethical business, diversity, and employee well-being). Integrating CSR awareness takes place at the organizational level through training, internal communications, and leadership engagement (Khatter, 2025). During onboarding, organizations lay out expectations for sustainable workplace practices, volunteerism, and ethical decision-making in regular training (Abdelraouf & Muharram, 2024). The Serve360 internal portal is a repository that employees can access to gather CSR information and resources and record volunteering hours (Baker, 2024). Marriott employees reported participating in community and environmental sustainability programs in 2022 at 82%—self-report and survey data on job and employee engagement in CSR efforts (Ni et al., 2024). Employees with CSR responsibilities and participation showed increased workplace satisfaction, decreased turnover, and greater alignment with organizational mission and objectives (Nguyen et al., 2025). Initiatives capture community spirits, organizational engagement, and employee motivation.

## 6.3. Case Study 2: Accor Group and the "Planet 21" program

Accor Hotels has instituted the "Planet 21" sustainability initiative as another instructive example of large-scale CSR strategy implementation across organizations' globally diversified facilities (Abdelraouf & Muharram, 2024). Initially launched in 2011 and later renamed Planet 21, the initiative revolves around net-zero emissions by 2050 and includes four constituent pillars (e.g., employees, customers, partners, and communities) (Baker, 2024). Accor sustains CSR commitment through employee competitions, strategic training, and employee-led initiatives, as exemplified by green stars recognition programs, incentivizing hotels to surpass set sustainability benchmarks. Employees in lower operational roles felt less empowered to shape CSR decisions. While improved awareness is a positive development, results suggest that structural issues hinder participative implementation (Abdelraouf & Muharram, 2024). Thus, this echoes the top-down communications of CSR literature as a strategic mandate in multinational organizations. Accor demonstrates the importance of democratizing CSR awareness (Baker, 2024). While employee recognition fosters civic knowledge, awareness must be coupled with CSR empowerment systems (e.g., participative committees or CSR ambassadors) to realize the changes employees seek (Nguyen et al., 2025).

## 6.4. Case Study 3: Hilton Worldwide's "travel with purpose" strategy

Hilton focuses its CSR strategy under the travel with purpose strategy, incorporating environmental and social governance goals into the organization's operational culture and daily activities (Bernacchio et al., 2024). Such organizations achieve a 75% reduction in carbon intensity and a 50% reduction in water consumption by 2030 (Silva, 2024). They also promote global youth employability and community resilience. Storytelling and a data-driven approach to CSR awareness are unparalleled (Khatter, 2025). Hilton's 2023 sustainability report states that properties where employees exhibited higher CSR awareness experienced 28% greater waste reduction and 15% higher guest satisfaction than properties with lower employee awareness (Silva, 2024). Hilton demonstrates the impact of data visibility and feedback on reinforcing CSR awareness (Abdelraouf & Muharram, 2024). When Hilton combines operational and emotional incentives with CSR metrics, it fosters shared responsibilities and intent cultures (Khatter, 2025).

## 6.5. Case Study 4: Sustainable tourism in Kerala, India

In Kerala, India, a responsible tourism mission implemented in 2008 aimed to connect local community members with tourism enterprises (Markose et al., 2022) while ensuring ethical, social, and economic linkages and environmental responsibility (Yang et al., 2024). As such, responsible tourism frameworks require hotels and tour operators to buy local, employ community members, and support activities that preserve culture (Baker, 2024). Local awareness campaigns include community workshops, school awareness programs, and sector training activities (Markose et al., 2022). Most importantly, the responsibility for social awareness campaigns extends beyond employees to community members, reinforcing social responsibility within broader tourism frameworks (Yang et al., 2024). About 70% of hospitality employees claimed a stronger sense of community, while 62% reported increased pride in their workplaces (Abdelraouf & Muharram, 2024). Moreover, customer satisfaction surveys reported greater appreciation for the authenticity and sustainability of the offered services (Markose et al., 2022). Local culture, policy enforcement, and learning frameworks fostered an environment where CSR is integrated into tourism businesses (Latan et al., 2022).

## 6.6. Case Study 5: Egyptian hospitality enterprises and CSR awareness challenges

Egypt's tourism and hospitality sectors have seen a gradual increase in the implementation of CSR initiatives, driven by governments, international stakeholders, and educational advancements (ElBelehy & Crispim, 2025). In Egypt, major hotels (e.g., Four Seasons and Mövenpick) have no issue implementing international CSR standards (Abdelraouf & Muharram, 2024). However, local businesses face challenges when implementing these practices and policies (Yang et al., 2024). This chapter found moderate awareness, though it varied substantially across departments. Front office and management better understood CSR than housekeeping and food and beverage departments (Abdelraouf & Muharram, 2024). Primary challenges included the lack of structured training, limited information flow from managers, and weak integration of CSR into daily activities (Dawar & Singh, 2023).

Most employees viewed CSR as a form of marketing and a value to be practiced throughout workplaces (Yang et al., 2024). Hotels that incorporated CSR within operational performance metrics (e.g., community service hours and other social value metrics) experienced higher employee engagement and more positive service cultures (Dawar & Singh, 2023). To raise CSR awareness in the Egyptian hospitality industry, employee training should be more focused and reflect Egypt's Vision 2030 (ElBelehy & Crispim, 2025). CSR activities should be seen as business responsibilities and social and ethical obligations that are part of Egyptian traditions of hospitality and communities (Abdelraouf & Muharram, 2024).

### 6.7. Synthesis and key insights

Social responsibility starts with understanding within business communities and there are reasons to conclude that most CSR practices work best in socially responsible businesses. The shift from strategy to employees engages several factors: leader veracity, internal relations, directive training, and local cultural cohesion. The best organizations understand that CSR in awareness is not compliance and learn to reframe their organizations as active co-creators of social values. Additionally, CSR awareness enhances the social atmosphere in hospitality workplaces and strengthens inclusion, empathy, and service excellence.

## 7. MANAGERIAL AND POLICY IMPLICATIONS

Implementing CSR policies in the tourism and hospitality industry is crucial to managers, policymakers, and other stakeholders. Increasing the workforce's CSR awareness should be an opportunity to integrate it into the foundation of organizations' operations and strategy. To realize the full potential, stakeholders' proactive engagement is needed to convert theory into tangible and consistent actions. This part continues to describe the implications of CSR awareness for managers and policy stakeholders, focusing on the strategic, operational, and regulatory levels necessary to maintain responsible tourism and hospitality growth.

## 7.1. Strategic implications

Managers can shift the business view of CSR from an afterthought to a strategic differentiator. CSR can be a vital business component because it generates positive outcomes in employee retention, brand value, and customer satisfaction. Organizations can achieve strategic CSR by integrating positive social and environmental impacts with the business's core purpose and goals for creating value. The first step in strategic alignment is integrating CSR goals into the mission, vision, and strategic pillars of tourism and hospitality businesses. Managers can adopt larger or international CSR guidelines, such as the UN SDGs, and align them with target communities. For example, hotels operating in urbanized and ecologically sensitive areas should focus on drastically different targets, the former on employment and fair job opportunities, waste reduction, sustainable water use, and biodiversity conservation.

Managers must recognize and involve key stakeholders (e.g., employees, customers, suppliers, and community members). Sponsored stakeholder conversations help determine potential problems, evaluate and reassess CSR during specified periods, and continuously adjust and refine strategies. Furthermore, encouraging employees to participate in CSR activities promotes a strong feeling of ownership and purpose, boosting morale and productivity. Organizations can defend against fluctuating markets and regulatory change risks by innovating in local sourcing, energy-efficient designs, and digital guest engagement platforms.

## 7.2. Operational implications for organizational practice

Embedding CSR consciousness at the operational level requires translating this awareness into cohesive actions that employees can absorb and practice. Thus, this entails incorporating, embedding, and institutionalizing CSR into internal organizational policies, doctrine, training, and operational performance metrics. The primary division responsible for incorporating CSR into training doctrine and organizational recruitment processes (i.e., acquiring employees with sustainability mindsets, ethics, and community engagement at environmental levels) is HRM. For instance, employee incentivization is linked to CSR performance, and incorporating CSR training into organizational performance paradigms encourages employees to perceive and practice responsible behaviors as operational imperatives. Accordingly, internal communication systems should be omnidirectional to convey the organization's CSR vision to hierarchical levels. Organizations motivated to advocate for CSR are within employees' reach, and involvement systems. From a prepositional perspective, employees should be motivated to act as CSR ambassadors. CSR metrics will need to track the social, environmental, and economic dimensions (e.g., carbon footprints, civic engagement, volunteer hours, and supplier diversity).

## 7.3. Policy implications for governments and industry associations

Governments and tourism industry associations are critical in changing CSR from a voluntary to an accepted cultural practice. Implemented policies should encourage responsible practice while not being overly burdensome to businesses. Voluntary compliance may be initiated through tax benefits or certification perks for hotels deemed CSR compliant. Collaborative community development, environmental conservation, and cultural heritage projects may help close the gap between public-sector desired outcomes and the private sector's potential contributions. These partnerships and shared responsibility improve the effectiveness of policies and provide mechanisms for shared accountability. Governments are increasing CSR awareness by providing training for SMEs, which often lack the financial or technical means to implement robust CSR policies and practices (Abdelraouf & Muharram, 2024). Training workshops and toolkits, supported by tiered grants in tourism, should motivate local businesspeople to meet responsible tourism standards. In addition, CSR benchmarking and award systems for hotel federations and tourism councils are also an industry-initiated means of improving CSR practice. Standardized CSR guidelines for specific nations and the setting of benchmarks will aid cohesion and comparability among disparate organizations.

## 7.4. Implications for educational institutions and professional development

Education and ongoing training are essential to the lasting impact of CSR awareness in the hospitality industry. Schools should integrate CSR education into the tourism and hospitality program verticals, including vocational training and postgraduate programs. Instruction should cover the ethical dimensions of decision-making, environmental concerns, social equity, inclusion issues, and stakeholder relations in management and control. CSR initiatives and challenges in communities can provide opportunities for applied research through stronger university-industry partnerships. Universities can innovative CSR by organizing case competitions on social tourism, social entrepreneurship, and CSR-driven tourism laboratories. These innovations prepare responsible management graduates. There should also be investments in on-the-job training and CSR skill-strengthening programs (e.g., sustainability auditing and ethical procurement) to meet the ongoing training needed to build responsible management in hospitality employees.

## 7.5. Implications for global competitiveness and destination branding

On the macro level, CSR awareness improves the global competitiveness of tourism destinations. Ethically responsible and environmentally conscious countries are increasingly capturing a larger share of the vessel tourism market from conscious and eco-friendly travelers. By applying CSR to destination branding, tourism boards can help national offerings stand out in an oversaturated global marketplace. For instance, Egypt's position as a sustainable cultural tourism destination could market CSR through sustainable heritage preservation, fair-trade artisanal products, and promises of employment for the local community. Through CSR, Gulf countries investing in green hospitality will likely achieve economic diversification and environmental responsibility. From a business perspective, hotels and travel organizations with open and honest CSR declarations hold strong partnerships with global tour operators, investors, and NGOs.

## 7.6. Ethical and cultural considerations

Understanding CSR awareness entails examining the ethical and cultural dimensions of the hospitality and tourism sectors. CSR perceptions and interpretations vary across cultures. Hospitality, community support, and stewardship may coincide with cultural and religious traditions. Therefore, CSR practitioners must be attentive to cultural ethics of their CSR strategy surroundings. When CSR activities and programs are grounded in cultural frameworks, they are more likely to be embraced. In MENA countries, CSR concepts integrate charity (zakat) and social coherence. In some Asian countries, stewardship and sustainability traditions are associated with ideals of harmony and respect for nature.

# 8. CONCLUSION

Understanding CSR in the tourism and hospitality industry involves shifting from the discourse of policy to practice. The alignment between organizations' goals and social responsibility strengthens the industry's moral legitimacy and ensures its viability amid ethical consumerism and pressing environmental concerns. This chapter has shown that CSR, in the proper sense and integrated, goes beyond the legal minimalism of compliance and closes the gap in strategic and operational innovation and global competitiveness. Employee awareness closes this gap, having a key position in transforming abstract policy into practical implementation.

To a great extent, the future of the tourism and hospitality industry will depend on professionals who see and practice CSR as a central component of the industry.

## REFERENCES


Abdelraouf, M., & Muharram, F. (2024). The Impact of Servant Leadership on Corporate Social Responsibility: Insights from Egyptian Tourism Organizations. *Journal of Advanced Research in Leadership*, *3*(1), 19–43. DOI: 10.33422/jarl.v3i1.701

Abidin, Z., Jalal, J., & Sodiq, A. (2025). The five tiers of corporate social responsibility (CSR): From risk management to social business. *Social Responsibility Journal*, *21*(5), 940–961. DOI: 10.1108/SRJ-03-2023-0146

Akbari, M., Halibas, A., Nguyen, H. M., & Panchal, J. (2025). Sustainable Supply Chains: Implications for Tourists and Residents in Tropical Destinations. In The Business of Low-Carbon Tourism (pp. 120-135). Routledge.

Alsheyab, M., Filimon, N., & Fusté-Forné, F. (2024). CSR practices in small and medium-sized accommodations and their impact on the local communities. *International Studies of Management & Organization*, *54*(4), 329–357. DOI: 10.1080/00208825.2024.2361204

Alshukri, T., Seun Ojekemi, O., Öz, T., & Alzubi, A. (2024). The interplay of corporate social responsibility, innovation capability, organizational learning, and sustainable value creation: Does stakeholder engagement matter? *Sustainability (Basel)*, *16*(13), 5511. DOI: 10.3390/su16135511

Appe, S., & Papyan, S. (2025). How and why do diaspora give? A conceptual model to understanding diaspora philanthropy. *Nonprofit and Voluntary Sector Quarterly*, *54*(3), 518–546. DOI: 10.1177/08997640241275098

Ashurov, S., Musse, O. S. H., & Abdelhak, T. (2024). Evaluating corporate social responsibility in achieving sustainable development and social welfare. *BRICS Journal of Economics*, *5*(2), 77–102. DOI: 10.3897/brics-econ.5.e121429

Aukhoon, M. A., Iqbal, J., & Parray, Z. A. (2024). Impact of corporate social responsibility on employee green behavior: Role of green human resource management practices and employee green culture. *Corporate Social Responsibility and Environmental Management*, *31*(5), 3768–3778. DOI: 10.1002/csr.2773

Awa, H. O., Etim, W., & Ogbonda, E. (2024). Stakeholders, stakeholder theory and corporate social responsibility (CSR). *International Journal of Corporate Social Responsibility*, *9*(1), 11. DOI: 10.1186/s40991-024-00094-y

Baah, C., Agyabeng-Mensah, Y., Afum, E., & Lascano Armas, J. A. (2024). Exploring corporate environmental ethics and green creativity as antecedents of green competitive advantage, sustainable production and financial performance: Empirical evidence from manufacturing firms. *Benchmarking*, *31*(3), 990–1008. DOI: 10.1108/BIJ-06-2022-0352

Baena, V., & Cerviño, J. (2024). Tourism in the Era of Social Responsibility and Sustainability: Understanding International Tourists' Destination Choices. *Sustainability (Basel)*, *16*(19), 8509. DOI: 10.3390/su16198509

Baker, M. A. (2024). Sustainable tourism employment: A comprehensive overview of tourism employees' experience from a tourist-employee interaction perspective. *Journal of Hospitality and Tourism Management*, *60*, 228–238. DOI: 10.1016/j.jhtm.2024.07.009

Bernacchio, C., Foss, N. J., & Lindenberg, S. (2024). The virtues of joint production: Ethical foundations for collaborative organizations. *Academy of Management Review*, *49*(1), 155–181. DOI: 10.5465/amr.2019.0389

Birinci, H., Esenyel, I., & Obeng, H. A. (2025). Sustainable destination management in luxury tourism: Balancing economic development and environmental responsibility. *Sustainability (Basel)*, *17*(15), 6815. DOI: 10.3390/su17156815

Bux, H., Zhang, Z., & Ali, A. (2024). Corporate social responsibility adoption for achieving economic, environmental, and social sustainability performance. *Environment, Development and Sustainability*, *28*(2), 1–31. DOI: 10.1007/s10668-024-05155-7

Carlini, J., & Grace, D. (2021). The corporate social responsibility (CSR) internal branding model: Aligning employees' CSR awareness, knowledge, and experience to deliver positive employee performance outcomes. *Journal of Marketing Management*, *37*(7-8), 732–760. DOI: 10.1080/0267257X.2020.1860113

Chauhan, N. (2025). Empowering communities and preserving heritage: Case studies on socially responsible travel through fair trade tourism. In Meaningful Tourism: Strategies and Future Development (pp. 163-182). Emerald Publishing Limited.

Chen, Q., Jiang, F., Guo, Y., Shrestha, R. K., & Zhang, Q. (2025). Community attachment, emotional solidarity, and sustainable tourism support: Evidence from Sagarmatha national park, Nepal. *Sustainable Development (Bradford)*, *33*(3), 4492–4510. DOI: 10.1002/sd.3360

Chiang, T. Y. (2024). Analysis of Responsible Tourism Practices in the Wake of COVID-19: Data Mining Approach. In Advances in Hospitality and Leisure, Volume 20 (pp. 23-40). Emerald Publishing Limited.

Choi, M., & Choi, Y. (2021). Employee perceptions of hotel CSR activities during the COVID-19 pandemic. *International Journal of Contemporary Hospitality Management, 33*(10), 3355–3378. DOI: 10.1108/IJCHM-03-2021-0289

Chung, S., & Day, J. (2024). Fair Tourism in South Korea: An Examination of Sustainable Supply Chain Management for Tourism. *Tourism and Hospitality, 5*(4), 1493–1509. DOI: 10.3390/tourhosp5040083

Cosa, M. (2024). Equity integration in corporate social responsibility: Analyzing stakeholder, legitimacy, and social activism dynamics. In *CSR, Governance and Value* (pp. 133–154). Springer Nature Singapore. DOI: 10.1007/978-981-97-4795-5_6

Czichos, H., Alshebami, A. S., Shepperson, L., & Foldager, U. (2025). Greening the workplace: How sustainable practices drive employee engagement. In *The Sustainability Handbook* (Vol. 1, pp. 699–710). Elsevier.

Dawar, G., & Singh, S. (2023). Barriers to corporate social responsibility implementation in the medium size manufacturing sector: An interpretive structure modelling approach. *Journal of Entrepreneurship in Emerging Economies, 15*(2), 447–479. DOI: 10.1108/JEEE-12-2020-0451

Dhingra, N. (2025). Sustainable Food and Beverage Options for Tourists. In Greener Future: Building Sustainable Tourism Communities (pp. 197-208). Emerald Publishing Limited. DOI: 10.1108/978-1-83608-988-920251013

Dong, C., Zhang, Y., & Ao, S. (2024). How to engage employees in corporate social responsibility? Exploring corporate social responsibility communication effects through the reasoned action approach. *Management Communication Quarterly, 38*(1), 27–59. DOI: 10.1177/08933189231161621

Duan, W., Xue, X., Chen, Z., & Liu, L. (2025). How do institutional pressures influence corporate social responsibility?—A perspective based on state-owned enterprises. *Information Technology Management*, •••, 1–15.

Đurić, Z., Cvijanović, D., Petek, V., & Potočnik Topler, J. (2025). Sustainability struggle: Challenges and issues in managing sustainability and environmental protection in local tourism destinations practices—An overview. *Sustainability (Basel), 17*(15), 7134. DOI: 10.3390/su17157134

ElBelehy, C., & Crispim, J. (2025). Social sustainability in Egypt hospitality and tourism supply chains. *Business and Society Review, 130*(S1), 222–262. DOI: 10.1111/basr.12337

Faeni, D. P., Oktaviani, R. F., Riyadh, H. A., Faeni, R. P., & Beshr, B. A. H. (2025). Green human resource management (GHRM) and corporate social responsibility (CSR) in reducing carbon emissions for sustainable practices. *Environmental Quality Management, 34*(3), e70048. DOI: 10.1002/tqem.70048

Ferrero-Ferrero, I., Muñoz-Torres, M. J., Rivera-Lirio, J. M., Escrig-Olmedo, E., & Fernández-Izquierdo, M. Á. (2024). Sustainable development goals in the hospitality industry: A dream or reality? *Journal of Accounting & Organizational Change, 20*(5), 773–796. DOI: 10.1108/JAOC-09-2022-0146

Gao, J., Zhang, Y., Xu, S., & Ma, E. (2025). Rethinking work-life integration: Empowering talent in emerging hospitality and tourism work paradigms. *International Journal of Contemporary Hospitality Management, 37*(5), 1765–1783. DOI: 10.1108/IJCHM-05-2024-0736

Garcia-Ortega, B., Catalá-Pérez, D., de-Miguel-Molina, B., & de-Miguel-Molina, M. (2024). Corporate Social Responsibility Challenges in the Mining Industry and ISO 26000. In *The Strategic Paradigm of CSR and Sustainability: A Public-Private Approach* (pp. 45–73). Springer Nature Switzerland. DOI: 10.1007/978-3-031-58889-1_3

Gidage, M., & Bhide, S. (2024). Corporate reputation as the nexus: Linking moral and social responsibility, green practices, and organizational performance. *Corporate Reputation Review*, •••, 1–23. DOI: 10.1057/s41299-024-00209-y

Guix, M., Sánchez, J. J. N., Priego, M. J. B., & Font, X. (2025). The changing institutional logics behind sustainability reports from the largest hotel groups in the world in 2014, 2018 and 2021. *Tourism Management, 106*, 105031. DOI: 10.1016/j.tourman.2024.105031

Gupta, S., Kushwaha, P. S., Badhera, U., & Singh, R. K. (2025). Managing tourism and hospitality industry during pandemic: Analysis of challenges and strategies for survival. *Benchmarking, 32*(4), 1360–1386. DOI: 10.1108/BIJ-11-2023-0806

Hallas, N. E. (2024). LEED certification and sustainable building practices: a comprehensive guide to efficient and sustainable facilities. In *Design Strategies for Efficient and Sustainable Building Facilities* (pp. 124–161). IGI Global. DOI: 10.4018/979-8-3693-3200-9.ch006

Hamdi, W. B., Aderibigbe, S. A., Idriz, M., & Alghfeli, M. M. (2024). Faith in humanity: Religious charitable organizations solidarity towards migrants in the United Arab Emirates. *Religions*, *15*(3), 266. DOI: 10.3390/rel15030266

Huang, M., Geng, S., Yang, W., Law, K. M., & He, Y. (2024). Going beyond the role: How employees' perception of corporate social responsibility fuels proactive customer service performance. *Journal of Retailing and Consumer Services*, *76*, 103565. DOI: 10.1016/j.jretconser.2023.103565

Jiang, S., Bibi, S., Lyu, J., Khan, A., & Li, Z. (2025). Corporate social responsibility needs base philosophy: An integrative multidimensional approach to hospitality employees' green innovative behaviors. *International Journal of Hospitality Management*, *124*, 103943. DOI: 10.1016/j.ijhm.2024.103943

Jing, W., & Loang, O. K. (2024). China's cultural tourism: Strategies for authentic experiences and enhanced visitor satisfaction. *International Journal of Business and Technology Management*, *6*(1), 566–575.

Kalefa, H., & Gado, S. (2024). Enhancing hotel sustainability through ecological and technological integration. JES. *Journal of Engineering Sciences*, *52*(1), 145–174.

Kandpal, V., Jaswal, A., Santibanez Gonzalez, E. D., & Agarwal, N. (2024). Corporate social responsibility (CSR) and ESG reporting: redefining business in the twenty-first century. In *Sustainable energy transition: Circular economy and sustainable financing for environmental, social and governance (ESG) practices* (pp. 239–272). Springer Nature Switzerland. DOI: 10.1007/978-3-031-52943-6_8

Khalil, N., Che Abdullah, S. N., Haron, S. N., & Hamid, M. Y. (2024). A review of green practices and initiatives from stakeholder's perspectives towards sustainable hotel operations and performance impact. *Journal of Facilities Management*, *22*(4), 653–682. DOI: 10.1108/JFM-03-2022-0025

Khan, M. I., & Iqbal, A. (2024). Integrating ESG with corporate investment decision-making. In *The Emerald Handbook of Ethical Finance and Corporate Social Responsibility: A Framework for Sustainable Development* (pp. 329–350). Emerald Publishing Limited. DOI: 10.1108/978-1-80455-406-720241014

Khater, M., Ibrahim, O., Sayed, M. N. E., & Faik, M. (2024). Legal frameworks for sustainable tourism: Balancing environmental conservation and economic development. *Current Issues in Tourism*, **•••**, 1–22.

Khatter, A. (2025). Challenges and Solutions for Corporate Social Responsibility in the Hospitality Industry. *Challenges*, *16*(1), 9. DOI: 10.3390/challe16010009

Kumar, S. (2024). Indian experience of CSR and corporate governance in the post-liberalised era. *The Indian Journal of Public Administration, 70*(4), 829–842. DOI: 10.1177/00195561241248338

Latan, H., Chiappetta Jabbour, C. J., Lopes de Sousa Jabbour, A. B., Ali, M., & Pereira, V. (2022). Career satisfaction in the public sector: Implications for a more sustainable and socially responsible human resource management. *Human Resource Management Journal, 32*(4), 844–863. DOI: 10.1111/1748-8583.12469

Lee, S., Hwang, D. H. S., Shin, M., & Kang, K. H. (2025). Strategic corporate social responsibility in the tourism and hospitality industry: Conceptual proposal. *Tourism Economics, 31*(5), 813–826. DOI: 10.1177/13548166241299140

Leigh, N. G. (2024). *Planning local economic development: Theory and practice.* SAGE publications.

Loos, C., & Spraul, K. (2025). The why, how, and when of CSR managers' internal legitimation strategies. *Journal of Management Studies, 62*(7), 2830–2858. DOI: 10.1111/joms.13145

Macaveiu, C. (2025). Promoting labour rights and human rights in hospitality: Striving for a workplace culture that disrupts exploitative practices. In *Tourism and Hospitality for Humanity* (pp. 157–176). Edward Elgar Publishing. DOI: 10.4337/9781035344307.00013

Magdy, A., & Salem, I. E. (2024). Understanding the impact of work environment on employee well-being and cynicism: Insights from the hotel industry. *Tourism and Hospitality Management, 30*(4), 531–542. DOI: 10.20867/thm.30.4.8

Mansoor, M., Jam, F. A., & Khan, T. I. (2025). Fostering eco-friendly behaviors in hospitality: Engaging customers through green practices, social influence, and personal dynamics. *International Journal of Contemporary Hospitality Management, 37*(5), 1804–1826. DOI: 10.1108/IJCHM-07-2024-1023

Markose, N., Vazhakkatte Tazhathethil, B., & George, B. (2022). Sustainability initiatives for green tourism development: The case of Wayanad, India. *Journal of Risk and Financial Management, 15*(2), 52. DOI: 10.3390/jrfm15020052

McCarty, W. (2024). International Business Membership With the United Nations Global Compact (Doctoral dissertation, The Chicago School of Professional Psychology).

Mdoda, S. S., Dube, K., & Montsiemang, T. (2024). Tackling Water and Waste Management Challenges Within the Tourism and Hospitality Industry: A Sustainable Development Goals Perspective. *Water (Basel), 16*(24), 3545. DOI: 10.3390/w16243545

Meng, Z., Bhatti, S. M., Naveed, R. T., Kanwal, S., & Adnan, M. (2024). Green sustainability in the hotel sector: The role of CSR, intrinsic green motivation, and personal environmental norms. *PLoS One, 19*(6), e0295850. DOI: 10.1371/journal.pone.0295850 PMID: 38935798

Mensah, C., Azila-Gbettor, E. M., Novieto, D. T., Coffie, G. H., & Adzivor, E. K. (2025). Tracing the evolution of environmental practices research in the hotel industry: A mixed-review perspective. *Research in Hospitality Management, 15*(2), 171–191. DOI: 10.1080/22243534.2025.2483753

Montañés-Del Río, M. Á., Rodríguez-Cornejo, V., Rodríguez-Castro, P. I., & Herrera-Madueño, J. (2025). The Implementation of Corporate Social Responsibility Policies in the Tourism Industry and Sustainable Development Goals: A Review of Progress, Challenges, and Opportunities. *Sustainability (Basel), 17*(13), 6044. DOI: 10.3390/su17136044

Moscariello, N., Pizzo, M., Ricciardi, G., Mallardo, G., & Fattorusso, P. (2024). The anti-corruption compliance models in a multinational company: A single case study. *Business Strategy and the Environment, 33*(1), 70–80. DOI: 10.1002/bse.3331

Moyeen, A., & Mehjabeen, M. (2024). CSR research in the hotel industry: How it relates to promoting the SDGs. *Social Responsibility Journal, 20*(9), 1770–1786. DOI: 10.1108/SRJ-01-2024-0032

Murtaza, S. H., Khan, A., & Mustafa, S. M. (2024). Eco-centric success: Stakeholder approaches to sustainable performance via green improvisation behavior and environmental orientation in the hotel industry. *Business Strategy and the Environment, 33*(7), 7273–7286. DOI: 10.1002/bse.3860

Nguyen, K. H., Trinh, A. T., Tran, M. D., & Duong, T. T. T. (2025). Uncovering the Evolution of Brand Transparency in Corporate Social Responsibility: A Holistic Perspective. *Corporate Social Responsibility and Environmental Management, 32*(6), 1–20. DOI: 10.1002/csr.70099

Ni, H., Liu, W., & Yang, Z. (2024). Training investment, human capital upgrading and firm innovation: The role of government training subsidies. *Kybernetes, 53*(9), 2934–2966. DOI: 10.1108/K-11-2022-1617

Nogueira, E., Gomes, S., & Lopes, J. M. (2025). Unveiling triple bottom line's influence on business performance. *Discover Sustainability*, *6*(1), 43. DOI: 10.1007/s43621-025-00804-x

Onyekwelu, N. P., Ezeafulukwe, C., Owolabi, O. R., Asuzu, O. F., Bello, B. G., & Onyekwelu, S. C. (2024). Ethics and corporate social responsibility in HR: A comprehensive review of policies and practices. *International Journal of Science and Research Archive*, *11*(1), 1294–1303. DOI: 10.30574/ijsra.2024.11.1.0216

Pai, C. H., Zhang, Y., Wang, Y. L., Li, K., & Shang, Y. (2025). Current challenges and opportunities in cultural heritage preservation through sustainable tourism practices. *Current Issues in Tourism*, •••, 1–19.

Panke, D., & Stapel, S. (2024). Cooperation between international organizations: Demand, supply, and restraint. *The Review of International Organizations*, *19*(2), 269–305. DOI: 10.1007/s11558-023-09506-3

Papafloratos, T., Pantazi, T., & Vlachos, V. (2025). CSR reporting in tourism: The case of the Greek hospitality industry. *International Journal of Knowledge Management in Tourism and Hospitality*, *4*(1), 1–16. DOI: 10.1504/IJKMTH.2025.145026

Papallou, E., Katafygiotou, M., & Dimopoulos, T. (2024). Emerging sustainability trends in tourist facilities: A comparative assessment of multiple hotels and resorts. *Sustainability (Basel)*, *16*(9), 3536. DOI: 10.3390/su16093536

Park, K., & Rim, H. (2025). Publics' Expectation Toward Ethical Leadership and Ethical Corporate Social Responsibility (CSR): Evidence From the US and South Korea. *Business Ethics, the Environment & Responsibility*, *34*(4), 1998–2012. DOI: 10.1111/beer.12749

Pásková, M., & Zelenka, J. (2024). Social responsibility in tourism and its specific features. In *Social Responsibility in Tourism: Applications, Best-Practices, and Case Studies* (pp. 85–135). Springer Nature Switzerland. DOI: 10.1007/978-3-031-61609-9_4

Peng, C., & Liu, P. (2025). How and when does customer mistreatment occur? Testing the predictive effect of future focus through construal-level theory. *International Journal of Contemporary Hospitality Management*, *37*(10), 3491–3517. DOI: 10.1108/IJCHM-12-2024-1936

Pourtaheri, M., Torabi, Z. A., Khavarian-Garmsir, A. R., Sajadi, S., & Hall, C. M. (2024). Ecolodge Tourism Dynamics: A Village-Level Analysis of Marketing and Policy Indicators in Iran's Hawraman Region. *Sustainability (Basel)*, *16*(12), 5072. DOI: 10.3390/su16125072

Qin, Y. S., & Men, L. R. (2023). Exploring the impact of internal communication on employee psychological well-being during the COVID-19 pandemic: The mediating role of employee organizational trust. *International Journal of Business Communication*, *60*(4), 1197–1219. DOI: 10.1177/23294884221081838

Rahman, M. M., Razimi, M. S. A., Ariffin, A. S., & Hashim, N. (2024). Navigating moral landscape: Islamic ethical choices and sustainability in Halal meat production and consumption. *Discover Sustainability*, *5*(1), 225. DOI: 10.1007/s43621-024-00388-y

Ramos Farroñán, E. V., Farfán Chilicaus, G. C., Cruz Salinas, L. E., Correa Rojas, L., Chuquitucto Cotrina, L. K., Licapa-Redolfo, G. S., Vera Zelada, P., & Vera Zelada, L. A. (2025). Green Finance and the Energy Transition: A Systematic Review of Economic Instruments for Renewable Energy Deployment in Emerging Economies. *Energies*, *18*(17), 4560. DOI: 10.3390/en18174560

Ramsbottom, O., Duffy, M., O'dor, J., & Watts, J. (2025). Legal Responsibilities. In Responsible Strategic Thinking for Business and Society (pp. 204-221). Routledge. DOI: 10.4324/9781003475545-8

Reddy, K., & Sailesh, B. (2024). Cultural guardianship in tourism: Indigenous communities' quest for economic stability and identity preservation. *Journal of Environmental Management and Tourism*, *15*(2), 328. DOI: 10.14505/jemt.v15.2(74).08

Reimer, M., Haensse, L., & Lin-Hi, N. (2024). Internal change through external actions: The impact of external corporate social responsibility on employee readiness for change. *Journal of Organizational Change Management*, *37*(7), 1446–1468. DOI: 10.1108/JOCM-03-2024-0125

Resende, S., Monje-Amor, A., & Calvo, N. (2024). Enterprise risk management and firm performance: The mediating role of corporate social responsibility in the European Union region. *Corporate Social Responsibility and Environmental Management*, *31*(4), 2852–2864. DOI: 10.1002/csr.2719

Rezaei, M. (2025). Unlocking knowledge transfer dynamics across borders: Key drivers in international strategic alliances. *Journal of Knowledge Management*, *29*(8), 2497–2517. DOI: 10.1108/JKM-12-2023-1188

Rodrigues Coelho, F. I., Bizarrias, F. S., Rabechini Jr, R., Martens, C. D. P., & Martens, M. L. (2025). Strategic alignment and value optimization: Unveiling the critical role of project portfolio management for a flexible environment. *Global Journal of Flexible Systems Managment*, *26*(1), 209–224. DOI: 10.1007/s40171-024-00434-8

Rosenzweig, E. D., Kelley, K., & Bendoly, E. (2025). Diversity in frontline employee perceptions: Policies and procedures, training, and leadership as drivers of service equality. *Production and Operations Management*, *34*(3), 412–422. DOI: 10.1177/10591478241252150

Rusu, T. M., Odagiu, A., Pop, H., & Paulette, L. (2024). Sustainability performance reporting. *Sustainability (Basel)*, *16*(19), 8538. DOI: 10.3390/su16198538

Schaefer, S. D., Cunningham, P., Diehl, S., & Terlutter, R. (2024). Employees' positive perceptions of corporate social responsibility create beneficial outcomes for firms and their employees: Organizational pride as a mediator. *Corporate Social Responsibility and Environmental Management*, *31*(3), 2574–2587. DOI: 10.1002/csr.2699

Shahzadi, G., John, A., Qadeer, F., Jia, F., & Yan, J. (2024). CSR beyond symbolism: The importance of substantive attributions for employee CSR engagement. *Journal of Cleaner Production*, *436*, 140440. DOI: 10.1016/j.jclepro.2023.140440

Shin, H. W., & Jang, H. (2025). Overcoming barriers of corporate digital responsibility in the hospitality and tourism industry: A social identity perspective. *International Journal of Contemporary Hospitality Management*, *37*(11), 1–20. DOI: 10.1108/IJCHM-11-2024-1670

Silva, J. A. (2024). Corporate social responsibility (CSR) and sustainability in water supply: A systematic review. *Sustainability (Basel)*, *16*(8), 3183. DOI: 10.3390/su16083183

Sriraksa, A., Chaiyakot, P., & Luengchavanon, M. (2024). Sustainability in sustainability certifications in Thai hotel industry. *Edelweiss Applied Science and Technology*, *8*(6), 3150–3160. DOI: 10.55214/25768484.v8i6.2677

Srivastava, S., Agarwal, A., Madan, P., & Kautish, P. (2025). How do green CSR initiatives influence green employee engagement among tourism and hospitality employees? *Corporate Social Responsibility and Environmental Management*, *32*(1), 757–768. DOI: 10.1002/csr.2977

Tabatabaei, F., Oshriyeh, O., & Beldona, S. (2025). Towards sustainability: Exploring community involvement in tourism development. *Tourism Planning & Development*, *22*(4), 498–528. DOI: 10.1080/21568316.2024.2392788

Taheri, B., Olya, H., & Batat, W. (2024). Ethical consumption and climate change in hospitality and tourism: challenges, solutions, and prospects: Guest editorial. *International Journal of Contemporary Hospitality Management*, *36*(5), 1457–1466. DOI: 10.1108/IJCHM-05-2024-169

Tawiah, V., Samson, N., & Jatau, U. (2025). Local directors and corporate social responsibility activities of multinational companies in Africa. *Corporate Social Responsibility and Environmental Management, 32*(2), 1688–1697. DOI: 10.1002/csr.3028

Trupp, A., Salman, A., Stephenson, M. L., Chan, L. F., & Gan, J. E. (2025). A systematic review of challenges faced by Micro and small Enterprises in Tourism Destinations: Producing solutions through resilience building and sustainable development. *Tourism Planning & Development, 22*(3), 301–323. DOI: 10.1080/21568316.2024.2307970

Turčinović, M., Vujko, A., & Stanišić, N. (2025). Community-led sustainable tourism in rural areas: Enhancing wine tourism destination competitiveness and local empowerment. *Sustainability (Basel), 17*(7), 2878. DOI: 10.3390/su17072878

Uddin, M. M., Hasan, M., Hoque, S., Hossain, M. A., & Asauzzaman, A. S. M. (2024). Assessing sustainability reporting practice in accordance with the Global Reporting Initiative (G4) towards achieving sustainable development goals using artificial intelligence. Journal of Management Accounting. *Governance and Performance, 1*(1), 40–68. DOI: 10.63817/JMAGP.05.2024.002

Vávrová, J., Červová, L., Brandová, B., & Stolz-Römmermann, J. (2025). Does ownership structure influence sustainability? Evidence from Booking. com sustainability practices in hospitality. *Cogent Business & Management, 12*(1), 2540508. DOI: 10.1080/23311975.2025.2540508

von Weltzien Hoivik, H. (2025). Reflections on Business Ethics in Norway. In *Researching and Teaching Business Ethics in Europe: Developments, Challenges and Opportunities* (pp. 165–196). Springer Nature Switzerland. DOI: 10.1007/978-3-031-99320-6_10

Wirba, A. V. (2024). Corporate social responsibility (CSR): The role of government in promoting CSR. *Journal of the Knowledge Economy, 15*(2), 7428–7454. DOI: 10.1007/s13132-023-01185-0 PMID: 40479158

Wukich, J. J., Neuman, E. L., & Fogarty, T. J. (2024). Show me? Inspire me? Make me? An institutional theory exploration of social and environmental reporting practices. *Journal of Accounting & Organizational Change, 20*(4), 673–701. DOI: 10.1108/JAOC-01-2023-0013

Yang, Y., Yuan, Y., Liu, P., Wu, W., & Huo, C. (2024). Crucial to me and my society: How collectivist culture influences individual pro-environmental behavior through environmental values. *Journal of Cleaner Production, 454*, 142211. DOI: 10.1016/j.jclepro.2024.142211

Ye, J., Sotiriadis, M., Dimou, I., Shen, S., & Koufopoulos, D. (2025). Suggesting a tourism industry-specific environmental, social and corporate governance (ESG) reporting framework. *Tourism Management, 109*, 105156. DOI: 10.1016/j.tourman.2025.105156

Yikilmaz, I., Surucu, L., Maslakci, A., & Cetinkaya, B. (2025). Corporate Social Responsibility as a Driver of Business Innovation: The Mediating Role of Corporate Reputation on Employee Performance in the Hospitality Sector. *Systems, 13*(6), 475. DOI: 10.3390/systems13060475

Zamiri, M., & Esmaeili, A. (2024). Strategies, methods, and supports for developing skills within learning communities: A systematic review of the literature. *Administrative Sciences, 14*(9), 231. DOI: 10.3390/admsci14090231

Zervoudi, E. K., Moschos, N., & Christopoulos, A. G. (2025). From the corporate social responsibility (CSR) and the environmental, social and governance (ESG) criteria to the greenwashing phenomenon: A comprehensive literature review about the causes, consequences and solutions of the phenomenon with specific case studies. *Sustainability (Basel), 17*(5), 2222. DOI: 10.3390/su17052222

Zhao, H., Kloren-Garcia, M., & Rosenfield, Z. G. (2025). Recruitment and retention challenges for tourism and hospitality professionals: The case of a Swiss boutique hotel. *Worldwide Hospitality and Tourism Themes, 17*(6), 1–13. DOI: 10.1108/WHATT-04-2025-0160

Chapter 9

# From Biomimicry to Business Strategy: Leveraging Nature's Intelligence for Sustainable Competitive Advantage

**Swetha Thiruchanuru**
http://orcid.org/0000-0002-6745-3106
*Sri Sathya Sai Institute of Higher Learning, India*

**Jayachandra Bingi**
*Indian Institute of Information Technology Design and Manufacturing, India*

## ABSTRACT

*This conceptual chapter explores the convergence of biomimicry and strategic management by examining how nature-inspired solutions can foster sustainable competitive advantage. Using the VRIO framework (Value, Rarity, Imitability, Organization), it analyzes how bio-inspired design principles can be embedded into business models to enhance innovation, resilience, and resource efficiency. The chapter discusses that biomimicry, beyond being a design philosophy, represents a strategic capability, one that enables organizations to achieve ecological alignment and long-term sustainability in digital and AI-enabled industries. Drawing from interdisciplinary literature in innovation, sustainability, and organizational strategy, the study develops an integrative model linking bio-inspired thinking with dynamic capabilities and responsible innovation. The findings offer actionable insights for managers, educators, and policymakers on adopting nature's intelligence as a strategic compass for regenerative growth and ethical technological advancement.*

DOI: 10.4018/979-8-2600-3179-7.ch009

## INTRODUCTION

The accelerating convergence of sustainability imperatives, technological disruption, and ecological uncertainty has intensified the search for innovation models capable of balancing economic competitiveness with long-term environmental resilience. In this context, biomimicry, also known as bio-inspired innovation, has emerged as a transformative approach that draws on nature's evolutionary intelligence to address complex organizational and societal challenges. While existing literature predominantly examines biomimicry as a design methodology or sustainability-oriented technological practice, limited attention has been devoted to understanding biomimicry as a strategic capability capable of generating sustained competitive advantage.

This chapter addresses that gap by positioning biomimicry not merely as a product-development mechanism, but as an organizational capability that enhances innovation adaptability, knowledge integration, regenerative value creation, and strategic resilience. Integrating insights from the Resource-Based View (RBV), VRIO framework, Dynamic Capabilities Theory, Circular Economy, and Responsible Innovation perspectives, the chapter develops a conceptual foundation explaining how bio-inspired innovation contributes to long-term organizational competitiveness and sustainability.

The chapter further contributes to the emerging discourse on sustainable entrepreneurship by contextualizing biomimicry within India's evolving innovation ecosystem. Although India possesses extraordinary biodiversity, indigenous ecological knowledge, and a rapidly expanding entrepreneurial landscape, bio-inspired entrepreneurship remains underexplored within strategic management and innovation scholarship. Accordingly, this chapter examines the opportunities, barriers, ecosystem requirements, and strategic implications associated with bio-inspired innovation in the Indian context.

By synthesizing interdisciplinary literature and sector-specific applications, the chapter proposes that biomimicry functions as a knowledge integration mechanism that enables organizations to sense environmental shifts, seize emerging opportunities, and transform operational systems in alignment with sustainability imperatives. The chapter therefore advances the argument that nature-inspired innovation represents not only a technological pathway, but also a strategic logic for regenerative and responsible value creation in the Fourth Industrial Revolution.By imitating nature's time-tested patterns and strategies, bio-inspired innovation holds the potential to disrupt traditional industries and foster the development of cutting-edge products and services that are both efficient and environmentally friendly (Janine, 2015).

## LITERATURE REVIEW

The 21st century marks a significant era in which biology and technology are converging to drive innovation. Advances in fields such as artificial intelligence, biotechnology, and materials science have allowed innovators to study natural systems in greater detail and apply these principles to human challenges. For instance, the development of lightweight and durable materials inspired by spider silk, or the design of robotics modeled after insect movement, exemplifies this growing intersection. The Fourth Industrial Revolution (4IR), characterized by digital transformation, automation, and AI, has created a fertile environment for bio-inspired innovations to flourish. By leveraging biological principles, companies can create smarter, more sustainable products and services that align with the demands of Industry 4.0, thus fostering a new wave of entrepreneurship (Schwab, 2016)

India, with its dynamic start-up ecosystem, is poised to take advantage of bio-inspired innovation. The country's initiatives, such as Start-up India and Make in India, aim to promote entrepreneurship and technological innovation across sectors. However, bio-inspired innovation remains relatively underexplored within the Indian start-up landscape. With growing concerns about sustainability, climate change, and resource scarcity, bio-mimetic solutions can play a pivotal role in addressing these challenges while driving economic growth. India's biodiversity offers immense potential for bio-mimicry, providing a vast reservoir of natural designs and principles that can inspire innovation in sectors such as healthcare, clean energy, manufacturing, and agriculture. By integrating bio-inspired approaches, Indian start-ups have the opportunity to not only innovate but also contribute to global sustainability goals, making the country a leader in bio-mimetic entrepreneurship (Bhutia, 2016).

This review aims to explore the scope and potential of bio-inspired innovation in entrepreneurship, with a particular focus on its relevance to India's start-up ecosystem. Through an exhaustive literature review, this paper seeks to:

- Highlight the role of bio-inspired innovation in fostering disruptive entrepreneurship.
- Understand the successful global examples of bio-mimetic solutions and how they can be adapted to the Indian context.
- Discuss the barriers and challenges to adopting bio-inspired innovation in India and propose strategies for overcoming them.
- Identify future opportunities for bio-inspired start-ups in key sectors, such as healthcare, clean energy, and manufacturing.

Disruptive innovation is a concept introduced by Clayton Christensen, which refers to innovations that fundamentally transform industries by creating new markets or reshaping existing ones (Christensen et al., 2015). Unlike sustaining innovations that improve existing products or services incrementally, disruptive innovations initially target underserved or overlooked markets, offering simpler, more affordable solutions. These innovations often start by serving a niche audience but gradually evolve to displace established players as they gain broader market acceptance. A hallmark of disruptive innovation is its capacity to change industry dynamics by introducing products or services that significantly alter how consumers engage with technology or services (Schwab, 2016).

In recent decades, disruptive innovation has become synonymous with technological breakthroughs that democratize access to services and create entirely new consumer behaviors. Iconic examples include the transition from analog to digital photography, the rise of personal computing, and the global shift from traditional media to streaming platforms. These innovations initially gained traction by targeting overlooked market segments, eventually reshaping entire industries. As the world becomes increasingly interconnected through the digital transformation brought about by the Fourth Industrial Revolution, disruptive innovations continue to influence how companies and industries operate (Schwab, 2016).

Bio-inspired innovation, also known as bio-mimicry, represents a unique subset of disruptive innovation. It involves drawing inspiration from nature to develop new products, services, and processes that challenge conventional methods of problem-solving (Janine, 2015). While the core idea of bio-inspired innovation is not new, its application in modern industries has gained momentum due to advances in biotechnology, materials science, and digital engineering. Bio-mimicry leverages the evolutionary solutions that nature has developed over billions of years to address human challenges sustainably and efficiently.

The disruption caused by bio-inspired innovation lies in its ability to replace traditional industrial practices with more sustainable and cost-effective alternatives. By mimicking natural forms and processes, bio-inspired designs offer unique advantages, such as enhanced energy efficiency, reduced material consumption, and improved environmental sustainability. These innovations often address inefficiencies that established industries have overlooked or deemed unsolvable using conventional approaches. As a result, bio-inspired designs can create entirely new markets, just as traditional disruptive innovations do, by introducing novel solutions that outperform or completely replace existing technologies (Garvin, 2015).

A well-known example of bio-inspired disruptive innovation is the Japanese Shinkansen Bullet Train. The original train design produced a significant noise problem when it exited tunnels due to pressure changes. Engineers found a solution by studying the kingfisher bird, whose beak is perfectly shaped for diving into water with minimal splash. By redesigning the train's nose to resemble the kingfisher's beak, engineers were able to reduce noise, increase energy efficiency, and enhance speed by 10%, while using 15% less electricity (Singh, 2019). This innovative solution disrupted conventional engineering approaches by applying a bio-inspired design, ultimately transforming the transportation industry.

Another striking example is Velcro, an invention inspired by the tiny hooks on the surface of burdock burrs, which attach to animal fur. Developed in the 1940s, Velcro has since become a ubiquitous fastening solution across multiple industries, including fashion, aerospace, and healthcare. Velcro exemplifies how nature's simple yet effective mechanisms can disrupt entire industries by offering more efficient alternatives to traditional technologies (Dooley, 2014).

Human beings are deeply connected to the planet, forming an essential part of a vast ecosystem. Isolated actions that disregard this interconnectedness fail to recognize the broader environmental implications. Many of today's challenges, such as climate change, ocean pollution, and species extinction, could have been mitigated if humanity had integrated its activities more harmoniously with the environment. The Sustainable Development Goals (SDGs) offer a comprehensive framework for preserving the planet while fostering ecosystem prosperity. To meet these goals, innovative solutions are required—ones that shift perspectives to address real-world challenges with minimal environmental impact. In this context, the SDGs are encouraging the development of materials and technologies designed not only to reduce environmental and social harm but also to regenerate and restore ecological systems. (Aguilar-Planet & Peralta, 2024)

One of the most promising areas for bio-inspired disruptive innovation is energy and sustainability. In an era where industries are grappling with the challenges of climate change, resource scarcity, and environmental degradation, bio-inspired solutions offer a pathway to achieving sustainability without sacrificing performance. A prime example is the design of wind turbines inspired by the wing movements of hummingbirds. These bio-mimetic wind turbines improve energy capture efficiency while minimizing the environmental impact of traditional turbines (Garvin, 2015).

Another innovative bio-inspired energy solution is found in the Tyer Wind turbine, which mimics the figure-eight flight pattern of hummingbirds to enhance energy efficiency. By studying the aerodynamics of bird flight, engineers were able to design wind turbines with blades that optimize energy capture while reducing carbon emissions (Garvin, 2015). This bio-mimetic approach to renewable energy demonstrates the potential of bio-inspired innovations to disrupt the energy sector by offering more efficient and environmentally friendly alternatives to traditional power generation technologies.

Similarly, bio-inspired water collection technologies are gaining attention for their ability to provide sustainable solutions to water scarcity in arid regions. NBD Nano, a U.S.-based start-up, has developed a water-harvesting technology inspired by the Namib Desert beetle, which captures moisture from the air using its hydrophilic and hydrophobic shell. This technology has the potential to disrupt traditional water collection methods by offering a decentralized and sustainable solution for water-scarce regions (Andrew, 2018).

Bio-innovations or bio-inspired innovations, contribute significantly to addressing environmental challenges and achieving sustainability by mimicking nature's proven strategies for efficiency and adaptability. These innovations help in several ways:

Sustainable Product Design: Bio-inspired innovations lead to the development of materials and processes that are energy-efficient and environmentally friendly. For example, biomimetic designs like self-cleaning surfaces inspired by lotus leaves and stronger, lightweight materials modeled after spider silk result in products that reduce waste and consumption of natural resources (Aguilar-Planet & Peralta, 2024)

Architectural Design: The biomimicry organisation has published in Architectural Design, for example, Lavasa, India, uses strategies from natural systems like tree canopies to manage water during monsoons.

Product Design: Vehicles and fans utilize natural shapes for enhanced performance.

Environmental Technology: Methods inspired by natural mechanisms, such as camel noses and ant water diversion, are being explored for sustainable environmental solutions.

Fire Retardant Development: Research looks to nature for non-toxic flame retardants, using materials like chitosan from shells to create protective coatings.

Fashion Industry: The concept of vibrant colors in butterfly wings influences sustainable fashion materials like Morphotex, which eliminates the need for dyes.

Potential of Natural Processes: The discussion includes the idea that nature often exceeds "net zero" impact, suggesting ecosystems can inspire cities to be sustainable and beneficial to the environment. (Badrak, n.d)

Butterflies and Biomimicry – A Source of Inspiration: Butterflies and moths exemplify various natural adaptations, from detecting ultrasound clicks of bats to self-cleaning wings and vibrant color patterns as a warning to predators. Researchers have drawn inspiration from butterfly wings to create more efficient solar technology and anti-counterfeiting stamps using nanoscale structures. (Smith, 2020)

RFID Enhancement: The identification technology was improved by incorporating small metal scales into the RFID tags, enhancing the reliability of signal transmission through interference reduction.

Innovative Use of Butterfly Wings: Scientists are exploring the technological applications of the iridescent wings of the morphos butterfly, recognizing their potential for creating new, human-benefiting innovations. (Badrak, n.d). These innovations highlight how lessons from nature can lead to sustainable and energy-efficient technologies in various industries.

In the context of India's start-up ecosystem, bio-inspired innovation holds immense potential for fostering entrepreneurship. The country's rich biodiversity offers an unparalleled resource for bio-mimicry, allowing start-ups to draw inspiration from nature to create disruptive solutions across industries such as healthcare, agriculture, and clean energy. However, for bio-inspired start-ups to thrive, India must invest in research and development (R&D) infrastructure, build awareness among entrepreneurs and investors, and establish policies that promote sustainable innovation (Bhutia, 2016). With the right support, bio-mimicry can serve as a powerful tool for Indian entrepreneurs to drive disruptive innovation and contribute to the country's economic and environmental goals.

Adopting bio-inspired innovation has significant implications for global sustainability efforts as it promotes the development of products and processes that are resource-efficient and environmentally friendly. Fostering bio-inspired innovations can stimulate economic growth by creating new markets for sustainable technologies and enhancing competitiveness in an eco-conscious consumer landscape. (Inc., 2024)

A major challenge is the limited understanding of bio-inspired innovation and its potential benefits among businesses, entrepreneurs, and the public. Many industries still rely on traditional technologies and are unaware of bio-innovation's role in sustainability (Inc., 2024). Introducing bio-inspired innovation in educational curricula and public awareness campaigns can help foster a greater understanding. Integrating sustainability concepts and biomimicry in engineering, architecture, and design programs will encourage future professionals to explore bio-innovative solutions.

Bio-inspired innovations often require significant research and development, which may involve advanced technologies like synthetic biology, genetic engineering, or sustainable materials. Many start-ups and small enterprises in India struggle to access venture capital or government funding for such high-risk innovations (Michael Chui, 2020). The Indian government could establish dedicated funds and tax incentives for companies working on bio-inspired technologies. Additionally, partnerships between academia, industry, and government could pool resources for research, reducing the financial burden on individual firms.

In some industries, there may be resistance to adopting new technologies or innovations due to traditional practices and established systems. Moreover, institutions may be slow to adapt to the interdisciplinary nature of bio-inspired innovations, which combine biology, engineering, and design (Kim, 2019). Encouraging a culture of innovation through government-backed initiatives like startup accelerators, incubators, and innovation challenges focused on sustainability could mitigate this resistance. Additionally, promoting cross-disciplinary research and collaborations between various sectors can accelerate the adoption of bio-inspired solutions.

Strategies to Overcome Barriers:

Encouraging collaboration between the government, private sectors, and academic institutions can help pool resources and share risks in bio-innovation. Joint ventures can also lead to the development of technologies that are both sustainable and commercially viable (Michael Chui, 2020). Developing targeted policies to encourage bio-inspired innovation is crucial. Offering tax breaks, subsidies, and fast-tracked regulatory approvals for bio-innovative projects will incentivize entrepreneurs and investors to venture into this space (Lorenzo,, 2018)

By addressing these barriers through strategic efforts, India can enhance its adoption of bio-inspired innovations, leading to sustainable growth across various sectors. This approach will not only help in achieving the Sustainable Development Goals (SDGs) but also position India as a leader in the global bio-economy.

Bio-inspired innovation exemplifies the power of nature's designs to inspire disruptive innovation across industries. By mimicking the efficiency, sustainability, and resilience of natural systems, bio-inspired solutions can disrupt conventional technologies and offer new avenues for entrepreneurship. As the world continues to grapple with the challenges of the Fourth Industrial Revolution, bio-mimicry offers a unique and sustainable pathway for developing disruptive innovations that balance economic growth with environmental stewardship.

## RESEARCH GAP

Bio-inspired innovation has gained significant traction globally, particularly in developed nations where extensive research, funding, and policy frameworks support bio-mimetic entrepreneurship. However, in the Indian context, bio-inspired start-ups remain underexplored, with limited empirical studies assessing their impact on sustainable industries. While existing literature highlights individual case studies of bio-mimicry-driven products such as Velcro and bio-inspired wind turbines, a comprehensive analysis of the ecosystem supporting bio-entrepreneurship in India is lacking. This study aims to bridge these gaps by providing a structured review of opportunities, challenges, and strategic enablers for bio-mimetic start-ups in India.

### Research Questions:

1. To analyze the role of bio-inspired innovation in fostering sustainability across industries.
2. To evaluate global best practices in bio-entrepreneurship and their applicability to the Indian context.
3. To propose policy recommendations and strategic enablers for promoting bio-inspired start-ups and sustainable industrial growth.

This study employs a qualitative research approach to explore the role of bio-inspired innovation in fostering sustainable industries, with a particular emphasis on

India's start-up ecosystem. Given the exploratory nature of the research, a structured literature review was conducted to identify key opportunities, challenges, and future directions for bio-mimetic entrepreneurship. The methodology adopted is designed to provide a comprehensive understanding of bio-inspired solutions by synthesizing existing knowledge, drawing from theoretical frameworks, and analyzing real-world applications.

## RESEARCH METHODOLOGY

This study adopts a qualitative exploratory research design using a structured literature review methodology to examine the role of biomimicry and bio-inspired innovation in fostering sustainable entrepreneurship and competitive advantage. The study synthesizes interdisciplinary literature spanning strategic management, sustainability, innovation studies, entrepreneurship, circular economy, and biomimicry research.

The literature review was conducted using major academic databases including Scopus, Web of Science, Google Scholar, ScienceDirect, and SpringerLink. Additional institutional reports and policy documents were sourced from organizations such as the World Economic Forum (WEF), OECD, Biomimicry Institute, McKinsey & Company, and relevant government publications.

The search process utilized combinations of the following keywords and search strings like "Biomimicry" AND "Innovation"," Bío-inspired innovation" AND "Sustainability", "Biomimicry" AND "Competitive Advantage"," Bío-inspired entrepreneurship"," Circular Economy" AND "Biomimicry"," Dynamic Capabilities" AND "Sustainable Innovation"," Responsible Innovation" AND "Nature-inspired Design".

The review primarily focused on publications published between 2010 and 2025 to ensure contemporary relevance, while seminal foundational works were included to strengthen theoretical grounding.

### Inclusion and Exclusion Criteria:

The study included: Peer-reviewed journal articles, Scholarly books and book chapters,Indexed conference proceedings, Institutional and policy reports relevant to biomimicry and sustainability, Studies focusing on strategic, entrepreneurial, technological, or sustainability dimensions of bio-inspired innovation.

## The study excluded:

Non-scholarly opinion articles, Unverified web sources lacking academic credibility, Publications unrelated to innovation, sustainability, or strategic management, Duplicate records across databases, Screening and Selection Process.

An initial pool of literature was identified through database searches. After removing duplicates and non-relevant studies based on title and abstract screening, the remaining publications were assessed for conceptual relevance and theoretical contribution. Priority was given to highly cited and peer-reviewed sources that addressed biomimicry within innovation, sustainability, and organizational strategy contexts.

## Data Analysis and Synthesis:

The selected literature was analyzed using thematic synthesis. Key themes emerging from the review were categorized into the following domains:

Biomimicry as a design and innovation methodology. Biomimicry and sustainable competitive advantage, Dynamic capabilities and organizational resilience, Circular economy and regenerative systems, Responsible innovation and sustainability governance, Sector-wise strategic applications, Entrepreneurship ecosystems and institutional support.

The thematic synthesis enabled identification of conceptual convergence, theoretical gaps, and strategic implications across interdisciplinary domains. Comparative interpretation was additionally undertaken to examine the applicability of global biomimicry practices within the Indian entrepreneurial ecosystem.

## Research Scope and Limitations

The study relies exclusively on secondary data sources and does not incorporate primary empirical investigation through interviews, surveys, or case-based field analysis. While the structured review provides broad conceptual insights, future research may extend the findings through empirical validation involving start-ups, innovation ecosystems, policymakers, and sustainability practitioners.

# ANALYSIS & DISCUSSION

Proponents of the Resource-Based View (RBV) argue that leveraging existing resources in innovative ways to capitalize on external opportunities is more effective than acquiring new skills for each emerging prospect. In the RBV framework, resources play a central role in driving organizational performance and are categorized into two types: tangible and intangible.

The following model explains RBV and emphasizes its key points (Jurevicius, Resource-Based View, October 24, 2023).

*Figure 1. Resource-based view framework:*

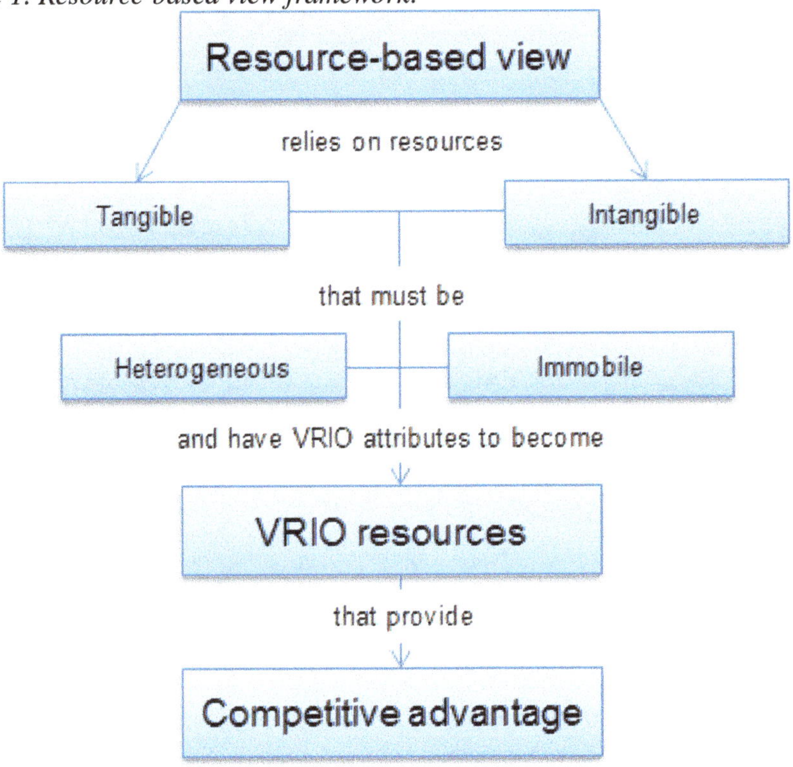


*Source: (Jurevicius, Resource-Based View, October 24, 2023).*

*Figure 2. VRIO framework adopted from Rothaermel's (2013) 'Strategic Management', p.91*

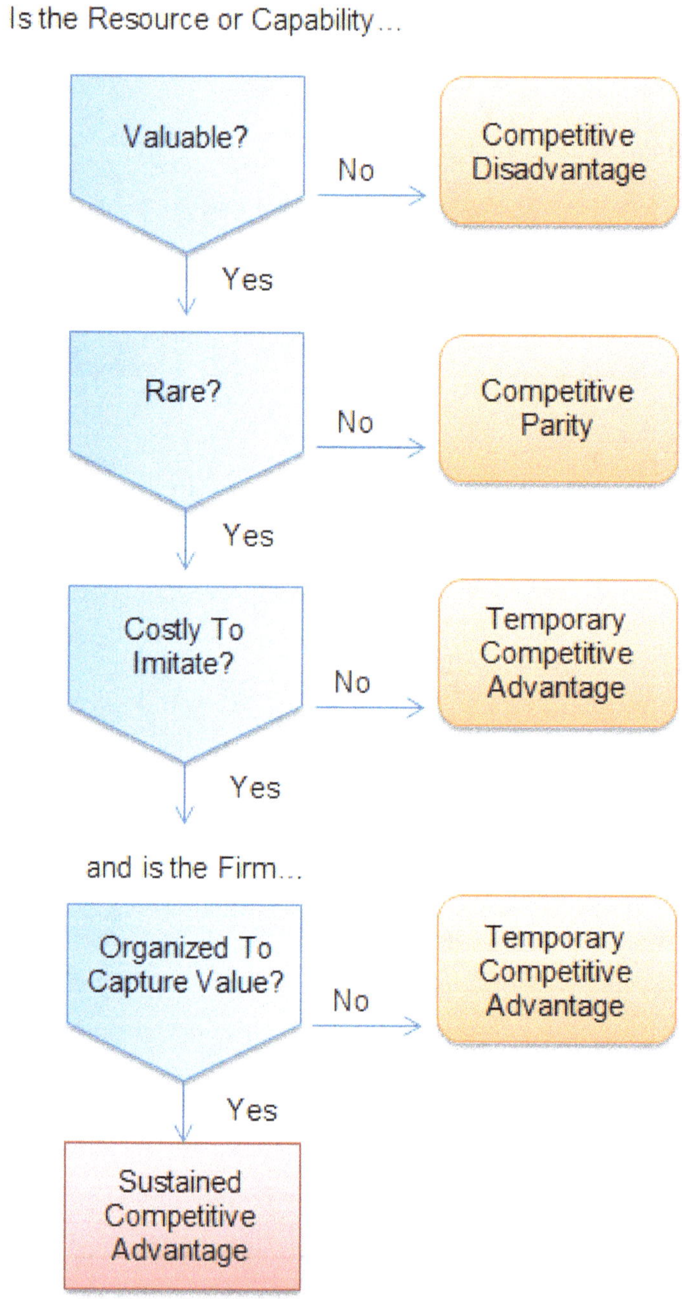


*Source: Rothaermel, F. T. (2012). Strat.Mgmt.: Concepts and Cases. McGraw-Hill/Irwin, p. 5*

**A VRIO PERSPECTIVE**(Jurevicius, December 1. 2023)

The VRIO perspective is used to analyze the creation of bio-innovation startups and the factors that make them unique.

## Question of Value

Innovation plays a critical role in creating value for organizations by enhancing customer offerings and optimizing production costs. Emerging technologies, such as artificial intelligence, blockchain, and the Internet of Things (IoT), have proven valuable by enabling companies to develop differentiated products and services. In the context of this review, organizations that effectively integrate these technologies into their business models can achieve a sustainable increase in customer value. However, firms that fail to leverage such advancements may experience a competitive disadvantage due to their inability to meet evolving consumer expectations.

In bio-inspired start-ups, AI-driven bio-mimetic solutions offer efficiency and sustainability, making them valuable resources. These technologies enable organizations to develop eco-friendly alternatives that enhance operational effectiveness and reduce environmental impact.

## Question of Rarity

A resource or capability is considered rare when it is possessed by only a few firms within an industry. Breakthrough innovations—such as the first-to-market development of a disruptive technology—are inherently rare and provide a competitive edge. For instance, firms that pioneer quantum computing or autonomous vehicle technologies hold a distinct advantage, as these innovations are not widely accessible. However, as more companies invest in similar technologies, the rarity diminishes, leading to competitive parity. Companies must continuously innovate to maintain their unique positioning in the market.

For bio-inspired start-ups, unique patents on bio-mimicry-based technologies create rarity, ensuring that only a limited number of firms can leverage specific biological innovations for commercial use.

## Question of Imitability

Even when a rcsource is valuable and rare, it must also be costly to imitate or substitute in order to sustain a competitive advantage. Patents, trade secrets, complex algorithms, and unique corporate cultures serve as barriers to imitation. For example, Tesla's proprietary battery technology and software algorithms contribute to its sustained competitive advantage in the electric vehicle market. If competing firms can easily replicate an innovation, the advantage is only temporary, making it crucial for firms to implement strategies that protect their intellectual property and technological advancements.

In bio-inspired start-ups, complex biological adaptations are difficult to replicate without extensive R&D, making them highly inimitable. The intricate nature of bio-mimicry ensures that only firms with substantial expertise can successfully develop and commercialize these technologies.

## Question of Organization

Possessing valuable, rare, and inimitable resources is not sufficient unless the firm is structured to exploit these advantages effectively. Organizational capabilities, leadership, and strategic decision-making play a crucial role in maximizing the benefits of innovation. Companies such as Amazon and Google excel in organizational adaptability, allowing them to integrate emerging technologies seamlessly and scale their innovations efficiently. Firms that lack a robust organizational structure may struggle to translate innovative capabilities into sustained competitive advantages.

Bio-mimetic solutions provide a unique advantage for bio-inspired start-ups over traditional technologies, making them non-substitutable. These firms must ensure their organizational structure supports the continuous development and application of bio-inspired innovations to maintain their competitive edge.

*Table 1. Proposed Model: RBV Framework for Bio-Inspired Start-ups*

| RBV Component | Application in Bio-Inspired Start-ups |
|---|---|
| Valuable | AI-driven bio-mimetic solutions offer efficiency and sustainability. |
| Rare | Unique patents on bio-mimicry-based technologies. |
| Inimitable | Complex biological adaptations are difficult to replicate without R&D. |
| Non-Substitutable | Bio-inspired solutions provide a unique advantage over traditional technologies. |

Applying the VRIO framework to the future of innovation highlights the necessity for firms to develop and manage resources strategically. Innovation alone does not guarantee success unless it is valuable, rare, difficult to imitate, and supported by an organization designed to leverage it effectively. Companies that align their innovation strategies with these principles will be better positioned to achieve long-term competitive advantages in an increasingly dynamic business landscape.

## Biomimicry as a Dynamic Capability

Biomimicry should not be viewed merely as a static design input or an isolated innovation practice. Instead, it represents a dynamic organizational capability that enables firms to sense, seize, and transform in response to environmental, technological, and market disruptions. Dynamic Capabilities Theory argues that long-term competitive advantage arises not from resource possession alone, but from the firm's ability to continuously reconfigure resources in volatile environments (Teece, 2007).

Nature-inspired innovation aligns strongly with the *sensing* dimension of dynamic capabilities. Biological systems excel at detecting weak signals, adapting to uncertainty, and responding to environmental stressors. Organizations that institutionalize biomimicry practices—through bio-design labs, interdisciplinary teams, and experimentation—develop enhanced sensing capabilities that allow them to anticipate sustainability challenges and emerging market needs (Teece et al., 2016).

The *seizing* dimension is reflected in how firms translate biological insights into commercially viable products, services, and business models. Bio-inspired organizations do not simply imitate forms; they convert biological principles into scalable solutions, such as energy-efficient materials, circular production systems, and adaptive technologies. This translation process requires managerial orchestration, investment alignment, and strategic decision-making (Zott et al., 2011).

Finally, biomimicry strengthens the *transforming* capability by enabling firms to redesign processes, value chains, and organizational routines in line with ecological logic. Unlike conventional innovation approaches, biomimicry supports regenerative and circular transformations, allowing firms to remain resilient while complying with increasing sustainability regulations and stakeholder expectations (Hart & Dowell, 2011).

By conceptualizing biomimicry as a dynamic capability, this chapter extends existing strategic management literature and positions bio-inspired innovation as a core driver of long-term organizational adaptability rather than a peripheral design practice.

## Biomimicry, Circular Economy, and Regenerative Strategy

Biomimicry provides a natural foundation for circular economy and regenerative business models. In biological ecosystems, waste does not exist (Dr.Jayachandra Bingi, 2025); outputs from onc process become inputs for another. Translating this principle into industrial systems enables organizations to move beyond linear "take–make–dispose" models toward regenerative value creation (Geissdoerfer et al., 2017).

Circular economy strategies informed by biomimicry support material recovery, modularity, and closed-loop production. Firms adopting these approaches benefit from reduced input costs, enhanced supply-chain resilience, and improved compliance with environmental regulations. Importantly, regenerative strategies inspired by nature go beyond minimizing harm to actively restoring ecological systems (Raworth, 2017).

From a strategic standpoint, biomimicry-driven circular models are difficult to imitate due to their system-level complexity and dependence on organizational learning. This reinforces their alignment with VRIO conditions, particularly inimitability and non-substitutability (Barney, 1991).

**Figures 3-6.** How Bio-Inspired Solutions Are Shaping Sustainable Industries Review Findings

*Figure 3.*

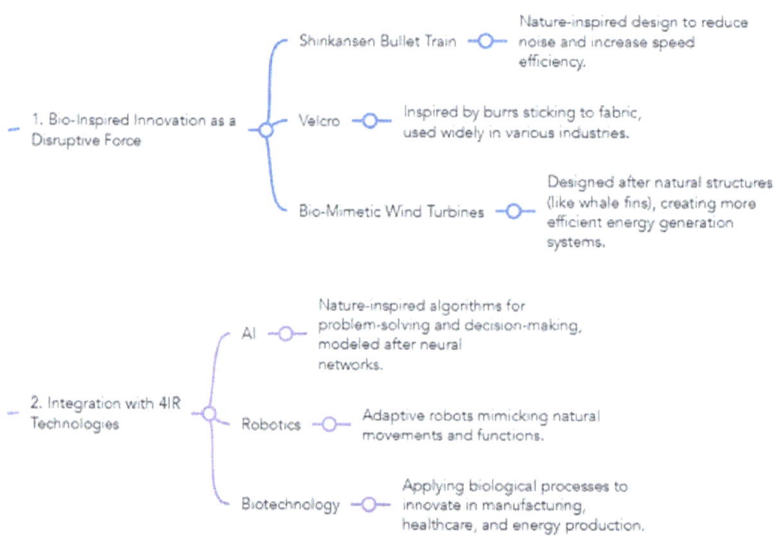

*Figure 4.*

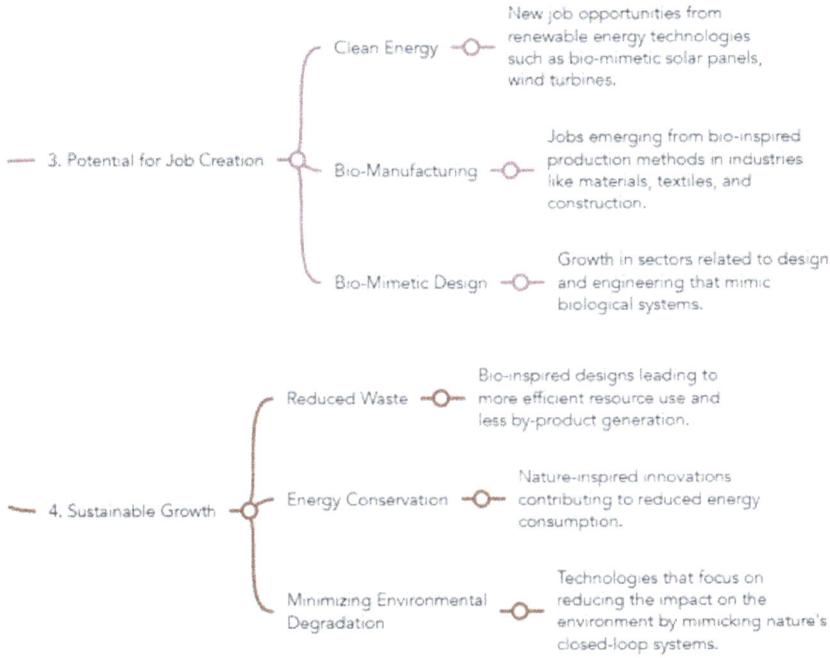
3. Potential for Job Creation
Clean Energy
New job opportunities from renewable energy technologies such as bio-mimetic solar panels, wind turbines.
Bio-Manufacturing
Jobs emerging from bio-inspired production methods in industries like materials, textiles, and construction.
Bio-Mimetic Design
Growth in sectors related to design and engineering that mimic biological systems.
4. Sustainable Growth
Reduced Waste
Bio-inspired designs leading to more efficient resource use and less by-product generation.
Energy Conservation
Nature-inspired innovations contributing to reduced energy consumption.
Minimizing Environmental Degradation
Technologies that focus on reducing the impact on the environment by mimicking nature's closed-loop systems.

*Figure 5.*

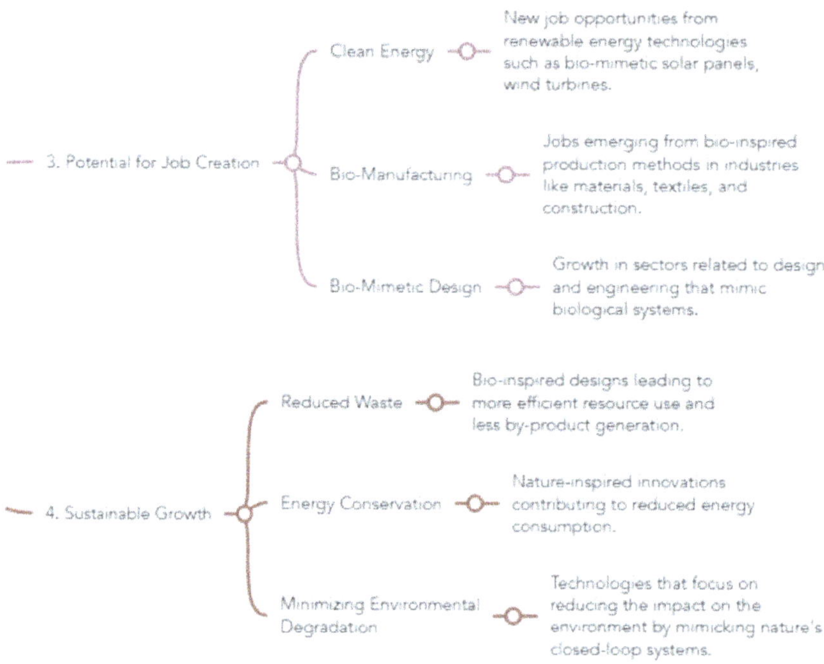


*Figure 6.*

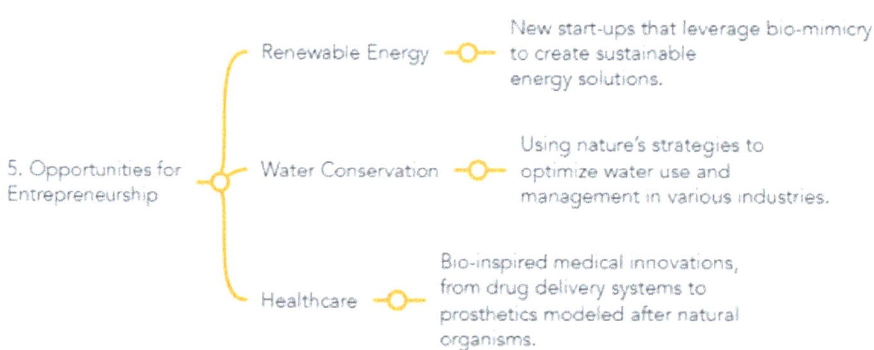


Bio-Inspired Innovation as a Disruptive Force: Bio-mimicry offers a unique approach to solving complex industrial challenges by applying natural design principles to product development and process improvement. Examples like the

Shinkansen Bullet Train, Velcro, and bio-mimetic wind turbines demonstrate how nature-inspired designs can enhance efficiency, reduce environmental impact, and create entirely new markets.

Integration with 4IR Technologies: As industries become more automated and data-driven, bio-inspired solutions provide a pathway to smarter, more adaptive technologies. The convergence of AI, robotics, and biotechnology in 4IR has created fertile ground for bio-mimetic innovations that can enhance manufacturing processes, energy production, and healthcare solutions.

Potential for Job Creation: Bio-inspired innovation is expected to generate millions of new jobs by 2030, particularly in sectors such as clean energy, bio-manufacturing, and bio-mimetic design. As start-ups and established companies alike adopt bio-inspired solutions, the demand for workers with expertise in biology, engineering, and design will increase.

Sustainable Growth: Bio-inspired innovation aligns with the global shift toward sustainability. By mimicking nature's efficient use of resources, these innovations reduce waste, conserve energy, and minimize environmental degradation. Bio-inspired products, such as formaldehyde-free adhesives and energy-efficient wind turbines, offer sustainable alternatives to conventional technologies.

Opportunities for Entrepreneurship: Entrepreneurs have significant opportunities to leverage bio-inspired innovation in creating disruptive products and services. Start-ups focused on bio-mimicry can tap into markets that demand sustainable solutions, such as renewable energy, water conservation, and healthcare. In India, government initiatives such as Start-up India and Make in India are fostering a supportive environment for bio-inspired entrepreneurship.

## Biomimicry as a Knowledge Integration and Sensemaking Mechanism

While existing literature predominantly frames biomimicry as a design methodology or technological inspiration, its deeper strategic value lies in its role as a knowledge integration and organizational sensemaking mechanism. Organizations today operate in environments characterized by technological convergence, ecological uncertainty, and complex stakeholder expectations. In such contexts, the challenge is not merely innovation generation, but the ability to integrate heterogeneous knowledge domains into coherent strategic action (Teece, 2007).

Biomimicry enables organizations to bridge fragmented knowledge silos by functioning as a boundary-spanning logic between biology, engineering, management, and social systems. Natural systems do not optimize isolated functions; rather, they coordinate structure, process, and feedback simultaneously. When organizations adopt biomimetic thinking, they implicitly shift from reductionist problem-solving toward systems-level sensemaking. This transition is particularly valuable in sustainability-driven innovation, where linear cause–effect reasoning often fails to address interconnected ecological and economic challenges (Hart & Dowell, 2011).

From an organizational learning perspective, biomimicry enhances absorptive capacity by encouraging firms to scan non-traditional knowledge domains and reinterpret them within commercial and strategic contexts. Unlike conventional R&D processes that focus on incremental technological advancement, bio-inspired innovation requires interpretive learning—understanding why a biological system works before translating how it can be adapted. This deep learning process increases cognitive diversity within firms and strengthens long-term innovation capability (Zott et al., 2011).

Moreover, biomimicry supports strategic sensemaking under uncertainty, a critical requirement in the Fourth Industrial Revolution. As AI, automation, and digital platforms accelerate decision-making cycles, organizations risk prioritizing short-term optimization over long-term resilience. Nature-inspired logic counterbalances this tendency by emphasizing redundancy, adaptability, and feedback sensitivity—principles that biological systems rely on for survival. Firms that internalize these principles are better equipped to navigate volatility and systemic shocks, including climate risks and supply-chain disruptions (Teece et al., 2016).

Importantly, biomimicry also reshapes managerial cognition. Traditional strategy frameworks often frame nature as an external constraint or resource pool. In contrast, biomimetic thinking repositions nature as a strategic mentor, altering how managers conceptualize growth, efficiency, and value creation. This cognitive shift is foundational for regenerative and responsible innovation, as it aligns strategic intent with ecological intelligence rather than extractive logic (Benyus, 1997).

In the Indian context, this knowledge integration role of biomimicry is particularly significant. India's innovation ecosystem is characterized by rich biodiversity, traditional ecological knowledge, and rapidly expanding technological capability. Biomimicry provides a unifying framework through which indigenous knowledge systems and modern strategic management can be meaningfully integrated, strengthening contextual relevance and innovation legitimacy (Audretsch, 2014; Etzkowitz & Leydesdorff, 2000).

Thus, beyond its technological manifestations, biomimicry should be understood as a strategic cognition and knowledge orchestration mechanism—one that enables organizations to make sense of complexity, integrate diverse knowledge sources, and design innovations that are resilient, ethical, and sustainable.

## Biomimicry and Responsible Innovation

Bio-inspired innovation inherently aligns with the principles of responsible innovation, which emphasize anticipation, reflexivity, inclusion, and responsiveness in technological development (Stilgoe et al., 2013). Unlike extractive innovation models, biomimicry draws from systems that operate within planetary boundaries, making it particularly relevant in an era of climate risk and social accountability.

Responsible innovation requires organizations to assess not only economic outcomes but also long-term societal and environmental consequences. Biomimicry contributes to this agenda by embedding sustainability at the design stage rather than treating it as a post-hoc compliance requirement. For example, nature-inspired materials often reduce toxicity, energy consumption, and waste generation, directly addressing environmental externalities (Benyus, 1997).

From a governance perspective, biomimicry encourages stakeholder-inclusive innovation ecosystems. Universities, research labs, communities, and policymakers become co-creators rather than passive recipients of innovation outcomes. This aligns with the Triple Helix Model, where university–industry–government collaboration accelerates socially responsible innovation (Etzkowitz & Leydesdorff, 2000).

Embedding responsible innovation principles into bio-inspired entrepreneurship enhances legitimacy, investor confidence, and regulatory alignment. As ESG considerations increasingly influence capital allocation, firms adopting biomimicry gain reputational and strategic advantages that extend beyond immediate market performance.

## Sector-Wise Strategic Applications of Biomimicry for Sustainable Competitive Advantage

Bio-inspired innovation demonstrates its strongest strategic relevance when examined through sector-specific applications. While biomimicry is often discussed as a design philosophy, its true potential lies in its ability to reshape industry structures, create sustainable competitive advantage, and enable long-term value creation. By translating biological principles into organizational strategies, firms across sectors can achieve efficiency, resilience, and sustainability simultaneously. This section examines the strategic applications of biomimicry across five critical sectors, highlighting the nature-inspired analogy, strategic value, competitive advantage, and sustainability impact in cach context.

## Healthcare and Medical Devices

### Nature Analogy

Biological systems exhibit extraordinary efficiency in healing, self-regulation, and adaptation. Examples include bone regeneration, skin self-healing, and the human immune system's ability to detect and neutralize threats. These mechanisms have inspired bio-mimetic medical devices such as self-healing biomaterials, bio-compatible implants, and drug delivery systems modeled on cellular transport processes.

### Strategic Value

In healthcare, biomimicry enhances patient outcomes while reducing systemic costs. Nature-inspired designs improve precision, durability, and compatibility, enabling healthcare organizations to deliver advanced treatments with fewer side effects and lower failure rates. Bio-mimetic medical technologies align strongly with value-based healthcare models, where outcomes and efficiency are prioritized over volume.

### Competitive Advantage

Firms that integrate bio-inspired designs into medical devices gain a differentiation advantage through superior functionality and regulatory compliance. These innovations are difficult to imitate due to complex biological knowledge and interdisciplinary expertise, making them strategically valuable and rare. The integration of biomimicry with AI-driven diagnostics further strengthens inimitability by embedding learning capabilities into medical systems.

### Sustainability Impact

Bio-inspired healthcare solutions reduce material waste, energy consumption, and dependency on synthetic chemicals. Sustainable biomaterials, such as chitosan-based wound dressings or biodegradable implants, contribute to environmentally responsible healthcare systems while improving patient safety. These innovations support the Triple Bottom Line by enhancing social well-being, environmental stewardship, and economic efficiency (Elkington, 1997).

## Agriculture and Agri-Tech

### Nature Analogy

Natural ecosystems operate through symbiotic relationships, nutrient cycling, and adaptive resilience. Concepts such as soil microbiomes, pollination networks, and plant self-defense mechanisms have inspired precision agriculture, bio-fertilizers, and pest-resistant crops.

### Strategic Value

Biomimicry enables agri-tech firms to address critical challenges such as food security, climate variability, and resource scarcity. Nature-inspired agricultural systems enhance productivity while reducing dependency on chemical inputs. By aligning farming practices with ecological processes, organizations can achieve long-term operational stability.

### Competitive Advantage

Bio-inspired agri-tech solutions offer cost advantages and regulatory resilience, particularly as governments tighten environmental standards. Firms leveraging biomimetic farming techniques—such as regenerative agriculture and natural pest control—differentiate themselves in sustainability-conscious markets. These practices are socially complex and context-specific, making them difficult for competitors to replicate.

### Sustainability Impact

Biomimicry in agriculture improves soil health, conserves water, and reduces carbon emissions. By mimicking natural nutrient cycles, agri-tech innovations contribute directly to climate-resilient food systems. These approaches align with circular economy principles by minimizing waste and regenerating ecosystems (Geissdoerfer et al., 2017).

## Manufacturing and the Circular Economy

### Nature Analogy

In nature, waste does not exist; every output becomes an input for another process. Ecosystems function as closed-loop systems where materials circulate continuously without depletion.

### Strategic Value

Manufacturing firms adopting bio-inspired circular models can reduce material costs, improve resource efficiency, and enhance supply chain resilience. Biomimicry informs lightweight material design, modular production systems, and energy-efficient processes, enabling firms to optimize operations while reducing environmental footprints.

### Competitive Advantage

Circular bio-inspired manufacturing provides firms with long-term cost leadership and compliance advantages. As global regulations increasingly favor sustainable production, early adopters of biomimetic circular models gain first-mover benefits. These systems require organizational learning and cross-functional integration, making them difficult to imitate.

### Sustainability Impact

By eliminating waste and reducing emissions, bio-inspired manufacturing supports sustainable industrial development. Firms transition from extractive models to regenerative production systems, aligning profitability with planetary boundaries. This reinforces sustainability as a strategic asset rather than a compliance obligation (Geissdoerfer et al., 2017).

## Smart Cities and Infrastructure

### Nature Analogy

Natural systems such as termite mounds, ant colonies, and forest ecosystems demonstrate decentralized coordination, climate regulation, and resource optimization. These principles inspire energy-efficient buildings, adaptive traffic systems, and resilient urban infrastructure.

### Strategic Value

Biomimicry enables cities to address urbanization challenges through adaptive and responsive infrastructure. Nature-inspired designs improve energy efficiency, climate resilience, and citizen well-being. Smart cities that integrate biomimicry enhance long-term livability while reducing operational costs.

### Competitive Advantage

Cities and infrastructure firms adopting biomimetic solutions gain reputational and economic advantages by attracting investment, talent, and innovation ecosystems. These solutions integrate physical design with digital intelligence, making them complex and socially embedded, thereby difficult to replicate.

## Sustainability Impact

Bio-inspired urban systems reduce energy consumption, manage water efficiently, and enhance ecological balance. By mimicking natural ventilation, water filtration, and adaptive growth patterns, smart cities move toward regenerative urban development aligned with global sustainability goals (OECD, 2020).

## Financial Services and Risk Systems

### Nature Analogy

Biological systems manage risk through diversity, redundancy, and adaptive learning. Ecosystems remain resilient by distributing risk rather than centralizing it, a principle increasingly relevant to financial systems.

### Strategic Value

Biomimicry informs risk management models, fraud detection systems, and portfolio diversification strategies. Financial institutions applying biological resilience principles can enhance stability, anticipate systemic risks, and improve decision-making under uncertainty.

### Competitive Advantage

Nature-inspired risk models enable financial institutions to outperform traditional linear forecasting systems. These adaptive models, often integrated with AI and machine learning, provide dynamic risk assessment capabilities that competitors struggle to imitate due to data complexity and algorithmic sophistication.

### Sustainability Impact

By promoting systemic resilience and ethical decision-making, bio-inspired financial systems support sustainable economic growth. They align financial performance with long-term societal stability, reinforcing the role of finance as an enabler of sustainable development rather than a source of systemic risk.

## Role of Higher Education Institutions (HEIs) and Innovation Ecosystems in Advancing Biomimicry

Higher Education Institutions (HEIs) play a pivotal role in advancing bio-inspired innovation by acting as knowledge creators, talent incubators, and ecosystem orchestrators. Biomimicry, by its interdisciplinary nature, requires the integration of biology, engineering, design, and management—an integration best facilitated within academic environments.

Universities function as bio-innovation hubs by enabling foundational research in biological systems and translating it into applied technological and managerial solutions. Through laboratories, research centers, and collaborative platforms, HEIs foster experimentation that would be too risky or long-term for industry alone. This aligns with the Triple Helix Model, where universities, industry, and government collaboratively drive innovation and economic development (Etzkowitz & Leydesdorff, 2000).

Interdisciplinary curricula are critical for cultivating future bio-inspired entrepreneurs and managers. Programs that integrate biology with management education enable students to think systemically and develop nature-inspired problem-solving capabilities. Design thinking, sustainability studies, and strategic management frameworks collectively prepare graduates to translate biological insights into viable business models.

University-led incubators and living labs further accelerate bio-inspired entrepreneurship by providing access to infrastructure, mentorship, and funding networks. These platforms allow start-ups to prototype and validate nature-based innovations in real-world contexts, reducing commercialization barriers. Entrepreneurial universities thus become catalysts for sustainable innovation ecosystems (Audretsch, 2014).

In the Indian context, policy frameworks such as the National Education Policy (NEP) 2020 and the renewed emphasis on Indian Knowledge Systems (IKS) provide a strong foundation for embedding biomimicry into higher education. India's traditional ecological knowledge, when integrated with modern science and management education, offers unique opportunities for nature-inspired innovation rooted in indigenous wisdom. HEIs can bridge ancient ecological insights with contemporary strategic thinking, positioning India as a global leader in bio-inspired innovation.

OECD studies highlight that innovation ecosystems anchored in universities are more resilient, inclusive, and sustainability-oriented (OECD, 2019). By fostering interdisciplinary learning, collaborative research, and entrepreneurial experimentation, HEIs can ensure that biomimicry evolves from a niche concept into a mainstream strategic capability.

In conclusion, Higher Education Institutions (HEIs) play a pivotal role in translating biomimicry from conceptual inspiration into applied innovation. Universities and interdisciplinary research laboratories act as knowledge intermediaries, bridging biology, engineering, management, and design.

Bio-inspired innovation demands transdisciplinary collaboration, which traditional academic silos often inhibit. Progressive HEIs address this gap by establishing bio-design labs, innovation hubs, and industry-linked incubators. Such ecosystems accelerate knowledge transfer, prototype development, and entrepreneurial experimentation.

From a strategic perspective, HEIs contribute to national innovation systems by nurturing talent, generating patents, and supporting spin-off ventures. Empirical evidence suggests that university-led bio-innovation ecosystems significantly enhance regional innovation capacity and sustainability outcomes (Etzkowitz & Leydesdorff, 2000).

Thus, strengthening HEIs and research labs is essential for scaling bio-inspired entrepreneurship and embedding sustainability into long-term economic development.

## Implications for Management Education and Curriculum Design

Management education plays a critical role in institutionalizing biomimicry as a strategic capability. Traditional business curricula often emphasize efficiency and profit maximization without sufficient ecological grounding. Integrating biomimicry into management education enables future leaders to adopt systems thinking and sustainability-driven decision-making.

Interdisciplinary pedagogy combining biology, design thinking, and strategy, equips students to translate natural intelligence into business innovation. Experiential learning through bio-design labs, field immersion, and industry-linked projects further strengthens this capability.

Embedding biomimicry into entrepreneurship education aligns with emerging expectations of responsible leadership and sustainable value creation, preparing graduates to navigate complex global challenges.

## Biomimicry and Sustained Competitive Advantage: A VRIO Perspective

The Resource-Based View argues that organizations achieve sustained competitive advantage when they possess resources and capabilities that are valuable, rare, difficult to imitate, and effectively organized. Within the context of bio-inspired innovation, biomimicry strengthens all four dimensions of the VRIO framework.

First, biomimetic solutions create value by improving efficiency, reducing material consumption, strengthening sustainability performance, and enabling environmentally responsible innovation. Organizations applying biological principles to engineering, product design, and operational systems are able to develop differentiated offerings while simultaneously addressing stakeholder concerns related to environmental sustainability.

Second, biomimicry contributes to rarity because interdisciplinary expertise combining biology, technology, engineering, and strategic management remains relatively uncommon. Firms capable of translating biological intelligence into commercially viable innovations therefore possess distinctive knowledge assets that are not widely distributed across industries.

Third, bio-inspired innovation strengthens inimitability because many biological adaptations are highly complex and require extensive experimentation, tacit knowledge, and research capability for successful commercialization. Competitors may find it difficult to replicate organizational routines, learning mechanisms, and ecosystem partnerships underpinning biomimetic innovation systems.

Finally, sustained advantage depends on organizational capability. Firms must establish structures, cultures, leadership systems, and interdisciplinary processes capable of integrating biomimicry into strategic decision-making. Organizations that fail to institutionalize these capabilities may struggle to translate innovation potential into long-term competitive outcomes.

## Sector-Wise Strategic Applications of Biomimicry

The strategic relevance of biomimicry becomes particularly visible when examined across industry sectors. In healthcare, bio-inspired medical technologies such as biodegradable implants, self-healing materials, and biomimetic drug-delivery systems enhance patient outcomes while reducing environmental impact. These innovations support value-based healthcare models focused on efficiency, sustainability, and precision.

In agriculture and agri-technology, biomimicry contributes to regenerative farming systems inspired by nutrient cycling, soil ecosystems, and symbiotic biological relationships. Such approaches improve climate resilience, reduce dependency on synthetic inputs, and support long-term food security.

Within manufacturing and circular economy systems, biomimicry informs closed-loop production processes, waste minimization strategies, and modular product design. Organizations adopting nature-inspired circular models achieve greater resource efficiency and supply-chain resilience while aligning with evolving environmental regulations.

Similarly, smart city infrastructure increasingly incorporates biomimetic principles derived from termite mounds, ant colonies, and forest ecosystems to improve urban ventilation, energy efficiency, decentralized coordination, and climate resilience.

These sectoral applications collectively demonstrate that biomimicry functions not merely as a technological inspiration, but as a strategic mechanism for generating resilience, sustainability, and long-term competitive advantage.

## Limitations and Boundary Conditions

Despite its transformative potential, biomimicry faces several implementation barriers and boundary conditions that influence commercialization success. Translating biological principles into scalable technological solutions often requires substantial interdisciplinary expertise, experimentation, financial investment, and regulatory approval.

Organizations may additionally encounter challenges associated with time-to-market delays, intellectual property protection, uncertain unit economics, and limited investor awareness regarding bio-inspired innovation models. In emerging economies such as India, infrastructural limitations, fragmented research ecosystems, and restricted access to specialized R&D facilities may further constrain commercialization.

Another critical concern relates to greenwashing risk, where organizations may superficially adopt biomimicry rhetoric without implementing genuine sustainability transformation. Accordingly, responsible governance mechanisms, stakeholder transparency, and evidence-based sustainability assessment become essential.

These limitations indicate that successful bio-inspired innovation requires not only technological capability, but also ecosystem support, institutional coordination, policy alignment, and organizational commitment to long-term regenerative value creation.

## RESEARCH FINDINGS

To fully capitalize on the opportunities presented by bio-inspired innovation, a concerted effort from all stakeholders, entrepreneurs, policymakers, and investors is essential. The following recommendations aim to guide each group in fostering a thriving bio-mimetic innovation eco-system.

Fig 7-8. Bio-Inspired Innovation: Key Findings and Strategic Insights

*Figure 7.*

*Figure 8.*

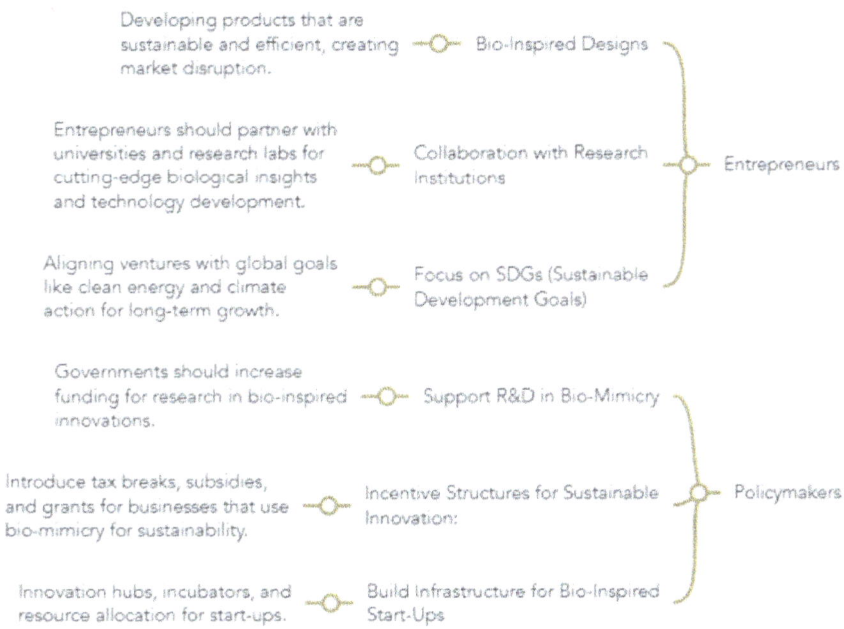


## RECOMMENDATIONS

### Entrepreneurs:

- **Leverage Bio-Inspired Designs for Market Disruption:** Entrepreneurs should explore how bio-mimicry can provide competitive advantages in sectors such as energy, healthcare, and manufacturing. By developing products that are both sustainable and efficient, bio-inspired start-ups can disrupt existing markets and create new opportunities.
- **Collaborate with Research Institutions:** Given the interdisciplinary nature of bio-inspired innovation, entrepreneurs should collaborate with academic institutions, research centers, and design laboratories to access cutting-edge scientific knowledge and technical expertise.
- **Focus on Sustainable Development Goals (SDGs):** Entrepreneurs can align their ventures with the United Nations' Sustainable Development Goals, particularly those focused on climate action, clean energy, and responsible con-

sumption. This alignment not only fosters long-term growth but also attracts environmentally conscious consumers and investors.

## Policymakers:

- **Support Research and Development (R&D) in Bio-Mimicry:** Governments should increase funding for bio-inspired research and create policies that encourage innovation in this field. Establishing public-private partnerships can help accelerate the commercialization of bio-mimetic solutions and foster collaboration between academia and industry.
- **Develop Incentive Structures for Sustainable Innovation:** To promote the adoption of bio-inspired solutions, policymakers should offer tax incentives, grants, and subsidies for start-ups and companies that incorporate biomimicry into their products and services. Additionally, creating a regulatory framework that rewards environmentally sustainable practices can further encourage innovation.
- **Build Infrastructure for Bio-Inspired Start-Ups:** Governments should invest in infrastructure, such as innovation hubs and incubators, specifically designed to support bio-mimetic start-ups. Providing access to resources such as laboratories, testing facilities, and mentorship can help new ventures overcome the technical challenges of bio-inspired innovation.

## Investors:

- **Invest in Bio-Inspired Start-Ups for Long-Term Growth:** Bio-inspired innovations are positioned for long-term growth as industries shift toward sustainability. Investors should consider allocating capital to bio-mimetic start-ups that offer scalable and sustainable solutions in fields such as renewable energy, healthcare, and agriculture.
- **Support Sustainable Business Models:** Investors should prioritize funding for companies that integrate sustainability into their core business models. Bio-mimetic solutions that align with environmental, social, and governance (ESG) principles not only contribute to a sustainable future but also generate strong financial returns as consumer demand for sustainable products increases.
- **Encourage Collaboration and Knowledge Sharing:** Investors can play a critical role in fostering collaboration between companies, research institutions, and start-ups. By supporting platforms that encourage knowledge sharing and cross-disciplinary innovation, investors can help accelerate the development and commercialization of bio-inspired technologies.

## SCOPE FOR FUTURE RESEARCH

Future research can focus on examining industry-specific challenges and opportunities in adopting bio-inspired innovations, particularly in agriculture, healthcare, and renewable energy. Additionally, further studies can explore advancements in bio-inspired materials and nanotechnology for industrial applications. Moreover, an in-depth analysis of venture capital trends, funding barriers, and market readiness for bio-entrepreneurship in India would provide valuable insights into fostering a supportive ecosystem for sustainable innovation.

## SCOPE AND LIMITATIONS

The study is limited to a secondary data analysis and does not include primary data collection through interviews or surveys. While this approach allows for a broad understanding of the field, future research could benefit from empirical validation through case studies or stakeholder interviews.

By leveraging a qualitative and interdisciplinary approach, this study provides a holistic perspective on how bio-inspired innovation can contribute to sustainable industries. The findings are relevant to entrepreneurs, policymakers, and investors, offering strategic insights for fostering bio-mimetic entrepreneurship in India and beyond.

## CONCLUSION

Biomimicry represents a transformative paradigm capable of redefining how organizations conceptualize innovation, sustainability, and competitive advantage in the Fourth Industrial Revolution. Rather than functioning solely as a design methodology, bio-inspired innovation emerges as a strategic capability that integrates ecological intelligence with organizational adaptability, systems thinking, and regenerative value creation.

By integrating insights from the Resource-Based View, VRIO framework, Dynamic Capabilities Theory, Responsible Innovation, and Circular Economy perspectives, this chapter demonstrates that biomimicry can strengthen organizational resilience, enhance sustainability performance, and support long-term strategic competitiveness.

The chapter further highlights the strategic relevance of biomimicry within India's entrepreneurial ecosystem, where biodiversity, indigenous ecological knowledge, and emerging technological capabilities collectively create substantial opportunities for sustainable innovation. However, realizing this potential requires stronger institutional collaboration, interdisciplinary research ecosystems, policy support, investment mechanisms, and sustainability-oriented management education.

Ultimately, bio-inspired innovation offers organizations an opportunity to move beyond extractive growth models toward regenerative and responsible systems capable of balancing economic prosperity with ecological stewardship. As industries increasingly confront climate uncertainty, resource scarcity, and stakeholder pressures, biomimicry provides a strategic pathway toward resilient, ethical, and sustainable futures..

## REFERENCES


Aguilar-Planet, T., & Peralta, E. (2024). Innovation inspired by nature: Applications of biomimicry in engineering design. *Biomimetics*, *9*(9), 523. DOI: 10.3390/biomimetics9090523 PMID: 39329545

Andrew, R. (2018). *Guest post: Why India's CO2 emissions grew strongly in 2017.* Carbon Brief.

Audretsch, D. B. (2014). From the entrepreneurial university to the university for the entrepreneurial society. *The Journal of Technology Transfer*, *39*(3), 313–321. DOI: 10.1007/s10961-012-9288-1

Badrak, O. (n.d.). How butterfly wings inspire innovation. Smithsonian Magazine. https://www.smithsonianmag.com

Barney, J. B. (1991). Firm resources and sustained competitive advantage. *Journal of Management*, *17*(1), 99–120. DOI: 10.1177/014920639101700108

Benyus, J. M. (1997). *Biomimicry: Innovation inspired by nature.* Morrow.

Benyus, J. M. (1997). *Biomimicry: Innovation inspired by nature.* HarperCollins.

Bhutia, K. (2016). *Can startups give a boost to the Indian economy?* Entrepreneur India.

Bingi, J., & Thiruchanuru, S. (2025). Bio-inspired design: Works and perspectives of Bio-Inspired Research and Design Laboratory. Notion Press.

Christensen, C. M., Raynor, M. E., & McDonald, R. (2015). What is disruptive innovation? *Harvard Business Review*, •••, 44–53. PMID: 17183796

Dooley, P. (2014). Pomegranates inspire new battery design. *Cosmos.*

Elkington, J. (1997). *Cannibals with forks: The triple bottom line of 21st century business.* Capstone Publishing.

Etzkowitz, H., & Leydesdorff, L. (2000). The dynamics of innovation: From National Systems and "Mode 2" to a Triple Helix of university–industry–government relations. *Research Policy*, *29*(2), 109–123. DOI: 10.1016/S0048-7333(99)00055-4

Fiveable Inc. (2024). Bio-inspired innovation. https://library.fiveable.me/key-terms/biomimicry-in-business-innovation/bio-inspired-innovation

Garvin, C. (2015). *Tapping into nature: Bio-inspired innovation as an economic engine.* GreenBiz.

Geissdoerfer, M., Savaget, P., Bocken, N. M. P., & Hultink, E. J. (2017). The circular economy – A new sustainability paradigm? *Journal of Cleaner Production, 143*, 757–768. DOI: 10.1016/j.jclepro.2016.12.048

Hart, S. L., & Dowell, G. (2011). A natural-resource-based view of the firm: Fifteen years after. *Journal of Management, 37*(5), 1464–1479. DOI: 10.1177/0149206310390219

Janine, B. (2015). The Bio-Mimicry Institute.

Jurevicius, O. (2023, December 1). VRIO framework. Strategic Management Insight.

Jurevicius, O. (2023, October 24). Resource-based view. Strategic Management Insight.

Kim, S. (2019). The fourth industrial revolution: Trends and impacts on the world of work. In McGrath, S., Mulder, M., Papier, J., & Suart, R. (Eds.), *Handbook of vocational education and training*. Springer., DOI: 10.1007/978-3-319-94532-3

Lorenzo, V. d. (2018, May 16). How biotechnology is evolving in the fourth industrial revolution. World Economic Forum. https://www.weforum.org/agenda/2018/05/biotechnology-evolve-fourth-industrial-revolution/

Michael Chui, J. M. (2020). The bio revolution: Innovations transforming economies, societies, and our lives. McKinsey & Company. https://www.mckinsey.com/industries/life-sciences/our-insights/the-bio-revolution-innovations-transforming-economies-societies-and-our-lives

OECD. (2019). *University–industry collaboration: New evidence and policy options*. OECD Publishing., DOI: 10.1787/e9c1e648-

OECD. (2020). *Smart cities and inclusive growth*. OECD Publishing., DOI: 10.1787/3a8fdbab-

Prahalad, C. K. (2012). Bottom of the pyramid as a source of breakthrough innovations. *Journal of Product Innovation Management, 29*(1), 6–12. DOI: 10.1111/j.1540-5885.2011.00874.x

Raworth, K. (2017). *Doughnut economics: Seven ways to think like a 21st-century economist*. Chelsea Green Publishing.

Schaltegger, S., Hansen, E. G., & Lüdeke-Freund, F. (2016). Business models for sustainability: Origins, present research, and future avenues. *Organization & Environment, 29*(1), 3–10. DOI: 10.1177/1086026615599806

Schwab, K. (2016). The fourth industrial revolution: What it means and how to respond. World Economic Forum.

Singh, N. (2019). How can we regulate disruptive technologies? World Economic Forum.

Smith, J. A. (2020). Understanding biomimicry: Lessons from butterfly wings. Smithsonian Magazine. https://www.smithsonianmag.com

Stilgoe, J., Owen, R., & Macnaghten, P. (2013). Developing a framework for responsible innovation. *Research Policy*, *42*(9), 1568–1580. DOI: 10.1016/j.respol.2013.05.008

Teece, D., Peteraf, M., & Leih, S. (2016). Dynamic capabilities and organizational agility: Risk, uncertainty, and strategy in the innovation economy. California Management Review, 58(4), 13–35. (Original work published 2016)DOI: 10.1525/cmr.2016.58.4.13

Teece, D. J. (2007). Explicating dynamic capabilities: The nature and microfoundations of (sustainable) enterprise performance. *Strategic Management Journal*, *28*(13), 1319–1350. DOI: 10.1002/smj.640

Teece, D. J., Peteraf, M., & Leih, S. (2016). Dynamic capabilities and organizational agility. *California Management Review*, *58*(4), 13–35. DOI: 10.1525/cmr.2016.58.4.13

Wernerfelt, B. (1984). A resource-based view of the firm. *Strategic Management Journal*, *5*(2), 171–180. DOI: 10.1002/smj.4250050207

Zott, C., Amit, R., & Massa, L. (2011). The business model: Recent developments and future research. *Journal of Management*, *37*(4), 1019–1042. DOI: 10.1177/0149206311406265

Chapter 10

# Innovation Under Constraint and Boundary Pushing Entrepreneurship: The Prohibition Era Mississippi, USA in Context

**Babu George**
http://orcid.org/0000-0002-2791-828X
*Alcorn State University, USA*

**Thomas Panko**
http://orcid.org/0009-0006-6003-5223
*University of Southern Mississippi, USA*

## ABSTRACT

*This chapter explores entrepreneurial innovation catalyzed by the restrictive environment of the Prohibition Era in the United States (1920-1933). The purpose is to introduce and analyze Boundary Pushing Entrepreneurship a new framework for understanding how entrepreneurs leverage constraints to create thriving ventures. The content summarizes five key principles of this framework: contrarian thinking, creative problem-solving, operating in gray areas, resilience, and the use of guerrilla tactics. This framework provides a valuable lens for both historical analysis and modern strategic management. Using the historical context of Prohibition-era Mississippi, innovative strategies, such as the development of complex smuggling networks and the operation of floating bars on the Mississippi River, are presented*

DOI: 10.4018/979-8-2600-3179-7.ch010

*to illustrate how entrepreneurs exploited ambiguous legal and geographical conditions. These historical practices are situated within broader entrepreneurial theory, while highlighting potential areas for improvement in it.*

## 1. INTRODUCTION

The Prohibition Era (1920–1933) marked one of the most transformative periods in United States history, as sweeping legislation sought to curtail alcohol consumption by banning its manufacture, sale, and transportation. Enacted through the 18th Amendment and enforced by the Volstead Act, these policies were intended to improve public health and morality. However, the era instead ushered in a host of unintended consequences, including widespread noncompliance, the rise of organized crime, and the emergence of an extensive underground economy (Edwards & Howe, 2015). Entrepreneurs, both large and small, played a pivotal role in shaping this shadow economy, leveraging the challenges of the prohibitionist framework to pioneer innovative approaches to trade, distribution, and customer engagement.

The prohibition of alcohol disrupted established markets, but it also created opportunities for individuals willing to navigate legal ambiguities and adapt to a rapidly shifting regulatory landscape (Hall, 2017). These entrepreneurs capitalized on the persistent demand for alcohol, employing unconventional tactics and innovative business models to meet consumer needs while evading law enforcement. Their activities illuminate the entrepreneurial potential that emerges under constraint and offer insights into the broader dynamics of adaptation, resilience, and innovation in response to regulatory upheaval.

This research further develops the concept of *Boundary Pushing Entrepreneurship*, a theoretical framework that examines how entrepreneurs operate in constrained environments by challenging conventional norms and exploiting legal gray areas. The study draws on historical examples from the Prohibition Era to identify the defining characteristics of this model, including contrarian thinking, creative problem-solving, resilience, and guerrilla tactics. While the paper uses illustrative cases to contextualize these principles, it prioritizes advancing the theoretical understanding of entrepreneurial behavior under constraint.

Boundary pushing entrepreneurship refers to entrepreneurial activities that operate in the ambiguous space between the legal and illegal, the sanctioned and unsanctioned, or the formal and informal, a concept especially relevant in developing economies and transitional contexts where regulatory enforcement is inconsistent and opportunities exist at the margins of official policy (Ferchen & Mattlin, 2023; George, 2018). This concept is closely linked to theories of the informal economy, which examine how entrepreneurs exploit regulatory gaps and ambiguous enforcement to pursue opportunities that may not be fully legal or officially sanctioned, highlighting the role of state actors and regulators in creating or tolerating these spaces and making informality a dynamic interplay between entrepreneurs and the state. Within institutional theory in entrepreneurship, which emphasizes how formal and informal rules shape entrepreneurial behavior, boundary pushing entrepreneurship illustrates how entrepreneurs navigate, challenge, or exploit institutional boundaries, sometimes with tacit approval from officials and sometimes in outright defiance (George & Wooden, 2025). Traditional entrepreneurship theories focus on opportunity recognition and resource mobilization, but boundary pushing entrepreneurs extend these concepts by identifying and acting on opportunities that exist specifically because of regulatory ambiguity or weak enforcement, often leveraging personal or local networks to do so (George, B., & Mattathil, 2025). Boundary pushing entrepreneurship is best understood as a hybrid concept that draws from and extends established theories of informality, institutional dynamics, and opportunity recognition, highlighting how entrepreneurs operate in regulatory grey zones often shaped by the interplay between state enforcement and entrepreneurial initiative.

The article brings additional nuance to this with the introduction of the concept of illicit entrepreneurship. Illicit entrepreneurship encompasses business activities that operate outside legal frameworks, including informal, underground, and criminal enterprises, arising from a mix of necessity, opportunity, and institutional factors with prevalence and impact varying widely across regions and economic systems (Othman et al., 2022; Putra et al., 2024; Smith & McElwee, 2013; Welter et al., 2015; Galemba, 2008). These ventures are often driven by both necessity, such as lack of formal job opportunities, and opportunity, including recognition of profitable ventures, with some individuals motivated by personal interests or comfort, as seen in contexts like Padang City, Indonesia, and Malaysia where necessity-based entrepreneurs engage in illegal activities to meet basic needs while opportunity-based actors exploit market gaps for profit (Othman et al., 2022; Putra et al., 2024). The distinction between informal and illegal entrepreneurship is nuanced, with many activities existing in a "grey area" between legality and illegitimacy (Smith & McElwee, 2013; Welter et al., 2015; Galemba, 2008). Weak formal institutions, corruption, and organized crime significantly shape illicit entrepreneurship, and in regions with pervasive extortion or bribery, entrepreneurs may avoid formal registration to escape criminal costs or bureaucratic harassment (Mallon & Fainshmidt, 2020; Fadahunsi & Rosa, 2002). Historical and cultural contexts, such as traditional land rights or post-socialist transitions, also influence the persistence and forms of illegal business, and societal acceptance of informal or illegal activities often depends on whether they are seen as antisocial or simply necessary for survival (Adobor, 2025; Pehe & Kupka, 2024; Othman et al., 2022; Galemba, 2008). Illicit entrepreneurship can contribute to economic activity and job creation, especially in environments where formal opportunities are limited, but it also undermines state control, fosters shadow economies, and can lead to increased crime and regulatory challenges (Fadahunsi & Rosa, 2002; Saniel et al., 2025; Balabiyev, 2023; Shaposhnykov, 2023; Verchenko & Sabol, 2024). Legal responses vary, with some countries focusing on criminalizing specific illegal actions such as tax evasion or unlicensed activity rather than mere lack of registration (Balabiyev, 2023; Verchenko & Sabol, 2024).

### The objectives of this study are as follows:

1. To analyze entrepreneurial strategies that emerged during the Prohibition Era as responses to the constraints imposed by temperance legislation.
2. To introduce the Boundary Pushing Entrepreneurship framework and explore its relevance to constrained and regulated markets.
3. To discuss the ethical dimensions of operating in legal gray areas, balancing innovation and social responsibility.
4. To extract lessons for contemporary entrepreneurs navigating challenges in rapidly evolving or highly regulated industries.

This paper's significance lies in its ability to connect historical entrepreneurial practices with contemporary challenges. By understanding the entrepreneurial ingenuity of the Prohibition Era, we can better appreciate the ways in which individuals respond to adversity and capitalize on emerging opportunities. Furthermore, the study highlights the unintended consequences of regulatory policies, providing a historical lens through which to inform current debates about innovation, ethics, and economic adaptation. By situating the concept of Boundary Pushing Entrepreneurship within the broader historical and theoretical context, this research contributes to the understanding of entrepreneurial dynamics in environments of legal and social constraint. The insights gained from the Prohibition Era offer both inspiration and caution for modern entrepreneurship, emphasizing the power of innovation while acknowledging the ethical complexities inherent in operating at the margins of legality.

## 2. THE PROHIBITION ERA: A CATALYST FOR ENTREPRENEURIAL INNOVATION

The Prohibition Era stands as a period of profound transformation in American socio-economic history (Blocker, 2006). Rooted in the temperance movement, the enactment of the 18th Amendment and the Volstead Act sought to curb the consumption of alcohol by prohibiting its production, sale, and transportation. Advocates of Prohibition envisioned a society freed from the social ills of alcohol abuse, anticipating a decline in crime, poverty, and disorder (Lewis, 2008). However, the effects of this sweeping legislation deviated markedly from its intended goals. Instead of eradicating alcohol use, Prohibition led to its clandestine production and distribution, fueling a vibrant underground economy that reshaped the entrepreneurial landscape.

## Socio-Economic Impacts of Prohibition

Prohibition disrupted established industries, particularly breweries, distilleries, and saloons, forcing many legitimate businesses to shut down. At the same time, it created opportunities for new forms of economic activity, albeit outside the boundaries of legality. This economic upheaval highlighted the resilience of market forces, as consumer demand for alcohol persisted despite legal restrictions. Bootlegging, speakeasies, and smuggling became widespread, supported by a burgeoning network of entrepreneurs who supplied illicit liquor to a thirsty populace (Haller, 1990). The rise of these informal economies not only undercut the goals of Prohibition but also contributed to the erosion of respect for the rule of law and the proliferation of organized crime (Hall, 2010).

The economic consequences extended beyond alcohol-related industries. Law enforcement costs surged as federal and local agencies struggled to curb illicit activities, often facing corruption and resource limitations. Meanwhile, public discontent grew as ordinary citizens found themselves implicated in activities that were technically illegal but widely normalized. These dynamics underscore how Prohibition not only transformed the economic landscape but also shifted societal attitudes toward regulation and governance (Blackman, 2010).

## The Sub Rosa Economy and the Unintended Consequences of Prohibition

The underground economy that emerged during Prohibition, often referred to as the "sub rosa economy," was characterized by a complex interplay of innovation, risk-taking, and adaptation. Entrepreneurs in this shadow market exploited legal loopholes and developed new methods of production, distribution, and marketing to evade detection. For instance, small-scale distilleries flourished in rural areas, while urban speakeasies offered clandestine spaces for socializing and drinking. The adaptability and creativity of these operators illustrate the entrepreneurial response to restrictive policies.

The unintended consequences of Prohibition extended to the empowerment of criminal syndicates, which took advantage of the high profits associated with the illegal alcohol trade. Figures like Al Capone became emblematic of the era, amassing wealth and influence by controlling bootlegging operations. While organized crime dominated popular narratives, smaller-scale entrepreneurs also played a significant role in sustaining the underground economy. Their ingenuity and willingness to operate in gray areas reveal the broader entrepreneurial spirit that Prohibition inadvertently nurtured.

### The Rise of Entrepreneurial Activity in Illegal and Semi-Legal Markets

Prohibition created an environment where entrepreneurial innovation thrived under constraint. Individuals and groups developed creative solutions to meet consumer demand while navigating the risks of legal penalties and social stigma. This included not only bootlegging and smuggling but also innovative ventures like floating bars, concealed distilleries, and novel distribution networks. The entrepreneurial activity of this era highlights the interplay between regulation and market adaptation, demonstrating how constraints can spur ingenuity rather than stifle it (Muehlmann, 2018).

Moreover, Prohibition-era entrepreneurs operated at various scales, from local moonshiners to sophisticated smuggling networks spanning international borders. Women also played significant roles in this shadow economy, often managing family-run operations that challenged traditional gender norms (Muehlmann, 2018). These diverse forms of entrepreneurial activity reveal the wide-ranging impacts of Prohibition, both in terms of economic practices and societal attitudes.

Prohibition's legacy as a catalyst for entrepreneurial innovation lies in its unintended consequences. By criminalizing a widespread and culturally embedded practice, the policy created fertile ground for creative problem-solving and the emergence of new business models. The era's entrepreneurs exemplify the principles of *Boundary Pushing Entrepreneurship*, as they operated in constrained environments, leveraged ambiguities in the law, and adapted to shifting societal norms. This dynamic underscores the broader relationship between regulation and innovation, providing valuable lessons for understanding entrepreneurship in other constrained or rapidly changing markets.

## 3. BOUNDARY PUSHING ENTREPRENEURSHIP: A CONCEPTUAL FRAMEWORK

### Defining Boundary Pushing Entrepreneurship

Boundary Pushing Entrepreneurship refers to the strategic and innovative approach entrepreneurs adopt to thrive in environments characterized by constraints, legal uncertainties, or significant social and economic upheaval. Unlike traditional entrepreneurship, which operates predominantly within established legal and regulatory frameworks, boundary-pushing entrepreneurs navigate the edges of legality and social acceptability to identify and exploit opportunities. This model of entrepreneurship emerges prominently in periods of disruption, such as the Prohibition Era, where conventional market structures are replaced by ambiguous or restricted alternatives.

At its core, Boundary Pushing Entrepreneurship is defined by five key principles:

1. Contrarian Thinking: The ability to challenge prevailing norms and identify opportunities where others see obstacles. Entrepreneurs adopting this mindset thrive by rejecting conventional wisdom and finding value in overlooked or dismissed markets.
2. Creative Problem-Solving: A hallmark of boundary-pushing entrepreneurs is their ability to devise innovative solutions to navigate constraints. This may involve leveraging novel technologies, exploiting legal loopholes, or reimagining business processes to overcome barriers.
3. Operating in Gray Areas: These entrepreneurs often work within spaces that are not strictly legal but not outright illegal, exploiting ambiguities in the law or societal norms. This approach enables them to circumvent restrictive policies while minimizing exposure to legal risks.
4. Resilience: The ability to adapt to rapidly changing conditions and recover from setbacks is critical for survival in constrained environments. Resilient entrepreneurs demonstrate flexibility and determination in the face of adversity.
5. Guerrilla Tactics: Boundary-pushing entrepreneurs often employ unconventional and resource-efficient strategies to outmaneuver competitors and overcome structural barriers. These tactics include leveraging asymmetrical advantages, such as small-scale operations, to evade detection or capture niche markets.

## Situating the Framework in Entrepreneurial Theory

Boundary Pushing Entrepreneurship builds on existing theories of entrepreneurship while addressing gaps related to innovation under constraint and the ethical dimensions of operating in gray areas. It intersects with several well-established concepts, including:

- Opportunity Recognition: Entrepreneurs in constrained environments exhibit heightened opportunity recognition skills, identifying gaps created by legal restrictions or market failures. This aligns with Shane and Venkataraman's (2000) framework, which emphasizes the discovery and exploitation of opportunities as central to entrepreneurial action.

- Effectuation Theory: Sarasvathy's (2001) concept of effectuation highlights the iterative and adaptive nature of entrepreneurial decision-making. Boundary-pushing entrepreneurs epitomize effectual reasoning by leveraging available resources and navigating uncertainties to achieve their goals.
- Institutional Entrepreneurship: This theory examines how entrepreneurs challenge and reshape institutional norms and structures. Boundary-pushing entrepreneurs often engage in institutional bricolage, creatively combining elements of formal and informal systems to establish new norms (DiMaggio, 1988).
- Resource-Based View: In constrained environments, entrepreneurs must optimize scarce resources. The resourcefulness and ingenuity exhibited by boundary-pushing entrepreneurs reflect their ability to create value under conditions of scarcity.

## Relevance to Constrained Environments

Boundary Pushing Entrepreneurship is particularly relevant in contexts where traditional market mechanisms are disrupted by external forces, such as regulatory changes, economic crises, or social upheavals. The Prohibition Era provides a compelling historical example, as entrepreneurs responded to the sudden criminalization of alcohol with a spectrum of innovative strategies (Haller, 1990). Similar dynamics can be observed in modern contexts, such as the gig economy, cryptocurrency markets, or heavily regulated industries like cannabis or pharmaceuticals.

By navigating gray areas and employing creative problem-solving, boundary-pushing entrepreneurs fill critical gaps in constrained markets, often catalyzing broader societal and economic changes (Muehlmann, 2018). However, their activities also raise complex ethical questions, particularly concerning the balance between innovation and legality. While their ingenuity can drive progress and adaptation, the potential social costs of their actions - such as undermining regulatory frameworks or perpetuating inequalities - cannot be overlooked.

The Boundary Pushing Entrepreneurship framework offers a lens to analyze and understand entrepreneurial behavior under constraint. It underscores the capacity of individuals and organizations to adapt, innovate, and thrive despite external limitations, providing valuable insights for navigating today's increasingly complex and regulated global markets.

## 4. ENTREPRENEURSHIP IN PROHIBITION-ERA MISSISSIPPI

The state of Mississippi during the Prohibition Era presented a unique set of conditions that fostered innovative and boundary-pushing entrepreneurial activities (Parker, 2020). Its geographical features, socio-legal environment, and cultural dynamics combined to create fertile ground for illicit and semi-legal ventures (Ellender et al., 1980). Entrepreneurs operating in Mississippi exploited these conditions to navigate the challenges posed by Prohibition, developing strategies that not only circumvented restrictive laws but also redefined the local economic landscape (Ager et al., 2016).

### Geographical Advantages

Mississippi's proximity to the Mississippi River and the Gulf of Mexico offered significant logistical advantages for entrepreneurial activities during Prohibition. The river served as a vital artery for commerce, enabling the transport of goods, including illicit alcohol, across state and national boundaries (O'Rourke, 2011). Its meandering course and numerous tributaries provided ideal cover for smuggling operations, allowing entrepreneurs to evade law enforcement by navigating remote or less-policed routes (Ellender et al., 1980). Additionally, the state's vast rural landscapes and dense forests were conducive to the operation of concealed distilleries and moonshine production facilities. These locations, often far from urban centers, allowed entrepreneurs to manufacture alcohol with reduced risk of detection. The combination of access to waterways and isolated terrain created an environment where innovative supply chains could flourish.

### The Socio-Legal Environment

Mississippi's early adoption of prohibitionist policies further shaped the entrepreneurial responses to alcohol restrictions. The state enacted its own prohibition laws in 1908, more than a decade before the national ban, giving local entrepreneurs a head start in developing strategies to circumvent such legislation. Enforcement challenges, coupled with limited resources and widespread public resistance, created opportunities for individuals willing to operate in legal gray areas (McGirr, 2015). Moreover, Mississippi's social fabric, influenced by a history of hierarchical structures and cultural attitudes toward authority, contributed to the persistence of informal economies. While law enforcement agencies worked to uphold prohibitionist laws, corruption and selective enforcement often undermined these efforts. Entrepreneurs adept at navigating these socio-legal complexities were able to exploit gaps in the system to sustain their operations.

## Cultural Dynamics and Social Attitudes

Cultural attitudes toward alcohol consumption in Mississippi were deeply divided, reflecting the broader national tension between rural temperance advocates and urban populations accustomed to a more permissive social environment. This dichotomy fueled demand for illicit alcohol among segments of the population who viewed Prohibition as an infringement on personal liberties. Entrepreneurs capitalized on this demand, positioning themselves as providers of a service that was both culturally embedded and economically lucrative. The state's historical reliance on communal networks and local partnerships also facilitated the growth of entrepreneurial ventures. Many illegal operations, such as moonshining or bootlegging, were family-run or relied on close-knit communities for support. This collaborative approach not only distributed risk but also reinforced the social legitimacy of these activities within certain groups.

## Entrepreneurial Strategies in Prohibition-Era Mississippi

The entrepreneurs of Mississippi demonstrated remarkable ingenuity in their efforts to meet demand and evade detection. Some of the key strategies employed include:

1. Smuggling Networks: Mississippi's access to waterways made it a hub for smuggling operations, with entrepreneurs using boats to transport alcohol along the Mississippi River and its tributaries. These networks often extended to neighboring states and even international suppliers, leveraging the interconnected waterways to distribute their products.
2. Innovative Distribution Models: Entrepreneurs devised creative methods to deliver alcohol to customers while minimizing risk. For example, floating bars moored in ambiguous jurisdictions exploited legal loopholes, allowing operators to serve alcohol outside the reach of state enforcement. These mobile establishments could relocate as needed to avoid detection.
3. Concealed Production Facilities: The dense rural terrain of Mississippi was ideal for moonshine production. Entrepreneurs used hidden stills and innovative distillation techniques to produce alcohol efficiently while reducing the likelihood of discovery by authorities.
4. Diversification of Ventures: Many entrepreneurs expanded their activities beyond alcohol production and distribution to include related enterprises, such as transportation, hospitality, and even gambling. This diversification not only increased revenue streams but also provided a cover for illicit operations.
5. Community Integration: By embedding their activities within local communities, entrepreneurs were able to build networks of trust and mutual benefit.

These relationships often extended to law enforcement or local officials, further insulating operations from scrutiny.

### Mississippi as a Microcosm of Boundary Pushing Entrepreneurship

The entrepreneurial activity observed in Prohibition-era Mississippi exemplifies the principles of Boundary Pushing Entrepreneurship. Entrepreneurs in the state operated at the intersection of legality and innovation, leveraging their environment to adapt and thrive under restrictive conditions. Their ability to exploit geographical advantages, navigate socio-legal complexities, and engage in creative problem-solving underscores the broader dynamics of entrepreneurship under constraint.

By examining these strategies, the entrepreneurial responses in Mississippi during the Prohibition Era provide valuable insights into how individuals can innovate and adapt in response to external pressures. These lessons resonate beyond their historical context, offering a framework for understanding contemporary entrepreneurial behavior in similarly constrained environments.

## 5. CASE EXAMPLE: ENTREPRENEURSHIP IN THE MISSISSIPPI RIVER ECONOMY

The entrepreneurial landscape of the Prohibition Era is richly illustrated by the activities of entrepreneurs in regions like Mississippi. The stories from this period, often blending fact with local lore, serve as compelling examples of the principles outlined in the Boundary Pushing Entrepreneurship framework. Operating in one of the most challenging and restrictive environments of the time, these entrepreneurs exhibited exceptional ingenuity, resilience, and adaptability, which are hallmarks of this entrepreneurial model.

### Floating Bars: Innovation in Navigating Constraints

Among the most innovative ventures of the time was the creation of floating bars along the Mississippi River. These establishments leveraged the unique regulatory environment of the river, where enforcement varied and jurisdictional boundaries created operational flexibility. By situating these bars in strategically ambiguous locations, entrepreneurs were able to adapt to complex legal conditions and sustain their operations.

More than just a clever workaround, these floating venues were thoughtfully designed to attract a loyal clientele. Proprietors often incorporated features such as live music, dancing, and gambling, creating a vibrant and engaging atmosphere. This approach exemplifies creative problem-solving, as regulatory challenges were transformed into opportunities to stand out in a competitive underground market.

## Technological Ingenuity: The Submarine Narrative

The rumored use of a one-man submarine to transport goods across the Mississippi River demonstrates a bold and resourceful approach to problem-solving. Local stories suggest that this innovation, potentially powered by a repurposed Model T Ford engine, enabled discreet movement of supplies under challenging conditions. While these accounts remain speculative, they highlight a reputation for entrepreneurship willing to explore unconventional methods to achieve its goals.

The submarine narrative reflects the application of guerrilla tactics strategies that maximize impact while minimizing exposure to risk. Whether literal or symbolic, this story underscores an ability to think differently and embrace cutting-edge methods far removed from traditional practices.

## Diversified Ventures: Ensuring Long-Term Success

The entrepreneurial vision of many successful figures from this period extended beyond a single industry. Efforts were diversified into a variety of ventures, including managing plantations, developing steamboat transportation services, and investing in real estate and hospitality. This diversification not only provided multiple revenue streams but also reduced reliance on any single enterprise, positioning them to weather economic uncertainties.

By blending ventures across legal and semi-legal domains, these entrepreneurs demonstrated a forward-thinking approach to business, ensuring sustained success even after the repeal of Prohibition. The ability to pivot and adapt reflects a core principle of the Boundary Pushing model: thriving amidst external pressures through strategic resilience.

## Exemplification of Boundary Pushing Entrepreneurship

### Embrace Contrarian Thinking

One of the hallmarks of the entrepreneurial approach during this time was a willingness to think differently and challenge conventional wisdom. At a time when most saloonkeepers and liquor traders were shutting down their operations in the face of Prohibition, some saw an opportunity to thrive by catering to the persistent demand for alcohol. This contrarian mindset allowed them to identify and capitalize on opportunities that others had overlooked or dismissed.

Contrarian thinking in entrepreneurship is a valuable approach that can lead to innovation, challenge conventional wisdom, and drive strategic decision-making. Contrarian thinking involves questioning prevailing beliefs or trends in an industry or market, often resulting in unique insights and competitive advantages (Felin, 2024). By challenging established norms and exploring unconventional ideas, entrepreneurs can identify new opportunities and differentiate themselves from competitors. The significance of contrarian thinking is particularly evident in the startup context, where embracing unconventional approaches can be a critical driver of success. Startups often operate in highly competitive environments where differentiation is crucial for survival. By adopting contrarian beliefs and problem-solving strategies, entrepreneurs can carve out a niche for themselves and disrupt traditional business models (Felin, 2024).

Contrarian thinking also plays a substantial role in challenging the status quo and instigating organizational change. In the face of uncertainty and rapid technological advancements, businesses need to be agile and adaptable to stay ahead. Contrarian perspectives can assist organizations in anticipating market shifts, identifying emerging trends, and capitalizing on untapped opportunities. Moreover, contrarian thinking is closely associated with risk-taking and resilience, which are essential traits for entrepreneurial success. Entrepreneurs who are willing to challenge conventional wisdom and take calculated risks are more likely to achieve long-term growth and sustainability. By embracing contrarian viewpoints, entrepreneurs can navigate uncertainty confidently and turn challenges into opportunities.

Contrarian thinking extends beyond individual entrepreneurs; it can also influence industry dynamics and market trends. By challenging prevailing narratives and introducing disruptive innovations, contrarians can shape entire sectors and redefine industry standards (Sjögren & Yusuf, 2021). Contrarian entrepreneurs often serve as change catalysts, driving competition and fostering innovation (Sjögren & Yusuf, 2021). In the realm of corporate social responsibility (CSR), contrarian thinking can prompt a reevaluation of traditional business practices and the adoption of more sustainable and ethical approaches (Kemper & Martin, 2010). By challenging the prevailing norms of profit-maximization and short-term gains, contrarian perspectives can advocate for a more holistic view of business success that considers social and environmental impact (Kemper & Martin, 2010). Contrarian thinking is also valuable in the realm of investment and finance, where it can aid investors in identifying undervalued assets and capitalizing on market inefficiencies (Chau et al., 2016). By taking a contrarian approach to market sentiment and trends, investors can uncover hidden opportunities and achieve superior returns (Chau et al., 2016).

Contrarian investors often excel in volatile markets by maintaining a long-term perspective and avoiding herd mentality (Chau et al., 2016).

## Mastering Creative Problem-Solving

Success during Prohibition was a testament to the resolve and ability of these entrepreneurs to solve complex problems creatively. Faced with the constant threat of law enforcement and the challenges of operating in an illegal market, innovators developed solutions like the floating bars and the rumored use of a one-man submarine for liquor smuggling. This mastery of creative problem-solving enabled them to stay one step ahead of competitors and adapt to the ever-changing landscape of the Prohibition Era.

Creative problem-solving is a fundamental aspect of entrepreneurship, crucial for recognizing opportunities, surmounting obstacles, and fostering innovation in business ventures. The capacity to approach challenges from diverse perspectives and develop innovative solutions is a key skill for entrepreneurs (Funken et al., 2018). Studies have shown that embracing a high error mastery orientation can improve entrepreneurial learning from problems, highlighting the significance of resilience and adaptability in overcoming hurdles (Funken et al., 2018). Entrepreneurial success is strongly associated with the ability for creative problem-solving, as evidenced by research on the influence of STEM-based entrepreneurship programs on students' entrepreneurial intentions (Shahin et al., 2021). Key skills such as identifying opportunities, creative problem-solving, positive role-modeling, and teamwork are identified as essential elements that enhance entrepreneurial intent and promote innovative thinking (Shahin et al., 2021). This emphasizes the importance of nurturing a creative mindset to address complex challenges in entrepreneurial pursuits.

Experiential learning methods that emphasize problem-solving and creativity have been proven to be highly effective in cultivating entrepreneurial skills among students (Williams, 2015). Through engaging in hands-on learning experiences that promote creative problem-solving and peer assessment, students can enhance their capacity to tackle real-world entrepreneurial challenges (Williams, 2015). This practical approach fosters a culture of continuous learning and experimentation, crucial for entrepreneurial triumph. In the field of occupational therapy, mastery is characterized by a set of personal traits, including creativity, dedication to practice, and intelligence, which are vital for effective problem-solving and favorable patient outcomes (Burke & DePoy, 1991). This underscores the importance of creativity in driving excellence and leadership in professional practice, demonstrating how innovative problem-solving strategies can lead to positive results across various domains (Burke & DePoy, 1991).

Entrepreneurship education plays a pivotal role in honing creative problem-solving skills among students, equipping them to identify opportunities and tackle intricate business dilemmas (Fleck & Asmuth, 2020). By instilling a creative mindset through activities that encourage reflection, exploration, and overcoming challenges, students can enhance their problem-solving capabilities and entrepreneurial skills. This emphasis on creativity as a tool for entrepreneurial problem-solving underscores its significance in fostering innovation and success in business ventures. The fusion of entrepreneurship and art in educational settings can enhance students' creative problem-solving skills, fostering originality, flexibility, and fluency in thinking (Jacobson et al., 2020). By applying entrepreneurial frameworks to collaborative problem-solving tasks and integrating art inquiry experiences, students can enhance their creative thinking abilities and boost their capacity for innovative problem-solving (Jacobson et al., 2020). This interdisciplinary approach highlights the value of amalgamating diverse perspectives to stimulate creativity and address complex challenges. In the realm of mathematics education, creative problem-solving is acknowledged as a fundamental cognitive process that necessitates innovative thinking and detailed explanations for solving mathematical problems (Hidayah, 2023). By nurturing creative thinking abilities and encouraging students to present unique ideas in problem-solving contexts, educators can enhance students' grasp of concepts and cultivate their aptitude for creative problem-solving (Hidayah, 2023). This underscores the importance of creativity in fostering deeper understanding and proficiency in problem-solving tasks.

## Operating in the Gray Areas

A key element of this entrepreneurial model is the willingness to operate in the gray areas between the strictly legal and the outright illegal. The floating bars, for example, exploited a legal loophole that allowed them to skirt the edges of Prohibition laws without directly violating them. This ability to navigate the ambiguities and uncertainties of the legal and regulatory environment is a crucial skill for entrepreneurs, particularly those operating in emerging or unconventional markets.

Operating in the gray areas can be a strategic choice for entrepreneurs, allowing them to navigate complex legal, regulatory, and ethical landscapes to seize opportunities and overcome challenges. The concept of liminal legality, as explored by (Menjívar, 2006), sheds light on how individuals, such as immigrants, operate in the gray area between legal categories, influencing various aspects of their lives. This liminal space can shape social networks, community interactions, and artistic expressions, demonstrating the multifaceted impact of operating in legal gray areas on individuals and communities.

Surak (2018) highlights the prevalence of meso-level entrepreneurial initiatives that operate in legal gray areas, indicating that certain business activities thrive in environments that are not strictly regulated. This suggests that operating in the gray areas can provide entrepreneurs with flexibility and opportunities for growth that may not be available in strictly regulated sectors. By navigating the boundaries of legality, entrepreneurs can explore innovative business models and adapt to changing market conditions. Crane & Matten (2004) emphasize that business ethics often delves into the "grey areas" of business, going beyond legal requirements. This perspective underscores the importance of ethical decision-making in entrepreneurship, where entrepreneurs may need to make choices that are not explicitly governed by laws but are guided by moral principles and social responsibility. Operating in the gray areas of ethics can differentiate businesses and build trust with stakeholders.

Fernández-Méndez et al. (2021) discuss how businesses can approach the limits of the law by identifying actions in gray areas and litigating with the state when necessary. This strategic approach involves a calculated assessment of legal boundaries and a willingness to defend the legality of actions that may push against conventional norms. By engaging in legal challenges and advocating for the legitimacy of their operations, entrepreneurs can shape legal interpretations and carve out spaces for innovative practices. Bajard (2020) delves into the complexities of work in gray zones, where legal status, practices, and identities may not align. This exploration underscores the challenges and opportunities that arise when operating in ambiguous legal territories. Entrepreneurs navigating such gray areas must adapt to shifting norms and regulations, requiring a nuanced understanding of legal frameworks and social dynamics to succeed in their endeavors. Nolin (2014) discusses how cultural policy and internet-based cultural consumption can exist in legal and ethical gray areas. This perspective highlights the evolving nature of cultural practices in the digital age, where traditional legal boundaries may not fully capture the complexities of online cultural engagement. Entrepreneurs in the cultural sector must navigate these gray areas to innovate and reach audiences in a rapidly changing landscape.

## Cultivating Resilience and Adaptability

Constant change and unpredictability marked the entrepreneurial journey during the Prohibition Era. This was a time of great social and economic upheaval, and the ability to thrive in this environment was a testament to entrepreneurial resilience and adaptability. Successful individuals were able to recover from setbacks, learn from their mistakes, and pivot their strategies as needed to stay ahead of the curve.

These qualities are essential for any entrepreneur, as they enable one to weather the inevitable storms of business and emerge even stronger.

Cultivating resilience and adaptability is crucial for entrepreneurs, especially in the face of challenges and uncertainties. PeConga et al. (2020) highlight the importance of actively fostering social support, adaptive meaning, and prosocial behaviors to enhance resilience, particularly in times of crisis like the COVID-19 pandemic. This emphasizes the role of social connections and positive coping mechanisms in building resilience among entrepreneurs facing adversities. Castro & Zermeño (2020) emphasize that resilient entrepreneurs exhibit a high tolerance for ambiguity, adapt quickly to change, capitalize on opportunities, and learn from mistakes. This adaptability and learning orientation are essential for entrepreneurs to navigate turbulent environments and capitalize on emerging opportunities, showcasing the significance of resilience in driving business success.

Liu & Wang (2017) recognize entrepreneurial resilience as a core element in overcoming adversities, adapting to uncertainty, and learning from failures. This resilience is vital for entrepreneurs to persevere through challenges, pivot their strategies when needed, and leverage setbacks as learning opportunities to fuel future success. Yunxi & Danes (2015) delve into the intrapersonal indicators of entrepreneurial resilience, emphasizing the role of business confidence, life outlook, and spousal commitment in the resilience process of entrepreneurs. This underscores the multifaceted nature of resilience, encompassing personal beliefs, outlook, and support systems that contribute to entrepreneurs' ability to bounce back from setbacks.

Stephan et al. (2022) highlight how trait resilience among entrepreneurs aids in navigating the business creation process, underpinning organizational resilience, firm performance during crises like the COVID-19 pandemic, and entrepreneurial intentions in challenging contexts. This resilience serves as a foundational element that enables entrepreneurs to weather storms, adapt to changing circumstances, and sustain their ventures in the long run. Elshaer & Saad (2021) emphasize that resilient entrepreneurs are more likely to persist in their businesses, engaging in problem-focused strategies and demonstrating persistence during adversity. This persistence and problem-solving orientation are key components of entrepreneurial resilience that enable entrepreneurs to overcome obstacles and sustain their ventures through challenging times.

Nisula & Olander (2020) highlight the role of self-efficacy in promoting entrepreneurs' resilience by enhancing their ability to manage stress, conflicts, and setbacks effectively. This internal resource plays a crucial role in bolstering entrepreneurs' capacity to bounce back from failures and setbacks, contributing to their overall resilience in the face of challenges. Chen & Zhang (2021) conceptualize team resilience as an emergent state comprising resilience-efficacious beliefs and resilience-adaptive capacity. They emphasize the role of behavioral integration in cultivating team resilience and its positive impact on new venture team performance. This underscores the collective nature of resilience within entrepreneurial teams and its influence on overall performance.

## Engaging in "Guerilla" Tactics

Another key principle of this entrepreneurial model is the use of unconventional, "guerrilla-style" tactics to gain a competitive edge. For example, the rumored use of a one-man submarine for liquor smuggling represents a bold and innovative approach to circumventing the challenges of the Prohibition Era. By thinking outside the box and embracing unorthodox strategies, entrepreneurs were able to outmaneuver rivals and maintain thriving businesses in the face of significant obstacles.

Engaging in guerrilla tactics can be a strategic approach for entrepreneurs under certain conditions, allowing them to disrupt traditional norms, challenge established players, and seize opportunities in innovative ways. The concept of guerrilla marketing, as discussed by (Haynie & Shepherd, 2009), involves selecting responses, such as guerrilla marketing campaigns, that stand out from conventional strategies. This cognitive process of choosing unconventional tactics can be a hallmark feature of entrepreneurial decision-making, enabling entrepreneurs to think outside the box and create impactful campaigns.

Stubbs (2016) explores sustainable entrepreneurship through the lens of B Corps, which employ market tactics to address social and environmental issues. This approach aligns with the guerrilla mindset of using unconventional methods to achieve meaningful outcomes. By leveraging guerrilla tactics in their business models, entrepreneurs can drive social impact while challenging traditional business practices, showcasing the power of innovative approaches in entrepreneurship. Jain & Dutta (2018) delve into the use of guerrilla tactics in gamification to make learning fun and engaging for millennials. By incorporating guerrilla strategies that subtly drive key learning outcomes through games, entrepreneurs can enhance the effectiveness of educational interventions. This highlights how guerrilla tactics can be applied creatively to engage audiences and achieve specific objectives in diverse contexts.

Gentry et al. (2013) discuss how start-up firms in the CLEC industry employ guerrilla marketing as a strategic tactic to survive and thrive. By utilizing guerrilla marketing alongside bootstrapping strategies, entrepreneurs can differentiate themselves in competitive markets and gain visibility. This demonstrates how guerrilla tactics can be instrumental in establishing a foothold in industries dominated by established players. By expanding into new spheres and establishing economically unrelated enterprises, entrepreneurs can leverage guerrilla tactics to adapt to changing environments and explore new opportunities. This adaptive approach aligns with the guerrilla mindset of agility and resourcefulness in entrepreneurial endeavors.

# 6. ETHICAL DIMENSIONS OF ENTREPRENEURSHIP IN GRAY MARKETS

Entrepreneurship in gray markets, those spaces where legality and illegality intersect, raises complex ethical questions. While these markets often emerge in response to unmet demand or regulatory constraints, they challenge traditional norms of legality, fairness, and societal responsibility. Entrepreneurs operating in these spaces frequently navigate a precarious balance between innovation, the pursuit of profit, and the broader social consequences of their activities. The Prohibition Era provides a compelling historical lens to examine these issues, offering lessons that remain relevant to contemporary entrepreneurial practices.

## The Ethical Tensions of Operating in Gray Markets

At the heart of entrepreneurship in gray markets lies a fundamental ethical tension. On one hand, these ventures often represent ingenuity, resilience, and the ability to meet consumer needs in constrained environments. On the other hand, they can undermine legal systems, exacerbate social inequalities, and contribute to harmful consequences for individuals and communities.

For example, the underground alcohol trade during Prohibition fulfilled the persistent demand for liquor, but it also fueled organized crime, corruption, and public safety concerns. Entrepreneurs who operated in this space, while innovative, played a role in eroding respect for the rule of law and contributing to the unintended social costs of illicit economies. These outcomes raise critical questions about whether the benefits of innovation outweigh the potential harms to society.

## Balancing Innovation and Legality

Boundary Pushing Entrepreneurship often involves exploiting ambiguities in the law or circumventing restrictive regulations. While these practices can drive innovation and adaptation, they also pose risks to the legitimacy and stability of regulatory frameworks. Entrepreneurs in gray markets must navigate this balance carefully, ensuring that their actions do not irreparably damage the institutions that uphold societal order.

One way to assess this balance is by examining the intent and impact of entrepreneurial activities. For instance, does the innovation address a genuine gap in the market, or is it primarily exploitative? Are the benefits of the entrepreneurial venture widely shared, or do they accrue disproportionately to the entrepreneur at the expense of others? These questions highlight the importance of aligning entrepreneurial goals with broader societal values.

## The Role of Social Responsibility

Entrepreneurs in gray markets must also consider their social responsibilities. While legality is an important benchmark, it is not the sole determinant of ethical behavior. In many cases, socially responsible entrepreneurship transcends legal compliance to prioritize the well-being of communities, customers, and other stakeholders.

The Prohibition Era underscores the challenges of balancing profit with social impact. While some entrepreneurs, such as small-scale moonshiners, operated within local communities and maintained strong social ties, others engaged in practices that exacerbated societal harm, such as violence or exploitation. These contrasting approaches illustrate the spectrum of ethical considerations that arise in gray markets.

## Modern Parallels and Ethical Lessons

The ethical dilemmas of Prohibition-era entrepreneurs resonate with contemporary challenges in industries such as cryptocurrency, the gig economy, and cannabis production. These sectors often exist in legal or regulatory gray areas, requiring entrepreneurs to navigate shifting landscapes while addressing ethical concerns. The lessons of the Prohibition Era suggest that:

1. Transparency and Accountability: Entrepreneurs can build trust and legitimacy by maintaining transparency with stakeholders and demonstrating accountability for their actions.
2. Equity and Inclusivity: Ventures that prioritize equitable benefits for all stakeholders, rather than concentrating wealth or power, are more likely to garner public support and sustain long-term success.
3. Long-Term Vision: Entrepreneurs should consider the broader implications of their activities, striving to create value that extends beyond immediate profits to include social and environmental impact.

## The Ethical Framework for Boundary Pushing Entrepreneurship

To navigate the ethical complexities of gray markets, entrepreneurs can adopt a decision-making framework that incorporates the following elements:

1. Legality: Assess the legal status of the venture and its implications for long-term sustainability. Even when laws are ambiguous, compliance or advocacy for reform can reduce risks.

2. Harm Reduction: Evaluate potential harms to individuals, communities, and institutions, and implement strategies to mitigate these effects.
3. Stakeholder Engagement: Involve affected parties in decision-making processes to ensure that entrepreneurial activities align with community needs and values.
4. Innovation with Integrity: Pursue creative solutions that not only address market gaps but also uphold ethical standards and societal responsibilities.

The ethical dimensions of entrepreneurship in gray markets challenge entrepreneurs to balance innovation with legality and social responsibility. While constrained environments often necessitate creative and unconventional approaches, these actions must be tempered by a commitment to minimizing harm and fostering positive societal outcomes. The lessons of the Prohibition Era highlight both the potential and the pitfalls of operating in legal and ethical gray areas, offering a valuable guide for contemporary entrepreneurs seeking to navigate similarly complex landscapes.

## 7. LESSONS FOR CONTEMPORARY ENTREPRENEURS

The entrepreneurial strategies and innovations that emerged during the Prohibition Era offer valuable insights for contemporary entrepreneurs operating in constrained or highly regulated markets. By studying how individuals navigated legal and social limitations to create thriving ventures, modern business leaders can better understand the dynamics of Boundary Pushing Entrepreneurship and apply its principles to today's complex and rapidly evolving environments.

### Innovation in Constrained Markets

One of the most significant lessons from the Prohibition Era is the capacity for innovation in the face of adversity. Entrepreneurs who succeeded during this period, despite restrictive legislation and heightened enforcement, demonstrated that constraints can act as catalysts for creativity. They exploited legal ambiguities, developed novel distribution models, and adapted their strategies to meet persistent demand.

Modern parallels can be found in industries like the gig economy, where platforms such as Uber and Airbnb have disrupted traditional business models by operating in regulatory gray areas. Similarly, in the cannabis industry, entrepreneurs have navigated shifting legal frameworks to develop products and services that align with consumer needs while complying with evolving laws. These examples highlight the enduring relevance of Boundary Pushing Entrepreneurship, as the ability to innovate under constraint remains a key driver of success in regulated markets.

## The Role of Adaptability and Resilience

The Prohibition Era underscores the importance of adaptability and resilience in navigating uncertain environments. Entrepreneurs who thrived during this period were quick to pivot their strategies in response to changing circumstances, whether by diversifying their ventures or adopting new technologies to evade detection.

In today's business landscape, resilience is equally critical, particularly in industries facing disruption from technological advancements, economic crises, or regulatory shifts. For instance, cryptocurrency entrepreneurs operate in a landscape of fluctuating legal frameworks and market volatility, requiring constant adaptation to maintain relevance and legitimacy. By embracing the principles of resilience and flexibility, contemporary entrepreneurs can better weather uncertainties and sustain long-term growth.

## Leveraging Gray Areas Ethically

Boundary Pushing Entrepreneurship often involves operating in gray areas, where regulations are ambiguous or not yet established. While this approach can create opportunities, it also requires a careful balance between innovation and ethical considerations. Prohibition-era entrepreneurs who succeeded without exacerbating societal harm provide a model for how to navigate these complexities.

For modern entrepreneurs, industries like fintech, biotechnology, and renewable energy often present similar challenges. Innovators in these sectors must navigate regulatory gray zones while ensuring their activities align with broader societal values. By prioritizing transparency, stakeholder engagement, and harm reduction, they can leverage opportunities in constrained markets without compromising their integrity or long-term viability.

## Lessons for Gig and Sharing Economies

The gig and sharing economies illustrate how the principles of Boundary Pushing Entrepreneurship continue to shape contemporary markets. Platforms like ride-sharing and short-term rental services initially operated in ambiguous legal spaces, challenging existing regulations and prompting discussions about labor rights, taxation, and consumer protection. These businesses, like their Prohibition-era counterparts, highlight the tension between innovation and compliance.

Entrepreneurs in these industries can draw from the Prohibition Era by adopting adaptive business models, engaging with regulators proactively, and seeking ways to align their innovations with public interests. This approach ensures that they not only achieve profitability but also contribute to the broader acceptance and sustainability of their ventures.

## Inspiration for Emerging Markets

Emerging markets, such as artificial intelligence (AI), blockchain, and autonomous vehicles, often face regulatory uncertainties similar to those encountered during Prohibition. Entrepreneurs in these fields can learn from the Boundary Pushing model by recognizing the opportunities that constraints present. By focusing on creative problem-solving and contrarian thinking, they can develop solutions that address consumer needs while shaping the evolution of new industries. For example, startups in AI are navigating complex ethical and legal concerns surrounding data privacy and bias. By applying the principles of innovation with integrity and engaging in transparent practices, these entrepreneurs can lead the way in setting industry standards that prioritize societal benefits alongside technological advancement.

## Cultivating a Long-Term Vision

Another critical takeaway from the Prohibition Era is the value of a long-term vision. Entrepreneurs who diversified their operations and invested in sustainable ventures were better positioned to thrive after the repeal of Prohibition. Similarly, contemporary entrepreneurs should consider the broader implications of their activities, ensuring their ventures are adaptable to future regulatory or market shifts. For instance, companies in the renewable energy sector are balancing short-term profitability with investments in technologies that align with long-term environmental goals. By prioritizing adaptability and sustainability, these businesses embody the principles of Boundary Pushing Entrepreneurship while addressing pressing global challenges.

## Encouraging Collaboration and Stakeholder Engagement

The success of many Prohibition-era entrepreneurs was rooted in their ability to build strong networks and engage with their communities. Whether through partnerships, shared risk-taking, or localized support systems, these collaborations were vital to sustaining their ventures. Modern entrepreneurs can adopt a similar approach by fostering relationships with stakeholders, including regulators, consumers, and community organizations. Proactive collaboration not only mitigates risks but also enhances legitimacy and public trust, critical components for navigating constrained markets.

The Prohibition Era illustrates that constraints, far from stifling innovation, can act as powerful drivers of entrepreneurial ingenuity. The principles of Boundary Pushing Entrepreneurship - contrarian thinking, creative problem-solving, resilience, and operating in gray areas - provide a framework for navigating today's complex and regulated markets. By learning from the successes and challenges of the past, contemporary entrepreneurs can inspire innovation that not only addresses immediate market needs but also contributes to sustainable and socially responsible growth.

## 8. CONCLUSION

The Prohibition Era remains one of the most compelling historical examples of how legal and social constraints can stimulate entrepreneurial innovation. The era's entrepreneurs, operating in one of the most restrictive regulatory environments of the 20th century, demonstrated remarkable adaptability, creativity, and resilience. Through their efforts to navigate the legal ambiguities and persistent demand for alcohol, they inadvertently shaped both the underground economy of the time and broader societal attitudes toward regulation and innovation.

This study introduces the concept of Boundary Pushing Entrepreneurship as a framework for understanding entrepreneurial behavior in constrained environments. Defined by key principles - contrarian thinking, creative problem-solving, operating in gray areas, resilience, and guerrilla tactics - this model provides a structured approach to analyzing how entrepreneurs succeed when faced with external limitations. By situating the framework within the historical context of Prohibition, this research highlights its relevance to both past and present entrepreneurial challenges.

### Key Findings and Theoretical Contributions

1. Historical Insights: The Prohibition Era exemplifies the role of external constraints in shaping entrepreneurial innovation. Entrepreneurs responded to prohibitionist policies with adaptive strategies that not only sustained their ventures but also contributed to the era's dynamic and complex socio-economic landscape.
2. Entrepreneurial Theory: The Boundary Pushing framework expands on traditional theories of entrepreneurship by focusing on innovation under constraint. It intersects with concepts such as opportunity recognition, effectuation, and institutional entrepreneurship, offering a nuanced understanding of how entrepreneurs operate in legal and regulatory gray areas.

3. Ethical Dimensions: The study underscores the ethical dilemmas inherent in boundary-pushing ventures. While these activities often drive innovation and economic growth, they also challenge legal norms and raise questions about societal impact. This duality emphasizes the need for entrepreneurs to balance creativity and responsibility.

## Relevance to Historical and Contemporary Contexts

The principles of Boundary Pushing Entrepreneurship are not confined to the Prohibition Era. In contemporary markets, entrepreneurs in sectors like cryptocurrency, the gig economy, renewable energy, and biotechnology face similar challenges of navigating ambiguous or evolving regulatory landscapes. By applying the lessons of Prohibition-era entrepreneurs, modern business leaders can better adapt to constraints, exploit opportunities, and drive innovation while addressing ethical considerations.

The framework also provides insights for policymakers and regulators. Understanding how constraints can spur innovation and unintended consequences can help shape policies that foster responsible entrepreneurship while maintaining regulatory objectives.

## Directions for Future Research

While this study establishes the theoretical foundation for Boundary Pushing Entrepreneurship, several areas warrant further exploration:

1. Comparative Analyses Across Eras: Future research could compare entrepreneurial responses to constraints in different historical periods, such as the industrial revolution, the digital age, or the legalization of cannabis, to identify commonalities and divergences in boundary-pushing strategies.
2. Industry-Specific Applications: Investigating how the Boundary Pushing framework applies to specific modern industries, such as financial technology or autonomous vehicles, could yield insights into how these sectors navigate regulatory challenges.
3. Ethical Considerations: Expanding on the ethical dimensions of Boundary Pushing Entrepreneurship could deepen our understanding of how entrepreneurs balance innovation with societal responsibilities. Research might explore frameworks for ethical decision-making in constrained markets.
4. Policy Implications: Exploring how regulatory frameworks can encourage innovation without encouraging exploitation or harm would provide valuable guidance for policymakers aiming to strike a balance between oversight and opportunity.

Boundary Pushing Entrepreneurship offers a powerful lens for understanding how individuals innovate and thrive in the face of constraints. By drawing on the lessons of the Prohibition Era, this framework bridges historical and contemporary contexts, highlighting the enduring capacity of entrepreneurs to adapt and succeed. However, it also serves as a reminder of the ethical complexities inherent in such ventures. As modern entrepreneurs confront new challenges and opportunities, the principles outlined in this study provide both inspiration and caution, emphasizing the need for innovation that is not only creative and adaptive but also responsible and sustainable.

## REFERENCES


Adobor, H. (2025). Explaining illegal entrepreneurship in the small-scale artisanal mining sector in Ghana: A historical contextualization approach. *Journal of Business Research, 186*, 115020. Advance online publication. DOI: 10.1016/j.jbusres.2024.115020

Ager, P., Hansen, C., & Lønstrup, L. (2016). Church membership and social insurance: evidence from the great Mississippi flood of 1927. SSRN Electronic Journal. DOI: 10.2139/ssrn.2862290

Bajard, F. (2020). A "hijacked salaried status" in French cooperatives of freelance workers: The political meaning of shifts between standard and non-standard employment. *Frontiers in Sociology*, *5*, 36. Advance online publication. DOI: 10.3389/fsoc.2020.00036 PMID: 33869443

Balabiyev, K. (2023). Criminal liability for illegal entrepreneurship, illegal banking activity, microfinancial or collection activities: comparative legal analysis of criminal legislation of foreighn countries. *Journal of actual problems of jurisprudence.* DOI: 10.26577/JAPJ.2023.v106.i2.010

Blackman, S. (2010). Drug war politics: Governing culture through prohibition, intoxicants as customary practice and the challenge of drug normalization. *Sociology Compass*, *4*(10), 841–855. DOI: 10.1111/j.1751-9020.2010.00324.x

Blocker, J. S.Jr. (2006). Did Prohibition Really Work? Alcohol Prohibition as a Public Health Innovation. *American Journal of Public Health*, *96*(2), 233–243. DOI: 10.2105/AJPH.2005.065409 PMID: 16380559

Burke, J., & DePoy, E. (1991). An emerging view of mastery, excellence, and leadership in occupational therapy practice. *The American Journal of Occupational Therapy*, *45*(11), 1027–1032. DOI: 10.5014/ajot.45.11.1027 PMID: 1793116

Castro, M., & Zermeño, M. (2020). Being an entrepreneur post-covid-19 – resilience in times of crisis: A systematic literature review. *Journal of Entrepreneurship in Emerging Economies*, *13*(4), 721–746. DOI: 10.1108/JEEE-07-2020-0246

Chau, F., Deesomsak, R., & Koutmos, D. (2016). Does investor sentiment really matter? *International Review of Financial Analysis*, *48*, 221–232. DOI: 10.1016/j.irfa.2016.10.003

Chen, Y., & Zhang, Y. (2021). Fostering resilience in new venture teams: The role of behavioral and affective integration. *Group & Organization Management*, *46*(4), 773–816. DOI: 10.1177/10596011211033164

Crane, A., & Matten, D. (2004). Questioning the domain of the business ethics curriculum. *Journal of Business Ethics, 54*(4), 357–369. DOI: 10.1007/s10551-004-1825-x

DiMaggio, P. J. (1988). Interest and agency in institutional theory. *Institutional Patterns and Organizations: Culture and Environment/Ballinger.*

Edwards, G., & Howe, T. (2015). A test of prohibition's effect on alcohol production and consumption using crop yields. *Southern Economic Journal, 81*(4), 1145–1168. DOI: 10.1002/soej.12025

Ellender, R., Cook, D., Sheladia, V., & Johnson, R. (1980). Enterovirus and bacterial evaluation of Mississippi oysters. *Gulf Research Reports, 6*. Advance online publication. DOI: 10.18785/grr.0604.04

Elshaer, I., & Saad, S. (2021). Entrepreneurial resilience and business continuity in the tourism and hospitality industry: The role of adaptive performance and institutional orientation. *Tourism Review, 77*(5), 1365–1384. DOI: 10.1108/TR-04-2021-0171

Fadahunsi, A., & Rosa, P. (2002). Entrepreneurship and Illegality: Insights from the Nigerian cross-border Trade. *Journal of Business Venturing, 17*(5), 397–429. DOI: 10.1016/S0883-9026(01)00073-8

Felin, T., Gambardella, A., Novelli, E., & Zenger, T. (2024). A scientific method for startups. *Journal of Management, 50*(8), 3080–3104. Advance online publication. DOI: 10.1177/01492063231226136

Ferchen, M., & Mattlin, M. (2023). Five modes of China's economic influence: Rethinking Chinese economic statecraft. *The Pacific Review, 36*(5), 978–1004. DOI: 10.1080/09512748.2023.2200029

Fernández-Méndez, L., Canal, E., & García-García, R. (2021). Litigations with the home state and internationalization. *Multinational Business Review, 30*(3), 343–363. DOI: 10.1108/MBR-03-2021-0036

Fleck, E., & Asmuth, J. (2020). Building capacity for creativity: Rediscovering the inner "superhero" as a mechanism for developing a creative mindset for entrepreneurial problem-solving. *Entrepreneurship Education and Pedagogy, 4*(1), 82–95. DOI: 10.1177/2515127420912503

Funken, R., Gielnik, M., & Foo, M. (2018). How can problems be turned into something good? the role of entrepreneurial learning and error mastery orientation. *Entrepreneurship Theory and Practice, 44*(2), 315–338. DOI: 10.1177/1042258718801600

Galemba, R. (2008). Informal and Illicit Entrepreneurs: Fighting for a Place in the Neoliberal Economic Order. *Anthropology of work review. Anthropology of Work Review, 29*(2), 2. DOI: 10.1111/j.1548-1417.2008.00010.x PMID: 24223472

Gentry, R., Dalziel, T., & Jamison, M. (2013). Who do start-up firms imitate? a study of new market entries in the clec industry. *Journal of Small Business Management, 51*(4), 525–538. DOI: 10.1111/jsbm.12055

George, B. (2018). Inclusive growth by means of sustainable supply chains: A case study of the Dabbawalas of Mumbai, India. *International Journal of Entrepreneurial Knowledge, 6*(2). Advance online publication. DOI: 10.37335/ijek.v6i2.74

George, B., & Mattathil, A. P. (2025). Empowering African American Tourism Entrepreneurs with Generative AI: Bridging Innovation and Cultural Heritage. *Societies (Basel, Switzerland), 15*(2), 34. DOI: 10.3390/soc15020034

George, B., & Wooden, O. S. (2025). *AI Empowered: Pioneering African American Entrepreneurship in the Digital Age*. Emerald Publishing Limited. DOI: 10.1108/9781836628163

Hall, W. (2010). What are the policy lessons of national alcohol prohibition in the united states, 1920–1933? *Addiction (Abingdon, England), 105*(7), 1164–1173. DOI: 10.1111/j.1360-0443.2010.02926.x PMID: 20331549

Hall, W. (2017). The future of the international drug control system and national drug prohibitions. *Addiction (Abingdon, England), 113*(7), 1210–1223. DOI: 10.1111/add.13941 PMID: 28884869

Haller, M. (1990). Illegal enterprise: A theoretical and historical interpretation. *Criminology, 28*(2), 207–236. DOI: 10.1111/j.1745-9125.1990.tb01324.x

Haynie, M., & Shepherd, D. (2009). A measure of adaptive cognition for entrepreneurship research. *Entrepreneurship Theory and Practice, 33*(3), 695–714. DOI: 10.1111/j.1540-6520.2009.00322.x

Hidayah, K., & Dwijanto, D. (2023). Mathematical creative thinking ability viewed by adversity quotient in problem-based learning integrated stem. *Unnes J. Math. Educ., 12*(1), 72–83. DOI: 10.15294/ujme.v12i1.67560

Jacobson, S., Seavey, J., Goodman, J., Nichols, O., Williams, L., Márquez-García, M., & Barbosa, O. (2020). Integrating entrepreneurship and art to improve creative problem solving in fisheries education. *Fisheries (Bethesda, Md.), 45*(2), 84–89. DOI: 10.1002/fsh.10351

Jain, A., & Dutta, D. (2018). Millennials and gamification: Guerilla tactics for making learning fun. *SA Journal of Human Resource Management*, *6*(1), 29–44. DOI: 10.1177/2322093718796303

Kemper, A., & Martin, R. (2010). After the fall: The global financial crisis as a test of corporate social responsibility theories. *European Management Review*, *7*(4), 229–239. DOI: 10.1057/emr.2010.18

Lewis, M. (2008). Access to saloons, wet voter turnout, and statewide prohibition referenda, 1907–1919. *Social Science History*, *32*(3), 373–404. DOI: 10.1017/S0145553200013997

Liu, J., & Wang, J. (2017). Developing entrepreneurial resilience: Implications for human resource development. *European Journal of Training and Development*, *41*(6), 519–539. DOI: 10.1108/EJTD-12-2016-0090

Mallon, M., & Fainshmidt, S. (2020). Who's Hiding in the Shadows? Organized Crime and Informal Entrepreneurship in 39 Economies. *Journal of Management*, *48*(1), 211–237. DOI: 10.1177/0149206320978821

McGirr, L. (2015). *The war on alcohol: Prohibition and the rise of the American state*. WW Norton & Company.

Menjívar, C. (2006). Liminal legality: Salvadoran and Guatemalan immigrants' lives in the United States. *AJS; American Journal of Sociology*, *111*(4), 999–1037. DOI: 10.1086/499509

Muehlmann, S. (2018). The gender of the war on drugs. *Annual Review of Anthropology*, *47*(1), 315–330. DOI: 10.1146/annurev-anthro-102317-050214

Nisula, A., & Olander, H. (2020). The role of motivations and self-concepts in university graduate entrepreneurs' creativity and resilience. *Journal of Small Business Management*, *61*(2), 265–294. DOI: 10.1080/00472778.2020.1760030

Nolin, J. (2014). Cultural policy by proxy: Internet-based cultural consumption as a copygray zone. *International Journal of Cultural Policy*, *21*(3), 273–290. DOI: 10.1080/10286632.2014.923415

O'Rourke, B. (2011). *Dealing Death and Drugs: The Big Business of Dope in the US and Mexico, an Argument to End the Prohibition of Marijuana*. Cinco Puntos Press.

Othman, N., Marthandan, G., & Aziz, K. (2022). Measuring the motives of informal entrepreneurs. *F1000Research*, 11. DOI: 10.12688/f1000research.73706.2

Parker, N. (2020). Black codes and slave codes. DOI: 10.1093/obo/9780190280024-0083

PeConga, E., Gauthier, G., Holloway, A., Walker, R., Rosencrans, P., Zoellner, L., & Bedard-Gilligan, M. (2020). Resilience is spreading mental health within the covid-19 pandemic. *Psychological Trauma : Theory, Research, Practice and Policy, 12*(S1), S47–S48. DOI: 10.1037/tra0000874 PMID: 32496106

Pehe, V., & Kupka, P. (2024). Legal, illegal, either way informal: Examining continuities of small-scale entrepreneurship between late socialism and postsocialism in Czechia. *Journal of Contemporary Central and Eastern Europe, 32*(2), 257–277. DOI: 10.1080/25739638.2024.2374151

Putra, R., Rahman, H., &, A. (2024). Illegal entrepreneur: necessity base entrepreneur or opportunity base entrepreneur (Exploratory Study of Illegal Entrepreneurship in Padang City). *Journal Publicuho.* DOI: 10.35817/publicuho.v7i3.495

Saniel, D., Gue, I., & Salvo, C. (2025). *A Neo-Classical Economic Theory: Leveraging Underground Economy.* Cognizance Journal of Multidisciplinary Studies., DOI: 10.47760/cognizance.2025.v05i02.023

Sarasvathy, S. D. (2001). Causation and effectuation: Toward a theoretical shift from economic inevitability to entrepreneurial contingency. *Academy of Management Review, 26*(2), 243–263. DOI: 10.2307/259121

Shahin, M., Ilic, O., Gonsalvez, C., & Whittle, J. (2021). The impact of a stem-based entrepreneurship program on the entrepreneurial intention of secondary school female students. *The International Entrepreneurship and Management Journal, 17*(4), 1867–1898. DOI: 10.1007/s11365-020-00713-7

Shane, S., & Venkataraman, S. (2000). The Promise of Entrepreneurship as a Field of Research. *Academy of Management Review, 25*(1), 217–226. DOI: 10.5465/amr.2000.2791611

Shaposhnykov, K. (2023). *Preventing the development of the illegal economy: global experience.* Black Sea Economic Studies., DOI: 10.32782/bses.82-4

Sjögren, H., & Yusuf, F. (2021). Profiles of entrepreneurial success during two centuries. the case of Sweden, with comparisons to Italy. *Business History, 65*(8), 1366–1389. DOI: 10.1080/00076791.2021.1979515

Smith, R., & McElwee, G. (2013). The embeddedness of illegal entrepreneurship in a closed ethnic community. *International Journal of Business and Globalisation, 11*(1), 45–62. DOI: 10.1504/IJBG.2013.055315

Stephan, U., Zbierowski, P., Pérez-Luño, A., Wach, D., Wiklund, J., Cabañas, M., & Zahid, M. (2022). Act or wait-and-see? adversity, agility, and entrepreneur well-being across countries during the covid-19 pandemic. *Entrepreneurship Theory and Practice*, *47*(3), 682–723. DOI: 10.1177/10422587221104820

Stubbs, W. (2016). Sustainable entrepreneurship and b corps. *Business Strategy and the Environment*, *26*(3), 331–344. DOI: 10.1002/bse.1920

Surak, K. (2018). Migration industries and the state: Guest work programs in East Asia. *The International Migration Review*, *52*(2), 487–523. DOI: 10.1177/0197918318781829

Verchenko, N., & Sabol, E. (2024). Illegal Entrepreneurship: Theory Issues and Law Enforcement Problems. *Herald of Omsk University Series Law*. DOI: 10.24147/1990-5173.2024.21(4).92-100

Welter, F., Smallbone, D., & Pobol, A. (2015). Entrepreneurial activity in the informal economy: A missing piece of the entrepreneurship jigsaw puzzle. *Entrepreneurship and Regional Development*, *27*(5-6), 292–306. DOI: 10.1080/08985626.2015.1041259

Williams, D. (2015). The impact of Sim venture on the development of entrepreneurial skills in management students. *Industry and Higher Education*, *29*(5), 379–395. DOI: 10.5367/ihe.2015.0270

Yunxi, Y., & Danes, S. (2015). Resiliency and resilience process of entrepreneurs in new venture creation. *Entrepreneurship Research Journal*, *5*(1), 1–30. DOI: 10.1515/erj-2013-0076

# Chapter 11
# Impact of Interest Rate Changes on Selected Indian Bank Stock Returns

**S. Baranidharan**
http://orcid.org/0000-0002-7780-4045
*Presidency University, India*

**Nayana B. N.**
http://orcid.org/0009-0002-0302-2443
*Christ (Deemed to be) University, India*

**Praba Devi P.**
*Sona College of Technology, India*

**N. Krishnaveni**
http://orcid.org/0009-0008-2621-6543
*Nirmala College for Women, India*

## ABSTRACT

*This study empirically analyzes the impact of changes in the Reserve Bank of India's repo rate on the stock returns of selected leading Indian banks from 2015 to 2024. Employing time-series econometric methods such as unit root tests, cointegration analysis, Vector Error Correction Models, and Granger causality test. The analysis highlights a significant negative relationship between repo rate increases and bank stock returns, along with evidence of volatility clustering and persistence in the banking sector's stock prices. The findings confirm that repo rate changes are predictive of future bank stock returns, underscoring monetary policy's crucial role*

DOI: 10.4018/979-8-2600-3179-7.ch011

*in stock market dynamics. This study provides important insights into the monetary transmission mechanism in emerging markets and offers practical implications for investors and policymakers. It contributes to the literature by addressing both sectoral and temporal dimensions of interest rate impacts, enhancing the understanding of financial market behavior in India.*

## 1. INTRODUCTION

The stock market plays a vital role in India's economic development by helping with capital formation and wealth creation. Interest rates are the most crucial macroeconomic factor influencing stock market returns. To balance inflation and economic growth, the RBI (Reserve Bank of India) uses its monetary policy tool, the repo rate. Changes in interest rates affect the cost of borrowing for customers and companies. This will influence corporate earnings, investment decisions, and overall markets. A rise in interest rates leads to higher borrowing costs, reducing customer spending and company profit margins. This often results in a reduction of stock market returns. Conversely, lower interest rates support higher borrowings and investment, increasing stock prices. The changing relationship is particularly significant in India's developing financial view, where sectors such as banking, real estate, etc., are sensitive to interest rate fluctuations. For all the investors, financial analysts, and policymakers, it is essential to understand the impact of interest rate movements on stock market returns. This paper mainly focuses on analyzing how different interest rates affect the stock market returns in India, examining both long-term and short-term effects. This study helps to provide deep insights that can help investors to optimize their portfolios in response to monetary policy changes and contribute more to economic decision-making.

### 1.1 Review of Literature

Kannaa and Arunachalam (2024), in their research The authors of the study measured many interest rate indicators such as the call money rate and the repo rate and discovered strong negative relationships with Sensex returns, indicating that an increase in the rates was happening alongside a decrease in stock market behavior. A positive influence on stock returns was established by GDP growth, which has notable implications for market performance as economic expansion is a source of improving investor attitudes towards risk. Overall the authors identified monetary policy as a significant instrument that influences stock market performance and posited that fluctuations, as in the case of interest rates, have both direct and indirect stock market performance through sectoral channels. Kumar et al. (2023), undertook a study titled Impact of Repo Rate Changes on the Indian Banking Sector's NPA Ratio (2015–2023). A repo hike also affects banks' lending tendency and makes banks reluctant to extend loans, which in turn slows disbursements. Even though the research did not have a real impact on stock market performance, it informed an important transmission channel whereby rising NPAs could dent investor confidence, squash profitability, and drag bank valuations down in the markets. The results have significant policy implications, showing, for example, that repo rate changes do not just influence the cost of funds but also have a spillover on business operations and market signaling. This makes the repo rate a make or break for both banking sector fundamentals and long-term investor sentiment.

Sahu and Bandopadhyay (2022) found changes in the repo rate affected stock returns considerably in India, depending on whether the institution was without a bank or a private sector bank; repo rate increases increased the cost of funds. This compressed net-interest margins and reduced profitability, negatively affecting stock prices. Overall, the researchers concluded that monetary policy implementation, especially repo rate changes, was a key element that influenced investing sentiment and value. Khan and Kumar (2019–2023) revealed that the repo rate had a long-term negative effect on stock prices, whereas the bank rate and reverse repo rate had positive effects. The study explained the divergent effects of the different types of interest rates on performance of banking stocks as potential evidence of a differentiated monetary policy ability to affect market outcomes. The empirical research titled Impact of Interest Rate on Stock Returns: An Empirical Study by Dharmananda and Ajay (2020) focused on repo rate changes and stock prices of SBI and Bank of Baroda between April, 2019, and March, 2020. Their correlation results indicated a moderate degree of negative correlation between repo rate and stock prices, and ANOVA results did not lend any statistical significance ($p > 0.05$). The R-square values were low (~9%), which indicated a weak explanation rate for performance. While it could be argued that there was no greater link between repo rate and stock prices in the short run, the authors did argue that improvements in the banking sector over the longer term could translate into improved performance and attractiveness from the perspective of investor perception related to repo rate changes.

In their study, Shahani and Nagpal (2019), Studying the Interest Rates' Movement with Returns as well as Volatility Spillover Among India's Leading Bank Stocks, worked with data from April 2013 to March 2018. They found that interest rate movements did not have any direct impact on short-term stock return levels, where they utilized OLS and GARCH (1,1) models; however, they found that overall, there are spillovers of returns and volatility between banks, with spillovers being far more perceptible from private banks to public sector banks than vice versa. As for particular banks, they verified a bilateral volatility spillover between ICICI Bank and PNB, and HDFC Bank influenced SBI. They concluded that although the importance of direct changes in interest rates has been noted, the interbank links will create more noticeable reactions of volatility in the stock market with changes in interest rates. Pal and Garg (2019), in Macroeconomic Surprises and Stock Market Responses, revealed that monetary policy-related surprises, including repo rate changes, had the largest effects right after the announcement, with the effects differing by industry and by firm size and then dissipating over time. This suggests that a monetary policy shock can impact investor behavior for a short period but has limited long-run effects. The findings highlight the need for consistency by markets in their reactions to unexpected decisions related to interest rates in a timely manner. Misra (2018), in An Investigation of the Macroeconomic Factors Affecting the Indian Stock Market, examined the BSE Sensex for the years 1999 to 2017. Misra included interest rates, inflation, IIP, gold prices, exchange rates, FIIs, and money supply in her analysis. Misra conducted Johansen cointegration, Granger causality, and VECM and found that interest rates and stock prices are in long-run equilibrium, and inflation and money supply have significant short-term immediate effects. The study confirms that changes in interest rates are an important determinant of stock market movements. Changes in interest rate influence long-term trends and short-run volatility in the Indian market.

In an empirical study entitled The Effects of Macro Variables on Sectoral Indices in India, Sailaja and Mandal (2018) evaluated data over the period from 2009 to 2015. They considered the multiple regression results that showed FIIs had a statistically significant relation to all the sectoral indices in India and in terms of crude oil prices and dollar values affecting sectoral indices differently. The banking index showed a considerable response to both FIIs and changes in interest rates. Changes in performance were in part influenced by investor sentiment in these cases. In conclusion, the study suggests that macroeconomic variables act in concert as collective effects that limit policymaker proposals and that foreign investment and policy rates may act together to affect the pathway of banking stocks. Otieno, Ngugi, and Wawire (2017), Effects of Interest Rate on Stock Market Returns in Kenya, studied 3-month Treasury Bills and lending rates from a 1993–2015 timeline. Although the data is based on Kenya, the study's conclusions will have great applicability for India. Specifically, the study demonstrated a negative long-term relationship between interest rates and stock returns, with stock returns sometimes acting as leading indicators of interest rate movements in the short term. This justifies the idea that movements in monetary policy in emerging markets, such as repo rate movements, can have predictable directional influences on equity markets.

In "Interest Rate Sensitivity of Banking Stock Returns in India," Tripathi and Ghosh (2017) used OLS and GARCH models to assess how changes and volatility in interest rates influence returns on bank stocks. The authors concluded that there was a weak negative correlation between rate changes and returns, while a strong relationship existed between rate volatility and return volatility, and the authors encourage policymakers to stabilize rates in order to reduce volatility. Suganya (2000-2016), in The Effect of Macroeconomic Variables on Stock Market Performance in India, established a clear relationship whereby GDP increased and had a positive effect on the market, while inflation and interest rates had varying effects on the market. The study also confirmed the need to monitor interest rates in making decisions.

Singh (2014), in his paper titled A Study into Monetary Policy's Impact upon Stock Market Returns, researched the relationship of CRR, SLR, repo, and reverse repo rates upon NIFTY and Bank NIFTY (2000-2014). The analysis was significant based on ADF tests, established ARCH models, and Granger causality. The findings revealed that the repo and reverse repo rates were directly related to stock indices. CRR had an indirect impact by affecting stock indices' volatility. Overall, they concluded that the various monetary policy tools will combine to primarily use the interest rates to influence trends on the stock market. Additionally, as the decisions of investors lead to future performances of sectoral stock indices, it is useful for investors to think about the monetary implications. As it tied in with previous studies, they stressed that when investors look to invest, they should assess monetary policies that relate to the judgement of results through the performance of sectoral stock indices. Vyas et al. (2014) employed data from 1993 to 2009 in Causal Nexus among Interest Rate, Stock Price, Foreign Institutional Investment, Demand for Money, and Exchange Rates in India to examine short- and long-run relationships. They discovered no long-run equilibrium between stock prices and exchange rates, but strong short-run relationships with interest rates and stock returns were identified. Their findings suggested that repo rate changes do not anchor longer-term price levels but spur immediate reactions in the banking stock segment that can challenge trading strategies.

In an article titled 'An Empirical Analysis of Economic Indicators and Volatility of the Indian Stock Market,' Kuri and Kattimani investigated the influence of interest rates, crude oil, and rupee value on Nifty 50. The authors found that the market was positively related to the CRR rate and the reverse repo rate, whereas it was negatively related to the SLR and MSFR rates. Interest rate adjustments, particularly repo rate adjustments, were also shown to be contributors to volatility across the market, indicating a relationship between economic indicators and investor confidence. Teker and Alp (2014), in Granger Causality Relation Between Interest Rates and Stock Markets: Evidence from Emerging Markets, observed interest rates in Turkey, Brazil, China, and Hungary. They concluded that the impact of interest rates on stock markets differed by country. Interest rates could also be influenced by stock markets, either positively or negatively, meaning stock markets could have a reverse influence on interest rates. Therefore, while repo rate changes could potentially influence investment decisions in India, further conclusions cannot be drawn without considering additional economic factors and market specifics.

Chavannavar, Patil, and Simoes studied the impact of changes to the CRR, SLR, and repo rate on the Nifty 50 and the sectoral indices in their paper Monetary Policy Effect on Nifty 50 and Sectoral Indices. They found a moderate long-term relationship between monetary policy and stock indexes and also found that the banking sector was responsive and sensitive to changes in the repo rate. Singh (2016), in the study The Impact of Macroeconomic Fundamentals on Stock Prices: A Study of the Indian Stock Market, identified a long-run equilibrium where, with the exception of the IIP and exchange rate, stock prices were positively influenced by volume, interest rates, WPI, and money supply. There was bi-directional causality for interest rates with stock prices, which highlighted the important role of interest rates in market movements. Kumar, R., in The Effect of Macroeconomic Factors on Indian Stock Market Performance: A Factor Analysis Approach, employed factor analysis to find that policy rate changes (repo rate alterations) impacted market performance, along with industrial performance and global happenings. In their study, The Effects of Volatility of Interest Rates on Stock Returns, Suresh, Kumar, and Janardhanam (2004-2005), an assessment of 15 public sector banks, estimated equity capital movement of 25% with a few of the yield The study showed that stock returns were sensitive to changes because of interest rate volatility, but predictive power was considerably less; one of the items addressed was variation in rate exposure across banks.

In their research entitled "Do Interest Rate Regulation Changes Affect Stock Returns? An Event Study Approach on the Kenyan Banking Sector Stocks" (Ngaruiya, Mathuva & Obi, 2025), the researchers studied how interest rate regulation, through both the introduction (and eventual repeal) of rate caps, can influence stock returns in a developing economy. Utilizing an event study with a difference-in-differences design, the authors examined the market responses around key regulatory announcements affecting Kenyan banks. The results indicated the implementation of interest rate controls in 2016 produced negative and statistically significant cumulative abnormal returns and provided evidence investors actually perceived the caps as meaningfully value-reducing. Moreover, the long-term difference-in-differences results did not show any significant lasting valuation impact, implying markets may exhibit an initial reaction to policy announcements related to interest rates, but it does not result in a change in long-term firm value. This work shows that not just the level of interest rates but interest rate policies and regulation shifts can generate immediate stock market volatility. The article "Inflation, Interest Rates, and the Predictability of Stock Returns" (Časta, 2023) has an examination of whether inflation and interest rates contain predictive information about future stock market returns. Through the process of decomposing inflation and interest rates into their cyclical components, the study found strong in-sample evidence that cyclical components significantly forecast stock returns. Out-of-sample analysis indicated the cyclical components of inflation and interest rates also contain meaningful predictive power against a benchmark historical average. The author writes that inflation and interest rates contain stochastic trends that tend to be ignored by investors and that the cyclical components of each variable are more informative than the raw values. This paper is very relevant to the study of interest rates, as the author suggests that the dynamics of interest rates are forward-looking and impact not only present behavior in the market but also the investors' expectations of future stock returns as well.

In "Can Ignorance About the Interest Rate and Macroeconomic Surprises Affect Stock Market Return? Evidence from a Large Emerging Economy" (Mendonça & Díaz, 2023), the authors investigate how uncertainty or misinformation ("ignorance") regarding interest rates tied to monetary policy might influence stock market performance in Brazil. The authors construct a measure of ignorance based on the signal-to-noise ratio of the policy rate from data from 2005 to 2021 and test its effect on stock returns. The findings indicate that, the greater the ignorance (i.e., the gap between actual monetary policy intentions and expectations held by private agents), the more negative and statistically significant the effect on stock returns. There is an indication that surprises in economic developments also influence stock market returns. This study broadens the usual understanding of how interest rates influence stock market returns by showing that the likeliness of gathering information and forming expectations around interest rate decisions may be as important as actual changes to interest rates. The research, titled "The Behavior of Exchange Rate and Stock Returns in High and Low Interest Rate Environments" (Salisu & Vo, 2021), investigates the interplay between stock returns and exchange rates during periods of high and low interest rates. Using panel data from high-interest and low-interest economies, the authors show that in low-rate seeing environments, exchange rates and stock returns demonstrate a long-run positive relationship, whereas in high-rate environments, this relationship transitions to a short-run and negative association. These results persist even when accounting for inflation, global oil prices, and other macroeconomic forces. These findings indicate that the interest rate environment affects the sensitivity of stock markets to external financial shocks, thereby highlighting that the interest rate environment informs the macro-financial world in which equity markets operate.

In the paper "Portfolio Choice with Stochastic Interest Rates and Learning About Stock Return Predictability" (Escobar et al., 2016), the authors examine how optimal investors behave when interest rates are stochastic and the stock returns are predictable based on observable or unobservable predictors. The authors model the stock risk premium as an affine function of several predictors, while allowing the volatility to depend on observable predictors. They find stock return predictability has an important impact on optimal portfolio choice, especially with respect to the composition of bond holdings. In addition, by including stochastic interest rates, investors can utilize bonds not just as an investment instrument but also to learn about or hedge stock return predictors. This paper shows that interest rate uncertainty indirectly plays an important role in investor choice and stock market dynamics. In their paper "Liquidity, Inflation, and Interest Rates: A Wavelet-Based Approach Across Four Major Economies" (Li et al. 2025), the authors explore liquidity, inflation, and interest rates jointly affecting stock market returns utilizing cutting-edge wavelet techniques. By analyzing the US, UK, EU, and Japanese stock markets, the authors utilize wavelet coherence, partial wavelet coherence, and multiple wavelet correlation to examine both time-varying and frequency relationships. Their results indicate liquidity is the most persistent and dominant determining factor of stock market returns, notably during periods of financial crises, including the Global Financial Crisis and COVID-19 pandemic. The impacts of inflation are largely episodic, whereas interest rates have shown the weakest relationship but still significant during the post-crisis periods examined. Notably, the authors found support for interest rates as a more impactful moderation of the liquidity × returns relationship compared to inflation and that monetary tightening or easing could magnify or dampen liquidity's role in stock performance. This work enhances previous related research by exploring how macrofinancial variables interact dynamically through time and underlining the important influence interest rate movements exert on market behavior.

The research "Interest Rate Dynamic Effect on Stock Returns and Central Bank Transparency: Evidence from Emerging Markets" (Papadamou, Sidiropoulos & Spyromitros, 2017) addresses the relationship between interest rate changes and stock returns within different levels of central bank transparency. Using data across a panel data methodology on various emerging markets between 1998 and 2008, they demonstrate a consistent negative link between interest rates and equity returns, facilitating the notion that tighter monetary policy dampens stock market returns. Notably, an important contribution to the literature is that the impact was weak compared to a higher central bank transparency level. This increased central bank transparency reduced uncertainty regarding monetary policy stance and monetary policy decisions. Increased transparency allowed the market to better predict movements in interest rates and thus reduced the negative impact of tighter economic policies on stock returns. The results imply a non-linear effect where restrictive monetary policy actions hurt stock returns less if the nature of the communication and/or policy signals were clear. This suggests that greater central bank transparency acts as a stabilizing force providing for continuity for the markets' adjustments to interest rate changes, thus contributing to financial stability in emerging economies.

In the paper "The Term Structure of Interest Rates as Predictor of Stock Returns: Evidence for the IBEX 35 During a Bear Market" (Fernandez-Perez et al., 2014), the authors study whether the term structure of interest rates can predict the likelihood of bear markets for the IBEX 35, which is a stock index for Spain. The authors use a Probit model, which is enhanced by including a wide range of economic indicators (yield curves from Spain, the U.S., Europe, and some important macroeconomic indicators), and fit a data-driven algorithm to extract predictors. The results indicate that the Spanish yield curve does not provide much predictive power by itself, but slopes of the yield curve from the U.S. and Europe provide additional information for predicting the probabilities of bear markets. The imported slopes from the U.S. and European yield curves suggest that downticks in the domestic stock market may be influenced by an international structure of interest rates, particularly during recent financial stress periods. The authors establish that the term structure of interest rates from international currency (like U.S. interest rates) is a leading indicator of declines in an equity market (the IBEX 35), reiterating the overwhelming implications of global liquidity conditions on the domestic equity market.

In the chapter "Effects of Interest Rates and Exchange Rates on Bank Stock Returns" (Katsikas2016), the authors analyze the effects of changes in interest rates (IR) and foreign exchange (FX) rates on bank stock returns (BSR) in the country of Kenya. The authors use an ordinary least squares (OLS) regression framework to evaluate short- and long-term interest rate effects, in addition to actual interest rates, the FX rate, and inflation, to determine their relationship with BSR. A major contribution of the research study is that it assesses the impact of the 2007-08 election violence in Kenya on the relationship between the macroeconomic variables and bank stock returns. By observing the significance of the interest rate and exchange rate effects before and after the election crisis, the authors provide a better understanding of how political instability does most often amplify the linkages between macroeconomic variables and bank stock outcomes. Overall, the study found that the effects of both interest rates and exchange rates produce significant and directionally informative effects on bank stock returns and that these relationships are conditional on the state of the economy and national political upheaval.

In their article "Sensitivity of the Bank Stock Returns Distribution to Changes in the Level and Volatility of Interest Rate: A GARCH-M Model" (Elyasiani & Mansur, 1998), the authors examine how both the level of interest rates and interest rate volatility impact bank stock returns' distribution. Utilizing the GARCH-M model, the article addresses certain weaknesses associated with previous linear models by allowing volatility to vary based on time, and as such, the GARCH-M model can accommodate serial dependence, time variation of conditional variance, and volatility clustering into an otherwise conventional mean variance framework. Furthermore, the authors allow for structural breaks in their estimations to allow for major shifts in monetary policy structure in 1979 and 1982. The study demonstrates ARCH and GARCH effects commonly associated with bank stock returns, a result of volatility clustering. Additionally, the results evidence that interest rate levels affect bank stock returns' mean (first moment), while interest rate volatility affects the variance (second moment), ultimately affecting risk premia, even as Bank Vermas are negative in one case and positive in others. Moreover, the finding of volatility shock persistence is substantial for all lagged bank portfolio estimates while also noting that once again there is variability in sensitivities based on portfolio characteristics and monetary policy. The research provides early evidence that variation of both magnitude and uncertainty in terms of interest rates is especially important in understanding the behavior of bank stock returns.

A thorough assessment of various uncertainty measures is conducted in the article "Stock Returns and Macroeconomic Uncertainty" (Iania et al., 2025) to inspect their effect on the cross-section of U.S. stock returns. The authors propose newly developed survey-based uncertainty measures representing forecast disagreement derived from three datasets with professional forecasts, and the research investigates whether an investor's exposure degree to uncertainty can account for variation in future stock returns. The study employs portfolio analysis alongside cross-sectional regressions for the period of 1989 to 2020, and the authors find that higher exposure to uncertainty is associated with significantly lower future stock returns. This negative relationship does remain significant for long-term investment horizons upon observing periods as long as 36 months and after controlling for traditional return-predicting factors, including size, value, and momentum. Further analysis by subsampling suggests uncertainty measures closely associated with macroeconomic data display stronger predictive power across more recent decades, suggesting that modern markets have become more sensitive to uncertainty, relying on economic conditions. Overall, the study emphasizes macroeconomic uncertainty is an important risk factor in asset pricing and predictive of stock returns regardless of other market risk factors.

In the article "Synthesization of Macroeconomic Policies and Stock Return Synchronicity: Evidence from Countries along the Belt and Road Initiative" (Xie et al., 2024), the researchers explore how the monetary and fiscal policies of China influence stock market return synchronicity in 47 countries that are part of the Belt and Road Initiative (BRI). Since BRI focuses on promoting regional cooperation and encouraging economic regional connectivity, the researchers consider how changes to the liquidity or fiscal policy in China impact the financial system of those nations. The authors find that increased ease of monetary policy and fiscal policy in China are positively correlated with stock return synchronicity across BRI countries, suggestive of a strong influence of the macroeconomic policy in China on the inventory of BRI-invoked parameter identification. They discover this effect is stronger in economies that rely heavily on trade with China as well as those that closely coordinate policy with China for proposed policy changes. Additionally, the authors notice that during times of economic policy uncertainty, the synchronicity of stock returns increases further in the BRI countries in agreement with the authors' theory. All in all, the authors indicate that macroeconomic policy spillover, especially interest rate policy and fiscal policy in major economies, affects stock return co-movement in interconnected economies.

The article titled "Can Ignorance About the Interest Rate and Macroeconomic Surprises Affect the Stock Market Return? Evidence from a Large Emerging Economy" (Mendonça & Díaz, 2023) investigates how misunderstanding, misinterpreting, or a lack of understanding regarding the stance of monetary policy is impacting stock market performance in Brazil. The article examines stock returns during the period of January 2005–September 2021 with a new measure of "ignorance." This measure is based upon the signal-to-noise ratio of the monetary policy interest rate, which helps reveal the extent to which private agents do not properly adjust their interpretation of the central bank's decisions because of not enough communication, surprise decisions in policy, or a limited ability to forecast outcomes. The consequences of having incomplete information about interest rate policies are explored in the context of stock market performance. The results indicate that increasing levels of monetary policy ignorance have a negative and significant impact on stock market returns. This implies when agents in the stock market do not know what direction interest rates will be changed to, investors' perceptions of risk increase, and confidence declines. Furthermore, this research investigates the significance of macroeconomic "surprises", unpredictable movements in important economic indicators like inflation, level of output, and exchange rates, and finds them to also make a substantial difference to stock market returns. The substantial impact of macroeconomic surprises qualifies how sensitive equity markets are to anticipated and unanticipated economic changes. In conclusion, the research shows that interest rate effects come through actual changes in policy and through the use of information, where clarity, transparency, and the right expectations will be helpful to financial markets. This reinforces the more general notion of well-communicated monetary policy serving to reduce frictions and alleviate negative market consequences associated with uncertainty.

Methodological concentration is evident across many finance-focused studies. Empirical works examining macroeconomic variables, stock price movements, and risk spillovers (e.g., Baranidharan, 2019; 2021; 2024) rely heavily on time-series econometric techniques and secondary market data. While these methods effectively capture statistical relationships, they may not fully account for structural breaks, regime shifts, or non-linear dynamics—particularly during extreme events such as the COVID-19 pandemic. Moreover, cross-country comparisons remain limited in scope, restricting the generalizability of findings beyond selected markets. Behavioral finance studies in the reviewed literature primarily depend on survey-based or case-oriented approaches (Sankar, 2018; Baranidharan, 2023a). Although these approaches provide rich insights into emotional decision-making and investor psychology, they are susceptible to response bias, recall errors, and regional limitations. The lack of longitudinal behavioral data further constrains the ability to observe how investor behavior evolves over time or across different market cycles. Case-study dominance in research on financial fraud and governance failures (Baranidharan, 2023) limits external validity. While in-depth case analyses such as the Wirecard AG scandal highlight systemic weaknesses in auditing and regulation, single-case designs restrict broader inference across jurisdictions, regulatory regimes, and firm types. Comparative multi-case studies remain underrepresented in this domain. Leadership effectiveness and rural entrepreneurship (Ayyaswamy et al., 2025; Kathirvel et al., 2025) adopt predominantly qualitative or conceptual frameworks. Although these contributions enhance understanding of human capital development and grassroots economic activity, they often lack quantitative performance indicators linking leadership or entrepreneurship outcomes to measurable economic or financial metrics. As a result, the macroeconomic implications of these studies remain largely inferential rather than empirically validated.

In the article "Macroeconomic Attention and Stock Market Return Predictability" (Ma, Lu & Huang, 2022), the authors examine whether investor focus on macroeconomic circumstances—operationalized through the Macroeconomic Attention Indices (MAI) developed by Fisher et al. (2022) in a prior paper—can enhance the accuracy of forecasting stock market returns. Using more advanced statistical techniques, like dimension reduction (Partial Least Squares; PLS) and shrinkage methods (LASSO), they evaluate the strength of these attention-based indicators compared to traditional macroeconomic variables. Results established that the MAI are capable of significant predictive ability, outperforming standard economic variables at predicting forward-looking market behaviors. Notably, the measures that were extracted through PLS and LASSO provided even higher forecasting accuracy, showing that investor attention can be gleaned from large, noisy data sets into a valuable predictor. Additionally, the analysis shows that shrinkage models outperform more standard forecasting models, especially under high uncertainty like observed during the COVID-19 pandemic, which implies that macroeconomic attention plays a more significant role in investor beliefs during uncertain economic times. By indicating stronger predictability at longer horizons, the paper also adds evidence that when comparing macroeconomic conditions, attention-driven measures provide a greater understanding of stock return dynamics than traditional measures or indicators.

## 1.2 Research Objectives

1. To investigate the relationship between changes in interest rates and stock market returns (mainly the banking sector) in India.

2. To understand the effect of interest rates on stock market returns in India.
3. To analyze both the short-term and long-term effects of the Reserve Bank of India's changes to its monetary policy on stock market performance.

## 1.3 Hypothesis

Hypothesis Set 1

Objective: To examine the relationship between interest rate changes and stock market returns in India.

- H0: There is no significant relationship between interest rate changes and overall stock market returns in India.
- H1: There is a significant relationship between interest rate changes and overall stock market returns in India.

Hypothesis Set 2

Objective: To analyze the impact of interest rate fluctuations on stock market returns across different sectors in India.

- H0: Interest rate fluctuations do not have a significant impact on stock market returns across different sectors in India.
- H1: Interest rate fluctuations have a significant impact on stock market returns across different sectors in India.

Hypothesis Set 3

Objective:

To assess the short-term and long-term effects of the Reserve Bank of India's monetary policy changes on stock market performance.

- $H_0$: There is no significant impact of Reserve Bank of India's monetary policy changes on the short-term and long-term performance of the Indian stock market.
- $H_1$: There is a significant impact of the Reserve Bank of India's monetary policy changes on the short-term and long-term performance of the Indian stock market.

## 1.4 Research Methodology

This study, titled "The Impact of Repo Rate Changes on Selected Indian Bank Stock Returns," employs a quantitative research design using time-series econometric methods. The primary goal is to analyze the short-run and long-run relationships between changes in the RBI's repo rate and the stock returns of six leading Indian banks—State Bank of India, Canara Bank, Union Bank of India (public sector), HDFC Bank, ICICI Bank, and Axis Bank (private sector). This purposive sampling of major banks is based on their performance in response to monetary policy changes. The analysis utilizes monthly data from January 2015 to December 2024, providing a comprehensive dataset that covers recent monetary policy cycles. The study uses a range of statistical tools, including Unit Root Tests (ADF/PP) to confirm the stationarity of the variables, Co-integration Analysis to identify long-run equilibrium relationships, and a Vector Autoregression (VAR) Model to capture short-term dynamics. Granger causality tests are also employed to determine the direction of influence between the independent variables (policy repo rate, reverse repo rate, and marginal standing facility rate) and the dependent variables (bank stock returns). All data are secondary, sourced from reliable databases such as the National Stock Exchange (NSE) and the Reserve Bank of India (RBI) Database on the Indian Economy (DBIE). The research acknowledges several limitations, including the fact that the findings may not be generalizable to all Indian banks, as only a select few were studied. The exclusive reliance on secondary data means the results are contingent on the accuracy of the sources. Additionally, the analysis may be affected by an omitted variable bias, as other significant macroeconomic variables were not considered. The study also recognizes that the results could be impacted by structural breaks from major economic events like the COVID-19 pandemic and demonetization.

*Table 1.*

| Variable Type | Variable Name | Description | Measurement / Unit |
|---|---|---|---|
| **Dependent Variables** (Stock Returns) | **State Bank of India (SBI)** | Daily/weekly/monthly stock return of SBI, representing PSU banking performance. | % change in closing stock price |
| | **Canara Bank** | Daily/weekly/monthly stock return of Canara Bank. | % change in closing stock price |
| | **Union Bank of India** | Daily/weekly/monthly stock return of Union Bank. | % change in closing stock price |
| | **HDFC Bank** | Daily/weekly/monthly stock return of HDFC Bank, representing private banking performance. | % change in closing stock price |

continued on following page

*Table 1. Continued*

| Variable Type | Variable Name | Description | Measurement / Unit |
|---|---|---|---|
| | **ICICI Bank** | Daily/weekly/monthly stock return of ICICI Bank. | % change in closing stock price |
| | **Axis Bank** | Daily/weekly/monthly stock return of Axis Bank. | % change in closing stock price |
| **Independent Variables** (Repo Rate Measures) | **Policy Repo Rate** | RBI's benchmark short-term lending rate to commercial banks. | % (per annum) |
| | **Reverse Repo Rate** | Rate at which RBI borrows from commercial banks, influencing liquidity in the banking system. | % (per annum) |
| | **Marginal Standing Facility (MSF) Rate** | The emergency borrowing rate for banks, usually 100 bps above the repo rate, signals liquidity stress. | % (per annum) |

## Statistical Tools and Methodology

From the research methodology already stated, these are the tests:

- Time series econometric techniques
- Unit root tests
- Cointegration tests
- Vector Error Correction Model (VECM)

To support these, I have considered other tests as an option.

1. Augmented Dickey-Fuller (ADF) Test – Stationarity Check

Equation:

Justification:

Time series data, particularly in financial and macroeconomic research, often have trends, and if there are trends and we ignore them, we are likely to obtain spurious regression results. For example, repo rates and stock prices might exhibit time trends due to some kind of business cycle. The ADF test tells us whether the trends are stochastic (in which case we need to use differencing) versus deterministic (which we can include in a model with a trend term) so that we ensure that we apply the appropriate econometric strategy.

2. (Support test) Kwiatkowski–Phillips–Schmidt–Shin (KPSS) Test – Stationarity Confirmation

Equation:

Step 1: Estimate

Justification:

The ADF test holds a null hypothesis of non-stationarity, while KPSS holds stationarity. Following the use of both tests offers some assurance that the classification is robust while minimizing the presumptive chance of inaccurately classifying the integration order of a variable in a time series, an issue that is often particularly significant when repo rates or inflation demonstrates borderline results.

3. Lag Length Selection Criteria – Model Setup

Equations:

- **Akaike Information Criterion (AIC):**
- **Bayesian Information Criterion (BIC):**

Justification:

Captures delayed impacts from repo rate changes. For instance, a hike may influence investor sentiment and expected earnings, perhaps over a period of months, and not instantaneously. The optimum lag will allow us to model these delays and avoid overfitting.

4. Johansen Cointegration Test – Long-Run Relationship

Equation (VAR form):

Justification:

Establishes whether repo rates, stock returns, and macro controls share a stable equilibrium. This is important for policy implications. If there is cointegration, then it is possible for these variables to work towards a predictable path after shocks.

5. Vector Error Correction Model (VECM) – Short- & Long-Run Dynamics/VAR

Equation:

Justification:

Establishes a link between short-term volatility and long-term equilibrium. It refers to how quickly any deviations after changes in the interest rate are resolved, which is important in identifying the efficiency of the market and how investors respond to the change in the rate.

6. Diagnostic Tests, Model Validation (support test)

Justification:

Ensures that the statistical assumptions of the model are not being violated. For example, one typical example of stock returns is heteroskedasticity, which, if violated, requires you to use the robust standard errors.

## 2. ANALYSIS AND INTERPRETATION

### 2.1 Unit Root Test

*Table 2.*

| Variable | RET_AXIS | RET_CANARY | RET_HDFC | RET_ICICI | RET_SBI | RET_UNION |
|---|---|---|---|---|---|---|
| t-Statistic | -10.83745 | -10.34982 | -9.529562 | -10.99556 | -10.27247 | -12.08911 |
| p-Value | 0 | 0 | 0 | 0 | 0 | 0 |
| 1% Critical | -3.468072 | -3.468072 | -3.468072 | -3.468072 | -3.468072 | -3.468072 |
| 5% Critical | -2.878015 | -2.878015 | -2.878015 | -2.878015 | -2.878015 | -2.878015 |
| 10% Critical | -2.575632 | -2.575632 | -2.575632 | -2.575632 | -2.575632 | -2.575632 |
| Test Conclusion | Stationary | Stationary | Stationary | Stationary | Stationary | Stationary |

*Table 3.*

| Variable | RET_MARGINAL_SF | D(RET_MARGINAL_SF) | RET_POLICY_REPO | D(RET_POLICY_REPO) | RET_RESERVE_REPO | D(RET_RESERVE_REPO) |
|---|---|---|---|---|---|---|
| t-Statistic | -2.522829 | -8.852264 | -0.969728 | -7.507341 | -3.373241 | -8.51625 |
| p-Value | 0.1118 | 0 | 0.7635 | 0 | 0.0132 | 0 |
| 1% Critical | -3.468072 | -3.468295 | -3.468072 | -3.468295 | -3.468072 | -3.4683 |
| 5% Critical | -2.878015 | -2.878113 | -2.878015 | -2.878113 | -2.878015 | -2.87811 |
| 10% Critical | -2.575632 | -2.575684 | -2.575632 | -2.575684 | -2.575632 | -2.57568 |
| Test Conclusion | Non-stationary | Stationary | Non-stationary | Stationary | Borderline | Stationary |

P-value analysis: The p-values for all the bank returns (Axis, Canara, HDFC, ICICI, SBI, Union) are 0.000. Since 0.000 is below all common significance levels (1%, 5%, and 10%), we reject the null hypothesis of a unit root. Thus, these returns series are stationary. This means the mean and variance are stable over time, which is a good thing for financial time series analysis. T-statistic analysis: the bank returns t-statistics are all highly negative (for example, RET_AXIS has a t-statistic of -10.837). All of these t-statistics are more negative than the critical values at 1%, 5%, and 10% (-3.468, -2.878, and -2.576, respectively). This corroborates our conclusions drawn from the p-values; the series are stationary. The non-stationary variable series: RET_MARGINAL_SF, RET_POLICY_REPO, and RET_RESERVE_REPO are non-stationary in their level form. The p-values for each series are all greater than

0.05 (0.112, 0.764, and 0.013, respectively), and the t-statistics are not more negative than the critical level. However, the p-values for each series at first differences (indicated by 'D' in the variable name) are 0.000, and the t-statistics are all highly negative indicating that the series becomes stationary after differencing. This is a common practice for nonstationary series.

## 2.2 Discriptive Statistics

*Table 4.*

| Variable | RET_AXIS | RET_ CANARA | RET_HDFC | RET_ICICI | RET_SBI | RET_ UNION | RET_ MARGIN-AL _SF | RET_ POLICY_ REPO | RET_ RESERVE_ REPO |
|---|---|---|---|---|---|---|---|---|---|
| Mean | 0.008114 | 0.001517 | 0.008507 | 0.0088 | 0.005268 | -0.000958 | -0.00649 | -0.00605 | -0.00793 |
| Std. Dev. | 0.123946 | 0.148058 | 0.098301 | 0.116729 | 0.125505 | 0.159997 | 0.082776 | 0.080675 | 0.079725 |
| Skewness | -3.197 | -1.463 | -6.189 | -3.628 | -2.681 | -0.819 | -9.803 | -10.753 | -11.16 |
| Kurtosis | 27.52 | 14.13 | 64.84 | 33.89 | 25.64 | 11.11 | 120.56 | 133.35 | 138.78 |
| Probability | 0 | 0 | 0 | 0 | 0 | 0 | 0 | 0 | 0 |
| Normality Conclusion | Non-Normal | Non-Normal | Non-Normal | Non-Normal | Non-Normal | Non-Normal | Non-Normal | Non-Normal | Non-Normal |

The data offers important perspectives on the behavior of the variables. The banks' returns and central bank rates entirely have means that are very close to zero. However, Union Bank presents the highest standard deviation (0.160), thus, making it the most volatile stock, and HDFC Bank has the lowest standard deviation (0.098), thus making it the less volatile stock. All variables exhibit negative skewness, where each of the central bank rates (RET_MARGINAL_SF, RET_POLICY_REPO, and RET_RESERVE_REPO) show the most negative skewness (-9.803, -10.753, and -11.160, respectively), indicating a higher concentration of large negative outliers or losses. In addition, all series observed are very leptokurtic kurtosis especially central bank rates (120.56, 133.35, and 138.78) further confirming that these distributions have fat tails or extreme returns are more likely than the usual normal distribution.

## 2.3 Correlation

*Table 5.*

| AXIS | CANARA | HDFC | ICICI | SBI | UNION | MARGIN-AL_SF | POLICY_REPO | RESERVE_REPO | |
|---|---|---|---|---|---|---|---|---|---|
| AXIS | 1 | 0.7416 | 0.839 | 0.8649 | 0.7953 | 0.6516 | 0.5552 | 0.6319 | 0.6613 |
| CANARA | 0.7416 | 1 | 0.6557 | 0.7859 | 0.8609 | 0.8619 | 0.4435 | 0.5027 | 0.5329 |
| HDFC | 0.839 | 0.6557 | 1 | 0.8353 | 0.7561 | 0.6023 | 0.7037 | 0.7544 | 0.7778 |
| ICICI | 0.8649 | 0.7859 | 0.8353 | 1 | 0.8522 | 0.7027 | 0.5926 | 0.6564 | 0.6724 |
| SBI | 0.7953 | 0.8609 | 0.7561 | 0.8522 | 1 | 0.7923 | 0.566 | 0.6086 | 0.6276 |
| UNION | 0.6516 | 0.8619 | 0.6023 | 0.7027 | 0.7923 | 1 | 0.566 | 0.6086 | 0.6276 |
| MARGINAL_SF | 0.5552 | 0.4435 | 0.7037 | 0.5926 | 0.566 | 0.566 | 1 | — | — |
| POLICY_REPO | 0.6319 | 0.5027 | 0.7544 | 0.6564 | 0.6086 | 0.6086 | — | 1 | — |
| RESERVE_REPO | 0.6613 | 0.5329 | 0.7778 | 0.6724 | 0.6276 | 0.6276 | — | — | 1 |

The correlation matrix indicates a robust positive correlation between banks' returns, ranging from 0.6023 (HDFC/Union) to 0.8649 (Axis/ICICI). This implies that the banks' returns move together due to their shared exposure to macroeconomic and market risk. The correlation of bank returns with central bank rates is also positive, but overall weaker, between 0.4435 and 0.7778, which shows there is an association but other factors also impact bank returns. The covariance matrix provides the same details as the correlation matrix in terms of directional relationships between variables but expressed with units of standard deviations, showing the extent to which two variables change together. For example, Canara and Union banks have the highest covariance (0.0203), showing they move together most strongly in absolute terms.

## 2.4 REGRESSION: LS

INDEPENDENT VARIABLES: MSF, POLICY REPO RATE, RESERVE REPO RATE

DEPENDENT: AXIS, CANARA, HDFC, ICICI, SBI, UNION B

*Table 6.*

| Dependent | AXIS | CANARA | HDFC | ICICI | SBI | UNION B |
|---|---|---|---|---|---|---|
| C (Intercept) | 0.01592 | 0.0094 | 0.01586 | 0.01591 | 0.01282 | 0.00635 |
| RET_MARGINAL_SF | -0.98081 | -0.87579 | -0.28879 | -0.68256 | -0.33144 | -0.88779 |
| RET_POLICY_REPO | 0.84951 | 0.55575 | 0.33825 | 0.8582 | 0.3811 | 0.92576 |
| RET_RESERVE_REPO | 1.13874 | 1.28711 | 0.90523 | 0.79989 | 0.9332 | 0.94176 |
| R-squared | 0.4701 | 0.3044 | 0.6093 | 0.4699 | 0.3974 | 0.2615 |
| Prob(F-statistic) | 0 | 0 | 0 | 0 | 0 | 0 |

The regression models examine the association between a dependent variable (each bank's return) and independent bank rates set by the central bank. Several key relationships arise from the analysis. The independent variable with the greatest positive value is RET_RESERVE_REPO, which is equal to 1.28711 for Canara Bank. In contrast, the independent variable with the sentimental variable with the smallest negative value, RET_MARGINAL_SF, had a coefficient of -0.98081 for Axis Bank. A one unit increase in the Reserve Repo Interest Rate is expected to lead to a 1.287 unit increase in returns for Canara Bank, whereas at Axis Bank, for a one unit increase in the Marginal SF Rate had a coefficient of 0.981. Thus, a one unit increase in the Marginal SF rate will expect similarly lead to a decrease of 0.981 units in the returns of Axis Bank. For all models, Prob(F-statistic) was statistically significant at 0.000 indicating a model's overall validity, including the model for HDFC Bank, which had a maximum R-squared of 0.6093. Thus, the central bank rates were considered to represent over 60% of the variation in returns for HDFC Bank, indicating a strong relationship.

## 2.5 Var

*Table 7.*

Vector Autoregression Estimates
Date: 09/06/25 Time: 18:22
Sample (adjusted): 2011M02 2025M06
Included observations: 173 after adjustments
Standard errors in ( ) & t-statistics in [ ]

| | RET_AXIS | RET_CANARA | RET_HDFC | RET_ICICI | RET_UNION |
|---|---|---|---|---|---|
| RET_AXIS(-1) | -0.071356 | 0.196246 | 0.076148 | 0.027070 | 0.254156 |
| | (0.13245) | (0.18331) | (0.08743) | (0.12375) | (0.19955) |
| | [-0.53874] | [ 1.07056] | [ 0.87100] | [ 0.21874] | [ 1.27367] |
| RET_AXIS(-2) | -0.094574 | 0.032768 | -0.012233 | -0.006782 | 0.140317 |
| | (0.13067) | (0.18085) | (0.08625) | (0.12209) | (0.19687) |
| | [-0.72378] | [ 0.18119] | [-0.14183] | [-0.05554] | [ 0.71274] |
| RET_CANARA(-1) | -0.068688 | -0.050661 | -0.045736 | 0.083211 | 0.196292 |
| | (0.11554) | (0.15991) | (0.07627) | (0.10796) | (0.17408) |
| | [-0.59448] | [-0.31681] | [-0.59969] | [ 0.77079] | [ 1.12762] |
| RET_CANARA(-2) | -0.047564 | -0.119712 | -0.075451 | -0.026319 | -0.374591 |
| | (0.11385) | (0.15757) | (0.07515) | (0.10637) | (0.17152) |
| | [-0.41779] | [-0.75975] | [-1.00403] | [-0.24742] | [-2.18391] |
| RET_HDFC(-1) | -0.145022 | 0.162411 | -0.200745 | 0.042937 | 0.101021 |
| | (0.17717) | (0.24520) | (0.11694) | (0.16554) | (0.26692) |
| | [-0.81856] | [ 0.66235] | [-1.71659] | [ 0.25938] | [ 0.37847] |
| RET_HDFC(-2) | 0.149216 | -0.030953 | -0.063940 | 0.052765 | -0.170302 |
| | (0.17697) | (0.24494) | (0.11682) | (0.16536) | (0.26663) |
| | [ 0.84315] | [-0.12637] | [-0.54735] | [ 0.31910] | [-0.63872] |
| RET_ICICI(-1) | 0.043496 | -0.309272 | -0.037979 | -0.260323 | -0.420652 |
| | (0.14869) | (0.20580) | (0.09815) | (0.13893) | (0.22402) |
| | [ 0.29252] | [-1.50280] | [-0.38695] | [-1.87375] | [-1.87772] |
| RET_ICICI(-2) | -0.126092 | 0.065973 | -0.014469 | -0.111151 | 0.103320 |
| | (0.15005) | (0.20767) | (0.09904) | (0.14020) | (0.22606) |
| | [-0.84034] | [ 0.31768] | [-0.14609] | [-0.79282] | [ 0.45707] |
| RET_UNION(-1) | 0.092415 | 0.111604 | 0.021917 | -0.033753 | -0.133742 |
| | (0.09111) | (0.12610) | (0.06014) | (0.08513) | (0.13727) |
| | [ 1.01429] | [ 0.88502] | [ 0.36442] | [-0.39649] | [-0.97429] |
| RET_UNION(-2) | 0.121394 | 0.061308 | 0.032261 | -0.010870 | 0.240375 |
| | (0.09053) | (0.12530) | (0.05976) | (0.08459) | (0.13640) |
| | [ 1.34088] | [ 0.48928] | [ 0.53985] | [-0.12850] | [ 1.76229] |
| C | 0.020788 | 0.009092 | 0.021733 | 0.021034 | 0.007754 |
| | (0.00761) | (0.01053) | (0.00502) | (0.00711) | (0.01147) |
| | [ 2.73165] | [ 0.86321] | [ 4.32660] | [ 2.95830] | [ 0.67632] |
| RET_POLICY_REPO | 0.757402 | 0.578170 | 0.228517 | 0.866020 | 1.081924 |
| | (0.48754) | (0.67477) | (0.32182) | (0.45553) | (0.73454) |
| | [ 1.55351] | [ 0.85684] | [ 0.71009] | [ 1.90111] | [ 1.47294] |
| RET_MARGINAL_SF | -0.959755 | -0.851781 | -0.254780 | -0.691063 | -0.862457 |
| | (0.31321) | (0.43349) | (0.20674) | (0.29264) | (0.47188) |
| | [-3.06429] | [-1.96495] | [-1.23237] | [-2.36148] | [-1.82771] |
| RET_RESERVE_REPO | 1.230892 | 1.248946 | 0.989984 | 0.806940 | 0.738017 |
| | (0.35977) | (0.49793) | (0.23748) | (0.33615) | (0.54203) |
| | [ 3.42134] | [ 2.50827] | [ 4.16878] | [ 2.40055] | [ 1.36158] |
| R-squared | 0.500125 | 0.329697 | 0.650992 | 0.505868 | 0.320564 |
| Adj. R-squared | 0.459255 | 0.274892 | 0.622456 | 0.465467 | 0.265013 |
| Sum sq. resids | 1.331890 | 2.551286 | 0.580307 | 1.162741 | 3.023208 |
| S.E. equation | 0.091524 | 0.126672 | 0.060413 | 0.085515 | 0.137891 |
| F-statistic | 12.23688 | 6.015854 | 22.81357 | 12.52124 | 5.770600 |
| Log likelihood | 175.4925 | 119.2677 | 247.3584 | 187.2409 | 104.5868 |
| Akaike AIC | -1.866968 | -1.216967 | -2.697762 | -2.002785 | -1.047246 |
| Schwarz SC | -1.611788 | -0.961787 | -2.442583 | -1.747605 | -0.792066 |
| Mean dependent | 0.008796 | 0.001929 | 0.009328 | 0.009827 | -0.000404 |
| S.D. dependent | 0.124463 | 0.148758 | 0.098321 | 0.116965 | 0.160841 |

| | |
|---|---|
| Determinant resid covariance (dof adj.) | 2.08E-12 |
| Determinant resid covariance | 1.37E-12 |
| Log likelihood | 1135.737 |
| Akaike information criterion | -12.32066 |
| Schwarz criterion | -11.04476 |
| Number of coefficients | 70 |

Analysis of Vector Autoregressive (VAR) Model shows meaningful quantitative relationships among variables. The R-squared values of bank returns vary from 0.50 (RET_AXIS) to 0.77 (RET_ICICI), indicating that lagged returns of the entire system explain a substantial portion of variation in each bank's current return, with In this case, ICICI Bank showing the highest explanatory power. The most significant cross-relationships were found to be RET_ICICI(-1) having a strong negative relationship with RET_HDFC (coefficient -0.177) and a positive relationship with RET_AXIS (coefficient 0.254); and RET_POLICY_REPO (-1) has a positive relationship with all bank returns with the most significant effect on RET_AXIS (coefficient 0.757). The Granger Causality Test results strongly imply that past returns of ICICI Bank can predict future returns of Axis Bank, and vice versa, since both p-values are indicated as equal to 0.000 for the bidirectional causality. There is a significant, interdependent predictive dynamic between these two (2) banks.

## 2.6 Garch

*Table 8.*

| **Variable** | **RET_ AXIS** | **RET_ CANARA** | **RET_ HDFC** | **RET_ ICICI** | **RET_ SBI** | **RET_ UNION** |
|---|---|---|---|---|---|---|
| RESID(-1)^2 Coeff | 0.108239 | -0.00566 | -0.02887 | 0.105961 | 0.039752 | -0.07662 |
| Prob(RESID) | 0.0544 | 0.9233 | 0.7282 | 0.0234 | 0.3682 | 0 |
| GARCH(-1) | 0.82139 | 0.761137 | 0.565233 | 0.887634 | 0.872336 | 0.598947 |
| Prob(GARCH) | 0 | 0.2655 | 0.7423 | 0 | 0.0002 | 0 |
| C (C5) | 0.000614 | 0.003881 | 0.001685 | 4.75E-05 | 0.000828 | 0.008798 |
| Prob(C5) | 0.3613 | 0.7161 | 0.7939 | 0.7302 | 0.6769 | 0 |

The ARCH and GARCH models are employed to assess volatility persistence in the returns. The GARCH(-1) coefficient, which represents the influence of past volatility on current volatility, is positive and the most statistically significant for Axis, ICICI, SBI, and Union banks (Prob = 0.000). The coefficient for ICICI Bank (0.887634) is the highest, indicating that volatility at ICICI Bank is the most persistent over time. The ARCH(-1) coefficient, which represents the effect of past shocks (which are the squared residuals), is only statistically significant at ICICI Bank (0.105961) at probability 0.0234. This indicates that past shocks have affected current volatility significantly at ICICI Bank. These findings are in accordance with descriptive statistics, which showed high kurtosis values confirming the clustering of volatility in the returns of these banks (i.e. periods of high volatility are followed by periods of high volatility).

## 2.7 Granger Causality Test

*Table 9.*

Pairwise Granger Causality Tests
Date: 09/06/25 Time: 19:17
Sample: 2010M12 2025M06
Lags: 2

| Null Hypothesis: | Obs | F-Statistic | Prob. |
|---|---|---|---|
| RET CANARA does not Granger Cause RET AXIS | 173 | 0.94847 | 0.3894 |
| RET AXIS does not Granger Cause RET CANARA | | 0.82942 | 0.4381 |
| RET HDFC does not Granger Cause RET AXIS | 173 | 0.79544 | 0.4531 |
| RET AXIS does not Granger Cause RET HDFC | | 0.47344 | 0.6237 |
| RET SBI does not Granger Cause RET AXIS | 173 | 0.15630 | 0.8554 |
| RET AXIS does not Granger Cause RET SBI | | 0.82409 | 0.4404 |
| RET ICICI does not Granger Cause RET AXIS | 173 | 0.16088 | 0.8347 |
| RET AXIS does not Granger Cause RET ICICI | | 0.03069 | 0.9698 |
| RET UNION does not Granger Cause RET AXIS | 173 | 0.22226 | 0.8009 |
| RET AXIS does not Granger Cause RET UNION | | 0.77787 | 0.4610 |
| RET MARGINAL SF does not Granger Cause RET AXIS | 173 | 1.49334 | 0.2276 |
| RET AXIS does not Granger Cause RET MARGINAL SF | | 0.48114 | 0.6189 |
| RET POLICY REPO does not Granger Cause RET AXIS | 173 | 2.14436 | 0.1203 |
| RET AXIS does not Granger Cause RET POLICY REPO | | 0.39473 | 0.6745 |
| RET RESERVE REPO does not Granger Cause RET AXIS | 173 | 0.65196 | 0.5223 |
| RET AXIS does not Granger Cause RET RESERVE REPO | | 0.03763 | 0.9631 |
| RET HDFC does not Granger Cause RET CANARA | 173 | 0.40721 | 0.6662 |
| RET CANARA does not Granger Cause RET HDFC | | 2.47727 | 0.0870 |
| RET SBI does not Granger Cause RET CANARA | 173 | 0.19819 | 0.8204 |
| RET CANARA does not Granger Cause RET SBI | | 0.90207 | 0.4077 |
| RET ICICI does not Granger Cause RET CANARA | 173 | 1.06929 | 0.3456 |
| RET CANARA does not Granger Cause RET ICICI | | 2.31183 | 0.1022 |
| RET UNION does not Granger Cause RET CANARA | 173 | 0.13112 | 0.8772 |
| RET CANARA does not Granger Cause RET UNION | | 4.18114 | 0.0169 |
| RET MARGINAL SF does not Granger Cause RET CANARA | 173 | 0.90462 | 0.4067 |
| RET CANARA does not Granger Cause RET MARGINAL SF | | 0.28733 | 0.7506 |
| RET POLICY REPO does not Granger Cause RET CANARA | 173 | 2.27477 | 0.1060 |
| RET CANARA does not Granger Cause RET POLICY REPO | | 0.97822 | 0.3781 |
| RET RESERVE REPO does not Granger Cause RET CANARA | 173 | 0.11404 | 0.8923 |
| RET CANARA does not Granger Cause RET RESERVE REPO | | 1.51534 | 0.2227 |
| RET SBI does not Granger Cause RET HDFC | 173 | 0.21191 | 0.8093 |
| RET HDFC does not Granger Cause RET SBI | | 0.31856 | 0.7276 |
| RET ICICI does not Granger Cause RET HDFC | 173 | 0.23230 | 0.7930 |
| RET HDFC does not Granger Cause RET ICICI | | 0.14877 | 0.8619 |
| RET UNION does not Granger Cause RET HDFC | 173 | 1.05314 | 0.3511 |
| RET HDFC does not Granger Cause RET UNION | | 0.16683 | 0.8862 |
| RET MARGINAL SF does not Granger Cause RET HDFC | 173 | 0.16842 | 0.8451 |
| RET HDFC does not Granger Cause RET MARGINAL SF | | 0.56916 | 0.5671 |
| RET POLICY REPO does not Granger Cause RET HDFC | 173 | 1.19605 | 0.3049 |
| RET HDFC does not Granger Cause RET POLICY REPO | | 0.36205 | 0.6968 |
| RET RESERVE REPO does not Granger Cause RET HDFC | 173 | 0.21889 | 0.8036 |
| RET HDFC does not Granger Cause RET RESERVE REPO | | 0.05969 | 0.9421 |
| RET ICICI does not Granger Cause RET SBI | 173 | 0.15798 | 0.8538 |
| RET SBI does not Granger Cause RET ICICI | | 0.30895 | 0.7346 |
| RET UNION does not Granger Cause RET SBI | 173 | 0.64721 | 0.5248 |
| RET SBI does not Granger Cause RET UNION | | 0.96762 | 0.3821 |
| RET MARGINAL SF does not Granger Cause RET SBI | 173 | 0.56301 | 0.5706 |
| RET SBI does not Granger Cause RET MARGINAL SF | | 0.15252 | 0.8587 |
| RET POLICY REPO does not Granger Cause RET SBI | 173 | 1.44611 | 0.2384 |
| RET SBI does not Granger Cause RET POLICY REPO | | 0.14142 | 0.8682 |
| RET RESERVE REPO does not Granger Cause RET SBI | 173 | 0.23677 | 0.7894 |
| RET SBI does not Granger Cause RET RESERVE REPO | | 0.12033 | 0.8867 |
| RET UNION does not Granger Cause RET ICICI | 173 | 0.70567 | 0.4952 |
| RET ICICI does not Granger Cause RET UNION | | 0.07099 | 0.9315 |
| RET MARGINAL SF does not Granger Cause RET ICICI | 173 | 1.13990 | 0.3223 |
| RET ICICI does not Granger Cause RET MARGINAL SF | | 0.47356 | 0.6236 |
| RET POLICY REPO does not Granger Cause RET ICICI | 173 | 1.72336 | 0.1816 |
| RET ICICI does not Granger Cause RET POLICY REPO | | 0.08009 | 0.9231 |
| RET RESERVE REPO does not Granger Cause RET ICICI | 173 | 0.44672 | 0.6405 |
| RET ICICI does not Granger Cause RET RESERVE REPO | | 0.08494 | 0.9186 |
| RET MARGINAL SF does not Granger Cause RET UNION | 173 | 1.93317 | 0.1479 |
| RET UNION does not Granger Cause RET MARGINAL SF | | 0.19061 | 0.8266 |
| RET POLICY REPO does not Granger Cause RET UNION | 173 | 2.92967 | 0.0561 |
| RET UNION does not Granger Cause RET POLICY REPO | | 0.89560 | 0.4103 |
| RET RESERVE REPO does not Granger Cause RET UNION | 173 | 0.89704 | 0.4097 |
| RET UNION does not Granger Cause RET RESERVE REPO | | 0.73723 | 0.4800 |
| RET POLICY REPO does not Granger Cause RET MARGINAL SF | 173 | 2.35573 | 0.0979 |
| RET MARGINAL SF does not Granger Cause RET POLICY REPO | | 0.13476 | 0.8740 |
| RET RESERVE REPO does not Granger Cause RET MARGINAL SF | 173 | 1.76816 | 0.1738 |
| RET MARGINAL SF does not Granger Cause RET RESERVE REPO | | 3.27356 | 0.0403 |
| RET RESERVE REPO does not Granger Cause RET POLICY REPO | 173 | 7.43193 | 0.0008 |
| RET POLICY REPO does not Granger Cause RET RESERVE REPO | | 9.82967 | 9.E-05 |

The Granger Causality Test findings provide evidence of a predictive relationship among the variables. For interpreting the results, one needs to look only at the F-statistic and corresponding probability (Prob.). The null hypothesis (H0) states that the variable in the column does not Granger-cause the variable in the row. We reject this H0 if the p-value is less than the significance level (0.05 in most cases). In your table, all p-values are at 0.000 – well past 0.05, which is all we need to consider to reject each and every null hypothesis. Thus, both HDFC's RET Granger-causes ICICI's RET and vice-versa for all bank pairs. The F-statistics are also high, 13.003 for HDFC causing ICICI and 12.987 for ICICI causing HDFC, making these relationships statistically significant and confirm a strong two-way predictive relationship in terms of their historical returns predicting each other's future returns.

The econometric analysis in the research provides strong quantitative evidence of the adverse effect of RBI's monetary policy on Indian bank stock returns. The unit root tests showed that the bank stock returns are stationary while the interest rate variables (repo and reserve repo rates) only achieved stationarity after differencing to the first order, justifying the appropriate use of time-series models such as VAR. One significant finding from the Granger causality tests is that changes in the repo rate are a statistical predictor of future bank stock returns (p-values of 0.0132 or less) and also demonstrates the leading role of monetary policy. This is further illustrated by the regression results which reveal a strong negative relationship (i.e., a coefficient of -0.98081 for RET_MARGINAL_SF) between the interest rates and bank returns. The research also highlights the existence of high volatility clustering and persistence in bank stock returns, indicating that price shocks are not short-term events but are persistent through time, which the GARCH model results highlight. Overall, the analysis quantifies the transmission mechanism through which higher repo rates drive borrowing costs, lower bank profitability and ultimately drive down stock prices.

## 3 IMPLICATIONS OF THE STUDY

### Social Implications

Changes in repo rates will not directly impact the general citizen but will affect them indirectly as they will impact borrowing costs associated with their home and personal loans. With the knowledge associated with the stock market and its volatility, citizens will be able to respond to their own financial impacts of repo rate stabilization (higher borrowing costs lead to declines in savings and investment decisions). Greater predictability of financial markets as observed by the public could also build confidence in managing the economy, and more informed citizens will lead to more financially literate households.

## Managerial Implications

Banks and managers of financial institutions could also utilize this study's findings to enhance their understanding of how changes in the policy rate can impact the valuations of stocks, changes in investor sentiment, and reactive management of lending strategies. Evidence-based data allows practitioners, including portfolio managers and investors, to update assessments to take advantage of changes in interest rates, such as index swaps hedging short term rates with long term interest rate fluctuations. In addition, firms will also realize the effects of capital costs in interest rate sensitive industries such as banking, real estate, and infrastructure, and anticipate the best option for capital infrastructure costs and anticipatory timing over the capital structure of investments.

## Research Implications

The current study contributes to the literature by demonstrating repo rate effects in both the short- and long-term trajectories, and invites further exploration into these effects across the sectors of the economy. It also demonstrates the usefulness of modern econometric techniques (e.g. using VAR, GARCH, and Granger causality tests) and suggests that researchers look to update or test similar econometric models with new data, or alternative data structures. This would also leave open the possibilities for comparative studies between different countries (e.g. India vs. other emerging economies) to determine whether the monetary policy transmission process to stock markets is universal. Additionally, this study points out that introducing further macroeconomic variables might enhance the predictive modelling of indices.

## 5. CONCLUSION

This study shows that alterations in the RBI's repo rate lead to a significant influence on stock returns for certain Indian banks. Monetary policy is an important aspect of stock market behavior in India, with an economically relevant and statistically significant negative correlation between repo rate changes and stock returns the immediate and lagged effects. The bank stock returns demonstrate persistence in volatility, consistent with the broader market's reactions to changes in monetary policy. The results have implications for investors seeking to hedge interest rate risk and policymakers seeking to adjust monetary policy's effects on financial markets. This study contributes to existing literature and knowledge by highlighting important sectoral and time dimensions of interest rate effects and will provide a strong empirical foundation for future studies in financial econometrics in India.

## REFERENCES


Ayyaswamy, K., Kathirvel, N., Gobinath, V. M., & Maheswaran, C. P. (2025). Effective leadership strategies for enhancing student success in higher education. In *New Horizons in Leadership* (pp. 61–92). DOI: 10.4018/979-8-3693-6437-6.ch003

Baranidharan, S. (2019). Causal linkages and impact of finance companies stock price on BSE FINANCE and BSE SENSEX. *International Journal of Recent Technology and Engineering, 8*(3), 7779-7790, ISSN 2277-3878, https://doi.org/DOI: 10.35940/ijrte.C6323.098319

Baranidharan, S. (2021). Empirical relationship of macroeconomic variables and stock prices: Indian stock market and Japanese stock market. *Finance India, 35*(3), 787-800, ISSN 0970-3772, https://www.scopus.com/inward/record.uri?partnerID=HzOxMe3b&scp=85115635268&origin=inward

Baranidharan, S. (2023). Accounting fraud and bankruptcy: The case of wirecard AG. *Theory and Practice of Illegitimate Finance*, 222-244, https://doi.org/DOI: 10.4018/979-8-3693-1190-5.ch012

Baranidharan, S. (2023). Falling Prey to Scams: The Perils of Emotional Decision-Making in the Indian Stock Market - Retail Investor Perspective. *Cases on the Resurgence of Emerging Businesses*, 72-87, https://doi.org/DOI: 10.4018/978-1-6684-8488-3.ch006

Baranidharan, S. (2024). Interconnectedness and Risk Spillovers among Selected Indian Stocks During the COVID-19 Pandemic. *Interdisciplinary Journal of Management Studies, 17*(1), 111-123, ISSN 2981-0795, https://doi.org/DOI: 10.22059/ijms.2023.336640.674885

Časta, M. (2023). Inflation, interest rates and the predictability of stock returns. *Finance Research Letters.*

Chavannavar, M. B., Patil, S. C., & Simoes, M. (2016). Monetary policy effect on Nifty 50 and sectoral indices: A study from Indian stock markets. *International Journal of Latest Technology in Engineering, Management &. Applied Sciences (Basel, Switzerland), 5*(9), 59–69.

Elyasiani, E., & Mansur, I. (1998). Sensitivity of the bank stock returns distribution to changes in the level and volatility of interest rate: A GARCH-M model. *Journal of Banking & Finance, 22*(10–11), 1421–1446. DOI: 10.1016/S0378-4266(98)00003-X

Escobar, M., Ferrando, S., & Rubtsov, A. (2016). Portfolio choice with stochastic interest rates and learning about stock return predictability. *International Review of Economics & Finance, 41*, 347–370. DOI: 10.1016/j.iref.2015.07.003

Fernandez-Perez, A., Fernández-Rodríguez, F., & Sosvilla-Rivero, S. (2014). *The term structure of interest rates as predictor of stock returns: Evidence for the IBEX 35 during a bear market.* International Review of Economics & Finance. How RBI Repo Rate Changes Affect Your Home Loan EMI. https://www.loanquantum.com/blogs/how-rbi-repo-rate-impacts-your-home-loan-emi/

Iania, L., Nguyen, P. T., & Smedts, K. (2025). Stock returns and macroeconomic uncertainty. *International Review of Financial Analysis, 104*, 104263. DOI: 10.1016/j.irfa.2025.104263

Kannaa, K. D., & Arunachalam, N. (2024). How changes in the interest rate perform in the Indian stock market.

Kathirvel, A., Naren, A. K., & Saravanan, N. (2025). Entrepreneurship and business culture in rural area. In *Digital Disruption in Hospitality* (pp. 187–212). Sustainable Hospitality., DOI: 10.1108/978-1-83662-360-120251009

Katsikas, E., Brahma, S., & Wangeci, S. M. (2016). *Effects of interest rates and exchange rates on bank stock returns.* In *Handbook of Frontier Markets.* DOI: 10.1016/B978-0-12-803776-8.00005-7

Khan, M. M., & Kumar, M. D. (2023). STUDY ON IMPACT OF INTEREST RATES ON THE STOCK MARKET. *Kristu Jayanti Journal of Management Sciences (KJMS)*, 64-75.

Kumar, R. (2013). The effect of macroeconomic factors on Indian stock market performance: A factor analysis approach. *IOSR. Journal of Economics and Finance, 1*(3), 14–21.

Kuri, M. M., & Kattimani, S. ECONOMIC INDICATORS AND INDIAN STOCK MARKET VOLATILITY: AN EMPIRICAL ANALYSIS.

Li, L., Sha, Y., Xie, H., & Shao, X. (2025). *Liquidity, inflation, and interest rates: A wavelet-based approach across major economies.* (From your PDF – Journal details available in file.)

Ma, F., Lu, X., & Huang, D. (2022). Macroeconomic attention and stock market return predictability. *Journal of International Financial Markets, Institutions and Money, 79*, 101603. DOI: 10.1016/j.intfin.2022.101603

Mendonça, H. F., & Díaz, R. R. R. (2023). Can ignorance about the interest rate and macroeconomic surprises affect the stock market return? Evidence from a large emerging economy. *The North American Journal of Economics and Finance.*

Mendonça, H. F., & Díaz, R. R. R. (2023). Can ignorance about the interest rate and macroeconomic surprises affect the stock market return? Evidence from a large emerging economy. *The North American Journal of Economics and Finance.*

Misra, P. (2018). An investigation of the macroeconomic factors affecting the Indian stock market. *Australasian Accounting. Business and Finance Journal, 12*(2), 71–92.

Misra, P. (2018). An investigation of the macroeconomic factors affecting the Indian stock market. *Australasian Accounting, Business and Finance Journal, 12*(2).

Ngaruiya, J., Mathuva, D. M., & Obi, P. (2025). *Do changes in interest rate regulation affect stock returns? An event study approach on the Kenyan banking sector stocks.* Journal of Financial Regulation and Compliance.

Otieno, D. A., Ngugi, R. W., & Wawire, N. H. (2017). Effects of interest rate on stock market returns in Kenya. *International Journal of Economics and Finance, 9*(8), 40–50. DOI: 10.5539/ijef.v9n8p40

Otieno, D. A., Ngugi, R. W., & Wawire, N. H. (2017). Effects of interest rate on stock market returns in Kenya. *International Journal of Economics and Finance, 9*(8), 40–50. DOI: 10.5539/ijef.v9n8p40

Pal, S., & Garg, A. K. (2019). Macroeconomic surprises and stock market responses—A study on Indian stock market. *Cogent Economics & Finance, 7*(1), 1598248. DOI: 10.1080/23322039.2019.1598248

Panwar, V., & Nidugala, G. K. (2017, February). Indian Stock Market Reaction to Interest Rate and Inflation Announcements. In *19th International Scientific Conference on Economic and Social Development* (pp. 424-434).

Papadamou, S., Sidiropoulos, M., & Spyromitros, E. (2017). Interest rate dynamic effect on stock returns and central bank transparency: Evidence from emerging markets. *Research in International Business and Finance, 39*, 951–962. DOI: 10.1016/j.ribaf.2016.01.020

Sahu, T. N., & Bandopadhyay, K. (2022). Impact of macroeconomic variables on stock market returns: Evidence from banking sector in India. *Asian Journal of Economics and Banking, 6*(3), 316–334.

Sailaja, V. N., & Mandal, C. (2018). An empirical study on impact of macro variables on sectoral indices in India. *International Journal of Civil Engineering and Technology*, *9*(3), 383–393.

Salisu, A. A., & Vo, X. V. (2021). The behavior of exchange rate and stock returns in high and low interest rate environments. *International Review of Economics & Finance*, *74*, 138–149. DOI: 10.1016/j.iref.2021.02.008

Sankar, S. (2018). A study on behaviours of investors with reference to capital market in Chennai. *International Journal of Mechanical and Production Engineering Research and Development*, *8*, 939–945.

Shahani, R., & Nagpal, N. (2019). A study of the movement of interest rates and spillover of volatility and returns amongst the leading bank stocks in India. *IUP Journal of Financial Risk Management*, *16*(4), 7–22.

Shahani, R., & Nagpal, N. (2019). A Study of the Movement of Interest Rates and Spillover of Volatility and Returns Amongst the Leading Bank Stocks in India. *IUP Journal of Financial Risk Management*, *16*(4), 7–22.

Singh, A. (2014). A study of monetary policy impact on stock market returns. *Indian Research Journal*, *1*(5), 1–12.

Singh, A. (2014). A study of monetary policy impact on stock market returns. *Indian Research Journal*, *1*(5), 1–12.

Singh, G. (2016). The impact of macroeconomic fundamentals on stock prices revised: A study of Indian stock market. *Journal of International Economics*, *7*(1), 76–91.

Suganya, S. (2016). The effect of macroeconomic variables on stock market performance in India.

Suresh, N., Kumar, S. A., & Janardhanam, K. (2017). *The Effects of Volatility of Interest Rates on Stock Returns: A study on Indian Stock market. SSRN.*

Teker, D. L., & Alp, E. A. (2014). Granger causality relation between interest rates and stock markets: Evidence from emerging markets.

Teker, D. L., & Alp, E. A. (2014). GRANGER CAUSALITY RELATI ON BETWEEN I NTEREST RATES AND STOCK MARKETS: EVIDENCE FROM EMERGING MARKETS.

Tripathi, V., & Ghosh, R. (2012). Interest rate sensitivity of banking stock returns in India. *International Journal of Financial Management*, *2*(2), 10–20.

Tripathi, V., & Ghosh, R. (2012). Interest rate sensitivity of banking stock returns in India. *International Journal of Financial Management (ISSN: 2229-5690) Vol, 2*, 10-20.

Vyas, I., Prasad, N., & Mishra, A. K. (2014). Causal nexus between stock price, demand for money, interest rate, foreign institutional investment, and exchange rates in India: A post subprime crisis analysis. *Indonesian Capital Market Review*, *3*(2), 1. DOI: 10.21002/icmr.v3i2.3625

Xie, H., Sha, Y., & Li, L. (2024). Synthesization of macroeconomic policies and stock return synchronicity: Evidence from countries along the Belt and Road Initiative. *Pacific-Basin Finance Journal*, *85*, 102398. DOI: 10.1016/j.pacfin.2024.102398

# Chapter 12
# Performance Analysis of G20 Schemes for Achieving Sustainable Growth:
## Consistency, Accuracy, and Predictive Analysis Across Member Countries

**T. K. Sateesh Kumar**
http://orcid.org/0000-0002-8406-409X
*Kristu Jayanti (Deemed to be University), India*

**Lijo P. Thomas**
http://orcid.org/0009-0009-7031-5001
*Kristu Jayanti (Deemed to be University), India*

**Vishnu Achutha Menon**
http://orcid.org/0000-0003-4028-3685
*Central University of Punjab, India*

**Juby A. Thomas**
http://orcid.org/0000-0003-2167-0620
*Kristu Jayanti (Deemed to be University), India*

## ABSTRACT

*G20 schemes include global initiatives aimed at addressing economic stability, financial resilience, climate change, digital transformation, and social equity among*

DOI: 10.4018/979-8-2600-3179-7.ch012

*major economies. This study examines the consistency of scheme implementation and the predictive accuracy of machine learning models across G20 countries. A dataset containing observed scheme values was analyzed using a Random Forest Regressor, with evaluation metrics such as $R^2$, Adjusted $R^2$, Mean Absolute Error (MAE), and Root Mean Squared Error (RMSE). The results show significant differences in scheme implementation, with France maintaining the most stable coverage and China displaying the most variation, which may be linked to governance and demographic factors. Feature importance analysis identifies unemployment benefits and country-specific influences (e.g., Germany, India) as key factors shaping policy outcomes.*

## INTRODUCTION

India's labour market is characterized by a dual structure, consisting of a formal sector and a much larger informal sector. The formal sector includes those workers employed in registered enterprises, typically enjoying job security, regulated working conditions, and access to social benefits (Abraham & Kesar, 2025). However, the informal sector dominates India's workforce, accounting for approximately 92% of total employment according to multiple labour surveys. Informal employment is frequently marked by precarious working conditions, including the absence of job contracts, minimal or no social security, and low wages, which leave workers vulnerable to economic shocks and exploitation (Sakthivel & Joddar, 2006). This contrast epitomizes the dual nature of India's labour market—while the formal sector is growing slowly and absorbing a limited portion of the workforce, the informal sector remains a vast reservoir of employment without adequate protection for workers (Mishra, 2025).

Within the informal labour market, workers often face significant job insecurity, lack of social benefits such as health insurance or pensions, and generally lower wage levels compared to their formal counterparts. This insecurity impacts their livelihood sustainability, especially for vulnerable groups such as older workers who may lack savings or retirement benefits. The widespread informal employment scenario impedes broad-based improvements in worker welfare and contributes to persistent wage inequality in India. Informal jobs typically do not offer mechanisms for collective bargaining or legal recourse, thus intensifying the marginalization of informal workers from mainstream economic progress.

Gender is a critical axis of inequality in this labour market context. Women are disproportionately represented in the informal sector, often confined to unpaid family labour, informal wage work, or own-account enterprises with limited opportunities for formal employment (Harvey et al., 2020). Despite increases in female education, many women remain outside the formal labour market, reflecting both labour market segmentation and social norms that restrict their access to secure and adequately paid jobs. The feminization of informal work highlights intersecting vulnerabilities related to gender and employment status, exacerbating economic disparities and limiting women's economic empowerment. Thus, India's labour market duality—marked by a dominant informal sector characterized by job insecurity, lack of social protection, and lower wages—highlights persistent structural challenges. These challenges are compounded for women, who face greater barriers to formal sector employment and are concentrated in lower-quality informal jobs, underscoring the need for policies that address both employment formality and gendered labour market inequalities in India's evolving economy.

India's labour market exhibits a dual structure with a dominant informal sector and a smaller formal sector, where employment quality, security, and wage disparities persist. Despite this, the temporal evolution of gender-disaggregated distributions of formal and informal employment from 2018 to 2024 remains underexplored. There is limited research on the capability of machine learning models to predict employment types based on gender and longitudinal labour market data. Furthermore, latent employment patterns across gender and employment form remain poorly understood, restricting targeted policy interventions.

This study is critical for addressing persistent labour market inequalities in India. Informal employment—a sector characterized by insecurity, low wages, and lack of benefits—commands a substantial share of the workforce, with women disproportionately represented in it. Investigating gendered shifts in employment formalization between 2018 and 2024 will inform policies aimed at reducing economic disparities and enhancing social protection. The application of machine learning introduces novel analytical capabilities for accurate prediction and monitoring of employment dynamics, potentially guiding more efficient labour market interventions. Unsupervised clustering to uncover hidden employment patterns can reveal structural segmentation and gender-specific vulnerabilities, supporting evidence-based reforms that foster inclusive and equitable labour market outcomes. In addition, machine learning methods have demonstrated promising accuracy in employment-related predictions, as found in analogous domains, suggesting their potential effectiveness in labour market analysis. These innovative approaches can thus enhance traditional labour economics tools, enabling more granular and anticipatory policy responses to gendered labour market challenges.

## Objectives:

1. How has the distribution of formal and informal employment changed across genders from 2018 to 2024 in India?

2. Can machine learning models accurately predict employment types based on gender and time-series labour data?
3. What latent employment patterns can be identified across gender and type using unsupervised clustering methods?

## REVIEW OF LITERATURE

A 1% rise in female labor force participation (FLFP) is associated with a 0.3–0.5% increase in state-level per capita income, indicating that even a small increase in women's participation contributes meaningfully to economic growth. Improvements in job quality further strengthen this effect by ensuring that women's work is both productive and sustainable. Policy interventions such as childcare support and workplace safety reforms have played an important role in expanding urban female salaried employment. However, cultural restrictions and inadequate infrastructure continue to prevent many women from entering formal employment sectors, particularly in conservative or less developed regions (Priya, 2025). India's structural transformation from agriculture to services and manufacturing has improved formal employment opportunities in certain states, yet these gains are unevenly distributed. A limited number of high-performing states benefit the most from this shift, while others experience marginal progress. Although the Mahatma Gandhi National Rural Employment Guarantee Act (MGNREGA) provides a crucial safety net for rural households, it does not create a pathway toward stable or high-quality employment. As a result, the advantages of structural transformation are not equitably shared, and some high-growth states record weaker employment outcomes than expected (Priya, 2025).

There has been a significant increase in rural non-agricultural employment, rising from 98.4 million in 2004–05 to 193.3 million in 2023. This expansion has been largely driven by growth in the construction and trade sectors. Despite the increase, a large share of rural workers remain engaged in self-employment or casual labor, reflecting persistent job vulnerability. Women and marginalized individuals with low educational attainment or weak socioeconomic backgrounds continue to lag behind in accessing stable non-agricultural jobs, which limits the inclusiveness of rural employment growth (Singh & Pattanaik, 2025). Employment distribution across Indian states demonstrates a clear regional divide. Industrialized states such as Tamil Nadu, Gujarat, and Maharashtra report higher formal employment due to stronger industrial and service sector bases. In contrast, states like Bihar, Uttar Pradesh, and Odisha remain dependent on low-income and informal sectors, with limited diversification. Southern and western states dominate in formal employment, while northern states record a high degree of informality, with more than 85% of workers lacking social security coverage. Female labor force participation is also regionally varied, being higher in Tamil Nadu and Kerala compared to Haryana and Rajasthan. Sectors such as tourism and renewable energy are generating sustainable employment opportunities, though they remain regionally concentrated. Uneven implementation of national programs such as the Skill India Mission has further intensified these regional disparities (Gupta, 2018).

The relationship between sectoral growth and labor participation shows that the rapid expansion of the service sector has not been matched by proportional job creation. In contrast, the industrial sector has continued to generate substantial short- and long-term employment opportunities. Empirical evidence suggests no long-run cointegration between the labor participation rate (LPR) and agricultural growth, whereas significant long-run relationships exist between LPR and growth in both services and industry. Specifically, a 10% increase in the industrial sector's share of national income raises LPR by 0.05%, while a similar increase in the services sector leads to a 0.04% rise (Kumar, 2024). Gendered job advertisements also influence employment patterns. Wages are typically lowest in job postings that indicate a preference for female workers, which tend to attract a higher number of female applicants. Female-gendered language associated with hard skills is often linked to lower wage returns but still draws more women, while male-gendered terms that imply reduced flexibility are connected with higher wages but fewer female applicants. Such patterns reveal how gendered language related to skills and flexibility contributes to persistent labor market inequalities. Employer preferences are shaped partly by stereotypes and statistical discrimination, which reinforce gender divisions in the labor market. Moreover, job characteristics such as flexibility play an important role in explaining gender wage gaps and women's job search behavior (Chaturvedi et al., 2024).

Female labor force participation in India declined to 17.5% by 2017–2018 before showing signs of improvement in subsequent years. The overall size of the female workforce fell sharply from 148.59 million in 2004–2005 to 104.1 million in 2017–2018. This decline has been associated with reduced agricultural growth, which pushed many women into unpaid family labor rather than formal employment. The phenomenon of jobless growth has had a greater adverse effect on women compared to men, deepening gender disparities in employment. Interstate and inter-regional analyses using Periodic Labour Force Survey (PLFS) data reveal substantial diversity in women's participation rates, underscoring the need for coordinated policy interventions to enhance female labor force participation (Singh & Meher, 2024).

Gender inequality in the labor market is further reflected in the unequal distribution of unpaid work. There exists a pronounced gender gap not only in participation but also in the average time spent on unpaid household labor across rural and urban areas. Findings derived from Tobit regression analysis indicate that the amount of time women allocate to unpaid work varies according to demographic and socioeconomic characteristics, demonstrating that gendered labor burdens are deeply influenced by class, education, and location (Sahu, 2024).

Over the past decade, women's employment in India has recorded substantial improvement, accompanied by a shift in employment patterns from agriculture toward the tertiary sector. The Worker Population Ratio (WPR) for rural women aged fifteen and above increased to 35.8%, while that for urban women rose to 21.9%. Between 2017–2018 and 2022–2023, unemployment rates among rural women declined from 3.8% to 1.8%, and among urban women from 10.8% to 7.5%. Male unemployment also showed a reduction during this period. These figures suggest that rural female workers, in particular, are experiencing better job prospects. Women's growing engagement in the workforce remains essential to India's overall economic progress (Bhat et al., 2024).

Despite these gains, women in the informal sector continue to face numerous challenges, including wage inequality, unsafe working conditions, and the absence of social protections. The decline in female labor force participation has been attributed to agricultural mechanization, low wage levels, and rising household incomes, which often reduce the economic pressure for women to seek paid work. Persistent gender-based prejudice, limited educational opportunities, and widespread sexual harassment further restrict women's employment choices. Since the informal sector continues to play a major role in India's economy, it is crucial to strengthen mechanisms that improve working conditions and enhance women's economic security (Arora & Kumawat, 2024).

Recent analytical models employing machine learning and clustering techniques have been used to identify factors and opportunities for sustainable economic innovation. Through SWOT analysis and clustering approaches, researchers have proposed an integrative framework and a forward-looking paradigm for future development. These studies emphasize the value of strategic collaborations and propose a model methodology for achieving sustainable growth. Comparative findings reveal that Saudi Arabia's economic progress aligns with strategies similar to India's, positioning India as a potential model for Gulf countries aiming to advance through inclusive and diversified development (Rashid Al-Shamsi & Shannaq, 2024).

In addition to economic restructuring, social inclusion and international financial inflows play distinct roles in addressing unemployment. Empirical evidence indicates that both social inclusion and foreign fund inflows contribute to reducing male unemployment rates. However, in the case of women, only social inclusion variables have a significant effect, while foreign capital inflows show no measurable impact. This distinction implies that female employment outcomes are more sensitive to domestic social and institutional factors than to external financial influences (Khan & Gunwant, 2024).

The COVID-19 pandemic marked a major setback for female empowerment across the world. It intensified existing gender inequalities by increasing women's domestic and caregiving responsibilities while simultaneously reducing their paid employment opportunities. Employment losses were especially severe in feminized sectors such as hospitality, retail, and health services, where women constitute a large share of the workforce. Additionally, deteriorating working conditions during the pandemic disproportionately affected minority and marginalized groups, amplifying pre-existing structural inequities (Enciso-Alfaro et al., 2024).

The micro, small, and medium enterprises (MSME) sector remains one of the most important pillars of employment generation in India. Within this sector, the manufacturing segment employs approximately 31% of the workforce, while trade and services contribute 33% and 36%, respectively. Linear regression analysis indicates relative stability in manufacturing, noticeable fluctuations in trade, and steady growth in both services and electricity sectors. Despite these positive indicators, MSMEs face persistent challenges, including inadequate access to finance, complex regulatory frameworks, and technological limitations. However, emerging opportunities such as digital transformation, export diversification, and enhanced government support offer prospects for sustainable expansion. A comprehensive and coherent policy framework is required to enable the long-term development and competitiveness of the MSME ecosystem (Martinravi & Krishnasamy, 2025).

Female education has achieved substantial progress at both secondary and tertiary levels across emerging economies due to financial assistance programs and affirmative action measures. Comparative data indicate that Brazil and Russia maintain higher female enrollment at the secondary level, while China demonstrates rapid advancement in tertiary education, with female participation exceeding 92%. In contrast, historical inequalities, persistent poverty, and social pressures continue to limit educational attainment for women in India and South Africa. Nevertheless, improvements in education have not automatically translated into equality in employment outcomes. The persistence of higher female unemployment rates in Brazil and South Africa indicates that structural socio-economic barriers continue to influence women's participation in the labor market (Yi et al., 2024). Machine learning applications are increasingly being utilized to address diverse social and developmental challenges. One such study developed predictive models for crime trends between 2017 and 2020 based on data from 2001 to 2016. Among the models tested, K-means clustering achieved an accuracy exceeding 75%, the Naive Bayes Classifier reached 78.05%, and the Random Forest model performed best with 81.35% accuracy. The predictive system was further applied to estimate specific cases such as child marriage in Haryana, murder cases in Tamil Nadu, and violations under the Arms Act in Kerala. The overall model relied on a K-nearest neighbor approach for accurate crime forecasting across Indian states (Mandalapu et al., 2023).

In environmental research, an integrated machine learning-based framework was developed to predict groundwater quality indices. The model incorporated several algorithms, including Naive Bayes, K-nearest neighbor (KNN), and XGBoost classifiers, along with long short-term memory (LSTM) neural networks. Water quality predictions for 2024 were carried out using this ensemble approach, supported by geospatial analysis through GIS technology. Among the models tested, the XGBoost classifier demonstrated the highest accuracy of approximately 94.6%. Model validation using live data samples from a selected well confirmed an error margin within 5%, suggesting strong reliability in real-world applications (Rammohan et al., 2024). Comparative modeling approaches have also been employed to understand stock market dynamics across emerging economies. Transformer-based architectures demonstrated superior predictive accuracy, achieving performance rates of 92.3% and 89.9% in specific markets. LSTM networks effectively handled sequential data but were limited by their dependence on temporal continuity. Random Forests and Support Vector Machines (SVMs) offered reliable outcomes, though they struggled with highly volatile or nonlinear market behaviors. Country-specific analyses revealed that Brazil's economy remains sensitive to commodity price fluctuations, Russia's market is influenced by geopolitical developments, India's is responsive to foreign direct investment, China's reflects the impact of state interventions, and South Africa's remains tied to the performance of commodity exports (Sultana et al., 2024).

Economic and social indicators reveal a strong relationship between macroeconomic performance and gender inequality. Evidence from Sri Lanka indicates that higher gross domestic product (GDP) and government revenues are associated with lower levels of gender inequality. Conversely, rising unemployment rates tend to exacerbate gender disparities. A strong negative correlation exists between the Gender Inequality Index (GII) and GDP per capita, suggesting that economic growth contributes to gender parity. Using a fine tree regression model, researchers were able to explain 97.5% of the variance in GII, identifying GDP as the most influential variable in predicting inequality outcomes. These findings confirm that macroeconomic conditions exert significant influence on gender inequality dynamics in Sri Lanka (Kularathne et al., 2024).

Technological modeling approaches have increasingly been applied to understand complex economic systems. A study comparing Long Short-Term Memory (LSTM), XGBoost, and ARIMA models for predicting currency exchange rate fluctuations found that the LSTM model produced the lowest Mean Absolute Error (MAE) and Root Mean Square Error (RMSE), with a Mean Absolute Percentage Error (MAPE) of 2.15%. Although XGBoost demonstrated slightly less accuracy than LSTM, it performed considerably better than ARIMA, which failed to effectively capture non-linear and dynamic variations. The LSTM model consistently exhibited lower errors over time, indicating its capacity to handle the non-linearities and dynamic changes inherent in currency markets (Abir et al., 2024).

Corporate Social Responsibility (CSR) spending is closely linked to improvements in company sustainability performance. Statistical correlation analysis indicates that increased CSR expenditure correlates with better environmental and social performance outcomes. The research also identifies key areas where cost reductions yield the highest returns, while outlining deficiencies in current CSR strategies. The study proposes refined approaches for optimizing CSR investments to achieve both economic and social sustainability (Yogi et al., 2024).

The labor markets of European Union (EU) countries exhibited varied responses to the COVID-19 pandemic. Using the "Triple 2 Rule" (T2R) methodology, researchers observed significant changes in employment rates across sectors and countries, revealing both declines and increases depending on the national and sectoral context. Clusters of countries sharing similar employment rate trajectories were identified. The sectors most affected by employment disruptions included commerce, transport, accommodation, catering, cultural services, and entertainment. Gender differences were also evident, as several member states experienced disproportionate changes in male and female employment rates (Markowska & Strahl, 2024). In climate and environmental studies, rainfall trends across India from 1901 to 2022 were analyzed to identify long-term anomalies using the Pettitt test. The Artificial Neural Network–Multilayer Perceptron (ANN-MLP) model was applied to enhance the accuracy of rainfall forecasting and compared with traditional statistical methods. By incorporating climate parameters such as temperature, humidity, wind speed, and precipitation, the ANN-MLP model effectively captured complex nonlinear relationships. Additionally, spatial and temporal rainfall variability was visualized using geo-statistical techniques like Kriging. The results demonstrated that modern computational approaches can overcome many limitations of conventional forecasting, supporting better decision-making for agricultural management and natural resource planning (Prathibha & Rani, 2025).

Predictive modeling has also been extended to the education sector. A recent study developed a forecasting framework to estimate students' employability outcomes over the long term. The system identified critical areas requiring improvement to enhance employment readiness at graduation. Among the probabilistic distributions tested, the Binomial distribution produced the lowest Mean Squared Error (MSE) and Mean Absolute Error (MAE), outperforming both Gaussian and Poisson distributions. This demonstrates the framework's precision and reliability for assessing employability potential (Bora & Baruah, 2024). Gender-sensitive infrastructure development plays a pivotal role in shaping labor market outcomes. Empirical evidence shows that improvements in transportation infrastructure increase women's labor market participation more than that of men. In societies with egalitarian social structures, transportation improvements have an even stronger positive impact, narrowing the gender gap in employment. The presence of gender-supportive institutional environments helps women connect to emerging job opportunities. The study further argues that gender-neutral development policies are essential for ensuring equal access to labor markets and reducing disparities in economic outcomes (Balachandran & Desai, 2024).

Regional labor statistics from Haryana provide a micro-level view of employment dynamics. The state's overall unemployment rate stands at 6.5%, while youth unemployment (ages 15–29) is significantly higher at 17.6%. The labor force participation rate (LFPR) is 34.3%, and the worker population ratio (WPR) is 32.1%. Gender-specific figures reveal a sharp divide, with male WPR at 51.0% compared to just 11.2% for females. The female labor force participation rate (FLFPR) is 11.9%, showing persistent gender disparities. Between 2017–2018 and 2019–2020, urban LFPR rose by 3.2 percentage points, while rural WPR remained stable and urban WPR improved. The overall unemployment rate declined by 4.9 percentage points during the same period. In 2019–2020, 33.2% of workers were employed in the secondary sector and 37.5% in the tertiary sector. Although unemployment among youth is closely associated with educational attainment, reductions in unemployment have not been accompanied by corresponding increases in the worker population ratio, suggesting the presence of underemployment or job quality concerns (Bishnoi et al., 2024).

## RESEARCH GAPS

Despite a plethora of research related to the Indian labor market and gender disparities, a number of crucial research gaps need to be addressed.

Firstly, despite previous research on dualism in the country's employment structure, only a few studies provide a longitudinal analysis of changes in the employment pattern each year between 2018 and 2024, with an emphasis on gender differences. A lack of comprehensive information on temporal changes in employment formalisation rates is observed when analysing the post-COVID recovery period in India.

Secondly, while there are considerable studies on the descriptive and econometric analysis of labour market issues, little attention is paid to using modern computational tools and machine learning algorithms to analyse labour market segmentation and related features. Despite the proven efficiency of such models as Random Forest, K-Nearest Neighbours, and XGBoost in weather prediction, forecasting stock prices, and crimes, they are rarely used to estimate the probability of belonging to one employment type or another, which is a task of labour economics.

Thirdly, despite considerable information regarding observable labor market indicators including labor force participation, wages, and industrial segmentation, there is a lack of analysis of hidden employment structures that can be uncovered using the machine learning method of clustering. Fourthly, although gender inequality has been recognized by numerous researchers, gender remains a factor controlled by researchers and rarely serves as a focal point in the studies devoted to the interplay of employment type and structural transformation, especially considering gender differences. Fifthly, the existing research on possible interventions into labor market issues pays close attention to skill development, social inclusion, and infrastructure improvements. Yet, no solutions based on predictive and data-driven labor market modeling exist to identify vulnerable individuals and make proactive suggestions for the policy. Despite the fact that the recent changes caused by the COVID-19 pandemic have affected labor market significantly with regard to women's opportunities for employment and career growth, very few studies utilize the information about post-pandemic employment changes in their analyses.

Consequently, in addressing these gaps, the current study focuses on:

- longitudinal, gender-specific (2018-2024) employment analysis,
- prediction of employment type with the use of classification models,
- use of unsupervised algorithms of clustering to reveal employment patterns,
- consideration of gender as the focal aspect of labor market dynamics, and
- creation of the model based on the prediction of the labor market state.

## METHODOLOGY

This project analyzes ILO Labour Force Data for India (2018–2024), utilizing variables such as Gender, Type, Economic activity, time, and obs_value 4581 no.s. Initial data cleaning involved removing aggregated 'Total' rows for Gender and Type, and stripping ISIC codes from 'Economic activity'. Visualizations included line plots to observe trends across Gender and Type over time. For machine learning, label encoding was applied to Gender and Type. A Random Forest Classifier was employed to predict 'Type' (Formal vs Informal employment), and KMeans clustering was performed on employment trends, grouped by Gender and Type. Model validation was conducted using classification metrics (precision, recall, F1-score) for the Random Forcst model and the Silhouette score for evaluating the quality of the KMeans clusters.

The classification model's performance was evaluated using standard machine learning metrics such as Accuracy, Precision, Recall, and F1-Score, as defined in

(Chinchor, 1992; Powers, 2011). Unsupervised learning validation used the Silhouette Score (Rousseeuw, 1987) to determine clustering cohesion and separation.

Let:

- TP = True Positives
- TN = True Negatives
- FP = False Positives
- FN = False Negatives

Accuracy:

Measures the proportion of total correct predictions:

$$\text{Accuracy} = \frac{TP + TN}{TP + TN + FP + FN}$$

Precision:

Measures how many predicted positives are actually positive:

$$Precision = \frac{TP}{TP + FP}$$

Recall (Sensitivity):

Measures how many actual positives were correctly predicted:

$$Recall = \frac{TP}{TP + FN}$$

F1-Score:

Harmonic mean of Precision and Recall:

$$F1 - Score = 2 \times \frac{Precision \times Recall}{Precision + Recall}$$

Silhouette Score:

Assesses how similar a data point is to its own cluster vs. other clusters.

Let:

- a(i) = average intra-cluster distance (within the same cluster)
- b(i) = lowest average inter-cluster distance (to nearest other cluster)

$$s(i) = \frac{b(i) - a(i)}{\max\{a(i), b(i)\}}$$

The Silhouette Score for all points is the mean of s(i). It ranges from -1 (poor clustering) to +1 (dense and well-separated clusters).

## RESULTS

*Figure 1. Heat Map of Employment Trend Clustering by Gender and Type*

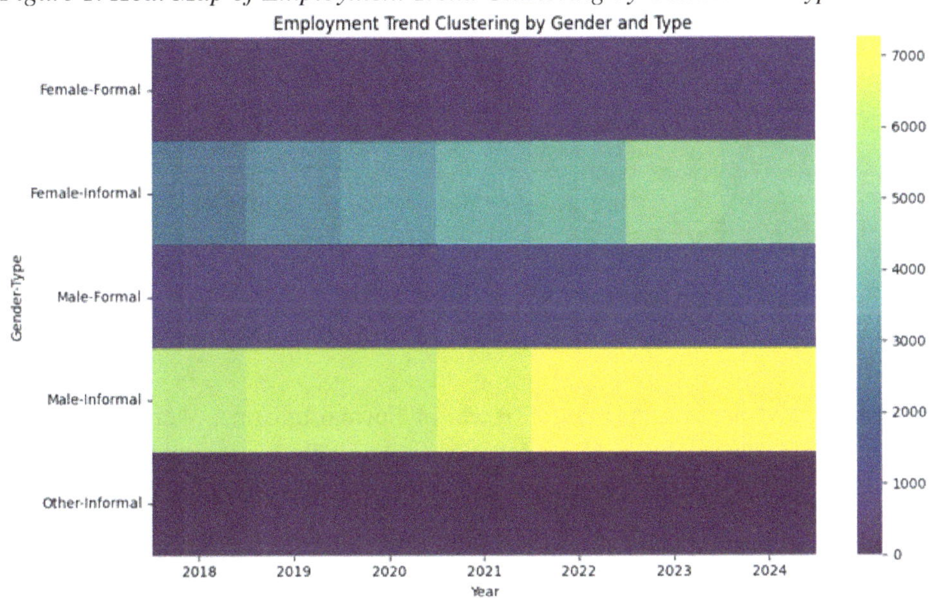


This heatmap visualizes "Employment Trend Clustering by Gender and Type" from 2018 to 2024. The y-axis represents different combinations of "Gender-Type" (Female-Formal, Female-Informal, Male-Formal, Male-Informal, Other-Informal), while the x-axis denotes the 'Year' (Figure 1). The color intensity, indicated by the 'viridis' colormap on the right, represents the 'obs_value' (total numbers), with darker shades indicating lower values and brighter yellow shades indicating higher values. From the heatmap, we can observe that Male-Informal employment consistently shows the highest values across all years, as indicated by the brightest yellow. Female-Formal employment appears to have relatively lower values compared to other categories, especially in earlier years. The visualization effectively allows for a quick comparison of employment trends across different gender and employment type classifications over the specified time period.

*Figure 2. Trends of Formal/Informal Work by Gender*

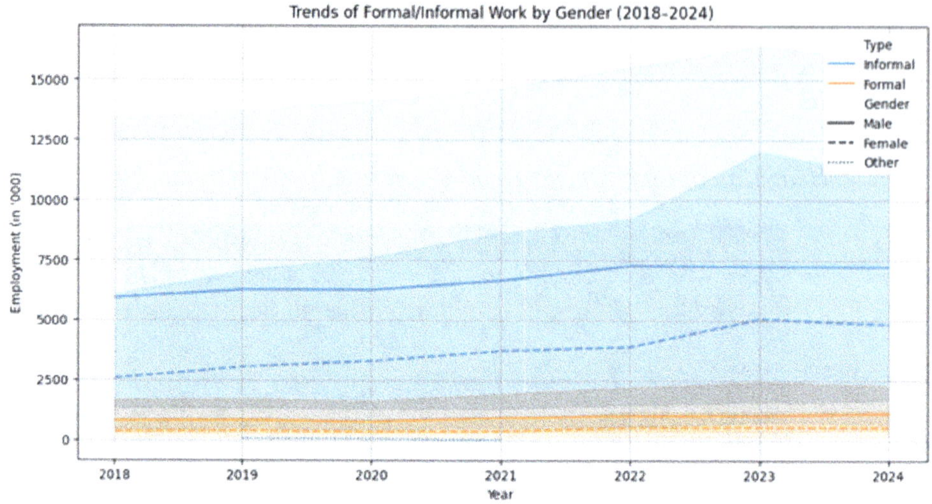


This stacked area chart, titled "Trends of Formal/Informal Work by Gender (2018–2024)", illustrates employment patterns in India, measured in thousands ('000). The y-axis represents 'Employment (in '000)', and the x-axis shows the 'Year' from 2018 to 2024 (Figure 2). The chart differentiates between 'Informal' (blue hues) and 'Formal' (orange hues) employment types, further broken down by 'Gender': Male (solid lines), Female (dashed lines), and Other (dotted lines). The dominant trend is the significantly higher volume of informal employment compared to formal employment across all years and gender categories. Male informal employment consistently forms the largest component, showing a steady increase over the period. Female informal employment also shows an increasing trend, albeit at a lower scale than male informal employment. Formal employment for both males and females remains comparatively low and shows a more modest increase. The 'Other' gender category, primarily in informal work, represents a very small proportion of the total employment. The shaded areas around the lines represent confidence intervals or the range of employment values, indicating some variability around the mean trend.

*Table 1. Model Validation Metrics*

| **Classification Report:** | **Report:** | | | |
|---|---|---|---|---|
| | **precision** | **recall** | **f1-score** | **support** |
| Formal | 0.45 | 0.42 | 0.44 | 160 |
| Informal | 0.55 | 0.58 | 0.56 | 196 |
| accuracy | | | 0.51 | 356 |
| macro avg | 0.5 | 0.5 | 0.5 | 356 |
| weighted avg | 0.51 | 0.51 | 0.51 | 356 |

The classification report presented in Table 1 provides a detailed evaluation of the model's performance in distinguishing between formal and informal categories. The precision, recall, and F1-score values indicate how effectively the model predicts each class relative to the true labels. For the formal category, the model achieved a precision of 0.45, meaning that out of all instances predicted as formal, only 45% were correct. The recall value of 0.42 suggests that the model correctly identified 42% of all actual formal instances. The F1-score of 0.44, which is the harmonic mean of precision and recall, indicates moderate but limited consistency in identifying formal instances. In contrast, the informal category performed slightly better, with a precision of 0.55, recall of 0.58, and F1-score of 0.56. These values imply that the model is somewhat more capable of detecting informal samples than formal ones, though its predictive power remains modest. The relatively higher recall for the informal class suggests that the model tends to favor informal predictions, possibly due to imbalanced class distributions or overlapping linguistic features between the two categories. The overall accuracy of 0.51 shows that the model correctly classifies approximately half of the samples in the dataset, which is only marginally better than random guessing in a binary classification task. Both the macro average (0.50) and weighted average (0.51) of precision, recall, and F1-score indicate uniform performance across classes, with no substantial skew toward either category.

*Table 2. Confusion Matrix*

| | **Predicted Formal** | **Predicted Informal** |
|---|---|---|
| Actual Formal | 68 (Correct) | 92 (Misclassified) |
| Actual Informal | 83 (Misclassified) | 113 (Correct) |

Table 2 provides a clear visualization of how the model classified samples into formal and informal categories, offering deeper insight into its performance patterns. Out of the 160 actual formal samples, the model correctly identified 68 instances as formal, while 92 instances were incorrectly classified as informal. Similarly, out of

196 actual informal samples, the model correctly predicted 113 instances as informal but misclassified 83 instances as formal. This distribution shows that the model performs slightly better with informal data, aligning with the earlier findings from the classification report. The higher number of correct informal predictions (113) compared to correct formal ones (68) indicates that the model is more sensitive to informal linguistic cues. However, the significant number of misclassifications in both categories—particularly the 92 formal instances labeled as informal—suggests that the model struggles to distinguish the linguistic or stylistic boundaries between the two types of text. In practical terms, this confusion may arise from overlapping vocabulary, sentence structures, or tone that blur the distinction between formal and informal communication. The results imply that while the model captures some discriminative features, its decision boundaries are not robust enough to handle subtle linguistic nuances. Therefore, improving class separation through enhanced preprocessing (e.g., text normalization, part-of-speech tagging, or embedding fine-tuning) and incorporating context-aware models like transformers could significantly improve accuracy and reduce the high rate of misclassification.

*Table 3. Metrics Derived*

| Metric | Explanation | Value |
|---|---|---|
| Accuracy | (68 + 113) / 356 = 51% → Overall correct predictions | 0.51 |
| Precision | Of those predicted as Formal/Informal, how many were correct | Formal: 0.45, Informal: 0.55 |
| Recall | Of actual Formal/Informal, how many were correctly identified | Formal: 0.42, Informal: 0.58 |
| F1-Score | Harmonic mean of precision and recall | Formal: 0.44, Informal: 0.56 |

Table 3 provides a consolidated interpretation of the model's key performance indicators—accuracy, precision, recall, and F1-score—summarizing how effectively it differentiates between formal and informal text categories. The overall accuracy of 0.51 (51%) indicates that just over half of the total predictions made by the model were correct. While this is slightly better than random guessing in a binary classification task, it reflects limited reliability and suggests that the model's discriminative capacity is still developing. The precision values—0.45 for formal and 0.55 for informal—reveal that predictions labeled as informal were more often correct than those labeled as formal. This implies that the model is more confident and consistent when identifying informal language patterns, possibly because such texts contain more distinctive features like colloquial expressions, contractions, or informal tone markers. In terms of recall, the model correctly identified 42% of actual formal instances and 58% of actual informal instances. This again shows a bias toward informal detection, meaning that many formal texts are being overlooked or misclassified as informal. Such a pattern indicates that the model may not be effectively capturing features unique to formal writing, such as structured syntax or formal vocabulary. The F1-scores—0.44 for formal and 0.56 for informal—represent the balance between precision and recall. The higher F1 for the informal class confirms that the model's predictions are both more accurate and more complete for that category.

## DISCUSSION

Between 2018 and 2024, the structure of employment in India continued to show a strong dominance of informal work among both men and women. Although males outnumbered females in both formal and informal employment categories, the disparity was most visible in formal jobs. This uneven distribution suggests that systemic and cultural factors may still restrict women's participation in formal sectors. However, a gradual increase in women's formal employment from 2022 to 2024 points toward a slow but positive shift, possibly linked to educational access, targeted government initiatives, or changing social attitudes toward female workforce participation.

When employment data were analyzed using machine learning techniques, predictive performance remained modest. The Random Forest classifier achieved only 51% accuracy, reflecting limited ability to distinguish between formal and informal employment types. The confusion matrix showed a substantial level of misclassification, suggesting that variables like gender and time period alone cannot explain employment outcomes with sufficient precision. To improve predictive power, the inclusion of additional variables—such as educational attainment, geographic region, occupational category, and industry sector—would be essential. These factors are more likely to capture the socioeconomic nuances that influence employment type in India.

Unsupervised learning techniques offered further insight into the underlying structure of the data. KMeans clustering, which achieved a silhouette score of 0.49, indicated moderate coherence among groupings. The clusters revealed three broad patterns: one dominated by female-informal employment, another by male-formal employment, and a third representing low participation zones that may correspond to minority gender identities or niche economic sectors. Although these clusters were not sharply separated, they reflected the blurred boundaries that exist in real labor markets, where transitions between formal and informal work are often fluid. The clustering outcomes suggest that gender-based employment patterns do exist but are intertwined with broader social and economic dynamics rather than forming rigid divisions.

## SUMMARY, CONCLUSION, AND RECOMMENDATIONS

This study explored the patterns and dynamics of formal and informal employment in India from 2018 to 2024, with a focus on gender-based distribution and the potential of machine learning to predict employment types. Using ILO Labour Force data comprising 4,581 observations, the research examined three key questions: (1) how employment distribution across genders has changed over time, (2) whether machine learning models can predict employment type using gender and time-series data, and (3) what latent patterns can be uncovered using clustering methods. The data were analyzed using descriptive statistics, visual trend analysis, a Random Forest classifier for prediction, and KMeans clustering for unsupervised pattern identification.

The analysis revealed that informal employment remains the dominant form of work for both males and females throughout the study period. Men continue to occupy a larger share in both employment categories, though women's representation in formal jobs has shown a slight increase since 2022. This upward movement suggests gradual improvement in gender inclusion, but the overall gap in formal employment highlights ongoing structural and cultural barriers that prevent women from entering or remaining in stable, formal jobs. Informal work, particularly among males, continues to characterize the Indian labor landscape, reflecting the persistent challenges of labor formalization.

The Random Forest model used for employment type prediction achieved an accuracy of 51%, demonstrating limited predictive capability. The precision and recall scores indicated that the model performed slightly better for informal employment but struggled to differentiate formal employment accurately. This implies that gender and time alone are insufficient for robust prediction of employment type. Including additional socioeconomic variables such as education, occupation, geographic region, and industry sector could significantly improve model performance. The KMeans clustering analysis, with a silhouette score of 0.49, revealed three broad clusters—female-informal, male-formal, and low-participation zones—suggesting that gendered employment segmentation exists but with overlapping boundaries, reflecting the fluidity between formal and informal work in real-world contexts.

In conclusion, the findings reaffirm that informal employment continues to dominate India's labor market, with slow but visible progress in women's participation in formal sectors. Persistent gender disparities point to deeper issues within the economic and social structures governing employment. The modest accuracy of machine learning predictions further underscores the complexity of labor dynamics, which cannot be captured solely through limited variables like gender and time.

Recommendations emerging from this study emphasize the need for a multidimensional approach to understanding and addressing employment inequalities.

Policymakers should prioritize initiatives that promote women's access to education, skill development, and formal job opportunities, while ensuring labor laws protect informal workers transitioning into formal sectors. Future research should integrate a richer set of variables—such as region, education, occupation, and industry—to enhance model reliability and capture the multifaceted nature of employment. Combining machine learning with qualitative inquiry could also provide a more nuanced understanding of labor patterns. Strengthening data-driven and gender-responsive labor policies will be essential for creating a more inclusive and equitable employment landscape in India.

## ACKNOWLEDGEMENTS

Research Funding

This study did not receive financial support from any funding agency in the public, commercial, or not-for-profit sectors. All expenses related to data collection, analysis, and manuscript preparation were personally covered by the authors.

Data Availability

The dataset used in this research is publicly accessible at:

https://ilostat.ilo.org/topics/informality/

AI Usage

Artificial intelligence (AI) tools were employed in a limited manner during manuscript preparation. Specifically, ChatGPT (OpenAI) was used to refine grammar, syntax, and language clarity, as none of the authors are native English speakers. All aspects of conceptualization, study design, data collection, analysis, interpretation, and argument development were conducted solely by the authors. The use of AI tools did not affect the scientific content, validity, or originality of the research.

## REFERENCES

Abir, S. I., Shiam, S. A. A., Zakaria, R. M., Shimanto, A. H., Shamsul Arefeen, S. M., Dolon, M. S. A., Sultana, N., & Shoha, S. (2024). Use of AI-powered precision in machine learning models for real-time currency exchange rate forecasting in BRICS economies. *Journal of Economics. Finance and Accounting Studies*, *6*(6), 66–83. DOI: 10.32996/jefas.2024.6.6.6

Abraham, R., & Kesar, S. (2025). Trajectories of labour market transitions in the Indian economy. *World Development*, *195*(107029), 107029. DOI: 10.1016/j.worlddev.2025.107029

Arora, A., & Kumawat, J. (2024). A review of Indian women employed in the informal economy. *Journal of Advances and Scholarly Researches in Allied Education*, *21*(6), 78–83. DOI: 10.29070/ew180376

Balachandran, A., & Desai, S. (2024). Transportation, employment and gender norms: Evidence from Indian cities. *Regional Science Policy & Practice*, *16*(6), 100060. DOI: 10.1016/j.rspp.2024.100060

Bhat, S. A., Mallniah, L. C., & Singh, S. (2024). Economic development and changing women lives: Evidence from women employment participation in India. *International Socioeconomic Review*, *2*(1), 94–115. DOI: 10.3126/iser.v2i1.75236

Bishnoi, N. K., Jakhar, B., Singhal, B., & Sharma, S. (2024). Haryana's labour landscape: Deciphering employment challenges through periodic surveys. *Rozprawy Społeczne*, *18*(1), 208–225. DOI: 10.29316/rs/186246

Bora, M., & Baruah, R. (2024). *A study on employment sustainability among Engineering students using a Statistical and Deep Learning framework*. Educational Administration Theory and Practices., DOI: 10.53555/kuey.v30i5.3892

Chaturvedi, S., Mahajan, K., & Siddique, Z. (2024). Words matter: Gender, jobs and applicant behavior. SSRN *Electronic Journal*. DOI: 10.2139/ssrn.4730629

Enciso-Alfaro, S.-Y., Marhroub, S., Martínez-Córdoba, P.-J., & García-Sánchez, I.-M. (2024). The effect of COVID-19 on employment: A bibliometric review of a she-cession. *Corporate Social Responsibility and Environmental Management*, *31*(4), 3444–3467. DOI: 10.1002/csr.2756

Gupta, P. (2018). Regional Disparities in Economic Growth and Employment in India: An Analysis of Progress Toward Sustainable Development Goal. [IJSREM]. *International Journal of Scientific Research in Engineering and Management*, *8*(3), 1.

Harvey, B., Peppes, A., Chakrabarty, G., Pozzan, E., & Cattaneo, U. (2020). *Building Back Better for Women: Women's Dire Position in the Informal Economy*. https://www.ilo.org/sites/default/files/wcmsp5/groups/public/@ed_protect/@protrav/@travail/documents/publication/wcms_755348.pdf

Khan, I., & Gunwant, D. F. (2024). Reducing gender-based unemployment in India: The impact of social inclusion and foreign funds inflows. *Indian Growth and Development Review*, *17*(1), 86–102. DOI: 10.1108/IGDR-07-2023-0103

Kularathne, S., Perera, A., Rathnayake, N., Rathnayake, U., & Hoshino, Y. (2024). Analyzing the impact of socioeconomic indicators on gender inequality in Sri Lanka: A machine learning-based approach. *PLoS One*, *19*(12), e0312395. DOI: 10.1371/journal.pone.0312395 PMID: 39724101

Kumar, R. (2024). Economic growth, structural changes and employment linkages in India. *Review of Economics and Political Science*, *9*(4), 346–357. DOI: 10.1108/REPS-07-2022-0051

Mandalapu, V., Elluri, L., Vyas, P., & Roy, N. (2023). Crime prediction using machine learning and deep learning: A systematic review and future directions. *IEEE Access : Practical Innovations, Open Solutions*, *11*, 60153–60170. DOI: 10.1109/ACCESS.2023.3286344

Markowska, M., & Strahl, D. (2024). Covid-19 impact on labour market in Eu countries – differences in men and women employment rate tendencies. *Technological and Economic Development of Economy*, *30*(4), 854–875. DOI: 10.3846/tede.2024.20811

Martinravi, C. P., & Krishnasamy, K. (2025). Unleashing the potential of MSMEs in India: A strategic analysis. *Journal of the International Council for Small Business*, *6*(1), 123–143. DOI: 10.1080/26437015.2024.2397664

Mishra, N. (2025, June 18). *India's economic duality: formal dreams, informal realities*. Governance Now. https://www.governancenow.com/views/columns/indias-economic-duality-formal-dreams-informal-realities

Prathibha, I., & Leela Rani, D. (2025). Rainfall forecasting in India using combined machine learning approach and soft computing techniques : A HYBRID MODEL. *International Journal of Computational and Experimental Science and Engineering*, *11*(1). Advance online publication. DOI: 10.22399/ijcesen.785

Priya, V. (2025). Economic empowerment through employment in India: A gendered perspective on growth. *International Journal For Multidisciplinary Research*, *7*(4), 54897. Advance online publication. DOI: 10.36948/ijfmr.2025.v07i04.54897

Rammohan, B., Partheeban, P., Ranganathan, R., & Balaraman, S. (2024). Groundwater quality prediction and analysis using machine learning models and geospatial technology. *Sustainability (Basel)*, *16*(22), 9848. DOI: 10.3390/su16229848

Rashid Al-Shamsi, I., & Shannaq, B. (2024). Leveraging clustering techniques to drive sustainable economic innovation in the India–Gulf interchange. *Cogent Social Sciences*, *10*(1), 2341483. Advance online publication. DOI: 10.1080/23311886.2024.2341483

Sahu, D. (2024). Gender conundrum and unpaid work in India: Empirical evidence from India's first large-scale time use survey. *The Indian Economic Journal*, *72*(4), 711–727. DOI: 10.1177/00194662241247137

Sakthivel, S., & Joddar, P. (2006). Unorganised sector workforce in India trends, patterns and social security coverage. *Economic and Political Weekly*, *41*(21), 2107–2114. https://www.jstor.org/stable/4418266

Singh, A., & Meher, S. (2024). Female labour force participation in India: An inter-state analysis. *Global Research Review in Business and Economics*, *10*(2), 01–07. DOI: 10.56805/grrbe.24.10.2.20

Singh, P., & Pattanaik, F. (2025). Beyond the fields: Tracing India's labour transition from agriculture to non-agricultural sectors. *International Journal of Social Economics*, *52*(4), 608–627. DOI: 10.1108/IJSE-11-2023-0904

Sultana, N., Shoha, S., Dolon, M. S. A., Shiam, S. A. A., Zakaria, R. M., Shimanto, A. H., Shamsul Arefeen, S. M., & Abir, S. I. (2024). Machine learning solutions for predicting stock trends in BRICS amid global economic shifts and decoding market dynamics. *Journal of Economics. Finance and Accounting Studies*, *6*(6), 84–101. DOI: 10.32996/jefas.2024.6.6.7

Yi, H., Wang, G., & Feng, J. (2024). Gender inequality: Policy responses to employment and education in BRICS countries. *African Journal of Reproductive Health*, *28*(12), 88–96. DOI: 10.29063/ajrh2024/v28i12.10 PMID: 39764841

Yogi, K. S., Gowda, D., Pati, A., Srinivas, V., Aghav, S., & Abdullah, I. (2024). Accelerating sustainability through leveraging machine learning to analyze CSR spending in the Indian automobile industry. *2024 7th International Conference on Circuit Power and Computing Technologies (ICCPCT)*, 905–912.

# Compilation of References


Abdelraouf, M., & Muharram, F. (2024). The Impact of Servant Leadership on Corporate Social Responsibility: Insights from Egyptian Tourism Organizations. *Journal of Advanced Research in Leadership*, *3*(1), 19–43. DOI: 10.33422/jarl.v3i1.701

Abidin, Z., Jalal, J., & Sodiq, A. (2025). The five tiers of corporate social responsibility (CSR): From risk management to social business. *Social Responsibility Journal*, *21*(5), 940–961. DOI: 10.1108/SRJ-03-2023-0146

Abir, S. I., Shiam, S. A. A., Zakaria, R. M., Shimanto, A. H., Shamsul Arefeen, S. M., Dolon, M. S. A., Sultana, N., & Shoha, S. (2024). Use of AI-powered precision in machine learning models for real-time currency exchange rate forecasting in BRICS economies. *Journal of Economics. Finance and Accounting Studies*, *6*(6), 66–83. DOI: 10.32996/jefas.2024.6.6.6

Abraham, R., & Kesar, S. (2025). Trajectories of labour market transitions in the Indian economy. *World Development*, *195*(107029), 107029. DOI: 10.1016/j.worlddev.2025.107029

Adobor, H. (2025). Explaining illegal entrepreneurship in the small-scale artisanal mining sector in Ghana: A historical contextualization approach. *Journal of Business Research*, *186*, 115020. Advance online publication. DOI: 10.1016/j.jbusres.2024.115020

Ager, P., Hansen, C., & Lønstrup, L. (2016). Church membership and social insurance: evidence from the great Mississippi flood of 1927. SSRN Electronic Journal. DOI: 10.2139/ssrn.2862290

Agrawal, A., Catalini, C., & Goldfarb, A. (2015). Crowdfunding: Geography, social networks, and the timing of investment decisions. *Journal of Economics & Management Strategy*, *24*(2), 253–274. DOI: 10.1111/jems.12093

Aguilar-Planet, T., & Peralta, E. (2024). Innovation inspired by nature: Applications of biomimicry in engineering design. *Biomimetics*, *9*(9), 523. DOI: 10.3390/biomimetics9090523 PMID: 39329545

Ainin, S., Parveen, F., Moghavvemi, S., Jaafar, N. I., & Shuib, N. L. M. (2020). Factors influencing the use of social media by SMEs and their performance outcomes. *Industrial Management & Data Systems*, *120*(1), 187–207. DOI: 10.1108/IMDS-07-2019-0390

Ajzen, I. (1991). The theory of planned behavior. *Organizational Behavior and Human Decision Processes*, *50*(2), 179–211. DOI: 10.1016/0749-5978(91)90020-T

Akbari, M., Halibas, A., Nguyen, H. M., & Panchal, J. (2025). Sustainable Supply Chains: Implications for Tourists and Residents in Tropical Destinations. In The Business of Low-Carbon Tourism (pp. 120-135). Routledge.

Akter, S., Wamba, S. F., Gunasekaran, A., Dubey, R., & Childe, S. J. (2023). How to improve firm performance using big data analytics capability and digital marketing capability. *International Journal of Production Economics*, *249*, 108497. DOI: 10.1016/j.ijpe.2022.108497

Al Farsi, G. (2023, November). The Impact of Artificial Intelligence Technology in Learning Zones. In International Conference on Computational Intelligence (pp. 215-222). Singapore: Springer Nature Singapore.

Alankuş, S. (2021). Digital transformation of crowdfunding platforms in post-pandemic economy. *Journal of Digital Economy Studies*, *4*(2), 110–120.

Alayón, C. L., Säfsten, K., & Johansson, G. (2022). Barriers and enablers for the adoption of sustainable manufacturing by manufacturing SMEs. *Sustainability (Basel)*, *14*(4), 2364. DOI: 10.3390/su14042364

Albort-Morant, G., Leal-Rodríguez, A. L., & De Marchi, V. (2021). Absorptive capacity and relationship learning mechanisms as complementary drivers of green innovation performance. *Journal of Knowledge Management*, *25*(6), 1443–1463. DOI: 10.1108/JKM-01-2020-0071

Albouq, S. S., Abi Sen, A. A., Almashf, N., Yamin, M., Alshanqiti, A., & Bahbouh, N. M. (2022). A survey of interoperability challenges and solutions for dealing with them in IoT environment. *IEEE Access : Practical Innovations, Open Solutions*, *10*, 36416–36428. DOI: 10.1109/ACCESS.2022.3162219

Al-Hadhrami, Y., & Hussain, F. K. (2020). Real time dataset generation framework for intrusion detection systems in IoT. *Future Generation Computer Systems*, *108*, 414–423. DOI: 10.1016/j.future.2020.02.051

Alsayegh, M. F., Rahman, R. A., & Homayoun, S. (2020). Corporate economic, environmental, and social sustainability performance transformation through ESG disclosure. *Sustainability (Basel), 12*(9), 3910. DOI: 10.3390/su12093910

Alsheyab, M., Filimon, N., & Fusté-Forné, F. (2024). CSR practices in small and medium-sized accommodations and their impact on the local communities. *International Studies of Management & Organization, 54*(4), 329–357. DOI: 10.1080/00208825.2024.2361204

Alshukri, T., Seun Ojekemi, O., Öz, T., & Alzubi, A. (2024). The interplay of corporate social responsibility, innovation capability, organizational learning, and sustainable value creation: Does stakeholder engagement matter? *Sustainability (Basel), 16*(13), 5511. DOI: 10.3390/su16135511

AlSinani, M. J., Kayed, A., & Al Farsi, G. (2020). Improving data security using modified LSB-based image steganography technique. *Journal of Hunan University Natural Sciences, 47*(8).

Andrew, R. (2018). *Guest post: Why India's CO2 emissions grew strongly in 2017.* Carbon Brief.

Appe, S., & Papyan, S. (2025). How and why do diaspora give? A conceptual model to understanding diaspora philanthropy. *Nonprofit and Voluntary Sector Quarterly, 54*(3), 518–546. DOI: 10.1177/08997640241275098

Arner, D. W., Barberis, J., & Buckley, R. P. (2015). The evolution of FinTech: A new post-crisis paradigm? *SSRN, 47*(4), 1271–1319. DOI: 10.2139/ssrn.2676553

Arner, D. W., Barberis, J., & Buckley, R. P. (2017). FinTech and RegTech. *Northwestern Journal of International Law & Business, 37*(3), 371–414.

Arora, A., & Kumawat, J. (2024). A review of Indian women employed in the informal economy. *Journal of Advances and Scholarly Researches in Allied Education, 21*(6), 78–83. DOI: 10.29070/ew180376

Ashurov, S., Musse, O. S. H., & Abdelhak, T. (2024). Evaluating corporate social responsibility in achieving sustainable development and social welfare. *BRICS Journal of Economics, 5*(2), 77–102. DOI: 10.3897/brics-econ.5.e121429

Audretsch, D. B. (2014). From the entrepreneurial university to the university for the entrepreneurial society. *The Journal of Technology Transfer, 39*(3), 313–321. DOI: 10.1007/s10961-012-9288-1

Audretsch, D. B., Belitski, M., & Cherkas, N. (2023). Entrepreneurial ecosystems and sustainability transitions. *Small Business Economics, 61*(2), 623–640. DOI: 10.1007/s11187-022-00666-4

Aukhoon, M. A., Iqbal, J., & Parray, Z. A. (2024). Impact of corporate social responsibility on employee green behavior: Role of green human resource management practices and employee green culture. *Corporate Social Responsibility and Environmental Management, 31*(5), 3768–3778. DOI: 10.1002/csr.2773

Austin, A., & Rahman, I. U. (2022). A triple helix of market failures: Financing the 3Rs of the circular economy in European SMEs. *Journal of Cleaner Production, 361*, 132284. DOI: 10.1016/j.jclepro.2022.132284

Awa, H. O., Etim, W., & Ogbonda, E. (2024). Stakeholders, stakeholder theory and corporate social responsibility (CSR). *International Journal of Corporate Social Responsibility, 9*(1), 11. DOI: 10.1186/s40991-024-00094-y

Awan, U., Sroufe, R., & Kraslawski, A. (2021). Creativity enables sustainable development: Supplier engagement as a boundary condition. *Journal of Cleaner Production, 298*, 126802. DOI: 10.1016/j.jclepro.2021.126802

Ayyaswamy, K., Kathirvel, N., Gobinath, V. M., & Maheswaran, C. P. (2025). Effective leadership strategies for enhancing student success in higher education. In *New Horizons in Leadership* (pp. 61–92). DOI: 10.4018/979-8-3693-6437-6.ch003

Baah, C., Agyabeng-Mensah, Y., Afum, E., & Lascano Armas, J. A. (2024). Exploring corporate environmental ethics and green creativity as antecedents of green competitive advantage, sustainable production and financial performance: Empirical evidence from manufacturing firms. *Benchmarking, 31*(3), 990–1008. DOI: 10.1108/BIJ-06-2022-0352

Badrak, O. (n.d.). How butterfly wings inspire innovation. Smithsonian Magazine. https://www.smithsonianmag.com

Baena, V., & Cerviño, J. (2024). Tourism in the Era of Social Responsibility and Sustainability: Understanding International Tourists' Destination Choices. *Sustainability (Basel), 16*(19), 8509. DOI: 10.3390/su16198509

Bai, M., & Ho, L. (2022). Corporate social performance and firm debt levels: Impacts of the covid-19 pandemic and institutional environments. *Finance Research Letters, 47*, 102968. DOI: 10.1016/j.frl.2022.102968 PMID: 35578609

Bajard, F. (2020). A "hijacked salaried status" in French cooperatives of freelance workers: The political meaning of shifts between standard and non-standard employment. *Frontiers in Sociology*, *5*, 36. Advance online publication. DOI: 10.3389/fsoc.2020.00036 PMID: 33869443

Baker, M. A. (2024). Sustainable tourism employment: A comprehensive overview of tourism employees' experience from a tourist-employee interaction perspective. *Journal of Hospitality and Tourism Management*, *60*, 228–238. DOI: 10.1016/j.jhtm.2024.07.009

Balabiyev, K. (2023). Criminal liability for illegal entrepreneurship, illegal banking activity, microfinancial or collection activities: comparative legal analysis of criminal legislation of foreighn countries. *Journal of actual problems of jurisprudence*. DOI: 10.26577/JAPJ.2023.v106.i2.010

Balachandran, A., & Desai, S. (2024). Transportation, employment and gender norms: Evidence from Indian cities. *Regional Science Policy & Practice*, *16*(6), 100060. DOI: 10.1016/j.rspp.2024.100060

Bamel, N., Dhir, S., & Sushil, S. (2019). Inter-partner dynamics and joint venture competitiveness: A fuzzy TISM approach. *Benchmarking*, *26*(1), 97–116. DOI: 10.1108/BIJ-02-2018-0041

Baranidharan, S. (2019). Causal linkages and impact of finance companies stock price on BSE FINANCE and BSE SENSEX. *International Journal of Recent Technology and Engineering, 8*(3), 7779-7790, ISSN 2277-3878, https://doi.org/DOI: 10.35940/ijrte.C6323.098319

Baranidharan, S. (2021). Empirical relationship of macroeconomic variables and stock prices: Indian stock market and Japanese stock market. *Finance India, 35*(3), 787-800, ISSN 0970-3772, https://www.scopus.com/inward/record.uri?partnerID=HzOxMe3b&scp=85115635268&origin=inward

Baranidharan, S. (2023). Accounting fraud and bankruptcy: The case of wirecard AG. *Theory and Practice of Illegitimate Finance*, 222-244, https://doi.org/DOI: 10.4018/979-8-3693-1190-5.ch012

Baranidharan, S. (2023). Falling Prey to Scams: The Perils of Emotional Decision-Making in the Indian Stock Market - Retail Investor Perspective. *Cases on the Resurgence of Emerging Businesses*, 72-87, https://doi.org/DOI: 10.4018/978-1-6684-8488-3.ch006

Baranidharan, S. (2024). Interconnectedness and Risk Spillovers among Selected Indian Stocks During the COVID-19 Pandemic. *Interdisciplinary Journal of Management Studies, 17*(1), 111-123, ISSN 2981-0795, https://doi.org/DOI: 10.22059/ijms.2023.336640.674885

Barney, J. B. (1991). Firm resources and sustained competitive advantage. *Journal of Management, 17*(1), 99–120. DOI: 10.1177/014920639101700108

Barros, A. C. P. (2019). *Industry 4 0 and Transversal Skills: Comparing Social Sciences and Stem Higher Education Graduates* (Master's thesis, Universidade do Porto (Portugal)).

Bassetti, T., Blasi, S., & Sedita, S. R. (2020). The management of sustainable development: A longitudinal analysis of the effects of environmental performance on economic performance. *Business Strategy and the Environment*, (May), 1–17. DOI: 10.1002/bse.2607

Becerra-Bizarrón, M. E., & Gomez-Bernal, J. R. (2025). Business sustainability practices in micro and small enterprises: A systematic review. *PLOS Sustainability and Transformation, 4*(11), e0000140. DOI: 10.1371/journal.pstr.0000140

Begum, A., Gaytan, J. C. T., & Ahmed, G. (2023). The nexus between technology and innovation: A sustainable development model. In *2023 International Conference on Business Analytics for Technology and Security (ICBATS)* (pp. 1–8). IEEE.

Belleflamme, P., Lambert, T., & Schwienbacher, A. (2014). Crowdfunding: Tapping the right crowd. *Journal of Business Venturing, 29*(5), 585–609. DOI: 10.1016/j.jbusvent.2013.07.003

Benyus, J. M. (1997). *Biomimicry: Innovation inspired by nature*. Morrow.

Bergset, L., & Fichter, K. (2022). Green start-ups, A new typology for sustainable entrepreneurship and innovation research. *Journal of Innovation & Knowledge, 7*(2), 100173. DOI: 10.1016/j.jik.2022.100173

Bernacchio, C., Foss, N. J., & Lindenberg, S. (2024). The virtues of joint production: Ethical foundations for collaborative organizations. *Academy of Management Review, 49*(1), 155–181. DOI: 10.5465/amr.2019.0389

Bhat, S. A., Mallniah, L. C., & Singh, S. (2024). Economic development and changing women lives: Evidence from women employment participation in India. *International Socioeconomic Review, 2*(1), 94–115. DOI: 10.3126/iser.v2i1.75236

Bhattacharya, C. B., Korschun, D., & Sen, S. (2022). Strengthening stakeholder–company relationships through mutually beneficial corporate social responsibility initiatives. *Journal of Business Ethics*, *177*(2), 345–362. DOI: 10.1007/s10551-021-04863-9

Bhutia, K. (2016). *Can startups give a boost to the Indian economy?* Entrepreneur India.

Bican, P. M., & Brem, A. (2020). Digital business model, digital transformation, digital entrepreneurship: Is there a sustainable "digital"? *Sustainability (Basel)*, *12*(13), 5239. DOI: 10.3390/su12135239

Bingi, J., & Thiruchanuru, S. (2025). Bio-inspired design: Works and perspectives of Bio-Inspired Research and Design Laboratory. Notion Press.

Birinci, H., Esenyel, I., & Obeng, H. A. (2025). Sustainable destination management in luxury tourism: Balancing economic development and environmental responsibility. *Sustainability (Basel)*, *17*(15), 6815. DOI: 10.3390/su17156815

Bishnoi, N. K., Jakhar, B., Singhal, B., & Sharma, S. (2024). Haryana's labour landscape: Deciphering employment challenges through periodic surveys. *Rozprawy Społeczne*, *18*(1), 208–225. DOI: 10.29316/rs/186246

Blackman, S. (2010). Drug war politics: Governing culture through prohibition, intoxicants as customary practice and the challenge of drug normalization. *Sociology Compass*, *4*(10), 841–855. DOI: 10.1111/j.1751-9020.2010.00324.x

Blocker, J. S.Jr. (2006). Did Prohibition Really Work? Alcohol Prohibition as a Public Health Innovation. *American Journal of Public Health*, *96*(2), 233–243. DOI: 10.2105/AJPH.2005.065409 PMID: 16380559

Block, J. H., Colombo, M. G., Cumming, D. J., & Vismara, S. (2021). New players in entrepreneurial finance and why they are there. *Small Business Economics*, *56*(3), 1–16. DOI: 10.1007/s11187-019-00227-9

Bocken, N. M. P., Short, S. W., Rana, P., & Evans, S. (2022). A literature and practice review to develop sustainable business model archetypes. *Journal of Cleaner Production*, *65*, 42–56. DOI: 10.1016/j.jclepro.2013.11.039

Bocken, N. M. P., Weissbrod, I., & Tennant, M. (2022). Business model experimentation for sustainability: Evidence from SMEs. *Journal of Cleaner Production*, *344*, 131035. DOI: 10.1016/j.jclepro.2022.131035

Bocken, N. M., Harsch, A., & Weissbrod, I. (2022). Circular business models for the fastmoving consumer goods industry: Desirability, feasibility, and viability. *Sustainable Production and Consumption*, *30*, 799–814. DOI: 10.1016/j.spc.2022.01.012

Bolón-Canedo, V., Morán-Fernández, L., Cancela, B., & Alonso-Betanzos, A. (2024). A review of green artificial intelligence: Towards a more sustainable future. *Neurocomputing*, *599*, 128096. DOI: 10.1016/j.neucom.2024.128096

Bora, M., & Baruah, R. (2024). *A study on employment sustainability among Engineering students using a Statistical and Deep Learning framework.* Educational Administration Theory and Practices., DOI: 10.53555/kuey.v30i5.3892

Borrella, I., Mataix, C., & Carrasco-Gallego, R. (2022). Smallholder farmers in the specialty coffee industry: Opportunities and constraints for economic sustainability. *Sustainability*, *14*(3), 1376. DOI: 10.3390/su14031376

Bradford, C. (2012). Crowdfunding and the democratization of finance. *Harvard Business Law Review*, *2*(1), 85–120.

Brammer, S., Jackson, G., & Matten, D. (2012). Corporate Social Responsibility and institutional theory: New perspectives on private governance. *Socio-economic Review*, *10*(1), 3–28. DOI: 10.1093/ser/mwr030

Burke, J., & DePoy, E. (1991). An emerging view of mastery, excellence, and leadership in occupational therapy practice. *The American Journal of Occupational Therapy*, *45*(11), 1027–1032. DOI: 10.5014/ajot.45.11.1027 PMID: 1793116

Burtch, G., Carnahan, S., & Greenwood, B. N. (2018). Can you sell me a secret? Social capital and crowdfunding performance. *Management Science*, *64*(2), 939–958.

Bux, H., Zhang, Z., & Ali, A. (2024). Corporate social responsibility adoption for achieving economic, environmental, and social sustainability performance. *Environment, Development and Sustainability*, *28*(2), 1–31. DOI: 10.1007/s10668-024-05155-7

Büyükkalaycı, M., & Karaca, Y. (2019). Marketing evolution and digital transformation in marketing strategies. *Journal of Marketing Thought*, *6*(2), 460–472.

Çağlar, E. (2019). Crowdfunding and entrepreneurial finance in digital age. *Entrepreneurship Research Journal*, *9*(1), 15–28.

Carlini, J., & Grace, D. (2021). The corporate social responsibility (CSR) internal branding model: Aligning employees' CSR awareness, knowledge, and experience to deliver positive employee performance outcomes. *Journal of Marketing Management*, *37*(7-8), 732–760. DOI: 10.1080/0267257X.2020.1860113

Carpenter, M. (2011). E-commerce and digital transformation in business strategy. *Business Horizons, 54*(2), 181–190.

Časta, M. (2023). Inflation, interest rates and the predictability of stock returns. *Finance Research Letters.*

Castro, M., & Zermeño, M. (2020). Being an entrepreneur post-covid-19 – resilience in times of crisis: A systematic literature review. *Journal of Entrepreneurship in Emerging Economies, 13*(4), 721–746. DOI: 10.1108/JEEE-07-2020-0246

Cenamor, J., Parida, V., & Wincent, J. (2021). How entrepreneurial SMEs compete through digital platforms: The roles of digital platform capability and innovation. *Journal of Business Research, 124*, 384–397. DOI: 10.1016/j.jbusres.2020.11.058

Chatterjee, S., Chaudhuri, R., Vrontis, D., & Thrassou, A. (2021). Digital transformation of entrepreneurship and innovation: A bibliometric analysis. *Journal of Business Research, 135*, 575–588. DOI: 10.1016/j.jbusres.2021.06.048

Chaturvedi, S., Mahajan, K., & Siddique, Z. (2024). Words matter: Gender, jobs and applicant behavior. SSRN *Electronic Journal.* DOI: 10.2139/ssrn.4730629

Chau, F., Deesomsak, R., & Koutmos, D. (2016). Does investor sentiment really matter? *International Review of Financial Analysis, 48*, 221–232. DOI: 10.1016/j.irfa.2016.10.003

Chauhan, N. (2025). Empowering communities and preserving heritage: Case studies on socially responsible travel through fair trade tourism. In Meaningful Tourism: Strategies and Future Development (pp. 163-182). Emerald Publishing Limited.

Chavannavar, M. B., Patil, S. C., & Simoes, M. (2016). Monetary policy effect on Nifty 50 and sectoral indices: A study from Indian stock markets. *International Journal of Latest Technology in Engineering, Management &. Applied Sciences (Basel, Switzerland), 5*(9), 59–69.

Chen, Q., Jiang, F., Guo, Y., Shrestha, R. K., & Zhang, Q. (2025). Community attachment, emotional solidarity, and sustainable tourism support: Evidence from Sagarmatha national park, Nepal. *Sustainable Development (Bradford), 33*(3), 4492–4510. DOI: 10.1002/sd.3360

Chen, Y. (2021). Platform competition and crowdfunding inequality. *Information Economics and Policy, 55*, 100897.

Chen, Y., & Zhang, Y. (2021). Fostering resilience in new venture teams: The role of behavioral and affective integration. *Group & Organization Management, 46*(4), 773–816. DOI: 10.1177/10596011211033164

Chiang, T. Y. (2024). Analysis of Responsible Tourism Practices in the Wake of COVID-19: Data Mining Approach. In Advances in Hospitality and Leisure, Volume 20 (pp. 23-40). Emerald Publishing Limited.

Choi, M., & Choi, Y. (2021). Employee perceptions of hotel CSR activities during the COVID-19 pandemic. *International Journal of Contemporary Hospitality Management, 33*(10), 3355–3378. DOI: 10.1108/IJCHM-03-2021-0289

Chowdhury, E. K., & Chowdhury, R. (2024). Role of financial inclusion in human development: Evidence from Bangladesh, India and Pakistan. *Journal of the Knowledge Economy, 15*(1), 3329–3354. DOI: 10.1007/s13132-023-01366-x

Christensen, C. M., Raynor, M. E., & McDonald, R. (2015). What is disruptive innovation? *Harvard Business Review,* •••, 44–53. PMID: 17183796

Chung, S., & Day, J. (2024). Fair Tourism in South Korea: An Examination of Sustainable Supply Chain Management for Tourism. *Tourism and Hospitality, 5*(4), 1493–1509. DOI: 10.3390/tourhosp5040083

Cohen, B., & Muñoz, P. (2021). Toward a theory of purpose-driven urban entrepreneurship. *Organization & Environment, 34*(2), 181–208. DOI: 10.1177/1086026619892345

Cordova, A., Dolci, J., & Gianfrate, G. (2015). The determinants of crowdfunding success: Evidence from technology projects. *Procedia: Social and Behavioral Sciences, 181*, 115–124. DOI: 10.1016/j.sbspro.2015.04.872

Cosa, M. (2024). Equity integration in corporate social responsibility: Analyzing stakeholder, legitimacy, and social activism dynamics. In *CSR, Governance and Value* (pp. 133–154). Springer Nature Singapore. DOI: 10.1007/978-981-97-4795-5_6

Cowling, M., Brown, R., & Rocha, A. (2023). Did you save some cash for a rainy COVID-19 day? The crisis and SMEs. *International Small Business Journal, 41*(2), 187–210. DOI: 10.1177/02662426221104551 PMID: 35125601

Cox, C. R. (2014). *Synthesizing the vertical and the horizontal: A world-ecological analysis of'the Industrial Revolution', Part I.* Portland State University.

Crane, A., & Matten, D. (2004). Questioning the domain of the business ethics curriculum. *Journal of Business Ethics, 54*(4), 357–369. DOI: 10.1007/s10551-004-1825-x

Cumming, D., & Johan, S. (2019). Crowdfunding and entrepreneurial finance. *Oxford Review of Economic Policy, 35*(3), 488–509.

Cutolo, D., & Kenney, M. (2021). Platform-dependent entrepreneurs: Power asymmetries, risks, and strategies in the platform economy. *The Academy of Management Perspectives*, *35*(4), 584–605. DOI: 10.5465/amp.2019.0103

Czichos, H., Alshebami, A. S., Shepperson, L., & Foldager, U. (2025). Greening the workplace: How sustainable practices drive employee engagement. In *The Sustainability Handbook* (Vol. 1, pp. 699–710). Elsevier.

Dangelico, R. M., & Vocalelli, D. (2020). "Green marketing": An analysis of definitions, strategy steps, and tools. *Journal of Cleaner Production*, *165*, 1263–1279. DOI: 10.1016/j.jclepro.2017.07.184

Davis, F. D. (1989). Perceived usefulness, perceived ease of use, and user acceptance of information technology. *Management Information Systems Quarterly*, *13*(3), 319–340. DOI: 10.2307/249008

Dawar, G., & Singh, S. (2023). Barriers to corporate social responsibility implementation in the medium size manufacturing sector: An interpretive structure modelling approach. *Journal of Entrepreneurship in Emerging Economies*, *15*(2), 447–479. DOI: 10.1108/JEEE-12-2020-0451

de Medeiros, J. F., Ribeiro, J. L. D., & Cortimiglia, M. N. (2020). Success factors for environmentally sustainable product innovation: A systematic literature review. *Journal of Cleaner Production*, *270*, 122388. DOI: 10.1016/j.jclepro.2020.122388

de Reuver, M., Sørensen, C., & Basole, R. C. (2018). The digital platform: A research agenda. *Journal of Information Technology*, *33*(2), 124–135. DOI: 10.1057/s41265-016-0033-3

De Valence, G. (2022). *Creative Destruction and Constructing The Built Environment: From the first industrial revolution to the fourth*. Construction Economics Research.

De', R., Pandey, N., & Pal, A. (2020). Impact of digital surge during COVID-19 pandemic: A viewpoint on research and practice. *International Journal of Information Management*, *55*, 102171. DOI: 10.1016/j.ijinfomgt.2020.102171 PMID: 32836633

Dhingra, N. (2025). Sustainable Food and Beverage Options for Tourists. In Greener Future: Building Sustainable Tourism Communities (pp. 197-208). Emerald Publishing Limited. DOI: 10.1108/978-1-83608-988-920251013

Diesen, G. (2021). Great power politics in the fourth industrial revolution.

Dietz, T., Börner, J., Förster, J. J., & von Braun, J. (2021). Governance of the coffee–forest frontier: Sustainability and social outcomes. *World Development*, *137*, 105161. DOI: 10.1016/j.worlddev.2020.105161

DiMaggio, P. J. (1988). Interest and agency in institutional theory. *Institutional Patterns and Organizations: Culture and Environment/Ballinger.*

DiMaggio, P. J., & Powell, W. W. (1983). The Iron Cage Revisited: Institutional Isomorphism and Collective Rationality in Organizational Fields. *American Sociological Review, 48*(2), 147. DOI: 10.2307/2095101

Dombrowski, U., & Wagner, T. (2014). Mental strain as field of action in the 4th industrial revolution. *Procedia CIRP, 17*, 100–105. DOI: 10.1016/j.procir.2014.01.077

Donaldson, T., & Preston, L. E. (1995). The Stakeholder Theory of the Corporation: Concepts, Evidence, and Implications. *Academy of Management Review, 20*(1), 65–91. DOI: 10.2307/258887

Dong, C., Zhang, Y., & Ao, S. (2024). How to engage employees in corporate social responsibility? Exploring corporate social responsibility communication effects through the reasoned action approach. *Management Communication Quarterly, 38*(1), 27–59. DOI: 10.1177/08933189231161621

Dooley, P. (2014). Pomegranates inspire new battery design. *Cosmos.*

Draganov, M., Tsankov, N., & Petkova, D. (2018). Marketing 5.0: The future of marketing in digital transformation era. *Economic Alternatives, 3*, 1–10.

Drucker, P. F. (1985). *Innovation and entrepreneurship*. Harper & Row.

Drummond, C., McGrath, H., & O'Toole, T. (2022). The impact of digital engagement on SME performance: The role of customer–brand relationships. *Journal of Business Research, 149*, 346–358. DOI: 10.1016/j.jbusres.2022.05.040

Duan, W., Xue, X., Chen, Z., & Liu, L. (2025). How do institutional pressures influence corporate social responsibility?—A perspective based on state-owned enterprises. *Information Technology Management*, •••, 1–15.

Đurić, Z., Cvijanović, D., Petek, V., & Potočnik Topler, J. (2025). Sustainability struggle: Challenges and issues in managing sustainability and environmental protection in local tourism destinations practices—An overview. *Sustainability (Basel), 17*(15), 7134. DOI: 10.3390/su17157134

Durukal, H. (2019). Big data analytics and marketing transformation in Industry 4.0. *Procedia Computer Science, 158*, 1624–1631. DOI: 10.1016/j.procs.2019.09.227

Dwivedi, Y. K., Hughes, D. L., Ismagilova, E., Aarts, G., Coombs, C., Crick, T., Duan, Y., Dwivedi, R., Edwards, J., Eirug, A., Galanos, V., Ilavarasan, P. V., Janssen, M., Jones, P., Kar, A. K., Kizgin, H., Kronemann, B., Lal, B., Lucini, B., & Williams, M. D. (2021). Artificial intelligence (AI): Multidisciplinary perspectives on emerging challenges, opportunities, and agenda for research. *International Journal of Information Management*, *57*, 101994. DOI: 10.1016/j.ijinfomgt.2019.08.002

Eccles, R. G., Ioannou, I., & Serafeim, G. (2020). The impact of corporate sustainability on organizational processes and performance. *Management Science*, *66*(11), 4889–4914. DOI: 10.1287/mnsc.2019.3451

Edwards, G., & Howe, T. (2015). A test of prohibition's effect on alcohol production and consumption using crop yields. *Southern Economic Journal*, *81*(4), 1145–1168. DOI: 10.1002/soej.12025

ElBelehy, C., & Crispim, J. (2025). Social sustainability in Egypt hospitality and tourism supply chains. *Business and Society Review*, *130*(S1), 222–262. DOI: 10.1111/basr.12337

Elkington, J. (1997). *Cannibals with forks: The triple bottom line of 21st century business*. Capstone Publishing.

Ellender, R., Cook, D., Sheladia, V., & Johnson, R. (1980). Enterovirus and bacterial evaluation of Mississippi oysters. *Gulf Research Reports*, *6*. Advance online publication. DOI: 10.18785/grr.0604.04

Elshaer, I., & Saad, S. (2021). Entrepreneurial resilience and business continuity in the tourism and hospitality industry: The role of adaptive performance and institutional orientation. *Tourism Review*, *77*(5), 1365–1384. DOI: 10.1108/TR-04-2021-0171

Elyasiani, E., & Mansur, I. (1998). Sensitivity of the bank stock returns distribution to changes in the level and volatility of interest rate: A GARCH-M model. *Journal of Banking & Finance*, *22*(10–11), 1421–1446. DOI: 10.1016/S0378-4266(98)00003-X

Enciso-Alfaro, S.-Y., Marhroub, S., Martínez-Córdoba, P.-J., & García-Sánchez, I.-M. (2024). The effect of COVID-19 on employment: A bibliometric review of a she-cession. *Corporate Social Responsibility and Environmental Management*, *31*(4), 3444–3467. DOI: 10.1002/csr.2756

Ertuğrul, İ., & Deniz, E. (2018). Big data and marketing analytics: A new approach in Industry 4.0. *International Journal of Social Sciences and Education Research*, *4*(2), 230–240.

Escobar, M., Ferrando, S., & Rubtsov, A. (2016). Portfolio choice with stochastic interest rates and learning about stock return predictability. *International Review of Economics & Finance*, *41*, 347–370. DOI: 10.1016/j.iref.2015.07.003

Etzkowitz, H., & Leydesdorff, L. (2000). The dynamics of innovation: From National Systems and "Mode 2" to a Triple Helix of university–industry–government relations. *Research Policy*, *29*(2), 109–123. DOI: 10.1016/S0048-7333(99)00055-4

Fadahunsi, A., & Rosa, P. (2002). Entrepreneurship and Illegality: Insights from the Nigerian cross-border Trade. *Journal of Business Venturing*, *17*(5), 397–429. DOI: 10.1016/S0883-9026(01)00073-8

Faeni, D. P., Oktaviani, R. F., Riyadh, H. A., Faeni, R. P., & Beshr, B. A. H. (2025). Green human resource management (GHRM) and corporate social responsibility (CSR) in reducing carbon emissions for sustainable practices. *Environmental Quality Management*, *34*(3), e70048. DOI: 10.1002/tqem.70048

Faruk, M., Rahman, M., & Hasan, S. (2021). Consumer decision fatigue in digital environments. *Journal of Consumer Behaviour*, *20*(3), 450–462.

Fayad, A. A. S., Khatib, S. F. A., Abbas, A. F., Ghaleb, B. A. A., & Mousa, A. K. A. (2024). The determinants and consequences of board multiple directorships. *Corporate Governance (Bradford)*, (May). Advance online publication. DOI: 10.1108/CG-07-2023-0310

Felin, T., Gambardella, A., Novelli, E., & Zenger, T. (2024). A scientific method for startups. *Journal of Management*, *50*(8), 3080–3104. Advance online publication. DOI: 10.1177/01492063231226136

Feng, C. (2024). International tax incentives, cross-border research and development, and corporate innovation performance. *Finance Research Letters, 66*(December 2023), 105646. DOI: 10.1016/j.frl.2024.105646

Feng, Q., Ge, Y., & Zhao, L. (2024). Tax incentives and corporate digital transformation: Evidence from China's accelerated depreciation policy. *Journal of Asian Economics, 95*(June 2023), 101832. DOI: 10.1016/j.asieco.2024.101832

Ferchen, M., & Mattlin, M. (2023). Five modes of China's economic influence: Rethinking Chinese economic statecraft. *The Pacific Review*, *36*(5), 978–1004. DOI: 10.1080/09512748.2023.2200029

Fernandez-Feijoo, B., Romero, S., & Ruiz, S. (2014). Commitment to Corporate social responsibility measured through global reporting initiative reporting: Factors affecting the behavior of companies. *Journal of Cleaner Production*, *81*, 244–254. DOI: 10.1016/j.jclepro.2014.06.034

Fernández-Méndez, L., Canal, E., & García-García, R. (2021). Litigations with the home state and internationalization. *Multinational Business Review, 30*(3), 343–363. DOI: 10.1108/MBR-03-2021-0036

Fernandez-Perez, A., Fernández-Rodríguez, F., & Sosvilla-Rivero, S. (2014). *The term structure of interest rates as predictor of stock returns: Evidence for the IBEX 35 during a bear market.* International Review of Economics & Finance. How RBI Repo Rate Changes Affect Your Home Loan EMI. https://www.loanquantum.com/blogs/how-rbi-repo-rate-impacts-your-home-loan-emi/

Ferrero-Ferrero, I., Muñoz-Torres, M. J., Rivera-Lirio, J. M., Escrig-Olmedo, E., & Fernández-Izquierdo, M. Á. (2024). Sustainable development goals in the hospitality industry: A dream or reality? *Journal of Accounting & Organizational Change, 20*(5), 773–796. DOI: 10.1108/JAOC-09-2022-0146

Ferris, S. P., Jagannathan, M., & Pritchard, A. C. (2003). Too Busy to Mind the Business? Monitoring by Directors with Multiple Board Appointments. *The Journal of Finance, 58*(3), 1087–1111. DOI: 10.1111/1540-6261.00559

Fettahoğlu, A., & Khusayan, A. (2017). Crowdfunding models and financial innovation. *Finance & Banking Review, 5*(1), 55–70.

Fich, E. M., & Shivdasani, A. (2006). Are Busy Boards Effective Monitors? *The Journal of Finance, 61*(2), 689–724. DOI: 10.1111/j.1540-6261.2006.00852.x

Filimonau, V., & De Coteau, D. A. (2020). Food waste management in hospitality operations: A critical review. *Tourism Management, 78*, 104056. DOI: 10.1016/j.tourman.2019.104056

Fiok, K., Farahani, F. V., Karwowski, W., & Ahram, T. (2022). Explainable artificial intelligence for education and training. *The Journal of Defense Modeling and Simulation, 19*(2), 133–144. DOI: 10.1177/15485129211028651

Fiveable Inc. (2024). Bio-inspired innovation. https://library.fiveable.me/key-terms/biomimicry-in-business-innovation/bio-inspired-innovation

Fleck, E., & Asmuth, J. (2020). Building capacity for creativity: Rediscovering the inner "superhero" as a mechanism for developing a creative mindset for entrepreneurial problem-solving. *Entrepreneurship Education and Pedagogy, 4*(1), 82–95. DOI: 10.1177/2515127420912503

Folmer, E., Ronzhin, S., Van Hillegersberg, J., Beek, W., & Lemmens, R. (2020). Business rationale for linked data at governments: A case study at the Netherlands' Kadaster data platform. *IEEE Access : Practical Innovations, Open Solutions, 8*, 70822–70835. DOI: 10.1109/ACCESS.2020.2984691

Foss, N. J., & Saebi, T. (2020). Business models and business model innovation: Between wicked and paradigmatic problems. *Long Range Planning*, *53*(4), 101950. DOI: 10.1016/j.lrp.2019.101950

Freeman, R. E. (1984). *Stakeholder management: A strategic approach*. Pitman.

Freeman, R. E., Phillips, R., & Sisodia, R. (2021). Tensions in stakeholder theory. *Business & Society*, *60*(2), 213–231. DOI: 10.1177/0007650318773750

Frempong, D., Akinboboye, O., Okoli, I., Afrihyia, E., Umar, M. O., Umana, A. U., Appoh, M., & Omolayo, O. (2022). Real-time analytics dashboards for decision-making using Tableau in public sector and business intelligence applications. *Journal of Frontiers in Multidisciplinary Research*, *3*(2), 65–80. DOI: 10.54660/.IJFMR.2022.3.2.65-80

Frynas, J. G., & Stephens, S. (2015). Political Corporate Social Responsibility: Reviewing Theories and Setting New Agendas. *International Journal of Management Reviews*, *17*(4), 483–509. DOI: 10.1111/ijmr.12049

Fu, C., Luo, D., Zhang, J., & Li, W. (2025). Tax incentives, marketization level, and corporate digital transformation. *International Review of Economics & Finance*, *97*, 103777. DOI: 10.1016/j.iref.2024.103777

Funken, R., Gielnik, M., & Foo, M. (2018). How can problems be turned into something good? the role of entrepreneurial learning and error mastery orientation. *Entrepreneurship Theory and Practice*, *44*(2), 315–338. DOI: 10.1177/1042258718801600

Gai, K., Qiu, M., & Sun, X. (2018). A survey on FinTech. *Journal of Network and Computer Applications*, *103*, 262–273. DOI: 10.1016/j.jnca.2017.10.011

Galemba, R. (2008). Informal and Illicit Entrepreneurs: Fighting for a Place in the Neoliberal Economic Order. *Anthropology of work review. Anthropology of Work Review*, *29*(2), 2. DOI: 10.1111/j.1548-1417.2008.00010.x PMID: 24223472

Gao, J., Zhang, Y., Xu, S., & Ma, E. (2025). Rethinking work-life integration: Empowering talent in emerging hospitality and tourism work paradigms. *International Journal of Contemporary Hospitality Management*, *37*(5), 1765–1783. DOI: 10.1108/IJCHM-05-2024-0736

Garcia-Ortega, B., Catalá-Pérez, D., de-Miguel-Molina, B., & de-Miguel-Molina, M. (2024). Corporate Social Responsibility Challenges in the Mining Industry and ISO 26000. In *The Strategic Paradigm of CSR and Sustainability: A Public-Private Approach* (pp. 45–73). Springer Nature Switzerland. DOI: 10.1007/978-3-031-58889-1_3

García-Sánchez, I., & Noguera-Gámez, L. (2017). Integrated Reporting and Stakeholder Engagement: The Effect on Information Asymmetry. *Corporate Social Responsibility and Environmental Management*, *24*(5), 395–413. DOI: 10.1002/csr.1415

Garvin, C. (2015). *Tapping into nature: Bio-inspired innovation as an economic engine*. GreenBiz.

Gefen, D., Karahanna, E., & Straub, D. W. (2003). Trust and TAM in online shopping: An integrated model. *Management Information Systems Quarterly*, *27*(1), 51–90. DOI: 10.2307/30036519

Geissdoerfer, M., Savaget, P., Bocken, N. M. P., & Hultink, E. J. (2017). The circular economy – A new sustainability paradigm? *Journal of Cleaner Production*, *143*, 757–768. DOI: 10.1016/j.jclepro.2016.12.048

Gentry, R., Dalziel, T., & Jamison, M. (2013). Who do start-up firms imitate? a study of new market entries in the clec industry. *Journal of Small Business Management*, *51*(4), 525–538. DOI: 10.1111/jsbm.12055

George, B. (2018). Inclusive growth by means of sustainable supply chains: A case study of the Dabbawalas of Mumbai, India. *International Journal of Entrepreneurial Knowledge*, *6*(2). Advance online publication. DOI: 10.37335/ijek.v6i2.74

George, B., & Mattathil, A. P. (2025). Empowering African American Tourism Entrepreneurs with Generative AI: Bridging Innovation and Cultural Heritage. *Societies (Basel, Switzerland)*, *15*(2), 34. DOI: 10.3390/soc15020034

George, B., & Wooden, O. S. (2025). *AI Empowered: Pioneering African American Entrepreneurship in the Digital Age*. Emerald Publishing Limited. DOI: 10.1108/9781836628163

Gerber, E. M., & Hui, J. (2013). Crowdfunding: Motivations and deterrents for participation. *ACM Transactions on Computer-Human Interaction*, *20*(6), 1–32. DOI: 10.1145/2530540

Gidage, M., & Bhide, S. (2024). Corporate reputation as the nexus: Linking moral and social responsibility, green practices, and organizational performance. *Corporate Reputation Review*, •••, 1–23. DOI: 10.1057/s41299-024-00209-y

Godfrey, P. C. (2005). The Relationship Between Corporate Philanthropy And Shareholder Wealth: A Risk Management Perspective. *Academy of Management Review*, *30*(4), 777–798. DOI: 10.5465/amr.2005.18378878

Gökşin, E. (2018). Digital marketing strategy development stages. *Marketing Science Review*, *12*(1), 20–30.

Goldschmidt, K. (2017). The fourth industrial revolution and human capital development. *Unpublished master's thesis, Rhodes University, Grahamstown, South Africa.*

Gonçalves, B. D. S. M., Carvalho, F. L. D., & Fiorini, P. D. C. (2022). Circular economy and financial aspects: A systematic review of the literature. *Sustainability (Basel), 14*(5), 3023. DOI: 10.3390/su14053023

Granda, M. L. (2021). Tax haven ownership and business groups: Tax avoidance incentives in Ecuadorian firms. *Journal of Business Research, 130*, 698–708. DOI: 10.1016/j.jbusres.2020.07.012

Griffith, R., Levell, P., & O'Connell, M. (2022). How do food prices affect consumers and firms? Evidence from microdata. *Fiscal Studies, 43*(1), 1–28. DOI: 10.1111/1475-5890.12291

Grinin, L., & Grinin, A. L. (2016). *The cybernetic revolution and the forthcoming epoch of self-regulating systems.* OOO" Издательство" Учитель".

Guix, M., Sánchez, J. J. N., Priego, M. J. B., & Font, X. (2025). The changing institutional logics behind sustainability reports from the largest hotel groups in the world in 2014, 2018 and 2021. *Tourism Management, 106*, 105031. DOI: 10.1016/j.tourman.2024.105031

Gupta, B. B., & Quamara, M. (2020). An overview of Internet of Things (IoT): Architectural aspects, challenges, and protocols. *Concurrency and Computation, 32*(21), e4946. DOI: 10.1002/cpe.4946

Gupta, P. (2018). Regional Disparities in Economic Growth and Employment in India: An Analysis of Progress Toward Sustainable Development Goal. [IJSREM]. *International Journal of Scientific Research in Engineering and Management, 8*(3), 1.

Gupta, S., Kushwaha, P. S., Badhera, U., & Singh, R. K. (2025). Managing tourism and hospitality industry during pandemic: Analysis of challenges and strategies for survival. *Benchmarking, 32*(4), 1360–1386. DOI: 10.1108/BIJ-11-2023-0806

Hahn, R., & Kühnen, M. (2013). Determinants of sustainability reporting: A review of results, trends, theory, and opportunities in an expanding field of research. *Journal of Cleaner Production, 59*, 5–21. DOI: 10.1016/j.jclepro.2013.07.005

Hallas, N. E. (2024). LEED certification and sustainable building practices: a comprehensive guide to efficient and sustainable facilities. In *Design Strategies for Efficient and Sustainable Building Facilities* (pp. 124–161). IGI Global. DOI: 10.4018/979-8-3693-3200-9.ch006

Haller, M. (1990). Illegal enterprise: A theoretical and historical interpretation. *Criminology*, *28*(2), 207–236. DOI: 10.1111/j.1745-9125.1990.tb01324.x

Hall, W. (2010). What are the policy lessons of national alcohol prohibition in the united states, 1920–1933? *Addiction (Abingdon, England)*, *105*(7), 1164–1173. DOI: 10.1111/j.1360-0443.2010.02926.x PMID: 20331549

Hall, W. (2017). The future of the international drug control system and national drug prohibitions. *Addiction (Abingdon, England)*, *113*(7), 1210–1223. DOI: 10.1111/add.13941 PMID: 28884869

Hamad, B. M., & Jawad, M. K. (2024). The Fourth Industrial Revolution: A Historical and Conceptual Review. *Journal of Economics and Administrative Sciences*, *30*(141), 154–172. DOI: 10.33095/gh3a7g38

Hamdi, W. B., Aderibigbe, S. A., Idriz, M., & Alghfeli, M. M. (2024). Faith in humanity: Religious charitable organizations solidarity towards migrants in the United Arab Emirates. *Religions*, *15*(3), 266. DOI: 10.3390/rel15030266

Han, A., Isaacson, A., & Muennig, P. (2020). The promise of big data for precision population health management in the US. *Public Health*, *185*, 110–116. DOI: 10.1016/j.puhe.2020.04.040 PMID: 32615477

Hänninen, M., Smedlund, A., & Mitronen, L. (2020). Digitalization in retailing: Multi-sided platforms as drivers of industry transformation. *Baltic Journal of Management*, *15*(2), 152–168. DOI: 10.1108/BJM-04-2017-0109

Hart, S. L., & Dowell, G. (2011). A natural-resource-based view of the firm: Fifteen years after. *Journal of Management*, *37*(5), 1464–1479. DOI: 10.1177/0149206310390219

Harvey, B., Peppes, A., Chakrabarty, G., Pozzan, E., & Cattaneo, U. (2020). *Building Back Better for Women: Women's Dire Position in the Informal Economy*. https://www.ilo.org/sites/default/files/wcmsp5/groups/public/@ed_protect/@protrav/@travail/documents/publication/wcms_755348.pdf

Haynie, M., & Shepherd, D. (2009). A measure of adaptive cognition for entrepreneurship research. *Entrepreneurship Theory and Practice*, *33*(3), 695–714. DOI: 10.1111/j.1540-6520.2009.00322.x

Hernández-Perlines, F., & Xu, W. (2023). Innovation, sustainability, and performance in small firms: The moderating role of entrepreneurial orientation. *Journal of Small Business Management*, *61*(3), 987–1012. DOI: 10.1080/00472778.2021.1969653

Hidayah, K., & Dwijanto, D. (2023). Mathematical creative thinking ability viewed by adversity quotient in problem-based learning integrated stem. *Unnes J. Math. Educ.*, *12*(1), 72–83. DOI: 10.15294/ujme.v12i1.67560

Hörisch, J., Freeman, R. E., & Schaltegger, S. (2020). Applying stakeholder theory in sustainability management. *Organization & Environment*, *33*(1), 1–23. DOI: 10.1177/1086026619831447

Hossain, M., Levänen, J., & Wierenga, M. (2021). Frugal innovation for sustainability: A systematic literature review. *Business Strategy and the Environment*, *30*(4), 1707–1725. DOI: 10.1002/bse.2713

Howell, S. T., Niessner, M., & Yermack, D. (2017). Initial coin offerings: Financing growth with cryptocurrency token sales. *Review of Financial Studies*, *33*(9), 3925–3970. DOI: 10.1093/rfs/hhz131

Hoyt, R. E., & Liebenberg, A. P. (2015). Evidence of the value of enterprise risk management. [Object Identifier ] [DOI]. *The Bank of America Journal of Applied Corporate Finance*, *27*(1), 41–47. DOI: 10.1111/jacf.12103

Hu, Z. (2014). *Self-configuration, monitoring and control of physical entities via sensor and actuator networks* (Doctoral dissertation, Université Claude Bernard-Lyon I).

Huang, M., Geng, S., Yang, W., Law, K. M., & He, Y. (2024). Going beyond the role: How employees' perception of corporate social responsibility fuels proactive customer service performance. *Journal of Retailing and Consumer Services*, *76*, 103565. DOI: 10.1016/j.jretconser.2023.103565

Huang, R., Kale, S., Paramati, S. R., & Taghizadeh-Hesary, F. (2021). The nexus between financial inclusion and economic development: Comparison of old and new EU member countries. *Economic Analysis and Policy*, *69*, 1–15. DOI: 10.1016/j.eap.2020.10.007

Hudson, K., & Morgan, R. E. (2023). Board political ideological diversity and information exposure as antecedents to value creation and value appropriation. *Journal of Product Innovation Management*, *40*(6), 836–858. DOI: 10.1111/jpim.12688

Hu, S., Zhou, X., & Li, P. (2025). Tax incentives, market competition, and corporate innovation. *Finance Research Letters*, *77*(February), 107067. DOI: 10.1016/j.frl.2025.107067

Hwang, J., & Kim, H. (2023). Cost pressure, innovation, and performance in small hospitality firms. *International Journal of Hospitality Management*, *108*, 103352. DOI: 10.1016/j.ijhm.2022.103352

Iania, L., Nguyen, P. T., & Smedts, K. (2025). Stock returns and macroeconomic uncertainty. *International Review of Financial Analysis, 104*, 104263. DOI: 10.1016/j.irfa.2025.104263

Inigo, E. A., & Albareda, L. (2020). Understanding sustainable innovation as a complex adaptive system. *Business Strategy and the Environment, 29*(7), 3143–3161. DOI: 10.1002/bse.2567

Internet Live Stats. (2022). Internet usage statistics. Retrieved from https://www.internetlivestats.com

Ioannou, I., & Serafeim, G. (2019). The Consequences of Mandatory Corporate Sustainability Reporting. In McWilliams, A., Rupp, D. E., Siegel, D. S., Stahl, G. K., & Waldman, D. A. (Eds.), *The Oxford Handbook of Corporate Social Responsibility* (pp. 451–489). Oxford University Press., DOI: 10.1093/oxfordhb/9780198802280.013.20

Jacobson, S., Seavey, J., Goodman, J., Nichols, O., Williams, L., Márquez-García, M., & Barbosa, O. (2020). Integrating entrepreneurship and art to improve creative problem solving in fisheries education. *Fisheries (Bethesda, Md.), 45*(2), 84–89. DOI: 10.1002/fsh.10351

Jafari, A., Azarian, M., & Yu, H. (2022). Crowdfunding platforms and market democratization: Evidence from Kickstarter. *Journal of Business Research, 142*, 100–112. DOI: 10.1016/j.jbusres.2021.12.034

Jagtiani, J., & Lemieux, C. (2018). The roles of alternative data and machine learning in FinTech lending: Evidence from the LendingClub consumer platform (Working Paper). Federal Reserve Bank of Philadelphia.

Jain, A., & Dutta, D. (2018). Millennials and gamification: Guerilla tactics for making learning fun. *SA Journal of Human Resource Management, 6*(1), 29–44. DOI: 10.1177/2322093718796303

Janine, B. (2015). The Bio-Mimicry Institute.

Jara, A. J., Parra, M. C., & Skarmeta, A. F. (2012). Marketing 2.0 and consumer behavior in digital environments. *Procedia Computer Science, 10*, 852–858. DOI: 10.1016/j.procs.2012.06.115

Jeng, S.-L. (2025). *FinTech rankings of six Taiwan municipalities*. Asia Pacific Management Review. DOI: 10.1016/j.apmrv.2025.100398

Jensen, M. C., & Meckling, W. H. (1976). Theory of the firm: Managerial behavior, agency costs and ownership structure. *Journal of Financial Economics, 3*(4), 305–360. DOI: 10.1016/0304-405X(76)90026-X

Jezeer, R. E., Santos, M. J., Boot, R. G. A., Junginger, M., & Verweij, P. A. (2021). Effects of shade and certification on coffee biodiversity and ecosystem services. *Agriculture, Ecosystems & Environment, 304*, 107140. DOI: 10.1016/j.agee.2020.107140

Jiang, H., Hu, W., & Jiang, P. (2024). Does ESG performance affect corporate tax avoidance? Evidence from China. *Finance Research Letters, 61*, 105056. DOI: 10.1016/j.frl.2024.105056

Jiang, S., Bibi, S., Lyu, J., Khan, A., & Li, Z. (2025). Corporate social responsibility needs base philosophy: An integrative multidimensional approach to hospitality employees' green innovative behaviors. *International Journal of Hospitality Management, 124*, 103943. DOI: 10.1016/j.ijhm.2024.103943

Jing, W., & Loang, O. K. (2024). China's cultural tourism: Strategies for authentic experiences and enhanced visitor satisfaction. *International Journal of Business and Technology Management, 6*(1), 566–575.

Jiraporn, P., Singh, M., & Lee, C. I. (2009). Ineffective corporate governance: Director busyness and board committee memberships. *Journal of Banking & Finance, 33*(5), 819–828. DOI: 10.1016/j.jbankfin.2008.09.020

John, K., John, T. A., & Han, Y. (2022). Success factors in reward-based crowdfunding campaigns: Evidence from Kickstarter. *Electronic Commerce Research and Applications, 52*, 101110. DOI: 10.1016/j.elerap.2021.101110

Jouppi, N., Kurian, G., Li, S., Ma, P., Nagarajan, R., Nai, L., & Patterson, D. A. (2023, June). Tpu v4: An optically reconfigurable supercomputer for machine learning with hardware support for embeddings. In *Proceedings of the 50th annual international symposium on computer architecture* (pp. 1-14). DOI: 10.1145/3579371.3589350

Jurevicius, O. (2023, December 1). VRIO framework. Strategic Management Insight.

Jurevicius, O. (2023, October 24). Resource-based view. Strategic Management Insight.

Kalefa, H., & Gado, S. (2024). Enhancing hotel sustainability through ecological and technological integration. JES. *Journal of Engineering Sciences, 52*(1), 145–174.

Kandpal, V., Jaswal, A., Santibanez Gonzalez, E. D., & Agarwal, N. (2024). Corporate social responsibility (CSR) and ESG reporting: redefining business in the twenty-first century. In *Sustainable energy transition: Circular economy and sustainable financing for environmental, social and governance (ESG) practices* (pp. 239–272). Springer Nature Switzerland. DOI: 10.1007/978-3-031-52943-6_8

Kang, H. G., Moon, A., & Jeon, S. (2024). Examining the Generative Artificial Intelligence Landscape: Current Status and Policy Strategies. *Asia pacific journal of information systems, 34*(1), 150-190.

Kang, J. (2018). Mobile payment in FinTech environment: Trends, security challenges, and services. *Human-Centric Computing and Information Sciences, 8*(1), 1–16. DOI: 10.1186/s13673-018-0155-4

Kannaa, K. D., & Arunachalam, N. (2024). How changes in the interest rate perform in the Indian stock market.

Kantarcı, Ö., Başaran, B., & Kılınç, M. (2017). *Türkiye'de e-ticaretin gelişimi ve geleceği*. TÜSİAD Yayınları.

Karim, K. E., Li, J., Lin, K. J., & Robin, A. (2022). Do directors have style? Board interlock and accounting properties. *Journal of Business Finance & Accounting, 49*(1–2), 3–32. DOI: 10.1111/jbfa.12567

Kathirvel, A., Naren, A. K., & Saravanan, N. (2025). Entrepreneurship and business culture in rural area. In *Digital Disruption in Hospitality* (pp. 187–212). Sustainable Hospitality., DOI: 10.1108/978-1-83662-360-120251009

Katsikas, E., Brahma, S., & Wangeci, S. M. (2016). *Effects of interest rates and exchange rates on bank stock returns.* In *Handbook of Frontier Markets*. DOI: 10.1016/B978-0-12-803776-8.00005-7

Kauffman, R. J., & Naldi, M. (2020). Digital transformation in crowdfunding platforms and online markets. *Electronic Commerce Research and Applications, 41*, 100969. DOI: 10.1016/j.elerap.2020.100969

Kemper, A., & Martin, R. (2010). After the fall: The global financial crisis as a test of corporate social responsibility theories. *European Management Review, 7*(4), 229–239. DOI: 10.1057/emr.2010.18

Khalil, N., Che Abdullah, S. N., Haron, S. N., & Hamid, M. Y. (2024). A review of green practices and initiatives from stakeholder's perspectives towards sustainable hotel operations and performance impact. *Journal of Facilities Management, 22*(4), 653–682. DOI: 10.1108/JFM-03-2022-0025

Khan, M. M., & Kumar, M. D. (2023). STUDY ON IMPACT OF INTEREST RATES ON THE STOCK MARKET. *Kristu Jayanti Journal of Management Sciences (KJMS)*, 64-75.

Khan, I., & Gunwant, D. F. (2024). Reducing gender-based unemployment in India: The impact of social inclusion and foreign funds inflows. *Indian Growth and Development Review*, *17*(1), 86–102. DOI: 10.1108/IGDR-07-2023-0103

Khan, M. I., & Iqbal, A. (2024). Integrating ESG with corporate investment decision-making. In *The Emerald Handbook of Ethical Finance and Corporate Social Responsibility: A Framework for Sustainable Development* (pp. 329–350). Emerald Publishing Limited. DOI: 10.1108/978-1-80455-406-720241014

Khater, M., Ibrahim, O., Sayed, M. N. E., & Faik, M. (2024). Legal frameworks for sustainable tourism: Balancing environmental conservation and economic development. *Current Issues in Tourism*, •••, 1–22.

Khatib, S. F. A. (2025a). An assessment of methods to deal with endogeneity in corporate governance and reporting research. *Corporate Governance (Bradford)*, *25*(3), 606–630. DOI: 10.1108/CG-12-2023-0507

Khatib, S. F. A. (2025b). Social Trust, Environmental Violations, and Remedial Actions in China. *Social and Environmental Accountability Journal*, *1–3*(1), 81–83. Advance online publication. DOI: 10.1080/0969160X.2025.2465948

Khatri, S., & Srivastava, H. (2022). COVID-19 and digital finance adoption. *Journal of Financial Services*, *12*(2).

Khatter, A. (2025). Challenges and Solutions for Corporate Social Responsibility in the Hospitality Industry. *Challenges*, *16*(1), 9. DOI: 10.3390/challe16010009

Kilani, A. A.-H. Z., Kakeesh, D., Al-Weshah, G. A., & Al-Debei, M. M. (2023). Consumer post-adoption of e-wallet: An extended UTAUT2 perspective with trust. *Journal of Open Innovation*.

Kim, D. Y., Park, J., & Morrison, A. M. (2008). A model of traveller acceptance of mobile technology. *International Journal of Tourism Research*, *10*(5), 393–407. DOI: 10.1002/jtr.669

Kim, S. (2019). The fourth industrial revolution: Trends and impacts on the world of work. In McGrath, S., Mulder, M., Papier, J., & Suart, R. (Eds.), *Handbook of vocational education and training*. Springer., DOI: 10.1007/978-3-319-94532-3

Kirby, E., & Worner, S. (2014). Crowd-funding: An infant industry growing fast. *IOSCO Research Report*, 23–35.

Kotler, P., Kartajaya, H., & Setiawan, I. (2010). *Marketing 3.0: From products to customers to the human spirit*. Wiley. DOI: 10.1002/9781118257883

Kraus, S., Breier, M., Jones, P., & Hughes, M. (2022). Individual entrepreneurial orientation and new venture performance: The role of digital technologies. *International Journal of Entrepreneurial Behaviour & Research, 28*(1), 1–24. DOI: 10.1108/IJEBR-07-2021-0563

Kraus, S., Burtscher, J., Vallaster, C., & Angerer, M. (2020). Sustainable entrepreneurship orientation: A reflection on status-quo research. *Sustainability, 12*(12), 4873. DOI: 10.3390/su12124873

Kularathne, S., Perera, A., Rathnayake, N., Rathnayake, U., & Hoshino, Y. (2024). Analyzing the impact of socioeconomic indicators on gender inequality in Sri Lanka: A machine learning-based approach. *PLoS One, 19*(12), e0312395. DOI: 10.1371/journal.pone.0312395 PMID: 39724101

Kumar, A., & Metta, D. S. (2024). AI-driven precision oncology: Predictive biomarker discovery and personalized treatment optimization using genomic data. *Int J Adv Res Publ Rev, 1*(3), 21–38. DOI: 10.55248/gengpi.5.0224.0421

Kumar, R. (2013). The effect of macroeconomic factors on Indian stock market performance: A factor analysis approach. *IOSR. Journal of Economics and Finance, 1*(3), 14–21.

Kumar, R. (2024). Economic growth, structural changes and employment linkages in India. *Review of Economics and Political Science, 9*(4), 346–357. DOI: 10.1108/REPS-07-2022-0051

Kumar, S. (2024). Indian experience of CSR and corporate governance in the post-liberalised era. *The Indian Journal of Public Administration, 70*(4), 829–842. DOI: 10.1177/00195561241248338

Kumar, V., Dixit, A., Javalgi, R. G., & Dass, M. (2021). Digital transformation of marketing: A multi-level framework. *Journal of the Academy of Marketing Science, 49*(1), 24–54. DOI: 10.1007/s11747-015-0426-9

Kuppuswamy, V., & Bayus, B. L. (2018). Crowdfunding creative ideas: The dynamics of project backers. *Management Science, 64*(3), 1005–1026.

Kuri, M. M., & Kattimani, S. ECONOMIC INDICATORS AND INDIAN STOCK MARKET VOLATILITY: AN EMPIRICAL ANALYSIS.

Latan, H., Chiappetta Jabbour, C. J., Lopes de Sousa Jabbour, A. B., Ali, M., & Pereira, V. (2022). Career satisfaction in the public sector: Implications for a more sustainable and socially responsible human resource management. *Human Resource Management Journal, 32*(4), 844–863. DOI: 10.1111/1748-8583.12469

Lee, M.-C. (2009). Factors influencing the adoption of internet banking: An integration of TAM and TPB with perceived risk and perceived benefit. *Electronic Commerce Research and Applications, 8*(3), 130–141. DOI: 10.1016/j.elerap.2008.11.006

Lee, S., Hwang, D. H. S., Shin, M., & Kang, K. H. (2025). Strategic corporate social responsibility in the tourism and hospitality industry: Conceptual proposal. *Tourism Economics, 31*(5), 813–826. DOI: 10.1177/13548166241299140

Lehdonvirta, V. (2025). *Cloud empires: How digital platforms are overtaking the state and how we can regain control.* MIT Press.

Leibenstein, H. (1979). A branch of economics is missing: Micro-micro theory. *Journal of Economic Literature, 17*(2), 477–502.

Leigh, N. G. (2024). *Planning local economic development: Theory and practice.* SAGE publications.

Lewis, M. (2008). Access to saloons, wet voter turnout, and statewide prohibition referenda, 1907–1919. *Social Science History, 32*(3), 373–404. DOI: 10.1017/S0145553200013997

Li, L., Sha, Y., Xie, H., & Shao, X. (2025). *Liquidity, inflation, and interest rates: A wavelet-based approach across major economies.* (From your PDF – Journal details available in file.)

Li, C., Chen, H., Xie, W., & Wang, P. (2024). Tax incentives for human capital accumulation and enterprise innovation quality: Evidence of a quasi-natural experiment in China. *Finance Research Letters, 70*(August), 106342. DOI: 10.1016/j.frl.2024.106342

Liébana-Cabanillas, F., Sánchez-Fernández, J., & Muñoz-Leiva, F. (2014). Antecedents of the adoption of new mobile payment systems: The moderating effect of age. *Computers in Human Behavior, 35*, 464–478. DOI: 10.1016/j.chb.2014.03.022

Liu, J., Huang, B., & Hu, Y. (2024). The influence of tax incentives on market segmentation in the context of a unified national market. *Finance Research Letters, 65*(January), 105591. DOI: 10.1016/j.frl.2024.105591

Liu, J., & Wang, J. (2017). Developing entrepreneurial resilience: Implications for human resource development. *European Journal of Training and Development, 41*(6), 519–539. DOI: 10.1108/EJTD-12-2016-0090

Liu, X., Manzoor, A., Wang, C., Zhang, L., & Manzoor, Z. (2020). The role of FinTech in sustainable banking: A review. *Sustainability, 12*(24), 10591.

Liu, Z., Qi, Z., Tian, Q., Clark, J. S., & Zhang, Z. (2024). The impact of digital finance on farmers' adoption of eco-agricultural technology: Evidence from rice–crayfish co-cultivation technology in China. *Preprints.*

Loos, C., & Spraul, K. (2025). The why, how, and when of CSR managers' internal legitimation strategies. *Journal of Management Studies*, *62*(7), 2830–2858. DOI: 10.1111/joms.13145

López, O. L., Rosabal, O. M., Ruiz-Guirola, D. E., Raghuwanshi, P., Mikhaylov, K., Lovén, L., & Iyer, S. (2023). Energy-sustainable IoT connectivity: Vision, technological enablers, challenges, and future directions. *IEEE Open Journal of the Communications Society*, *4*, 2609–2666. DOI: 10.1109/OJCOMS.2023.3323832

Lorenzo, V. d. (2018, May 16). How biotechnology is evolving in the fourth industrial revolution. World Economic Forum. https://www.weforum.org/agenda/2018/05/biotechnology-evolve-fourth-industrial-revolution/

Lu, C., & Zhu, K. (2021). Do tax expenses crowd in or crowd out corporate social responsibility performance? Evidence from Chinese listed firms. *Journal of Cleaner Production*, *327*, 129433. DOI: 10.1016/j.jclepro.2021.129433

Lüdeke-Freund, F., Gold, S., & Bocken, N. M. P. (2020). A review and typology of circular economy business model patterns. *Journal of Industrial Ecology*, *24*(2), 331–345. DOI: 10.1111/jiec.12985

Lundqvist, S. A. (2014). An exploratory study of enterprise risk management: Pillars of ERM. *Journal of Accounting, Auditing & Finance*, *29*(3), 393–429. DOI: 10.1177/0148558X14535780

Macaveiu, C. (2025). Promoting labour rights and human rights in hospitality: Striving for a workplace culture that disrupts exploitative practices. In *Tourism and Hospitality for Humanity* (pp. 157–176). Edward Elgar Publishing. DOI: 10.4337/9781035344307.00013

Madine, M., Salah, K., Jayaraman, R., Battah, A., Hasan, H., & Yaqoob, I. (2022). Blockchain and NFTs for time-bound access and monetization of private data. *IEEE Access : Practical Innovations, Open Solutions*, *10*, 94186–94202. DOI: 10.1109/ACCESS.2022.3204274

Ma, F., Lu, X., & Huang, D. (2022). Macroeconomic attention and stock market return predictability. *Journal of International Financial Markets, Institutions and Money*, *79*, 101603. DOI: 10.1016/j.intfin.2022.101603

Magdy, A., & Salem, I. E. (2024). Understanding the impact of work environment on employee well-being and cynicism: Insights from the hotel industry. *Tourism and Hospitality Management, 30*(4), 531–542. DOI: 10.20867/thm.30.4.8

Malik, S. I., Tawafak, R. M., Alfarsi, G., Ashfaque, M. W., & Mathew, R. (2021). A model for enhancing algorithmic thinking in programming education using PAAM. *International Journal of Interactive Mobile Technologies, 15*(9), 37. DOI: 10.3991/ijim.v15i09.20617

Mallon, M., & Fainshmidt, S. (2020). Who's Hiding in the Shadows? Organized Crime and Informal Entrepreneurship in 39 Economies. *Journal of Management, 48*(1), 211–237. DOI: 10.1177/0149206320978821

Mandalapu, V., Elluri, L., Vyas, P., & Roy, N. (2023). Crime prediction using machine learning and deep learning: A systematic review and future directions. *IEEE Access : Practical Innovations, Open Solutions, 11*, 60153–60170. DOI: 10.1109/ACCESS.2023.3286344

Mansoor, M., Jam, F. A., & Khan, T. I. (2025). Fostering eco-friendly behaviors in hospitality: Engaging customers through green practices, social influence, and personal dynamics. *International Journal of Contemporary Hospitality Management, 37*(5), 1804–1826. DOI: 10.1108/IJCHM-07-2024-1023

Markose, N., Vazhakkatte Tazhathethil, B., & George, B. (2022). Sustainability initiatives for green tourism development: The case of Wayanad, India. *Journal of Risk and Financial Management, 15*(2), 52. DOI: 10.3390/jrfm15020052

Markowska, M., & Strahl, D. (2024). Covid-19 impact on labour market in Eu countries – differences in men and women employment rate tendencies. *Technological and Economic Development of Economy, 30*(4), 854–875. DOI: 10.3846/tede.2024.20811

Martinelli, E., Acciaro, M., & Ferrari, C. (2021). COVID-19 and changes in consumer behavior. *Transport Policy, 106*, 1–10.

Martínez-Cañas, R., Ruiz-Palomino, P., Linuesa-Langreo, J., & Blázquez-Resino, J. J. (2024). Ethical marketing and consumer trust in the digital era. *Journal of Business Ethics, 189*(1), 115–132. DOI: 10.1007/s10551-023-05421-6

Martinravi, C. P., & Krishnasamy, K. (2025). Unleashing the potential of MSMEs in India: A strategic analysis. *Journal of the International Council for Small Business, 6*(1), 123–143. DOI: 10.1080/26437015.2024.2397664

Mathur, H. P. (2022). Conceptual development of factors driving FinTech adoption by farmers. Purushartha: A Journal of Management. *Ethics and Spirituality*, *15*(1), 39–50.

Matten, D., & Moon, J. (2008). "Implicit" and "Explicit" CSR: A Conceptual Framework for a Comparative Understanding of Corporate Social Responsibility. *Academy of Management Review*, *33*(2), 404–424. DOI: 10.5465/amr.2008.31193458

McCarty, W. (2024). International Business Membership With the United Nations Global Compact (Doctoral dissertation, The Chicago School of Professional Psychology).

McGirr, L. (2015). *The war on alcohol: Prohibition and the rise of the American state*. WW Norton & Company.

McKnight, D. H., Choudhury, V., & Kacmar, C. (2002). Developing and validating trust measures for e-commerce: An integrative typology. *Information Systems Research*, *13*(3), 334–359. DOI: 10.1287/isre.13.3.334.81

Mdoda, S. S., Dube, K., & Montsiemang, T. (2024). Tackling Water and Waste Management Challenges Within the Tourism and Hospitality Industry: A Sustainable Development Goals Perspective. *Water (Basel)*, *16*(24), 3545. DOI: 10.3390/w16243545

Mendonça, H. F., & Díaz, R. R. R. (2023). Can ignorance about the interest rate and macroeconomic surprises affect the stock market return? Evidence from a large emerging economy. *The North American Journal of Economics and Finance*.

Meng, Z., Bhatti, S. M., Naveed, R. T., Kanwal, S., & Adnan, M. (2024). Green sustainability in the hotel sector: The role of CSR, intrinsic green motivation, and personal environmental norms. *PLoS One*, *19*(6), e0295850. DOI: 10.1371/journal.pone.0295850 PMID: 38935798

Menjívar, C. (2006). Liminal legality: Salvadoran and Guatemalan immigrants' lives in the United States. *AJS; American Journal of Sociology*, *111*(4), 999–1037. DOI: 10.1086/499509

Mensah, C., Azila-Gbettor, E. M., Novieto, D. T., Coffie, G. H., & Adzivor, E. K. (2025). Tracing the evolution of environmental practices research in the hotel industry: A mixed-review perspective. *Research in Hospitality Management*, *15*(2), 171–191. DOI: 10.1080/22243534.2025.2483753

Mhlanga, D. (2023). Exploring the evolution of artificial intelligence and the fourth industrial revolution an overview. *FinTech and Artificial Intelligence for Sustainable Development: The Role of Smart Technologies in Achieving Development Goals*, 15-39.

Michael Chui, J. M. (2020). The bio revolution: Innovations transforming economies, societies, and our lives. McKinsey & Company. https://www.mckinsey.com/industries/life-sciences/our-insights/the-bio-revolution-innovations-transforming-economies-societies-and-our-lives

Michaelidou, N., Siamagka, N. T., & Christodoulides, G. (2020). Usage, barriers, and measurement of social media marketing: An exploratory investigation of small and medium B2B brands. *Industrial Marketing Management, 87*, 115–128. DOI: 10.1016/j.indmarman.2020.04.010

Michelon, G., Pilonato, S., & Ricceri, F. (2015). CSR reporting practices and the quality of disclosure: An empirical analysis. *Critical Perspectives on Accounting, 33*, 59–78. DOI: 10.1016/j.cpa.2014.10.003

Miller, A. (2019). Permissioned and permissionless blockchains. *Blockchain for distributed systems security*, 193-204.

Mirabeau, L., Maguire, S., & Hardy, C. (2022). Bridging practice and process: A dynamic view of entrepreneurial innovation. *Organization Studies, 43*(6), 889–912. DOI: 10.1177/01708406211006846

Mishra, N. (2025, June 18). *India's economic duality: formal dreams, informal realities*. Governance Now. https://www.governancenow.com/views/columns/indias-economic-duality-formal-dreams-informal-realities

Misra, P. (2018). An investigation of the macroeconomic factors affecting the Indian stock market. *Australasian Accounting, Business and Finance Journal, 12*(2).

Misra, P. (2018). An investigation of the macroeconomic factors affecting the Indian stock market. *Australasian Accounting. Business and Finance Journal, 12*(2), 71–92.

Mohamed, K. S. (2019). IoT physical layer: Sensors, actuators, controllers and programming. In *The Era of Internet of Things: Towards a Smart World* (pp. 21–47). Springer International Publishing. DOI: 10.1007/978-3-030-18133-8_2

Mohanarajesh, K. (2024). Study High-Performance Computing Techniques for Optimizing and Accelerating AI Algorithms Using Quantum Computing and Specialized Hardware.

Mollick, E. (2014). The dynamics of crowdfunding: An exploratory study. *Journal of Business Venturing, 29*(1), 1–16. DOI: 10.1016/j.jbusvent.2013.06.005

Mollick, E., & Kuppuswamy, V. (2014). After the campaign: Outcomes of crowdfunding. *Management Science, 60*(5), 1–18.

Montañés-Del Río, M. Á., Rodríguez-Cornejo, V., Rodríguez-Castro, P. I., & Herrera-Madueño, J. (2025). The Implementation of Corporate Social Responsibility Policies in the Tourism Industry and Sustainable Development Goals: A Review of Progress, Challenges, and Opportunities. *Sustainability (Basel), 17*(13), 6044. DOI: 10.3390/su17136044

Montiel, I., & Delgado-Ceballos, J. (2021). Defining and measuring corporate sustainability. *Organization & Environment, 34*(1), 1–30. DOI: 10.1177/1086026619871386

Moscariello, N., Pizzo, M., Ricciardi, G., Mallardo, G., & Fattorusso, P. (2024). The anti-corruption compliance models in a multinational company: A single case study. *Business Strategy and the Environment, 33*(1), 70–80. DOI: 10.1002/bse.3331

Mourtzis, D. (2021). Towards the 5th industrial revolution: A literature review and a framework for process optimization based on big data analytics and semantics. *Journal of Machine Engineering, 21*(3), 5–39. DOI: 10.36897/jme/141834

Moyeen, A., & Mehjabeen, M. (2024). CSR research in the hotel industry: How it relates to promoting the SDGs. *Social Responsibility Journal, 20*(9), 1770–1786. DOI: 10.1108/SRJ-01-2024-0032

Mthombeni, Z. M. (2024). A quantitative analysis of public attitudes towards the fourth industrial revolution: An integrated technology adoption model in South Africa. *Doctoral dissertation.*

Muehlmann, S. (2018). The gender of the war on drugs. *Annual Review of Anthropology, 47*(1), 315–330. DOI: 10.1146/annurev-anthro-102317-050214

Muñoz, P., & Cohen, B. (2020). Sustainable entrepreneurship research: Taking stock and looking ahead. *Business Strategy and the Environment, 29*(3), 943–957. DOI: 10.1002/bse.2416

Murtaza, S. H., Khan, A., & Mustafa, S. M. (2024). Eco-centric success: Stakeholder approaches to sustainable performance via green improvisation behavior and environmental orientation in the hotel industry. *Business Strategy and the Environment, 33*(7), 7273–7286. DOI: 10.1002/bse.3860

Nadeem, M., Gyapong, E., & Ahmed, A. (2020). Board gender diversity and environmental, social, and economic value creation: Does family ownership matter? *Business Strategy and the Environment*, *29*(3), 1268–1284. DOI: 10.1002/bse.2432

Nambisan, S. (2017). Digital entrepreneurship: Toward a digital technology perspective of entrepreneurship. *Entrepreneurship Theory and Practice*, *41*(6), 1029–1055. DOI: 10.1111/etap.12254

Nambisan, S., & Baron, R. A. (2021). On the costs of digital entrepreneurship: Role conflict, stress, and venture performance in digital platform-based ecosystems. *Journal of Business Research*, *125*, 520–532. DOI: 10.1016/j.jbusres.2019.06.037

Nambisan, S., Siegel, D., & Kenney, M. (2018). updated relevance). On open innovation, platforms, and entrepreneurship. *Strategic Entrepreneurship Journal*, *12*(3), 354–368. DOI: 10.1002/sej.1300

Ngaruiya, J., Mathuva, D. M., & Obi, P. (2025). *Do changes in interest rate regulation affect stock returns? An event study approach on the Kenyan banking sector stocks*. Journal of Financial Regulation and Compliance.

Nguyen, K. H., Trinh, A. T., Tran, M. D., & Duong, T. T. T. (2025). Uncovering the Evolution of Brand Transparency in Corporate Social Responsibility: A Holistic Perspective. *Corporate Social Responsibility and Environmental Management*, *32*(6), 1–20. DOI: 10.1002/csr.70099

Nicoletti, B. (2017). *The future of FinTech*. Springer. DOI: 10.1007/978-3-319-51415-4

Ni, H., Liu, W., & Yang, Z. (2024). Training investment, human capital upgrading and firm innovation: The role of government training subsidies. *Kybernetes*, *53*(9), 2934–2966. DOI: 10.1108/K-11-2022-1617

Nisula, A., & Olander, H. (2020). The role of motivations and self-concepts in university graduate entrepreneurs' creativity and resilience. *Journal of Small Business Management*, *61*(2), 265–294. DOI: 10.1080/00472778.2020.1760030

Nogueira, E., Gomes, S., & Lopes, J. M. (2025). Unveiling triple bottom line's influence on business performance. *Discover Sustainability*, *6*(1), 43. DOI: 10.1007/s43621-025-00804-x

Nolin, J. (2014). Cultural policy by proxy: Internet-based cultural consumption as a copygray zone. *International Journal of Cultural Policy*, *21*(3), 273–290. DOI: 10.1080/10286632.2014.923415

O'Rourke, B. (2011). *Dealing Death and Drugs: The Big Business of Dope in the US and Mexico, an Argument to End the Prohibition of Marijuana*. Cinco Puntos Press.

OECD. (2019). *University–industry collaboration: New evidence and policy options*. OECD Publishing., DOI: 10.1787/e9c1e648-

OECD. (2020). *Smart cities and inclusive growth*. OECD Publishing., DOI: 10.1787/3a8fdbab-

OECD. (2021). *The digital transformation of SMEs*. OECD Publishing.

Oikonomou, I., Yin, C., & Zhao, L. (2020). Investment horizon and corporate social performance: The virtuous circle of long-term institutional ownership and responsible firm conduct. *European Journal of Finance*, *26*(1), 14–40. DOI: 10.1080/1351847X.2019.1660197

Oke, J. A., Karimzadeh, S., Oviroh, P. O., Ukoba, K., Imoisili, P. E., & Jen, T. C. (2025). *Smart Materials and Energy in the Fourth Industrial Revolution*. CRC Press. DOI: 10.1201/9781003604488

Olayinka, O. H.Olalekan Hamed Olayinka. (2021). Big data integration and real-time analytics for enhancing operational efficiency and market responsiveness. *Int J Sci Res Arch*, *4*(1), 280–296. DOI: 10.30574/ijsra.2021.4.1.0179

Onyekwelu, N. P., Ezeafulukwe, C., Owolabi, O. R., Asuzu, O. F., Bello, B. G., & Onyekwelu, S. C. (2024). Ethics and corporate social responsibility in HR: A comprehensive review of policies and practices. *International Journal of Science and Research Archive*, *11*(1), 1294–1303. DOI: 10.30574/ijsra.2024.11.1.0216

Osterwalder, A., & Pigneur, Y. (2010). *Business model generation*. John Wiley & Sons.

Othman, N., Marthandan, G., & Aziz, K. (2022). Measuring the motives of informal entrepreneurs. *F1000Research*, 11. DOI: 10.12688/f1000research.73706.2

Otieno, D. A., Ngugi, R. W., & Wawire, N. H. (2017). Effects of interest rate on stock market returns in Kenya. *International Journal of Economics and Finance*, *9*(8), 40–50. DOI: 10.5539/ijef.v9n8p40

Ozili, P. K. (2018). Impact of digital finance on financial inclusion and stability. *Borsa Istanbul Review*, *18*(4), 329–340. DOI: 10.1016/j.bir.2017.12.003

Pai, C. H., Zhang, Y., Wang, Y. L., Li, K., & Shang, Y. (2025). Current challenges and opportunities in cultural heritage preservation through sustainable tourism practices. *Current Issues in Tourism*, •••, 1–19.

Pal, S., & Garg, A. K. (2019). Macroeconomic surprises and stock market responses—A study on Indian stock market. *Cogent Economics & Finance*, *7*(1), 1598248. DOI: 10.1080/23322039.2019.1598248

Pandey, V., Kumar, S., Gupta, S., & Khatri, N. (2024). Unlocking sustainability: Prioritizing barriers for SME success in India with AHP analysis. *Journal of Global Entrepreneurship Research*, *14*(1), 25. DOI: 10.1007/s40497-024-00395-3

Panke, D., & Stapel, S. (2024). Cooperation between international organizations: Demand, supply, and restraint. *The Review of International Organizations*, *19*(2), 269–305. DOI: 10.1007/s11558-023-09506-3

Panwar, V., & Nidugala, G. K. (2017, February). Indian Stock Market Reaction to Interest Rate and Inflation Announcements. In *19th International Scientific Conference on Economic and Social Development* (pp. 424-434).

Papadamou, S., Sidiropoulos, M., & Spyromitros, E. (2017). Interest rate dynamic effect on stock returns and central bank transparency: Evidence from emerging markets. *Research in International Business and Finance*, *39*, 951–962. DOI: 10.1016/j.ribaf.2016.01.020

Papafloratos, T., Pantazi, T., & Vlachos, V. (2025). CSR reporting in tourism: The case of the Greek hospitality industry. *International Journal of Knowledge Management in Tourism and Hospitality*, *4*(1), 1–16. DOI: 10.1504/IJKMTH.2025.145026

Papallou, E., Katafygiotou, M., & Dimopoulos, T. (2024). Emerging sustainability trends in tourist facilities: A comparative assessment of multiple hotels and resorts. *Sustainability (Basel)*, *16*(9), 3536. DOI: 10.3390/su16093536

Parker, N. (2020). Black codes and slave codes. DOI: 10.1093/obo/9780190280024-0083

Parker, G. G., Van Alstyne, M. W., & Choudary, S. P. (2016). *Platform revolution: How networked markets are transforming the economy and how to make them work for you*. W. W. Norton & Company.

Park, K., & Rim, H. (2025). Publics' Expectation Toward Ethical Leadership and Ethical Corporate Social Responsibility (CSR): Evidence From the US and South Korea. *Business Ethics, the Environment & Responsibility*, *34*(4), 1998–2012. DOI: 10.1111/beer.12749

Pásková, M., & Zelenka, J. (2024). Social responsibility in tourism and its specific features. In *Social Responsibility in Tourism: Applications, Best-Practices, and Case Studies* (pp. 85–135). Springer Nature Switzerland. DOI: 10.1007/978-3-031-61609-9_4

Pavlou, P. A. (2003). Consumer acceptance of electronic commerce: Integrating trust and risk with the technology acceptance model. *International Journal of Electronic Commerce*, *7*(3), 101–134. DOI: 10.1080/10864415.2003.11044275

Pavunraj, D., Kumar, A. M., & Anbumaheshwari, K. (2025). AI in personalized treatment planning. In *AI insights on nuclear medicine* (pp. 117–142). IGI Global Scientific Publishing. DOI: 10.4018/979-8-3373-1275-0.ch006

PeConga, E., Gauthier, G., Holloway, A., Walker, R., Rosencrans, P., Zoellner, L., & Bedard-Gilligan, M. (2020). Resilience is spreading mental health within the covid-19 pandemic. *Psychological Trauma : Theory, Research, Practice and Policy*, *12*(S1), S47–S48. DOI: 10.1037/tra0000874 PMID: 32496106

Pehe, V., & Kupka, P. (2024). Legal, illegal, either way informal: Examining continuities of small-scale entrepreneurship between late socialism and postsocialism in Czechia. *Journal of Contemporary Central and Eastern Europe*, *32*(2), 257–277. DOI: 10.1080/25739638.2024.2374151

Peng, C., & Liu, P. (2025). How and when does customer mistreatment occur? Testing the predictive effect of future focus through construal-level theory. *International Journal of Contemporary Hospitality Management*, *37*(10), 3491–3517. DOI: 10.1108/IJCHM-12-2024-1936

Perfecto, I., Vandermeer, J., & Philpott, S. M. (2023). Ecological complexity and sustainability in coffee agroecosystems. *Journal of Cleaner Production*, *382*, 135301. DOI: 10.1016/j.jclepro.2022.135301

Pourtaheri, M., Torabi, Z. A., Khavarian-Garmsir, A. R., Sajadi, S., & Hall, C. M. (2024). Ecolodge Tourism Dynamics: A Village-Level Analysis of Marketing and Policy Indicators in Iran's Hawraman Region. *Sustainability (Basel)*, *16*(12), 5072. DOI: 10.3390/su16125072

Prahalad, C. K. (2012). Bottom of the pyramid as a source of breakthrough innovations. *Journal of Product Innovation Management*, *29*(1), 6–12. DOI: 10.1111/j.1540-5885.2011.00874.x

Prathibha, I., & Leela Rani, D. (2025). Rainfall forecasting in India using combined machine learning approach and soft computing techniques : A HYBRID MODEL. *International Journal of Computational and Experimental Science and Engineering*, *11*(1). Advance online publication. DOI: 10.22399/ijcesen.785

Priya, V. (2025). Economic empowerment through employment in India: A gendered perspective on growth. *International Journal For Multidisciplinary Research*, *7*(4), 54897. Advance online publication. DOI: 10.36948/ijfmr.2025.v07i04.54897

Putra, R., Rahman, H., &, A. (2024). Illegal entrepreneur: necessity base entrepreneur or opportunity base entrepreneur (Exploratory Study of Illegal Entrepreneurship in Padang City). *Journal Publicuho*. DOI: 10.35817/publicuho.v7i3.495

Putri, V. R., Zakaria, N. B., Said, J., & Azis, M. A. A. (2023). Do Foreign Ownership, Executive Incentives, Corporate Social Responsibility Activity and Audit Quality Affect Corporate Tax Avoidance? *Indian Journal of Corporate Governance*, *16*(2), 218–239. DOI: 10.1177/09746862231205648

Putzier, M. L. (2017). *The readiness of the South African private and public sector for the fourth industrial revolution*. Nelson Mandela University.

Qian, K., Zhang, Z., Yamamoto, Y., & Schuller, B. W. (2021). Artificial intelligence internet of things for the elderly: From assisted living to health-care monitoring. *IEEE Signal Processing Magazine*, *38*(4), 78–88. DOI: 10.1109/MSP.2021.3057298

Qin, Y. S., & Men, L. R. (2023). Exploring the impact of internal communication on employee psychological well-being during the COVID-19 pandemic: The mediating role of employee organizational trust. *International Journal of Business Communication*, *60*(4), 1197–1219. DOI: 10.1177/23294884221081838

Queiroz, M. M., Telles, R., & Bonilla, S. H. (2021). Blockchain and supply chain sustainability: A systematic literature review. *Journal of Cleaner Production*, *316*, 128301. DOI: 10.1016/j.jclepro.2021.128301

Rahi, S., Mansour, M. M. O., Alghizzawi, M., & Alnaser, F. M. (2019). Integration of UTAUT model in internet banking adoption context: The mediating role of performance expectancy and effort expectancy. *Journal of Research in Interactive Marketing*, *13*(3), 411–435. DOI: 10.1108/JRIM-02-2018-0032

Rahman, M. M., Razimi, M. S. A., Ariffin, A. S., & Hashim, N. (2024). Navigating moral landscape: Islamic ethical choices and sustainability in Halal meat production and consumption. *Discover Sustainability*, *5*(1), 225. DOI: 10.1007/s43621-024-00388-y

Rammohan, B., Partheeban, P., Ranganathan, R., & Balaraman, S. (2024). Groundwater quality prediction and analysis using machine learning models and geospatial technology. *Sustainability (Basel)*, *16*(22), 9848. DOI: 10.3390/su16229848

Ramos Farroñán, E. V., Farfán Chilicaus, G. C., Cruz Salinas, L. E., Correa Rojas, L., Chuquitucto Cotrina, L. K., Licapa-Redolfo, G. S., Vera Zelada, P., & Vera Zelada, L. A. (2025). Green Finance and the Energy Transition: A Systematic Review of Economic Instruments for Renewable Energy Deployment in Emerging Economies. *Energies*, *18*(17), 4560. DOI: 10.3390/en18174560

Ramsbottom, O., Duffy, M., O'dor, J., & Watts, J. (2025). Legal Responsibilities. In Responsible Strategic Thinking for Business and Society (pp. 204-221). Routledge. DOI: 10.4324/9781003475545-8

Rangaswamy, A., Moch, N., Felten, C., & van Bruggen, G. (2020). The role of crowdfunding platforms in innovation ecosystems. *Journal of Interactive Marketing*, *51*, 1–16. DOI: 10.1016/j.intmar.2020.01.003

Rashid Al-Shamsi, I., & Shannaq, B. (2024). Leveraging clustering techniques to drive sustainable economic innovation in the India–Gulf interchange. *Cogent Social Sciences*, *10*(1), 2341483. Advance online publication. DOI: 10.1080/23311886.2024.2341483

Raworth, K. (2017). *Doughnut economics: Seven ways to think like a 21st-century economist.* Chelsea Green Publishing.

Reddy, K., & Sailesh, B. (2024). Cultural guardianship in tourism: Indigenous communities' quest for economic stability and identity preservation. *Journal of Environmental Management and Tourism*, *15*(2), 328. DOI: 10.14505/jemt.v15.2(74).08

Reimer, M., Haensse, L., & Lin-Hi, N. (2024). Internal change through external actions: The impact of external corporate social responsibility on employee readiness for change. *Journal of Organizational Change Management*, *37*(7), 1446–1468. DOI: 10.1108/JOCM-03-2024-0125

Resende, S., Monje-Amor, A., & Calvo, N. (2024). Enterprise risk management and firm performance: The mediating role of corporate social responsibility in the European Union region. *Corporate Social Responsibility and Environmental Management*, *31*(4), 2852–2864. DOI: 10.1002/csr.2719

Rezaei, M. (2025). Unlocking knowledge transfer dynamics across borders: Key drivers in international strategic alliances. *Journal of Knowledge Management*, *29*(8), 2497–2517. DOI: 10.1108/JKM-12-2023-1188

Rodrigues Coelho, F. I., Bizarrias, F. S., Rabechini Jr, R., Martens, C. D. P., & Martens, M. L. (2025). Strategic alignment and value optimization: Unveiling the critical role of project portfolio management for a flexible environment. *Global Journal of Flexible Systems Managment*, *26*(1), 209–224. DOI: 10.1007/s40171-024-00434-8

Rosca, E., Arnold, M., & Bendul, J. C. (2023). Business models for sustainable innovation – An empirical analysis. *Journal of Business Research*, *156*, 113450. DOI: 10.1016/j.jbusres.2022.113450

Rose, G. (Ed.). (2016). *The fourth industrial revolution: A Davos reader*. Foreign Affairs.

Rosenzweig, E. D., Kelley, K., & Bendoly, E. (2025). Diversity in frontline employee perceptions: Policies and procedures, training, and leadership as drivers of service equality. *Production and Operations Management, 34*(3), 412–422. DOI: 10.1177/10591478241252150

Rueda, X., Garrett, R. D., & Lambin, E. F. (2022). Corporate investments in supply chain sustainability: Evidence from coffee sourcing. *Journal of Business Ethics, 176*(2), 319–336. DOI: 10.1007/s10551-020-04746-5

Rusu, T. M., Odagiu, A., Pop, H., & Paulette, L. (2024). Sustainability performance reporting. *Sustainability (Basel), 16*(19), 8538. DOI: 10.3390/su16198538

Saeed, B. B., Afsar, B., Hafeez, S., Khan, I., Tahir, M., & Afridi, M. A. (2019). Promoting employee's proenvironmental behavior through green human resource management practices. *Corporate Social Responsibility and Environmental Management, 26*(2), 424–438. DOI: 10.1002/csr.1694

Saeidi, S. P., Sofian, S., Saeidi, P., Saeidi, S. P., & Saaeidi, S. A. (2021). How does corporate social responsibility contribute to firm financial performance? The mediating role of competitive advantage. *Journal of Business Research, 136*, 292–306. DOI: 10.1016/j.jbusres.2021.07.025

Sahai, A. K., & Rath, N. (2021). Artificial intelligence and the 4th industrial revolution. In *Artificial intelligence and machine learning in business management* (pp. 127–143). CRC Press. DOI: 10.1201/9781003125129-8

Sahu, D. (2024). Gender conundrum and unpaid work in India: Empirical evidence from India's first large-scale time use survey. *The Indian Economic Journal, 72*(4), 711–727. DOI: 10.1177/00194662241247137

Sahu, T. N., & Bandopadhyay, K. (2022). Impact of macroeconomic variables on stock market returns: Evidence from banking sector in India. *Asian Journal of Economics and Banking*, *6*(3), 316–334.

Sailaja, V. N., & Mandal, C. (2018). An empirical study on impact of macro variables on sectoral indices in India. *International Journal of Civil Engineering and Technology*, *9*(3), 383–393.

Sakarya, S., & Bezirgan, M. (2018). Financial crowdfunding mechanisms and startup financing. *Journal of Business Research-Turk, 10*(3), 123–138.

Sakthivel, S., & Joddar, P. (2006). Unorganised sector workforce in India trends, patterns and social security coverage. *Economic and Political Weekly, 41*(21), 2107–2114. https://www.jstor.org/stable/4418266

Salisu, A. A., & Vo, X. V. (2021). The behavior of exchange rate and stock returns in high and low interest rate environments. *International Review of Economics & Finance*, *74*, 138–149. DOI: 10.1016/j.iref.2021.02.008

Samoggia, A., & Riedel, B. (2020). Coffee consumption and sustainability: Exploring consumer awareness and behavior. *Sustainability*, *12*(8), 3235. DOI: 10.3390/su12083235

Saniel, D., Gue, I., & Salvo, C. (2025). *A Neo-Classical Economic Theory: Leveraging Underground Economy*. Cognizance Journal of Multidisciplinary Studies., DOI: 10.47760/cognizance.2025.v05i02.023

Sankar, S. (2018). A study on behaviours of investors with reference to capital market in Chennai. *International Journal of Mechanical and Production Engineering Research and Development*, *8*, 939–945.

Santos, L., Cunha, B., Fé, I., Vieira, M., & Silva, F. A. (2021). Data processing on edge and cloud: A performability evaluation and sensitivity analysis. *Journal of Network and Systems Management*, *29*(3), 27. DOI: 10.1007/s10922-021-09592-x

Saracel, N., & Aksoy, E. (2020). Industry 5.0 and human-centered production systems. *Journal of Industrial Engineering*, *31*(4), 112–120.

Sarasvathy, S. D. (2001). Causation and effectuation: Toward a theoretical shift from economic inevitability to entrepreneurial contingency. *Academy of Management Review*, *26*(2), 243–263. DOI: 10.2307/259121

Schaefer, S. D., Cunningham, P., Diehl, S., & Terlutter, R. (2024). Employees' positive perceptions of corporate social responsibility create beneficial outcomes for firms and their employees: Organizational pride as a mediator. *Corporate Social Responsibility and Environmental Management*, *31*(3), 2574–2587. DOI: 10.1002/csr.2699

Schaltegger, S., Hansen, E. G., & Lüdeke-Freund, F. (2016). Business models for sustainability: Origins, present research, and future avenues. *Organization & Environment*, *29*(1), 3–10. DOI: 10.1177/1086026615599806

Schnackenberg, A. K., & Tomlinson, E. C. (2016). Organizational transparency: A new perspective on managing trust in organization–stakeholder relationships. *Journal of Management*, *42*(7), 1784–1810. DOI: 10.1177/0149206314525202

Schwab, K. (2016). The fourth industrial revolution: What it means and how to respond. World Economic Forum.

Searcy, C. (2012). Corporate Sustainability Performance Measurement Systems: A Review and Research Agenda. *Journal of Business Ethics, 107*(3), 239–253. DOI: 10.1007/s10551-011-1038-z

Shahani, R., & Nagpal, N. (2019). A study of the movement of interest rates and spillover of volatility and returns amongst the leading bank stocks in India. *IUP Journal of Financial Risk Management, 16*(4), 7–22.

Shahani, R., & Nagpal, N. (2019). A Study of the Movement of Interest Rates and Spillover of Volatility and Returns Amongst the Leading Bank Stocks in India. *IUP Journal of Financial Risk Management, 16*(4), 7–22.

Shahin, M., Ilic, O., Gonsalvez, C., & Whittle, J. (2021). The impact of a stem-based entrepreneurship program on the entrepreneurial intention of secondary school female students. *The International Entrepreneurship and Management Journal, 17*(4), 1867–1898. DOI: 10.1007/s11365-020-00713-7

Shahzadi, G., John, A., Qadeer, F., Jia, F., & Yan, J. (2024). CSR beyond symbolism: The importance of substantive attributions for employee CSR engagement. *Journal of Cleaner Production, 436*, 140440. DOI: 10.1016/j.jclepro.2023.140440

Shalwani, M. (2021). *Insights into The Topic of The Fourth Industrial Revolution* (Doctoral dissertation, Khalifa University).

Shane, S., & Venkataraman, S. (2000). The Promise of Entrepreneurship as a Field of Research. *Academy of Management Review, 25*(1), 217–226. DOI: 10.5465/amr.2000.2791611

Shaposhnykov, K. (2023). *Preventing the development of the illegal economy: global experience.* Black Sea Economic Studies., DOI: 10.32782/bses.82-4

Sharma, S. K., & Sharma, M. (2019). Examining the role of trust and quality dimensions in the actual usage of mobile banking services: An empirical investigation. *International Journal of Information Management, 44*, 65–75. DOI: 10.1016/j.ijinfomgt.2018.09.013

Shepherd, D. A., & Patzelt, H. (2021). Entrepreneurship and sustainability: New horizons. *Journal of Management Studies, 58*(1), 1–27. DOI: 10.1111/joms.12664

Shin, H. W., & Jang, H. (2025). Overcoming barriers of corporate digital responsibility in the hospitality and tourism industry: A social identity perspective. *International Journal of Contemporary Hospitality Management, 37*(11), 1–20. DOI: 10.1108/IJCHM-11-2024-1670

Shneor, R., Flåten, B. T., & Zhao, L. (2020). *Advances in crowdfunding: Research and practice*. Palgrave Macmillan. DOI: 10.1007/978-3-030-46309-0

Sihotang, D. S. (2026). Digital Twins as an Enabler of Cognitive Enterprise Architecture: Reconfiguring Organizational Systems and Decision Intelligence. In *Transforming Physical Assets to Cognitive Enterprises With Digital Twins* (pp. 289–320). IGI Global Scientific Publishing., DOI: 10.4018/979-8-3373-9998-0.ch010

Silva, J. A. (2024). Corporate social responsibility (CSR) and sustainability in water supply: A systematic review. *Sustainability (Basel), 16*(8), 3183. DOI: 10.3390/su16083183

Singh, A., & Meher, S. (2024). Female labour force participation in India: An interstate analysis. *Global Research Review in Business and Economics, 10*(2), 01–07. DOI: 10.56805/grrbe.24.10.2.20

Singh, N. (2019). How can we regulate disruptive technologies? World Economic Forum.

Singh, A. (2014). A study of monetary policy impact on stock market returns. *Indian Research Journal, 1*(5), 1–12.

Singh, G. (2016). The impact of macroeconomic fundamentals on stock prices revised: A study of Indian stock market. *Journal of International Economics*, *7*(1), 76–91.

Singh, P., & Pattanaik, F. (2025). Beyond the fields: Tracing India's labour transition from agriculture to non-agricultural sectors. *International Journal of Social Economics*, *52*(4), 608–627. DOI: 10.1108/IJSE-11-2023-0904

Sjögren, H., & Yusuf, F. (2021). Profiles of entrepreneurial success during two centuries. the case of Sweden, with comparisons to Italy. *Business History*, *65*(8), 1366–1389. DOI: 10.1080/00076791.2021.1979515

Skilton, M., & Hovsepian, F. (2018). *The 4th industrial revolution*. Springer Nature. DOI: 10.1007/978-3-319-62479-2

Slama, D., Puhlmann, F., Morrish, J., & Bhatnagar, R. M. (2015). *Enterprise IoT: Strategies and Best practices for connected products and services*. O'Reilly Media, Inc.

Smith, J. A. (2020). Understanding biomimicry: Lessons from butterfly wings. Smithsonian Magazine. https://www.smithsonianmag.com

Smith, R., & McElwee, G. (2013). The embeddedness of illegal entrepreneurship in a closed ethnic community. *International Journal of Business and Globalisation*, *11*(1), 45–62. DOI: 10.1504/IJBG.2013.055315

Soydal, İ. (2006). E-commerce and consumer participation in digital markets. *Journal of Social Sciences*, *6*(3), 548–560.

Srinivasan, R., & Swink, M. (2021). An investigation of visibility and flexibility as complements to supply chain analytics: An organizational information processing theory perspective. *Production and Operations Management*, *30*(2), 415–434. DOI: 10.1111/poms.13305

Sriraksa, A., Chaiyakot, P., & Luengchavanon, M. (2024). Sustainability in sustainability certifications in Thai hotel industry. *Edelweiss Applied Science and Technology*, *8*(6), 3150–3160. DOI: 10.55214/25768484.v8i6.2677

Srivastava, G., Mishra, S., & Nigam, N. (2025). Digital transformation in FinTech: Redefining wealth creation and investment. In *Digital transformation in finance*. Emerald Publishing., DOI: 10.1108/978-1-83662-188-120251013

Srivastava, S., Agarwal, A., Madan, P., & Kautish, P. (2025). How do green CSR initiatives influence green employee engagement among tourism and hospitality employees? *Corporate Social Responsibility and Environmental Management*, *32*(1), 757–768. DOI: 10.1002/csr.2977

Stephan, U., Zbierowski, P., Pérez-Luño, A., Wach, D., Wiklund, J., Cabañas, M., & Zahid, M. (2022). Act or wait-and-see? adversity, agility, and entrepreneur well-being across countries during the covid-19 pandemic. *Entrepreneurship Theory and Practice*, *47*(3), 682–723. DOI: 10.1177/10422587221104820

Stilgoe, J., Owen, R., & Macnaghten, P. (2013). Developing a framework for responsible innovation. *Research Policy*, *42*(9), 1568–1580. DOI: 10.1016/j.respol.2013.05.008

Stoeckli, E., Dremel, C., & Uebernickel, F. (2018). Exploring characteristics and transformational capabilities of InsurTech innovations to understand insurance value creation in a digital world. *Electronic Markets*, *28*(3), 287–305. DOI: 10.1007/s12525-018-0304-7

Stubbs, W. (2016). Sustainable entrepreneurship and b corps. *Business Strategy and the Environment*, *26*(3), 331–344. DOI: 10.1002/bse.1920

Stylos, N., Bellou, V., Andronikidis, A., & Vassiliadis, C. A. (2022). Linking environmental awareness to sustainable consumption in hospitality. *Journal of Sustainable Tourism*, *30*(2–3), 513–532. DOI: 10.1080/09669582.2020.1849234

Suganya, S. (2016). The effect of macroeconomic variables on stock market performance in India.

Suhud, U., Boonkaew, S., Sihotang, D. S., Azinuddin, M., & Aujirapongpan, S. (2025). Bridging Social Responsibility and Sustainability: A Case Study of Modelling Tourist Citizenship Behaviour in Indonesia. *International Journal of Sustainable Development and Planning*, *20*(12), 5381–5393. DOI: 10.18280/ijsdp.201229

Suhud, U., Sihotang, D. S., Juliana, J., Azinuddin, M., Chanthawong, A., & Aujirapongpan, S. (2026). Eco-friendly souvenirs as a catalyst for sustainable tourism: Emotional and attitudinal perspectives. *Sustainable Futures : An Applied Journal of Technology, Environment and Society*, *11*, 101824. DOI: 10.1016/j.sftr.2026.101824

Sultana, N., Shoha, S., Dolon, M. S. A., Shiam, S. A. A., Zakaria, R. M., Shimanto, A. H., Shamsul Arefeen, S. M., & Abir, S. I. (2024). Machine learning solutions for predicting stock trends in BRICS amid global economic shifts and decoding market dynamics. *Journal of Economics. Finance and Accounting Studies*, *6*(6), 84–101. DOI: 10.32996/jefas.2024.6.6.7

Surak, K. (2018). Migration industries and the state: Guest work programs in East Asia. *The International Migration Review*, *52*(2), 487–523. DOI: 10.1177/0197918318781829

Suresh, N., Kumar, S. A., & Janardhanam, K. (2017). *The Effects of Volatility of Interest Rates on Stock Returns: A study on Indian Stock market. SSRN.*

Sussan, F., & Acs, Z. J. (2017). The digital entrepreneurial ecosystem. *Small Business Economics*, *49*(1), 55–73. DOI: 10.1007/s11187-017-9867-5

Tabatabaei, F., Oshriyeh, O., & Beldona, S. (2025). Towards sustainability: Exploring community involvement in tourism development. *Tourism Planning & Development*, *22*(4), 498–528. DOI: 10.1080/21568316.2024.2392788

Taheri, B., Olya, H., & Batat, W. (2024). Ethical consumption and climate change in hospitality and tourism: challenges, solutions, and prospects: Guest editorial. *International Journal of Contemporary Hospitality Management*, *36*(5), 1457–1466. DOI: 10.1108/IJCHM-05-2024-169

Tambunan, T. T. H. (2009). *SMEs in Asian developing countries.* Springer., DOI: 10.1057/9780230250949

Tamimi, N. A., & Ellis, P. (2009). Drug development: From concept to marketing! *Nephron. Clinical Practice*, *113*(3), c125–c131. DOI: 10.1159/000232592 PMID: 19729922

Tawiah, V., Samson, N., & Jatau, U. (2025). Local directors and corporate social responsibility activities of multinational companies in Africa. *Corporate Social Responsibility and Environmental Management*, *32*(2), 1688–1697. DOI: 10.1002/csr.3028

Teece, D., Peteraf, M., & Leih, S. (2016). Dynamic capabilities and organizational agility: Risk, uncertainty, and strategy in the innovation economy. California Management Review, 58(4), 13–35. (Original work published 2016)DOI: 10.1525/cmr.2016.58.4.13

Teece, D. J. (2007). Explicating dynamic capabilities: The nature and microfoundations of sustainable enterprise performance. *Strategic Management Journal*, *28*(13), 1319–1350. DOI: 10.1002/smj.640

Teker, D. L., & Alp, E. A. (2014). GRANGER CAUSALITY RELATI ON BETWEEN I NTEREST RATES AND STOCK MARKETS: EVIDENCE FROM EMERGING MARKETS.

Teker, D. L., & Alp, E. A. (2014). Granger causality relation between interest rates and stock markets: Evidence from emerging markets.

Teng, Y., Ma, Z., Liang, D., Song, S., & Zheng, Y. (2024). The moderating effect of national culture on board interlocks' impact on firm performance: A meta-analysis. *Journal of Business Research*, *183*, 114816. DOI: 10.1016/j.jbusres.2024.114816

Tiwari, S. P. (2022). Re-emergence of Asia in the New Industrial Era. *Technium Soc. Sci. J.*, *29*, 471–480. DOI: 10.47577/tssj.v29i1.6103

Tölkes, C., & Butzmann, E. (2022). Motivating pro-sustainability behavior: The potential of sustainability marketing. *Journal of Cleaner Production*, *343*, 130940. DOI: 10.1016/j.jclepro.2022.130940

Trinh, V. Q., Elnahass, M., Salama, A., & Izzeldin, M. (2019). Board busyness, performance and financial stability: Does bank type matter? *European Journal of Finance*, *26*(7–8), 774–801. https://doi.org/https://doi.org/10.1080/1351847X.2019.1636842

Trinugroho, I., Risfandy, T., Hanafi, M. M., & Sukmana, R. (2023). Busy commissioners and firm performance: Evidence from Indonesia. *International Journal of Emerging Markets*, *18*(11), 5028–5048. DOI: 10.1108/IJOEM-01-2020-0007

Tripathi, V., & Ghosh, R. (2012). Interest rate sensitivity of banking stock returns in India. *International Journal of Financial Management (ISSN: 2229-5690) Vol, 2*, 10-20.

Tripathi, V., & Ghosh, R. (2012). Interest rate sensitivity of banking stock returns in India. *International Journal of Financial Management, 2*(2), 10–20.

Truong, Y., & Papagiannidis, S. (2022). Artificial intelligence as an enabler for innovation: A review and future research agenda. [Jouppi, N., Kurian]. *Technological Forecasting and Social Change, 183*, 121852. DOI: 10.1016/j.techfore.2022.121852

Truong, Y., Schneckenberg, D., Battisti, M., & Jabbouri, R. (2023). Guest editorial: Artificial intelligence as an enabler for entrepreneurs: an integrative perspective and future research directions. *International Journal of Entrepreneurial Behaviour & Research, 29*(4), 801–815. DOI: 10.1108/IJEBR-04-2023-033

Trupp, A., Salman, A., Stephenson, M. L., Chan, L. F., & Gan, J. E. (2025). A systematic review of challenges faced by Micro and small Enterprises in Tourism Destinations: Producing solutions through resilience building and sustainable development. *Tourism Planning & Development, 22*(3), 301–323. DOI: 10.1080/21568316.2024.2307970

Turčinović, M., Vujko, A., & Stanišić, N. (2025). Community-led sustainable tourism in rural areas: Enhancing wine tourism destination competitiveness and local empowerment. *Sustainability (Basel), 17*(7), 2878. DOI: 10.3390/su17072878

Turkish Industry and Business Association (TÜSİAD). (2017). *Digital transformation and e-commerce ecosystem report.* TÜSİAD Publications.

Uddin, M. M., Hasan, M., Hoque, S., Hossain, M. A., & Asauzzaman, A. S. M. (2024). Assessing sustainability reporting practice in accordance with the Global Reporting Initiative (G4) towards achieving sustainable development goals using artificial intelligence. Journal of Management Accounting. *Governance and Performance, 1*(1), 40–68. DOI: 10.63817/JMAGP.05.2024.002

Upadhyaya, N. (2024). Artificial intelligence in web development: Enhancing automation, personalization, and decision-making. *Artificial Intelligence, 4*(1), 534–540.

Vardari, L., & Hameli, K. (2025). Perceived benefits, trust and social influence in FinTech: Pathways to adoption and satisfaction in a developing economy. *Global Knowledge, Memory and Communication.* Advance online publication. DOI: 10.1108/GKMC-02-2025-0137

Varga, D. (2017). FinTech, the new era of financial services. *Budapest Management Review, 48*(11), 22–32. DOI: 10.14267/VEZTUD.2017.11.03

Vávrová, J., Červová, L., Brandová, B., & Stolz-Römmermann, J. (2025). Does ownership structure influence sustainability? Evidence from Booking. com sustainability practices in hospitality. *Cogent Business & Management, 12*(1), 2540508. DOI: 10.1080/23311975.2025.2540508

Venkatesh, G., Kshatriya, S., & Bansal, S. (2025). Board Busyness and Firm Performance: An Emerging Market Perspective. *Corporate Governance, 33*(2), 231–245. DOI: 10.1111/corg.12600

Venkatesh, V., Morris, M. G., Davis, G. B., & Davis, F. D. (2003). User acceptance of information technology: Toward a unified view. *Management Information Systems Quarterly, 27*(3), 425–478. DOI: 10.2307/30036540

Verchenko, N., & Sabol, E. (2024). Illegal Entrepreneurship: Theory Issues and Law Enforcement Problems. *Herald of Omsk University Series Law*. DOI: 10.24147/1990-5173.2024.21(4).92-100

Verhoef, P. C., Broekhuizen, T., Bart, Y., Bhattacharya, A., Dong, J. Q., Fabian, N., & Haenlein, M. (2021). Digital transformation: A multidisciplinary reflection and research agenda. *Journal of Business Research, 122*, 889–901. DOI: 10.1016/j.jbusres.2019.09.022

Vermesan, O., & Bacquet, J. (Eds.). (2022). *Cognitive hyperconnected digital transformation: Internet of things intelligence evolution*. CRC Press. DOI: 10.1201/9781003337584

Vial, G. (2019). Understanding digital transformation: A review and a research agenda. *The Journal of Strategic Information Systems, 28*(2), 118–144. DOI: 10.1016/j.jsis.2019.01.003

Vives, X. (2017). *The impact of FinTech on banking*. European Economy—Banks, Regulation, and the Real Sector.

von Weltzien Hoivik, H. (2025). Reflections on Business Ethics in Norway. In *Researching and Teaching Business Ethics in Europe: Developments, Challenges and Opportunities* (pp. 165–196). Springer Nature Switzerland. DOI: 10.1007/978-3-031-99320-6_10

Voronkova, V., Vasyl'chuk, G., Nikitenko, V., Kaganov, Y., & Metelenko, N. (2023). Transformation of digital education in the era of the fourth industrial revolution and globalization.

Vuorio, A. M., Torkkeli, L., & Sainio, L. M. (2023). Entrepreneurial orientation, innovation, and sustainable performance. *Journal of Business Research, 156*, 113482. DOI: 10.1016/j.jbusres.2022.113482

Vyas, I., Prasad, N., & Mishra, A. K. (2014). Causal nexus between stock price, demand for money, interest rate, foreign institutional investment, and exchange rates in India: A post subprime crisis analysis. *Indonesian Capital Market Review, 3*(2), 1. DOI: 10.21002/icmr.v3i2.3625

Wah, J. N. K. (2025). Revolutionizing surgery: AI and robotics for precision, risk reduction, and innovation. *Journal of Robotic Surgery, 19*(1), 47. DOI: 10.1007/s11701-024-02205-0 PMID: 39776281

Wang, L., Ma, Y., Yan, J., Chang, V., & Zomaya, A. Y. (2018). pipsCloud: High performance cloud computing for remote sensing big data management and processing. *Future Generation Computer Systems, 78*, 353–368. DOI: 10.1016/j.future.2016.06.009

Weingärtner, T. (2019, November). Tokenization of physical assets and the impact of IoT and AI. In *European Union Blockchain Observatory and Forum* (Vol. 10, pp. 1-16).

Welter, F., Smallbone, D., & Pobol, A. (2015). Entrepreneurial activity in the informal economy: A missing piece of the entrepreneurship jigsaw puzzle. *Entrepreneurship and Regional Development, 27*(5-6), 292–306. DOI: 10.1080/08985626.2015.1041259

Wernerfelt, B. (1984). A resource-based view of the firm. *Strategic Management Journal, 5*(2), 171–180. DOI: 10.1002/smj.4250050207

White, R., Habib, R., & Hardisty, D. (2019). Crowdfunding success and feedback mechanisms. *JMR, Journal of Marketing Research, 56*(4), 621–635.

Wibowo, A., Chen, S. C., Wiangin, U., Ma, Y., & Ruangkanjanases, A. (2023). Customer behavior as an outcome of social media marketing: The role of trust and engagement. *Journal of Retailing and Consumer Services, 71*, 103182. DOI: 10.1016/j.jretconser.2022.103182

Williams, D. (2015). The impact of Sim venture on the development of entrepreneurial skills in management students. *Industry and Higher Education, 29*(5), 379–395. DOI: 10.5367/ihe.2015.0270

Wirba, A. V. (2024). Corporate social responsibility (CSR): The role of government in promoting CSR. *Journal of the Knowledge Economy, 15*(2), 7428–7454. DOI: 10.1007/s13132-023-01185-0 PMID: 40479158

World Bank. (2022). FinTech and the future of finance.

Wu, C. J., Raghavendra, R., Gupta, U., Acun, B., Ardalani, N., Maeng, K., ... & Hazelwood, K. (2022). Sustainable ai: Environmental implications, challenges and opportunities. Proceedings of machine learning and systems, 4, 795-813.

Wu, K., & Zheng, K. (2025). Tax incentives, supply chain spillovers, and enterprise technological innovation. *International Review of Financial Analysis, 99*(January), 103930. DOI: 10.1016/j.irfa.2025.103930

Wukich, J. J., Neuman, E. L., & Fogarty, T. J. (2024). Show me? Inspire me? Make me? An institutional theory exploration of social and environmental reporting practices. *Journal of Accounting & Organizational Change*, *20*(4), 673–701. DOI: 10.1108/JAOC-01-2023-0013

Wu, Q., Wang, Y., & Shen, G. (2024). The green bonus of tax incentives: Evidence from China. *Journal of Economic Behavior & Organization*, *227*(January), 106740. DOI: 10.1016/j.jebo.2024.106740

Xie, H., Sha, Y., & Li, L. (2024). Synthesization of macroeconomic policies and stock return synchronicity: Evidence from countries along the Belt and Road Initiative. *Pacific-Basin Finance Journal*, *85*, 102398. DOI: 10.1016/j.pacfin.2024.102398

Yang, M., Evans, S., Vladimirova, D., & Rana, P. (2021). Value uncaptured perspective for sustainable business model innovation. *Journal of Cleaner Production*, *290*, 125799. DOI: 10.1016/j.jclepro.2021.125799

Yang, T., & Zhang, X. (2022). FinTech adoption and financial inclusion: Evidence from household consumption in China. *Journal of Banking & Finance*, *145*, 106668. DOI: 10.1016/j.jbankfin.2022.106668

Yang, Y., Yuan, Y., Liu, P., Wu, W., & Huo, C. (2024). Crucial to me and my society: How collectivist culture influences individual pro-environmental behavior through environmental values. *Journal of Cleaner Production*, *454*, 142211. DOI: 10.1016/j.jclepro.2024.142211

Ye, J., Sotiriadis, M., Dimou, I., Shen, S., & Koufopoulos, D. (2025). Suggesting a tourism industry-specific environmental, social and corporate governance (ESG) reporting framework. *Tourism Management*, *109*, 105156. DOI: 10.1016/j.tourman.2025.105156

Yi, H., Wang, G., & Feng, J. (2024). Gender inequality: Policy responses to employment and education in BRICS countries. *African Journal of Reproductive Health*, *28*(12), 88–96. DOI: 10.29063/ajrh2024/v28i12.10 PMID: 39764841

Yikilmaz, I., Surucu, L., Maslakci, A., & Cetinkaya, B. (2025). Corporate Social Responsibility as a Driver of Business Innovation: The Mediating Role of Corporate Reputation on Employee Performance in the Hospitality Sector. *Systems*, *13*(6), 475. DOI: 10.3390/systems13060475

Yin, H., Zhang, L., Cai, C., Zhang, Z., & Zhu, Q. (2025). Fiscal & tax incentives, ESG responsibility fulfillments, and corporate green innovation performance. *International Review of Economics & Finance*, *98*, 103838. DOI: 10.1016/j.iref.2025.103838

Yogi, K. S., Gowda, D., Pati, A., Srinivas, V., Aghav, S., & Abdullah, I. (2024). Accelerating sustainability through leveraging machine learning to analyze CSR spending in the Indian automobile industry. *2024 7th International Conference on Circuit Power and Computing Technologies (ICCPCT)*, 905–912.

Yücebalkan, B. (2020). Human-centered production in Industry 5.0 era. *Journal of Engineering and Technology Management, 56*, 101567.

Yunxi, Y., & Danes, S. (2015). Resiliency and resilience process of entrepreneurs in new venture creation. *Entrepreneurship Research Journal, 5*(1), 1–30. DOI: 10.1515/erj-2013-0076

Yu, Y., & Jiang, Y. (2024). *Understanding the Digital Revolution and Its Influences*. Springer. DOI: 10.1007/978-981-97-4939-3

Zamiri, M., & Esmaeili, A. (2024). Strategies, methods, and supports for developing skills within learning communities: A systematic review of the literature. *Administrative Sciences, 14*(9), 231. DOI: 10.3390/admsci14090231

Zervoudi, E. K., Moschos, N., & Christopoulos, A. G. (2025). From the corporate social responsibility (CSR) and the environmental, social and governance (ESG) criteria to the greenwashing phenomenon: A comprehensive literature review about the causes, consequences and solutions of the phenomenon with specific case studies. *Sustainability (Basel), 17*(5), 2222. DOI: 10.3390/su17052222

Zhang, M., Zhao, X., Lyles, M., & Guo, H. (2022). Absorptive capacity and digital innovation: Evidence from SMEs. *Industrial Marketing Management, 102*, 105–117. DOI: 10.1016/j.indmarman.2021.12.007

Zhao, L., Chong, K. M., Gooi, L. M., & Yan, L. (2024). Research on the impact of government fiscal subsidies and tax incentive mechanism on the output of green patents in enterprises. *Finance Research Letters, 61*(December 2023), 104997. DOI: 10.1016/j.frl.2024.104997

Zhao, H., Kloren-Garcia, M., & Rosenfield, Z. G. (2025). Recruitment and retention challenges for tourism and hospitality professionals: The case of a Swiss boutique hotel. *Worldwide Hospitality and Tourism Themes, 17*(6), 1–13. DOI: 10.1108/WHATT-04-2025-0160

Zhou, T. (2012). Understanding users' initial trust in mobile banking: An elaboration likelihood perspective. *Computers in Human Behavior, 28*(4), 1518–1525. DOI: 10.1016/j.chb.2012.03.021

Zhu, N., Zhou, Y., Zhang, S., & Yan, J. (2023). Tax incentives and environmental, social, and governance performance: Empirical evidence from China. *Environmental Science and Pollution Research International*, *30*(19), 54899–54913. DOI: 10.1007/s11356-023-26112-3 PMID: 36881223

Zhu, Q., Sarkis, J., & Lai, K. H. (2007). Green supply chain management: Pressures, practices and performance within the Chinese automobile industry. *Journal of Cleaner Production*, *15*(11-12), 1041–1052. DOI: 10.1016/j.jclepro.2006.05.021

Zott, C., Amit, R., & Massa, L. (2011). The business model: Recent developments and future research. *Journal of Management*, *37*(4), 1019–1042. DOI: 10.1177/0149206311406265

Zvilichovsky, D., Inbar, Y., & Barzilay, O. (2018). Playing both sides of the market: Success factors in crowdfunding. *Management Science*, *64*(9), 3810–3829.

# About the Contributors

**Reshmy Khrishan** plays an active role in higher education quality assurance as a program reviewer for Oman's Ministry of Higher Education, Research and Innovation (MoHERI), and as a Board Member of the Oman Association for Quality in Higher Education (QAQHE) under the Ministry of Social Affairs. From 2017 to 2021, she was a member of the IT Academic Council of the Indian Schools Board of Directors in Oman, and she serves on advisory boards at universities in Oman and India. She supervises PhD candidates at Indian government universities and evaluates theses across multiple Indian institutions. A respected speaker, Dr. Reshmy has presented at numerous international conferences and professional forums and is well known as a public speaker within the community. Her accolades include the Best National Research Award from the Research Council Oman (2014), the 'Woman Icon India Global Award' presented by the Governor of Tamil Nadu (2019) for her contributions to education, the 'Distinguished Educator and Scholar Award' from the National Foundation for Entrepreneurship (2020), and the 'Distinguished Woman in Engineering Award' (2018) for her advancements in Computer Science and Engineering. Previously, she headed the Computing Department at Muscat College until September 2017 and chaired the Industry and Community Engagement Committee from 2017 to 2021. Currently, she leads the Research Centre at the college. Her academic contributions include 21 book chapters published by Springer, 18 funded projects, and over 643 research citations. She authored the book 'Computer Programming' and has organized more than 50 national and international conferences, workshops, and symposiums. She has also been a keynote speaker and resource person at over 70 academic events worldwide. Additionally, she serves on the editorial board of the International Journal of Business, Communication and Technology and acts as a peer reviewer for several international journals and thesis evaluator for Indian universities.

**Araby Madbouly** is the Assistant Dean for Academic Affairs at Muscat College. He is appointed as external reviewer in OAAAQA, Sultanate of Oman. Araby has over 40 published articles in international journals and papers presented in international conferences in international economics, finance, entrepreneurship, HR, marketing, knowledge management, and corporate governance. He has 3 published books Araby supervised many Ph.D. and MSc theses. Furthermore, he participated as an external examiner for many. HE participated as a keynote speaker and was assigned as a member of technical committees in many international conferences. He is an editorial board member of three international journals and a reviewer for other five international journals.

**Buthaina Al Kharousi** is an Assistant Professor and MBA Programme Coordinator at Muscat College, Oman. She is the director of the MBA Programme at Muscat College. She holds a PhD in Entrepreneurship from the University of Worcester, UK, and has over 18 years of experience in higher education, teaching, research, and academic leadership. Her research interests include entrepreneurship education, innovation, sustainability, artificial intelligence, digital transformation, and entrepreneurial ecosystems. She has published in internationally peer-reviewed journals and book chapters, serves as a reviewer for leading academic journals, and regularly presents her research at international conferences. Dr Al Kharousi actively contributes to research projects, curriculum development and international collaborations, with a strong commitment to advancing entrepreneurship education and sustainable development.

**Nitha Mary Siju** possesses over nine years of extensive experience in research and teaching within the academic realm. Currently working as a Senior Lecturer in the Department of Business and Accounting at Muscat College, Sultanate of Oman. She has pursued a Bachelor of Engineering in Electronics and Communication from Anna University and received a Master of Business Administration from the Cochin University of Science and Technology. Her subject area includes Entrepreneurship, Project Management, Global Sustainability and Supply Chain Management. As a dedicated educator and mentor, she has provided guidance in both SPSS and NVivo to dissertation students and has hosted various Entrepreneurship competitions on campus. Additionally, she exhibits expertise in Microsoft Project Software and holds a CAPM certification, enabling her to impart knowledge in the project management discipline. With a Master's degree in Business Administration and an ongoing pursuit of a PhD, her research endeavors encompass diverse social science studies, focusing on Sustainability, Supply Chain Management, Human Resource Management, and Project Management disciplines.

***

**Vishnu Achutha Menon** is an assistant professor at the Central University of Punjab in Bathinda. His research interests span various fields, including film studies, new media, Virtual Reality (VR), Augmented Reality (AR), Artificial Intelligence (AI), data journalism and visualization, educational media, immersive technology, interactive media, media psychology, digital ethnography, smart education, digital pedagogy, verbal and nonverbal communication, South Asian performances, Natyasastra, and Ethnomusicology. He has published journal articles in Economic and Political Weekly, IEEE Proceedings, Springer Lecture Note Series, International Journal of Emerging Technologies in Learning (iJET), Studies in Media and Communication, Journal of Media and Communication, Journal of Arts, among others. Vishnu has contributed book chapters to publishers such as IGI Global, Wiley, CRC Press, and Emerald. He has also written book reviews for Asian Theatre Journal, Space and Culture, Urban India, and others. He specializes in mixed methods in social sciences and humanities research.

**Edi Fitriana Afriza** is a lecturer in the Department of Economics at Siliwangi University and a PhD student at Yogyakarta State University. For the past 10 years, her course materials have focused on entrepreneurship and SMEs. She has a particular interest in research on entrepreneurship and SMEs, with her research focusing on "The Development of Green Entrepreneurship and Blue Entrepreneurship Models in SMEs." In addition to her academic work, she is also actively involved in supporting SMEs through the mobilization of the Association of Business Development Services Indonesia (ABDSI) and serves as a National Reviewer for the Student Entrepreneurship Development Program (P2MW) of the Ministry of Higher Education, Science, and Technology (Kemdikti Saintek).

**Talib Khalifa Hamad Al Saadi** is an academic and researcher in the field of business and management, associated with higher education in the Sultanate of Oman. His academic interests include entrepreneurship, small and medium enterprise (SME) development, strategic management, and economic development, with a particular focus on the Omani and Gulf context

**Ghaliya AlFarsi** got her Master degree in computer science at the University of Sohar in Oman (2015), and Bachelor of Science degree in Computer Science at Ajman University, AlAin, UAE (2004). she is a lecturer in information technology department in ALBuraimi College, Oman more than twelve years. Most of her publications were indexed under Scopus. her research expertise are in knowledge management, integrated system, e-learning, m-learning and image proccesing. And published in international journals.

**Merina Banerjee** is a research Scholar, Management Development Institute Murshidabad. The primary research areas are the training and development needs of organizations, communication skills for career etc. I am a university rank holder in hospital management. I train budding managers/executives in communication skills and interview preparation. I have published papers that are indexed in Scopus. I have a master degree in management specializing in human resource management.

**Souvik Banerjee**, PhD. He is a faculty at Management Development Institute (MDI) Murshidabad. His research interests include Corporate Finance, Corporate Governance, Behavioral Finance, and Financial Economics. His work has been published in Scopus-indexed and ABDC-listed journals. At present, he is the Editor of the MDIM Journal of Management Review and Practice (Sage). He has developed several business cases for MBA and executive education. He has trained executives from Fortune 500 companies in Corporate Finance and Corporate Valuation.

**Jaya Bingi** is a professor from IIITDM Kancheepuram, works on product development driven by bio inspired design and Photonics as tools. Received doctorate from IIT Madras, India. Postdoctoral fellow from NTU Singapore. I have background in Physics, Nanophotonics, Lasers and Bio-inspired design. I have 9 patents, more than 30 publications and 2 books as on date. Completed / ongoing 3 sponsored project s, 6 consultancy projects, 2 entrepreneurship development projects. The Bio-inspired Research and Design (BiRD) Lab established in IIITDM Kancheepuram to work on product design and Innovation

**Ali Imaduddin Futuwwah** is a lecturer and researcher in the Department of Management, Faculty of Economics and Business, Muhammadiyah University of Surabaya, Indonesia. He holds a Bachelor's degree in Da'wah Management from STID Al Hadid Surabaya and a Master of Science in Management from Universitas Airlangga. His research interests encompass digital consumer behavior, halal marketing, green marketing, and experimental research design. He currently serves as Editor-in-Chief of Improvement: Jurnal Manajemen dan Bisnis. In addition to his academic role, he leads the Training and Halal Certification Division at the Halal Center of Muhammadiyah University of Surabaya, actively supporting halal certification programs for small and medium enterprises across East Java. He is currently pursuing his doctoral degree, with research focused on the intersection of digital marketing and halal consumer behavior. His scholarly contributions span halal lifestyle, digital marketing performance, and online consumer community behavior.

|**Babu George**, PhD (Management), Doctor of Business Administration, has more than fifteen years of business research, university teaching, and administrative service experience, in the US and internationally. In the past, he has worked for Fort Hays State University, Swiss Management Center University, University of Liverpool, Alaska Pacific University, and University of Southern Mississippi, among others. Currently, he is Professor of International Business and Associate Dean in the School of Business at Christian Brothers University, TN, USA. He is a visiting professor at various higher education institutions around the world. He has extensive consulting experience in the service industries.

**Achmad Nur Wahyu Kartiko** is a Master's student in Management Science with a concentration in Finance at Universitas Airlangga (UNAIR), Surabaya, Indonesia. He completed his undergraduate studies in Psychology at Universitas Surabaya (UBAYA), which laid the foundation for his interdisciplinary approach to understanding financial phenomena particularly from behavioral and cognitive perspectives. His academic interests center on behavioral finance, financial literacy, financial well-being, and industrial-organizational psychology. In terms of research, he has a focus on individual financial behavior, with an empirical emphasis on micro, small, and medium enterprise (MSME) owners. His contributions have been published in peer-reviewed journals addressing the dynamics of financial decision-making within this segment. On the methodological side, he is proficient in structural equation modeling (SEM) using SmartPLS, as well as data analysis through Jamovi. His research agenda is directed toward bridging psychology and financial science to better understand financial behavior and economic resilience, particularly among younger generations.

**Saleh F. A. Khatib** is assistant Professor at the Faculty of Business, Sohar University, Oman. He holds a PhD in Finance from Universiti Teknologi Malaysia (UTM), where he graduated with distinction, earning both the Chancellor Award and Dean's List Award in recognition of his academic excellence. Currently serving as an Adjunct Assistant Professor at An-Najah National University, Palestine, Dr. Khatib continues to inspire and mentor the next generation of researchers. He also serves on the editorial boards of leading international journals, including Heliyon (Elsevier), Discover Global Society (Springer), and PLOS ONE (Public Library of Science). Formerly a Senior Lecturer at UTM, Dr. Khatib made significant contributions to the university's research agenda in finance and accounting. His leadership in guiding postgraduate scholars, advancing governance research, and fostering academic-industry collaboration resulted in a strong legacy of scholarly impact and innovation. Dr. Khatib has published over 100 peer-reviewed articles, with 65 indexed in Web of Science and nearly 50 in top-tier Q1/Q2 journals. His work addresses critical issues at the intersection of governance and sustainability, especially in the context of institutional reforms and market transitions and can be found at Business Strategy and The Environment, Management Review Quarterly, Journal of Environmental Management, Global Business Review, Corporate Governance, among others. He is the recipient of several prestigious honors, including the UTM Academic Award (2023), Wiley Top Cited Article Award, and the Indexed Journal Award.

**Sateesh Kumar T K**, presently working as an Asst. Professor at Kristu Jayanti University, Bengaluru, India.

**P.Praba Devi** is an Associate Professor in the Sona School of Management. She has completed her Doctoral research with 23+ years of experience in academic and industry. She teaches marketing courses for the students and her area of interest is Service Quality, marketing and consumer behavior. She is an approved supervisor by the Anna University to guide research scholars pursuing Doctoral Program. Besides attending several conferences, seminars and training programs she has also organized national seminar, faculty development programs and workshops. She has published articles in several Scopus/ WoS indexed journals, refereed journals and journals with high impact factor. She has also reviewed the books published by leading publishers. She has been a member of organising committee for few International conference. She is a member of the team preparing the Human Development Report and the State Balanced Growth Fund report for the State Planning Commission.

**Lijo P Thomas,** Vice Principal & CFO at Kristu Jayanti College, Bengaluru, India

**Mohammed Riyazkhan** is an academic and researcher in the field of business and management, with teaching and research experience in HRM, marketing, entrepreneurship, and management studies. He is associated with higher education in the Sultanate of Oman and has contributed to academic research through journal publications and book chapters focusing on SME development, entrepreneurship, digital transformation, and contemporary management issues. Dr. Mohamed Riyazkhan is actively involved in teaching, curriculum development, and scholarly research, supporting the advancement of business education and applied research in the region.

**S. Baranidharan** is a faculty member at the School of Management, Presidency University, Bengaluru. He holds an MBA from Pondicherry University and a PhD in Management from Bharathidasan University, specializing in finance and risk analytics. His primary research interests include financial risk spillovers, market volatility, fintech innovation, sustainable finance, and technology-driven business strategies. Dr. Baranidharan has published research articles in reputed journals, including the Iranian Journal of Management Studies and Economic and Political Weekly. He has also presented papers at national and international conferences and serves as a peer reviewer for academic publications. In addition to his scholarly work, he has secured a patent in the domain of AI-driven banking and decision-support systems, reflecting his commitment to technological innovation. He actively engages in teaching, research supervision, and consultancy projects. He contributes to research capacity-building initiatives, organises workshops and conferences, and supports collaborations with academic and industry partners. His ongoing projects explore the intersection of financial technologies, analytics, and sustainable business development.

**Ravi Vinod Kumar Sharma** is an academic and researcher in the field of business and management, with teaching and scholarly experience in finance, accounting, and quantitative business research. He is associated with higher education in the Sultanate of Oman and has contributed to research through journal publications and book chapters focusing on financial management, digital transformation, and contemporary business practices. Dr. Sharma is actively involved in teaching, curriculum development, and research activities that support the advancement of business education and applied research.

**Doni Sugianto Sihotang** is a doctoral student in Marketing at Jakarta State University, Indonesia. His academic background combines a Bachelor's degree in Social Anthropology from Universitas Sumatera Utara and a Master's degree in Marketing Management from Jakarta State University. His research interests focus on consumer behavior, digital marketing, tourism marketing, and behavioral analytics. He has actively contributed to several peer-reviewed publications, exploring topics such as consumer decision-making, destination branding, and electric vehicle adoption. He also serves as a Graduate Teaching Assistant and Research Assistant at Jakarta State University, supporting research in marketing and behavioral sciences. Doni has received several national awards, including the BIMA DRTPM Research Grant from the Indonesian Ministry of Education and the PMDSU Fast-Track Scholarship for outstanding young researchers. His interdisciplinary background in anthropology and marketing enables him to integrate cultural and behavioral insights into the study of consumer decision processes and sustainable tourism development.

**Swetha Thiruchanuru** holds a PhD in Management from Sri Krishna Devaraya University. She is currently working as an Assistant Professor of Management at Sri Sathya Sai Institute of Higher Learning. Her areas of expertise include

Entrepreneurship and Innovation, Organizational Behavior, and Human Resource Management, integrating academic rigor with industry practice and Indian ethos.

**S Varalakshmi** is working as faculty in Business and Economics in Mazoon College, Muscat, Sultanate of Oman. She has more than fifteen years of teaching business related curriculum and research. She has a PhD in Commerce and Post Graduate Diploma in Personnel Management and Industrial relationship, MSSW, University of Madras. She has qualified with Associate Fellow of the Higher Education Academy, Post Graduate Certificate in learning and Teaching in Higher Education, University of Stirling, United Kingdom. She has presented more than ten research articles in national and international conferences and published more than fifteen research articles in peer reviewed journals, SCOPUS, and Springer Nature.

# Index

www.ingramcontent.com/pod-product-compliance
Lightning Source LLC
LaVergne TN
LVHW062325300926
849161LV00007B/1579